Greenwich Readers

Crime, Deviance and Society

Crime, Deviance and Society

Selected Debates

edited by

SUSAN CAFFREY

SENIOR LECTURER IN SOCIOLOGY
UNIVERSITY OF GREENWICH

and

GARY MUNDY

RESEARCH STUDENT
UNIVERSITY OF GREENWICH

 Greenwich University Press

First published in 1996 by
Greenwich University Press
Unit 42
Dartford Trade Park
Butterly Avenue
Dartford
Kent DA1 1JG
United Kingdom

British Library Cataloguing-in-Publication Data
A CIP catalogue record for this book is available from the British Library

ISBN 1 874529 91 4

Designed and produced for Greenwich University Press by Angela Allwright.

Contents

Introduction

What is normal? What is deviant? Who are the criminals in a changing society? These are questions that frequently emerge in discussions about crime. The readings included here address these issues and provide a critical look at the different theoretical explanations of why people commit crimes or why they become deviant. Other questions looked at include issues of whether or not crime is an inevitable part of human society. Are the unemployed more criminal than the employed? Should we value deviants, are they catalysts for social change?[1] The selection has been chosen from both established positions and more recent material that gives us the basis of criminological and sociological thought in this area.

They also demonstrate, as Jock Young[2] has argued, that criminological theory has a habit of repeating itself. One can see, in the work of the psychologist Eysenck for example, elements of biological determinism which was the basis of Lombroso's work developed in the nineteenth century. This means that the established approaches to crime are not included merely for their historical interest, but also because they underpin many contemporary theories about criminality, in particular recent forms of positivism and the realist criminology.

The article by Jock Young, 'Thinking seriously about crime', gives readers an especially useful set of models of criminology. The article focuses on the way theorists have certain assumptions about human nature and the social order. These assumptions are important because they shape the development of these models. The article focuses attention on the origins of the models and also shows the way these models inform more recent approaches and debates about the place of crime and deviance in society.

This collection focuses upon changes and developments in the way in which criminal and deviant behaviour has been theorised. By addressing these different theories one can reflect upon them and appreciate their value and limitations. One can see the value of a structural explanation, and also acknowledge that human agency must be given appropriate recognition. As Downes and Rock[3] say '. . . no theory can be assessed intelligently until it can be regarded with sympathy.'

An attempt has been made to include material which gives both insight into and a critical appreciation of the contrasting theories. For example, the contrast between the approach to the criminal which is inherent in varieties of positivism and that provided by people such as David Matza[4] and Howard Becker[5]. When one compares these one can see that there are very different kinds of knowledge, often conflictual, even though they are related to the same type of behaviour.

Matza argues that positivistic approaches to crime fail to 'appreciate' the criminal. By this he means that in focusing upon the 'cause' of criminality, positivism (whether social, psychological or biological) overlooks an important element of criminal behaviour, that is, the meanings which such actions have to the criminal. It is argued that without such an understanding one only has a partial understanding of the processes involved in criminal activity.

The first set of readings directs attention at some of the early explanations of crime. Whilst classical criminology sought to understand crime as a product of an absence of deterrence or effective control, positivist approaches saw criminality in terms of the pathological conditions of the criminal actor. Classicism assumes that human nature is based upon free will, whereas positivism works from the assumption that human beings are determined by influences outside their control.

Under classicism the criminal was seen as culpable for his or her actions and this led to a system of 'just deserts' for crimes that were committed. On the other hand, the policy implications of positivism were that people needed treatment following their criminal actions rather than punishment. Thus the readings selected draw out the major differences between these approaches and the implications which they have for developing particular policies and legal frameworks for dealing with criminality.

An attempt has been made to place those early approaches in a contemporary context. The readings by Taylor *et al*[6], Young[7] and Matza[8] place the classical and positivistic approaches to crime in a critical light. The readings highlight the shortcomings of these theoretical positions but at the same time show how their general principles can still be found within criminological theory. The work of Farrington[9] shows through his empirical work, particularly among young people, the value of positivism in developing an understanding of the 'criminal career'.

The readings address general explanatory positions that attempt to produce universal theoretical arguments for explaining crime. Attention is also given to the reasons for specific types of crime and specific types of offenders. Focus is given to the work of Durkheim[10] and how he addresses the relationship of society to particular types of criminal and deviant activity. Here the issue of punishment and the maintenance of boundaries between normal and criminal behaviour is of particular importance. One of the most interesting debates is whether it is possible to have a crime free society. Durkheim looks at whether crime is inevitable and addresses various social facts in order to reach an answer to this question.

When we are addressing the issue of social order we are also addressing the issue of why some people deviate. This is a particularly important issue when looking at the reasons why men are more likely to be convicted of criminal offences. One way of addressing this issue is to see why women are more likely to abide by existing norms and social rules. Hobbes's[11] answer to the problem of social order entailed the fear of the ruler. This answer, if related to women particularly, leads to another question; why are women more likely than men to regard themselves as being at the mercy of fearful situations?

These themes are followed up by Steven Box in his piece, 'Deviance, Latent Functions and Society'[12] which draws our attention to the relationship of power to the creation of particular types of rules. Box also uses Durkheim's idea that crime is a product of the relationship between the individual subject and the different kinds of social integration. In particular he shows why people are content to see others punished. He says that 'most ordinary people are plagued by two doubts: Is the social world in which I live normal?' and, 'In the social world in which I live, am I normal?' He argues that because of these doubts the majority of people are ready to accept that the people who have been selected for punishment are in fact guilty. It puts at the back of most people's minds the possibility that they may be one of the deviants.

Punishment can also serve societal functions in terms of demarcating boundaries of acceptable and unacceptable behaviour. This theme is followed up in a particularly critical way by Bianchi[13]. He attempts to arrive at a position on punishment that transcends the idea of the necessity of a social ritual of condemnation. Bianchi argues that the use of punitive forms of reaction to crime should be abolished or at least restricted to the most minimal use. The use of punitive sanctions is seen as being one which is too often used for the interests of a powerful minority rather than for its represented function as being for the 'public good'. He wants to show that reaction to crime need not be punitive. He believes that detention should be only for the most dangerous offenders. Bianchi argues that it is society that is instrumental in producing the offender and therefore should take on a more positive role by introducing practices which attempt to resolve the conflicts between offenders and society.

The set of readings that deal with corporate crime have been selected as they raise questions that are often overlooked. This arises when there are discussions about the nature of criminality in contemporary society. In particular, there is a tendency for the media and political rhetoric to give a higher profile to 'street crime', as opposed to corporate crime. However, it is not an area that criminological theory can ignore. The readings that deal with corporate crime are ones that focus upon the differences and similarities in relation to 'conventional' or 'street crime'.

Edwin Sutherland[14] wanted to show that the theory he developed for white collar criminality was applicable to any area of deviance which one chooses to focus attention upon. Sutherland's concept of 'differential association' is one which he saw as being a universally applicable process. He showed that all those who enter into criminal activity go through this process. Thus Sutherland's approach gives us a theoretical model for understanding all criminality. In fact, he would argue that in his model all forms of human behaviour can be understood. There is value in this model. However, the major shortcoming is that his concept of human nature seems to be one which is reactive to external events, particularly when it is applied to criminals.

The readings by Hazel Croall[15] and Steven Box[16] focus upon the different way in which corporate crime is perceived and dealt with by the institutions of the Criminal Justice System. Croall and Box argue against some of the commonplace myths around corporate crime, that it is less prevalent and less socially damaging than street crime. They show why crime in its corporate form is not subjected to the same kinds of concerns that surround street crime.

The next two readings have been grouped together under the title of 'strain theory' as they both have a strong relation to the theory of 'strain' as developed by Merton[17]. Although it has been used in different ways, both of the readings use ideas which can be traced back to Merton and which he had, for the most part, gained from Durkheim. Durkheim developed his concept of anomie in relation to division of labour and subsequently suicide. This gave him a partial explanation of criminality.

Leonard[18] takes a critical look at Merton's concept of anomie in relation to gender and crime. Box[19], in his piece entitled 'Why Should Recession Cause Crime to Increase?' addresses the relationship between inequality and crime, showing how different criminologists and sociologists have tackled this issue. He focuses our attention upon the way in which economic changes can give rise to social conditions that are conducive to criminal activity. In order to show the value of the different positions an attempt is made at producing a synthesis of them.

Those articles that consider the relationship between subculture and crime focus upon the insights that can be gained through understanding the meanings which criminal and deviant behaviour have to social actors. The articles by Clarke et al[20] and Dick Hobbs[21] draw attention to the subculture of young working-class males. Their general argument is that criminal activity is not devoid of meaning, but rather gains its meanings through the development of subcultural groups. These groups are ones that transmit alternative values to those who enter into them. Both of the readings argue that one cannot fully understand such subcultural groupings and the meanings that they develop without also taking account of the wider social structures in which they emerge. In particular, it is important to ask why these groups arise out of a working-class culture. Moreover, it is questioned as to how far working-class culture is based upon oppositional values and how far is it based upon a culture that is derived from the dominant culture. These two texts provide somewhat different answers to these questions.

When turning to the labelling approach, we can see the value that the questioning of the meanings of criminal and deviant behaviour has for theorising about its occurrence. Labelling theories focus on the meaning of the act, not so much to the actor but to the social group in which it occurs. Jock Young in 'Thinking Seriously About Crime. . .' gives us a working analysis of the approach. Ken Plummer's 'Misunderstanding Labelling Perspectives'[22] outlines the general approach of labelling theory to the understanding of crime. Plummer also produces a defence of the labelling approach in the light of criticisms that have been made of it. He wants to show that labelling theory is more sophisticated than it is often given credit for and that it is an approach which still has much to offer criminological understanding.

The labelling approach, and that of Becker in particular, concentrates on the application of rules to so-called deviant acts rather than the quality of the act. This means that the act is ignored. Putting a fist in someone's face is an act by itself that the labelling theorists are not interested in: rather Becker wishes to concentrate on the application of the rules following the act. In the case of the act just described it is only when the act is seen in a particular context and certain rules applied that the act becomes meaningful. In the case of the act taking place in the boxing ring then the Queensbury rules apply. What is interesting for the labelling theorist is whether the act violates the Queensbury rules of boxing or not. If, on the other hand, the act takes place in the street then the rules associated with the criminal law will apply. In both examples the act for the labelling theorists only becomes meaningful when there is an application of rules. However, this means that the labelling approach has to cope with the problem of relativism. We have the situation where no particular act can be seen as intrinsically deviant. It seems from the labelling perspective that one act of deviance cannot be distinguished from another. Traffic violation, for example, is seen in the same way as robbery if both are apprehended by the law enforcement agencies. A related criticism comes from the way that they seem to assume that the deviant or criminal is a naive subject. As the New Criminologists[23] say about the labelling approach, the deviants seem not to know when an act is deviant until a label has been imposed upon it.

The other major criticism arises from Becker's concepts of 'secret deviance' and the 'falsely accused'. In the case of the secret deviant this means that the person applies a set of rules to their own act. This means that the secret deviant knows that they are committing a deviant act. The reality of the secret deviant means that the separation of the act and the application of the rules can only be achieved analytically. In the actual case of the secret deviant they are united, because the secret deviant is both aware of performing the act and the application of the rules when that act is performed. The problem of the falsely accused is one where the charge of breaking a rule has been successfully made, but despite this a deviant or criminal act has not occurred, hence the subject is falsely accused. For the labelling theorist this is a problem, because becoming deviant only requires the application of the label following the breaking of a rule. So those individuals who have been successfully labelled as deviant cannot be distinguished from those who have similarly been successfully labelled and who have committed a deviant act. This creates a problem for the labelling theorist because the theory does not help one to understand the difference between the falsely accused and the others. In the real world, for example, black youths who are successfully accused and have committed a criminal act remain analytically the same as those who have not.

Plummer says these criticisms come from the need to reconcile that which cannot be reconciled. That is the idea that deviance is both relativist and absolutist. He believes it is possible to come to terms with the problems associated with the labelling approach, and develops an analytical distinction between (i) 'societal deviance' and (ii) situational deviance.

Societal deviance focuses on the way society has certain expectations of what deviance is. In these cases there is seen to be a consensus about those deviant acts; for example, murder, child molesting, suicide, etc. Situational deviance, on the other hand, focuses on the ways in which individual actors wish to negotiate those deviant labels, and the way other actors try to construct new ways of seeing these acts. Societal deviance is applied to those laws and norms of a society which, if broken, bring about a deviant state. Thus, homosexuality falls under the category of societal deviance. However, those deviants themselves will set up rules that are appropriate for homosexuals and when these rules are broken, those rule-breakers will be seen as deviants. This is a case of situational deviance. So there is a process whereby members of a subculture create rules and determine when they have been broken.

Plummer wants the sociologist to investigate not just the actions of acknowledged deviants, but the ways in which so-called normal actions have deviant actions within them. So, within routine work in the factory, for example, there will be deviant acts.

In the case of drug-takers they are considered to be deviant from the perspective of society. However, from the perspective of their subculture a different set of rules will apply; there will be actions that will be considered normal and there will be those which will be considered deviant. What Plummer is doing is bringing out into the open the complexity of both the constructing and breaking of rules. This can be seen as the strength of labelling theory.

Plummer also wants to show that there are other advantages with the labelling approach. In particular there is the possibility of having a blending of categories, which show us the connections between acts that were formally seen as different. Thus, the owners of unguarded factory machinery that had caused death should be put in the same category as other people who are considered responsible for causing death.

The collection concludes by going back to more general, explanatory models of theorising about crime. Paul Hirst's 'Marx and Engels on Law, Crime and Morality'[24] and Frank Pearce's 'The State, Law and Order in Complex Societies'[25], examine what marxist social theory has to offer to an understanding of crime. Paul Hirst criticizes the 'New Criminology' for its attempts to integrate Marx into criminological theory. He argues that the works of Marx can only be used in relation to the concepts that he defined in his texts, for example modes and relations of production. A specific analysis of crime was not part of Marx's theoretical arguments, and Hirst argues that it is a 'distortion' of Marx's work to use it in such a manner.

Frank Pearce addresses other limitations of the marxist approach to crime. In order to do this Pearce focuses upon the idealism apparent in marxist criminology. This approach to crime assumes that crime would disappear with the advent of socialist relations of production. In order to further the debate Pearce uses the work of Durkheim to raise issues that surround the relationship between human nature and societal type.

There have been new developments since the debate in the 1970s between the New Criminologists and Paul Hirst on the place of marxism within criminological theory. In particular, there has been the emergence of 'realist' criminology. Jock Young's 'The Ten Points of Realism' lays down the principles of the realist approach to understanding crime and is one that is both a synthesis and critique of the history of criminology. Realist approaches attempt to move away from the mono-causal explanations of crime and criminal behaviour. Jock Young sees this mono-causal explanation as being prevalent within the field of criminology. He believes it has been detrimental to a fuller understanding of criminal activity and the development of an appropriate social policy to manage crime.

The theoretical positions presented within these readings often oppose one another. When they are read with the realist approach in mind, one's attention is drawn to important theoretical issues. In particular, those issues that might be overlooked in attempting to provide a single theory of crime. It is a good idea to read this selection in relation to the critical insights that the 'realist' perspective gives us. Perhaps the reason this is particularly important is that those theories that base their practices on the 'natural scientific method' have to limit their frame of reference and field of study in order to come up with clear answers. What this method overlooks is that there are essential issues when attempting to understand crime which are not amenable, clear cut causes.

Acknowledgement

We wish to express our thanks to Elizabeth Lebas and Professor Michael Kelly for their helpful comments on an ealier draft.

Susan Caffrey and Gary Mundy
April 1996

Notes

1. The term 'deviance' is different from the categopry of 'criminal'. Deviance refers to an action or actor who has placed themselves outside the norms of the group to which they belong. This does not necessitate any criminal action as such. For example, a gang member might be considered 'deviant' in terms of the group's norms if they did not involve themselves in criminal behaviour of some kind. 'Deviance' is a sociological category, whereas 'criminal' is primarily a legal one.

2. Young, J. 'Recent Pradigms in Criminology', in Maguire, M. *et al.*, (eds.) *The Oxford Handbook of Criminology*, 1994.

3. Downes, D. & Rock, P. *Understanding Deviance*, Revised 2nd. ed. 1995.

4. Matza, D. 'Correction and Appreciation'.

5. Becker, H. *Outsiders*, 1963.

6. Taylor, I. *et al.*, 'The Appeal of Positivism'.

7. Young, J. 'Thinking Seriously About Crime: Some Models of Criminology'.

8. Matza, D. 'Correction and Appreciation'.

9. Farrington, D.P. 'Human Development and Criminal Careers'.

10. Durkheim, E. *The Rules of Sociological Method*, 1964.

11. Hobbes, T. *Leviathan*, 1957.

12. Box, S. 'Deviance, Latent Functions and Society'.

13. Bianchi, H. 'Abolition: Assensus and Sanctuary'.

14. Sutherland, E. 'A Theory of White Collar Crime'.

15. Croall, H. 'Criminology and the Problem of White Collar Crime'.

16. Box, S. 'Crime, Power and Ideological Mystification'.

17. Merton, R. 'Social Structure and Anomie', in *Social Theory and Social Structure*, 1963.

18. Leonard, E. 'Anomie Theory'.

19. Box, S. 'Why Should Recession Cause Crime to Increase?'.

20. Clarke, J. *et al.*, 'Subcultures, Cultures and Class'.

21. Hobbs, D. 'The Adolescent Entrepreneur: Youth, Style and Cultural Inheritance'.

22. Plummer, K. 'Misunderstandind Labelling Perspectives'.

23. Taylor, I., Walton, P. and Young, J. *The New Criminology*, 1973.

24. Hirst, P. 'Marx and Engels on Law, Crime and Morality'.

25. Pearce, F. 'The State, Law and Order in Complex Societies'.

Bibliography

Becker, H. (1963) *Outsiders: Studies in the Sociology of Deviance*, Free Press, New York.

Durkheim, E. (1964) *The Rules of Sociological Method*, Free Press, New York.

Eysenck, H. (1970) *Crime and Personality*, Paladin, London.

Hobbes, T. (1962) *Leviathan*, Macmillan, New York.

Merton, R. (1963) 'Social Structure and Anomie', in *Social Theory and Social Structure*, Free Press, Glencoe.

Taylor, I., Walton, P. & Young, J. (1973) *The New Criminology*, Routledge & Kegan Paul, London.

Young, J. (1994) 'Incessant Chatter: Recent Paradigms in Criminology', in Maguire, M., Morgan, R. & Reiner, R. (eds.) *The Oxford Handbook of Criminology*, Clarendon Press, Oxford.

Publisher's note

The contents of the readings in this anthology have been reproduced as they appear in the publications from which they are taken. In the majority of cases footnotes are included as are references which are original to this volume. Otherwise, references can be found in the publications in which the readings first appeared.

Early Explanations of Crime

1.   The Appeal of Positivism
Ian Taylor, Paul Walton and Jock Young

Two types of questions can be asked of any theory: what is its explanatory power and what is its appeal? We wish to remove ourselves from that comfortable school of thought which believes that theories compete with each other in some scholarly limbo, heuristic facility being the only test of survival. We need to explain why certain theories, despite their manifest inability to come to terms with their subject-matter, survive — and indeed, as in the case of positivism, flourish. In the [last] chapter we criticized the capacity of positivism to explain deviancy. In this chapter we will, first of all, discuss the appeal of positivism. What benefits does this manner of viewing the social universe have as an ideology for protecting the interests inherent in the *status quo* and distorting the information perceived by its adherents?

We intend, therefore, to elucidate the ideological strengths of the central aspects of positivist thought.

The consensus world view

To insist that there is a consensus in society obviates all discussion of the possibility of fundamental conflicts of value and interest. There is only one reality and deviancy is envisaged as a lack of socialization into it. It is a meaningless phenomenon, the only proper response to which can be therapeutic. In one stroke, ethical questions concerning the present order and the reaction against the deviant are removed, for the humanitarian task of the expert becomes that of bringing the miscreant back into the consensual fold.

The determinism of behaviour

To argue that there is a consensus in society and a determination of behaviour allows the positivist to present an absolute situation (uncomplicated by the exercise of choice) for both normals and deviants. The 'normal man in the street' has no option but to conform, for he is, given his adequate socialization, impelled to do so and as there is only one monolithic reality, no 'choices' exist outside of the consensus. Similarly, the deviant does not choose an alternative mode of life: he is propelled by factors beyond his control. The possible attractiveness of deviant realities is thus subtly defused: for no one could possibly freely choose them. The inevitable deduction from this, that punishment is inappropriate, merely serves to fill the positivist with the sense of his own rationality and humanitarianism.

The science of society

The evocation of natural science presents the positivist with a powerful mode of argument. For the system of thought which produces miracles of technology and medicine is a prestigious banner under which to fight. It grants the positivist the gift

Ian Taylor, Paul Walton and Jock Young: 'The Appeal of Positivism' from THE NEW CRIMINOLOGY (Routledge, 1973), pp. 31–61; 65–66.

of 'objectivity'; it bestows on his pronouncements the mantle of 'truth'; it endows his suggestions of therapy, however threatening to individual rights and dignity, with the air of the inevitable. Thus Eysenck counters criticisms that his behaviourist techniques smack of brainwashing, in the following fashion (1969, p. 690):

> I think the major objection to the proposals I have outlined is that they smack of treating human beings as if they were nothing but biological organisms subject to strictly deterministic rules; this Pavlovian revolution, coming on top of the Copernican and Darwinian ones, is too much for the self-esteem of many people. Undesirable the fact may be, but that is not sufficient reason for rejecting it as a fact, one would need better reasons to change one's scientific judgement. And where there is (1) a recognised social need, and (2) a recognised body of scientific knowledge which looks likely to be able to create a technology to cope with that need, it needs little in the way of precognitive ability to forecast that in the course society will use this knowledge and create this technology.

The meshing of interests

All three of these strands: consensus, determinism and scientism, give weight to positivist rhetoric. What is necessary at this juncture, is to explain why this mode of thought is taken up by the positivist and how the interests of the practitioner and the politician mesh together. It is important, at the outset, to realize that at the simplest level the positivist, by placing himself in the middle of the posited consensus, defends the reality of his own world. For example, Dr R. Cockett (Regional Psychologist to the Home Office Prison Department) writes of working-class drug-takers in the Ashford Remand Centre (1971, p. 142): '[they] were shown to be rather more suspicious and withdrawn than non-drugtakers, more emotionally tense and excitable, and more radical or less conservative in temperament, but to have relatively poor self-sentiment formation — persistence, will-power, social effectiveness and leadership'. This was coupled with: 'less emotional maturity and tolerance of frustration', 'intrapunativeness' and 'a tendency towards paranoid feeling'.

Such 'discoveries' are commonplace in the literature of all forms of deviant behaviour. But behind the neutral language lies, in Cockett's own words, 'what is popularly understood by "inadequacy" and "weakness of character" '(p. 144). It is a simple translation to interpret hedonistic and expressive subcultures as not cultures at all but merely as aggregates of inadequate individuals who are excitable, have a low tolerance of frustration, maturity, etc. Moreover, it is sleight of hand which can conjure what some would term repression into a 'tendency towards paranoid feeling'. All of this reinforces the middle-class professional world of the expert; his stable employment and marriage, deferred gratification and planning are all indices of his own 'strong' personality and social 'adequacy'. By making statements about the deviant he is, inevitably, making valuations about his own world.

Further, the social universe of the expert, like so many others in a complex industrial society, is extremely segregated. He is, therefore, blinkered from receiving information at odds with his world view. As one of the present authors put it (Young, 1971b, pp. 72–3):

The [experts] must explain what is perceived as unusual in terms of the values associated by their audience as usual. In this process, utilising the theoretical ploys listed, they circumscribe and negate the reality of values different from their own. They do not explain, they merely *explain away*. They are well-trained men, but the rigour of their training has enabled them to view the world only from the narrow-blinkered perspective of their own discipline. The fragmentation of knowledge concomitant with specialisation has encouraged the strict compartmentalisation of analysis. . . . As a result such experts can, from the vantage of their cloistered chauvinism, scarcely grasp the totality of the social world even in terms of their own values let alone take a critical stance outside of these values. We are producing what Lucien Goldmann has described as the specialist who is simultaneously illiterate and a graduate of a university.

But ideas do not exist in a vacuum; if there are retailers of ideas there are also buyers; and we must now examine the nexus existing between expert, bureaucrat and politician. The emergence of large-scale bureaucracies in every sphere of social activity has given rise to the demand for co-ordination and predictability within enterprises and the precise determination of consumer and public responses. The 'normal' man must be understood in terms of his roles as consumer and voter. At the same time the emergence of alternative realities outside of the official consensus must be defused of their potential to deny consciously, or unconsciously, the ends of the system they threaten to disrupt.[1] The deviant himself is in a more powerful position in a tightly co-ordinated system. Hans Eysenck recognizes this well, for in an article urging the greater need for social conditioning (1969, p. 688), he backs up his argument by noting a trend which is so 'important and serious . . . that our whole future may rest on our ability to expedite it.' Namely:

What seems to be happening is that society is getting more and more closely knitted together, due to our advancing technology: production is nearing the point where it is nation-wide, particularly in consumer goods like motor cars and such like, and distribution too is getting organized in larger and larger complexes. In other words, there is greater and greater dependence on cooperation between very large groups of people — which do not need to be in close proximity to each other, or even to know of each other's existence. Yet if even a small section within one of the coordinated complexes fails — the tally clerks at the docks, say, or the women sewing covers at Ford's, the whole nexus breaks down, and far-reaching consequences are experienced over a wide area . . . . It is hardly necessary to belabour the main point here made; it is too obvious to require much documentation. The problem to be discussed is: how can we engineer a social consent which will make people behave in a socially adapted, law-abiding fashion, which will not lead to a break-down of the intricately interwoven fabric of social life? Clearly we are failing to do this: the ever-increasing number of unofficial strikes, the ever-increasing statistics of crime of all sorts, the general alienation on which so many writers have commented are voluble witnesses to this statement. The psychologist would answer that what was clearly required was a technology of consent — that is, a generally applicable method of inculcating suitable habits of socialised conduct into the citizens (and particularly the future citizens) of the country in question — or preferably the whole world.

For the politician and the planner, positivism provides a model of human nature which, in its consensual aspects, allows the world 'as it is' to remain unquestioned and, in its determinist notion of human action, offers the possibility of rational planning and control. Thus Jack Douglas (1970, p. 269) writes:

> Positivistic social science provides the administrator of the official organisations with a completely deterministic metaphysics of man and his actions in society. If he chooses to practise the willing suspension of disbelief — to have faith — in the specific theories of this positivistic social science, it also provides him with specific explanations of behaviour which, in combination with deterministic metaphysics, give him a belief that he can *control* the public responses which will be used to judge his own adequacy as an official. At the same time, use of the positivistic social sciences, which always make maximum use of the very prestigious mathematical forms of the natural sciences, provides the official with the very powerful rhetoric of science in justifying his complex ways to the suspicious public. And, if the 'right' effects are not forthcoming from the operations of his agency, he will be well covered by the 'scientific' justifications for the actions with such unfortunate consequences.

The expertise of the positivist comes to be used as scientific justification for political and commercial action and he himself, in line with his own edicts, is bereft of any role in questioning the aims of such activities (Douglas, 1970, p. 267):

> Insofar as social scientists do not initiate and become personally involved in the practical action aimed at solving problems but, rather, await the summons to involvement from men of practical affairs, they not only allow but force the men of practical affairs to define the problems, define the relevance of the social scientists, *define which social scientists* are to be consulted, define the structure of the advising situation, and then, most importantly, force them to pick and choose from that advice those parts which they can interpret in some way which 'helps' them, as they see it, to construct their intended course of practical action. Because of this, it is actually the metaphysics of everyday life or practical affairs which determines most of the impact of the social sciences on everyday life. What has normally happened so far, and what threatens to become even more prevalent, is that the men of practical affairs make use through this consulting process of the prestige of expert scientific knowledge in our society to achieve the goals which they set by the means which they determine: they use the social sciences as a front which helps them to control public opinions and, hence, public responses to what they intend to do.

In other words, during the course of the late nineteenth and early twentieth century, positivism has become institutionalized. Alex Comfort (1967) has pointed out how the growth of the medical profession has been accompanied by intervention in moral and personal spheres which are beyond the jurisdiction of the medical practitioner. C. Wright Mills (1943) has shown how the growth of the social work profession, sustained and infused with the terminology of psychoanalysis and other deterministic ideologies, has resulted in the translation of public issues into private problems. It is of no small significance that psychoanalysis, one of the major ideologies of an institutionalized positivism, was produced as a direct outgrowth of the medical profession, specifically as a result of the dissatisfaction of thinkers trained in the medical tradition (like Freud himself): since psychoanalysis, for all that it is a break with simple medical thought, remains impregnated with biological and physiological assumptions.

Thus, Freud's aim was to reduce explanations of pathology to explanations of neurophysiology. He believed, for instance, that schizophrenia was genetically determined; whilst even the more radical Reich, who combined his medical and psychoanalytical training with some grounding in a Marxist humanism, refused to treat homosexuals on similar grounds. Gouldner, in a recent attack on 'welfare state sociology' (1968), has argued that American sociology — whether traditionally positivist or 'sceptical' — serves the important social and political function of displacing, in the process of making amenable for research and policy, the structures of power, domination and control.

The positivist's epistemological split between facts and values thus corresponds to his institutional role in society (cf. I. Taylor and Walton, 1970). In this his interests are well served, for, as Dennis Chapman astutely notes (1968, p. 23), to challenge the consensual definitions of crime and deviancy is to invite heavy penalties. . . . 'The penalties are: To be isolated from the mainstream of professional activity, to be denied resources for research, and to be denied official patronage with its rewards in material and status.'

Yet if such a philosophy has its uses for the politicians, this does not mean it is accepted wholeheartedly by them. Rather, it is used to back up arguments and proposals, it is selected for quotation at the appropriate, strategic time and place. For there is a fundamental conflict between the free will classicist's models held to by the legal profession and the determinist notions of the psychiatrist and the social worker. Total determinism palpably contradicts the 'feel' of human existence. More importantly, from the perspective of those in control, it is in contradiction with democratic ideology — given its implicit assumptions of moral choice, free selection of employment and rational voting for political candidates, etc. Determinism is, in the last analysis, from the social control point of view, a dangerous doctrine, for it removes from individuals the sense of striving towards the 'good' behaviour. As we shall see later, it tends to obliterate the distinction between what is (behavioural norms) and what should be (prescriptive norms). Other people (the therapist and the expert) can change 'what is' in the direction of what they perceive as 'what should be'. But the individual is not accountable for his actions and he is not likely on his own accord to change his behaviour without parallel change in significant determining factors (environmental or genetic). The resolution of the conflict between free will and determinism is achieved by the adoption of what we have termed neo-classicism. Namely, a qualitative distinction is made between the majority who are seen as capable of free choice and the minority of deviants who are determined.

We wish to turn, now, to the evolution of positivism and to the reasons for the emergence and continuing appeal of biological positivism in particular. The first attempts to tackle the problem of crime scientifically were social rather than biological. The transition between classicism and positivism was largely effected by the 'moral statisticians', Quetelet and Guerry, and is well exemplified in Guerry's assertion, made in 1863 (p. lvii), that:

> The time has gone by when we could claim to regulate society by laws established solely on metaphysical theories and a sort of ideal type which was thought to conform to absolute justice. Laws are not made for men in the abstract, for humanity in general, but for real men, placed in precisely determined circumstances.

Quetelet (a Belgian mathematician of wide intellectual concerns) and Guerry (a French lawyer) working independently, but almost simultaneously, had drawn very similar conclusions from the publication from 1827 onwards, of the first sets of national criminal statistics (in France). As the figures continued to be published, on an annual basis, it became more and more clear to Quetelet and Guerry, first, that the annual totals of recorded crime remained extraordinarily constant, and, second, that the contribution of the various types of crime to the annual total fluctuated hardly at all.

Such a discovery carried with it the clear implication that (officially recorded) crime was a regular feature of social activity, as distinct from being the product of individual (and therefore arbitrary) propensities to asocial activity. There was, then, some fundamental feature of the existing social arrangements that gave rise to regular outcomes; so that it must be possible, theoretically, to specify the causes with a view to eliminating the outcome. Quetelet's 'social physics' and Guerry's 'moral statistical analysis' were concerned, above all, therefore, with specifying the relationship between different features of the social arrangements and different (especially criminal) outcomes. In this respect, they have been said to have provided the groundwork for the much more thoroughgoing revolution in theory undertaken by Emile Durkheim some few years later.[2]

The work of Quetelet and Guerry stemmed from the publication of social statistics, these in turn being a reflection of concern with social unrest (cf. Morris, 1957, ch. 3). For the next half-century, the analysis of crime was in a sociological vein, ranging from the work of Mayhew to Bonger[3] and the audience was concerned with reform. Then, in 1876, Cesare Lombroso published *L'Uomo Delinquente* and the whole focus of analysis drastically changed from the social to the individual. As Lindesmith and Levin (1937, p. 661) put it:

> What Lombroso did was to reverse the method of explanation that had been current since the time of Guerry and Quetelet and, instead of

maintaining that institutions and traditions determined that nature of the criminal, he held that the nature of the criminal determined the character of institutions and traditions.

Indeed Terence Morris (1957, p. 41) has argued that:

> The founding of a school of 'criminal anthropology' seems to have resulted in the total or near total eclipse of the work of sociologists in the criminological field. The genetic theories of crime which have been subsequently replaced by psychological theories of crimes seem to have excited so much interest that sociological theories, particularly in Europe, have been of secondary importance.

What caused this phenomenon? Lindesmith and Levin note how the genetic theories of Lombroso fitted in well with the rise of Darwinism. *The Origin of the Species* had been published in 1859 and Darwinian concepts had been applied in a wholesale manner throughout the social sciences. But, fundamentally, it involved the movement of the medical man into the field of crime with the corresponding ousting of the sociologically inclined (Lindesmith and Levin, 1937, pp. 668–9):

> The growth of the Lombrosian myth is to be accounted for, basically, not so much in terms of the acceptance or rejection of theories or methods of research as in terms of a changing personnel. After Lombroso's attempt to appropriate criminology to biology and medicine had attracted wide publicity in Europe, physicians and psychiatrists were attracted to the problem in greater numbers and gradually displaced in public attention and prestige the magistrates, prison authorities, lawyers, philanthropists, journalists, and social scientists who had previously dominated the field, although it should be noted that physical factors in crime had been noted and studied long before Lombroso made his abortive attempt to make them the sole or the chief causes. The Lombrosian myth arose, therefore, as a result of the 'seizure of power', so to speak, by the medical profession. Medical men compiled medical bibliographies and traced the history of criminology as a branch of medicine through the works of Gall, Lavater, Pinel, Morel, Esquirol, Maudsley, etc., ignoring the voluminous sociological literature. Sociologists have uncritically accepted this medical conception of the history of criminology, and they too have ignored the older sociological tradition of Guerry and Quetelet.

This would seem to be an accurate appraisal of events with the proviso that, as we have argued, the positivist movement was severely curtailed by the classicist positions of both lawyers and politicians. It was sociological positivism (not magistrates, lawyers and prison authorities) which was ousted. Lindesmith and Levin (1937, p. 670) proceed to answer a more fundamental question: why was support for such a seizure so forthcoming:

> For more than a century before criminal anthropology came into existence society's responsibility for its criminal classes had been recognised and embodied in the legislation of all civilised countries. It may be that the

theory of the born criminal offered a convenient rationalisation of the failure of preventive effort and an escape from the implications of the dangerous doctrine that crime is an essential product of our social organisation. It may well be that a public, which had been nagged for centuries by reformers, welcomed the opportunity to slough off its responsibilities for this vexing problem.

Leon Radzinowicz (1966, pp. 38–9) concurs with this and clearly indicates the superior ideological efficacy of biological positivism:

> This way of looking at crime as the product of society was hardly likely to be welcome, however, at a time when a major concern was to hold down the 'dangerous classes'. The concept of the dangerous classes as the main source of crime and disorder was very much to the fore at the beginning of the nineteenth century. They were made up of those who had so miserable a share in the accumulating wealth of the industrial revolution that they might at any time break out in political revolt as in France. At their lowest level was the hard core of parasites to be found in any society, ancient or modern. And closely related to this, often indistinguishable from it, were the 'criminal classes'.
>
> It served the interests and relieved the conscience of those at the top to look upon the dangerous classes as an independent category, detached from the prevailing social conditions. They were portrayed as a race apart, morally depraved and vicious, living by violating the fundamental law of orderly society, which was that a man should maintain himself by honest, steady work. In France they were commonly described as nomads, barbarians, savages, strangers to the customs of the country. English terminology was, perhaps, less strong and colourful, but the meaning was fundamentally similar.

Biological determinism, then, has a greater appeal than sociological positivism in that it removes any suggestion that crime may be the result of social inequalities. It is something essential in the nature of the criminal and not a malfunctioning of society. In addition, it achieves the utter decimation of the possibility of alternative realities. For the biologically inferior is used synonymously with the asocial. The analysis focuses on the individual who is unable to be social; thus atomized, he poses no threat to the monolithic reality central to positivism. For no individual alone can create an alternative reality and his asocial nature ensures that he is a mere blemish on conventional reality.

We need to examine briefly several examples of biological positivism in brief before turning to a fuller discussion of the work of Hans Eysenck and the derivative theory of Gordon Trasler. Eysenck will be dealt with in detail, and his theory used as the exemplar of biological positivism — its most developed formulation. We shall be concerned there to examine both the ideological appeal and the explanatory sufficiency of the most sophisticated statement in this whole tradition. It is our contention that Eysenck's breadth of approach and complexity of argument make him the most worthy twentieth-century successor to Lombroso. First, then, let us turn to Lombroso, and to the minor theorists working in his tradition.

Lombroso

Cesare Lombroso, the founding father of the biological positivist school, is best known for his notion of the atavistic criminal. These born criminals were seen to be reversions to earlier evolutionary periods, and to earlier levels of organic development. Atavism was suggested first by Darwin (1871, p. 137) when he wrote: 'With mankind some of the worst dispositions which occasionally without any assignable cause make their appearance in families, may perhaps be reversions to a savage state, from which we are not removed by many generations.'

Lombroso first claimed to have discovered the 'secret' of criminality when he was examining the skull of the famous brigand Vihella. He described his flash of inspiration in the following terms (1911, p. xiv):

> This was not merely an idea, but a flash of inspiration. At the sight of that skull, I seemed to see all of a sudden, lighted up as a vast plain under a flaming sky, the problem of the nature of the criminal — an atavistic being who reproduces in his person the ferocious instincts of primitive humanity and the inferior animals. Thus were explained anatomically the enormous jaws, high cheek bones, prominent superciliary arches, solitary lines in the palms, extreme size of the orbits, handle-shaped or sensile ears found in criminals, savages and apes, insensibility to pain, extremely acute sight, tattooing, excessive idleness, love of orgies, and the irresistible craving for evil for its own sake, the desire not only to extinguish life in the victim, but to mutilate the corpse, tear its flesh and drink its blood.

Atavistic man could be recognised by a series of physical stigmata: abnormal dentition, asymmetry of face, supernumerary nipples, toes, fingers, large ears, eye defects, inverted sex characteristics, tattooing, etc. Lombroso compared criminals to control groups of soldiers and found significant differences in the incidence of such stigmata. In a later investigation of the anatomical characteristics of anarchists, he found that 31 per cent of his sample in Paris, 40 per cent in Chicago, and 34 per cent in Turin had stigmata whereas in the ranks of other 'extremist' political movements under 12 per cent were found to have such 'blemishes'.

His theory was first spelt out in *L'Uomo Delinquente* in 1876 but by the time of the publication in 1897 of the fifth edition, he, in the face of criticism, was insisting less strongly on the atavistic nature of all criminality. The born criminal as such was in the minority: to this atavistic type were now to be added:

(a) the epileptic criminal

(b) the insane criminal

(c) a large corps of occasional criminals who may have a trace of atavism and degeneration, may be precipitated into crime by association with criminal elements, or may have poor education, or may be inspired by patriotism, love, honour or political ideals.

In the face of criticism, Lombroso hinted at (and sometimes expanded on) a large number of 'environmental influences'. Moreover, like all thoroughgoing positivists, he was willing to see the influence of atavism or degeneracy as a matter of degree. As we argued in [chapter 1], the sharp distinction between criminal and non-criminal (the idea of differentiation that Matza alleges to be characteristic of criminological positivism) is often ruled out in relatively sophisticated positivist accounts — largely as a result of their concern for quantification.

The major shortcomings of Lombrosian theory can be summarized as follows:

Technical

Lombroso's statistical techniques (reflecting the level of development in the mathematics of his time) were totally inadequate. His results have been shown, repeatedly, to be statistically insignificant (cf. Goring, 1913).

Physical stigmata

It has been often remarked, and demonstrated, that physical stigmatization is often the direct result of social environment, for example, of poor nutrition. Tattooing, which is perhaps Lombroso's most laughable example, is clearly the result of cultural fashions which have tended to have been concentrated in the lower classes (i.e., amongst those most 'at risk' of criminal apprehension).

Genetic theory

Modern genetic theory has totally ruled out the possibility of an evolutionary throwback to earlier more primitive species.

Social evaluation

Individuals with pronounced physical stigmata may be evaluated differently from those without such visible markings by others in the course of ongoing social interaction. A self-fulfilling prophecy, therefore, in which the individual carries out the other's expectations of him, is entirely possible (Goffman, 1968, ch. 4). Further, as one recent English study has shown (Walsh, 1969), individuals who are generally socially stigmatized in this fashion tend to be more likely to be arrested.

Crime rates

Biological variation alone cannot begin to explain the variation in crime rates (e.g., across cultures, time and class) and has nothing to offer in the explanation of how (and why) law arises.

Body types in biological positivism

A direct derivative of Lombroso's work is the investigation of the relationship between criminality and body shape. Pioneers in this field were Ernst Kretschmer (1921) and William Sheldon (1940).

Building on Kretschmer's endeavours, Sheldon differentiated between three body types: the endomorphic (soft and round), the mesomorphic (hard and round) and the ectomorphic (fragile and thin). He argued that a particular temperament corresponded to each of these individual types: the endomorph being predominantly slow, comfort-loving and extraverted; the mesomorph aggressive and active; and the ectomorph self-restrained and introverted.[4] A statistically significant application of Sheldon's typology by the Gluecks (1950; 1956) found that there were twice as many mesomorphs amongst delinquents than could have occurred by chance, and half as many ectomorphs. In Germany a more recent development of this kind of theory by Klaus Conrad (1963) studied the percentage changes in body build as a child grows up. He calculated head to body length against age, and found that, on average, children were more mesomorphic and adults more ectomorphic.[5] Thus, adult mesomorphs were said to resemble children of a mean age of eight years whereas ectomorphs more resembled adults. Conrad concluded that mesomorphs are on a lower level of 'ontogenetic development' than ectomorphs. This notion of level of ontogenetic development is reminiscent of Lombrosian 'atavism'. Conrad further suggested that mesomorphs are more immature psychologically — and, in this, his theory goes close to that of Eysenck who also utilizes the notion of body shape and quotes Conrad's results approvingly.[6]

The criticisms of this school centre around the social origins of body type: the ways in which a particular somatype is to be explained. It may well be that lower-working-class children, who are more likely to be found in the criminal statistics, are also by virtue of diet, continual manual labour, physical fitness and strength, more likely to be mesomorphic than ectomorphic. Further, it is probably also the case that admission to delinquent subcultures is dependent on bodily appearance. As Don Gibbons (1968, p. 134) puts it:

> It could be argued that delinquent subcultures recruit new members selectively, placing a premium upon agile, muscular boys . . . excessively fat or overtly thin and sickly youngsters make poor candidates for the rough and tumble world of delinquent behaviour, so they are excluded. . . . If so, this is a social process, not a biologically determined pattern of behaviour.

The fact that many of the studies in this tradition have used inmates as subjects (and come up with significant results) may, of course, reflect only a tendency for mesomorphs to be incarcerated more than ectomorphs.[7]

The XYY chromosome theory[8]

A recent and well-publicized genetic theory of crime attempts to establish a connection between the possession of an XYY set chromosome complement and criminality.

The normal complement of chromosomes for the female is XX and for the male XY. However, in rare cases, a chromosome may be absent, or there may be additional chromosomes. For example, the combination XXY occurs 1.3 times per 1,000 male babies and XYY, 1.0 times per 1,000 male babies. In a very few instances, the combinations XYYY, XXYY and XXXYY occur.[9]

The first sex chromosome abnormality to be investigated was that of XXY males. Termed 'Klinefelter's Syndrome', this complement was found to be associated with the degeneration of testes during adolescence, with low intelligence and to be over-represented amongst inmates of institutions for the subnormal.

It was generally believed that because XXYY cases appeared to manifest traits similar to Klinefelter's Syndrome (i.e., XXY), and that, because XYY cases had mild mental defects, the extra Y chromosome was of very little significance. Then, in 1962, Court Brown found that the rate of delinquency amongst his patients who had sex chromosomal abnormalities was significantly high (p. 508). In Sheffield, Casey *et al.* (1966), following up this suggestion, searched for sex chromosome abnormalities amongst mentally abnormal patients, institutionalized in special security conditions and thought to be potentially criminal. They found twice as many sex chromosome abnormalities amongst this population as amongst 'normal defectives', and ten times as many as in the 'normal' population. But, most significantly, a large proportion had XXYY chromosomes. Now since the excess of sex chromosome abnormalities in these institutions could almost wholly be accounted for by the XXYY cases, it seemed that such patients had a special tendency to be delinquent. It was also noted that they were unusually tall.

Since in these respects these patients had the features of the more common XXY Klinefelter's Syndrome, it could be deduced that the extra height and the greater delinquency involvement was a product of the extra Y chromosome (which constituted the difference between XXY abnormality and XXYY aberrations of these particular patients).

On this assumption, Price *et al* (1966, p. 565)[10] undertook chromosome counts on all available male patients in a special security institution in Scotland and found that XYY males were (a) not physically exceptional except in terms of height, (b) that their genitalia appeared to be well developed (in contrast to Klinefelter's Syndrome), and (c) that there was some evidence of slight mental deficiency. Since there was evidence of abnormal height amongst XXX females, it was concluded that the *extra* Y chromosome was responsible for increasing an individual's height.

In a subsequent investigation (1967, pp. 533–6), Price's team found that those patients with an extra Y chromosome tended, first, to be severe psychopaths; second, to be convicted at a younger age than other psychopaths; third, to commit crimes against property rather than against the person; and, finally, to come from backgrounds where there was no real evidence of crime. The extra Y chromosome, therefore, seemed to be positively linked to increased height and psychopathy.

The XYY sex chromosome theory is extraordinary in that it makes the remarkable claim to be able to pinpoint the precise genetic basis for a particular criminal disposition. In all other respects it is manifestly a very crude theory which (unlike the version of biological positivism expounded by Eysenck) does not even attempt to explain or even to indicate the mechanisms whereby these genetic differences are translated into behavioural differences (i.e., into different orientations to social action). The theory is also very restrictive in that its explanations — such as they are — apply only to a tiny proportion of all offenders.[11]

The limitations of sex chromosome abnormality theory are similar to the limitations of theories of body-type. As Hunter astutely pointed out in a letter to the *Lancet* (1966, p. 984):

Even if their behaviour was no more aggressive than XXY males, it might be that because of their great height and build they would present such a frightening picture that the courts and psychiatrists would be biased to direct them to special hospitals for community safety. The bias might be further aggravated by the associated intellectual abnormality. This factor might find expression in the raised incidence of XYY (and XXYY) males in special hospital groups.

Sarbin and Miller (1970) have pointed to the failure of the 'chromosomal theorists' to distinguish between the *efficient* causes of crime (the antecedents of the individual's performance of the illegal act) and the *formal* cause (the reasons for particular acts being stamped as illegal in the first place). As Lemert has argued elsewhere (1967, ch. 5), these two types of cause are only transitively related — the reasons for a person committing a criminal act may be entirely different in order and significance from the reasons for a particular law-breaker being arrested.

Sarbin and Miller point to the widespread occurrence of criminality throughout the population — and to the fact that one of the central concerns in contemporary criminology is an investigation of the processes of selection and sifting which result in only a small proportion of law-breakers being apprehended as such. It just is not possible to tell whether XYY chromosome males commit more illegal acts than XY (i.e., 'normal') males, until we are able to specify whether sex chromosome abnormalities are a part of the efficient or the formal 'causes' of crime. In fact, sex chromosomal theorists leave the formal causes of crime unexamined: and the formal causes may include what the police perceive as 'dangerousness'[12] — and thus relate (as Hunter suggested) to excessive height and mental defectiveness. It could also be the case, Sarbin and Miller suggest, that the number of XYY males located in the working class is disproportionately high (for reasons no one has explained):[13] if this is the case, then the fact that there is a disproportionate representation of XYY males in institutions may merely reflect the tendency of the police to apprehend working-class males (and the class-based nature of the law itself).

But this type of analysis alone, pertinent as it is, is essentially static. The bizarre appearance and behaviour of XYY males may be inextricably involved, in dialectical fashion, with the social labelling and stigmatization they experience; and their exclusion from 'normal' social interaction may (along with material deprivation associated with such handicaps) make it more likely that they will be attracted to illegitimate or illegal alternatives. That is, stigmatization of XYY individuals (the formal causes of *deviancy*) eventually engenders crime (the efficient causes of *deviancy*) — which, because of their unusual appearance, makes them more likely than other law-breakers to be arrested (the formal causes of *crime*). In short, biological abnormality is interpreted in such a fashion that is likely to result in the stigmatized person reacting to those who are responsible for interpreting his abnormality in a deviant fashion. Biological factors enter into crime only in an indirect respect: the crucial mediation which goes unexamined in positivistic accounts is the interpretation placed on biological characteristics.

15

We turn now to a biological theory which is a considerable advance on the theories just discussed. Both in analysing the mechanisms by which genetic potentialities are translated into criminal behaviour in particular, and social action in general, and in fully acknowledging the interplay of environmental factors, Hans Eysenck's formulations have a distinct advantage over other biological interpretations of society. Eysenck has extended his attention over a wide range of issues, and, in so doing, has allowed us the opportunity of discussing the fundamental attributes of biological positivism in its most developed form, namely its conception of human nature, social order, deviant behaviour and scientific method.

Eysenck

Conception of human nature

Man's primary motivation is the pursuit of pleasure and the avoidance of pain; to this extent Eysenck is in agreement with the classicist philosophers. He differs, however, in his dismissal of free will and rationality in human actors. For the stumbling block to this utilitarian notion of motivation is that the punishment of crime — by the inflicting of pain proportional to its consequences (as we have seen in Beccaria) — does not, in fact, eliminate criminality. The task of modern psychology, according to Eysenck, is to refurbish classical hedonism with positivistic refinements. First, he notes what he terms the principle of immediacy (1969, p. 689):

> To talk about a balance between pain and pleasure, as far as the consequences of a particular act are concerned, is similar to talking about two weights at opposite sides of a fulcrum; we need to consider not only the weights themselves but also the distance from the fulcrum at which they are suspended. A light weight far from the fulcrum may pull down a heavy one near it. In the case of pain and pleasure, what we have to consider is the temporal contiguity of these two resultant states to the action which produces them; the nearer in point of time the consequences are to the action, the more powerfully will they determine future actions. Thus an action followed by a small but immediate gratification will tend to be repeated, even though it is followed by a large but delayed painful consequence.

'Thus the negative effects of punishment are very much attenuated by the long period of time elapsing between crime and retribution. Furthermore, while the positive consequences of crime are fairly certain, the negative ones are very much less so' (Eysenck, 1965, p. 259). After all, as Eysenck points out, only a small proportion of crimes are cleared up and the chances of avoiding detection are often considerable. Man is seen here as a short-term hedonist; live today and enjoy yourself for you never know what tomorrow will bring.

What, then, can the positivist offer as a reasonable alternative in the control of crime? For punishment, because of its distance from the criminal deed and its probabilistic nature, has been manifestly ineffective. Eysenck (1965, pp. 260–1) turns to a concept of a distinctly non-utilitarian kind: the conscience. But he defuses it of any connotation of a striving towards values which are pursued for their own sake. Rather:

How does conscience originate? Our contention will be that conscience is simply a conditioned reflex. . . . What happens is that the young child, as he grows up, is required to learn a number of actions which are not, in themselves, pleasant or pleasurable and which in fact go counter to his desires and wishes. He has to learn to be clean and not to defecate and urinate whenever and wherever he pleases; he has to suppress the overt expression of his sexual and aggressive urges; he must not beat other children when they do things he does not like; he must learn not to take things which do not belong to him. In every society there is a long list of prohibitions of acts which are declared to be bad, naughty, and immoral, and which, although they are attractive to him and are self-rewarding, he must nevertheless desist from carrying out. As we have pointed out before, this is not likely to be achieved by any formal process of long-delayed punishment, because what is required to offset the immediate pleasure derived from the activity must be an immediate punishment which is greater than the pleasure and, if possible, occurs in closer proximity to the crime. In childhood it is possible for parents, teachers and other children to administer such punishment at the right moment of time; the child who does something wrong is immediately slapped, told off, sent upstairs, or whatever the punishment may be. Thus we may regard the evil act itself as the conditioned stimulus and we may regard the punishment — the slap, the moral shaming, or whatever the punishment may be — as the unconditioned stimulus which produces pain or, at any rate, some form of suffering and, therefore, of sympathetic response. On the principle of conditioning, we would now expect that after a number of repetitions of this kind, the act itself would produce the conditioned response; in other words, when the child is going to carry out one of the many activities which have been prohibited and punished in the past, then the conditioned autonomic response would immediately occur and produce a strong deterrent, being, as it were, unpleasant in itself. Thus the child would be faced with a choice between carrying on, obtaining the desired object but, at the same time (and perhaps even earlier), suffering from the unpleasant punishment administered by its conditioned autonomic system, or desisting from carrying out the act and thus avoiding this punishment. Provided that the conditioning process had been carried out efficiently and well, it is predictable, on psychological principles, that the choice would lie in the direction of desisting rather than carrying out the act. Thus the child acquires, as it were, an 'inner policeman' to help in controlling his atavistic impulses and to supplement the ordinary police force which is likely to be much less efficient and much less omnipresent.

This conception of conscience allows for the inbuilt punishments of the autonomic nervous system: anxiety and alarm, of which the classicists and criminologists were unaware. Thus behaviour is seen to be acquired in two ways:

(a) *learning* which is based on simple hedonism and involves the central nervous system. Problems are solved rationally through reinforcement: that which leads to pleasure is positively reinforced and those activities which give rise to pain are reinforced negatively. (This corresponds to *instrumental or operant conditioning*.) As we have seen the propinquity of pleasure is a major determinant of positive reinforcement.

(b)   *conditioning. Classical conditioning* operates not by direct reinforcement but by contiguity, and involves the autonomic nervous system. As we see from the last quotation, activities pleasurable in themselves are associated in a reflex fashion with unpleasurable autonomic experience.[14]

Therefore man's voluntary, rational activity comes to be seen as being solely concerned with the satisfaction of his individual and pre-social desires. The implementation of such impulses is learnt in a trial and error fashion, success bringing forth the positive reinforcement of the behaviour, and failure the negative (the so-called 'law of effect'). The model of learning is Darwinian in its mindlessness. The reason is the seat of striving for pleasure, as it were, a cunning which schemes to maximize its immediate satisfactions and minimize its pains. The conscience is a passive reflex which unthinkingly checks these hedonistic impulses by virtue of autonomic distress. A strange model of man, this, where reason has become the seat of the passions and conscience relegated to the viscera!

The ideological nature of this model is immediately apparent. What is pleasurable (the good) is unquestioned: it is a biological given which the organism will attempt to maximize. What restrictions occur are not created by the actors themselves but derive mysteriously from the normative order as it is. Man does not generate his own rules and oppose the rules of others, he is active only in that he attempts to reduce the tensions of displeasure and his desires for satisfaction.

Thus as far as the specific individual is concerned, his desires are not formulated by him, neither is the ability to curb them under his own control. His cathectic focus on certain objects is a function of 'rational learning', his inability to avoid 'anti-social' activities a result of lack of conditioning. The degree to which a person has been conditioned to avoid 'anti-social' behaviour is central to Eysenck's explanation of criminality. The measure of this conditioning is dependent on two variables:

(a)   the sensitivity of the autonomic nervous system which he has inherited.

(b)   the quality of the conditioning that he has received within his family in terms of their efficiency in utilizing adequate conditioning techniques.

Thus on top of the genetic potential of the person to become fully social is *added* the environmental variable of family of origin. It is noteworthy that both of these factors are sited in the early life of the individual. The ideological leverage of this is to deflect criticisms aimed at the origins of deviancy away from the present to the past history of the person or group concerned.

The differences in the autonomic nervous system give rise to variations in the individual's ability to be conditioned. That is, individuals range between those in whom it is easy to *excite* conditioned reflexes and whose reflexes are difficult to *inhibit,* to those whose reflexes are difficult to condition and easy to extinguish. This corresponds to Eysenck's major personality dimension of introversion to extraversion.[15] Once formed, by the end of early childhood, a biological potentiality is set up, measurable as a point on the introversion–extraversion continuum, which will determine the individual's propensity to crime.

In contrast to this, we wish to argue that man's action is not a mere attempt at reducing the tension between socialized desires and conditioned prohibitions: that an essential human characteristic is that man is both the product and the producer of society. At times he accepts, at times he reinterprets, at times he transcends and resists existing values. Much of his action in fact may be seen as tension-heightening rather than tension-reducing, in that he may find it necessary to act against social disapproval and early conditioning (negative reinforcement) in order to fulfil his ideals.[16]

The central and autonomic nervous systems are undoubtedly involved in the learning process — to deny this would be to deny that man has a body. But reason is not merely a set of deterministic reflexes — rather it is a consciousness of the world, an ability of the individual to give meaning to his universe, both to interpret and to creatively change the existing moral order. Man's reason, rather than being a conditioned amorality, is a conscious optimizing of choices. Similarly, autonomic responses of a conditioned nature doubtless occur but their meaning is dictated to by consciousness. A man may well feel autonomic anxiety when faced with the opportunity to steal and this may have been a product of early socialization but his action will take various courses — not necessarily of a tension-reducing nature. Thus he may:

(a)   feel anxiety and consciously agree that such an action is amoral, and, therefore, refuse to steal;

(b)   feel anxiety and consciously decide that despite all, stealing in this case is justified and, therefore, go ahead and steal despite autonomic distress;

(c)   feel anxiety and consciously (over time) resocialize himself into ridding himself of the 'hangovers' from his initial socialization.

As Gordon Allport (1955, pp. 34–5) suggests:

> The truth of the matter . . . is that the moral sense and life-styles of most people reach far beyond the confines of domestic and community mores in which they were first fashioned. If we look into ourselves we observe that our tribal morality seems to us somehow peripheral to our personal integrity. True, we obey conventions of modesty, decorum, and self-control, and have many habits that fashion us in part as mirror-images of our home, class, and cultural ways of living. But we know that we have selected, reshaped, and transcended these ways to a marked degree.

and again (p. 71):

> While applicable to the early stages of the growth of conscience, this theory is not convincing for later stages. For one thing, it is not often the violation of tribal taboos or of parental prohibitions that makes us as

adults feel most guilty. We now have our private codes of virtue and sin; and what we feel guilty about may have little relation to the habits of obedience we once learned. If conscience were merely a matter of self-punishment for breaking an established habit taught with authority, then we could not account for the fact that we do often discard codes imposed by parents and by culture, and devise codes of our own.

It is a failing in sociological theory that it has rarely examined concepts such as guilt and conscience. For this reason it exposes a weak flank both to behaviourist and Freudian critiques. It is therefore urgently necessary to distinguish between the reflexive guilt of an autonomic nature and the guilt arising from conflict of consciously embraced values and expedient behaviour.

Lastly, the phenomenon of expediency must be seen in the light, not of the failure of internal prohibitions learnt in the past, but as the avoidance of sanctions of a present and external nature. That is, the social reaction of the powerful bent on protecting their interests by the manipulation of material and social rewards. 'Positive and negative reinforcements' are not the autonomic response of a 'taken-for-granted' universe to conformity or deviation but meaningful attempts of the powerful to maintain and justify the *status quo* of wealth and interest.

Social order

Eysenck is faced with the problem of where the rules of society come from and how is it that society manages not to degenerate into a 'war of all against all'. Translated into his own terms: Who decides what is to be positively and negatively reinforced? This is the Achilles Heel of all individualistic utilitarian theory. Eysenck would not maintain that the pleasurable and the painful is derivative from inate biological drives. He is only too aware of the relative nature of human desires and likes.[17] They differ from society to society (1953, p. 179):

> The tendency to regard certain forms of conduct as natural and biologically innate is not logically absurd. It seems to be based in many cases, however, on an erroneous identification of that which is natural with that which is current in our society. This tendency to regard as natural (instinctively innate) that with which we are familiar is brought out very clearly in certain animal studies. We regard as instinctive and natural, for instance, the behaviour of cats who catch and kill mice and rats and feed on them. We may not regard this as ideal behaviour — in many cases we disapprove of a well-fed cat killing birds and other animals for no apparent purpose — but we regard this behaviour as innate and therefore natural and normal. Yet the evidence is fairly conclusive that it is nothing of the kind.

If values vary, then, presumably they must relate to the nature of the society within which they have evolved. A strict biological determinism would relate this either to racial characteristics or to a social Darwinian position concerned with the potentiality for human survival. But Eysenck is more sophisticated than this, for in 'The technology of consent' (1969, p. 690) (which we examined earlier in this chapter), he was willing to give social factors their due, arguing that human behaviour must be patterned around the technological imperatives of a society with a high division of labour: 'I think these developments are essential however, if society is to survive under the technological conditions created by physical and chemical science.'

Society, he constantly argues, is failing to adapt in a rational manner to the problems which face it. It is too permissive in its child-rearing practices (he is very critical of Dr Spock) and above all, it will not implement the conclusions of a scientific psychology. Thus he writes (1953, p. 175):

> Not so many have realised that a whole new approach to social and political problems may be in the making, an approach based on factual knowledge of human nature rather than on hypothetical beliefs and preconceived notions. Political parties generally seem to have exhausted the dynamic which once motivated them, and are looking around for new ideas and new conceptions. Might it not be that these new ideas and conceptions are to be found in a realistic appraisal of the potentialities, abilities, attitudes, and motives of the human beings who make up society? Where there is so much agreement among all parties about the *aims* of society, should not the disputes about *means* be handed over to scientific investigation? The solution of social problems can in principle at least be found in the same way as the solution to physical and chemical problems; we do not determine the atomic weight of gold, or the size of the moon, or the spectral colour of hydrogen by a counting of heads, and there appears no ground for assuming such a method to be any more effective in arriving at correct decisions about industrial productivity, or motivation, or other psychological problems.

Thus, for Eysenck in particular, and biological positivists in general, there is a general consensus in society and an élite which is capable of understanding the 'real' nature of human motivation.

Eysenck is critical of the *laissez-faire* nature of the social order and the pursuit of immediate satisfactions rather than their scientifically planned solution. His quarrel, it would seem, is with the very characteristics of human nature that he has empirically discovered. But he is a constant pessimist in that he believes untold blunders have been made in planning enterprises which did not conform to the basic 'facts' of human nature. Man will always pursue immediate pleasure unless he is conditioned to do otherwise. But who, then, are to be the far-seeing, 'unnatural' men who are able to transcend their narrow utilitarian natures and plan rationally for society in general? Presumably the psychologists — but, if this is true, it would demand that Eysenck's paradigm of behaviour does not apply to all men. Some, by virtue of their foresight, are able to create new norms more applicable to changed times. But behaviourism can only explain creativity by positive reinforcement. Thus Koestler (1964), in a brilliant demolition of behaviourist metaphysics, cites the following attempt at the explanation of creativity by the father of the behaviourist school, John Broadus Watson (1925, pp. 198ff):

> One natural question often raised is, how do we ever get new verbal creations such as poems or a brilliant essay? The answer is that we get them by manipulating words, shifting them about until a new pattern is hit upon. . . . How do you suppose Patou builds a new gown? Has he any 'picture in his mind' of what the gown is to look like when it is finished? He has not. . . . He calls his model in, picks up a new piece of silk, throws it around her, he pulls it in here, he pulls it out there. . . . He manipulates the material until it takes on the semblance of a dress. . . . Not until the new creation aroused admiration and commendation, both his own and others, would manipulation be complete — the equivalent of the rat's finding food . . . the painter plies his trade in the same way, nor can the poet boast of any other method.

But who is to supply such positive reinforcements if the innovation violates existing values? Eysenck himself cites incessantly the resistance and scorn poured on his own conclusions. It is difficult to understand how psychology managed to evolve in the context of political and public apathy. The creation of new norms, the innovation of scientific theories and artistic projects, the dynamics of social change are all inexplicable in terms of positivist theory. For, in reality, what will act as reinforcer for men is given by their purposive response to their situation, and the salience of a reinforcer for a human actor must therefore be explicable in terms of choices made freely but within conditions of material and social restraint. The valuation of what ought to be cannot be derived either from the imperatives of technology or the existing configuration of values.

Eysenck's insistence on following the 'facts' of human existence — whether technological necessity, the existing dominant values, or the essential psychological nature of man — places him in a contradictory position, for he is so often forced to recognise that these 'facts' can fall out of phase. Doggedly, however, he continues to deny human creativity and purpose, in deducing 'what ought to be' from 'what is'. He sees himself always in a different realm of being from the subjects he studies, he alone being able to criticize the existing order. It was precisely this kind of self-deceit that Marx was moved, in 1845, to describe in the following terms (Marx and Engels, 1968, p. 28):

> The materialist doctrine that men are products of circumstances and changed upbringing, forgets that it is men that change circumstances and that the educator himself needs educating. Hence this doctrine necessarily arrives at dividing society into two parts, of which one is superior to society.

Deviant behaviour

Eysenck views the description of an act as deviant as largely non-problematic — the consensus defines behaviour as normal or deviant, it being the psychologist's task merely to provide efficient means of treatment.[18] He does not fall into the trap of the biological determinists before him in suggesting that deviant behaviour is intrinsic in the biological nature of an individual. Thus he writes (1970 pp. 74–5):

> Nothing that has been said so far should lead the reader to imagine that environment plays no part at all in the causation of crime. . . . The very notion of criminality or crime would be meaningless without a context of learning or social experience and, quite generally, of human interaction. What the figures have demonstrated is that heredity is a very strong predisposing factor as far as committing crimes is concerned. But the actual way in which the crime is carried out, and whether or not the culprit is found and punished — these are obviously subject to the changing vicissitudes of everyday life. It would be meaningless to talk about the criminality or otherwise of a Robinson Crusoe, brought up and always confined by himself on a desert island. It is only in relation to society that the notion of criminality and of predisposition to crime has any meaning. While recognising therefore, the tremendous power of heredity, we would by no means wish to suggest that environmental influences cannot also be very powerful and important indeed.

Society defines what is criminal and non-criminal, and the social environment plays a large part in determining the degree of socialization a person has experienced. This answers well the critique of environmentalists that biological variation is insufficient to explain changes in the rate of crime.[19] We wish to argue that Eysenck's analysis is misguided not because of his omission of social factors but because he constructs a false notion of the interplay between biology and society. For Eysenck the interaction between society and the individual potential for deviance is *additive*. He has a *steady state* notion of biological potential — it is something which is fixed and measurable and follows a man throughout his life. Rather, we wish to suggest that man's consciousness is not a product of what society makes of his biological attributes. The distinctively human trait is to be able to stand back and interpret bodily constitution and social circumstances. Raw biological drives and passive acceptance of socially imposed labels is true only at birth and diminishes thereafter. His definitions of himself evolve not as a determinate result of the addition of social factors on to a biological substratum but rather as *praxis,* as the meaningful attempt by the actor to construct and develop his own self-conception.

Eysenck, in contrast, characterizes deviant behaviour as meaningless: it is behaviour outside of a monolithic consensus. It is perceived independently of any social context as the pathology of the isolated individual. Ronald Laing (1967, p. 17), writing about mental illness, has noted how such a procedure can make any behaviour seem unintelligible:

> Someone is gibbering away on his knees, talking to someone who is not there. Yes, he is praying. If one does not accord him the social intelligibility of his behaviour, he can only be seen as mad. Out of social context, his behaviour can only be the outcome of an unintelligible 'psychological' and/or 'physical' process, for which he requires treatment. This metaphor sanctions a massive ignorance of the social context within which the person was interacting.

In contrast to Eysenck, we wish to suggest that instead of seeing extraversion as a discrete trait characterized by absolute under-socialization, we should take it to represent meaningful behaviour by individuals which is judged by others, in this case the psychological testers, to be undesirable. It is under-socialization with respect to certain values: it is not absolute lack of values. Thus, if we examine Eysenck's characterization of extraverts and introverts (1970, p. 50) we are struck by the social valuations which lie just beneath the surface of his 'objective' descriptions:

> The typical extravert is sociable, likes parties, has many friends, needs to have people to talk to, and does not like reading or studying by himself. He craves excitement, takes chances, acts on the spur of the moment, and is generally an impulsive individual. He is fond of practical jokes, always has a ready answer, and generally likes change; he is care-free, easygoing, optimistic, and likes to 'laugh and be merry'. He prefers to keep moving and doing things, tends to be aggressive and loses his temper quickly; his feelings are not kept under tight control and he is not always a reliable person.

> The typical introvert is a quiet, retiring sort of person, introspective, fond of books rather than people: he is reserved and reticent except with intimate friends. He tends to plan ahead, 'looks before he leaps', and distrusts the impulse of the moment. He does not like excitement, takes matters of everyday life with proper seriousness, and likes a well-ordered mode of life. He keeps his feelings under close control, seldom behaves in an aggressive manner, and does not lose his temper easily. He is reliable, somewhat pessimistic, and places great value on ethical standards.

It is extraordinary how similar such a list is to Matza and Sykes's depiction of the difference between formal and subterranean values (1961):

Formal values: deferred gratification, planning, continuity to bureaucratic rules, routine, predictability, non-aggressive, self-centred.

Introversion: 'introspective', 'reserved', 'tends to plan ahead', 'distrusts impulse', 'does not like excitement', 'likes a well-ordered mode of life', 'keeps feelings under control', 'seldom behaves aggressively', 'reliable'.

Subterranean values: short-term hedonism, spontaneity, ego-expressivity, new experience, excitement, aggressive masculine role, peer-centred.

Extraversion: 'sociable', 'has many friends', 'craves excitement', 'takes chances', 'acts on spur of moment', 'impulsive', 'carefree' 'easygoing', 'likes change', 'aggressive'.

Matza and Sykes suggest that the subterranean values are held throughout society and usually find expression in leisure time and play. Further, they note how certain groups such as juvenile delinquents tend to accentuate these values at the expense of the formal values of work.

One of the authors of this present study has suggested that the accentuation of subterranean values is associated with the structural position and problems faced by certain social groups (Young, 1971a). Important amongst these are the lower working-class, represented minority groups and deviant youth cultures. These are also the groups most prone to contribute to the criminal statistics. Thus the existence of values which are contracultural and closely related to purposive criminal activities is interpreted by Eysenck as a reflection of psychological propensities (i.e., high extraversion) denoting the absence of social values. This extraversion–introversion scale may, in fact, in certain instances be accurately yet unwittingly gauging such value differences. However, crime is only related in certain instances to the subterranean values. The business criminal of the Mafia, the professional thief, the corporate criminal, the bank clerk embezzler are hardly likely to embrace the same values as the ghetto Negro and the juvenile vandal. Thus, the enterprise is doomed to failure: inconsistent results abound and 'significant' correlations where they occur merely result in false imputations of causality.

Scientific method

There has been a plenitude of critiques of Eysenck from within the ranks of positivism. Thus Hoghughi and Forrest (1970) point to the frequent finding that persistent young offenders are significantly more introverted than control groups (see also Little, 1963). Further, his research techniques have come under vehement criticism. As Richard Christie (1956, p. 450) put it:

> Errors of computation, uniquely biased samples which forbid any generalisations, scales with built-in biases which do not measure what they purport to measure, unexplained inconsistencies within the data, misinterpretations and contradictions of the relevant research of others, and unjustifiable manipulation of the data. Any one of Eysenck's many errors is sufficient to raise serious questions about the validity of his conclusions. *In toto,* absurdity is compounded upon absurdity, so that where the truth lies is impossible to determine.

It is not, however, our intention to enter into technical criticisms of Eysenck. For our argument would be, as we have outlined in the last section, that even if in some instances reliable correlations were found between extraversion and crime, these would be based on a causality of a social nature *not* of a theory based on the autonomic nervous system. This is not to deny the falsifiability of his theory — for if our argument is correct successful correlations will only be found to occur amongst a minority of criminals. Eysenck meanwhile, in order to keep pace with his critics, must desperately invoke new 'sophistications' of factor analysis and involve added complications and dimensions to his theory (e.g. Eysenck and Eysenck, 1970). Like a Ptolemaic astronomer, he must add epicycle after epicycle to keep the theory in line with the facts, until all parsimony is lost and the last vestige of scientific open-mindedness vanishes.

Our aim in this text is to concentrate on the criticisms of Eysenck's theory rather than to enter the internecine squabbles of positivism. For this reason we turn to his underlying notion of reductionism (1970, p.75):

> What will be suggested rather is that without an understanding of the way in which the innate criminality, the predisposition of the person to commit

a crime, is translated into reality, it will be very difficult, if not impossible, to carry out investigations into the environmental influences which determine criminality or lack of criminality in a given person. It will be argued that purely statistical studies, such as those which have customarily been carried out by sociologists and others, in an attempt to correlate such items as absence of the father, absence of the mother, poor conditions of upbringing, lack of home life, and so forth, with criminality, while interesting, lack any great causal importance because it is difficult to see just precisely how these various factors exert their influence. It is hoped that, by relating these factors to a general theory which also accounts for the way in which the hereditary causes work, we shall be able to produce a more satisfactory picture of the whole complex of causes which produce criminal behaviour in our modern world.

Eysenck's belief is that there are psychological and physiological laws which will explain social behaviour. Such reductionism supposedly increases the scientific validity of the analysis. Eysenck attempts to relate such measurable psychological and physiological states to 'objective' behaviour (1965, pp. 13–14, our emphasis):

> The 'mind', or the 'soul', or the 'psyche', are a little too immaterial to be investigated as such by any scientific procedures; what the psychologist deals with, in fact, is *behaviour* which is palpable enough to be observed, recorded and analysed. The hard-headed view is often criticized by people who say that this way of looking at things leaves out important qualities and aspects of humanity. Such an objection may or may not be true in the long run; this becomes almost a philosophical, rather than a scientific question, and there would be little point in arguing it here.

The 'meaning' of behaviour is thus somehow seen as obvious to the psychologist and valuable information can legitimately be obtained from animal studies where deviancy can be seen as a behavioural deviation subject to simple statistical calculation (Eysenck, 1965, p. 228):

> Too many similarities in conditioning and learning behaviour have been shown to exist when animals and human beings are compared, to deny a biological basis of considerable similarity for these various types of organisms, and if we maintain, as I think we must, that social behaviour is learned and conditioned very much as are other types of behaviour, then it is difficult to deny that a knowledge of these laws, whether derived from animal work or from human work, is an essential pre-requisite for an understanding of such behaviour.

Eysenck's assumption is that the meaning of an item of behaviour is non-problematic, and that to explain the physical basis of it is to explain it as a social phenomenon. But as Alasdair MacIntyre (1962) has succinctly put it:

> The same physical movements may constitute in different contexts quite different actions. So a man may go through the same physical movements involved in signing his name and be concluding a treaty or paying a bill,

which are quite different actions. But is not the man performing the same action in each case, namely signing his name? To this the answer is that writing one's name is never merely by itself an action: one is either signing a document or giving information or perhaps just doodling. All these are actions, but writing one's name is not. Equally, the same action may be constituted by quite different physical movements. Writing on paper, passing a coin, even saying words may all constitute the same action of paying a bill. When we talk about 'explaining human behaviour', we sometimes blur this distinction. Because there is no human action which does not involve physical movement we may suppose that to explain the movement is to explain the action.

Even if it were true that the physical basis of behaviour lay in the reflexes of the autonomic nervous system, it would not explain the nature of deviant action. To explain social phenomena demands social analysis involving the meaning that the behaviour has to the actor. The man who breaks the window of the British Embassy in Dublin might well have a poor autonomic response but both his lack of reflex and violent behaviour can only be understood in terms of the meanings he gave to the situation and the social context of the movement for a united Ireland. Indeed, as MacIntyre argues, causality in the social sciences is different from causality in the natural sciences in so far as the connection between mere behaviour and social action is to be found at the level of beliefs. Thus, the relationship between beliefs and action is 'inner and conceptual'. If, as with Eysenck, it is to be believed that one can reduce explanation of action to explanations in terms of the acquisition of conditioned reflexes which in their turn could be explained in terms of genetics, then the situation in which an act occurs and the meaning which an actor gives to his physical behaviour would be irrelevant. There is, however, a crucial epistemological break between biological and social explanation (and not a continuum of reductions). For *in social explanations causes are 'inner and conceptual'* — that is to say, the connection between physical movement and the outside world is in terms of what men believe (the purposes to which they hold). Thus men rob banks because they believe they may enrich themselves, not because something biologically propels them through the door of a bank. The fact that people may have different chromosomal configurations or are different biophysiological types may be of interest in accounting for constitutional differences between men, but it goes no way towards explaining deviancy as social action. The epistemology of social science is of a different order to that of a natural science: a social theory must have reference to men's teleology — their purposes, their beliefs and the contexts in which they act out these purposes and beliefs.

Behaviourist and positivist analyses contain no such epistemology. Indeed, their very appeal is to be explained in terms of their having a view of man as malleable and conditionable. The positivists refuse to question beliefs, since this would involve consideration of values, an area which they would see to be irrelevant to science. The appeal is made to the scientificity of physical explanation — the more physical the explanation, the more scientific it is. The positivist conception of science as exemplified in the work of Eysenck, is a conception of science which denies meaning to any action taken outside the consensus and thereby the established social order itself.

*   *   *   *   *

Conclusion

Biological positivism has, in the work of psychological positivists such as Eysenck and Trasler, reached a higher level of sophistication than in the work of simple genetic or physical type theorists. Social factors are taken into account, moral relativism mooted, and precise postulations of the manner in which genetic influences manifest themselves in behaviour is elaborated upon. No claim is made to explain the formal causes of crime (i.e., the reasons why certain acts are deviant and particular deviant actors are apprehended); the focus is exclusively placed on the efficient causes. Positivism as a doctrine is wedded to the position of taking social reaction for granted. Yet, as we have seen, Eysenck in a critical vein stumbles on the problem of social order. The explanation of the creation of value and thus the meaningful nature of both deviant action and social reaction, eludes a theory which utilizes a model of human nature where man is a passive actor. We would not deny the influence of autonomic responses in human behaviour but we would argue that their role must be seen in the context of human creativity and purpose. As Matza (1969, pp. 92–3) says:

> Capable of creating and assigning meaning, able to contemplate his surroundings and even his own condition, given to anticipating, planning and projecting man — the subject — stands in a different and more complex relation to circumstance. This distinctively human capacity in no way denies that human existence frequently displays itself in ways characteristic of lower levels. Frequently man is wholly adaptive, *as if* he were just an organic being. And sometimes, though very rarely, he is wholly reactive, *as if* a mere object. But mere reactivity or adaptation should not be confused with the distinctively human condition. They are better seen as an alienation or exhaustion of that condition. A subject actively addresses or encounters his circumstance; accordingly, his distinctive capacity is to reshape, strive towards creating, and actually to *transcend* circumstance. Such a distinctly human project is not always feasible, but the capacity always exists.

Our position in this critique is not one in which psychology is totally excluded or denied. But, as our argument evolves, it will become clear that the most pressing need is for a social psychology which is capable of situating the actions of men acting according to beliefs and values in their historical and structural contexts. Martin Nicolaus (1969) has said of social science: 'What kind of science is this, which holds true only when men hold still?' A social theory of deviance must attempt to deal with men who move.

Notes

1. For a discussion of 'the ethos of productivity' as a central tenet of consensual politics and the defusion in the mass media of realities which threaten it, see J. Young (1974; 1975).

2. Cf. Jack Douglas (1967, p. 21) in which Douglas, referring to *Suicide*, argues that 'Durkheim seems to have been at his best in developing the ideas he had taken from the moral statisticians.'

3. Cf. the account of Bonger's work in [chapter 7].

4. Note that each individual is scored, by Sheldon, on a seven point scale in terms of the extent to which he measures up to each ideal somatype. There is a quantitative continuum from extreme ectomorph to extreme endomorph with mesomorphs in the middle. Once again, sharp qualitative differences are disallowed.

5. Conrad, in fact, uses Kretschmer's distinction between the *pybric* and the *leptosomatic* body types, which corresponds roughly to Sheldon's distinction between the mesomorph and the endomorph.

6. Hans Eysenck in *Fact and Fiction in Psychology* (1965) quotes approvingly Sheldon's suggestion that mesomorph/endomorphs are more likely to be extraverted and ectomorphs to be introverted (Sheldon, 1940).

7. The tendency amongst biological positivists has been to use inmates as subjects (with outsiders as the control group). The convenience of this group for research purposes is obvious: few contact and refusal problems are likely to be encountered. The problem is however that biological positivists have tended to see inmates as generally representative of the potentially or actually criminal, rather than as a highly-sifted, processed and (therefore) unrepresentative section of those at risk of apprehension and incarceration.

8. For an illuminating critique of this debate, see Sarbin and Miller (1970).

9. The presence of a Y chromosome ensures that a baby is male, and, as we shall see, the chromosome debate is concerned entirely with male chromosomal abnormality. *Female* chromosome abnormality arises when there is an additional X chromosome, or when one X chromosome is missing, i.e., the XXX and XO combinations respectively.

10. The sex chromosome abnormality theory is also exceptional in that, unlike most of the contemporary positivist accounts, it does posit a qualitative difference between the criminal and the non-criminal: that is, in the possession or non-possession of the extra Y chromosome. Theories involving biological homeostasis, for example, biochemical theories of mental illness, might also do this. We will not be dealing with this area in this text.

11. Although this is not at all the impression one would gather from some discussions of the sex chromosomal debate in the mass media.

12. For an examination of this concept, see Sarbin (1969).

13. This is based on the article by S. Kessler and R. Moos, 'The XYY karyotype and criminality' (1970).

14. Eysenck and Trasler both base their theory of crime on classical conditioning and the autonomic nervous system. To them crime is seen as a lack of learning social norms in a conditioned fashion. An alternative behaviourist theory of crime is based primarily on rational learning (operant conditioning) and the central nervous system. Here crime is normal and social, learnt because it has been positively reinforced in the past. Such an approach is absent in Eysenck because he fails to consider the possibility of elaborate criminal values and techniques which can be learnt — rather, for him crime occurs as an outburst of pre-social covetousness, it is raw impulse unstemmed by the social reflexes of the conditioned conscience. For a discussion of a behaviourist theory based on operant conditioning, see [chapter 4], where we deal with Burgess and Akers's reformulation of Sutherland's principles.

15. The other two personality dimensions he uses are emotionality — stability and psychoticism — and normality, both of which, like introversion–extraversion, are based on the autonomic nervous system. We shall concentrate on introversion–extraversion for simplicity's sake.

16. This conception of man has some affinity with Gordon Allport's conception of the Leibnizean, creative nature of man, rather than the passive determined Lockean nature as exhibited in the work of Eysenck (see Allport, 1955). But, we shall argue later, the first theorist to operate with a fully social conception of man was Karl Marx.

17. See Eysenck, 1953, pp. 180 et seq., where he argues extensively for social relativism.

18. Note the tension here between Eysenck's élitism and his appeal to the consensus. The trained psychologist knows best for society and, therefore, presumably can ascertain who are the really socially dangerous deviants. Thus he can, as in 'The technology of consent' suggest that 'private' deviancy in the general realm is permissible yet the 'public' deviancy of strikes threatens the social system and demands ameliorative action.

19. A critique that stemmed from Ferri's attack on the work of Lombroso in the late nineteenth century.

2. Foundations: Beccaria and the Basis of Classicism

Bob Roshier

> Some tangible motives had to be introduced, therefore, to prevent the despotic spirit, which is in every man, from plunging the laws of society into its original chaos. These tangible motives are the punishments established against infractors of laws . . . These motives, by dint of repeated presentation to the mind, counterbalance the powerful impressions of the private passions that oppose the common good
>
> (Beccaria, 1963, p. 12).

By far the most significant figure responsible for the formulation of the principles of classical criminology was Cesare Beccaria (1738–94). Indeed, classical criminology is almost entirely constituted by the one, short book that he wrote, *Dei Delitti e delle Pene* in 1764 (Beccaria, 1963). It was not particularly its originality that distinguished it— it consisted mainly of ideas borrowed from the Enlightenment and from earlier social contract writers. Nor, evidently, was Beccaria himself a towering figure of his time; in fact, he was unknown when he wrote it, never wrote anything else of note and was an embarrassing failure in personal appearances to evangelise his cause. It has even been darkly insinuated by Paolucci (in Beccaria, 1963) that he may merely have been used as a front by his radical friends, the Verri brothers, who were too much in trouble with the authorities at the time to risk writing it themselves.

Whatever its origins, *Dei Delitti e delle Pene* is a masterpiece of compression, focusing its borrowed ideas into a comprehensive, coherent treatise on the iniquities of the contemporary European criminal justice systems and offering a systematic alternative. The iniquities that Beccaria had in mind were cruelty, arbitrariness and inefficiency (like all reformers he has, of course, been accused of gross exaggeration — see Paolucci in Beccaria, 1963); the alternatives he offered were humanity, consistency and rationality.

Cesare Beccaria: *On Crimes and Punishments*

Beccaria starts by looking at the justification of the right to punish; he concludes that it is to be found in the social contract whose central tenet he declares to be 'the greatest happiness of the greatest number' (it is possible that he is responsible for originating this particular cliché). The social contract involves our sacrificing a portion of our personal liberty to achieve this end, but *not* out of some innate desire for the common good, since 'If it were possible, every one of us would prefer that the compacts binding others do not bind us'. Rather, it is because, 'Weary of living in a continual state of war, and of enjoying liberty rendered useless by the uncertainty of preserving

Bob Roshier: 'Foundations: Beccaria and the Basis of Classicism' from *CONTROLLING CRIME: THE CLASSICAL PERSPECTIVE IN CRIMINOLOGY* (Open University Press, 1989), pp. 5–19.

it, [we] sacrifice a part so that [we] might enjoy the rest of it in peace and safety' (p. 11).[1]

So the social contract is selfishly motivated; it comes about through our rational ability to perceive a personal advantage from it. Consequently, it is precarious. Disincentives are also needed (to 'prevent reversion') in the form of punishments for law infractors. We would will this as part of the social contract because our own selfishness would enable us to see its necessity.

Punishments, however, must not exceed the minimum that is necessary to deter — we would not, Beccaria again argues, will it otherwise in the social contract. Thus, the 'humanitarianism' that informs his programme is also derived from selfish, rational motives; it stems from the fact that, since we can imagine ourselves breaking the contract, we can also imagine ourselves being the objects of punishment.

Beccaria's reputation for humanity comes from the famous sections that oppose the use of torture and of capital punishment. While his arguments about capital punishment are still of great relevance, it now seems rather odd that it could have been thought necessary to have to argue against the use of torture for extracting confessions. At the time Beccaria was writing, however, it was assumed that God and righteousness would prevent innocents from breaking under torture and falsely confessing. He points to the irrationality of this assumption and makes the seemingly rather obvious point that 'Torture . . . is an infallible means for absolving robust scoundrels and for condemning innocent persons who happen to be weak' (p. 32).

His opposition to capital punishment is, again, based on utilitarian and social contractual reasons. No rational person, he says, would enter into a social contract that would 'leave to other men the choice of killing him'. His alternative, 'perpetual servitude', is chosen because of its supposed greater effectiveness as a general deterrent rather than its lesser cruelty:

> To anyone raising the argument that perpetual servitude is as painful as death and therefore equally cruel, I will reply that, adding up all the moments of unhappiness of servitude, it may well be even more cruel; but these are drawn out over an entire lifetime, while the pain of death exerts its whole force in a moment. And precisely this is the advantage of penal servitude, that it inspires terror in the spectator more than in the sufferer (p. 48).

Beccaria was not, on the other hand, opposed to corporal punishment. This is much less often commented upon, probably because he mentions it in a rather throwaway fashion, losing it in a section almost entirely devoted to the argument that noblemen should receive the same punishments as people of the lower orders. For crimes which are 'attempts against the person' he says, 'the penalties . . . should always be corporal punishments' (p. 68). That is absolutely all he has to say on the matter. I shall return to the question of Beccaria's humanity later.

As the above quotation on 'perpetual servitude' suggests, Beccaria considered the purpose of punishment to be to deter, with the emphasis on general rather than individual deterrence. It is aimed at minds rather than bodies (though it uses bodies) and its *intent* is not to torment (though it may do so). Its overriding concern is with efficient crime control. Although this is quite different from retribution (an aim that Beccaria specifically rejects), he retains the idea, usually associated with retribution, that the punishment should be *proportional* to the crime — but not, he insists, proportional to its *sinfulness* (since only God can gauge that). It should, instead, be proportional to the *harm done to society*. All personal characteristics of offenders, including their subjective intent, should be excluded from consideration; the sole measure of the punishment should be the objective harm done. If we ask who is to gauge that (presumably not God), he gives the unhelpful and not a little pompous reply that it is 'known with clarity and precision only by some few thinking men in every nation and every age' (p. 64).

The reason that Beccaria gives for his requirement of proportionality is that 'If an equal punishment be ordained for two crimes that do not equally injure society, men will not be any more deterred from committing the greater crime, if they find a greater advantage associated with it' (p. 63). It is this feature of Beccaria's programme that has caused more problems than probably anything else, as we shall see later. Briefly, the problems are both practical and moral. On the practical side, Beccaria makes the quite unwarranted assumption that more serious crimes are more attractive and of necessity require more serious punishments to deter them than do lesser ones. The moral problem arises from Beccaria's insistence that all personal characteristics of offenders and circumstances of their offences should be excluded from consideration in determining punishments. This violates such deep-seated feelings of justice that it has proved to be unacceptable under any criminal law jurisdiction.

Two other requirements that Beccaria makes of punishments for them to be effective are that they should be *prompt* and *certain*. These two qualities make 'so much stronger and more lasting in the human mind . . . the association of these two ideas *crime* and *punishment*. . . The association of ideas is the cement that forms the fabric of the human intellect' (p.56). He attaches great importance to 'the association of ideas' and sees it as being most powerfully achieved where the punishment symbolises the offence as far as possible. Thus property offences should be dealt with by fines (to be earned by forced labour if the offender cannot pay) and violent offences by corporal punishment. Imprisonment, because of its invisibility (symbolism obviously requires public visibility) seems to be relegated to a relatively minor role, though he is not very clear on this. His opposition to capital punishment, on the other hand, does not seem to fit very well with the principle of symbolic representation — the public execution of murderers appears to satisfy all his requirements.

Beccaria concludes with a section on prevention, which he sees as being very much preferable to punishment — it increases aggregate utility, the happiness of the greatest number (or, rather, decreases their aggregate unhappiness). Prevention requires laws to be clear, simple and universally supported. It also seems to require a restriction of the scope of the criminal law and a readiness to consider decriminalisation:

> For one motive that drives men to commit a real crime there are a
> thousand that drives them to commit those indifferent acts which are

called crimes by bad laws; and if the probability of crimes is proportionate to the number of motives, to enlarge the sphere of crimes is to increase the probability of their being committed (p. 94).

Another important resource for the prevention of crime is the spread of enlightenment via education. 'Knowledge' says Beccaria 'breeds evil in reverse ratio to its diffusion' since 'no enlightened person can fail to approve the clear and useful public compacts of mutual security' which constitute the social contract (p. 95). Beccaria summarises his arguments in a 'general theorem':

> In order for punishment not to be, in every instance, an act of violence of one or of many against a private citizen, it must be essentially public, prompt, necessary, the least possible in the given circumstances, proportionate to the crimes, dictated by the laws (p. 99).

Beccaria and Bentham: utility and humanity

In Britain, the ideas of Beccaria are probably best known through their influence on Bentham. Certainly, Bentham acknowledged his debt to Beccaria. Almost all of the basic principles of his utilitarian programme in relation to the criminal justice system can be traced back to *Dei Delitti e delle Pene*. The most striking difference between them is in the amount they wrote — Beccaria so little and Bentham so much. If Beccaria's fault was brevity, then Bentham's was immense, often boring, detail (as exhibited, for example, in his celebrated attempt to specify all possible pains and pleasures).

One important distinction between the two writers is that Bentham became much more favourably disposed towards the prison as a medium of criminal reformation than Beccaria appeared to be (a point to which I shall return later). Hart (1983, p. 51) has drawn attention to a second important difference: Beccaria, he says, has 'a respect for the individual person' that is lacking in Bentham:

> I think that very often where Bentham and Beccaria differ in detail this is traceable to Beccaria's conviction that what may be done in the name of utility should be limited by consideration of what befits the dignity of man.

In that long-noted contradiction between the happiness of the greatest number and the 'natural' rights of the individual, Hart locates the two writers in quite different positions. This is an important distinction, since it relates to a fundamental dilemma in the classical conception of what is legitimate in punishing crime.

Clearly, what humanity there is in Bentham is very much aggregate humanity; his willingness to sacrifice individual humanity to achieve it is legendary. A good example (and one that affords an interesting comparison with Beccaria) is his attitude towards torture. Bentham was perfectly willing to countenance torture if it would reveal information that would prevent more injury and suffering than was used in obtaining it (Twining and Twining, 1973). Beccaria, as already noted, was famous for his opposition to torture. Tempting as this comparison is, however, it is not quite fair; they were talking about different things. Beccaria was opposing the use of torture for extracting confessions. His opposition was on utilitarian rather than humane grounds: it does not work; it 'absolves robust scoundrels' and condemns weak innocents. Indeed, Beccaria always avoided direct appeals to humanity or individual rights. Even in his opposition to capital punishment, as we have seen, his arguments are in terms of effectiveness and utility. He was not at all put off by the possibility that his alternative 'may well be even more cruel'. Nor was he averse to corporal punishments where the logic of his 'symbolic representation' thesis seemed to require it. Indeed, the logic seemed to require that such punishment should take place in public. Since it would have been unlikely that many property offenders would have been able to pay the fines that he advocated, they would mostly have been subjected to the forced labour that he proposed as the alternative. None of these examples suggests a particularly marked concern with the 'dignity of man'.

Beccaria's appearance of humanity is perhaps to some extent due to the fact that, unlike Bentham, he often glossed over the darker implications of his arguments. This, in turn, suggests that perhaps he found himself in a dilemma — caught between his naturally humane feelings and the logic of his unsentimental, utilitarian theory. Yet, on the other hand, his particular version of the social contract *allows* for both. The requirement of effective deterrence is potentially extremely harsh. It is moderated by the fact that since we are all naturally deviant given the chance, we can identify with offenders because we can imagine them being ourselves. This is why only the minimum necessary punishments are prescribed; we would not will it otherwise. The view that the punishments are, potentially, things that may happen to us provides a selfish (and, therefore, suitably utilitarian) basis for a concern with humanity and the rights of the individual offender. Beccaria uses just such an argument against capital punishment (in addition to his rational, effectiveness arguments); we simply would not enter into a social contract that gave someone the right to kill us. What is perhaps surprising, if it *is* the case that Beccaria was moved by humane sentiments towards the individual offender, is that he did not use this argument more often. Would we, for example, be happy with giving someone the right to administer corporal punishment to us (in public)? It seems that Beccaria did not often err, in his balancing of contradictory requirements, in favour of the rights of the individual against the achievement of effective deterrence via symbolic representation .

Whatever Beccaria's personal position, his vision of a social contract set up by people who can at least imagine themselves as the recipients of its punishments is in marked contrast to the later, positivist position that tended to see criminals as different kinds of people altogether. Ferri (1967, p. 7), in his criticisms of classical criminology and its influence, writing in 1917, was particularly concerned with its 'excessive solicitude for delinquents'. The vision of delinquents as a different species of being threatening society provided a potentially much more unfettered entitlement to take action against them than was allowable under Beccaria's version of the social contract that underpinned the classical theory.

Neoclassicism

Beccaria's classical criminology is universally attributed with a powerful influence over subsequent developments in the criminal justice systems of most European countries.

Paolucci claims (in Beccaria 1963, p. ix) that *Dei Delitti e delle Pene* has had 'more practical effect than any other treatise ever written in the long campaign against barbarism in criminal law and procedure'. And Monachesi (1960, p. 49) goes as far as to say that 'The reader will find proposed in his essay practically all of the important reforms in the administration of criminal justice and in penology which have been achieved in the civilised world since 1764'.

An abbreviated version of the general theorem with which Beccaria summarised his arguments was incorporated as Article VIII of the 'Declaration of the Rights of Man and of the Citizen', passed by the revolutionary National Assembly of France, on 26 August 1789. However, actual attempts to legislate and operate Beccaria's programme in Europe encountered a serious stumbling block, and the final outcome was invariably something significantly different from what he actually proposed. The main example was the French Code of 1791, where legislators consciously attempted to put his ideas into practice. The problem that soon emerged was Beccaria's insistence on the strict proportionality between offences and punishments, regardless of the circumstances of the offence or characteristics of the offender. This proved to be quite unacceptable, and the French Code moved progressively over the years towards allowing judges more and more discretion to vary punishments on precisely these grounds. The resulting system has come to be referred to as 'neoclassicism' — a retention of the assumption of free will, but with an allowance that it is sometimes freer than at other times and that the proportionality of punishments should be adjusted to these varying degrees of freedom. Neoclassicism, in this sense, became the basis of all European and Western criminal law jurisdictions and has remained so, more or less, to this day.

Even in Britain, with its relative isolation from, and suspicion of, continental legal thinking, Beccaria's ideas made some impression. In 1833 commissioners were appointed to rationalise the criminal law and procedure. Radzinowicz and Hood (1986, p. 726) have noted their obvious (and acknowledged) debt to Beccaria. But these ideas soon became diluted (very much along 'neoclassical' lines), 'Perhaps because of the English Common Law tradition that room should always be left to accommodate the peculiarities of individual cases' (ibid., p.727). Eventually, however, the whole project came to nothing. Any idea of codification was out of keeping with the English tradition of relatively unfettered judicial discretion and the elasticity of the common law. But despite this, the English system developed to incorporate 'neoclassical' assumptions very similar to those on the Continent.

The main individual characteristics that have been incorporated, under neoclassicism, as making a difference to the culpability of offenders have been age, mental capacity and intent (for instance, degree of premeditation). The reason for their inclusion is that they are seen as influencing (or being indicative of) the responsibility of offenders for their actions. They are expressive of the sentiments of retributive justice that Beccaria wished to exclude from consideration of punishments. He was solely concerned with whether punishments were effective as deterrents and not with whether they were 'fair' (though, as we shall see later, his views on deterrence were also problematic). Indeed, his insistence that punishments should only reflect the harm done to society and have nothing to do with subjective intent would seem to imply that the accident-prone should be treated the same as those who cause harm by design! Perhaps not surprisingly, no criminal justice system was able to take on such gross violations of widely-held sentiments of retributive justice.

Interestingly, although neoclassicism allowed individual differences to influence punishments on the grounds of justice, in doing so it paved the way for the later, positivist conception of the causes and treatment of crime. For in accepting that age and, more importantly, insanity could influence the degree of individuals' responsibility for their actions it was also accepting that in some cases, and to some extent at least, human actions could be seen as *determined*. Thus, it began to incorporate the principles of determinism and the differentiation of offenders from non-offenders that were to be the later hallmarks of positivist criminology.

Classicism and the prison

Neoclassicism represented, at least in part, a conscious attempt by reformers to put into practice Beccaria's ideas about the administration of criminal justice. On the other hand, the relationship between classical criminology and the major development in *penal* practice in the ensuing century — the rising dominance of the prison — is much more problematic. When I say 'relationship' I mean this in its purely formal sense; there is no attempt here to make any claim about possible causal relationships between ideas and practice.[2] But the formal relationship between classical criminology and the prison is of considerable importance since, it has been claimed, they embodied quite different ideas about the way to control crime. The most important exponent of this view has been Michel Foucault (1977). He claims that by the latter half of the eighteenth century the fading 'monarchical law' of the *ancien régime* was being confronted by two different alternatives: the programme of the 'reforming jurists' (classical criminology) and that of the advocates of the prison:

> Broadly speaking, one might say that, in monarchical law, punishment is a ceremonial of sovereignty; it uses the ritual marks of the vengeance that it applies to the body of the condemned man; and it deploys before the eyes of the spectators an effect of terror as intense as it is discontinuous, irregular and always above its own laws, the physical presence of the sovereign and of his power. The reforming jurists, on the other hand, saw punishment as a procedure for requalifying individuals as subjects, as juridical subjects; it uses not marks, but signs, coded sets of representations, which would be given the most rapid circulation and the most general acceptance possible by citizens witnessing the scene of punishment. Lastly, in the project for a prison institution that was then developing, punishment was seen as a technique for the coercion of individuals; it operated methods of training the body — not signs — by the traces it leaves, in the form of habits, in behaviour; and it presupposed the setting up of a specific power for the administration of the penalty (ibid., p. 130–1).

It was the prison, of course, which was to come out on top. Indeed, Beccaria's classical model, at least as far as the form and content of actual penal treatments are concerned, has never really been tried — if we are to accept Foucault's version of events.

There are two elements in Foucault's characterisation of the prison as an alternative model to that of classicism. First, there is the prison itself, as a physical entity — apparently given only a very minor role in the classical model. Second, there is the *aim* — the prison (according to Foucault), being concerned with transforming individual offenders into non-offenders via disciplinary training, classicism with utilising individual offenders to symbolise the offence and deter others. I think there is evidence to suggest that neither of these distinctions was, in practice, nearly as sharp as Foucault suggests.

To take the second element first, it does seem to be true that there is not much mention in Beccaria's book of reformative effects on the individual offender; he is far more concerned with frightening off potential offenders. Even where he does show an interest in 'education' it is, as we have seen, only as a preventive device aimed at the public at large. However, this does not mean that his position was incompatible with individual reformation; he just did not happen to consider it. Bentham, starting from almost identical premises as Beccaria, gets much nearer to it. Ignatieff (1978) suggests that Bentham like the prison reformer John Howard, also arrived at the idea of the corrigibility of man by re-education directed at the mind, albeit it by a different route. Bentham arrived at it via his belief in the universality of reason and hence the possibility of correctly socialising man's instinct for pleasure; Howard by his belief in original sin, guilt and the possibility of awakening man's consciousness of sin.

Anyway, whatever the ideas that inspired the advocates of the prison, it would obviously be very dangerous to assume that their ideas were automatically embodied in the actual operation of the prison system when it came into being. Garland (1985), in his detailed consideration of the Victorian prison system, concluded that, for Britain at least, Foucault's characterisation is wide of the mark. Individualised reformation as a dominant penal principle did not emerge here until the early part of the twentieth century, when positivist criminology was in the ascendant (though, again, that is not to suggest a simple causal relation). Garland puts Foucault as being around a century out in his characterisation! His analysis (Garland 1985b, p.32) concludes that the 'constraints of legal principle and political ideology' produced a system aimed at 'uniformity, equality of treatment and proportionality' in which concerns for individual reformation played only a very minor part. Thus Garland's version of the prison suggests the mixture of Beccarian classicism (proportionality for deterrent purposes) and retributive justice (proportionality according to desert) that, as we have seen, was the hallmark of neoclassicism. Foucault, of course, acknowledged that the reformative ideals that gave rise to the prison were a failure, in practice, from the start. Garland, however, seems to go rather further than this in suggesting that, in Britain at least, the emergent prison system never really embodied a 'reformative' alternative to classicism and neoclassicism at all.

The other distinction that Foucault makes relates to the significance of the institution of the prison itself. Again, at first reading, the evidence appears to be on his side: there is scarcely a mention of the prison in Beccaria's book. However, as we have seen earlier in relation to corporal punishment, it is instructive to look at the 'small print' in his writings. Beccaria's prescribed punishment for property crime was the fine. He recognised, however, that since most property crime was committed by the poor, they would not be able to pay fines. Consequently, they were to be subjected to forced labour to pay the equivalent. Let us examine the implications of this; property crime became by far the most common form of crime during the period in which the prison emerged; therefore forced labour would have become the most common punishment; forced labour requires incarceration (people tend not to turn up for it of their own free will). Would Beccaria's programme have looked much different in practice? The only real difference would have been that since Beccaria required his punishments to be public, his offenders would have laboured in the open air during the day rather than within the confines of their prison (presumably led out in chain-gangs). Even the particular architectural form of the prison, with its emphasis on facilitating supervision, discipline and hygiene, was hardly alien to the spirit of rationality and efficiency that inspired classicism. It was, after all, Bentham's 'panopticon' that provided the inspirational model.

It is true that Beccaria's classical programme has never been given a full trial (the image of his public floggings and toiling chain-gangs rather than his denial of capital punishment may help the liberal-minded to feel this less of a loss). But despite this, the prison does not appear to represent the radically different model that Foucault suggests. Rather, it seems that, in its usage at least, it can best be seen as having been incorporated into the neoclassical compromise which has dominated most Western criminal justice systems.

Conclusions: the basis of classicism

Beccaria's classical programme is a mixture of basic assumptions about the nature of human beings and the way they relate to crime and conformity, and empirical conclusions that he draws from these assumptions about how best to control crime. It is the former that constitute the 'classical perspective' and, in this final section, I want to try and extricate them and look at some of the problems that Beccaria's version of them encountered. In doing so I am not suggesting that I am delineating some objective essence of classicism. What follows is, of course, a personal selection.

I think the classical perspective can be seen as incorporating three fundamental assumptions about the nature of human beings that are crucial to its position on crime and conformity: *freedom, rationality and manipulability.*

Freedom

Like those who advocate retributive justice, Beccaria sees humans as free-willed and choice-making. It is important, however, to distinguish his use of the conception of human freedom. Under retributive justice punishment is justified because it is 'deserved' by free, choice-making individuals who are held responsible for their actions. As we have seen, Beccaria's justification for punishment was on quite different, purely utilitarian grounds: efficient crime control. His utilitarianism required a practical, socially useful justification for punishment; retribution was totally inadequate. A bonus of rejecting retribution, it seemed, was that he could avoid the particularly tricky problems raised in trying to assess subjective intent, desert and responsibility.

Perhaps Beccaria was also conscious of the incompatibility of retribution and deterrence as penal aims. It is certainly the case that sentencing practice to the present day has manifested an uneasy and uneven relationship between the two. But, as we saw in the discussion of neoclassicism, it was unrealistic to suppose that questions of intent and responsibility could be abandoned. To do so would not only be to abandon deep-seated conceptions of justice and desert, but to abandon the conception of 'guilt' itself. For Beccaria's conception of punishing purely in proportion to harm done failed to distinguish between 'crimes' committed intentionally, under duress or provocation, or even by accident.[3] The sense of injustice created by such a system would inevitably work against its deterrent effectiveness (Beccaria always acknowledged the importance of consent in producing compliance; it is difficult to imagine how his version of the social contract would have allowed such a system to operate).

Beccaria's attempt to avoid considerations of responsibility and desert must be regarded as something of a failure. Later on, positivists attempted to do the same by postulating a view of humans as determined in their actions by forces beyond their control. Whatever one may think of such a position, it at least had the merit of being internally consistent. Beccaria's attempt to avoid the issue while retaining the conception of free will was, perhaps, asking for trouble.

Rationality

According to classical criminology we mostly behave in a rational manner. The goal of our rationality is personal satisfaction; rational self-interest is the key motivational characteristic that governs our relationship with crime and conformity. Since crime, however it is defined in any particular society, always involves some degree of restraint on individual self-interest, our natural tendency is always towards deviation: we will, it seems, always choose the deviant alternative when it suits us and when we think we can get away with it. We appear to be selfish, cynical creatures; our greatest ambition in relation to rules of behaviour is to get other people to obey them so that our own cheating is even more productive.

It is odd that the holder of such a view of human beings could have appeared in history as a humanitarian and heroic opponent of cruelty and barbarism; it seems more appropriate to Hitler than to Beccaria. I have suggested earlier that part of Beccaria's reputation may have resulted from his glossing over the more unsavoury implications of his views, and the fact that his full programme has never really been put into practice; but this is not to deny that, in so far as he has been an influence, he has been a relatively benign one.

A more complex view of our selfishness emerges if we consider its crucial feature — its rationality — a little further. As we have seen, it is our rationality that enables us also to appreciate the personal advantages we would derive from a social contract that promotes self-denial and individual rights. Thus, we are simultaneously capable of altruism. True, it is an altruism grounded in selfishness, but that need not bother us (it can only lead into the usual teenage casuistry about altruism always being ultimately selfish). More important is the fact that our simultaneous selfish demands make it a precarious, situational altruism. It is this ambiguous, contradictory and fluctuating view of our relationship with deviance and conformity that makes the classical position so much more dynamic and plausible than subsequent versions.

Beccaria also implies that our rationality would enable us to agree on what constitutes social harm. It thus provides the basis for defining objective legal rules. In practice though, as we saw, Beccaria thought that most people had not developed their rational insight sufficiently for this to be the case — full rational insight had only been achieved by 'some few thinking men in every nation in every age'. The source of objective legal rules thus appears to be the fully developed rationality of the intellectual élites of different nations. But the implication is that through education we all have the potential to achieve the rational insight of the 'few thinking men' and that, if we did, we, too, would agree on the legal rules that would prevent social harm. Fully rational reasoning, then, would provide an objective, consensual determination of legal rules (though not, of course, any guarantee that we would not break them!).

Despite the possibility of there being objective legal rules, however, Beccaria was clearly not implying that existing legal systems, including that of his own society, necessarily embody them. His critique was open to the inclusion of the *content* as well as the administration of the law. There was certainly no implication in classical criminology, as there was to be in positivist, that we can ignore the content and operation of legal rules in addressing ourselves to the question of the causes and treatment of crime. If anything it is more open to criticism for *solely* addressing itself to these areas.

Manipulability

Although classical criminology clearly portrays humans as being free, responsible and choice-making, this does not preclude their being manipulated. The universally-shared human motive of rational self-interest makes human action predictable, generalisable and controllable. In its concern with manipulation, classical criminology was fully compatible with its successor, positivist criminology; they were both based on the belief that the primary purpose of the penal system was to control crime. However, their views on the way in which this could be achieved were quite different. In the classical version, we are manipulable only through threats or appeals; in the positivist it is through the alteration of mechanistic causal variables.

Beccaria's unwillingness to allow individual differences — whether in terms of personal characteristics or socio-economic position — to enter into considerations of punishment, also distanced him from the positivist version of human manipulability. Strangely enough, as we saw earlier, neoclassicism's inclusion of apparently incompatible retributive concerns provided a more direct link in this respect. Neoclassicism allowed that some offenders were less guilty than others because they were less responsible. When immaturity and, more especially, insanity came to be accepted as making people less responsible, this allowed for the possibility that, for some offenders at least, personal characteristics (or defects) could be seen as both differentiating them from other people and *causing* their criminality. This was to be precisely the starting assumption of positivist criminologists (although they were interested in these differences not because they justified different levels of desert, but because they suggested different types of treatment). To some extent, positivist criminology can be seen as incorporating both the classical concern with rational crime control, and the neoclassical concern with individual differentiation.

41

In general, the classical perspective contained a peculiarly narrow view of what it actually is that controls human behaviour. It was concerned solely with the formal legal apparatus and relied on a very specific mechanism of control (deterrence by making punishments proportional to crimes). I will be considering the empirical evidence on the effectiveness of this particular mechanism in [Chapter 9]. It has already been noted, however, that there is no particular reason inherent in the classical view of human motivation to assume that this is the only possible means of control. Beccaria just happened to think it was.

There was no consideration at all given to the possibility of disincentives operating in the informal social context, and a total neglect of social and economic *incentives* of all kinds. Leftist critics have suggested that this is because *any* consideration of the socio-economic context of crime would have proved an embarrassment to the classical position. Taylor, Walton and Young (1973), for example, argue that it would inevitably have raised unpalatable issues: that there *are* important socio-economic differences between people, and that these are relevant to crime causation; in other words, issues of *differentiation* and *social determinism* (inimical to the classical position) would have demanded attention. They suggest that the particular problem that confronted Beccaria was the observable fact that criminals were in one important respect clearly differentiated: they were mostly poor. This suggested poverty as both a cause and a rational reason for crime. They give (ibid., pp. 5–6) an example of how Beccaria deals with this problem (in a discussion of theft):

> He who endeavours to enrich himself with the property of others, should be deprived of part of his own. But this crime, alas! is commonly the effect of misery and despair; the crime of that unhappy part of mankind, to whom the right of exclusive property (a terrible and perhaps unnecessary right) has left but a bare existence. Besides, as pecuniary punishments may increase the number of robbers, by increasing the number of poor, and may deprive an innocent family of subsistence, the most proper punishment will be that kind of slavery, which alone can be called just; that is, which makes society, for a time, absolute master of the person, and labour of the criminal, in order to oblige him to repair, by this dependence, the unjust despotism he usurped over the property of another, and his violation of the social compact.

They interpret this as showing that Beccaria, through his commitment to a social contract that accepted the necessity of the inequities and poverty resulting from private property, was forced to overlook these as much more plausible reasons for crime than his own. Interestingly, Paolucci in his translation of Beccaria (1963, p. 74) (not the one used by Taylor, Walton and Young) adds the following footnote to the above passage:

> in a manuscript of Beccaria's own hand as well as in the first edition, Beccaria had written 'a terrible but perhaps necessary right' — that is to say, quite the opposite of 'a terrible and perhaps unnecessary right,' as found here.

The 'original' actually fits Taylor, Walton and Young's argument rather better than the amended version they quote above which implies at least the *possibility* of poverty as a cause of 'rational' crime. Vold and Bernard (1986, p. 29) are critical of Taylor, Walton and Young for not allowing that Beccaria could see crime as being sometimes rational and justified. But they are being rather generous; whatever Beccaria may have privately thought or hinted at, he never developed his position on these matters. At most, it suggests that he lacked the courage of his more radical convictions, rather than being a straightforward conservative. Certainly, his *intellectual* position would not have been jeopardised by such an extension of his arguments. His version of human freedom and motivation could easily have included poverty as a 'rational' reason for crime; and there was no necessary reason for him to equate his social contract with the status quo as far as property relations were concerned (after all, he did not equate it with the status quo in many other respects).

In general, there was nothing inherent in Beccaria's intellectual position to preclude a consideration of the socio-economic context of crime, any more than there was to necessitate his sole concentration on deterrence that was remarked on earlier. Indeed, it is an oddity that he seemed to see the criminal justice system as being the only aspect of the environment that influences individual decisions about whether it is worthwhile to commit crime or not.

Conclusion

A recent assessment has portrayed him as a cautious conservative who successfully redirected enlightenment thinking away from a potentially much more radical path: 'His sudden fame can be attributed to the relief of educated society that it was possible to hold rational "enlightened" views on human behaviour without having to accept radical materialism (Jenkins, 1984, p. 113). Jenkins argues that enlightenment thinking in Beccaria's time was 'advanced': atheistic and deterministic ideas proposing that humans are determined by their social environment, that morality is relative and that the justification for the existing social order was consequently bogus, were being openly espoused. He uses William Godwin and the Marquis de Sade as examples. Beccaria's offer of a less radical alternative, says Jenkins, had the effect of postponing the positivist revolution for over a century.

It is true that Beccaria seems careful not to offend. The introduction to his book contains a strong denial that he is an atheist, revolutionary or opponent of sovereign rulers. But this is hardly surprising; such things could get you into trouble (his 'promoters', the Verri brothers, were already in trouble). It is also true that most people would look fairly conventional, even today, when compared with de Sade. What is rather more strange is that Jenkins should portray the postponement of the positivist revolution as being an anti-radical step. After all, when it did come it initially avoided these political problems by the simple device of locating the determinants of crime in the individual's make-up (and for that reason the early version of positivism has been a firm favourite with rulers and governments ever since).

Certainly, positivism did also produce social determinist critiques of the existing order. But then, as I have argued earlier, there was nothing in the basic assumptions of classicism that necessarily prevented it from being equally critical. In both classical and positivist criminology, it is the particular way their basic assumptions are interpreted and developed that establishes their political and ideological positions.

Despite all the problems that have been discussed in relation to the basic assumptions of classical criminology, I have emphasised that they have stemmed mostly from the way they were interpreted, and from their underdevelopment. The assumptions themselves have remained more or less intact, and in [Part Two] I will return to them in developing a 'postclassical' perspective.

Notes

1. In this section, references where only a page number is given are to Beccaria (1963).

2. For a useful summary and critique of arguments about the ideological and material forces behind the emergence of the prison, see Ignatieff (1985).

3. For a definitive discussion of these problems in the context of a more recent, positivist attempt to abandon questions of the responsibility of criminals, see Kneale (1967).

References

Beccaria, C. (1963) *On crimes and punishments* (translated by H. Paolucci). Indianapolis: Bobbs-Merrill (first published, as *Dei Delitti e delle Pene,* in 1764).

Ignatieff, M. (1985) 'State, civil society and total institutions: A critique of recent histories of punishment'. In S. Cohen & A. Scull (Eds.), *Social control and the State*. Oxford: Blackwell.

Kneale, W. (1967) *The responsibility of criminals*. Oxford: Clarendon Press.

3. Thinking Seriously about Crime: Some Models of Criminology

Jock Young

Crime is a subject of perennial interest, and in recent years it has once again become a topic of major public debate. We are likely to encounter the 'conversation about crime' wherever we turn — in conversations at a bus stop, or in the pub, reading the 'News of the World' or the 'Guardian' or listening to a phone-in on the radio. These conversations will not only reflect the concern with what is commonly perceived as the ever-rising rate of crime, our feelings about what this means, and what ought to be done about it. They will also draw on a range of implicit explanations as to what causes crime, and a range of implications as to how to deal with it, even though we are not aware that we are using criminological theories and explanations of crime at all.

But there are important differences between 'popular theories' of crime and criminology. In particular, the latter:

(a) attempts to ground itself in an empirical knowledge of the patterns, incidences and variations in criminal behaviour, drawing on more systematic information;

(b) attempts to build a theoretical position systematically, so that the different parts of the theory fit coherently, ironing out inconsistencies and contradictions of position;

(c) attempts to be as comprehensive as it can — dealing with the different aspects and drawing these into a systematic account.

This does not mean that it is only criminologists who are capable of 'thinking seriously about crime'. Popular or lay discussions of crime may be well-ordered and thoughtful, and most criminological theories are better at explaining some aspects (or types) of crime than others.

In more popular discussions, we can often identify the points where people switch theories in mid-argument. For example, they sometimes define vandalism as a 'wilful act of damage' (implying conscious intent), but go on in the next breath to explain vandalism as a product of the vandal's poor home background (implying that the behaviour is determined). Another common 'switch' is between the explanation of crime and the policy conclusions that are drawn. For example, if it is true that vandalism is the product of poor family and home circumstances, then is it logical to propose that vandals should be harshly punished for acts which are determined by circumstances? If the principal cause of vandalism is 'bad home conditions', we should logically 'treat' the circumstances, not the individual vandal, if we want to get to the root of the problem.

Jock Young: 'Thinking Seriously about Crime: Some Models of Criminology' from CRIME AND SOCIETY, edited by Mike Fitzgerald, Gregor McLellan and Jennie Pawson, (Routledge in association with the Open University, 1981) pp. 248–274; 279–307. © The Open University, 1981.

Using criminological theories can be equally problematical. It is not uncommon for theories of crime to adopt different explanations for different types of crime and offender. Thus white-collar crime is theorised differently from working-class petty property crime. Indeed the variability of what is defined as crime has led some criminologists to question the search for a single, all-embracing theory which will explain all criminal activity. What is considered to be crime differs between and within societies over time. For example, the sale of alcohol was a legitimate activity in the USA at the turn of the century, was effectively criminalised during the Prohibition period, and is once more legitimate again. Throughout this period the activity remained the same, it was the legal status of the sale of alcohol that changed. It may well be that we should not require a single theory, no matter how systematic in form, to account for all the many different types of crime within a single explanatory framework. Criminological theories indeed differ precisely as to whether or not they assume a *single* explanation of crime in general to be either conceivable or useful.

In this article I shall introduce and consider six of the major paradigms within criminological theory. I shall show how some theories explain particular types of crime more adequately than others — and need not necessarily be faulted on this ground alone. The proposition that, though crime-in-general is universal, the types and patterns of crime are specific to particular societies at particular times is central to some of the theories that we review. The test of this *general* applicability may not be relevant for judging their value as it would for theories, for example, on a set of universal psychological or physiological features.

Each of the paradigms I shall consider has certain features or elements in common. For example, they all have a particular view of human nature or of social order, even though this may not be especially stated. In examining the six paradigms, then, I shall ask a number of questions about each one.

(a) What is their view of *human nature* in general?

(b) What picture do they present of the *social order* which crime challenges, abrogates or deviates from?

(c) Do they define crime as a 'natural', 'social' or 'legal' phenomenon?

(d) What is the *extent* and *distribution* of crime — is it general and 'normal', in all societies, or is crime a marginal and exceptional activity? Do all people commit crime or are there particular groups or individuals who engage in criminal activity?

(e) What are the principal *causes* of crime?

(f) What *policy deductions* do they draw as to how crime should be dealt with?

I shall ask these six questions to each of the major paradigms — classicism, positivism, conservatism, strain theory, new deviancy theory and marxism — which we examine in this article. The answers to questions which are provided by each paradigm will enable us to distinguish clearly between them.

It is important to remember that we are using these questions as a device for organising one's thoughts about crime. In posing them as dichotomies (Is the view of human nature a voluntaristic or deterministic one? Is the view of social order based on consensus or coercion?), we are deliberately applying the question to draw out and emphasise the difference between paradigms. Posing the questions as dichotomies does not necessarily mean that each theory wholly answers the questions with one alternative or the other.

It is also worth noting that the six paradigms are not of the same kind. Conservatism, for example, has been generally ignored in academic criminology, being regarded largely as a pragmatic and unelaborated way of thinking. The paradigms also have different historical developments; classicism dates back to the eighteenth century, while interest and work in new deviancy theory stems from the 1960s.

In this article, paradigms are presented ideal-typically. Just as I have emphasised differences between the paradigms, so I have minimised the variety of position *within* six theoretical models. Positivism, for example, contains many other strands besides that of 'individual positivism' on which this article focuses. Although the paradigms are presented sequentially, this does not imply that they have been developed in a series of discrete historical stages from classicism to marxism. Nor does it suggest that they were developed in a unilinear fashion. They are competing paradigms, each with its own intellectual history and each flourishing, with powerful support and a substantial body of research work, at the present time.

The dichotomies

(A) Human nature: voluntarism versus determinism

At the point of committing a crime, is the offender perceived as acting out of free-will (voluntarism) or is she/he seen as propelled by forces beyond his or her control (determinism)? This can be conceived of as a question of either whether the act was committed wilfully as part of a process of reasoning (i.e. was it a rational act, whether or not correct in its reasoning) or whether it was non-rational, invoking determining factors outside rational control. (Such factors can be either genetically or environmentally determined.)

(B) Social order: consensus or coercion

Theories of crime are the other side of the coin to theories of order. All criminological theory, at least implicitly, involves a theory of social order. Order in our society can be understood as based either on the consent of the vast majority (although a minority may be coerced by this consent) or largely by the coercion — subtle or blatant — of the majority by a powerful minority.

(C) Definition of crime: legal versus social

The definition of crime may be seen as obvious and taken for granted: it is behaviour or activities which break the legal code. Alternatively it may be argued that a more appropriate measure would be behaviour or activities that offend the social code of a particular community. The legal and social codes do not always coincide and can often conflict. One might argue that tax-evasion is illegal only on paper; in reality it is a normal activity indulged in by a large part of the population. Similarly, vandalism may be seen simply as a crime by virtue of the act of being illegal or else it may be seen as part and parcel of the spirited behaviour of young adolescent boys.

(D) The extent and distribution of crime: limited versus extensive

Is crime, as the official statistics suggest, a limited phenomenon committed by a small number of people, or are the statistics misleading in that law-breaking is an extensive phenomenon engaged in by a large proportion of the population? All criminological theories start from this key problem, although, as we shall see, they differ markedly in their use and interpretation of official crime statistics.

In Figure 1 I have constructed a series of Aztec pyramids, each representing the likelihood of going to prison depending on class, age, race and sex. As can be seen, the social characteristics which greatly increase the risk of incarceration are to be lower working class rather than middle class, young rather than old, black rather than white, and male rather than female. Thus — to take an example — whereas on an average day in 1960 only one in 450 Americans were in prison: one in 26 black men aged between twenty-five and thirty-four were behind bars. Serious crime, according to the statistics, is a minority phenomenon within which certain social categories most marginal to society are vastly over represented. We have used American statistics here because comparable British figures on race are non-existent and, on class, extremely limited (although one British study, interestingly, indicates that the likelihood of a labourer going to prison is identical to that in the USA — see Banks (1978)).

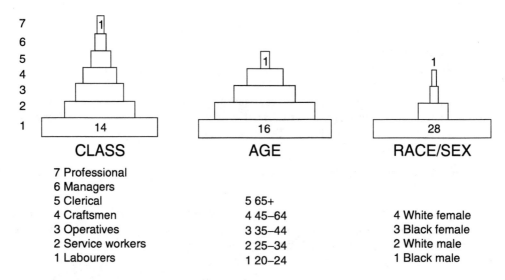

Figure 1   Odds on going to prison by class, age, race and sex.
Source: **American data derived from Wright (1973).**
Note: **a labourer is fourteen times more likely to go to prison than a professional; a 20- to 24-year-old is sixteen times more likely than a 65-year-old; a black male is twenty-eight times more likely than a white female.**

The prisoner is thus seen to be on the fringe of the economy — unemployed or a casual labourer, to have missed out on the educational system, to belong to a minority group.

(E) The causes of crime: individual versus society

The causes of crime may either be located primarily within the individual, whether in his or her personality, biological make-up or powers of reasoning, or be seen as essentially the product of the wider society within which the individual exists. For example, rape might be viewed either as a product of a gross genetically-determined personality disorder, or as a mode of conduct which is a direct product of the sexist nature of a patriarchal society and the way in which sexual encounters are usually understood and conducted by men.

(F) Policy: punishment versus treatment

Such a series of propositions regarding the nature of the criminal, the way social order is to be maintained, the definition and extent of crime and its root causes has, of course, implications for public policy. If, for instance, we view crime as a voluntary act of the individual, we would tend towards a policy of punishing him or her, whereas, if she/he is seen as acting under the compulsion of individual or social forces, the treatment of the criminal might seem to be inappropriate.

Classicism

Classicist theories of crime and punishment developed out of the Philosophy of the Enlightenment which swept Europe in the second half of the eighteenth century. Within a hundred years, most of the legal and penal systems of administration in Europe had been thoroughly remodelled in the light of classicist principles. Enlightenment thinkers were reacting strongly against the arbitrary systems of justice which prevailed during the ancien régime, and the severe and 'barbarous' codes of punishment by which the law was upheld in the period of feudalism and the absolutist monarchies. The rise of classicism is closely associated with the emergence of the free market and the beginnings of agrarian capitalism, and is best thought of as the philosophical outlook of the emerging bourgeoisie — the class that was rising to prominence in this new social order. The members of this new rising class not only sought to secure a privileged position for themselves in society, but aspired to refashion society itself along new lines. They demanded political rights hitherto denied them — they were political, as well as legal reformers in England, at the forefront of the movement to extend the franchise to the new propertied classes. They also demanded a legal system that would defend their interests and protect their 'rights and liberties' against the arbitrary power hitherto wielded exclusively by the aristocratic landed classes and the Crown. In England, they were the principal inheritors of the English Revolution of 1644 which limited the prerogative of the monarchy, and, even more, of the 'Glorious Settlement' of 1688 which settled the country under a constitutional monarchy and undermined the last vestiges of feudal power and authority.

The legal system they proposed had at its centre the concept of the 'free' and legal contract between free and equal individuals. 'Contract' for them was a practical necessity, for it was the relation which allowed men to hire the labour of others, to sell goods and acquire property, not according to rank and statute, but according only to the dictates of a free market. Modern civil law, which revolves around the concept of the contract, was first elaborated under these auspices. But 'contract' was also a grand conception of how society itself arose and how individuals were bound to one another within it, and therefore how their conduct ought to be regulated (i.e., the foundations of a new system of law).

Enlightenment philosophy centred on the 'sovereign individual'. Individuals were conceived as free and rational agents, capable of defining their own self-interests and of choosing rationally to temper their actions according to the dictates of Reason, a faculty lodged in each individual. They therefore thought of society, not as something sovereign which pre-dated the individual, but as something which individuals had contracted to establish for their own individual and mutual benefit. They expressed their legal claims in terms of the 'rights and liberties of the individual' — and sought to limit the power and prerogative of the state (which, in previous times, had been powerfully identified with aristocracy and Crown) to the defence of the rights, liberties and property, as well as the safety and security, of the individual. The preoccupation with individual rights and duties, and with the limited conception of the state, together with the centrality of property and the market, make Enlightenment classicism the source of many ideas and conceptions that were subsequently to be elaborated within liberal political theory and constitutional doctrine. Their influence has been carried into our own times within the 'liberal tradition'. Individuals were therefore 'free' to act according to the dictates of Reason and self-interest, except in so far as their actions limited the freedom of others, equally free, citizens. They should be rewarded proportionately to their energy, skill and efforts — and, conversely, punished proportionately, according to the social harm which they inflicted on other individuals.

The rights, liberties and freedoms which had previously belonged to the very few by virtue of birth, rank and title were now claimed by this rising class. But they laid claim to them, not in their own name, but as a 'universal' right. The American Declaration of Rights, a classic Enlightenment constitutional document, is entirely cast in this language of 'universal rights' — though there were many classes of persons (for example, the labouring poor and women) to whom, in fact, they did not conceive that they could apply. They were opposed to the arbitrary administration of justice in earlier times, which depended on the discretions and exceptions which 'great men' could make according to personal whim or inclination. They wanted, instead, a *universal* system of justice that would apply equally to all men. They wanted it to be a 'rational' system, derived not from the jumble of precedent and custom and tradition but from clearly-defined rational first principles, and set out in a systematic form. Its operations should be certain and predictable, so that men could calculate the 'benefits' and 'costs' of wrong-doing as they did the profit and loss of a financial transaction. They wished to abolish the irrational discrepancy between petty crimes, punished by the terrible engines of capital statute and torture, and devised in their place a scale of punishment proportional to the severity of the crime. Just as men were governed by Reason, so too ought the systems of government, legislation and law by which their common conduct was governed. The application of Reason, calculation and predictability to matters of legislation and law made them the forerunners of modern systems of administration.

The most celebrated classicist theorist is the eighteenth-century Italian writer, Cesare Beccaria; his work was enormously influential on Enlightenment thinkers, including English legal reformers like John Howard, whose writings led to the construction of new penal regimes based on imprisonment, Romilly, who led the attack on the capital statutes, and the founder of Utilitarianism and leading figure among the 'philosophical radicals', Jeremy Bentham. The first chapter of Beccaria's classic work, 'An Essay on Crimes and Punishments', serves well to introduce us to classicist principles in criminological theory (1801, pp. 5–6):

> Laws are the conditions, under which men, naturally independent, united themselves in society. Weary of living in a continual state of war, and of enjoying a liberty which became of little value, from the uncertainty of its duration, they sacrificed one part of it, to enjoy the rest in peace and security. The sum of all these portions of the liberty of each individual constituted the sovereignty of a nation; and was deposited in the hands of the sovereign, as the lawful administrator. But it was not sufficient only to establish this deposit; it was also necessary to defend it from the usurpation of each individual, who would always endeavour not only to take away from the mass his own portion, but to encroach on that of others. Some motives, therefore, that strike the senses, were necessary to prevent the despotism of each individual from plunging society into its former chaos. Such motives are the punishments established against the transgressors of the laws. I say, that motives of this kind are necessary; because experience shows that the multitude adopt no established principle of conduct; and because society is prevented from approaching to that dissolution (to which, as well as all other parts of the physical and moral world, it naturally tends), only by motives that are the immediate objects of sense, and which being continually presented to the mind, are sufficient to counter-balance the effect of the passions of the individual, which oppose the general good. Neither the power of eloquence nor the sublimest truths, are sufficient to restrain, for any length of time, those passions which are excited by the lively impressions of present objects.

This passage is based on several fundamental premises of the classicist school: the 'natural independence' and sovereignty of the individual; the binding together in society under the 'social contract', which yielded power to the monarch or state only in return for the protection of rights and the security of person and property; the 'associationist' psychology of human motivations which underpinned their legal and social theories; the need for law to prevent the pursuit of naked self-interest from plunging society into a competitive struggle — a 'war of all against all', as the political philosopher, Hobbes, put it. Beccaria's leading disciple in England was Bentham, who applied the rational calculus of his Utilitarian philosophy extensively to questions of law and punishment. Bentham sought to reform the archaic English system of justice according to rational principles, systematically applied. The legal code should be formalised, punishment made to bear directly on the individual, predictable and proportional to the offence. He reduced the complex issues concerning criminal motivation to the simple terms of his 'pleasure/pain' continuum. Punishment should be rational and impersonal. Bentham said of Beccaria that his was the 'first of any account which is uniformly censorial'.

Classicist thinking has been immensely influential on legal and criminological reasoning over the past two centuries: many modern ideas about crime — for example, the centrality in English law of the concept of individual responsibility — can be traced to classicist roots. It was rarely, however, anywhere put into practice in its pure form. Its implementation within the reform of both the criminal law and the administration of justice was more piecemeal and governed by pragmatic considerations than the pure classicists would have wanted. Classicism was subsequently further modified by the introduction, within its framework, of some principles drawn from positivism, the second major paradigm we shall examine: for example, a wider number of groups — children, the insane and feeble-minded — were recognised as being incapable of full rational responsibility for their actions, and the law was required to take some circumstantial factors and influences into account, modifying the pure classicist doctrine of 'free will'. The resulting amalgam of classicism and positivism — often labelled 'neoclassicism' — has, however, constituted the dominant criminological paradigm in Anglo-Saxon legal thought and practice, and is the main source of the eclectic synthesis which, as Radzinowicz and others have observed, has dominated British and North American criminology since.

What is interesting about the classicist paradigm is that it has the largest history of any contemporary criminological theory but still continues to be a major influence both on institutions of social control and in controversies in criminology. For example, a major debate within the last decade has been over the necessity of re-establishing classicist principles in terms of adult offenders (e.g., N. Morris, 1974; Fogel, 1975) and in the juvenile courts (e.g., A. Morris, 1978).

(A) Human nature

> Although free will may not exist perfectly, the criminal law is largely based upon its presumed vitality and forms the only foundation for penal sanctions. (Fogel, 1975, p. 183)

Within classicism, human nature is concurred as rational, free and governed by self-interest. Human beings are considered 'equal' in that they are all endowed with free-will and with the faculty of Reason. When cast in this universal framework, the theory disclaims distinctions of birth and aristocratic lineage, making its claims in the name of universal Man. In terms of its origins, this fitted well with the rising ambitions and fortunes of the emergent bourgeoisie who most fiercely espoused its principles. In practice, significant sections of the population — women, the labouring poor, the insane (even, at times, the great majority) — have not been assumed to meet the criteria of the full citizenship accorded only to the fully rational individual. Such exceptions are justified on the grounds that they are either *pre*-rational (e.g., children and juveniles) or *sub*-rational (the aged and infirm). The precise constituency of those excluded from the category of rational equals varies historically. The issue was and continues to be politically significant, since it related to the question of how far the reform of the franchise should go in extending full citizenship to the un-enfranchised.

There is a tension in the classicist conception of human nature between the rational self and the pursuit of self-interest. Using self-interest as a basic reference point in the analysis of human motivation gave the theory a firm, realistic — perhaps even materialistic — foundation: 'society' arose because the self-interest of individuals in the security of life and property over-rode the competitive drive to gain maximum advantage — there was no need to posit some wider, 'social' instinct or ideal. But, in order that individuals, all seeking to realise their interests, did not bring society to ruin, self-interest had to be tempered by Reason, which was something more than mere 'rational calculation'. This tension was never adequately resolved. Nevertheless, writers like Bentham believed that the motivation to commit or not to commit a crime for personal advantage could be so weighted — provided punishment was sufficiently severe and certain — that 'choosing to obey the law' would come to be seen as the most rational of the available choices. Punishment — or, as he called it, the 'science of pain' — should be so severe that the 'benefits' of crime were far outweighed by its 'costs'. Classicists are little concerned with the complexities of human motivation. They believed motivations could be calculated and influenced by external, objective arrangements.

(B) Social order

In the classicist conception, social order is based on the Social Contract. In their view, society did not pre-date the individual. Instead, individuals rationally calculated that they could best secure their mutual advantage by 'contracting together' to establish a sovereign state or power. In the face of the threat from external conquest or the 'war of all against all', they were prepared to sign away some part of their sovereign liberties to 'the Sovereign', in return (the basis of *the contract*) for the protection of person and property against crime and usurpation. But they believed that this sovereign power, the state, should play a limited role — accorded only that power necessary to protect individuals' rights and liberties. Coercion by the state should be limited to this minimum, based on a consensus between rational citizens. The exercise of power by the state is therefore justified only in so far as it satisfies the interests of its citizens by facilitating and maintaining justice — that is, by protecting the just rewards of labour and punishing justly those who offended against this order. In a modified form, this conception of a social order based on the Social Contract continues to be influential in contemporary thought and, together with the emphasis on the individual's rights and civil liberties and the doctrine of the limited state (itself constrained by the 'rule of law') forms the cornerstones of modern legal and constitutional traditions within the liberal perspective .

The classicist conception of social order assumed, of course, the formal equality of status between all individuals who merited the honour of full citizenship. However, the emphasis on private property, on the just rewards for entrepreneurial skill and the 'right' to accumulate wealth produced an actual social structure in which the basis of rights and benefits was very unequally distributed throughout society. This formal universalism underpinned the notion that 'all men' should be equal under the 'rule of law'. Classicism, however, failed both in theory and practice to square the significant divergencies between *formal* and *substantive* equality.

The rights which the law protected stemmed from and, ultimately, reverted to the individual citizens — the foundation stone of social order. Consent, once given, could also be withdrawn (though classicists differ as to the conditions under which the overthrow of the Sovereign or state is justified). In this sense, the bourgeois classes who subscribed to 'social contract' doctrine remained faithful to the Whig Revolutionary tradition that had overthrown the absolute monarchy in the 1640s — though they were rapidly gaining ascendency in the new social order which emerged in the wake of the Hanoverian settlement.

(C) Definition of crime

Crime is defined as that which violates the Social Contract: in this definition, behaviour which is detrimental, not to the state as such, but to the personal safety and property of those individuals in society whose decision to 'contract in' founded the authority of the state. This, and not the question of whether such behaviour is widespread or 'normal', is the main criterion. Thus, for Social Contract theorists, tax-evasion might be widespread and generally condoned as 'normal', but it would be necessary to legislate against it because it is anti-social and against social justice as they defined it. For them, 'legal' rather than 'natural' definitions are paramount in the definition of crime. They do not, therefore, subscribe to relativist conceptions of crime. They concentrate, not on circumstances and influences, but on the criminal *act* itself. If illegal, judged as the law defines it in the light of the Social Contract, then the act should be punished proportionally — with unwavering certainty, severity and impartiality. Neither the arbitrary exercise of terror nor the discretionary application of justice — so much a feature of judicial administration under the ancien régime or discretionary justice as practised in the modern courts — are acceptable to them.

The law, however, though certain and predictable, should not be involved in the control of any activities which do not harm others, do not contradict their self-interest or threaten the Social Contract. From this stems the long tradition in Anglo-Saxon law that, far from prescribing what the individual can and cannot do, it allows citizens to be free to do anything they like, provided only it is not proscribed by law. Liberty was sovereign: subject only to the law's constraints. Thus the law should not be extended to so-called 'consensual crimes' — crimes which are 'without identifiable victims' (e.g., prostitution, as it is viewed from their highly masculine-oriented world). Law and morality should be regarded as separate spheres: the one regulating public concerns, the sphere of the social contract; the other, the proper sphere of individual judgment and private reasoning. The civilised state is that which defines the minimal number of activities as crimes, and which permits moral diversity and individual variation — provided only that the Social Contract is protected.

(D) The extent and distribution of crime

Crime is the infringement of a legal code, not of a behavioural or social norm. The only acceptable method of ascertaining whether a particular act is, in fact, 'criminal' is *within* the legal process — that is, by 'due process of law'. 'Due process' was a founding conception of classicism because it preserved the rights of an ascendent class against the arbitrary exercise of justice and coercion by the state. Provided 'due process' is observed, and the certainty of detection improved (classicists strongly favour a regular and improved police), the criminal statistics can be taken as an accurate guide as to the true extent of criminality in a society. As Paul Tappan forcefully puts it (1970, p. 47):

> The behavior prohibited has been considered significantly in derogation of group welfare by deliberative and representative assembly, formally constituted for the purpose of establishing such norms; nowhere else in the field of social control is there directed a comparable rational effort to elaborate standards conforming to the predominant needs, desires and interests of the community . . .

> Adjudicated offenders represent the closest possible approximation to those who have in fact violated the law, carefully selected by the sieving of the due process of the law; no other province of social control attempts to ascertain the breach of norms with such rigor and precision.

This process of adjudication by due legal procedures represents the judgment by the court, not only as to whether in fact the act was committed by an individual, but — of crucial importance to classicism — whether the individual intended to commit the act, whether the accused was in his or her right mind (*mens rea*) and could thus be held responsible for his or her actions as a rational individual.

(E) Causes of crime

In the classicist paradigm, the whole conception of the 'causes of crime' relates to the question of rational motivation. Within the consensual majority, where Reason and self-interest are in a proper balance and the 'costs' of crime clearly outweigh the 'benefits', no one should ideally be tempted to commit crime since, by definition, this would be an *irrational* calculation. But for the labouring poor of the nineteenth century, for example, many instances could be conceived where 'benefits' were greater than 'costs', and crime was the result of a rational calculation — though harmful to the Social Contract. For this reason, punishment is at the centre of the classicist conception of justice: through legislation and the reform of penal regimes, punishment must be made so strict that the individual would be deterred from committing crime again.

To this rational calculus, significant exceptions are made, along the continuum of Reason. Rationality in its full sense — and hence full responsibility — could not be present where Reason is impaired (e.g., insanity) or where no 'intent' can be shown (accident). Somewhat against the main thrust of this thinking, certain marginal exceptions through mitigating circumstances can also be allowed as marginal excuses (e.g., under duress or provocation). Even so, they are attributed to errors or absence of Reason, rather than to the positive force of circumstances. The source of criminality is thus located within the rational, 'reasoning' individual.

Nevertheless, unsatisfactory laws, or a legal system lacking clear principles, can create crimes which should never be labelled as such, and unjust laws or inequitable punishments can exacerbate the extent of crime. The systematisation and proportionality of law and punishment — the reforms which the classicists champion — are supported as much for these as for more strictly 'humanitarian' reasons.

(F) Policy

Principles guiding the decision to imprison should be these:

1. *Parsimony*: the least restrictive (punitive) sanction necessary to achieve defined social purposes should be imposed.

2. *Dangerousness*: prediction of future criminality should be rejected as a base for determining that the convicted criminal should be imprisoned.

3. *Desert*: no sanction should be imposed greater than that which is 'deserved' by the last crime, or series of crimes, for which the offender is being sentenced.
   (N. Morris, 1974, p. xi)

> Here we will suggest that the law should deal only with a narrow aspect of the individual, that is, his criminal act or acts. We will urge that the law be applied uniformly to all offenders. We will spell out our principles of restraint, urging that criminal sanctions be imposed only when other remedies have proved inadequate.

> The whole person is not the concern of the law. Whenever the law considers the whole person it is more likely that it considers factors irrelevant to the purpose of delivering punishment. The other factors, by and large, have been and will certainly continue to be characteristics related to influence, power, wealth, and class. They will not be factors related to the needs or the treatment potentialities of the defendant.
> (American Friends Service Committee, 1971, pp. 146–7)

The central focus of classicist criminal policy is the criminal act itself. Criminals must 'choose' within the certain knowledge of detection — hence the requirement of a modernised and regular police force. Punishment must bear down directly on the responsibilities and calculations of the individual. Since the purpose of punishment is *not* to inflict arbitrary pain, or to make public retribution, but so to arrange things as to make obeying the law the most rational of choices, punishment must be made proportional to the actual social harm it causes, and limited to only that required to deter further criminal acts. Previous convictions of the actor are to be judged irrelevant to the particular act being judged by judicial process, since he or she must be punished only in relation to the specific action for which an accusation has been laid. The notion of using punishment to make a *general* example is anathema to classicism: the process must bear directly on the individual and the act. General deterrence puts the principle of social order (a subordinate or derived principle, a classicist doctrine) *above* that of justice to the individual (the sovereign or founding principle). Classicism is, of course, concerned to preserve the Social Contract: but, it argued, the most effective way of doing this is through the resolute pursuit of individual justice. Within 'due process', there should be a strict defence of the individual's legal rights — classicism strongly defends the 'presumption of innocence', for example. This concern for 'due judicial process' extends to the proportionate penalties in sentencing. Bentham hoped for a strict 'economy' of punishment — penalties and sentences strictly proportional to the offence. Thus modern neoclassicists strongly favour a fixed 'tariff system' of sentencing, as against the more discretionary system which prevails in, for example, English and American courts at this moment. (American Friends Service Committee, 1971, p. 124):

> We submit that many distortions and corruptions of justice — such as the discriminatory use of penal sanctions and the use of the criminal justice system to promote conformity and control classes of person — depend upon the existence of wide margins of discretionary power in the hands of police, district attorneys, judges, correctional administrators, parole boards, and parole agents. Therefore, discretion is at the core of the problem.

According to the principles of legal equality, crimes should be judged by a jury of one's peers — that is, by other rational and equal individuals. Judges should be guided by a clear and systematic legal code. And sentencing should be limited to applying a prior, agreed and fixed set of penalties — a tariff system — equally across the board, allowing only minor adjustments and discretions for 'mitigating circumstances'. Thus (Fogel, 1975, p. 254):

> We propose to inform the convict at the outset of the penalties for his crime. We would replace the present law with a series of determinate sentences, keyed to the present felony classification system. For each felony class, a fixed sentence is proposed, with a narrow range in mitigation or aggravation allowed around that definite figure to permit adjustments either for the facts of a particular case or for the seriousness of the offense as compared to others in the same class. In effect, then, a relatively small range of allowable prison terms would be associated with each offense. Whenever the court found imprisonment to be the appropriate disposition, it would select a fixed sentence from within that range and impose it. When a convicted person left the courtroom, he would know his actual sentence to be served less good time.

Neither inappropriate leniency nor undue harshness are permissible in the classicist economy of punishment. The first fails to achieve its effect; the latter introduces a personal and emotional element into a system which should be rational and impartial. Punishment should therefore be strictly applied, irrespective of the status or background of the accused, but also applied efficiently and effectively. Bentham, indeed, hoped to impose within the new penal regimes a very strict criterion of efficiency and cost-accounting: he was, for example, in favour of prisons which 'paid', but of regular public inspection as well. Punishment should be seen to be 'just' — but it should also be strict, regular and disciplined. Justice should be doled out without delay and to the maximum of offenders the police can apprehend. The law is an instrument, not only of control, but also of education. And 'educating the public' into the calculus of law-abidingness requires that irregularities, due to either lack of detection or evasion of penalties or irrational prison regimes, should be eliminated. Any deviation from strict disciplinary uniformity simply encourages crime, either through ineffective control or by propagating injustices which cause citizens to question the justice and impartiality of the Social Contract. In particular, modern classicists have directed their wrath against the prison regime on two counts: that prison life does not embody principles of justice and/or that it attempts to treat the individual rather than to punish him. David Fogel notes this in two of the central parts in his demands for justice (1975, p.184):

> The entire process of the criminal law must be played out in a milieu of justice. Justice-as-fairness represents the superordinate goal of all agencies of the criminal law.

> When correction becomes mired in the dismal swamp of preaching, exhorting, and treating ('resocialization') it becomes dysfunctional as an agency of justice. Correctional agencies should engage prisoners as the law otherwise dictates — as responsible, volitional and aspiring human beings.

Thus N. Morris notes sadly: 'The prison should, were the world not full of paradox, be a very paradigm of the rule of law' (1974, p. 21). Instead, due process ends at the point of imprisonment and the prison has become a lawless institution. The lawful educational role of the lawful prison is viewed by David Fogel as the central keynote of the neo-classicist 'justice model' (1977, pp. 126–7):

> The period of incarceration can be conceptualized as a time in which we try to reorient a prisoner to the lawful use of power. One of the more fruitful ways the prison can teach nonlaw-abiders to be law-abiding is to treat them in a lawful manner. The entire effort of the prison should be seen as an influence attempt based upon operationalizing justice. This is called the 'justice model.'

> It is a sad irony in our system of criminal justice that we insist on the full majesty of due process for the accused until he is sentenced to a prison, then justice is said to have been served. The entire case for a justice model rests upon the need to continue to engage the person in the quest for justice as he moves on the continuum from defendant-to-convict-to-free citizen.

Nor is justice achieved in the modern prison by instituting seemingly progressive treatment or rehabilitation processes. For these involve a dishonesty which conceals disproportionate punishment. (American Friends Service Committee, 1971, p. 24) :

> Thus the sleight of hand that transforms prisons into something else, such as 'civil institutions' for addicts and reformatories for juvenile delinquents, does not alter the coercive reality. . . .

> We believe there is much to be gained from honesty in our semantics. By characterizing all penal coercion as punishment, we emphasize rather than dilute the critical necessity of limiting it as much as possible.

Thus it is the twin obstacles to justice of arbitrary punishment or scientific treatment which classicism opposes.

Problems of classicism

The classicist contradiction

The principal contradiction at the heart of classicism has already been indicated. It is, in essence, the contradiction between formal and substantive equality. Classicism assumes that all 'men' are free, rational and equal. An impartial and universal system of justice can operate 'rationally' in such circumstances, where none has priority of rank or status, and no prior handicaps or advantages. But the real world does not in any way resemble this ideal model. Indeed, it cannot by definition, since classicism is rooted in a competitive model of man, where seeking advantage is precisely the most rational of motivations; and the principal purpose of the Social Contract is to defend the rights and liberties of 'men', above all the liberty to employ the labour of others, to acquire property and accumulate wealth. These generate, as the necessary consequence of a competitive system, massively unequal distribution of advantages and disadvantages. But classicism attempts to abstract from these real material conditions, and to posit a state of formal equality. It has therefore constantly to confront all the contradictions that flow from a legal philosophy based on formal equality which is required to operate 'justly' in conditions of substantive inequality. Many of the other problems in classicism flow from this central contradiction.

The necessity of punishment

If men are free, sovereign and rational, and the contract just, we may ask why individuals persist in violating the law at all? Should not Reason regularly prevail? The fact that it does not, necessitating just and swift, but also extensive and severe, punishment, means that the motivations and incentives to commit crime are arising from some aspect of society not accounted for within the rationalist calculus. One source is that very structure of substantive inequalities which the paradigm finds so difficult to explain or take into account. Another may be that the Social Contract is, in reality, more 'just' for some than it is for others — the others being, perhaps, the majority of those lacking an advantageous position within the system. The premise that what is good and just for individuals corresponds to the 'collective good' is assumed, not demonstrated.

The pyramid of crime

If all individuals are equally endowed with Reason, why is the incidence of criminal irrationalities not random? Why do the statistics take the shape of that pyramid shown in Figure 1, with the poor regularly committing so much more crime than the rich? Perhaps, in the light of this, formal equality is a sham, imposing a form of legal fairness on a system which regularly generates substantive inequalities: a world where, as Anatole France cynically put it, the 'law in all its majesty forbids both the rich and poor from sleeping under the bridges of the Seine'. Both may be equal 'in the sight of the law' — but nowhere else.

The problem of rational abstraction

Many of the problems with classicism derive from its tendency to abstract out the individual act from its circumstantial conditions and contexts. This tendency parallels that of attempting to isolate formal equality from its substantive circumstances. But men and women rarely make such strictly isolated individual calculations into which no trace of surrounding conditions enter. It is not only that we often act 'irrationally'. It is also that what is and is not 'rational' depends on the prevailing conditions and the circumstances from which calculations about human actions are made. Goals are very rarely formed in a void; and they are hardly ever motivated by pure self-interest. Classicists tend to resolve all these factors into the general faculty of Reason, but apart from a sort of built-in philosophical guarantee, they produce no convincing explanation of what this general faculty is or where it came from or how it modifies and tempers the competitive drive to self-advantage. Moreover, though they claim a universal Reason, their actual social calculations are based on a highly particular and differentiated notion of which groups in society are endowed with this universal faculty. In fact, it has often excluded a wide range of people in the population — the vast majority, including the lower orders and outcasts of society, women and children. They speak of Reason and Men as abstract universals, but they often mean the reasons of a very particular and limited number of particular men.

The problem of equivalence

In particular, no matter how one tries in abstract reasoning, in concrete terms, it is impossible to squeeze 'equivalence' out of the poor, who were clearly not equal. Beccaria himself touched upon the problem when he attempted to elaborate a punishment suitable for robbery (1801, pp. 80–1):

> He who endeavours to enrich himself with the property of another, should be deprived of part of his own. But this crime, alas! is commonly the effect of misery and despair — the crime of that unhappy part of mankind, to whom the right of exclusive property (a terrible and perhaps unnecessary right) has left but a bare existence. Besides as pecuniary punishments may increase the number of robbers, by increasing the number of poor, and may deprive an innocent family of subsistence, the most proper punishment will be that kind of slavery, which alone can be called just; that is, which makes society, for a time, absolute master of the person, and labour of the criminal, in order to oblige him to repair, by this dependence, the unjust despotism he usurped over the property of another, and his violation of the social compact.

Thus equivalence is impossible to squeeze out of the poor — indeed any attempt makes matters worse. Thus, the classicist justification of imprisonment arises as a solution to this problem of how to extract equivalence out of those who possess no property. Namely, that we equate the extent of property violation with its equivalence in time, and deprive the person of his or her liberty proportionally. But, however ingenious Beccaria's formulation and its repeated invocation through the centuries, it scarcely solves the problem of the impoverished dependents. For imprisonment likewise increases the number of poor but, more than this, by stigmatising the prisoner, it often denies him future employment, thus exacerbating his poverty. The equivalent formal punishment has, therefore, real substantive consequences in the lives of the offender and his dependents. For whereas the rich offender may be cushioned by his or her wealth, the poor offender, with the *same* sentence but little to fall back on, is punished in *fact* disproportionately.

Positivism

> We speak two different languages. For us, the experimental (i.e. inductive) method is the key to all knowledge; to them everything derives from logical deductions and traditional opinion. For them, facts should give place to syllogisms; for us the fact governs and no reasoning can occur without starting with facts, for them science needs only paper, pen and ink and the rest comes from a brain stuffed with more or less abundant reading of books made with the same ingredients. For us science requires spending a long time in examining the facts one by one, evaluating them, reducing them to a common denominator, extracting the central idea from them. For them a syllogism or an anecdote suffices to demolish a myriad of facts gathered through years of observation and analysis; for us the reverse is true (Ferri, 1901, p. 244)

> Psychology is no longer a subsidiary of philosophy, it refers no longer on common sense reflections of life, or on armchair theorizing; by becoming experimental it has made the first faltering steps towards becoming scientific . . . Admittedly these theories are much less powerful than those of physics, or astronomy, or chemistry, and they command less universal agreement; nevertheless they cannot be dismissed out of hand as useless and premature. Consider how quickly the older and more mature sciences outgrew their earlier theories and how, almost unnoticed, they changed the face of the world. Psychology has set out on the same road, and sooner or later society will have to take heed of its views. . . .

> Sooner or later, society will have to replace its happy-go-lucky, unreasoning ways of dealing with offenders by rational, scientific methods, firmly founded on painstaking observation and empirically-based theory; three thousand years of failure to solve the problem of crime would suggest even to the most conservative that the old ways might not be the best! (Eysenck, 1977, pp. 212–13)

Emerging in the nineteenth century, positivism attempted, under the influence of Darwinism, to carry through a radical change in the conception of man's place in nature. For just as Darwin's theories served to displace the human species out of the unique category of a divine creation into the wider evolutionary context of life on this planet, positivism's task was to show that human behaviour was understandable by the same scientific laws that governed all living activity. This 'positivist revolution' has seen a continuing struggle against 'metaphysical', 'pre-scientific' conceptions of human behaviour — in particular as represented by classicism and its notions of human rationality, equality and free-will.

Positivism's major attribute — from which its major characteristics may all be deduced — is in its insistence on the unity of the scientific method. That is, the premises and instruments which are so demonstrably successful in the study of the physical world and of animal biology are seen to be of equal validity and promise in the study of society and humans. Insisting on this premise, positivists have proceeded to propound methods for the quantification of behaviour, to acclaim the objectivity of the scientific expert and to assert the determinate, law-governed nature of human action. In so doing, positivist criminology creates almost a mirror image of classicism: free-will disappears under determinancy, equality bows before natural differences and expert knowledge, and human laws that are created become scientific laws that are discovered.

There have been many varieties of positivism both in criminology and in the social sciences in general. The particular version I wish to focus on in this section is by far the most prominent example, both in positivist theory and in practice. This theory admits that biological, physiological, psychological and social influences all contribute to the creation of the criminal but that it is in the *individual* that the fundamental predisposition to crime is situated. Furthermore, that the social order is consensual and that crime is a product of the under-socialisation of the individual into this consensus. This type of positivism — what could be termed individual positivism — is the focus of this analysis. It owes its prominence not only to its theoretical dominance but, even more, because it is the paramount type of theory used by practitioners. I will refer to other varieties of positivism at the end of this section.

(A) Human nature

> I think the major objection to the proposals I have outlined is that they smack of treating human beings as if they were nothing but biological organisms subject to strictly deterministic rules; this Pavlovian revolution, coming on top of the Copernican and Darwinian ones, is too much for the self-esteem of many people. Undesirable the fact may be, but that is not sufficient reason for rejecting it as a fact, one would need better reasons to change one's scientific judgment. And where there is (1) a recognised social need, and (2) a recognised body of scientific knowledge which looks likely to be able to create a technology to cope with that need, it needs little in the way of precognitive ability to forecast that in due course society will use this knowledge and create this technology. (Eysenck, 1969, p. 190)

All individual behaviour — however much this may violate human conceit — is a determined product of circumstances. Human beings have a basic animal nature which is more or less socialised into the values of society so that the line from the criminal to the law-abiding citizen is a continuum of degrees of socialisation. Therefore it is not a question of the 'criminal' and the 'normal' existing as separate categories of humanity but rather of everyone being a determined being, the major variable being the degree and efficacy of socialisation.

(B) Social order

Individual positivists would hold that there is a consensus in society which corresponds to the needs of the system. That is the values into which individuals are socialised are necessary to the orderly maintenance of the total society. Coercion should be limited to a minimum of cases where recalcitrant, 'under-socialised' individuals refuse to recognise their problems and are unwilling to be integrated into society.

To the positivist, the classicist contradiction between substantive and formal equality is a fiction based on the preposterous assumption of formal equality. People are substantially different — not in the sense of status — but in terms of their individual abilities and degree of socialisation. Here again, as with determinism, there is much resistance to scientific reality (Eysenck, 1977, p. 75):

> This general attitude is often supported by reference to political notions. It is said that all men are born equal and it is deduced from this that indeed all men have the same innate ability, the same good or poor degree of personality, the same propensity to crime, and so on. This, of course, is a misinterpretation of the old saying. What it means is simply that all men are equal before the law . . . It does not say anything whatsoever about their strength, their health or other features in which they may differ from each other, and in which, as we know perfectly well, they do in fact differ. However, the fact that this is a misunderstanding has in no way lessened the impact of the saying on the great majority of people who are strongly convinced that any innate differences in ability or in propensity to crime would set some kind of limit to the working of modern democracy.

In reality, an individual's final place in the social order reflects more or less the compound of his or her potentiality and the social skills which have been inculcated into them.

(C) Definition of crime

A hallmark of such positivism is the belief that there is a consensus of value in society that can be scientifically ascertained. Against this it can be judged whether an act is deviant or not. The word 'deviant' is preferable to 'criminal', as the latter merely refers to violations of legal codes which (a) may not reflect consensual values at all (e.g., tax evasion as normal behaviour), (b) do not encompass all acts of deviance (e.g., sexual promiscuity may be deviant but perfectly legal), or (c) are based on legal concepts which are unscientific reflecting metaphysical concepts of free-will and intent (i.e., they are classicist) .

(D) The extent and distribution of crime

However much the positivists would be sceptical of the crime statistics in that they are a product of an unscientific conceptualisation collected in a process which is unsystematic and non-exhaustive, they would not doubt their basic pyramidal shape and the variations indicated between different groups of people. That is, that the incidence of crime is indeed greater among blacks than whites, young than old, male than female, and is inversely proportional to class and education. Thus they would regard the official statistics as 'poor' data, yet data of relevance all the same. Whatever his or her scientific scruples, it is a rare positivist who will not make direct use of the criminal statistics.

(E) Causes of crime

> Every crime is the resultant of individual, physical and social conditions.
> (Ferri, 1893, p. 161)

Crime is a product of the undersocialisation of the individual. This can be a result of (a) an innate genetic or physiological incapacity of the individual to be easily socialised; (b) a family background which was ineffective in the use of socialisation techniques in its child-rearing practices; (c) a social milieu which lacked coherent and consistent consensual values. Each of these levels — the physical, the family and the social — will be seen to compound with each, to determine the socialisation of a specific individual. And it is noted that it is at the very bottom of the class structure, where the incidence of crime is greatest, that such 'defects' are most likely to occur. For it is there that the least capable individuals accumulate and pass on their inadequacies from generation to generation in a cycle of deprivation.

The causes of crime are thus rooted in defects in the past of the actor, in his or her determined antecedents. Crime itself is a reflection of these; as a product of undersocialisation it is an activity without meaning, a non-rational outburst of pre-social impulses.

None of this falls into the trap of suggesting that the *direction* or *shape* that crime takes is a biological pre-given. As Hans Eysenck astutely notes (1977, pp. 77, 79):

> criminality is a social concept, not a biological one. Indeed, what is criminal in one country may not be criminal in another; homosexuality is a crime in some American states but not in Germany. Similarly, what is a crime at one time may not be at another. It is a crime to kill people but only in peace time; during war time it becomes a citizen's duty to kill others . . .

> The very notion of criminality or crime would be meaningless without a context of learning or social experience and, quite generally, of human interaction. What the figures have demonstrated is that heredity is a very strong predisposing factor as far as committing crimes is concerned. But the actual way in which the crime is carried out, and whether or not the culprit is found and punished — these are obviously subject to the changing vicissitudes of everyday life. It would be meaningless to talk about the criminality or otherwise of a Robinson Crusoe, brought up and always confined by himself on a desert island. It is only in relation to society that the notion of criminality and of predisposition to crime has any meaning. While recognizing therefore, the tremendous power of heredity, we would by no means wish to suggest that environmental influences cannot also be very powerful and important indeed.

The criminal or deviant would be a rule-breaker in any culture — he would be a pacifist during wartime, an aggressor during peace. It is not necessary, therefore, for the positivist to explain the content of the norms that are violated, merely the propensity of the individual to violate them.

(F) Policy

> The classical school exhort men to study justice; the positivist school exhorts justice to study men. (Hamel, 1906, p. 265)

> The criminal justice of the future, administered by judges who have sufficient knowledge, not of Roman or civil law, but of psychology, anthropology and psychiatry, will have for its sole task to determine if the defendant is the material author of the established crime; and instead of brilliant logomachies by the prosecution and the defence in an effort to trick one another, there will be a scientific discussion on the personal and social condition of the offender in order to classify him in one or another anthropological class to which one or another form of indeterminate segregation will apply. (Ferri, 1901, p. 229)

If the criminal is determined and not responsible for his or her actions, it makes no sense to punish crime. Instead, we must replace punishment by *treatment*. We must substitute for the jury system of lay people a panel of experts who diagnose the condition of the *individual* and prescribe the appropriate treatment. The punitive response, as advocated by classicist and conservative theorists, is not only inapplicable, it actually exacerbates the socialisation problems of the deviant.

Prognosis for the criminal is based not so much on what he or she did (the *act*), not on who he or she is (the *actor*) but on his or her background (the *antecedents*). The vandal may cause £5 worth of damage or £50 worth, but to sentence him proportionately to the impact of the act (as the classicists would) is meaningless. What is necessary is to see if the vandalism sprang from a deep-seated malaise of socialisation or if it was the mere experimentation of a normal youth. And once diagnosis is made, the criminal must be treated for as long as is necessary. Sentences are therefore indeterminate, just as one's stay in hospital is indeterminate, and based on satisfactory treatment or 'cure' rather than on the fixed sentences of the classicists. Rehabilitation rather than punishment must be our priority. But to achieve this, it will be necessary to discard outmoded prejudices and thinking. As Hans Eysenck stridently put it (1977, p. 213):

> Modern psychology holds out to society an altogether different approach to criminality, an approach geared only to practical ends, such as the elimination of antisocial conduct, and not cluttered with irrelevant, philosophical, retributory and ethico-religious beliefs . . . We have now reached the point where we can hope to combat crime effectively; shall we have the courage and the wisdom to give up our ancient hates and fears, and grasp the opportunity?

Problems of positivism

The denial of authenticity

By asserting that deviancy is a non-rational, determinate product of undersocialisation, the positivists take all human volition and meaning away from activity. For example, they would argue that in advanced capitalist societies, as property ownership is the central cultural concern, then those who are undersocialised will be thieves. In Puritan New England, on the other hand, religious norms were paramount, and the undersocialised were adulterers and blasphemers. The danger here lies in stressing a consensual culture when all deviation is simply attributed to lack of socialisation. In reality the conflict over property in Western capitalism is not a function of lack of culture; it relates to the inequitable distribution of property in such societies. Sometimes such a conflict can be a result of a fully-formed oppositional culture (e.g., revolutionary socialism) or by an alternative culture which despises property (e.g., bohemian countercultures). More often, it will involve people accepting the dominant culture of success — yet, as they have limited opportunities to acquire property, taking up illegitimate means to achieve it (e.g., as depicted in strain theory, see below) or accepting the prevalent culture of individualism and engaging in a no-holds-barred competition with their fellows ('the cult of the individual'). In all these instances deviance is *cultural*, whether it is a deviant culture set against the wider culture, or the dominant culture itself encouraging deviance. One might not like the particular cultural manifestation, but that is another thing; it is not sufficient to label it a product of undersocialisation. Thus human deviance may be the result of:

Alternative value systems — contradictions in value, cynicism or hesitances about official values. Because positivism ignores human choice and creativity it becomes myopic to the diverse ways in which human beings cope with a given environment and the different cultures which they create in response to it.

The normal criminal — Acceptance of the dominant culture of success may exacerbate feelings of frustration as regards one's lot in life, and acceptance of the cult of individualism may encourage aggressive competition. Both these may lead to crime — but not only in the lower reaches of society. For studies of unreported crime invariably indicate that crime is widespread throughout the social structure (see Pearce, 1976; Reiman, 1979). This suggests that it is not merely the 'undersocialised' lower reaches of society which engender crime but also the 'socialised' top of the pyramid. This endemic deviancy would point to the conclusion that the total society might be 'pathological' in positivist terms. That, for example, there might be a close link between an acquisitive society and theft; between patriarchal sexist values and rape. It is 'normal' socialisation, then, that may lead to crime.

Both these instances suggest that the equation utilised by positivism, namely that crime equals the consensual society defining the rules and the predisposed individual breaking them, is woefully inadequate.

Denial of the classicist contradiction

By putting such an emphasis on the predisposed individual as the source of crime, positivism defuses the problem of the classicist contradiction. Thus it translates a major problem of capitalist order — how to cope with the conflict between the ideals of equal competition and the reality of unequal property distribution — into a function of the inequality of individuals. No matter whether one agrees with such competition or not, it is obvious that limitations in social mobility, access to educational opportunities, differentially distributed career prospects, etc., constantly belie the reality of such a meritocratic competition. It is substantive differences in *social* opportunities, as well as in individual capacities, that structure the actual material possibilities constraining individuals in our society. The insistence on equality in classicist thought is not a mere metaphysical mistake — rather it is an ideal which is constantly undermined by the reality of capitalist society.

Denial of freedom

The stress on determination denies the alternative possibilities facing the majority of human beings at each juncture of their lives. For although *total* determination is a human possibility, for example in the case of a heavily tranquillised prisoner in a high security prison, choices nearly always remain. Such an overstress on determinacy denies the role of consciousness in standing back and creating and assessing the means of interpreting and manoeuvring a particular set of material conditions. For example, even if it is absolutely correct that there is a high correlation between, for example, lower-working-class backgrounds and delinquency, this does not imply that the background *causes* delinquency. It merely implies that people in such an underprivileged determinant position in our type of society tend at a particular time to create a culture of delinquency as a means of attempting to cope with their predicament. Sometimes, in fact, these cultural responses to *given* conditions can rapidly change, witness the politicisation of prisoners at Attica, or the way in which particular individuals in their 'moral career' can explore different cultural means of understanding their position. For example, note how individuals such as Malcolm X moved from being a thief, to being a Black Muslim, to becoming a revolutionary, seeking actively to understand and surmount his problems as a ghetto black.

To prove that there are correlations between certain determinant positions and certain types of crimes (e.g., company directors and corporate tax-evasion) does not take meaning away from these activities, it merely provides us with the facts which we have to explain in terms of human choice and meaning.

This is not to deny that human beings confront material determinants which are experienced in the same way as the laws of the natural sciences.

Varieties of positivism: a critical comment

At the close of this section there is an important comment to be made which applies throughout the article. As noted in the introduction, one of our tasks is to examine the inconsistencies of structure in a theory. Now although the particular version of positivism we have examined is often presented as an internally coherent structure, that is, in fact, debatable. For example, starting from the central premise of the unity of scientific method, it is frequently assumed that the other characteristics of the theory are logically deducible — for example, that human action is determined and that there is a consensus of value in society. Now it is difficult to imagine a positivist criminology which does not assume human behaviour is determined — for it is not then predictably determined and scientific laws are inappropriate. But it is quite possible to imagine a positivism which denies the consensual nature of social order. Indeed such positions exist, for example:

Radical positivism — where the total society is seen to be disintegrating and a multiplicity of emerging cultures are occurring to challenge the old order. In this instance some types of crime could be construed as a 'healthy' innovative adaption to a pathological society (see Taylor, Walton and Young, 1973, pp. 14–19).

A *pluralistic positivism* — By a scientific survey of cultural norms, a positivist may come to the conclusion that there empirically exists in society a variety of normative standards. Indeed some of these subcultures may seem to be supportive of criminal behaviour. That is, a type of *sociological* positivism may emerge which argues that, in these cultures, it is the socialised, well-adjusted individual who is the criminal (e.g., Miller, 1958).

It is important to note, then, that certain aspects of the above critique strike at the heart of positivist theory, whereas others merely represent a critique of the specific variety presented here. Thus to argue that positivism denies the possibility of a plurality of value applies only to species of 'individual positivism', presented above, whereas criticisms regarding the denial of human volition apply to the total spectrum of positivist theories of human behaviour.

* * * * *

Strain theory

The [three] perspectives we have discussed have all focused on the individual. Although crime is seen as arising from some weakness in the binding between the individual and society, the impulse to criminal or deviant behaviour is located firmly in the individual. In classicism, temptation to break, and infractions of, the law occur because the chains of reason which bind the individual to the social contract are insufficiently developed. Within positivism, the socialisation of the individual is seen to be insufficient to constrain his or her natural impulses; whereas in conservative thought, tradition has been undermined and discipline relaxed to the extent that the individual feels little need to have self-sacrifices and limitations on his or her desires. In each theory crime or deviancy arises from the natural impulses of the individual as a result of a process of 'leakage' or weakness in the social order. Strain theory breaks with such theories because it rejects the notion that crime arises from innate drives or instincts of the individual, and insists that the impulse to crime is normal and socially induced.

(A) Human nature

In rejecting the notion of an innate human nature, strain theory moves towards a position which emphasises the social nature of a person's individuality. Human nature is not a pre-social 'given', but is created by the particular society within which the individual lives. There is not, therefore, a tension within the individual between the 'natural' self and 'social' self — for the self is a product of social order.

It is not only in the focus on the total society rather than the individual which distinguishes strain theory from classicism, positivism and conservatism. In addition, while its main thrust remains determinist, it attempts to break out of the rigid either–or dichotomies of determinism or free will which beset the previous theories. This it endeavours to do by picturing the human situation as that of rational problem-solving individuals placed in determined frameworks. In particular, the individual is seen to be inculcated with cultural goals and with a range of appropriate means and opportunities of achieving them. These determined 'givens' are the framework within which rational people make choices and decisions in order to attempt to solve the particular predicaments they face in their part of the social structure.

(B) Social order

Social order is maintained by the socialisation of people into a consensus of values which corresponds to the needs of the social system. Society is a functioning entity in which each part interrelates and supports the other. Such a *functionalist* notion of social order does not, however, preclude the examination of its dysfunctions. As Robert Merton, the leading exponent of strain theory, explained (1966, p. 817):

> The study of social problems requires sociologists to attend to the dysfunctions of patterns of behavior, belief and organization rather than focusing primarily or exclusively on their functions. It thus curbs any inadvertent or deliberate tendency in functional sociology to reinstitute the philosophy that everything in society works for 'harmony' and the 'good'.

It is at this juncture that strain theorists make their major innovation, for they note how, in order that social order may function, dysfunctional consequences are inevitable. Richard Cloward and Lloyd Ohlin graphically locate this process in their book 'Delinquency and Opportunity' (1960, pp. 81–2):

> A crucial problem in the industrial world is to locate and train the most talented persons in every generation irrespective of the vicissitudes of birth, to occupy technical work roles. Whether he is born into wealth or poverty, each individual, depending upon his ability and diligence, must be encouraged to find his 'natural level' in the social order. This problem is one of tremendous proportions . . .

> . . . One of the ways in which the industrial society attempts to solve this problem is by defining success-goals as potentially accessible to all, regardless of race, creed or socio-economic position. Great social rewards, it is said, are not limited to any particular segment or segments of the population but are available to anyone, however lowly his origins . . . The industrial society, in short, emphasizes *common* or universal success-goals as a way of ensuring its survival. If large masses of young people can be motivated to reach out for great social rewards, many of them will make the appropriate investment in learning and preparation, and a rough correlation between talent and ultimate position in the occupational hierarchy will presumably result.

> One of the paradoxes of social life is that the processes by which society seeks to ensure order sometimes result in disorder. If a cultural emphasis on unlimited success-goals tends to solve some problems in the industrial society, it also creates new ones. A pervasive feeling of position discontent leads men to compete for higher status and so contributes to the survival of the industrial order, but it also produces acute pressure for deviant behavior.

But the emphasis on the possibility of success constantly contradicts the actual opportunities facing people — particularly those lower in the class structure. Thus Merton notes (1964, p. 214) :

In this same society that proclaims the right, and even the duty, of lofty aspirations for all, men do not have equal access to the opportunity structure. Social origins do variously facilitate or hamper access to the forms of success represented by wealth or recognition or substantial power. Confronted with contradiction in experience, appreciable numbers of people become estranged from a society that promises them, in principle, what they are denied in reality.

It is out of such an estrangement that crime and deviance are seen to arise.

(C) Definition of crime

It is at this point that we should note that strain theory does not limit itself to mere economic crime. It has been applied not only to thieving and robbery but to vandalism, truancy, drug-addiction, mental illness, suicide and homicide (Clinard, 1964). The major thrust of the argument is that the means by which an industrial society maintains itself create the circumstances by which a wide range of disorder occurs. Thus it is in a plethora of indicators of dysfunction that strain theorists are interested. Indeed as functionalists they note that some examples of crime may be directly functional to the social order, being the result of 'normal' behaviour rather than strain, and should not be considered as major indications of disequilibrium. Strain theorists do not therefore limit themselves to using the official crime statistics, but rather see them along with other social indices as useful and usable.

(D) Extent and distribution of crime

Despite reservations about the immediate use of official statistics or studies limited to interpreting these figures alone, strain theorists would accept the general pyramidal 'shape' of crime and disorder: namely that there is an inverse correlation between class position and crime. Indeed the pyramid of crime is the basic empirical problematic of their theory. For it is at the bottom of society that the strain of blocked opportunities to shared cultural goals is greatest and where the highest amount of crime and deviancy should take place. The classicist contradiction regarding the fact that not all rational citizens will equally embrace the Social Contract is not a problem for strain theorists, rather the reverse: it is the basis of their explanation of disorder. Differences in wealth and property provide success goals and opportunities for their achievement to a much greater extent for the wealthy than for the poor. The classicist principles of a free and equal race for rewards are seen as essential for an industrial society to function, but the substantive inequalities of wealth give rise to frustration and deviance among the poor.

(E) Causes of crime

Deviance then is seen to be the result of a disjunction between the culturally induced aspirations of individuals and the structurally determined opportunities. The focus is not at all on the individual's antecedents, the actor, or the act, and it is a tension not within the individual, but between culture and structure. Such a tension is rooted in the total society, and in pointing to this strain theory recognises a fundamental irony in the social order (Matza, 1969, p. 77):

the irony of a virtue, ambition, promoting a vice, deviant behavior, contains an ellipsis. Ambition promotes deviation when it is institutionally frustrated. The latent feature of ambition that will yield a reversal and mock its virtue is the reality of class barriers and restrictions on social mobility. Such barriers and restrictions inhere in the very idea of ambition; by definition its only possible aim is to overcome them. Thus, ambition contains within itself the seed of institutional frustration.

Irony, as David Matza puts it, becomes a central tenet of such functionalist analysis.

But these dysfunctions are experienced not so much by isolated individuals as by whole groups of individuals in certain structural positions. It is here that strain theory introduces its concept of subculture. Thus David Downes (1966), in his study of working-class delinquency in Stepney and Poplar, invokes the definition of culture formulated by C.S. Ford, namely 'learned problem solutions'. That is, subcultural responses are jointly elaborated solutions to collectively experienced problems. Groups of people have both collective goals and legitimate means fixed for them by the determining agency of society. In their positions as housewives, or teenagers, or corporate executives, they evolve subcultures — specialised parts of the general culture suitable for their needs. Often these are deviant, but where there are significant discrepancies between aspiration and opportunity, deviant subcultures or *contracultures* occur. Deviant behaviour, then, is viewed as being a meaningful attempt to solve the problems faced by groups of individuals in particular structural positions — it is not a meaningful pathology. And here strain theory differs qualitatively from classicism, positivism and conservatism, for it *guarantees meaning to deviancy*.

(F) Policy

The policy arising from strain theory is to attempt to alleviate the disjunction between aspiration and opportunities, institutional means and structural goals. In its most characteristic form, this involves piecemeal social engineering in order to try and provide opportunities to lessen the 'strain'. Coercion should be at a minimum; what is necessary is to reform the structure of society so that a more egalitarian opportunity structure is engendered and the contradictions of classicism are lessened in *fact*.

In terms of treatment of the individual, punishment is obviously irreconcilable with this approach. What is necessary on the immediate level is to teach the individual skills that will allow people most profitably to use their opportunities and demonstrate that many subcultural 'solutions' are of limited usefulness.

Problems with strain theory

Problems of middle-class crime

Strain theory accepts the pyramid of crime and sees the high incidence of lower-working-class crime as a product of the greater strain experienced by those at the lower end of the class structure. As with positivism, surveys of unreported crime which show that crime is ubiquitous would seem to undermine the causal basis of strain theory. Against this it can be countered that what is vital for strain theory is merely a disjunction between aspirations and opportunities — people do not have to be *absolutely* deprived to suffer from feelings of frustration — they may be *relatively* deprived in terms of their aspirations and opportunities. Thus the income-tax fiddler may be middle class and relatively well-off — yet his aspirations may be still considerably higher than his opportunities. All this may be true, but what remains to be explained is why the powerful who make laws find it necessary to break them.

Denial of pluralism of value

Without our denying the existence in Western capitalist countries of a consensual ideology which stresses the equal possibilities of all to succeed, it is a fault in strain theory that it sees such values as monolithic and unquestioned. This is not to suggest, for example, a working-class consciousness which is clearly contrary to the status quo. It points to the widespread existence of contradictions in value, cynicism, fatalism, and disassociation from the major institutions — as well as outright rejection. Similarly, the attempt in strain theory to marry rational choice and determinancy fails because it allows human rationality only a foothold in the process. Rational problem-solving is seen to occur, first, in individuals attempting to link together the predetermined goals and opportunities that constrain them, and then, if this fails, in innovating means to achieve the same goals (e.g., stealing to acquire consumer goods, etc.), and only then, if all else fails, in the innovation of new goals and means (e.g., violent gangs, drug users with countercultural norms, etc.). The rational person is added onto the predetermined culture and structure — he or she is an added extra. Such a position considerably underestimates the rational undermining of accepted value and legitimate procedure which constantly occurs: negotiation of values, cross-cuts in means, reinterpretation of goals, cynical conformity, distancing of commitment, etc. In each case, human reason steps into the determining process — rebellion is rare, but so is the simple acceptance of the central values which the strain theorists describe. Normality and deviance are not separate watertight categories of behaviour, nor does normal behaviour automatically precede ventures into deviance. Rather, at times, they blend together, are mistaken for each other or are irrevocably interwoven into the actual patterns of social behaviour.

The limits of reform

It is important to ask how far opportunities can be provided to lessen 'strain' without necessitating a change in the system. The reformist principles of strain theory would suggest that widespread adaptation is possible — yet the actual experience of projects such as Mobilization for Youth would suggest that severe economic and social limits to such adaptations occur. The short-term goals of adjusting the individual to existing opportunity suggests strongly the adaptation of the individual to the status quo rather than an attempt at any fundamental changes.

Why is the system there in the first place?

Strain theory explains the classicist contradiction as resulting from the necessity for a high level of inculcated aspirations in order for the social system to function. It is extremely doubtful if such a stratagem is an international ploy on the part of the ruling class or — even if it were — if it would be the most efficient method of solving the problem of the recruitment of appropriate personnel to specific tasks. A system of selective recruitment and cooling out would seem more adequate — and is probably more accurate empirically.

The classicist contradiction between equality of opportunity and inequality of wealth is a means of legitimating the system. On a formal level it presents the notion of the open meritocratic society, while on a substantive level it preserves the existing class structure. This process of legitimation is, itself, a result of political pressure and conflict — the compromise of a half-finished struggle.

A satisfactory explanation of the structural roots of the contradiction and the nature of the 'strain' eludes these theorists. As Laurie Taylor nicely puts it (1971, p. 148):

> It is as though individuals in society are playing a gigantic fruit machine, but the machine is rigged and only some players are consistently rewarded. The deprived ones then either resort to using foreign coins or magnets to increase their chances of winning (innovation), or play on mindlessly (ritualism), give up the game (retreatism), or propose a new game altogether (rebellion). But in this analysis nobody appears to ask who put the machine there in the first place and who takes the profits. Criticism of the game is confined to changing the pay-out sequences so that the deprived can get a better deal (increasing educational opportunities, poverty programmes). What at first sight looks like a major critique of society ends up taking the existing society for granted. The necessity of standing outside the present structural/cultural configurations is not just the job for those categorized in the rebellion mode of adaptation — it is also the task of the sociologist.

New deviancy theory

This theoretical position emerged primarily in the 1960s and early 1970s, and has a close relationship with the libertarian currents widespread within Western capitalism in that period. Its influence was, and still is, widespread. Outside criminology theoretical parallels occur, for example, within anti-psychiatry and radical feminism. New deviancy theory was primarily a radical response to positivist domination of criminology, and attempted to recover the 'meaning' in human behaviour denied, or reduced to biological and physiological imperatives, in positivism.

(A) Human nature

The new deviancy theorists' conception of human nature is one which emphasises free-will and creativity. People create meaning in the world, and they, in striving towards diverse numbers of cultural goals, impart a multitude of interpretations to the social and physical world around them. Human behaviour must be understood on the level of meaning imparted to it by the people involved. Reality is not 'given' or predetermined: it is socially constructed. Human rationality relates to the logic and norms of a particular culture; it is relative rather than absolute. Human nature is then constantly open and existentially boundless, and cannot be delimited in terms of a pre-given essence, for human beings make their own world and transform their own nature.

73

Like strain theory, new deviancy theory attempts to marry voluntaristic and deterministic notions of human nature, but does so in almost a reverse fashion. In strain theory, human beings were seen to improvise rationally within their pre-given social framework. In new deviancy theory, human beings are born free, but lose their voluntaristic capacity in the structures that society lays down in order to control their behaviour.

(B) Social order

The basic image that new deviancy theory has of social order is that of a pluralism of values. Individuals live in an overlapping world of normative ghettos. In contrast to all previous theories, the notion of a consensus in society is challenged and replaced by the concept of a diversity of values. Consensus is a mystification, an illusion foisted on the public by the powerful. More precisely, it is an attempt by the powerful to foist their own particular value system on the diversity of groups within society. This is achieved, on the one hand, by their control over the major ideological apparatus within society (e.g., the mass media, education) and on the other, by their control and use of the repressive apparatus (e.g., the police, courts). It is the particular nature of this illusion that new deviancy theorists stress. They argue that the illusion is constructed first, by securing general agreement that there is a consensus rather than a diversity of values within a particular social order, and second, by insisting that this consensus — which is, in fact, the particular values of the powerful — is not a human but a natural construct to which any well-socialised person would *naturally* adhere. Thus what is in fact a human construct, a system of values created by a specific group of people, is presented as a 'thing', a reification having existence outside and above human creation. Such a position, as we have seen, is most characteristic of positivism — the main ideological enemy of new deviancy theory — but both classicism and conservatism embrace a similar notion of natural consensual values which all fully social individuals would share.

(C) Definition of crime

The most characteristic conception of the new deviancy theorists is their notion of *labelling*. Society, they argue, does not consist of a monolithic consensus but rather of a pluralistic array of values. For an action to be termed criminal or deviant demands not one, but two, activities: a group or individual must act in a particular fashion, and, second, another group or individual with different values must label the initial activity as deviant. Human beings acting creatively in the world constantly generate their own system of values. Unfortunately within the pluralistic order of society certain groups — variously and vaguely termed 'the powerful', 'the bureaucracy', 'the moral entrepreneur' — with more power than others, *enforce* their values upon the less powerful, labelling those who infringe their rules with stereotypical tags. Thus, people who in fact are existentially free, and evolve different values or experiment with various forms of behaviour, are labelled by the authorities as *in essence* 'a homosexual', 'a thief', or 'a psychopath'.

(D) Extent and distribution of crime

At the same time as emphasising the diversity of behaviour, the new deviancy theorists stress the ubiquity of deviance. It is not merely the poor who commit crime. Exposés of corporate activities and self-report studies of middle-class youth indicate the widespread nature of crime. But the theorists go further than this, for they stress not merely ubiquity and diversity but also, paradoxically, *similarity*. And it is through this observation that new deviancy theory obtains its radical purchase on the world. That is, while it recognises that the norms of sexual intercourse vary from one social group to another, it notes how they all involve aggression and male domination. Similarly, while it is true that economic relations involve a great diversity, they also ubiquitously involve theft. All men are rapists, all people are thieves. Categories blend into one another: marriage and prostitution, rape and 'normal' sexual intercourse, corporate income-tax fiddling and robbery, street violence and the violence of unguarded machinery in factories, the vandalism of the 'redevelopment' of the city and the vandalism of the kid in the telephone kiosk.

Whereas previous theories make clear lines between conformity and deviancy, these theorists suggest that not only is deviance relative to the values of the beholder but that behind conformist appearances lies an underlife of deviance.

For conformity *involves* deviance, the everyday life of the deviant involves infraction, and, of particular importance, the sanctimonious conformity of the powerful involves the violation of the laws which they themselves create.

What, then, are the new deviancy theorists to make of the pyramid of the official statistics? Simply, that it is a fabrication. It is a result of the prejudiced fashion in which the police and the courts discriminate against lower-working-class deviance and ignore the crimes of the powerful. The classicist contradiction between equality and property is a reality which is manifest not in the way in which the poor commit more crimes than the rich, but rather in the fact that the poor are more *vulnerable* to arrest and prosecution than the rich. The ubiquity of crime becomes a pyramid of official statistics because of the differential reaction of authority.

(E) Causes of crime

> In analysing cases of intended non-conformity, people usually ask about motivation: why does the person want to do the deviant thing he does? The question assumes that the basic difference between deviants and those who conform lies in the character of their motivations [. . .] Psychological theories find the cause of deviant motivations and acts in the individual's early experiences . . . sociological theories look for socially structured sources of 'strain' in the society, social positions which have conflicting demands placed upon them such that the individuals seek an illegitimate way of solving the problems their position presents them with. (Merton's famous theory of anomie fits this category.)

> But the assumption on which these approaches are based may be entirely false. There is no reason to assume that only those who finally commit a deviant act actually have the impulse to do so. It is much more likely that most people experience deviant impulses frequently. (Becker, 1963, p. 26)

If crime and deviancy are ubiquitous, it is not necessary to explain their origin. If previous theories have focused on the individual and structural antecedents of the criminal act (positivism and strain theory, respectively), on the act itself (classicism) and on the actor (conservatism), new deviancy theory focuses on *reaction*. It is the administration of crime, not its origins, which is the key to understanding the phenomena (Duster, 1970, p. 90):

> The person described as deviant in society may be considered deviant in only one way, but the community reaction to him can be total. For example, a pregnant high-school senior may be quite capable of finishing her studies successfully before graduation, but the total response, stigma, and ridicule may lead her to leave; a homosexual may be as competent as the next person in the government bureaucracy and similar in every other way except for his sexual appetite; but may be treated as though he was *totally* different.

The labelling process has two consequences: ideological and coercive. Troy Duster brings this out in his study of heroin addicts at the California Rehabilitation Center. Certain deviant aspects of the addict may be regarded as 'master statuses' from which a knowledge of the total identity of the individual, overriding all other characteristics of the person, may be deduced. The process is often self-fulfilling, for, once stigmatised, the heroin addict finds it very difficult to re-enter the ranks of normality. Further, Duster notes how the addicts, in order to be released at an early date, must in the therapeutic group accept the moral characterisation imposed by their attendant psychiatrists. Moreover, the identity and kinship which they develop in the institution reinforces their notion of themselves as men set apart from the normal by virtue of their postulated personality weaknesses. In fact, Duster argues, there is negligible difference between addict and normal, apart from social inferiority, *until* the deviancy amplification process occurs (1970, p. 247):

> The point to be made is that the addict supplied a drug without stigmatisation would make the case that has been presented: that he cannot be identified among 'normal' men without a chemical test, and could therefore lead that kind of social life which would negate the charge of psychic weakness.

Duster, in common with other labelling theorists, implicitly holds a view of the world which suggests that there is a plurality of forms of behaviour in society and therefore definitions of deviancy. None of these deviant forms is, however, particularly extreme until social reaction occurs and spirals the deviant into a gross and unnecessary position. He would suggest that heroin addiction is initially a peripheral deviancy which, because of the blinkering effect of the notion of the 'dope fiend' as a 'master status', is reacted to in a totally miscued and unnecessary fashion. Thus the very act of labelling, by materially limiting the future choices of the person and by being presented to the person as being the truth about his or her nature with all the force of authority, has a self-fulfilling effect. The old adages, 'once a thief always a thief', 'once a junkie always a junkie', *become* true not because, as earlier criminologists had maintained, this was the essence of the person involved but because the power of labelling transformed and cajoled people into acting and believing as *if* they possessed no freedom in the world. This observation is a pointed criticism of positivist notions of scientific laws that govern human behaviour. These 'laws', far from holding sway outside human control and purpose, are a *creation* of human interventions. If there is a correlation between broken homes and delinquency, it is not because the former *causes* the latter, but rather that delinquents from broken homes are differentially selected over their 'normal' compatriots to be arrested, prosecuted and to end up in the statistics. They are preferentially chosen because of the stereotype of them as typical 'delinquents'. Thus they become like this stereotype through the process of labelling in both its coercive and ideological aspects. The criminal *career* is a function of social reaction rather than a result of a predisposed essence.

(F) Policy

In strain theory we saw the irony of how the pursuit of *conformity* gives rise to deviance. Counterposed against this, in new deviancy theory, is the irony of *social control* giving rise to gross deviance. For much social control is seen to be irrational and dysfunctional. The prisons do not work — they have a high recidivism rate. The stigmatisation of the delinquent leads, in a man-made progression, to the hardened criminal. Those in power are not only wrongly intolerant of diversity, their overreaction creates a more intransigent deviance which further threatens their image of the monolithic consensual world and raises the level of coercive strategies necessary to maintain control. The key to controlling the 'crime problem', then, lies in the control of reaction against deviance, rather than in structural change.

For example, in 1967 in the United States, the President's Commission published 'The Challenge of Crime in a Free Society'. Among other things, this report suggested that major causes of crime were poverty, slum conditions and blocked opportunities (i.e., a strain-theory approach). It was from the new deviancy perspective that Jack Douglas assembled a series of essays in a reader, 'Crime and Justice in American Society', which mounted a critique against this conventional wisdom (1971, pp. xix–xx):

> The authors of this book also share many ideas on how Americans must go about reconstructing the foundations of their laws and legal procedures in order to increase the safety of their person and their property while at the same time increasing the sense of social justice and the degree of social order. It is particularly noteworthy in this respect that none of the essays argues that we must have any kind of socio-economic reordering of our society to produce these results. Whereas the crime commission report continually insisted we must end slum living and every other form of social ill before we can solve our worst problems connected with crime and injustice, these essays have little to say about the social reorganization of priorities and resources. I suspect most of us are in favor of more equitable social policies in one form or another, yet it has been our implicit assumption that the critical, basic, problems with our laws and legal practices are causing our most severe problems of crime and injustice. The presidential commission's choice of placing the blame for these problems on social imbalances became a way of absolving legislators and legal authorities from responsibility for their own failures to create and administer practicable and just laws and legal procedures. We do not

absolve them. We hold them to be most culpable, collectively and personally, for our most urgent problems of crime and injustice. They will continue to be so as long as they continue to administer and support the present system of unworkable and unjust laws and legal procedures. No amount of rhetoric, mystification, denial, or blame-gaming can change this fact.

What is to be done then about crime? Each of the two parts of the control process — ideological and coercive — must be tackled. Ideologically it must be recognised that advanced industrial countries are diverse in value, and what is necessary is what Becker and Horovitz (1971) termed 'a culture of civility'. That is, tolerance must replace moral indignation, and an awareness of the open nature of human action replace essentialist stereotypes and reified notions of value. In terms of coercion, there must be a de-escalation of punishment, a realisation of the insignificant nature of most primary deviance (deviance before it is amplified — when it is termed secondary deviance) and a resistance to the creation of moral panics over deviancy. This policy of *radical non-intervention* (E. Schur 1973) involves the decriminalisation of many offences, particularly the so-called 'crime without victims' (pornography, prostitution, gambling, etc.) and severely lowers penalties on most others. And for the remaining serious offenders (Douglas, 1971, pp. 42–3):

> it will probably be necessary to maintain a form of maximum isolation from the rest of society simply because the offender cannot be controlled by any other means. In such instances, Americans should investigate the possibilities of 'banishment' in which the recalcitrant offenders are allowed to run their own society, providing humane living conditions are maintained; banishment would absolve the rest of us from the guilt of dehumanizing our fellow human beings.

Problems with the new deviancy theory

Denial of structural causes

By granting human beings freedom in an absolute sense without acknowledging any material constraints, human purpose is reduced to the level of whimsy. By propounding a conception of human nature as being free and spontaneous before the intervention of the state sullied it, these theorists threw all the weight of their criticism on bad administration. It was a romantic theory of the noble deviant, expressive and creative, who was bowed under the fetters of state control.

Thus whereas positivist theory, however, distortedly, had emphasised the make-up of the individual and the structure of his or her social arrangements as generating deviancy (albeit ignoring the effects of social reaction), new deviancy theory accomplished precisely the reverse position. It romantically suggested that nothing was wrong with the structure of society and the individual psyche outside the maladministration of the state and heavy-handed control agencies. In this manner, the conflict endemic in a class society was glossed over and the basic causes of crime ignored.

Inadequate explanation of social reaction

Paradoxically for a theory which prides itself on introducing social reaction into the explanation of deviant behaviour, it is extremely limited in this respect. For the emphasis on maladministration rather than on structures ignores the structural causes of reaction. Hence reaction is regarded as a simple irrationality in terms of administration, and politics is seen as showing up dysfunctions in the ruling class and clarifying mistakes in logic. Against this I would argue that the control system does involve a logic and that this logic relates to the total social order. Therefore the resistance of our rulers to the 'rational' logic of labelling theory is scarcely a mere whim of irrationality.

Problem of the ubiquity of crime

The stress on the ubiquity of crime and the denial of structural causes do not leave any possibility of explaining differences in human behaviour between subcultures, over time and between countries. For although it may be true that all people commit crime, it is palpably obvious that they do not commit the same kinds of crime or to the same extent. Even deviancy theorists who argue that middle-class and working-class juvenile delinquency is identical, as are the real crime rates of blacks and whites and even men and women, are stopped short when asked about old people compared with young people. Such a search for a democratic crime statistic may be a laudable pursuit of equality, but it is very bad criminology.

Furthermore, whereas the new deviancy theorists have importantly stressed the differential vulnerability of people to arrest, they are wrong to pose this as an *alternative* to the differential propensity of people to commit crime. Surely, a study of differences in vulnerability and propensity would take us some of the way towards understanding the official statistics on crime?

Problem of political intervention

The strategy of non-intervention has serious flaws. At the most obvious level, the emphasis on maladministration rather than structure as the cause of problems in society blinds the theory to the root causes of the various crimes without victims. Because of this there is little attempt to suggest structural *as well as* legislative solutions to the problems.

Even if we take the empirical incidents most tailor-made for new deviancy theory, namely 'crimes without victims', problems arise. For if we examine a list of these crimes — prostitution, drug use, illegal gambling, pornography, abortion, homosexuality — the first thing to be noted is that it is a mixed bag. We are asked to agree in each case that there is no victim; we are asked to agree that it is irrational to intervene in so-called 'consensual crimes'. Why should we interfere, the new deviancy theorists ask us, with free individuals doing their own thing? Our answer to them must be clear: because individuals are not free, because it is precisely the structural determinants, which the labelling theorists chose to ignore, which imprison and enmesh human action and rationality. Furthermore, the exercise of power is not an inherent evil, for it can be used to combat the repressive institutions that surround us. It is because social intervention can have a progressive as well as a deleterious consequence that we must discriminate between 'crimes without victims' and separate these categories which are presented to us. To present consensus between partners as an argument for the innocuousness of an activity is to ignore that contractual agreement in a capitalist society is very often not an agreement between equals but one between those of unequal power. Nor is such a 'free contract' beset by merely material constraints; the ideological domination of bourgeois ideas and categories scarcely makes for a *rational* contract between free individuals.

If we turn then to the structural causes of 'crimes without victims', we shall be more capable of distinguishing between them. To do this we must place activities in their social and historical context, and not generalise upon such an abstract and spurious basis as 'consensual activities'.

When we move beyond 'crimes without victims', the problems become even greater. For although we might argue that we should leave the juvenile vandal alone, should we absolve the income-tax fiddler? And in discussing rape, we find a crucial contradiction in new deviancy theory. Consistent with their general theory, new deviancy theorists would argue that rape is ubiquitous and scarcely demands a causal explanation outside its assumption as normal male behaviour, but would, at the same time, hesitate to warn about false labelling or suggest that recent fears about rape are merely a moral panic which grossly over-estimates the threat.

At base, the politics of non-intervention overlook the genuine fears that people have about crime. By underplaying the dangers of crime in the streets and suggesting that all would be solved merely by the state de-escalating its reaction to the criminal, it ignores the profound malaise and destructive anti-social behaviour which exists in our cities and which is generated by the type of society we live in.

Marxism

The sixth theoretical perspective to be discussed is marxism. Although marxism has developed more sophisticated analyses of human nature and social order than the other traditions, its early contributions to the analysis of crime were limited. During the last decade, a Marxist criminology has emerged although the debates are at an early stage. In this development there has been a tendency both to reject some of the conceptual gains and to ignore the rational kernel and insights of non-marxist traditions in criminology.

(A) Human nature

> Men make their own history, but they do not make it just as they please;
> they do not make it under circumstances chosen by themselves, but under
> circumstances directly encountered, given and transmitted from the past.
> The tradition of all the dead generations weighs like a nightmare on the
> brain of the living. (Marx, 1969, p. 360)

For marxists, the dichotomy between human beings being depicted as having free-will (e.g., classicism or conservatism) or as being determined (e.g., in positivism) is false. Also they reject the notion of adding free-will at the end of a large series of determinants (e.g., strain theory) or the depiction of determinancy as a monopoly of social reaction impacting on the pure spirit (e.g., new deviancy theory). Human beings are both the producers and the products of history; they create institutions and meaning within a particular historical period which is, in the last instance, determined by the mode of production of the time. Furthermore, there is no pre-social essence of humanity as is postulated in the majority of non-marxist theories. The notion of an animal nature which will determine behaviour if 'society' does not intervene, or of an *a priori* human reason which exists outside of social context, is an absurdity. Rather, in their deviant behaviour and in their normal behaviour, in their reason or their unreason, in their individualism or in their collectivism, human beings are social beings. Thus (Marx, 1971. p. 189):

> Man is a *zoon politikon* in the most literal sense; he is not only a social animal, but an animal that can be individualised only within society. Production by a solitary individual outside society . . . is just as preposterous as the development of speech without individuals who live *together* and talk to one another.

Statements concerning the particular characteristics of social relationships, about, for example, the degree of individualism, rationality, freedom or determinancy must be historically grounded. That is, they must be generalisations not about all humanity in the abstract, but about specific historical periods. It is important to specify, then, problems of freedom and determinancy within capitalism.

(B) Social order

In 'Capital' (vol.1), Marx characterises the transition from feudalism to early capitalism as the imposition of the discipline 'necessary for the system of wage labour' (1976, pp. 899–900):

> The advance of capitalist production develops a working class which by education, tradition and habit looks upon the requirements of that mode of production as self-evident natural laws. The organization of the capitalist process of production, once it is fully developed, breaks down all resistance. The constant generation of a relative surplus population keeps the law of the supply and demand of labour, and therefore wages, within narrow limits which correspond to capital's valorization requirements. The silent compulsion of economic relations sets the seal on the domination of the capitalist over the worker.

The coercion necessary at the genesis of capitalism becomes supplanted by the silent compulsion of the market. The worker is doubly free — free to sell his labour and 'free' of the ownership of the means of production. That is, compared with feudal relationships, he is free — but it is a voluntary compulsion because he is forced to sell his labour in the market-place: he is free to be exploited. But not all the population are able to find employment; there is a 'relative surplus population' in capitalism which seem to maintain a market in labour — the ability of the employer to bid for labour among competing individuals selling their labour-power. Lastly, Marx notes how, through 'education, tradition, habit', people begin to accept this 'double freedom' as natural — as being an eternal part of human existence. The natural world of the voluntary compulsion of the market-place coupled with the daily discipline of the factory seal the fate of the worker. Marxism stresses the role of the work situation as the major focus of social control in capitalist society, while 'direct extra-economic force is still used only in exceptional cases'.

It is important to stress the double nature of freedom under capitalism. Marxism does not suggest that freedom is an illusion, but rather that the nature of capitalist reality is both opaque and contradictory. Unlike the new deviancy theory, it does not view support for the existing system as a mystification but as arising out of the nature of capitalist reality itself. As Maurice Godelier puts it (1972, p. 337), in a capitalist society,

> It is not the subject who deceives himself, but *reality* which deceives him, and the appearances in which the structure of the capitalists' production process conceals itself are the starting-point for individuals' conceptions.

In his discussion of the labour process in 'Capital', Marx outlines two contrasting spheres. On the one hand, the world as it appears from the level of the process of circulation (the market exchange of commodities, i.e., labour and wages) with the process of production (i.e., the production of surplus value); on the level of the sphere of circulation of commodities the worker freely sells his labour, he obtains the market equivalent for it, he is an equal before the law, he is not cheated by the individual capitalist. On the other hand, if we leave 'the noisy sphere of human rights' and enter 'the hidden abode of production', we find a different story: coercion and necessity replace freedom, substantive inequality replaces formal equality, exploitation replaces equivalence. The market economy creates of necessity real freedom, rationality and individualism, at least in *certain sections* of the population. Thus the immediate world of appearances (freedom, equality, equivalence) inverts and obfuscates reality (servitude, inequality, exploitation) but it is not a mere illusion. Such a double, opaque and contradictory structure of reality is characteristic of capitalism and throws up theories which stress one-sidedly either free-will or determinism. There is the rational basis of conformity in our society (as one-sidedly depicted in classicism) and there is the determinancy (as one-sidedly portrayed in positivism).

The dull compulsion of economic need, as an indirect coercion, exists throughout the workforce. What of direct coercion and the 'exceptional circumstances' of its use? Here, as Dario Melossi puts it, the exceptions are in fact 'the sphere of penal repression, that is, in the sphere of exceptions' (1976, p. 32). For the coercion at the genesis of capitalism continues with its development (p. 28):

> The way of the cross walked for some time by the proletariat punished for a social transition that they did not initiate or understand and which they opposed with all their force is, in a more developed moment, walked by the rebel, the criminal, by the ones Marx numbers among the lumpenproletariat.

Thus the data presented to the President's Commission indicate that the labourer is fourteen times more likely to go to prison than the professional, the person with less than four years education is eighteen times more likely to enter prison than the postgraduate, and the black male is five times more likely to go to prison than the white. Unemployment in particular correlates and covaries with imprisonment (Quinney, 1977, pp. 131–40; Janovic, 1977).

The pattern is clear: the major focus of the prison (i.e., direct coercion) is the workless, the reserve army of labour and those marginal to the workforce. Indeed in New York one out of every twenty blacks between the ages of 25 and 34 was actually *in* prison on an average day (Wright, 1973, p. 32).

The principles behind the control of the worker and the workless are the same. Whereas classicism portrays the history of punishment as the tale of men of good-will advancing steadily on humanitarian grounds under the banner of reason, marxism notes how classicist ideals are historically situated. Central to this debate is the work of the Bolshevik legal theorist Eugene Pashukanis (1978), who pointed out that concomitant with the rise of commodity production (involving the notion of abstract labour, the free and equal worker, the proportional correspondence of labour reward, and the concept of time as an abstract and general measure of values) arose precisely similar concepts in punishment. Namely, the notion of the abstract voluntaristic formally equal, legal actor who is punished proportionately to the cost of his crime by a fine or by the equivalent denial of his free time in prison. Thus the principles of reward which coax and give reason to the conformity of the worker in the factory are the same as the principles of punishment which are inflicted upon the recalcitrant. Just as the population must be convinced that utility to society is proportionately rewarded, they must also be made aware that lack of utility is effectively curbed and stigmatised. The pyramid of success must have a shadow of failure.

An image used by the new deviancy theorists was that of the iron fist and the velvet glove. Social control was at base naked coercion, a fist poised above the total population, but this was disguised and supplemented by a velvet glove of mystification. Material coercion and ideological delusion attempted to pacify the population, yet — and here was the irony of their critique — such a control mechanism was, in the last resort, dysfunctional. For labelling exacerbated rather than ameliorated deviancy.

How does marxism differ from this? I have pointed to its insistence on pinpointing the nature of coercion and consensus in a particular historical period — in this case capitalism — and on detailing how coercive means are differentially applied to the working population (the worker or the workless). Coercion is not a blanket category, but is directly applied to the workless while manifesting itself as an indirect pressure on those in work ('the dull compulsion of economic need'). Consensus is not a system of mystified ideas by which the ruling class deludes the population but arises out of the contradictory nature of reality itself. It is based on the *real* freedom and gains of capitalism that coexist and conceal coercion and exploitation; that is, the 'double freedom' of the worker under capitalism.

Marxists as well as new deviancy theorists are fascinated by the role of the prison as an instrument of social control.

What point, the new deviancy theorists ask, is there in such a *dysfunctional* system? It represents for them the prime symbol of administrative irrationality. But marxists, from the same empirical observation, come to exactly the opposite conclusion. They argue that the prison has two vital and efficient *functions* in capitalist society. The first is as a material deterrent, the second is as an ideological weapon. First, they point to the fact that although the focus of penal sanctions is on the workless, their real effort is on those in work. For the prisons do not control the future activities of their inmates; their presence controls the rest of the population. For the threat of being permanently excluded from reasonable work, of social stigmatisation and of immiseration holds the respectable working class, the honest citizen, constantly in check.

Second, by portraying crime as a monopoly of the emarginalised and the major problem of order in society, they deflect attention away from the crimes of the powerful and the exploitative nature of capitalism itself.

Marxist criminology does not only specify and differentiate the way in which coercive and consensual controls impact on the working and workless population; it views the system as an integrated whole. Thus:

(a) The 'reserve army of labour', a relatively immiserised pool of people out of work, affects the market position of those in work by posing a constant potential competition for jobs.

(b) The social conditions of the reserve army and the threat of those in work joining them allow the imposition of a rigorous discipline in the workplace.

(c) Both workless and those in work are rewarded and punished in terms of the same principles of proportionality; there is a continuum of reward and punishment within society.

(d) The prison's 'failure', in that it well-nigh irrevocably stigmatises the recalcitrant, serves as a first line of control for the workless and an important second line of control — after work itself — for those in work.

(e) The state in acting against the criminal serves to legitimate itself as the protector of universal interests in society.

(C) Definition of crime

With the exception of the new deviancy theory, all the theories discussed in this article assume that crime is any action which is severely against the interests of the majority of citizens. New deviancy theory disagrees here: crime is that behaviour which violates the interests of the powerful. How does marxism differ from this?

The basis for the political support of bourgeois society among the mass of the population is closely entwined with their fears of crime and disorder. Just as the ruling class takes working-class demands for justice and enmeshes them in the support of a class-ridden society, so, too, a real need for social order is similarly transmuted. The existence of a class society leads to desperation, demoralisation and a war of all against all. The working-class community suffers immensely from the criminals in its midst. Law gains its support not through a mere mystification of the working class, an ability to render people spellbound by its paraphernalia of pomp and authority. Legal institutions represent, it is true, the interest of the ruling class, but they are also much more than just this. As Herbert Marcuse put it (1971, p. 101):

> The state, being and remaining the state of the ruling class, sustains *universal* law and order and thereby guarantees at least a modicum of equality and security for the whole society. Only by virtue of these elements can the class state fulfil the function of 'moderating' and keeping within the bounds of 'order' the class conflicts generated by the production relations. It is this 'mediation' which gives the state the appearance of a universal interest over and above the conflicting particular interests.

The class society which creates social disorganisation also creates its partial palliative. Legal institutions also contain within them gains and concessions wrested from the bourgeoisie by the labour movement. Furthermore, they are a repository for the ideals of equality, justice and liberty which, however empty these remain as formal pronouncements outside the economic and political basis necessary to realise them, remain genuine ideals all the same. Conservative law-and-order campaigns therefore play on real needs for social order and embody genuine ideals, albeit in a distorted form. In this fashion, the criminal and the destructive elements of a class society are presented not as *result* of the present society but as the *cause* of its lack of harmony. The ideological impact of such an inversion of the real world is considerable.

As with our discussion of the contradictory nature of the work process in capitalism, we see in law similar opaque and contradictory phenomena. Thus bourgeois law arises in order to safeguard, contract and protect property: that is, to maintain equality in the realm of exchange while perpetuating and allowing for increasing accumulation at the level of production. The law offering equality of judgment and protection to all involves a contrast between formal equality on one level which obscures and perpetuates substantive inequality on the other. Thus, laws are passed which judge people as equal individuals, obscuring the fact that their inequitable class position makes them differentially vulnerable to commit crime in the first place. The formal equality of protection which laws give in the defence of the property of individuals, however, is simply the right of one class to perpetuate and extend its ownership of the means of production, thus rendering the working class both propertyless and unequal. Therefore to judge people equally is to act inequitably, to protect property equally is to extend inequality. Here again, bourgeois society creates crime which threatens the working class, and law maintains a degree of protection against the criminal. Also legal rights allow the individual to organise politically and they afford some protection against the intrusions of the ruling class and the state. Law not only legitimates ruling-class domination, it has a legitimate component to it, in terms of the protection of working-class interests. It is not, therefore, a mystification of the real interests of the powerful, as new deviancy theorists would maintain.

(D) The extent and distribution of crime

In marxist criminology, crime is seen to be endemic in the social order. The explanation of how the pyramid of crime emerges is, however, different from previous theories. In strain theory, the classicist contradiction between property (substantive equality) and formal equality of opportunity is seen to be the root cause of crime. With this, marxism would be in broad agreement. Contrary to this, new deviancy theory stresses that the main contradiction is between the formal equality of ideal justice and the substantive inequality of justice in practice. With this, no Marxist would quarrel. It must be stressed, however, that the two positions are not alternatives. For the pyramid of crime is not merely a figment of the differential reaction of the powerful. In a class society, despite the espousal of formal equalities of opportunity and of justice, substantive inequalities occur on *both* levels. As Jeffrey Reiman puts it (1979, pp. 7–8):

> There is evidence suggesting that the particular pressures of poverty lead poor people to commit a higher proportion of the crimes that people fear (such as homicide, burglary, and assault) than their number in the population.

> . . . if arrest records were brought in line with the real incidence of crime, it is likely that those who are well off would appear in the records far more than they do at present, even though the poor would still probably figure disproportionately in arrests for the crimes people fear. In addition to this, those who are well off commit acts that are not defined as crimes and yet that are as harmful or more so than the crimes people fear. Thus, if we had an accurate picture of who is really dangerous to society, there is reason to believe that those who are well off would receive still greater representation.

(E) Causes of crime

Contemporary capitalism makes a social contract based on effort and reward, the premise of citizenship being the provision of work and access to property and consumer goods. It is unable to employ the totality of the population: a proportion of individuals are marginalised. It is impossible to enmesh these people in the social control of the workplace as thus they are potentially a dangerous class. They have, unlike the stable workforce, little to lose from criminality. The judicial machinery must, therefore, be used to coerce them into subservience: it must fill the gap where work discipline is absent. The aetiology of crime and law-abiding behaviour has, therefore, the same root: the incorporation, or lack of it, of the population into the workforce. While this explains merely the propensity for crime among the workers, it does not root the actual motivation. Here again the motivation lies — as strain theory has indicated — in the classicist contradiction. The ever-present disparity between effort and reward, the emphasis on equal opportunities yet the unequal reality of a class society, the stress on individual competition yet the handicapped nature of the race — all militate to create a criminogenic milieu. Such contradictions are particularly hard on the marginalised groups who are denied full access to the consumer society. Thus, the very process which binds the worker to his bench turns the mind of the unemployed to forms of crime which have, in fact, a high rate of surveillance and apprehension.

Such a root cause of crime must be combined with an analysis of the effects of social reaction upon crime — as the new deviancy theorists one-sidedly argue. In fact Marx himself, in one of his rare discussions on crime, noted (1859):

> There must be something rotten in the very core of a social system which increases its wealth without decreasing its misery, and increases in crimes even more rapidly than in numbers . . . Violations of the law are generally the offspring of the economical agencies beyond the control of the legislator, but, as the working of the Juvenile Offenders' Act testifies, it depends to some degree on official society to stamp certain violations of its rules as crimes or as transgressions only. This difference of nomenclature, so far from being indifferent, decides on the fate of thousands of men, and the moral tone of society. Law itself may not only punish crime, but improvise it.

What of crimes of the powerful — how is it that those that make the rules are also persistent rule-breakers? The solution to this paradox is in the contradictory nature of law. Certain laws are passed by pressure of subordinate classes which act against the interests of the powerful (e.g., anti-monopoly legislation, progressive income tax measures, factory safety legislation). The extension of real power is exhibited in the degree of their actual implementation: for, as Reiman has indicated, the pyramid of crime is in part the product of the differential immunity of the powerful to prosecution.

What of the element of volition or determinism in the criminal act? Engels is quite clear about the nature of crime in *extreme circumstances*. It evolves from the demoralisation and brutalisation of exploitation in which 'the working-man becomes precisely as much a thing without volition as water . . . at a certain point all freedom ceases' (1969, p. 159).

How does this differ from a positivist theory of crime, which would invoke invariable laws of human behaviour? In the sense that Engels specifies particular brutalising circumstances. As Hall and Scraton indicate, however, Engels is not consistent in his writings on crime. For it also constituted the 'earliest, crudest and least fruitful form of rebellion' (Engels, 1969, p. 240). But even such an act of volition is soon enveloped in determinants (p. 240):

> The workers soon realized that crime did not help matters. The criminal could protest against the existing order of society, only singly, as one individual; the whole might of society was brought to bear upon each criminal and crushed him with its immense superiority.

A marxist criminology also points to the existence of determinants which as a product of human creation are not natural laws but at the same time come to dominate the lives of human beings. It is here that positivism has its validity. It is at the desperate end of the social spectrum where the overwhelming milieu precipitates people into highly determined roles where the tyranny of the organism is best displayed, and where the positivists, whether psychologists or biologists, come into their own. But this is a product of historical time and place — it is *not* a part of 'human nature' or 'man's essence' in the way that positivism might have us believe.

Such a position is critical of the manner in which the new deviancy theory rejected positivism. That is, in suggesting that positivism is wrong because it has an incorrect portrayal of human capacity — it denies human creativity — and that people who act in a determined fashion are acting like that because they are acting as *if* they were determined. It is wrong to confuse human potential with human reality or to regard the determination of human beings as a mistake in thought.

(F) Policy

It may be true that there are correlations between broken homes and vandalism — the task must be to remove the conditions that give rise to such associations. It may be true — as strain theory argues — that the contradiction between the ideals of equality and the reality of restricted opportunities gives rise to delinquency. Yet this classicist contradiction between formal equality and the substantive inequalities stemming from property is not solved, as the strain theorists would have it, by merely opening up more opportunities. For the unequal distribution of property and power in capitalism will always result in the privileged reproducing inequalities of opportunity areas. For marxists, the solution to the contradiction of classicism is to abolish, that is to create a world where formal *and* substantive inequalities disappear.

Problems of marxist criminology

Problem of specificity

The line of causality invoked by marxists is: capitalism leads to crime, and creates a series of problems in terms of specific times, places and groups. To say, for instance, that crime is endemic among corporate élites does not explain which corporate executives commit criminal acts and under what specific economic circumstances.

In part, this problem relates to the overconcentration of marxism on the total society rather than on the individual or group. Strain theory, with its emphasis on subculture as a historical entity wherein a group of individuals faced a shared set of circumstances, and new deviancy theory with its notion of 'moral career' — the biographical interaction of the individual with society — are more readily capable of dealing with the micro-level of analysis. In recent years the concept of subculture has been recontextualised and integrated into marxist analysis, particularly of youth cultures — and this is a fruitful line of development.

Problem of functionalism

There is a tendency in much marxist criminology to take up a position which could be called *left functionalist*. That is, phenomena are 'explained' by the role they are seen to play in maintaining capitalism. Dysfunctions, effects which create imbalances and disequilibria, are played down. We have noted in our discussion of strain theory how Merton recommended the study of crime and social problems as a corrective to this tendency in bourgeois structural functionalism, but no such strictures have been applied to functionalist tendencies in marxist criminology.

Problems of dealing with non-economic crimes

There is a tendency in marxist criminology to assume an obvious economic motive for criminal activities. This is untrue, even in the case of a professional robber, and, of course, it is inadequate in terms of rape or vandalism. What is needed here is a widening of theory and further specification and contextualisation as discussed earlier.

In terms of rape, for example, one would look for a marxist approach which was capable of analysing the notion of patriarchy and discussing the basis of gender differences and male aggression. In terms of juvenile delinquency one would look for a way in which economic deprivation is manifested in delinquent subcultures which involve vandalism and acts of physical violence. Once again, it is to subculture theory that one turns to find concepts that mediate between the study of the total society and the actual activities of delinquent individuals.

Problems of reform and strategy

Marxist criminology would argue that real progress in the elimination of crime will occur only if fundamental changes are wrought in the ownership of the means of production. Revolution, not reform, is the major item on the agenda. With this in mind, it is necessary to argue for changes in criminal justice which would help to transform rather than merely shore up the system. Such a strategy is difficult, for there is no such thing as a demand which is without contradictions. For example, we have shown elsewhere (Greenwood and Young, 1975) how the right to abortion as a formal demand conceals the substantial inequalities which force some women to have abortions. Progressive abortion legislation involves gain on the level of women's rights, but is simultaneously a control measure on the part of population-controllers. Reforms, because they emerge from a class-divided society, will always display such a two-sided nature. The strategic problem is how to discriminate systematically between 'negative reforms', which on the whole serve to open up the system to fundamental change, and 'positive reforms', which merely give legitimacy to the system and increase its stasis (see Mathieson, 1974).

Problem of crime under socialism

In classical marxism the excesses of deviance, and with them the need for law and the state, are seen to 'wither away'. A debate occurs within marxist criminology as to whether such a position is utopian. Thus Paul Hirst writes (1975, p. 240): 'One cannot imagine . . . the absence of the suppression of theft and murder, nor can one consider these controls as purely oppressive.' Such a debate has relevance to the whole problem of the causality of crime for, if it is true that all industrial societies will produce 'excessive' deviance, then part of the cause of crime is not only in capitalism but in the complex nature of industrial societies *per se*.

Conclusion

I have presented in this article six theories of crime and deviance, systematically comparing them on the central questions which any theory of order and of criminality must tackle. By examining the paradigms in this way, it is possible to differentiate clearly between them. But, as was suggested in the introduction, one must be careful how we compare the different theoretical approaches. In particular, we should bear the following in mind.

Ideal-type theories

I have constructed 'ideal' theories which have, to an extent, a high degree of internal consistency; so the answer to each question should follow logically from the answer to the others. In actual practice, however, one finds theorists who lack consistency and, of course, others whose writings are *in between* the theories so described.

Thus in the early 1970s many theorists both in Britain and the United States began to move from new deviancy theory towards marxism. As a result, much of this transitional work shows characteristics of both traditions (e.g., the essays in Taylor, Walton and Young, 1975). The purpose of placing theories into such ideal types is to create a usable vocabulary so that we can argue about crime in a serious and systematic fashion.

The myth of unilinear development

With the exception of conservatism — which strangely is rarely discussed in books on criminological theory — we have presented the theories in the order that is conventional in textbooks on criminology. That is classicism, positivism, strain theory, new deviancy theory and (perhaps) marxism. This is not to make the common textbook mistake of believing that they developed in a series of discrete historical stages from classicism to marxism, each representing a step in the rational progress towards the solution of the crime problem.

This is palpably untrue, for the following reasons:

There are many unilinear lines — the one presented here is the one conventional in *sociological* textbooks on criminology. Different experts would have different unilinear lines and each unilinear line of development would be hotly disputed by experts from other disciplines; e.g., a biologist interested in crime might see biological positivism as the function of a line of scientific achievement — scarcely a stage at the beginning of criminology. Thus Hans Eysenck views himself as being at the end of a lengthy and distinguished lineage, but his line crosses the one presented above only at the point of positivism.

Lack of dominance of any one theory — Rarely, if at all, does a theory dominate even select parts of the Academy, as the notion of unilinear development suggests. Rather, the situation is more that of competing paradigms. For instance, at the moment, academic criminology is presented with a wealth of eminently viable positions and excellent theoreticians in each of the theoretical traditions I have presented here. All these positions are flourishing and have powerful support and sound and substantial work as their basis. They can hardly be considered remnants of bygone theoretical ages! They all have long intellectual histories and social bases which belie the notion of the revolutionary development of theory in which earlier forms are dismissed and become defunct.

The myth of the new theory

Criminology, like the rest of the social sciences, suffers from much forgetfulness of its history, and fresh theories are rediscovered with a surprising naiveté (see Young, 1979). A major case in point is the so-called positivist revolution at the beginning of the century presented by leading exponents such as Enrico Ferri as a Copernican transformation of notions of human nature, social order and criminal policy. But, in fact, a flourishing positivist school occurred in the middle of the nineteenth century (see Lindesmith and Levin, 1937; Pearson, 1975). Or, more recently, the distinguished American legal scholar Isaac Balbus in 1977 'discovered' the commodity fetishist theory of law only to admit ruefully at the end of his work that he had come across a more sophisticated version of this theory written in 1924 by Eugene Pashukanis!

Now the point of pouring scorn on the 'new discoveries complex' is not to say that nothing new ever happens in theory or to detract from the work of the recent theorists. Theories, however recurrent, emerge in particular historical periods with special emphasis and advantages of their own. They play important roles in revitalising past discoveries, putting new stress on the interpretation of events and relating these to current happenings. What is annoying is the amnesia regarding the past and the perennial tendency to one-sided interpretations of social reality: voluntarism versus determinism; biological versus sociological reductionism, etc. The problem facing a theorist is to transcend such dichotomies, yet the tendency in terms of the fashionable theory of the moment is to swing backwards and forwards, to bob from one position to the other. Thus in sociological circles in the late 1960s, positivism became démodé and was replaced by a new deviancy theory which, far from transcending the position put forward by its opponent, merely inverted every facet of positivist theory, so that a mirror image resulted.

Theory and the real world

At the beginning of this article I stressed how academic theorisation about crime is not separate from lay discussions by the public at large. It merely reproduces in a more systematic and consistent form the discussions occurring in pubs and at bus-stops. But there is another sense in which there is an intimate relationship between academic criminology and the real world. That is, these ideas very often have an only too real institutional basis. For instance, it may not have escaped the reader that the juvenile court is an arena where positivist theories of crime are dominant and that the adult courts are the realm where classicist principles often hold sway.

From the seating arrangement in magistrates' courts to the design and layout of prisons, fundamental ideas about the causation of crime and the nature of justice come into play.

I have indicated how the study of crime is not a marginal concern to the citizen but plunges us immediately into fundamental questions of order and morality in society and to the examination of the very basis of the civilisation we live in.

Recent Developments of Early Theories

4. Human Development and Criminal Careers

David P. Farrington

The criminal career approach

The criminal career approach is not a criminological theory but a framework within which theories can be proposed and tested (see Blumstein *et al.* 1986; Blumstein and Cohen 1987). Dictionary definitions of the term 'career' specify two different concepts: a course or progress through life, and a way of making a living. The term is used in the first sense here. A 'criminal career' describes a sequence of offences committed during some part of an individual's lifetime, with no necessary suggestion that offenders use their criminal activity as an important means of earning a living.

The criminal career approach emphasizes the need to investigate such questions as why people start offending (onset), why they continue offending (persistence), why offending becomes more frequent or more serious (escalation), and why people stop offending (desistance). The factors influencing onset may differ from those influencing other criminal career features such as persistence, escalation, and desistance, if only because the different processes occur at different ages. Indeed, Farrington and Hawkins (1991) in the Cambridge Study found that there was no relationship between factors influencing prevalence (official offenders versus non-offenders), those influencing early versus later onset, and those influencing desistance after age 21; and Loeber *et al.* (1991) in the Pittsburgh Youth Study reported no relationship between factors influencing onset and those influencing escalation.

In order to understand the causes of offending, it is important to study developmental processes such as onset, persistence, escalation, and desistance. However, it is also important not to restrict this study narrowly to offending, but to study as well the onset, persistence, escalation and desistance of other types of anti-social behaviour. Loeber and LeBlanc (1990) used many other concepts to describe developmental processes in anti-social careers, including acceleration and deceleration, diversification, switching, stabilization, and de-escalation. For example, 'retention' (escalating to serious acts while still committing trivial acts) was more common than 'innovation' (escalating and giving up trivial acts).

The criminal career approach is essentially concerned with human development over time. Most criminological theories focus on instantaneous or cross-sectional differences between official offenders and non-offenders, or on cross-sectional correlates of the frequency or variety of self-reported offending. Furthermore, most criminological theories aim to explain offending when it is in full flow, in the teenage years. However, the criminal career approach focuses on within individual changes over time and on the predictors of longitudinal processes such as onset and desistance, recognizing that the same person can be an active offender at one age and a non-offender at another. It also aims to explain the development of offending over all ages.

Criminal career research seeks to investigate whether aggregate career features are the same as or different from individual features (Blumstein *et al.* 1988). For example, the age–crime curve over all individuals shows that the aggregate rate of offending increases to a peak in the teenage years and then decreases. The shape of this curve may reflect changes in the prevalence of offenders at each age (the proportion of individuals who offend, out of the total population), or changes in the frequency of offending (by those who are offenders at each age), or some combination of these. Most of the existing British and American evidence suggests that the aggregate peak age of offending primarily reflects variations in prevalence, and that individual offenders commit offences at a tolerably constant frequency during their criminal careers (Farrington 1986a). On this model, a 30-year-old offender commits offences at roughly the same rate as an 18-year-old offender, although offenders are more prevalent in the population of 18-year-olds than in the population of 30-year-olds. Therefore, the flat age–crime distribution for individual offending frequency is quite different from the peaked distribution for prevalence and from the peaked aggregate age–crime curve.

Putting this point in a slightly different way, a key issue in criminal career research is to determine how far aggregate changes with age or during the course of a criminal career reflect changes within individual offenders as opposed to changes in the composition of the offending population. For example, juvenile offenders primarily commit their crimes with others, whereas adult offenders primarily commit their crimes alone (Reiss and Farrington 1991). Does this finding mean that offenders change their methods of offending as they get older, switching from co-offending to lone offending? Or does it mean that one population of co-offenders desists (drop out) and is replaced by a new population of lone offenders? The answer to this kind of question, which arises very frequently, has important theoretical and policy implications. Generally, the evidence suggests that changes occur within one population of offenders at different ages, rather than some offenders desisting and being replaced at later ages by a new population of offenders.

Similarly, criminal career researchers emphasize that different career features may be differently related to age. It has already been pointed out that prevalence peaks in the teenage years but that the individual offending frequency may not. Blumstein *et al.* (1982) found that the residual length of a criminal career (the time remaining up to the point of desistance) peaked between ages 30 and 40. While teenage offenders are quite prevalent in the teenage population, the average teenage offender does not commit offences at a particularly high frequency and tends to have only a relatively short criminal career remaining. Hence, the peak prevalence in the teenage years does not imply that criminal justice measures such as incapacitation should be especially targeted on teenagers. In contrast, 30-year-old offenders are much less prevalent in the population of 30-year-olds, but the average 30-year-old offender tends to have a relatively long criminal career remaining. Looked at developmentally, 30-year-old offenders tend to be a subset of teenage offenders. Most teenage offenders desist from offending before age 30.

A key feature of the criminal career approach is its emphasis on the development of explicit mathematical models and the testing of quantitative predictions (for more details, see Farrington 1992a). These predictions are usually probabilistic rather than deterministic. The aim is to propose models that are simplifications of reality but that explain complex data. For example, it is unlikely that the individual offending frequency is exactly constant over time, but it is possible to fit criminal career data on this simple assumption. Most models are stochastic, assuming that the occurrence of measured offences (e.g., convictions) depends to some extent on chance processes.

* * * * *

Development of offending and anti-social behaviour

Prevalence at different ages

One of the distinctive contributions of criminal career research has been to demonstrate the high cumulative prevalence of arrests and convictions of males (for a review, see Visher and Roth 1986). For example, in Philadelphia, Wolfgang *et al.* (1987) found that 47 per cent of males were arrested for a non-traffic offence up to age 30, including 38 per cent of whites and 69 per cent of non-whites. In London, Farrington and West (1990) reported that 37 per cent of males were convicted for criminal offences up to age 32, when these were restricted to offences normally recorded in the Criminal Record Office. In Sweden, Stattin *et al.* (1989) discovered that one-third of males (and 7 per cent of females) were officially registered for non-traffic offences by age 30. The curves showing the cumulative prevalence up to age 25 of offending by working-class males in London and Stockholm were remarkably similar (Farrington and Wikström 1993).

The cumulative prevalence of self-reported offences is even higher. In the Cambridge Study, Farrington (1989c) showed that 96 per cent of the males had committed at least one of ten specified offences (including burglary, theft, assault, vandalism, and drug abuse) by age 32. Many males commit minor acts, especially in their teenage years, that might, strictly speaking, be classified as offences. In order to compare offenders and non-offenders, it is necessary to set a sufficiently high criterion for 'offending' (e.g., in terms of frequency, seriousness, or duration, or in terms of arrests or convictions) so that the vast majority of the male population are not classified as offenders. Alternatively, more and less serious offenders could be compared.

An important focus of criminal career research is the relationship between age and crime. Generally, the 'point prevalence' of offending at each age increases to a peak in the teenage years and then declines. The age–crime curve obtained by following up a cohort of people over time (the same people at different ages) is often different from the cross-sectional curve seen in official statistics (which reflects different people at different ages; see Farrington 1990a). Farrington (1986a) proposed a mathematical model for the age–crime curve, with three parameters. The first determined the speed of increase of the curve up to the peak, the second determined the speed of decrease of the curve after the peak, and the third determined the height of the peak.

In the Cambridge Study, the peak age for the prevalence of convictions was 17 (Farrington 1992b). The median age of conviction for most types of offences (burglary, robbery, theft of and from vehicles, shoplifting) was 17, while for violence it was 20 and for fraud 21. Similarly, in the Philadelphia cohort study of Wolfgang *et al.* (1987), the arrest rate increased to a peak at age 16 and then declined. In the Cambridge Study, the peak age of increase in the prevalence of offending was at 14, while the peak age of decrease was at 23. These times of maximum acceleration and deceleration in prevalence draw our attention to times in people's lives when important life events may be occurring that influence offending. They also indicate that the modal age of onset of offending is probably 14 and the modal age of desistance is probably 23.

Self-report studies also show that the most common types of offending decline from the teens to the twenties. In the Cambridge Study, the prevalence of burglary, shoplifting, theft of and from vehicles, theft from slot machines, and vandalism all decreased from the teens to the twenties, but the same decreases were not seen for theft from work, assault, drug abuse, and fraud (Farrington 1989c). For example, burglary (since the last interview) was admitted by 13 per cent at age 14, 11 per cent at age 18, 5 per cent at age 21, and 2 per cent at both age 25 and age 32. In their American National Youth Survey, Elliott *et al.* (1989) found that self-reports of the prevalence of offending increased from 11–13 to a peak at 15–17 and then decreased by 19–21.

The prevalence of other types of anti-social behaviour also varies with definitions and methods of measurement. According to the DSM-IIIR manual, about 9 per cent of American males and 2 per cent of American females under age 18 meet the diagnostic criteria for conduct disorder. The most extensive information about the prevalence of psychiatric disorders in children and adolescents was collected in the large-scale Ontario Child Health Study in Canada (Offord *et al.* 1989). This was a survey of about 3,300 children. About 7 per cent of males and 3 per cent of females aged 12–16 were conduct-disordered in the previous six months, according to reports by teachers and by the adolescents themselves.

Detailed figures for the prevalence of individual symptoms were provided by Offord *et al.* (1986). For example, for 12–16-year-olds, 10 per cent of males and 9 per cent of females admitted cruelty to animals, while 14 per cent of males and 8 per cent of females admitted destroying other people's things. In the same survey, Boyle and Offord (1986) provided detailed figures for the prevalence of smoking, drinking, and drug abuse. Extensive information about the prevalence of different anti-social symptoms at different ages between 4–5 and 15–16 can he found in Shepherd *et al.* (1971) for English children and in Achenbach and Edelbrock (1983) and Loeber *et al.* (1989) for American children.

According to the DSM-IIIR manual, about 3 per cent of American males and less than 1 per cent of American females meet the diagnostic criteria for adult anti-social personality disorder. However, the prevalence was greater than this in the large-scale Epidemiological Catchment Area project carried out in five sites in the United States. The lifetime prevalence was 7.3 per cent for males and 1.0 per cent for females (Robins *et al.* 1991).

Individual offending frequency

Since the pioneering research of Blumstein and Cohen (1979), much criminal career research has been concerned to estimate the individual offending frequency of active offenders during their criminal careers (for a review, see Cohen 1986). For example, on the basis of American research, Blumstein and Cohen concluded that the average active Index (more serious) offender committed about ten Index offences per year free, and that the individual offending frequency essentially did not vary with age. Furthermore, the average active Index offender accumulated about one arrest per year free.

The British and American studies reviewed by Farrington (1986a) indicated that the individual offending frequency did not vary greatly with age or during criminal careers. More recently, however, Loeber and Snyder (1990) concluded that it increased during the juvenile years up to age 16, and Haapanen (1990) found that it decreased during the adult years. Furthermore, in the Stockholm Project Metropolitan, Wikström (1990) showed that frequency peaked at age 15–17, and in retrospective self-report research with Nebraska prisoners Horney and Marshall (1991) concluded that it varied over time within individuals. Since there are several studies indicating on the contrary that frequency is stable with age (e.g., Home Office 1987; LeBlanc and Frechette 1989), more research is clearly needed to establish the conditions under which it is relatively stable or varies with age.

If periods of acceleration or deceleration in the individual offending frequency could be identified, and if the predictors of acceleration or deceleration could be established, as Farrington (1987b) suggested, these could have important implications for theory and policy. Barnett and Lofaso (1985) found that the best predictor of the future offending frequency in the Philadelphia cohort study was the past offending frequency.

There are many life events or conditions that might lead to an increase in the individual offending frequency. For example, using retrospective self-reports, Ball et al. (1981) found that Baltimore heroin addicts committed non-drug offences at a higher rate during periods of addiction than during periods when they were off opiates, suggesting that addiction caused an increase in offending. Using official records, Farrington et al. (1986b) showed that London males committed offences at a higher rate during periods of unemployment than during periods of employment. This difference was restricted to offences involving material gain, suggesting that unemployment caused a lack of money, which in turn caused an increase in offending to obtain money. However, neither of these studies adequately disentangled differences in prevalence from differences in frequency.

The individual offending frequency cannot be estimated from aggregate data simply by dividing the number of offences at each age by the number of arrested or convicted persons at each age, because some persons who have embarked on a criminal career may not sustain an official record at a particular age. Barnett et al. (1987) tested several mathematical models of the criminal careers of the Cambridge Study males, restricting the analyses to persons with two or more convictions. They found that models assuming that all offenders had the same frequency of offending were inadequate. Hence, they assumed that there were two categories of offenders, 'frequents' and 'occasionals'. The data showed that both categories incurred convictions at a constant (but different) rate during their active criminal careers. Barnett et al. did not suggest that there were in reality only two categories of offenders, but rather that it was possible to fit the actual data with a simple model assuming only two categories.

The average 'street time' interval between offences is the reciprocal of the individual offending frequency. Generally, this time interval decreases with each successive offence in a criminal career (e.g., Hamparian et al. 1978; Tracy et al. 1985). This decrease could mean either that the individual offending frequency was speeding up with each successive offence or that relatively low-frequency offenders were gradually dropping out of the offending population, so that this population was increasingly composed of high-frequency offenders at each successive offence transition. With the Philadelphia cohort data, Barnett and Lofaso (1985) concluded that offenders were not speeding up; offending frequencies stayed relatively constant over time, and the decreasing time intervals reflected a changing population of offenders.

Most prior studies of recidivism have used reconviction or no reconviction (or rearrest or no rearrest) within a short follow-up period of two or three years as the key dependent variable to be predicted. However, this is a rather insensitive measure. The individual offending frequency and the associated (reciprocal) time intervals between offences would be a more sensitive measure, and might give researchers a better chance of detecting the effect of sentencing or penal treatment on recidivism.

Onset

Criminal career research on onset using official records generally shows a peak age of onset between 13 and 15. For example, in the USA, Blumstein and Graddy (1982) found that the age of onset curve for arrests of both white and non-white males peaked at age 15. In the Swedish Project Metropolitan, Fry (1985) reported that the peak age of first arrest for both males and females was 13. In the Cambridge Study, the peak age of onset was 14; 4.6 per cent of the males were first convicted at that age (Farrington 1992b). The onset curves up to age 25 of working-class males in London and Stockholm were quite similar (Farrington and Wikström 1993).

Rather than presenting the onset rate with all persons in a cohort still alive as the denominator, it might be better to present a 'hazard' rate. This relates the number of first offenders to the number of persons still at risk of a first offence, excluding those with a previous onset. Farrington, Loeber, Elliott, et al. (1990) presented both hazard rates and onset rates for convictions in the Cambridge Study. The hazard rate showed a later peak at age 17; 5.5 per cent of the males still at risk were first convicted at that age. Basically, the peak hazard rate was later and greater than the peak onset rate because of the decreasing number of males still at risk of a first conviction with increasing age (the denominator). McCord (1990) showed how hazard rates varied according to social background variables. In the Cambridge Study, Farrington and Hawkins (1991) found that the best childhood predictors of an early versus a later onset of offending were: rarely spending leisure time with the father; high troublesomeness; authoritarian parents; and high psychomotor impulsivity.

In reality, and in a mathematical model, the true age of onset of offending will precede the age of the first conviction. By knowing the true individual offending frequency (which can be estimated from time intervals between offences), it is possible to estimate the true age of onset from the measured age of onset. For example, if the true individual offending frequency was two per year, and the measured age of onset (the first recorded offence) was 13.0 years, the true age of onset would be 12.5 years (since the average time to the first offence would be 0.5 years).

It would also be desirable to study sequences of onsets, to investigate how far the onset of one type of offence is followed by the onset of another type. The age of onset varies with different types of offences. In a study of Montreal delinquents, LeBlanc and Frechette (1989) discovered that shoplifting and vandalism tended to occur before adolescence (average age of onset 11), burglary and motor vehicle theft in adolescence (average onset 14–15), and sex offences and drug trafficking in the later teenage years (average onset 17–19). It is also well established that early substance abuse predicts later serious drug use. For example, Yamaguchi and Kandel (1984) showed that alcohol use preceded smoking cigarettes, which in turn preceded marijuana use, which in turn preceded other illicit drug use.

Judging from average ages of onset, the onset of shoplifting or vandalism might provide an early opportunity to detect future serious criminal offenders. However, the onset of childhood anti-social behaviour such as cruelty to animals might provide an even earlier indication. On the basis of retrospective reports by parents of clinic-referred boys, Loeber et al. (1992) found that rule-breaking at home tended to occur at a median age of onset of 4.5 years, then cruelty to animals (5.0), bullying (5.5), lying, stealing, fighting (6.0), vandalism (6.5), and eventually burglary (10.0). It is desirable to investigate whether these sequences of onsets occur within individuals. Onset sequences might suggest stages when interventions can be introduced to prevent escalation to more serious behaviour.

In the Cambridge Study, the average age of the first conviction was 17.5. The males first convicted at the earliest ages (10–13) tended to become the most persistent offenders, committing an average of 8.1 offences leading to convictions in an average criminal career lasting 9.9 years (Farrington 1992b). Similarly, Farrington and Wikström (1993), using-official records in Stockholm, and LeBlanc and Frechette (1989) using both self-reports and official records in Montreal, showed that the duration of criminal careers decreased with increasing age of onset. It is generally true that an early onset of anti-social behaviour predicts a long and serious anti-social career (Loeber and LeBlanc 1990). Reitsma-Street et al. (1985) found that anti-social teenagers in Ontario had initiated smoking, drinking, drug use, and sexual behaviour on average over two years before their non-anti-social siblings.

Clearly, an early age of onset foreshadows a long criminal career (see also Home Office 1987). Whether it also foreshadows a high frequency of offending is less clear. Hamparian et al. (1978), in a study of violent juveniles in Ohio, reported that there was a (negative) linear relationship between the age of onset and the number of offences. Neglecting the possibility of desistance, this suggests that the offending frequency may be tolerably constant between onset and the eighteenth birthday. However, Tolan (1987) found that the frequency of current self-reported offending was greatest for those with the earliest age of onset.

It is important to establish why an early age of onset predicts a long criminal career and a large number of offences. Following Gottfredson and Hirschi (1986), one possibility is that an early age of onset is merely one symptom of a high criminal potential, which later shows itself in persistent and serious offending. On this theory, an early age of onset has no effect on underlying theoretical constructs. Another possibility is that an early age of onset in some way facilitates later offending, perhaps because of the reinforcing effects of successful early offending or the stigmatizing effects of convictions. In other words, an early onset leads to a change in an underlying theoretical construct such as the probability of persistence. Nagin and Farrington (1992a) concluded that the inverse relationship between age of onset and persistence of offending in the Cambridge Study was entirely attributable to the persistence of a previously existing criminal potential, and that an early age of onset had no additional impact on persistence.

An onset offence of a particular type might predict a later frequent or serious criminal career. For example, the Home Office study (1987) showed that an onset offence of burglary or theft was particularly predictive of persistence in offending. This type of information might be useful in identifying at first arrest or conviction those at high risk of progressing into a persistent and serious criminal career.

Desistance

The true age of desistance from offending can only be determined with certainty after offenders die. In the Cambridge Study up to age 32, the average age of the last offence, according to official records, was 23.3. Since the average age of the first offence was 17.5, the average length of the recorded criminal career was 5.8 years, with an average of 4.5 recorded convictions per offender during this period (Farrington 1992b).

In the Philadelphia cohort study, Wolfgang et al. (1972) showed how the probability of reoffending (persistence as opposed to desistance) increased after each successive offence. This probability was 0.54 after the first offence, 0.65 after the second, 0.72 after the third, and reached an asymptote of 0.80 after six or more arrests. Assuming a probabilistic process with a probability p of persisting after each offence, and conversely a probability $(1-p)$ of desisting, the expected number of future offences after any given offence is $p/(1-p)$, which at the asymptote ($p = 0.80$) is 4. Several other researchers have replicated these results by showing the growth in the probability of recidivism after each successive offence (see Blumstein et al. 1985; Farrington and Wikström 1993).

Barnett et al. (1987) proposed a more complex mathematical model for the Cambridge Study data, aiming to explain time intervals between convictions as well as recidivism probabilities. They distinguished 'frequents' and 'occasionals' who differed both in their rates of offending and in their probabilities of desisting after each conviction. The longitudinal sequences of convictions were fitted best by assuming persistence probabilities after each conviction of 0.90 for frequents and 0.67 for occasionals.

These models assume that desistance does or does not occur immediately after each conviction. Hence there is an implicit assumption that something connected with the conviction (e.g., the penalty) has an effect, with a certain probability. An alternative model is that, after onset, desistance occurs continuously as an annual process. With this assumption in the London data, the annual rate of desistance for the frequents (0.11) was not significantly different from that of the occasionals (0.14). It is difficult to distinguish between these alternative models on the basis of conviction sequences alone. However, they have very different theoretical and policy implications.

Barnett *et al.* (1989) also carried out a predictive test of their model with the Cambridge Study data. The model was developed on conviction data between the tenth and twenty-fifth birthdays and tested on reconviction data between the twenty-fifth and thirtieth birthdays. Generally, the model performed well, but it seemed necessary to assume that there was some intermittency (desisting and later restarting) in criminal careers. Some of the frequents ceased offending at an average age of 19 and then restarted after a period of 7–10 years with no convictions. It is important to establish why this restarting occurs.

Several projects have explicitly investigated why offenders desist. For example, in the Cambridge Study, getting married and moving out of London both fostered desistance (Osborn 1980; West 1982). Shover (1985) explicitly asked retrospective questions about desistance to older men who had given up offending. The main reasons advanced for desistance focused on the increasing costs of crime (long prison sentences), the importance of intimate relationships with women, increasing satisfaction with jobs, and becoming more mature, responsible, and settled with age. Some policy implications of desistance research are that ex-offenders should be helped to settle down in stable marital relationships and in stable jobs, and helped to break away from their criminal associates.

Chronic offenders

In the Philadelphia cohort study, Wolfgang *et al.*(1972) showed that 6 per cent of the males (18 per cent of the offenders) accounted for 52 per cent of all the juvenile arrests, and labelled these 6 per cent the 'chronic offenders'. These 'chronics' accounted for even higher proportions of serious offences: 69 per cent of all aggravated assaults, 71 per cent of homicides, 73 per cent of forcible rapes, and 82 per cent of robberies. Frequency and seriousness of offending are generally related. Other researchers have essentially replicated these results. For example, in the Cambridge Study, Farrington (1983a) found that about 6 per cent of the males accounted for about half of all the convictions. Furthermore, when convictions of all family members (fathers, mothers, sons, and daughters) were added together, it was discovered that less than 5 per cent of the families accounted for half of all the convictions (West and Farrington 1977). In Stockholm, Wikström (1987) showed that only 1 per cent of Project Metropolitan cohort members (6 per cent of all offenders) accounted for half of all the crimes, while Pulkkinen (1988) in Finland found that 4 per cent of males and 1 per cent of females accounted for half of all the convictions.

The chronic offenders who account for a disproportionate number of all offences are clearly prime targets for crime prevention and control. However, a lot depends on how far they can be identified in advance. Blumstein *et al.* (1985) pointed out that Wolfgang *et al.* (1972) identified the chronics retrospectively. Even if all the arrested boys were truly homogeneous in their underlying criminal potential, chance factors alone would result in some of them having more arrests and others having fewer. Because of these probabilistic processes, those with the most arrests — defined after the fact as the chronics — would account for a disproportionate fraction of the total number of arrests. For example, if an unbiased dice were thrown thirty times and the five highest scores added up, these would account for a disproportionate fraction of the total score obtained in all thirty throws (thirty out of 105, on average; 16.7 per cent of the throws accounting for 28.6 per cent of the total score).

A key question is whether the chronic offenders differ prospectively from the non-chronic offenders in their individual offending frequency. Blumstein *et al.* (1985) investigated this in the Cambridge Study. They used a seven-point scale of variables measured at age 8–10, reflecting child anti-social behaviour, family economic deprivation, convicted parents, low intelligence, and poor parental child-rearing behaviour. Of fifty-five boys scoring four or more, fifteen were chronic offenders (out of twenty-three chronics altogether), twenty-two others were convicted, and only eighteen were not convicted. Hence, it was concluded that most of the chronics could have been predicted in advance on the basis of information available at age 10. It is true that only a minority of the high-scoring boys became chronics; however, as will be explained below, the remainder should not all be regarded as 'false positives' or mistakes in prediction.

Blumstein *et al.* (1985) developed a mathematical model in which all the London males were classified as 'innocents', 'desisters', or 'persisters'. The best fit to the recidivism probabilities in the survey was obtained by assuming that the probability of persisting after each conviction was 0.87 for persisters and 0.57 for desisters. The proportion of first offenders who were persisters was 28 per cent. Persisters and desisters differed in their *a priori* probabilities of persisting, not in their *a posteriori* number of convictions (as chronics did).

Interestingly, the number of predicted chronics among the offenders (thirty-seven scoring four or more on the seven-point scale) was similar to the hypothesized number of persisters (36.7) according to the mathematical model. Furthermore, the individual process of dropping out of crime of the predicted chronics closely matched the aggregate drop-out process for persisters predicted by the mathematical model with parameters estimated from aggregate recidivism data. Hence, the predicted chronics might be viewed as equivalent to the persisters. According to the mathematical model, because of probabilistic processes, 18.3 of the 36.7 persisters should survive to have six or more convictions by age 25 (and hence be classified as 'chronics'). Actually, fifteen of the thirty-seven offenders who were predicted to be chronics became actual chronics. The mathematical model shows that it is inappropriate to view the other twenty-two offenders as 'false positives', because this concept reflects deterministic prediction. Most of the discrepancy between predicted and actual chronics (18.4 in the model, out of the actual discrepancy of twenty-two) reflects probabilistic desistance processes rather than errors in identification.

Duration

There has been less research on the duration of criminal careers. Farrington and Wikström (1993) found that, up to age 25, working-class boys had similar average career lengths in London (3.9 years) and in Stockholm (3.5 years). As already mentioned, the boys first convicted at the earliest ages (10–13) in the Cambridge Study tended to be the most persistent offenders, with an average career length close to ten years up to age 32. Those first convicted at age 10–11 had an average career length of 11.5 years (Farrington 1992b). Over a quarter of all convicted males had criminal careers lasting longer than ten years. The average duration of criminal careers declined precipitously from age 16 (7.9 years) to age 17 (2.9 years), suggesting that those males first convicted as juveniles were much more persistent offenders than those first convicted as adults.

Barnett et al. (1987) estimated career lengths in the Cambridge Study using their mathematical model. On average, the frequents had a duration of 8.8 years and the occasionals had a duration of 7.4 years. (Both groups included only males with two or more convictions, in order to estimate time intervals between offences.) Hence, the frequents and occasionals did not differ much in their career lengths, although they differed considerably in their individual offending frequencies. Little is known about the predictors and correlates of criminal career duration.

Another important concept is the residual length of a criminal career at any given moment. Blumstein et al. (1982) used a life-table method to estimate residual career length and, as already mentioned, found that it increased to a peak between ages 30 and 40. One area where knowledge about residual career length is important is in estimating the incapacitative effects of imprisonment. If the average time served exceeds the residual career length, people would be imprisoned beyond the point at which they would have stopped offending anyway. Hence, valuable prison space might be wasted by incarcerating those who would in any case have desisted from offending.

Continuity

Generally, there is significant continuity between offending in one age range and offending in another. In the Cambridge Study, nearly three-quarters (73 per cent) of those convicted as juveniles at age 10–16 were reconvicted at age 17–24, in comparison with only 16 per cent of those not convicted as juveniles (Farrington 1992b). Nearly half (45 per cent) of those convicted as juveniles were reconvicted at age 25–32, in comparison with only 8 per cent of those not convicted as juveniles. Furthermore, this continuity over time did not merely reflect continuity in police reaction to crime. Farrington (1989c) showed that, for ten specified offences, the significant continuity between offending in one age range and offending in a later age range held for self-reports as well as official convictions.

Other studies (e.g., McCord 1991) show similar continuity. For example, in Sweden, Stattin and Magnusson (1991) reported that nearly 70 per cent of males registered for crime before age 15 were registered again between ages 15 and 20, and nearly 60 per cent were registered between ages 21 and 29. Also, the number of juvenile offences is an effective predictor of the number of adult offences (Wolfgang et al. 1987). Farrington and Wikström (1993) showed that there was considerable continuity in offending between ages 10 and 25 in both London and Stockholm.

It is not always realized that relative continuity is quite compatible with absolute change. In other words, the relative ordering of people on some underlying construct such as criminal potential can remain significantly stable over time, even though the absolute level of criminal potential declines on average for everyone. For example, Farrington (1990a) in the Cambridge Study showed that the prevalence of self-reported offending declined significantly between ages 18 and 32, but that there was a significant tendency for the worst offenders at 18 also to be the worst offenders at 32.

There are two major alternative reasons for the continuity between past and future offending (Nagin and Farrington 1992b). One is that it reflects a stable underlying construct such as criminal potential; this was termed the 'persistent heterogeneity' explanation. The second is that the commission of one crime leads to an increase in the probability of commission of future crimes, perhaps because of reinforcement or stigmatization; this was termed the 'state dependence' explanation. In predicting convictions during each age range in the Cambridge Study, the best model included age, intelligence, daring, convicted parents, and poor child-rearing, but did not include prior convictions. Hence, prior convictions did not predict future convictions independently of background factors and age, so that the persistent heterogeneity explanation was supported. In other words, the continuity between past and future convictions reflected continuity in an underlying criminal potential.

These results are in agreement with the idea that there tends to be persistence of an underlying 'anti-social personality' from childhood to the teenage years and into adulthood. Robins (e.g., 1986) has consistently shown how a constellation of indicators of childhood anti-social behaviour predicts a constellation of indicators of adult anti-social behaviour. In several longitudinal studies, the number of different childhood symptoms predicted the number of different adult symptoms, rather than there being a linkage between any specific childhood and adult symptoms (Robins and Wish 1977; Robins and Ratcliff 1978, 1980). Numerous other studies also show that childhood conduct problems predict later offending and anti-social behaviour (e.g., Loeber and LeBlanc 1990). For example, Spivack et al. (1986) in Philadelphia discovered that troublesome behaviour in kindergarten (age 3–4) predicted later police contacts; and Ensminger et al. (1983) in Chicago and Tremblay et al. (1988) in Montreal showed that ratings of aggressiveness by teachers and peers in the first grade (age 6–7) predicted self-reported offending at age 14–15.

Similarly, in the Cambridge Study there was evidence of continuity in anti-social behaviour from childhood to the teenage years. The anti-social personality scale at age 10 correlated 0.50 with the corresponding scale at age 14 and 0.38 with the scale at age 18 (Farrington 1991a). The second-best predictor of the anti-social tendency scale at age 18 was childhood troublesomeness (getting into trouble at school, e.g., for bad behaviour or laziness) at age 8–10, rated by peers and teachers (Farrington 1993b); the best predictor was having a convicted parent by age 10. With regard to specific types of anti-social behaviour, troublesomeness was the only factor measured at age 8–10 that significantly predicted bullying at both ages 14 and 18 (Farrington 1993d). Again, troublesomeness at age 8–10 was the best predictor of both truancy and aggression at age 12–14 in the secondary schools (Farrington 1980, 1989a).

There is also continuity in anti-social behaviour at younger ages. For example, Rose *et al.* (1989) in New York City found that externalizing scores on the Achenbach Child Behaviour Checklist (reflecting a broad-band anti-social syndrome; see Achenbach and Edelbrock 1983) were significantly correlated ($r = 0.57$) between ages 2 and 5. Furthermore, a mother's ratings of her boy's difficult temperament at age six months significantly predicted ($r = 0.31$) his externalizing scores at age 8 years in the Bloomington longitudinal survey (Bates *et al.* 1991). It might possibly be argued that these kinds of relationships reflected the stability of the parent's personality rather than of the child's behaviour, but similar results are obtained even with different data sources (parents at an earlier age and teachers later). In outer London, Richman *et al.* (1985) reported that behaviour problems tended to persist between ages 3 and 8, and in New Zealand White *et al.* (1990) showed that externalizing scores and being difficult to manage at age 3 predicted anti-social behaviour at age 11.

There is also continuity in anti-social behaviour from the teenage to the adult years. In the Cambridge Study, a measure of adult social dysfunction at age 32 was developed, based on (in the previous five years) convictions, self-reported offending, poor home conditions, poor cohabitation history, child problems, poor employment history, substance abuse, violence, and poor mental health (a high score on the General Health Questionnaire; see Farrington *et al.* 1988*a, b*, and Farrington 1989*b*). This measure of adult social dysfunction at age 32 was significantly predicted by the anti-social tendency measure at age 18 (Farrington 1993*b*). Similarly, a measure of anti-social personality at age 32 was developed which was comparable with the anti-social personality measures for earlier ages. Anti-social personality at age 18 correlated 0.55 with anti-social personality at age 32 (Farrington 1991*a*).

Expressing this another way, 60 per cent of the most anti-social quarter of males at age 18 were still in the most anti-social quarter fourteen years later at age 32. Bearing in mind the very great environmental changes between ages 18 and 32, as the males left their parental homes, went through a period of unstable living arrangements, and eventually settled down in marital homes, this consistency over time seems likely to reflect consistency in the individual's personality rather than consistency in the environment. It is often found that about half of any sample of anti-social children persist to become anti-social teenagers, and that about half of any sample of anti-social teenagers persist to become anti-social adults. Comparing the 0.55 correlation between ages 18 and 32 with the 0.38 correlation between ages 10 and 18, it is interesting that there was increasing stabilization of anti-social personality with age.

Zoccolillo *et al.* (1992), in a follow-up study of children who had been in care, also demonstrated the continuity between childhood conduct disorder (at age 9–12) and adult social dysfunction (at age 26) in the areas of work and social and sexual relationships. For example, 81 per cent of those with three or more symptoms of conduct disorder showed adult dysfunction in two or more areas, compared with only 21 per cent of those with 0–2 symptoms of conduct disorder. Approaching half (40 per cent) of the males with three or more symptoms of conduct disorder showed persistent anti-social behaviour after age 18 and fulfilled the psychiatric criteria for adult anti-social personality disorder.

The continuity in anti-social personality does not mean that it is not desirable to study influences on criminal career features such as onset and desistance. Unlike Gottfredson and Hirschi (1990), I would not argue that all criminal career features reflect only one underlying construct of criminal potential. Also, the persistence of anti-social personality does not mean that there is no scope for change. The correlations between measures of anti-social personality at different ages (e.g., the 0.55 correlation between 18 and 32), and the fact that only about half of anti-social children become anti-social adults, show that a great deal of relative change is occurring. This makes it possible to investigate factors that might encourage anti-social children to become less anti-social as they grow older, or that might foster early desistance.

There is specific as well as general continuity in anti-social behaviour from the teenage to the adult years. In the Cambridge Study, Farrington (1990a) developed measures of absolute change and relative consistency between ages 18 and 32. For example, the prevalence of marijuana use declined significantly, from 29 per cent at age 18 to 19 per cent at age 32. However, there was a significant tendency for the users at age 18 also to be users at age 32 (44 per cent of users at age 18 were users at age 32, whereas only 8 per cent of non-users at age 18 were users at age 32). Other researchers (e.g., Ghodsian and Power 1987) have also reported significant consistency in substance abuse between adolescence and adulthood.

In contrast, the prevalence of binge drinking and drunk driving increased significantly between ages 18 and 32, but there was again significant consistency over time; the prevalence of heavy smoking did not change significantly between ages 18 and 32, but there was again significant consistency over time. Therefore, relative consistency could coexist with absolute increases, decreases, or constancy in anti-social behaviour in the Cambridge Study. In the Netherlands, Verhulst et al. (1990) also reported relative stability and absolute changes in childhood anti-social behaviour.

There is usually specific as well as general continuity in aggression and violence from the teenage to the adult years. In the Cambridge Study, aggression at age 16–18 was the best predictor of fighting at age 32 (Farrington 1989a). Spouse assault at age 32 was significantly predicted by teacher-rated aggression at age 12–14, and by the anti-social personality measures at ages 14 and 18, but not (surprisingly) by aggression at age 18 (Farrington 1993a). Bullying at 32 was specifically predicted by bullying at 14 and 18 independently of the continuity between aggression at 14 and 18 and aggression at 32 (Farrington 1993d). Furthermore, a male's bullying at 14 and 18 predicted bullying by his child when he was 32, showing that there was intergenerational continuity in bullying. In their New York study, Eron and Huesmann (1990) also found that a boy's aggression at age 8 predicted not only his aggression and spouse assault at age 30 but also the aggressiveness of his child.

Specialization and escalation

In the Cambridge Study, Farrington (1991b) investigated how far violent offenders specialized. About one-third of the convicted males (fifty out of 153) were convicted of violence (assault, robbery, or threatening behaviour). They committed a total of eighty-five violent offences (an average of 1.7 each), but they also committed 263 non-violent offences (an average of 5.3 each). Only seven of the fifty violent offenders had no convictions for non-violent offences. Other researchers (e.g., Hamparian *et al.* 1978; Snyder 1988) have also found that the majority of recorded offences of violent offenders are non-violent. Farrington (1991*b*) tested a model that assumed that violent offences occurred at random in criminal careers. Since the data fitted this model, it was concluded that offenders did not specialize in violence. Furthermore, violent offenders and non-violent but persistent offenders were virtually identical in childhood, adolescent, and adult features. Hence, violent offenders are essentially frequent offenders.

Using criminal career data collected in the South East Prison Survey, Stander *et al.* (1989) investigated specialization with offence-to-offence transition matrices. Generally, these matrices did not change (were 'stationary') during the criminal career. Stander *et al.* studied whether the offending sequences could be viewed as a first-order Markov chain (i.e., whether the probability of one offence following another was not influenced by the prior offending history), but concluded that they could not. While there was a great deal of generality in offending, there was some specialization superimposed on it. Stander *et al.* used the Forward Specialization Coefficient of Farrington, Snyder, and Finnegan (1988) to quantify the degree of specialization. They found that sex offenders were the most specialized, and that specialization in fraud was especially marked for persistent offenders. Other criminal career research also suggests that there is a small degree of specificity superimposed on a great deal of generality or versatility in offending (see Farrington, Snyder, and Finnegan, 1988). There is also some indication of increasing specialization (decreasing diversification) with age.

There has been less research on escalation, partly because of the prevailing belief in versatility and in the fact that different types of offences seem to be committed almost at random during criminal careers. In the Philadelphia cohort study, Tracy *et al.* (1990) found that the average seriousness of offences increased as offenders became older and with each successive offence. More information about escalation, and especially about the predictors of escalation, is needed.

Co-offending and motives

Past criminal career research has mainly focused on prevalence, frequency, onset, desistance, duration, and specialization. However, there are many other features of offences that might be studied in criminal career research. These include whether a person commits an offence alone or with others; the location of the offence, and the distance travelled by offenders to commit it; motives for committing offences, including how far they are planned in advance; characteristics of victims; methods of committing crimes, including use of psychological or physical force; the offender's subjective probability of being caught by the police, convicted, and sentenced to imprisonment; and the offender's subjective utilities of the costs and benefits of offending. Except for the work of LeBlanc and Frechette (1989), there has been little research on these topics within the criminal career perspective, despite their potential relevance. Many distinctive features of offences might help in detecting offenders, for example through 'offender profiling' (e.g., Canter 1989), but I will focus here on co-offending and motives.

In the Cambridge Study, Reiss and Farrington (1991) found that about half of all offences were committed with (usually one or two) others, and that the incidence of co-offending was greatest for burglary and robbery. Co-offending declined steadily with age from 10 to 32. As already mentioned, this was not because co-offenders dropped out but because the males changed from co-offending in their teenage years to lone offending in their twenties. Males who committed their first offence with others tended to have a longer criminal career than those who committed their first offence alone, but this was largely because first offences with others tended to be committed at younger ages than first offences alone, and of course those with an early age of onset tended to have a longer criminal career. Transition matrices showed that there tended to be some consistency in co-offending or lone offending between one offence and the next.

Burglary, robbery, and theft from vehicles were especially likely to involve co-offenders. Generally, co-offenders were similar in age, sex, and race to the males themselves, and lived close to the males' homes and to the locations of the offences. However, the similarity between the males and their co-offenders, and their residential propinquity, decreased with age. Co-offending relationships tended not to persist for very long: rarely more than one year. About one-third of the most persistent offenders continually offended with less criminally experienced co-offenders, and hence appeared to be repeatedly recruiting others into a life of crime. Recruiting was especially common for burglary offences. (For a review of research on co-offending, see Reiss 1988.)

West and Farrington (1977) found that the most common motives given for property offences (46 per cent of self-reported offences, 43 per cent of offences leading to convictions) were utilitarian, rational, or economic ones: offences were committed for material gain. The next most common motives (31 per cent of self-reported offences, 22 per cent of conviction offences) might be termed hedonistic: offences were committed for excitement, for enjoyment, or to relieve boredom. In general, utilitarian motives predominated for most types of property offences such as burglary and theft, except that vandalism and motor vehicle theft were committed predominantly for hedonistic reasons, and shoplifting was partly utilitarian and partly hedonistic. Offences at younger ages (under 17) were relatively more likely to be committed for hedonistic reasons while offences at older ages (17 or older) were relatively more likely to be committed for utilitarian reasons.

These results are similar to those reported by Petersilia et al. (1978) in a retrospective survey of about fifty armed robbers imprisoned in California. The main motives given for their crimes committed in the juvenile years were thrills and peer influence, but the main motive given for their crimes committed in the adult years was to obtain money — for drugs or alcohol or to support themselves or their families. Similar findings were obtained by LeBlanc and Frechette (1989) in Montreal. (For a review of research on motivation, see Farrington 1993c.)

In the Cambridge Study, Farrington et al. (1982) also studied motives for aggressive acts (physical fights). They found that the key dimension was whether the male fought alone or in a group. In individual fights, the male was usually provoked, became angry, and hit out in order to hurt his opponent and to discharge his own internal feelings of tension. In group fights, the male often said that he became involved in order to help a friend or because he was attacked, and rarely said that he was angry. The group fights were more serious, occurring in bars or streets, and they were more likely to involve weapons, produce injuries, and lead to police intervention. Fights often occurred when minor incidents escalated because both sides wanted to demonstrate their toughness and masculinity and were unwilling to react in a conciliatory way. Similarly, Berkowitz (1978) interviewed convicted violent offenders and found that most incidents arose out of arguments and were angry outbursts intended primarily to hurt the victim; the second most frequent cause was a friend's need for assistance.

In the future, criminal career research should be expanded to study a wider range of career features. For example, if utilitarian motives increase and hedonistic motives decrease with age, is this because hedonistically motivated people stop offending (and if so why?) or because hedonistically motivated people change to become utilitarian (and if so why?)? Prospective longitudinal research would be needed to resolve these kinds of criminal career issues.

Influences on criminal careers

Risk factors

Risk factors are prior factors that increase the risk of occurrence of events such as the onset, frequency, persistence, or duration of anti-social behaviour. In order to establish the ordering of risk factors and criminal career features, longitudinal data are required. The focus in this chapter is on risk factors for the onset or prevalence of offending and anti-social behaviour. Few studies have examined risk factors for persistence or duration. However, in the Cambridge Study, Farrington and Hawkins (1991) investigated factors that predicted whether convicted offenders before age 21 persisted or desisted between ages 21 and 32. The best independent predictors of persistence included the boy rarely spending leisure time with his father at age 11–12, low intelligence at age 8–10, employment instability at age 16, and heavy drinking at age 18. Indeed, nearly 90 per cent of the convicted males who were frequently unemployed and heavy drinkers as teenagers went on to be reconvicted after age 21.

It is also difficult to decide whether any given risk factor is an indicator (symptom) or a possible cause of anti-social behaviour. The problems raised by impulsivity have already been mentioned. As other examples, do heavy drinking, truancy, unemployment, and divorce measure anti-social tendency, or do they cause (an increase in) it? It is important not to include a measure of the dependent variable as an independent variable in causal analyses, because this will lead to false (tautological) conclusions and an overestimation of explanatory or predictive power (see e.g., Amdur 1989).

It is not unreasonable to argue that some factors may be both indicative and causal. For example, long-term variations *between* individuals in anti-social tendency may be reflected in variations in alcohol consumption, just as short-term variations *within* individuals in alcohol consumption may cause more anti-social behaviour during the heavier drinking periods. The interpretation of other factors may be more clear-cut.

For example, being exposed as a child to poor parental child-rearing techniques might cause anti-social tendency but would not be an indicator of it; and burgling a house might be an indicator of anti-social tendency but would be unlikely to cause it (although it might be argued that, when an anti-social act is successful in leading to positive reinforcement, this reinforcement causes an increase in the underlying anti-social tendency).

Cross-sectional studies make it impossible to distinguish between indicators and causes, since they can merely demonstrate correlations between high levels of one factor (e.g., unemployment) and high levels of another (e.g., offending). However, longitudinal studies can show that offending is greater (within individuals) during some periods (e.g., of unemployment) than during other periods (e.g., of employment). Because within-individual studies have greater control over extraneous influences than between-individual studies, longitudinal studies can demonstrate that changes in unemployment within individuals cause offending with high internal validity in quasi-experimental analyses (Farrington 1988b; Farrington, Gallagher, Morley, et al. 1986). Longitudinal studies can also establish whether factors such as unemployment have the same or different effects on offending when they vary within or between individuals. Implications for prevention and treatment, which require changes within individuals, cannot necessarily be drawn from effects demonstrated only in between-individual (cross-sectional) research.

It is unfortunate that the static model of relationships between independent and dependent variables has dominated research and theories of offending and anti-social behaviour. This model may have a veneer of plausibility in a cross-sectional study, at least if problems of causal order are neglected. However, it is not easily applied to longitudinal or criminal career data, where all presumed explanatory constructs and all measures of anti-social behaviour and criminal career features change continuously within individuals over different ages. Relationships between an explanatory factor in one age range and a measure of anti-social behaviour in another age range may vary a great deal according to the particular age ranges, and this needs to be systematically investigated by researchers.

The major risk factors for offending and anti-social behaviour that are reviewed in this chapter are the individual difference factors of impulsivity and intelligence, and family, socio-economic, peer, school, community, and situational factors. These factors often have additive, interactive, or sequential effects, but I will consider them one by one.

Impulsivity

In the Cambridge Study, the boys nominated by teachers as lacking in concentration or restless, those nominated by parents, peers, or teachers as the most daring, and those who were the most impulsive on psychomotor tests all tended to be juvenile but not adult offenders (Farrington 1992c). Later self-report questionnaire measures of impulsivity (including such items as 'I generally do and say things quickly without stopping to think') were related to both juvenile and adult offending. Daring, poor concentration, and restlessness were all related to both official and self-reported delinquency (Farrington 1992d). Daring at age 8–10 was an important independent predictor of anti-social tendency at age 18 (Farrington 1993b) and of violence and spouse assault at age 32 (Farrington 1989*a*, 1993*a*). Poor concentration or restlessness at age 8–10 was an important independent predictor of adult social dysfunction at age 32 (Farrington 1993*b*).

Many other investigators have reported a link between the constellation of personality factors termed 'hyperactivity–impulsivity–attention deficit' or HIA (Loeber 1987) and offending. For example, Satterfield (1987) tracked HIA and matched control boys in Los Angeles between ages 9 and 17, and showed that six times as many of the HIA boys were arrested for serious offences. Similar results were reported by Gittelman *et al.* (1985) in New York . Other studies have shown that childhood hyperactivity predicts adolescent and adult anti-social behaviour and substance use (e.g., Barkley *et al.* 1990; Mannuzza, Klein, and Addalli, 1991; Mannuzza, Klein, Bonagura *et al.* 1991).

A key issue is how far HIA is a cause or an indicator of anti-social behaviour, and more specifically whether HIA and conduct disorder reflect the same or different underlying constructs (Taylor 1986). Farrington, Loeber, and Van Kammen (1990) in the Cambridge Study developed a combined measure of HIA at age 8–10 and showed that it significantly predicted juvenile convictions independently of conduct problems at age 8–10. Hence, it might be concluded that HIA is not merely another measure of anti-social personality, but is a possible cause, or an earlier stage in a developmental sequence. Richman *et al.* (1985) found that restlessness at age 3 predicted conduct disorder at age 8, while McGee *et al.* (1991) showed that hyperactivity at age 3 predicted a variety of child disorders at age 15. Other studies have also concluded that hyperactivity and conduct disorder are different constructs (e.g., McGee *et al.* 1985; Blouin *et al.* 1989). Similar constructs to HIA, such as sensation seeking, are also risk factors for delinquency (e.g., White *et al.* 1985); and Gottfredson and Hirschi (1990) argued that individual propensities to commit crimes and other types of anti-social acts arose from the similar construct of low self-control.

It has been suggested that HIA might be a behavioural consequence of a low level of physiological arousal. Offenders have a low level of arousal according to their low alpha (brain) waves on the EEG, or according to autonomic nervous system indicators such as heart rate, blood pressure, or skin conductance, or they show low autonomic reactivity (e.g., Venables and Raine 1987). In his Swedish longitudinal survey, Magnusson (1988) demonstrated that low adrenalin levels at age 13, reflecting low autonomic reactivity, were related to aggressiveness and restlessness at that age and to later adult offending. Olweus (1987) also found that aggressive juveniles in Sweden tended to have low adrenalin levels. The causal links between low autonomic arousal, consequent sensation seeking, and offending are brought out explicitly in Mawson's (1987) theory of transient criminality.

Heart rate was measured in the Cambridge Study at age 18. While a low heart rate correlated significantly with convictions for violence (Farrington 1987*a*), it was not significantly related to delinquency in general. In addition, being tattooed was highly related to self-reported and official offending in the Cambridge Study (Farrington 1992*d*). While the meaning of this result is not entirely clear, tattooing may reflect risk taking, daring, and excitement seeking.

Intelligence

Loeber and Dishion (1983) and Loeber and Stouthamer-Loeber (1987) extensively reviewed the predictors of male delinquency. They concluded that poor parental child-management techniques, offending by parents and siblings, low intelligence and educational attainment, and separations from parents were all important predictors. Longitudinal (and indeed cross-sectional) surveys have consistently demonstrated that children with low intelligence are disproportionately likely to become offenders. Low intelligence and attainment are also related to childhood anti-social behaviour (e.g., Rutter *et al.* 1970).

In the Cambridge Study, one-third of the boys scoring ninety or less on a non-verbal intelligence test (Raven's Progressive Matrices) at age 8–10 were convicted as juveniles, twice as many as among the remainder (Farrington 1992*d*). Low non-verbal intelligence was highly correlated with low verbal intelligence (vocabulary, word comprehension, verbal reasoning) and with low school attainment at age 11, and all of these measures predicted juvenile convictions to much the same extent. In addition to their poor school performance, delinquents tended to be frequent truants, to leave school at the earliest possible age (which was then 15) and to take no school examinations.

Low non-verbal intelligence was especially characteristic of the juvenile recidivists (who had an average IQ of 89) and those first convicted at the earliest ages (10–13). Furthermore, low intelligence and attainment predicted self-reported delinquency almost as well as convictions (Farrington 1992*d*), suggesting that the link between low intelligence and delinquency was not caused by the less intelligent boys having a greater probability of being caught. Similar results have been obtained in other projects (e.g. Moffitt and Silva 1988*a*; Wilson and Herrnstein 1985). Low intelligence and attainment predicted both juvenile and adult convictions (Farrington, 1992*c*). Low intelligence at age 8–10 was an important independent predictor of anti-social tendency at age 18 (Farrington 1993*b*) and of spouse assault at age 32 (Farrington 1993*a*), while early school leaving was an important independent predictor of anti-social personality at age 32 (Farrington 1992*e*). Low intelligence and attainment predicted aggression and bullying at age 14, and poor reading ability at age 18 was the best predictor of having a child bully at age 32 (Farrington 1989*a*, 1993*d*).

The key explanatory factor underlying the link between intelligence and delinquency is probably the ability to manipulate abstract concepts. People who are poor at this tend to do badly in intelligence tests such as the Matrices and in school attainment, and they also tend to commit offences, probably because of their poor ability to foresee the consequences of their offending and to appreciate the feelings of victims (i.e., their low empathy). Certain family backgrounds are less conducive than others to the development of abstract reasoning. For example, lower-class, poorer parents tend to talk in terms of the concrete rather than the abstract and tend to live for the present, with little thought for the future, as Cohen (1955: 96) pointed out many years ago. A lack of concern for future consequences, which is a central feature of Wilson and Herrnstein's (1985) theory, is also linked to the concept of impulsivity.

Modern research is studying not just intelligence but also detailed patterns of cognitive and neuropsychological deficit. For example, in a New Zealand longitudinal study of over 1,000 children from birth to age 15, Moffitt and Silva (1988b) found that self-reported delinquency was related to verbal, memory, and visual–motor integration deficits, independently of low social class and family adversity. Neuropsychological research might lead to important advances in knowledge about the link between brain functioning and offending. For example, the 'executive functions' of the brain, located in the frontal lobes, include sustaining attention and concentration, abstract reasoning and concept formation, anticipation and planning, self-monitoring of behaviour, and inhibition of inappropriate or impulsive behaviour (Moffitt 1990). Deficits in these executive functions are conducive to low measured intelligence and to offending. Moffitt and Henry (1989) found deficits in these executive functions especially for delinquents who were both anti-social and hyperactive.

Family factors

Loeber and Stouthamer-Loeber (1986) completed an exhaustive review of family factors as correlates and predictors of juvenile conduct problems and delinquency. They found that poor parental supervision or monitoring, erratic or harsh parental discipline, parental disharmony, parental rejection of the child, and low parental involvement with the child (as well as anti-social parents and large family size) were all important predictors.

In the Cambridge–Somerville study in Boston, McCord (1979) reported that poor parental supervision was the best predictor of both violent and property offenders. Parental aggressiveness (which included harsh discipline, shading into child abuse at the extreme) and parental conflict were significant precursors of violent offenders, while the mother's attitude (passive or rejecting) was a significant precursor of property offenders. Robins (1979), in her long-term follow-up studies in St Louis, also found that poor supervision and discipline were consistently related to later offending, and Shedler and Block (1990) in San Francisco reported that hostile and rejecting mothers when children were aged 5 predicted frequent drug abuse at age 18.

Other studies also show the link between family factors and offending. In a Birmingham survey, Wilson (1980) concluded that poor parental supervision was the most important correlate of convictions, cautions, and self-reported delinquency. In their English national survey of juveniles aged 14–15 and their mothers, Riley and Shaw (1985) found that poor parental supervision was the most important correlate of self-reported delinquency for girls, and the second most important for boys (after delinquent friends). Similarly, family dysfunction is related to conduct disorder (e.g., Offord et al. 1989).

In the Cambridge Study, West and Farrington (1973) found that harsh or erratic parental discipline, cruel, passive, or neglecting parental attitude, poor supervision, and parental conflict, all measured at age 8, all predicted later juvenile convictions. Farrington (1992d) reported that poor parental child-rearing behaviour (a combination of discipline, attitude, and conflict), poor parental supervision, and low parental interest in education all predicted both convictions and self-reported delinquency. Poor parental child-rearing behaviour was related to early rather than later offending (Farrington 1986*b*), and was not characteristic of those first convicted as adults (West and Farrington 1977). Hence, poor parental child-rearing behaviour may be related to onset but not persistence. Poor parental supervision was related to both juvenile and adult convictions (Farrington 1992*c*), and was the strongest correlate of anti-social personality at age 10 (Farrington 1992*e*).

Offenders tend to have difficulties in their personal relationships. The Cambridge Study males who were in conflict with their parents at age 18 tended to be juvenile offenders. Both juvenile and adult offenders tended to have poor relationships with their wives or cohabitees at age 32, or to have assaulted them, and they also tended to be divorced and/or separated from their children (Farrington 1992*c*).

In agreement with the hypothesis that being physically abused as a child foreshadows later violent offending (Widom 1989), harsh parental discipline and attitude at age 8 significantly predicted later violent as opposed to non-violent offenders in the Cambridge Study (Farrington 1978). However, more recent research showed that it was equally predictive of violent and frequent offending (Farrington 1991*b*).

Broken homes and early separations are also risk factors for offending. In the Newcastle Thousand Family Study, Kolvin *et al.* (1990) reported that parental divorce or separation up to age 5 predicted later convictions up to age 33. McCord (1982) carried out an interesting study of the relationship between homes broken by loss of the natural father and later serious offending. She found that the prevalence of offending was high for boys reared in broken homes without affectionate mothers (62 per cent) and for those reared in united homes characterized by parental conflict (52 per cent) irrespective of whether they had affectionate mothers. The prevalence of offending was low for those reared in united homes without conflict (26 per cent) or in broken homes with affectionate mothers (22 per cent).

These results suggest that it is not so much the broken home (or a single-parent female-headed household) which is criminogenic as the parental conflict which causes it. Similarly, Fergusson *et al.* (1992), in the Christchurch (New Zealand) Child Development Study, found that parental separation before a child was 10 did not predict self-reported offending independently of parental conflict, which was the more important factor. However, teenage child-bearing combined with a single-parent female-headed household seems conducive to the development of offending in children (Morash and Rucker 1989). Single-parent families tended to have conduct-disordered and substance-abusing children in the Ontario Child Health Study, although such families tended to overlap with and were difficult to disentangle from low-income families (Blum *et al.* 1988; Boyle and Offord 1986).

The importance of the cause of the broken home is also shown in the British national longitudinal survey of over 5,000 children born in one week of 1946 (Wadsworth 1979). Boys from homes broken by divorce or separation had an increased likelihood of being convicted or officially cautioned up to age 21 in comparison with those from homes broken by death or from unbroken homes. Remarriage (which happened more often after divorce or separation than after death) was also associated with an increased risk of offending.

In the Cambridge Study, both permanent and temporary (more than one month) separations before age 10 predicted convictions and self-reported delinquency, providing that they were not caused by death or hospitalization (Farrington 1992*d*). However, homes broken at an early age (under age 5) were not unusually criminogenic (West and Farrington 1973). Separation from a parent before age 10 predicted both juvenile and adult convictions (Farrington 1992*c*), and was an important independent predictor of adult social dysfunction and spouse assault at age 32 (Farrington 1993*a*, *b*). After anti-social personality at 10, it was the best predictor of anti-social personality at 14 (Farrington 1992*e*).

Criminal, anti-social, and alcoholic parents also tend to have delinquent sons, as Robins (1979) found. For example, in her follow-up study of over 200 black males in St Louis (Robins *et al.* 1975), arrested parents tended to have arrested children, and the juvenile records of the parents and children showed similar rates and types of offences. McCord (1977), in her thirty-year follow-up study of about 250 boys in the treatment group of the Cambridge–Somerville study, reported that convicted fathers tended to have convicted sons. Whether there is a specific relationship in her study between types of convictions of parents and children is not clear. McCord found that 29 per cent of fathers convicted for violence had sons convicted for violence, in comparison with 12 per cent of other fathers, but this may reflect the general tendency for convicted fathers to have convicted sons rather than any specific tendency for violent fathers to have violent sons. Craig and Glick (1968) in New York City also showed that the majority of boys who became serious or persistent delinquents (84 per cent) had criminal parents or siblings, in comparison with 24 per cent of the remainder. Criminal parents tended to have conduct-disordered children in the Ontario Child Health Study (Offord *et al.* 1989), and substance use by parents predicted substance use by children in the Rutgers Health and Human Development project (e.g., Johnson and Pandina 1991) and in the west of Scotland longitudinal study (Green *et al.*1991).

In the Cambridge Study, the concentration of offending in a small number of families was remarkable. As already mentioned, West and Farrington (1977) discovered that less than 5 per cent of the families were responsible for about half of the criminal convictions of all family members (fathers, mothers, sons, and daughters). West and Farrington (1973) showed that having a convicted mother, father, or brother by a boy's tenth birthday significantly predicted his own later convictions. Furthermore, convicted parents and delinquent siblings predicted self-reported as well as official offending (Farrington 1992*d*). Therefore, there is intergenerational continuity in offending.

Unlike most early precursors, a convicted parent was related less to offending of early onset (age 10–13) than to later offending (Farrington 1986*b*). Also, having a convicted parent predicted those juvenile offenders who went on to become adult criminals and those recidivists at age 19 who continued offending (West and Farrington 1977). Hence, a convicted parent seemed to be a risk factor for persistence rather than onset. Having a convicted parent was the best predictor of anti-social tendency at age 18 and of spouse assault at age 32, and was also an important independent predictor of bullying at age 14 and adult social dysfunction at age 32 (Farrington 1993*a*, *b*, *d*). After earlier measures of anti-social personality, a convicted parent was the best predictor of anti-social personality at 18 and 32 (Farrington 1992*e*). These results are concordant with the psychological theory (e.g., Trasler 1962) that anti-social behaviour develops when the normal social learning process, based on rewards and punishments from parents, is disrupted by erratic discipline, poor supervision, parental disharmony, and unsuitable (anti-social or criminal) parental models. However, some part of the link between anti-social parents and anti-social children may reflect genetic transmission (see e.g., Wilson and Herrnstein 1985; Eysenck and Gudjonsson 1989).

Just as early family factors predict the early onset or prevalence of offending, later family factors predict later desistance. For example, it is often believed that male offending decreases after marriage, and there is some evidence in favour of this (e.g., Bachman *et al*. 1978). In the Cambridge Study, there was a clear tendency for convicted males who got married at age 22 or earlier to be reconvicted less in the next two years than comparable convicted males who did not get married (West 1982). However, in the case of both the males and their fathers, convicted males tended to marry convicted females, and convicted males who married convicted females continued to offend at the same rate after marriage as matched unmarried males. Offenders who married convicted females incurred more convictions after marriage than those who married unconvicted females, independently of their conviction records before marriage. Hence, it was concluded that the reformative effect of marriage was lessened by the tendency of male offenders to marry females who were also offenders. Rutter (1989) has drawn attention to the importance of studying turning-points, such as marriage, in people's lives.

Socio-economic deprivation

Most delinquency theories assume that offenders come disproportionately from lower-class social backgrounds, and aim to explain why this is so. For example, Cohen (1955) proposed that lower-class boys found it hard to succeed according to the middle-class standards of schools, partly because lower-class parents tended not to teach their children to delay immediate gratification in favour of long-term goals. Consequently, lower-class boys joined delinquent subcultures by whose standards they could succeed. Cloward and Ohlin (1960) argued that lower-class children could not achieve universal goals of status and material wealth by legitimate means and consequently had to resort to illegitimate means.

Generally, the social class or socio-economic status (SES) of a family has been measured primarily according to rankings of the occupational prestige of the family breadwinner. Persons with professional or managerial jobs are ranked in the highest class, while those with unskilled manual jobs are ranked in the lowest. However, these occupational prestige scales may not correlate very highly with real differences between families in socio-economic circumstances. The scales often date from many years ago, when it was more common for the father to be the family breadwinner and for the mother to be a housewife. Because of this, it may be difficult to derive a realistic measure of SES for a family with a single parent or with two working parents (Mueller and Parcel 1981).

Over the years, many other measures of social class have become popular, including family income, educational levels of parents, type of housing, overcrowding in the house, possessions, dependence on welfare benefits, and family size. These may all reflect more meaningful differences between families in socio-economic deprivation than occupational prestige does. For example, in his California self-report survey of over 4,000 children, Hirschi (1969) concluded that offending was related to the family being on welfare and the father being unemployed, but not to the occupational or educational status of the father. Family size is highly correlated with other indices of socio-economic deprivation, although its relationship with delinquency may reflect child-rearing factors (e.g., less attention given to each child) rather than socio-economic influences.

In many criminological research projects, delinquents and non-delinquents are matched on SES, or SES is controlled first in regression analyses. This reflects a widespread belief in the importance of SES, but of course it often prevents the correctness of this belief from being tested. Unfortunately, as Thornberry and Farnworth (1982) pointed out, the voluminous literature on the relationship between SES and offending is characterized by inconsistencies and contradictions, and some reviewers (e.g., Hindelang et al. 1981) have concluded that there is no relationship between SES and either self-reported or official offending.

Beginning with the pioneering self-report research of Short and Nye (1957), it was common in the USA to argue that low social class was related to official offending but not to self-reported offending, and hence that the official processing of offenders was biased against lower-class youth. However, British studies have reported more consistent links between low social class and offending. In a British national survey, Douglas et al. (1966) showed that the prevalence of official juvenile delinquency in males varied considerably according to the occupational prestige and educational background of their parents, from 3 per cent in the highest category to 19 per cent in the lowest. Also, Wadsworth (1979) reported that offending increased significantly with increasing family size in this survey. A similar link between family size and anti-social behaviour was reported by Kolvin et al. (1988) in their follow-up study of Newcastle children from birth to age 33, by Rutter et al. (1970) in an Isle of Wight survey, and by Ouston (1984) in an inner London survey.

Numerous indicators of SES were measured in the Cambridge Study, both for the male's family of origin and for the male himself as an adult, including occupational prestige, family income, housing, employment instability, and family size. Most of the measures of occupational prestige (based on the Registrar-General's scale) were not significantly related to offending. However, in a reversal of the American results, low SES of the family when the male was aged 8–10 significantly predicted his later self-reported but not his official delinquency. Should we therefore conclude that official processing is biased in favour of lower-class youth?

More consistently, low family income, poor housing, and large family size predicted official and self-reported, juvenile and adult offending (Farrington 1992c, d). Large family size at age 10 was an important independent predictor of anti-social tendency at age 18 and teenage violence, while low family income at age 8 was the best independent predictor of adult social dysfunction (Farrington 1989a, 1993b). Low-income families also tended to have conduct-disordered children in the Ontario Child Health Study (Offord et al. 1989).

Socio-economic deprivation of parents is usually compared with offending by sons. However, when the sons grow up, their own socio-economic deprivation can be related to their own offending. In the Cambridge Study, official and self-reported delinquents tended to have unskilled manual jobs and an unstable job record at age 18. Just as an erratic work record of his father predicted the later offending of the Study male, an unstable job record of the male at age 18 was one of the best independent predictors of his convictions between ages 21 and 25 (Farrington 1986b). Also, having an unskilled manual job at age 18 was an important independent predictor of adult social dysfunction and anti-social personality at age 32 (Farrington 1992e, 1993b). Also, as already mentioned, the Study males were convicted at a higher rate when they were unemployed than when they were employed (Farrington et al. 1986b), suggesting that unemployment in some way causes crime, and conversely that employment may lead to desistance from offending.

It seems clear that socio-economic deprivation is an important risk factor for offending and anti-social behaviour. However, low family income, poor housing, and large family size are better measures and produce more reliable results than low occupational prestige.

Peer influence

The reviews by Zimring (1981) and Reiss (1988) show that delinquent acts tend to be committed in small groups (usually of two or three people) rather than alone. In the Cambridge Study, as already mentioned, most officially recorded juvenile offences were committed with others, but the incidence of co-offending declined steadily with age from 10 years onwards (Reiss and Farrington 1991). When the Study males had brothers of similar age, they tended to offend with their brothers. In Ontario, Jones et al. (1980) discovered that male delinquents tended to have a preponderance of brothers, and proposed that there was male potentiation of anti-social behaviour.

A major problem of interpretation is whether young people are more likely to commit offences while they are in groups than while they are alone, or whether the high prevalence of co-offending merely reflects the fact that, whenever young people go out, they tend to go out in groups. Do peers tend to encourage and facilitate offending, or is it just that most kinds of activities out of the home (both delinquent and non-delinquent) tend to be committed in groups? Another possibility is that the commission of offences encourages association with other delinquents, perhaps because 'birds of a feather flock together' or because of the stigmatizing and isolating effects of court appearances and institutionalization. It is surprisingly difficult to decide among these various possibilities, although most researchers argue that peer influence is an important factor. For example, the key construct in Sutherland and Cressey's (1974) theory is the number of persons in a child's social environment with norms and attitudes favouring delinquency.

There is clearly a close relationship between the delinquent activities of a young person and those of his friends. Both in the USA (Hirschi 1969) and in England (West and Farrington 1973), it has been found that a boy's reports of his own offending are significantly correlated with his reports of his friends' delinquency. In the American National Youth Survey of Elliott et al. (1985), having delinquent peers was the best independent predictor of self-reported offending in a multivariate analysis. In the same study, Agnew (1991) showed that this relationship was greatest for teenagers who were most strongly attached to their peers and felt most peer pressure.

Unfortunately, if delinquency is a group activity, delinquents will almost inevitably have delinquent friends, and this result does not necessarily show that delinquent friends cause delinquency. In other words, delinquent friends could be an indicator rather than a cause. Longitudinal research is needed to establish the causal ordering between delinquent friends and delinquency. In the American National Youth Survey, Elliott and Menard (1988) concluded that having delinquent peers increased a person's own offending and that a person's own offending also increased his likelihood of having delinquent peers. Hence, both effects seemed to be operating.

In the Cambridge Study, association with delinquent friends was not measured until age 14, and so this was not investigated as a precursor of offending (which began at age 10). However, it was a significant independent predictor of convictions at the young adult ages (Farrington 1986b) and of teenage violence at age 16–18 (Farrington 1989a). As already mentioned, the recidivists at age 19 who ceased offending differed from those who persisted, in that the desisters were more likely to have stopped going round in a group of male friends. Furthermore, spontaneous comments by the youths indicated that withdrawal from the delinquent peer group was seen as an important influence on ceasing to offend (West and Farrington 1977). Therefore, continuing to associate with delinquent friends may be an important factor in determining whether juvenile delinquents persist in offending as young adults or desist.

Delinquent peers are likely to be most influential where they have high status within the peer group and are popular. However, studies both in the USA (Roff and Wirt 1984) and in England (West and Farrington 1973) show that delinquents are usually unpopular with their peers. It seems paradoxical for offending to be a group phenomenon facilitated by peer influence, and yet for offenders and especially aggressive youths to be largely rejected by other adolescents (Parker and Asher 1987). However, it may be that offenders are popular in anti-social groups and unpopular in pro-social groups, or that rejected children band together to form adolescent delinquent groups (Hartup 1983).

School factors

It is clear that the prevalence of offending varies dramatically among different secondary schools, as Power *et al.* (1967) showed more than twenty years ago in London. However, what is far less clear is how much of the variation should be attributed to differences in school climates and practices, and how much to differences in the composition of the student body.

In the Cambridge Study, Farrington (1972) investigated the effects of secondary schools on offending by following boys from their primary schools to their secondary schools. The best primary-school predictor of offending was the rating of troublesomeness at age 8–10 by peers and teachers. The secondary schools differed dramatically in their official offending rates, from one school with 20.9 court appearances per 100 boys per year to another where the corresponding figure was only

0.3. However, it was very noticeable that the most troublesome boys tended to go to the high-delinquency schools, while the least troublesome boys tended to go to the low-delinquency schools.

All the schools had overlapping catchment areas. The low-delinquency-rate secondary schools were oversubscribed, because parents who were most interested in their children's education, who tended to have high-achieving, well-behaved children, were very concerned that their children should go to these schools. Taking account of reports from primary schools, the head teachers of these secondary schools could pick and choose the best children out of all the applicants, leaving the high-delinquency schools with lower-achieving, worse-behaved children. Hence, it was clear that most of the variation in delinquency rates among schools could be explained by differences in their intakes of troublesome boys. The secondary schools themselves had only a very small effect on the boys' offending.

The most famous study of school effects on offending was carried out, also in London, by Rutter *et al.* (1979). They studied twelve comprehensive schools, and again found big differences in official delinquency rates among them. Schools with high delinquency rates tended to have high truancy rates, low-ability pupils, and parents of low social class. However, the differences in delinquency rates among the schools could not be entirely explained by differences in the social class and verbal reasoning scores of the pupils at intake (age 11). Therefore, Rutter *et al.* argued, they must have been caused by some aspect of the schools themselves or by other, unmeasured factors.

In trying to discover which aspects of schools might be encouraging or inhibiting offending, Rutter *et al.* (1979) developed a measure of 'school process' based on school structure, organization, and functioning. This was related to school misbehaviour, academic achievement, and truancy independently of intake factors. However, it was not significantly related to delinquency independently of intake factors. Many aspects of the schools were not related to their delinquency rates: the age of the buildings, the number of students, the amount of space per student, the staff/student ratio, the academic emphasis (e.g., amount of homework or library use), the rate of turnover of teachers, the number of school outings, the care of the school buildings, and so on. The main school factors that were related to delinquency were a high amount of punishment and a low amount of praise given by teachers in class. However, it is difficult to know whether much punishment and little praise are causes or consequences of anti-social school behaviour, which in turn is probably linked to offending outside school.

The research of Rutter *et al.* (1979) does not show unambiguously that school factors influence offending. This is partly because of the small number of schools involved in the study (only nine containing boys), and partly because far more is known about individual-level risk factors for offending than about school-level risk factors. Because this was a pioneering study, important school-level risk factors may not have been measured. In order to advance knowledge about possible school effects on offending, longitudinal research is needed in which many factors are measured for primary school children, who are then followed up to a large number of secondary schools. This might make it possible convincingly to identify school factors that explained differences in offending rates independently of individual-level factors present at intake.

Community influences

Offending rates vary systematically with area of residence. For example, Clark and Wenninger (1962) compared four areas in Illinois and concluded that self-reported offending rates were highest in the inner city, lower in a lower-class urban area, lower still in an upper-middle-class urban area, and lowest of all in a rural farm area. In their national survey of American juveniles, Gold and Reimer (1975) also found that self-reported offending was highest for males living in the city centres and lowest for those living in rural areas. More recently, Shannon (1988) documented how police contact rates over a long period were highest in the inner city (of Racine, Wisconsin) and lowest in the more peripheral areas.

The classic studies by Shaw and McKay (1942, 1969) in Chicago and other American cities also showed that juvenile delinquency rates (based on where offenders lived) were highest in inner-city areas characterized by physical deterioration, neighbourhood disorganization, and high residential mobility. A large proportion of all offenders came from a small proportion of areas, which tended to be the most deprived. Furthermore, these relatively high delinquency rates persisted over time, despite the effect of successive waves of immigration and emigration of different national and ethnic groups in different areas. Shaw and McKay concluded that the delinquency-producing factors were inherent in the community: areas had persistently high offending rates partly because of the cultural transmission of anti-social values and norms from one generation to the next and partly because of the ineffective socialization processes to which children were exposed in deprived areas. Both of these factors were consequences of the social disorganization of an area, or the poor ability of local institutions to control the behaviour of local residents (Bursik 1988).

Jonassen (1949) criticized Shaw and McKay's conclusions about the unimportance of national and ethnic origins. He pointed out that it was desirable not only to compare delinquency rates of the same ethnic group in different areas (as Shaw and McKay did) but also to compare those of different ethnic groups in the same area. Jonassen argued that Shaw and McKay's published data showed that northern and western Europeans had lower delinquency rates than southern and eastern Europeans living in the same areas of Chicago. Jonassen also noticed that Shaw and McKay had found that orientals had low delinquency rates even when they lived in the most deteriorated areas of the city, whereas blacks had high delinquency rates in all areas where they lived (see also Gold 1987).

Later work has tended to cast doubt on the consistency of offending rates over time. Bursik and Webb (1982) tested Shaw and McKay's cultural transmission hypothesis using more recent data in Chicago and more sophisticated quantitative methods. They concluded that the ordering of area delinquency rates was not stable after 1950, but reflected demographic changes. Variations in delinquency rates in different areas were significantly correlated with variations in the percentages of non-whites, of foreign-born whites, and of overcrowded households. The greatest increase in offending in an area occurred when blacks moved from the minority to the majority, as indeed Jonassen (1949) and Short (1969) had noticed earlier. These results suggested that Shaw and McKay's ideas, about community values which persisted irrespective of successive waves of immigration and emigration, were incorrect. It was necessary to take account both of the type of area and of the type of individuals living in the area (e.g., Simcha-Fagan and Schwartz 1986).

Similar ecological studies have been carried out in the UK (for a review, see Baldwin 1979). For example, Wallis and Maliphant (1967) showed that in London official offender rates correlated with rates of local authority renting, percentage of land used industrially or commercially, population density, overcrowded households, the proportion of non-white immigrants, and the proportion of the population aged under 21. However, offender rates were negatively related to suicide and unemployment rates and not related to illegitimacy or mental illness rates. Power *et al*(1972) carried out a similar study in one lower-class London borough and found that official delinquency rates varied with rates of overcrowding and fertility and with the social class and type of housing of an area.

In Wallis and Maliphant's (1967) project, it was generally true that crime rates were higher in the inner city, and it is important to investigate why this is so. One of the most significant studies of inner-city and rural areas is the comparison by Rutter and colleagues (Rutter, Cox, *et al*. 1975; Rutter, Yule, *et al*. 1975) of 10-year-old children in inner London and in the Isle of Wight. They found a much higher incidence of conduct disorder in their inner London sample. However, they also showed that the differences between their inner-city and rural areas disappeared after they controlled for family adversity (based on parental conflict, family breakdown, criminal parents, and large family size). Rutter (1981) concluded that rates of conduct disorder were higher in inner London purely because family adversities were more common there. Any effects of inner-city residence on children's anti-social behaviour were indirect and sequential: communities affected families, which in turn affected children.

It is not invariably true that offender rates are highest in inner-city areas. Baldwin and Bottoms (1976) found that in Sheffield the key factor influencing where offenders lived was the type of housing. Offender rates were lowest in owner-occupied areas and highest in areas of council housing and private renting, and the high-crime areas were not all near the centre of the city. They concluded that council housing allocation policies played a role in creating areas with high offender rates. This again raises the issue of how far offender rates reflect the influence of the area or the kinds of individuals who happen to be living there.

Reiss (1986) pointed out that a key question was why crime rates of communities changed over time, and to what extent this was a function of changes in the communities or in the individuals living in them. Answering this question requires longitudinal research in which both communities and individuals are followed up. The best way of establishing the impact of the environment is to follow people who move from one area to another, thus using each person as his own control. For example, Osborn (1980) in the Cambridge Study found that moving out of London led to a significant decrease in convictions and self-reported offending. This decrease may have occurred because moving out led to a breaking up of co-offending groups, or because there were fewer opportunities for crime outside London. Also, Rutter (1981) showed that the differences between inner London and the Isle of Wight held even when the analyses were restricted to children reared in the same area by parents reared in the same area. This result suggests that the movement of problem families into problem areas cannot be the whole explanation of area differences in offending.

Clearly, there is an interaction between individuals and the communities in which they live. Some aspects of an inner-city neighbourhood may be conducive to offending, perhaps because the inner city leads to a breakdown of community ties or neighbourhood patterns of mutual support, or perhaps because the high population density produces tension, frustration, or anonymity. There may be many interrelated factors. As Reiss (1986) argued, high-crime areas often have a high concentration of single-parent female-headed households with low incomes, living in low-cost, poor housing. The weakened parental control in these families — partly caused by the fact that the mother had to work and left her children unsupervised — meant that the children tended to congregate on the streets. In consequence, they were influenced by a peer subculture that often encouraged and reinforced offending. This interaction of individual, family, peer, and neighbourhood factors may be the rule rather than the exception.

Situational factors

It is plausible to suggest that criminal and anti-social behaviour results from the interaction between an individual (with a certain degree of underlying anti-social tendency) and the environment (which provides criminal opportunities). Given the same environment, some individuals will be more likely to commit offences than others, and conversely the same individual will be more likely to commit offences in some environments than in others. Criminological research typically concentrates on either the development of criminal individuals or the occurrence of criminal events, but rarely on both.

As already mentioned, delinquents are predominantly versatile rather than specialized. Hence, in studying delinquents it seems unnecessary to develop a different theory for each different type of offender. In contrast, in trying to explain why offences occur, the situations are so diverse and specific to particular crimes that it probably is necessary to construct different explanations for different types of offences.

The most popular theory of offending events suggests that they occur in response to specific opportunities, when their expected benefits (e.g., stolen property, peer approval) outweigh their expected costs (e.g., legal punishment, parental disapproval). For example, Clarke and Cornish (1985) outlined a theory of residential burglary which included such influencing factors as whether a house was occupied, whether it looked affluent, whether there were bushes to hide behind, whether there were nosy neighbours, whether the house had a burglar alarm, and whether it contained a dog. Several other researchers have also proposed that offending involves a rational decision in which expected benefits are weighed against expected costs (e.g., Farrington and Kidd 1977; Cook 1980; Trasler 1986).

While it is obvious that offences require opportunities, it is also probable that some individuals are more likely than others to seek out and create opportunities for offending and to select suitable victims. The 'routine activities' theory of Cohen and

Felson (1979) attempts to explain how opportunities for crime arise and change over time. They argue that criminal opportunities vary with routine activities that provide for basic needs such as food and shelter. For example, the increase in the number of working women, coupled with the increase in the number of single-parent female-headed households, has created increasing numbers of houses left unoccupied during the day, thus providing more numerous opportunities for burglary.

In the Cambridge Study, as already mentioned, the most common motives given for offending were rational or utilitarian ones, suggesting that most property crimes were committed because the offenders wanted the stolen items (West and Farrington 1977). In addition, a number of cross-sectional surveys have shown that low estimates of the risk of being caught were correlated with high rates of self-reported offending (e.g., Erickson *et al.* 1977). Unfortunately, the direction of causal influence is not clear in cross-sectional research, since committing delinquent acts may lead to lower estimates of the probability of detection as well as the reverse. A number of studies carried out by Farrington and Knight (1980), using experimental, survey, and observational methods, suggested that stealing involved risky decision-making. Hence, it is plausible to suggest that opportunities for delinquency, the immediate costs and benefits of delinquency, and the probabilities of these outcomes, all influence whether people offend in any situation.

Theoretical and policy issues

Explaining the development of offending

In explaining the development of offending, a major problem is that most risk factors tend to coincide and tend to be interrelated. For example, adolescents living in physically deteriorated and socially disorganized neighbourhoods tend disproportionately also to come from families with poor parental supervision and erratic parental discipline and tend also to have high impulsivity and low intelligence. The concentration and co-occurrence of these kinds of adversities make it difficult to establish their independent, interactive, and sequential influences on offending and anti-social behaviour. Hence, any theory of the development of offending in the present state of knowledge is inevitably speculative.

A first step is to establish which factors predict offending independently of other factors. In the Cambridge Study, it was generally true that measures in each of six categories of variables (impulsivity, intelligence, parenting, anti-social family, socio-economic deprivation, child anti-social behaviour) predicted offending independently of measures in each other category (Farrington 1990*b*). For example, Farrington and Hawkins (1991) reported that the independent predictors of convictions between ages 10 and 20 included high daring, low school attainment, poor parental child-rearing, convicted parents, poor housing, and troublesomeness. Hence, it might be concluded that impulsivity, low intelligence, poor parenting, anti-social family, and socio-economic deprivation, despite their interrelations, all contribute independently to the development of delinquency. Any theory needs to give priority to explaining these results.

Some of the most important theories of delinquency have already been mentioned in [this chapter]. These include Cohen's (1955) status frustration–delinquent subculture theory, Cloward and Ohlin's (1960) opportunity–strain theory, Trasler's (1962) social learning theory, Hirschi's (1969) control–social bonding theory, Sutherland and Cressey's (1974) differential association theory, Wilson and Herrnstein's (1985) discounting future consequences theory, Clarke and Cornish's (1985) situational decision-making theory, and Gottfredson and Hirschi's (1990) self-control theory. The modern trend is to try to achieve increased explanatory power by integrating propositions derived from several earlier theories (e.g., Elliott *et al.* 1985; Hawkins and Weis 1985; Pearson and Weiner 1985). My own theory of offending and anti-social behaviour (Farrington, 1986*b*, 1992*c*, 1993*c*) is also integrative, and it distinguishes explicitly between the development of anti-social tendency and the occurrence of anti-social acts. The theory suggests that offending is the end result of a four-stage process: energizing, directing, inhibiting, and decision-making.

The main long-term energizing factors that ultimately lead to variations in anti-social tendency are desires for material goods, status among intimates, and excitement. The main short-term energizing factors that lead to variations in anti-social tendency are boredom, frustration, anger, and alcohol consumption. The desire for excitement may be greater among children from poorer families — perhaps because excitement is more highly valued by lower-class people than by middle-class ones, in turn because poorer children think they lead more boring lives, or because poorer children are less able to postpone immediate gratification in favour of long-term goals (which could be linked to the emphasis in lower-class culture on the concrete and present as opposed to the abstract and future).

In the directing stage, these motivations produce anti-social tendency if socially disapproved methods of satisfying them are habitually chosen. The methods chosen depend on maturation and behavioural skills; for example, a 5-year-old would have difficulty stealing a car. Some people (e.g., children from poorer families) are less able to satisfy their desires for material goods, excitement, and social status by legal or socially approved methods, and so tend to choose illegal or socially disapproved methods. The relative inability of poorer children to achieve goals by legitimate methods could be attributable to their tendency to fail in school and to have erratic, low-status employment histories. School failure in turn may often be a consequence of the unstimulating intellectual environment that lower-class parents tend to provide for their children, and their lack of emphasis on abstract concepts.

In the inhibiting stage, anti-social tendencies can be inhibited by internalized beliefs and attitudes that have been built up in a social learning process as a result of a history of rewards and punishments. The belief that offending is wrong, or a strong conscience, tends to be built up if parents are in favour of legal norms, if they exercise close supervision over their children, and if they punish socially disapproved behaviour using love-orientated discipline. Anti-social tendencies can also be inhibited by empathy, which may develop as a result of parental warmth and loving relationships. The belief that offending is legitimate, and anti-authority attitudes generally, tend to be built up if children have been exposed to attitudes and behaviour favouring offending (e.g., in a modelling process), especially by members of their family, by their friends, and in their communities.

In the decision-making stage, which specifies the interaction between the individual and the environment, whether a person with a certain degree of anti-social tendency commits an anti-social act in a given situation depends on opportunities, costs, and benefits, and on the subjective probabilities of the different outcomes. The costs and benefits include immediate situational factors such as the material goods that can be stolen and the likelihood and consequences of being caught by the police, as perceived by the individual. They also include social factors such as likely disapproval by parents or spouse, and encouragement or reinforcement from peers. In general, people tend to make rational decisions. However, more impulsive people are less likely to consider the possible consequences of their actions, especially consequences that are likely to be long delayed.

Applying the theory to explain some of the results reviewed here, children from poorer families are likely to offend because they are less able to achieve their goals legally and because they value some goals (e.g., excitement) especially highly. Children with low intelligence are more likely to offend because they tend to fail in school and hence cannot achieve their goals legally. Impulsive children, and those with a poor ability to manipulate abstract concepts, are more likely to offend because they do not give sufficient consideration and weight to the possible consequences of offending. Children who are exposed to poor child-rearing behaviour, disharmony, or separation on the part of their parents are likely to offend because they do not build up internal controls over socially disapproved behaviour, while children from criminal families and those with delinquent friends tend to build up anti-authority attitudes and the belief that offending is justifiable. The whole process is self-perpetuating, in that poverty, low intelligence, and early school failure lead to truancy and a lack of educational qualifications, which in turn lead to low-status jobs and periods of unemployment, both of which make it harder to achieve goals legitimately.

The onset of offending might be caused by increasing long-term motivation (an increasing need for material goods, status, and excitement), an increasing likelihood of choosing socially disapproved methods (possibly linked to a change in dominant social influences from parents to peers), increasing facilitating influences from peers, increasing opportunities (because of increasing freedom from parental control and increasing time spent with peers), or an increasing expected utility of offending (because of the greater importance of peer approval and lesser importance of parental disapproval). Desistance from offending could be linked to an increasing ability to satisfy desires by legal means (e.g., obtaining material goods through employment, obtaining sexual gratification through marriage), increasing inhibiting influences from spouses and cohabitees, decreasing opportunities (because of decreasing time spent with peers), and a decreasing expected utility of offending (because of the lesser importance of peer approval and the greater importance of disapproval from spouses and cohabitees).

The prevalence of offending may increase to a peak between ages 14 and 20 because boys (especially lower-class school failures) have high impulsivity, high desires for excitement, material goods, and social status between these ages, little chance of achieving their desires legally, and little to lose (since legal penalties are lenient and their intimates — male peers — often approve of offending). In contrast, after age 20, desires become attenuated or more realistic, there is more possibility of achieving these more limited goals legally, and the costs of offending are greater (since legal penalties are harsher and their intimates — wives or girlfriends — disapprove of offending).

Risk factors and prevention

Methods of preventing or treating anti-social behaviour should be based on empirically validated theories about causes. In this section, implications about prevention and treatment are drawn from some of the risk factors and likely causes of anti-social behaviour listed above. The major focus is on the early social prevention of offending. (For more extensive reviews of this topic, see Kazdin 1985; Gordon and Arbuthnot 1987; McCord and Tremblay 1992.) The implications reviewed here are those for which there is some empirical justification, especially in randomized experiments. The effect of any intervention on delinquency can be demonstrated most convincingly in such experiments (Farrington 1983b; Farrington, Ohlin, and Wilson 1986).

It is difficult to know how and when it is best to intervene, because of the lack of knowledge about developmental sequences, ages at which causal factors are most salient, and influences on onset, persistence, and desistance. For example, if truancy leads to delinquency in a developmental sequence, intervening successfully to decrease truancy should lead to a decrease in delinquency. On the other hand, if truancy and delinquency are merely different behavioural manifestations of the same underlying construct, tackling one symptom would not necessarily change the underlying construct. Experiments are useful in distinguishing between developmental sequences and different manifestations, and indeed Berg et al. (1979) found experimentally that decreases in truancy were followed by decreases in delinquency.

The ideas of early intervention and preventative treatment raise numerous theoretical, practical, ethical, and legal issues. For example, should prevention techniques be targeted narrowly on children identified as potential delinquents or more widely on all children living in a certain high-risk area (e.g., a deprived housing estate)? It would be most efficient to target the children who are most in need of the treatment. Also, some treatments may be ineffective if they are targeted widely, if they depend on raising the level of those at the bottom of the heap relative to everyone else. However, the most extreme group may also be the most resistant to treatment or difficult to engage, so there may be a greater pay-off from targeting those who are not quite the most in need. Also, it might be argued that early identification could have undesirable labelling or stigmatizing effects, although the most extreme cases are likely to be stigmatized anyway and there is no evidence that identification for preventative treatment is in itself damaging; the degree of stigmatization, if any, is likely to depend on the nature of the treatment. In order to gain political acceptance, it may be best to target areas rather than individuals.

The ethical issues raised by early intervention depend on the level of predictive accuracy and might perhaps be resolved by weighing the social costs against the social benefits. For example, Farrington et al. (1988a, b) found that three-quarters of vulnerable boys identified at age 10 were convicted. It might be argued that, if preventative treatment had been applied to these boys, the one-quarter who were 'false positives' would have been treated unnecessarily. However, if the treatment consisted of extra welfare benefits to families, and if it was effective in reducing the offending of the other three-quarters, the benefits might outweigh the costs and early identification might be justifiable. Actually, the vulnerable boys who were not convicted had other types of social problems, including few or no friends at age 8 and living alone in poor home conditions at age 32. Therefore, even the unconvicted males in the survey might have needed and benefited from some kind of preventative treatment designed to alleviate their problems.

Impulsivity and other personality characteristics of offenders might be altered using the set of techniques termed cognitive–behavioural interpersonal skills training, which has proved to be quite successful (e.g. Michelson 1987). For example, the methods used by Ross to treat juvenile delinquents (see Ross *et al.* 1988; Ross and Ross 1988) are solidly based on some of the known individual characteristics of delinquents: impulsivity, concrete rather than abstract thinking, low empathy, and egocentricity.

Ross believes that delinquents can be taught the cognitive skills in which they are deficient, and that this can lead to a decrease in their offending. His reviews of delinquency rehabilitation programmes (Gendreau and Ross 1979, 1987) show that those which have been successful in reducing offending have generally tried to change the offender's thinking. Ross carried out his own 'Reasoning and Rehabilitation' programme in Canada, which aimed to modify the impulsive, egocentric thinking of delinquents, to teach them to stop and think before acting, to consider the consequences of their behaviour, to conceptualize alternative ways of solving interpersonal problems, and to consider the impact of their behaviour on other people, especially their victims. He found (in a randomized experiment) that it led to a significant decrease in reoffending for a small sample in a nine-month follow-up period.

If low intelligence and school failure are causes of offending, then any programme that leads to an increase in school success should lead to a decrease in offending. One of the most successful delinquency prevention programmes was the Perry pre-school project carried out in Michigan by Schweinhart and Weikart (1980). This was essentially a 'Head Start' programme targeted on disadvantaged black children, who were allocated (approximately at random) to experimental and control groups. The experimental children attended a daily pre-school programme, backed up by weekly home visits, usually lasting two years (covering ages 3–4). The aim of the programme was to provide intellectual stimulation, to increase cognitive abilities, and to increase later school achievement.

The pre-school children were significantly better in elementary school motivation, school achievement at 14, teacher ratings of classroom behaviour at 6–9, self-reports of classroom behaviour at 15, and self-reports of offending at 15. Furthermore, a later follow-up study of this sample by Berrueta-Clement *et al.* (1984) showed that, at age 19, the experimental group was more likely to be employed, more likely to have graduated from high school, more likely to have received college or vocational training, and less likely to have been arrested. Hence, this pre-school intellectual enrichment programme led to decreases in school failure and to decreases in delinquency.

If poor parental supervision and erratic child-rearing behaviour are causes of delinquency, it seems likely that parent training might succeed in reducing offending.

Many different types of family therapy have been used (see e.g., Kazdin 1987), but the behavioural parent-management training developed by Patterson (1982) in Oregon is one of the most hopeful approaches. His careful observations of parent–child interaction showed that parents of anti-social children were deficient in their methods of child-rearing. These parents failed to tell their children how they were expected to behave, failed to monitor the behaviour to ensure that it was desirable, and failed to enforce rules promptly and unambiguously with appropriate rewards and penalties. The parents of anti-social children used more punishment (such as scolding, shouting, or threatening), but failed to make it contingent on the child's behaviour. Patterson attempted to train these parents in effective child-rearing methods, namely noticing what a child is doing, monitoring behaviour over long periods, clearly stating house rules, making rewards and punishments contingent on behaviour, and negotiating disagreements so that conflicts and crises did not escalate. His treatment has been shown to be effective in reducing stealing and anti-social behaviour by children over short periods in small-scale studies (Dishion et al. 1992; Patterson et al.1982, 1992).

If having delinquent friends causes offending, then any programme which reduces their influence or increases the influence of pro-social friends could have a reductive effect on offending. Several studies show that school children can be taught to resist peer influences encouraging smoking, drinking, and marijuana use. (For detailed reviews of these programmes, see Botvin 1990; Hawkins et al. 1992.) For example, Telch et al. (1982) in California employed older high-school students to teach younger ones to develop counter-arguing skills to resist peer pressure to smoke, using modelling and guided practice. This approach was successful in decreasing smoking by the younger students, and similar results were reported by Botvin and Eng (1982) in New York City. Murray et al. (1984) in Minnesota used same-aged peer leaders to teach students how to resist peer pressures to begin smoking, and Evans et al. (1981) in Houston used films with the same aim.

Using high-status peer leaders, alcohol and marijuana use can be reduced as well as smoking (e.g., Klepp et al. 1986; McAlister et al. 1980). Botvin et al. (1984) in New York compared the application of a substance use prevention programme by teachers and peer leaders. The programme aimed to foster social skills and teach students ways of resisting peer pressure to use these substances. They found that peer leaders were effective in decreasing smoking, drunkenness, and marijuana use, but teachers were not. A large-scale meta-analysis by Tobler (1986) of 143 substance-use prevention programmes concluded that programmes using peer leaders were the most effective in reducing smoking, drinking, and drug abuse. These techniques, designed to counter anti-social peer pressures, could also help to decrease offending.

Criminal careers and crime control

The implications of criminal career research relate mainly to crime control. With regard to prevalence, if offending is spread widely throughout the whole community, primary prevention measures targeting the 'root causes' of crime, such as those described above, are likely to be most appropriate. On the other hand, if offending is narrowly concentrated among a few problem families, then criminal justice measures such as rehabilitation, individual deterrence, and incapacitation might be more effective. There is some justification for both these approaches in criminal career research, since a high overall prevalence of offending coexists with a small minority of 'chronic' offenders who account for a substantial proportion of the crime problem.

Estimates of the magnitude of criminal career features such as the individual offending frequency and career duration are needed to assess criminal justice policies such as selective incapacitation (Blumstein *et al.* 1988). All studies of the individual offending frequency have concluded that it differs markedly between individuals. These differences were shown most graphically in the Rand research on self-reports of prisoners in California, Michigan, and Texas (Greenwood and Abrahamse 1982). While the majority of offenders reported relatively low offending rates, a small number reported exceptionally high rates. For example, over all active offenders the median offending frequency for burglary was five offences per year, but the top 10 per cent of burglars averaged at least 232 per year; and while the median offending frequency for robbery was again five per year, the top 10 per cent of robbers averaged at least 87 per year. Greenwood and Abrahamse (1982) developed a seven-point scale to investigate how far it was possible to predict the high-rate offenders, on the basis of previous convictions and incarceration, the juvenile record, drug use, and unemployment history. This scale proved to be very efficient in discriminating among the offenders. For example, for California burglars, the median annual burglary rate was 1.4 for those scoring 0–1 on the scale, 6.0 for those scoring 2–3, and 92.9 for those scoring 4–7. Their results were replicated in New Orleans by Miranne and Geerken (1991).

Greenwood and Abrahamse (1982) went on to assess the value of a sentencing policy of selective incapacitation that involved lengthening the time served by predicted high-rate offenders and shortening the time served by predicted low-rate offenders. For California robbers, they estimated that such a policy might achieve a 15 per cent reduction in the robbery rate together with a 5 per cent reduction in the population incarcerated for robbery. For California burglars, the best selective incapacitation policy required a 7 per cent increase in the prison population to achieve a 15 per cent decrease in crime. The conclusions about the benefits of selective incapacitation for California robbers were largely replicated in the reanalysis by Visher (1986), but she concluded that a 13 per cent decrease in crime might be achieved with no increase in the prison population. The results in Texas were less impressive, because of the lower offending frequencies.

Recommendations about selective incapacitation based on criminal career research have proved highly controversial. Several objections were raised (see Visher 1986), some focusing on the ethics of sentencing according to predicted behaviour. Also, it was pointed out that all the information was derived from self-reports, and that offenders would be unlikely to provide valid self-reports if their sentence length or time served were dependent on them. Furthermore, predictive efficiency had probably been overestimated in this research, because the prediction instrument had not been constructed in one sample and applied to a different (validation) sample.

Chaiken and Chaiken (1984) analysed the same data but came to different conclusions. They argued that the low-rate offenders could be identified more accurately than the high-rate ones. Hence, they advocated that the predicted low-rate offenders should be diverted from prison to community programmes, and that this could be done with minimal risk to the public. Also, Rolph and Chaiken (1987) showed that optimistic conclusions about selective incapacitation were not warranted when official records were used to identify high-rate serious offenders, because of inadequacies in the records, and Greenwood and Turner (1987) concluded that the seven-point scale did not correlate with past or future arrests as highly as with self-reports. One problem is that offending frequencies based on arrests can never be as skewed as those based on self-reports. For example, Greenwood and Turner showed that, in self-reports, the offending frequency of the top 10 per cent of offenders was more than fifteen times the median frequency, but in arrest data the offending frequency of the top 10 per cent was less than four times the median frequency. The self-report frequencies seem likely to be closer to the truth.

Two important policy implications might be drawn from the growth in persistence probabilities after each successive offence. The first is that, since a high proportion of offenders desist after the first or second offence, significant criminal justice system interventions might be delayed until the third offence (Wolfgang *et al.* 1972). Diversionary measures might be appropriate after the first or second offence. The second is that desistance is uncommon after six or more arrests, at least for juveniles. Indeed, Barnett and Lofaso (1985) argued that virtually all apparent desistance of the chronic offenders in Philadelphia was illusory, caused by the truncation of the data at the eighteenth birthday. The high probability of reoffending by persistent offenders shows that they are important targets for crime control measures.

An important implication of the generally low degree of specialization by offenders is that it will be difficult to prevent a particular type of offending by targeting a particular type of offender. For example, special incapacitative, individually deterrent, or rehabilitative sentences applied to persons convicted of violence will not necessarily have a disproportionate effect in reducing violent crimes, because frequent offenders currently convicted of non-violent crimes will be as likely to commit violent crimes in the future as persons currently convicted of violent crimes. It would be more effective to target frequent or chronic offenders rather than any particular type of offender.

Co-offending has important implications for crime control. If an offence is committed by a group, criminal justice measures targeted on one member of the group will not necessarily prevent the offending. It is important to investigate under what circumstances individually focused control efforts do or do not prevent offending. For example, measures targeted on group leaders might prevent group offending. The recruiters are primary targets for control measures, and more research is needed to establish how far recruiters can be identified at an early age and what are their characteristics. In so far as recruiters lead formerly innocent people into criminal careers, successful crime control measures targeted on recruiters could have a disproportionate impact on the prevalence of offending.

LeBlanc and Frechette (1989) argued that there were two types of offenders, situational and chronic, who required two types of intervention strategies. Situational offending was infrequent, opportunistic, and minor, whereas chronic offending was part of an anti-social lifestyle. They proposed that situational offenders should be treated with social tolerance, diversion, conciliation, protection, and support, whereas chronics needed judicial control, intensive supervision, and social re-education. Following their criminal career model of two types, it might be proposed that early social prevention measures should be used with situational (or occasional) offenders, and criminal justice measures should be used with chronic (or frequent) offenders. Further research is needed on when and how it is possible to distinguish between these two categories.

Conclusions

Research on criminal careers has greatly advanced knowledge about the prevalence, frequency, onset, persistence, and desistance of individual offending. For example, the peak age of offending in the teenage years primarily reflects a peak in prevalence; the individual offending frequency is relatively constant at different ages, and residual career length reaches a peak at age 30–40. The peak onset rate is at age 13–15, while the peak desistance rate is at age 21–25.

An early onset of offending predicts a long and serious criminal career, because of the persistence of an underlying criminal potential. In the Cambridge Study, more than a quarter of all convicted males had a recorded criminal career lasting more than ten years. A small group of chronic offenders account for a large proportion of the crime problem, and these chronics might have been identified with reasonable accuracy at age 10. Most offenders are versatile, but there is a small degree of specialization superimposed on a great deal of versatility. Co-offending and hedonistic motives decrease from the teens to the twenties, while lone offending and utilitarian motives increase.

The criminal career approach also has important implications for criminological theories, which should address developmental processes. The theory proposed here suggested that offending depended on energizing, directing, inhibiting, and decision-making processes. In addition to explaining differences between individuals in the prevalence or frequency of offending, theories should explain changes within individuals: why people start offending, why they continue or escalate their offending, and why they stop offending. For example, onset may depend primarily on poor parental child-rearing behaviour, persistence may depend on criminal parents and delinquent peers, and desistance may depend on settling down with spouses and cohabitees.

There are a number of ways in which criminal career research might be extended and improved. Existing research is largely based on official records of offending. Future projects are needed that obtain information about offending, including exact dates, by the self-report method in prospective longitudinal surveys. Existing research tends to group together all kinds of crimes, largely because of the versatility of offending; future research should devote more attention to studying different kinds of crimes separately. This is more feasible with self-reports than with official records (because of the low prevalence and frequency of any given offence type in official records). Existing research focuses mainly on males. More studies are needed that systematically compare different criminal career patterns of different categories of people (e.g., males versus females, whites versus blacks, lower class versus upper and middle class).

Existing research focuses on individuals, but there could also be studies of the criminal careers of larger units, such as families, gangs, communities, and places.

Offending is one element of a larger syndrome of anti-social behaviour that arises in childhood and tends to persist into adulthood, with numerous different behavioural manifestations. However, while there is continuity over time in anti-social behaviour, changes are also occurring. It is commonly found that about half of a sample of anti-social children go on to become anti-social teenagers, and about half of anti-social teenagers go on to become anti-social adults. More research is needed on factors that vary within individuals and that predict these changes over time. Research is especially needed on changing behavioural manifestations and developmental sequences at different ages. In particular, more efforts should be made to identify factors that protect vulnerable children from developing into anti-social teenagers.

A great deal has been learned in the last twenty years, particularly from longitudinal surveys, about risk factors for offending and other types of anti-social behaviour. Offenders differ significantly from non-offenders in many respects, including impulsivity, intelligence, family background, peer influence, and socio-economic deprivation. These differences may be present before, during, and after criminal careers. Since most is known about risk factors for prevalence and onset, more research is needed on risk factors for frequency, duration, escalation, and desistance. While the precise causal chains that link these factors with anti-social behaviour, and the ways in which these factors have independent, interactive, or sequential effects, are not known, it is clear that individuals at risk can be identified with reasonable accuracy.

Research is needed on methods of preventing and treating this anti-social personality syndrome. Some promising techniques were reviewed in this chapter: cognitive–behavioural interpersonal skills training, pre-school intellectual enrichment programmes, behavioural parent-management training, and peer influence programmes. However, the preventative effects on offending are often small in magnitude, demonstrated with small samples, and not proved to be long-lasting. Larger-scale tests of these techniques, using randomized experiments and long-term follow-up periods, are clearly warranted and needed. More systematic research is needed to establish with what samples and in what circumstances different techniques are optimally effective.

The major policy implications of criminal career research focus on criminal justice measures such as incapacitation, individual deterrence, and rehabilitation. It is essential for criminal justice decision-makers to know the likely future course of criminal careers for different categories of offenders, and to know how far these careers can be predicted. Special attention could be paid to categories of offenders who are likely to reoffend quickly, who are likely to commit serious offences in the future, and who are likely to have a long future criminal career. On the other hand, categories of offenders who are likely to desist, or who are likely to have a long interval before their next offence, might be treated differently.

Similarly, it is essential for sentencers to know the relative effects of different sentences on aspects of the future criminal career, after controlling for aspects of the past criminal career. This information would assist judges in selecting optimal sentences for different categories of offenders. Very few studies have even attempted to relate sentences to recidivism probabilities with minimal controls for other criminal career variables (one example is Walker *et al.* 1981). Also, few studies have investigated the impact of official processing as opposed to no official action, but Farrington (1977) found an increase in offending frequency after first convictions. This again suggests that first offenders might be better diverted than convicted.

To advance knowledge about human development and criminal careers, Farrington (1988*a*) argued that a new generation of multiple-cohort longitudinal studies was needed. For example, Tonry *et al.* (1991) recommended that seven cohorts should each be followed up for eight years, beginning during the pre-natal period (with a sample of pregnant women) and at ages 3, 6, 9, 12, 15, and 18. This kind of project would advance knowledge about the development of offending and other types of anti-social behaviour from before birth up to the mid-twenties, covering the major periods of onset, persistence, and desistance of criminal careers. One attraction of this design is that, by amalgamating data from adjacent cohorts, conclusions about twenty-five years of development could be drawn in a project taking only ten years from start to finish (including preparatory work, analysis, and writing up). Indeed, preliminary conclusions about development from before birth up to age 21 could be drawn in the first five years of the project. It is also important to include experimental interventions within longitudinal studies, to distinguish between causes and indicators and to investigate the effects of prevention or treatment measures on criminal career features (Farrington 1992*f*).

The Home Office currently focuses on short-term narrowly policy-orientated research and seems disinclined to sponsor long-term fundamental research on the development and causes of offending. Assuming that offending and anti-social behaviour are indicators of mental health problems, it would be highly desirable for a health funding body to take over as the lead agency for sponsoring this type of research. This is most obviously justifiable in studying violence, which is clearly a public health problem (Shepherd and Farrington 1993). As with offending and anti-social behaviour, investigations of the causes and prevention of cancer and heart disease often require prospective longitudinal studies, the identification of risk factors and developmental sequences, and randomized clinical trials to evaluate the success of methods of prevention and treatment.

[This chapter] shows that much has been learned in the past two decades about human development and criminal careers. With a major investment in new longitudinal studies, there can be considerable further advances in knowledge and theory, and consequent improvements in crime prevention and control. Because of the link between offending and numerous other social problems, any measure that succeeds in reducing offending will have benefits that go far beyond this. Any measure that reduces offending will probably also reduce alcohol abuse, drunk driving, drug abuse, sexual promiscuity, family violence, truancy, school failure, unemployment, marital disharmony, and divorce. It is clear that problem children tend to grow up into problem adults, and that problem adults tend to produce more problem children. Major efforts to advance knowledge about and reduce offending and anti-social behaviour are urgently needed.

5.   Bourgeois Ideology and the Origin of Determinism

Steve Rose and Richard Lewontin

It is hard to realize today the extent to which primary social relations in early feudal European society, lay between person and person rather than between persons and things. The relationships between lord and vassal, seigneur and serf, entailed mutual obligations that did not depend on an equitable exchange but were absolute on each party separately. Relations to material things — to wealth, land, tools, products, and the range of social activity of each individual, including work obligations, freedom of movement, and freedom to buy and sell — were an indissoluble whole determined for each person by the single fact of status relation. Serfs were tied to the land, but lords could not eject them because their connection to the land flowed from their social status. Once renewable at the death of either lord or vassal, fiefdoms gradually became hereditary and the arrangement they dictated inescapable.

Underlying this social system and legitimizing it was the ideology of grace and, later, of divine right. People held their position in the social hierarchy as the result of the conferral or denial of God's grace; kings claimed their absolute right to rule on the same basis. As grace was inherited through blood, the conferral of grace on the founder of a line was a sufficient *primum mobilum,* guaranteeing grace to biological heirs (although only if legitimate) and insuring stable social and economic relations within and between generations. Changes in position in the social hierarchy, like that of the noble Norman house of Bellême, which arose from a crossbowman of Louis d'Outre-Mer, were explained as being the result of conferrals or withdrawals of grace. Charles I was king of England, *Dei gratia,* but, as Cromwell wryly observed, grace had been removed from him, as evidenced by his severed head.

This static world of social relations legitimated by God reflected, and was reflected by, the dominant view of the natural world as itself static. Unlike the more modern view of an essentially progressive and changing world, the feudal universe was conceived as being held in an ever revolving daily and seasonal dance, with the sun, moon, and stars rotating like bright lights fixed to a series of crystal spheres at the center of which was our earth, on which humans themselves were the central part of God's creation. Nature and humanity existed in order to serve God and God's representatives on earth, the lords temporal and spiritual.

In such a world, social and natural change alike were to be discouraged. Just as the heavenly spheres were fixed, so was the social order. People knew their place, were born and lived in it; it was natural and, like nature itself, ever changing on the mundane, quotidian level and yet basically immutable in the larger scheme. In this precapitalist world, not yet dominated by the metaphor of the machine (in which all phenomena are reduced to their component cogs and pulleys, linked in linear chains of

Steve Rose, Leon Kamin and Richard Lewontin: 'Bourgeois Ideology and the Origin of Determinism' from *NOT IN OUR GENES* (Pelican Books, 1984), pp. 37–61.

cause and effect), it was possible to be much more tolerant of apparently contradictory or overlapping explanations. The causes of events did not have to be mutually consistent. Sickness could be a natural phenomenon in its own right or a visitation from the Lord. Objects were not individual, atomistic, and separate but fluid and varied, and could be transformed one into another. People could become wolves, lead transmute into gold, fair foul and foul fair. It was possible to believe, at one and the same time, both that living forms had each been created separately according to Biblical myth and had existed unchanged since those Edenic days, *and* that individuals were mutable. Myths abounded of hybrid beasts, half horse, half human; and of women who gave birth to monsters as a result of impressions fixed by some event during pregnancy.

Humanity's relationship to nature was not one of domination because the appropriate machinery of domination did not exist — but rather of coexistence, which demanded respect for and integration with the natural world within which human lives were embedded. This nature was static in the long run and capricious in the short, and any understanding of it, then, could not be based in the end on constant manipulation and transformation, the active techniques of scientific experimentation, but had to be expressed as passive appreciation. Explanations therefore were couched in terms of appeals to the authority of ancient writings, Biblical or Greek, and not on empirical data.

The rise of bourgeois society

It is clear that feudal society was quite unsuited to a growing mercantile, manufacturing, and eventually capitalist system. First, social and economic life had to become disarticulated so that each individual could play many different roles, confronting others sometimes as buyer, sometimes as seller; sometimes as producer, sometimes as consumer; and sometimes as owner, sometimes as user. The particular role played came to depend upon a momentary relation to objects of production and exchange, not upon lifelong social relations.

Second, individuals had to become "free," but only in particular senses. Ties to specific places or persons had to be eliminated, freeing workers to leave land and lord in order to become manufacturing laborers and to move about in commerce. Reciprocally, landowners had to be free to alienate the land, ejecting inefficient and unproductive systems of production. The enclosure acts that began in Britain as early as the thirteenth century and reached a peak in the late seventeenth and eighteenth centuries were designed to concentrate large tracts of land into intensively cultivated and grazed holdings. A consequence of the dispossession of tenants was the creation of a large mobile army of prospective wage laborers for a growing industry. Freedom also had to come in terms of the ownership of one's own body, what Macpherson calls "possessive individualism."[1] Large-scale industrial production is carried out by wage workers who sell their labor power to the owners of capital. For such a system to work, laborers must have possession of their own power of work; they must possess themselves and not be the possession of others.

Note, however, that such workers were predominantly male. To work efficiently under these new conditions, the old divisions of labor between men and women needed to be reinforced. Men worked outside the home as productive laborers, women inside as reproductive laborers. Their task was to provide constantly for the male worker the renewal, the re-creation his conditions of work demanded, as well as to rear the next generation of young workers. Only sometimes could women function directly as productive wage laborers in addition to their reproductive work. As the nineteenth century wore on, this division of labor was steadily strengthened. By contrast with feudal society, men were no longer the possession of others; however, if they possessed nothing else, they possessed their women. The social order was not merely capitalist but patriarchal as well.

The third requirement of developing economic relations was presumptive equality for the growing bourgeoisie. Entrepreneurs needed to acquire and dispose of both real and personal property, which required a legal system that would guarantee them redress against nobles and, above all, access to political power. In practice, this was achieved by the supremacy of a parliament of commoners.

The changing mode of production which the emergent capitalist order of the seventeenth century represented demanded solutions to a wholly new range of technical problems. A mercantile and trading society required new and more accurate navigational techniques for merchants' ships, new methods of extraction of raw materials, and new processes of handling these materials when extracted. The techniques for generating solutions to these problems, and the body of knowledge that accumulated as a result of solving them, represented one of the fundamental transitions in the history of humanity, the emergence of modern science, an emergence that can be dated surprisingly precisely to northwestern Europe in the seventeenth century.

The new scientific knowledge, unlike the old precapitalist forms of knowledge, was not passive but active. Whereas in the past philosophers had contemplated the universe, for science in the post-Newtonian world the test of theory was practice, a credo given ideological form by the writings of Francis Bacon. A steady acquisition of facts about the world and its experimental manipulation in the light of those facts were integral to the new theories. No longer was it adequate merely to quote the authority of the ancients; and if the ancient words of wisdom were not in accord with today's observations, they must be discarded. The new science, like the new capitalism, was part of the liberation of humanity from the shackles of feudal serfdom and human ignorance (the links are beautifully displayed in Brecht's *Galileo*). Even the most abstract pronouncements of physics, such as Newton's laws of motion, could be seen as arising out of the social needs of an emergent class.[2] Science was thus an integral part of the new dynamic of capital, even though the fuller articulation of the links between them would take another two centuries to develop.[3]

The articulation of bourgeois scientific ideology

It is relatively easy to see the social determinants of science and to show the forces that urge particular problems forward and retard others as thus expressive of social needs as perceived by a dominant class. What is less clear, however, is how the nature of scientific knowledge is itself structured by the social world. And yet some such correspondence must exist. To view the universe and to extract explanatory principles and unifying hypotheses from the rich confusion of phenomena and processes, one must systematize and use tools for systematization that are derived from the experience of the social world and of one's fellow students of the natural world.

It is precisely at this point that the concept of ideology becomes of paramount importance in making transparent the ways in which human understanding becomes refracted by the social order in which that understanding develops. To understand the concerns and modes of explanation of bourgeois science, one must understand the underpinnings of bourgeois ideology.

The radical reorganization of social relations that marked the rise of bourgeois economy had, as a concomitant, the rise of an ideology expressive of these new relations. This ideology, which dominates today, was both a reflection onto the natural world of the social order that was being built and a legitimizing political philosophy by which the new order could be seen as following from eternal principles. Long in advance of the revolutions and regicides of the seventeenth and eighteenth centuries that marked the final triumph of the bourgeois order, intellectuals and political pamphleteers were creating the philosophy to which these revolutions looked for justification and explanation.

It is hardly surprising, then, that the philosophical principles enunciated by the philosophers of the Enlightenment should turn out to be just those that corresponded with the demands of bourgeois social relations. The emphasis of the new bourgeois order on the twin ideas of freedom and equality provided the revolutionary rhetoric of the new class struggling to throw off the grips of church and aristocracy. It was a rhetoric that was to be liberatory, and yet finally, once the victory of the bourgeois class was assured, was to contain within itself the contradictions with which the bourgeois order is faced today.

The eighteenth-century accord between the bourgeois order and its ideology of scientific rationality is typified by the clandestinely published French *Encyclopedia*. Its editor was the physicist and mathematician d'Alembert, and the emphasis throughout was on a secular, rational analysis of both the physical world and human institutions. The motif of scientific rationality, as opposed to the religious themes of faith, the supernatural, and tradition, was obviously a primary requirement for the development of productive forces based on new technological discoveries. Labor, too, had to be reorganized and relocated, in workshops whose productive activities were based on calculations of efficiency and profit, not customary relations. The machine model of the universe gained intellectual hegemony, ceasing to be regarded as merely a metaphor and becoming, instead, the "self-evident" truth about how to look at the world.

The bourgeois view of nature

Thus the bourgeois view of nature shaped and was shaped by the science that it developed, organized along certain basic reductionist principles. The rise of modern physics, first with Galileo and then particularly with Newton, ordered and atomized the natural world. Beneath the surface world in all its infinite variety of colors, textures, and varied and transient objects, the new science found another world of absolute masses interacting with one another according to invariant laws that were as regular as clockwork. Causal relationships linked falling bodies, the motion of projectiles, the tides, the moon, and the stars. Gods and spirits were abolished or relegated merely to the "final cause" which set the whole clockwork machinery in motion. (Actually Newton himself remained both religious and mystic throughout his life, but that is one of the minor quirks of personal history: The effect of Newtonian thought was the reverse of Newton's personal philosophy.) The feudal world's universe thus became demystified and, in a manner, disenchanted as well.

This change did not occur without a struggle against those interests that the rising world view opposed. The threat to the Church when astronomers like Copernicus and Galileo sought to replace an earth-centered model of the motion of the heavenly bodies by a sun-centered one was not about cosmology alone, for the Church perceived it as a challenge to a Church-centered world order on earth which mirrored the heavens above. The astronomers, in the spirit of the new capitalism, were challenging heavenly and earthly understanding simultaneously, which was why Bruno, who was most explicit about this, was burned, while Galileo was allowed merely to recant and Copernicus to be published with a little proviso that heliocentrism was merely a theory that made calculations easier but which should not be confused with reality.

In the new world that emerged after Newton, once again heavenly and earthly orders were in seeming harmony. The new physics was dynamic and not static, as were the new processes of trade and exchange. The old world view was replaced with a set of new abstractions in which a series of abstract forces between atomistic and unchanging masses underlay all transactions between bodies. Drop a pound of lead and a pound of feathers from the Leaning Tower of Pisa and the lead will arrive at the ground first because the feathers will be more retarded by air pressure, frictional forces, and so forth. But in Galileo's and Newton's equations the pound of feathers and the pound of lead arrive simultaneously because the *abstract* pound of lead and pound of feathers are equivalent unchanging masses to be inserted into the theoretical equations of the laws of motion.

Sohn-Rethel[4] has pointed out how these abstractions paralleled the world of commodity exchange in which the new capitalism dealt. To each object there are attached properties, mass, or value which are equivalent to or can be exchange for objects of identical mass or value. Commodity exchange is timeless, unmodified by the frictions of the real world; for example, a coin does not change its value by passing from one hand to another, even if it is slightly damaged or worn in the process. Rather, it is an abstract token of a particular exchange value. It was not until the nineteenth century that this view could become fully dominant. The demonstration by Joule that all forms of energy and heat, electromagnetism and chemical reactions were interchangeable and related by a simple constant, the mechanical equivalent of heat (and the later demonstration by Einstein of the equivalence of matter and energy), corresponded to an economic reductionism whereby all human activities could be assessed in terms of their equivalents of pounds, shillings, and pence.[5]

Humans themselves ceased to be individuals with souls to be saved but became merely hands capable of so many hours of work a day, needing to be stoked with a given quantity of food so that the maximal surplus value could be extracted from their labor.

Dickens described that epitome of the nineteenth-century rising capitalist, Thomas Gradgrind of Coketown, as a man

> with a rule and a pair of scales, and the multiplication table always in his pocket, sir, ready to weigh and measure any parcel of human nature, and tell you exactly what it comes to. It is a mere question of figures, a case of simple arithmetic . . . Time itself for the manufacturer becomes its own machinery: so much material wrought up, so much food consumed, so many powers worn out, so much money made.[6]

For bourgeois society, nature and humanity itself had become a source of raw materials to be extracted, an alien force to be controlled, tamed, and exploited in the interests of the newly dominant class. The transition from the precapitalist world of nature could not be more complete.[7]

So far we have discussed science in general, or rather physics as though it were all of science. But how did the new mechanical and clockwork vision of the physicists affect the status of living organisms? Just as modern physics starts with Newton, so modern biology must begin with Descartes — philosopher, mathematician, and biological theorist.

In Part V of his *Discourses* of 1637, Descartes analogizes the world, animate and inanimate, to a machine (the *bête machine*). It is this Cartesian machine image that has come to dominate science and to act as the fundamental metaphor legitimating the bourgeois world view, whether of individuals or of the "solid machine" in which they are embedded. That the machine was taken as a model for the living organism and not the reverse is of critical importance. The machine is as much the characteristic symbol of bourgeois productive relations as the "body social" was of feudal society. Bodies are indissoluble wholes that lose their essential characteristics when they are taken into pieces.

> Life following life through creatures you dissect,
> You lose it in the moment you detect.[8]

Machines, on the contrary, can be disarticulated to be understood and then put back together. Each part serves a separate and analyzable function, and the whole operates in a regular, lawlike manner that can be described by the operation of its separate parts impinging on each other.

Descartes's machine model was soon extended from nonhuman to human organisms. It was clear that many — in fact most — human functions were analogous to those of other animals and therefore were also reducible to mechanics. However, humans had consciousness, self-consciousness, and a mind, which for Descartes, a Catholic, was a soul; and by definition the soul, touched by the breath of God, could not be mere mechanism. So there had to be two sorts of stuff in nature: matter, subject to the mechanical laws of physics; and soul, or mind, a nonmaterial stuff which was the consciousness of the individual, his or her immortal fragment. How did mind and matter interact? By way of a particular region of the brain, Descartes speculated, the pineal gland, in which the mind/soul resided when incorporate, and from which it could turn the knobs, wind the keys, and activate the pumps of the body mechanism.

So developed the inevitable but fatal dysjunction of Western scientific thought, the dogma known in the case of Descartes and his successors as "dualism." As we shall see, some sort of dualism is the inevitable consequence of any sort of reductionist materialism that does not in the end wish to accept that humans are "nothing but" the motion of their molecules. Dualism was a solution to the paradox of mechanism that would enable religion and reductionist science to stave off for another two centuries their inevitable final contention for ideological supremacy. It was a solution compatible with the capitalist order of the day because in weekday affairs it enabled humans to be treated as mere physical mechanisms, objectified and capable of exploitation without contradiction, while on Sundays ideological control could be reinforced by the assertion of the immortality and free will of an unconstrained incorporeal spirit unaffected by the traumas of the workaday world to which its body had been subjected. Today as well, dualism continually reemerges in persistent and various manners from the ashes of the most arid of mechanical materialism.

The development of a materialist biology

For the confident and developing science of the eighteenth and nineteenth centuries, dualism was but a stepping stone toward more thoroughgoing mechanical materialism. Although the analogies changed and became more sophisticated as physical science advanced — from clockwork and hydraulic to electrical and magnetic, and onward to telephone exchanges and computers — the main thrust remained reductionist. For the progressive rationalists of the eighteenth century, science was about cataloguing the states of the world. If a complete specification of all particles at a given time could be achieved, everything would become predictable. The universe was determinate, and the laws of motion applied precisely across a scale ranging from the atoms to the stars. Living organisms were not immune from these laws. The demonstration by Lavoisier that the processes of respiration and the sources of living energy were exactly analogous to those of the burning of a coal fire — the oxidation of foodstuffs in the body tissues — was perhaps the most striking vindication of this approach. It was the first time that a programmatic statement that life must be reducible to molecules could be carried into practice.

But progress in the identification of body chemicals was slow. The demonstration that the substances of which living organisms are composed are only "ordinary," albeit complicated, chemicals came early in the nineteenth century. The intractability of the giant biological molecules — proteins, lipids, nucleic acids — to the available analytical tools remained a stumbling block. The mechanists could make programmatic statements about how life was reducible to chemistry, but these were largely acts of faith. Not until a century after the first nonorganic synthesis of the simple body chemicals did the molecular nature and structures of the giant molecules began to be resolved (and really not until the 1950s did progress become very rapid). The last remaining faith that there would be some special "life force" operating among them which distinguished them absolutely from lesser, nonliving chemicals lingered until the 1920s.[9]

Nonetheless, a radically reductionist program characterized the statements of many of the leading physiologists and biological chemists of the nineteenth century. In 1845 four rising physiologists — Helmholtz, Ludwig, Du Bois Reymond, and Brucke — swore a mutual oath to account for all bodily processes in physiochemical terms.[10] They were followed by others: for instance, Moleschott and Vogt, thoroughgoing mechanical materialists who claimed that humans are what they eat, that genius is a question of phosphorus, and that the brain secretes thought as the kidney secretes urine; and Virchow,[11] one of the leading figures in the development of cell theory, who was also part of a long tradition of social thought which argued that social processes could be described by analogy with the workings of the human body.

It is important to understand the revolutionary intentions of this group. They saw their philosophical commitment to mechanism as a weapon in the struggle against orthodox religion and superstition. Several of them were also militant atheists, social reformers, or even socialists. Science would alleviate the misery of the poor and strengthen the power of the state against the capitalists — and even, to some measure, help democratize society. Their claims were part of the great battle between science and religion in the nineteenth century for supremacy as the dominant ideology of bourgeois society, a fight whose outcome was inevitable but whose final battlefield was not to be physiological reductionism but Darwinian natural selection. The best-known philosopher of the group was Feuerbach, and it was against his version of mechanical materialism that Marx launched his famous theses.[12]

The theses on Feuerbach proved the starting point for Marx's own — and more explicitly Engels's — long-running attempts to transcend mechanical materialism by formulating the principles of a materialist but nonreductionist account of the world and humanity's place within it: dialectical materialism. But within the dominant perspective of biology in the Western tradition, Moleschott's mechanical materialism was to win out, stripped of its millenarian goals and, by the late twentieth century, revealed as an ideology of domination. When today biochemists claim that "a disordered molecule produces a diseased mind,"[13] or psychologists argue that inner city violence can be cured by cutting out sections of the brains of ghetto militants, they are speaking in precisely this Moleschottian tradition.

To complete the mechanical materialist world picture, however, a crucial further step was required: the question of the nature and origin of life itself. The mystery of the relationship of living to nonliving presented a paradox to the early mechanists. If living beings were "merely" chemicals, it should be possible to recreate life from an appropriate physico-chemical mix. Yet one of the biological triumphs of the century was the rigorous demonstration by Pasteur that life only emerged from life; spontaneous generation did not occur. The resolution of this apparent paradox, which had led to many confused polemics between chemical reductionists and the residual school of biological vitalists who continued to oppose them, awaited the Darwinian synthesis, which was able to show that although life came from other living organisms and could not now arise spontaneously, each generation of living things changed, evolved, as a result of the processes of natural selection.

With the theory of evolution came a crucial new element in the understanding of living processes: the dimension of time.[14] Species were not fixed immemorially but were derived in past history from earlier, "simpler" or more "primitive," forms. Trace life back to its evolutionary origins and one could imagine a primordial warm chemical soup in which the crucial chemical reactions could occur. Living forms could coalesce from this prebiotic mix. Darwin speculated about such origins, although the crucial theoretical advances depended on the biochemist Oparin and the biochemical geneticist Haldane in the 1920s (both, incidentally, consciously attempting to work within a dialectical and nonmechanist framework). Experiments only began to catch up with theory from the 1950s onward.

In one sense, evolutionary theory itself represents the apotheosis of a bourgeois world view, just as its subsequent development reflects the contradictions within that world view. The breakdown of the old static feudal order and its replacement with a continually changing and developing capitalism helped introduce the concept of mutability into biology. The age-old daily and seasonal rhythms and the "simple" movement of life from birth through maturity to death had characterized feudalism, but now each generation experienced a world qualitatively different from that of its predecessors. This change was, for the rising eighteenth-century bourgeoisie, progressive. Time's arrow pointed forward irreversibly; it did not loop back upon itself. Understanding of both the earth and life upon it was transformed. Geology slowly came to recognize that the earth had evolved, rivers and seas had moved, layers of rock had been laid down in time sequences atop one another — not in accord with the Biblical myth of creation and the flood but in a steady and uniform sequence over many thousands or millions of years. The principle of uniformitarianism in the hands of such early nineteenth-century geologists as Lyell destroyed the Biblical date for the creation of the earth, 4004 B.C.

And what of life itself? The resemblances and differences of species, their apparent grading virtually one into the other, seemed to imply more than mere coincidence. The discovery of fossils in rock formations whose ages could be estimated implied that some species that had once existed were no longer extant, while new ones had emerged. The doctrine of evolutionism had become an inevitability. At first, in the hands of eighteenth- and early nineteenth-century zoological philosophers like Lamarck and Erasmus Darwin, evolution itself was progressivist, but not in discord with a higher godly design. For Lamarck, species perfected themselves by striving, by modifying their properties to environmental demands and passing these modifications on to their offspring, just as humans were no longer "fixed" in place but could ascend a social hierarchy by virtue — in the liberal myth — of their own efforts. For the elder Darwin evolution was change onward and upward, steadily toward an always more perfect and harmonious future.

It was for Charles Darwin, and the dourer context of the mid-nineteenth century, to frame the mechanisms for evolutionary change in terms of natural selection. Drawing on ideas earlier expressed in the human context by Malthus, he saw that the fact that individuals produced more offspring than survived, and that those better adapted to their environment were more likely to survive long enough to breed in their turn, provides a motor for evolutionary change. Further, Darwinian evolution by natural selection applied not merely to nonhuman species but, it was immediately apparent, to humans as well. It was this observation that set the stage for the final conflict of science with religion, despite the reluctance of many on both sides of the debate to get drawn into it. For, far more than the programmatic statements of the physiological mechanists, Darwinian theory was a direct challenge to the residual hold of Christianity as the dominant ideology of Western society and was seen as such by friend and foe alike.

In retreat since Newton, orthodox Christianity had fallen back into the belief in a God who was first cause of the natural world and still remained the day-to-day controller of life — and especially of human destiny. Darwinism wrested God's final hold on human affairs from his now powerless hands and relegated the deity to, at the best, some dim primordial principle whose will no longer determined human action.

The consequence was to change finally the form of the legitimating ideology of bourgeois society. No longer able to rely upon the myth of a deity who had made all things bright and beautiful and assigned each to his or her estate — the rich ruler in the castle or the poor peasant at the gate — the dominant class dethroned God and replaced him with science. The social order was still to be seen as fixed by forces outside humanity, but now these forces were natural rather than deistic. If anything, this new legitimator of the social order was more formidable than the one it replaced. It has, of course, been with us ever since.

Natural-selection theory and physiological reductionism were explosive and powerful enough statements of a research program to occasion the replacement of one ideolgy — of God — by another: a mechanical, materialist science. They were, however, at best only programmatic, pointing along a route which they could not yet trace. For example, in the absence of a theory of the gene, Darwinism could not explain the maintenance of inherited variation that was essential for the theory to work. The solution awaited the development of genetic theory at the turn of the twentieth century with the rediscovery of the experiments done by Mendel in the 1860s. This in turn produced the neo-Darwinian synthesis of the 1930s and the recurrent attempts to parcel out biological phenomena into discrete and essentially additive causes, genetic and environmental: the science of biometry.

The quantification of behavior

Moleschott's claim that the brain secretes thought as the kidney secretes urine was perhaps the most extreme of the materialist claims of the nineteenth century, but it expresses at the same time the ultimate goal of the philosophy. It was not merely life, but consciousness and human nature itself which must be brought within the reach of rulers, scales, and chemical furnaces. To achieve such a goal it was necessary first to have a theory of behavior, which was no longer seen as a continuous and only partially predictable flow of human action arising from the demands of the soul, of free will, and of the vagaries of human character, stuff for the novelist rather than the scientist; instead, behaviors — now in the plural — had to be seen as a series of discrete and separable units, each of which could be distinguished and analyzed. It was no longer enough to see the body alone as a machine; the role of the brain in organizing and controlling behavior became the center of research attention.

For one school, the brain was an integrative organ whose properties were in some way holistic functions of the entire mass of tissue. For another, these functions were atomized and localized in different regions. This latter was essentially the claim made by the phrenological school of Gall and Spurzheim beginning in Germany and France at the end of the eighteenth century. All human faculties, it claimed, could be broken down into discrete units — abilities such as mathematics or propensities such as love of music or of producing children (philoprogenitiveness).[15] Further, these different abilities and propensities were located in different regions of the brain, and their extent could be assessed from outside by looking at the shape of an individual head or skull. Despite a period of high fashion, phrenology's empirical claims were laughed out of court by the orthodox science of the mid-nineteenth century, but a crucial series of fundamental claims remained intact. These were of the existence of discrete measurable traits that could be localized to specific brain regions. By the end of the nineteenth century the localization school of neuropsychology was clear that different regions of the brain controlled different functions; clear as a result of the postmortem examination of brains of patients whose disabilities had been studied before death; by the somewhat macabre investigations of the behavior of soldiers dying of brain injuries in the battlefields of the Franco–Prussian War; and by experiments with animals. There were brain regions associated with sensory, motor, and association functions; with speech, memory, and affect. It followed that differences in behavior between individuals might be accounted for in terms of differences in structure of different brain regions. There was much dispute as to whether brain size as measured in life by head circumference, or after death by directly weighing, might be associated with intelligence or achievement — an obsession of a number of distinguished nineteenth-century neuroanatomists who anxiously surveyed their colleagues, and left their own brains for analysis by posterity. The systematic distortion of the evidence by nineteenth-century anatomists and anthropologists in attempts to prove that the differences in brain size between male and female brains were biologically meaningful, or that blacks have smaller brains than whites has been devastatingly exposed in a detailed reevaluation by Stephen J. Gould.[16]

The obsession with brain size continued well into the twentieth century. Both Lenin's and Einstein's brains were taken for study after death. Lenin's had an entire institute of brain research founded for its study; years of work could find nothing unusual about the brain, but the institute remains as a major research center. The point is that there are no sensible questions that neuroanatomy can address to the dead brain of however distinguished a scientist or politician.[17] There is virtually no observable relationship between the size or structure of an individual brain measured after death and any aspect of the intellectual performance of its owner measured during life. There are exceptions: In cases of specific brain damage due to illness, lesions, or tumors, or the brain shrinkage of senile dementia or alcoholism, though even here there are counterexamples.[18] But in general, once the effects of height, age, etc. have been allowed for, brain weight is related to body size. The search for the seat of differences in performance between individuals must move beyond the simple examination of brain structures.

Despite this, there remains a common assumption that there is a relationship between large heads and high brows and intelligence, an assumption that was made the basis of a criminological theory of types by the Italian Cesare Lombroso in the late nineteenth century. According to Lombroso, in an extension of the phrenological theorizing of the early part of the century, criminals could be identified by certain basic physiological features:

> The criminal by nature has a feeble cranial capacity, a heavy and developed jaw, projecting [eye] ridges, an abnormal and asymmetrical cranium . . . projecting ears, frequently a crooked or flat nose. Criminals are subject to [color blindness]; left-handedness is common; their muscular force is feeble. . . . Their moral degeneration corresponds with their physical, their criminal tendencies are manifested in infancy by [masturbation], cruelty, inclination to steal, excessive vanity, impulsive character. The criminal by nature is lazy, debauched, cowardly, not susceptible to remorse, without foresight, . . . his handwriting is peculiar . . . his slang is widely diffused. . . . The general . . . persistence of an inferior race type . . . [19]

Lombroso and his followers attempted to establish a system whereby a predisposition to engage in antisocial behavior could be predicted on the basis of physical characteristics; from surveys conducted in prisons he concluded among other things that murderers have "cold, glassy, blood-shot eyes, curly abundant hair, strong jaws, long ears and thin lips"; forgers are "pale and amiable, with small eyes and large noses; they become bald and grey-haired early"; and sex criminals have "glinting eyes, strong jaws, thick lips, lots of hair and projecting ears."[20]

A rational criminology thus became possible, a theory of criminal faces that was the obvious forerunner to today's belief in criminal chromosomes. The strength of Lombroso's typology is that it drew from current myths about the criminal and gave them apparent scientific support. The myths found their way routinely into mass culture, as in Agatha Christie, for instance. In an early book we find her clean-cut young upper-class English hero secretly observing the arrival of a Communist trade unionist at a rendezvous: "The man who came up the staircase with a soft-footed tread was quite unknown to Tommy. He was obviously of the very dregs of society. The low beetling brows, and the criminal jaw, the bestiality of the whole countenance were new to the young man, though he was a type that Scotland Yard would have recognised at a glance."[21] Lombroso would have recognized him too.

Implicit in such criminology is the belief that individual behaviors can be located as the fixed properties of individuals, as characteristic as their height or hair color. Also implicit within the research program that such a reductionist biological determinism maintains is the claim that it is possible to compare the behaviors of different individuals across some appropriate scale. Behaviors are not all-or-none. Like height, they are continuously distributed variables; individual A is more aggressive than individual B, or less so than C. If one could devise appropriate scales, like rulers for height, one should be able to plot the distribution of the entire population on a scale for aggression, criminality, or whatever. It is the belief in such a distribution that provides the rationale for thinking about IQ tests as measures of intelligence, which is discussed in [Chapter 5]. If all individuals within a population can be placed, for any particular trait, along a linear distribution, the famous bell-shaped "normal" curve is produced. Individuals who fall outside the majority portion of this distribution are abnormal, or deviant.

Because we take the concept of deviance so easily for granted, because it seems so "natural," it is important to remember how recently it has appeared in the history of bourgeois society. The concepts of criminality, madness, and indeed illness itself — their treatment by seclusion, in prisons, asylums, and hospitals — only developed slowly from the seventeenth century and with accelerating pace through the nineteenth century.[22] It is not that prior to the bourgeois revolution there was no theory of human nature. Typological theory argued that human temperament was fixed as a sort of titration of the four basic types — phlegmatic, bilious, choleric, and sanguine. Concepts of the fixity of human evil and of original sin clashed with the possibility of redemption through faith or good works. Certainly criminal codes existed, as did madness and disease. But medieval and early capitalist society tolerated a far greater range of human variation than was to be acceptable later. Peddlers and vagabonds, rogues and eccentrics were part of life's stage: consider the characters in a Breughel or Hogarth painting, or an eighteenth-century picaresque novel. The reductionist materialism of the nineteenth century sought to control, regularize, and limit this variation. Or think of the transition between the multitudinous richness of characters of an early Dickens novel like *Pickwick Papers* and the later accounts of the conformity of the new bourgeoisie portrayed in *Dombey and Son* or *Hard Times*. The social institutions of an industrial society could decreasingly tolerate deviance, which became a meaningful concept only when there was a norm, a concept of the average, from which people could be argued to deviate.[23]

The origin of behavior

Behaviors, then, in the reductionist view, may be quantified, distributed in relationship to a norm, or located in some way "in the brain." But how do they arise? This too was a major concern of nineteenth-century theorizing. We have shown how the inheritance of behavior, of human nature, forms a major theme of the Victorian novelists from Disraeli to Dickens and Zola. The theory that behaviors, even trivial ones, are inherited rather than acquired was clearly articulated by Charles Darwin in his book *The Expression of Emotion in Man and Animals*. In it, for instance he notes:

> A gentleman of considerable position was found by his wife to have the peculiar trick, when he lay fast asleep on his back in bed, of raising his right arm slowly in front of his face up to his forehead, then dropping it with a jerk so that the wrist fell heavily on the bridge of the nose. . . . Many years after his death his son married a lady who had never heard of the family incident. She however, observed precisely the same peculiarity of her husband, but his nose not being particularly prominent has never as yet suffered from a blow. . . . One of his children, a girl, has inherited the same trick.[24,25]

While Darwin was collecting anecdotes, Galton was measuring, quantifying, and attempting to define the laws of ancestral inheritance of such behaviors. The inheritance or otherwise of such foibles as Darwin records was not, of course, the central question. In genetic studies from Darwin's day to the present, most of the attention directed to human behavior has been concerned with two major themes: the inheritance of intelligence and the inheritance of mental illness or criminality. One of the major purposes of the collection of psychometric evidence (to be discussed in relation to IQ in [Chapter 5]) was to measure the degree to which any given behavior was inherited rather than environmentally shaped. The spurious dichotomization of nature and nurture begins here.

While the techniques used in *Hereditary Genius*[26] were crude, the questions asked and the methodology developed soon after were to remain practically unchanged for the century dividing Darwin and Galton from the modern generation of biological determinists. The sorry history of this century of insistence on the iron nature of biological determination of criminality and degeneracy, leading to the growth of the eugenics movement, sterilization laws, and the race science of Nazi Germany has frequently been told.[27] It is not our purpose here to retrace that history. Rather, we are concerned with the way in which the philosophy of reductionism, and its intimate intertwining with biological determinism, developed into the modern synthesis of sociobiology and molecular biology.

The central dogma: the core of the mechanistic program

The nineteenth-century themes of the chemicalization of physiology, the quantification of behavior, and the genetic theory of evolution would have remained only programmatic insights without the explosive growth of biological theory and method of the last thirty years. To substantiate them turned out to require more than slogans and mathematics. What were needed were the powerful new machines and techniques for the determination of the structure of the giant molecules, for observing the microscopic internal structure of the cells, and, above all, for studying the dynamic interplay of individual molecules within the cell. By the 1950s it had begun to be possible to describe and account for, in the mechanistic sense, the behavior of individual body organs — muscles, liver, kidneys, etc. — in terms of the properties and interchange of individual molecules: the mechanist's dream.

The grand unification between the concerns of the geneticists and those of the mechanistic physiologists came in the 1950s — the "crowning triumph" of twentieth-century biology, the elucidation of the genetic code. This required a theoretical addition to the mechanistic program, to be sure. Hitherto it had been sufficient to claim that a full accounting for the biological universe and the human condition was possible by an understanding of the trio of *composition* — the molecules the organism contains; *structure* — the ways these molecules are arranged in space; and *dynamics* — the chemical interchanges among the molecules. To this now needed to be added a fourth concept, that of *information*.

The concept of information itself had an interesting history, arising as it did from attempts during the Second World War to devise guided missile systems, and, through the 1950s and 1960s, in laying the theoretical infrastructure for the computer and electronics industries. The understanding that one could view systems and their actions in terms not merely of matter and the energy flow through it but in terms of information exchanges — that molecular structures could convey instructions or information one to the other — shook up a theoretical kaleidoscope, and in one sense made possible Crick, Watson, and Wilkins's recognition that the double helical structure of the DNA molecule could also carry genetic instructions across the generations. Molecules, the energetic interchanges between them, and the information they carried provided the mechanists' ultimate triumph, expressed in Crick's deliberate formulation of what he called the "central dogma" of the new molecular biology: "DNA →RNA →protein."[28,29] In other words, there is a one-way flow of information between these molecules, a flow that gives historical and ontological primacy to the hereditary molecule. It is this that underlies the sociobiologists "selfish gene" arguments that, after all, the organism is merely DNA's way of making another DNA molecule; that everything, in a preformationist sense that runs like a chain through several centuries of reductionism, is in the gene.

It is hard to overemphasize the ideological organizing function that this type of formulation of the mechanics of the transcription of DNA into protein fulfills. Long before Crick, the imagery of the biochemistry of the cell had been that of the factory, where functions were specialized for the conversion of energy into particular products and which had its own part to play in the economy of the organism as a whole. Some ten years before Crick's formulation, Fritz Lipmann, discoverer of one of the key molecules engaged in energy exchange within the body, ATP, formulated his central metaphor in almost pre-Keynesian economic terms: ATP was the body's energy currency. Produced in particular cellular regions, it was placed in an "energy bank" in which it was maintained in two forms, those of "current account" and "deposit account." Ultimately, the cell's and the body's energy books must balance by an appropriate mix of monetary and fiscal policies.[30]

Crick's metaphor was more appropriate to the sophisticated economies of the 1960s in which considerations of production were diminishing relative to those of its control and management. It was to this new world that information theory, with its control cycles, feedback and feed-forward loops, and regulatory mechanisms, was so appropriate; and it is in this new way that the molecular biologists conceive of the cell — an assembly-line factory in which the DNA blueprints are interpreted and raw materials fabricated to produce the protein end products in response to a series of regulated requirements. Read any introductory textbook to the new molecular biology and you will find these metaphors as a central part of the cellular description. Even the drawings of the protein synthesis sequence itself are often deliberately laid out in "assembly line" style. And the metaphor does not merely dominate the teaching of the new biology: It and language derived from it are key features of the way molecular biologists themselves conceive of and describe their own experimental programs.

And not merely molecular biologists. The synthesis of physiology and genetics that an information theory containing a double helix provided was steadily extended upward from individuals to populations and their origins. The integrated reductionist world views presented by biologically determinist writings like those of E. O. Wilson (*Sociobiology: The New Synthesis*) or Richard Dawkins (*The Selfish Gene*) draw explicitly on molecular biology's central dogma to define their commitment to the claim that the gene is ontologically prior to the individual and the individual to society,[31] and equally explicitly on a set of transferred economic concepts developed in the management of the increasingly complex capitalist societies of the sixties and seventies: Cost benefit analysis, investment opportunity costs, game theory, system engineering and communication and the like are all unabashedly transferred into the natural domain.

Drawn from inspection of the human social order, they define sociobiology's world view, and, as we should expect and as happened with Darwinism earlier, they are then reflected back as a justifier for that social order — as, for instance, when economists describe monetarist theories as in accord with the biological condition of humanity.[32] We shall see this process amply exemplified in [the chapters] that follow. For now, we want only to emphasize how the very transparency and explicitness of Crick's formulation of the "central dogma," and his quasi-religious choice of language in which to cast it, seize and restate the essential ideological concern of this mechanist tradition.

For the mechanical materialists the grand program begun by Descartes has now in its broad outline been completed. All that remains is the filling in of details. Even for the workings of so complex a system as the human brain and consciousness, the end is in sight. Immense amounts are known about the chemical composition and cellular structures of the brain, about the electrical properties of its individual units, and indeed of great masses of brain tissue functioning in harmony. We know how the analyzer cells of the visual system or the withdrawal reflex of a slug given an electric shock may be wired up, and about regions of the brain whose function is concerned with anger, fear, hunger, sexual appetite, or sleep. The mechanists' claims here are clear. In the nineteenth century, Darwin's supporter T. H. Huxley dismissed the mind as no more than the whistle of the steam train, an irrelevant spin-off of physiological function. Pavlov, in discovering the conditioned reflex, believed he had the key to the reduction of psychology to physiology, and one strand of reductionism has followed his lead. In this tradition, molecules and cellular activity cause behavior, and, as genes cause molecules, the chain that runs from particular unusual genes, say, to criminal violence and schizophrenia is unbroken.

Much of what follows in [this book] will be an explanation of the inadequacy of the claims for these causal chains, both on theoretical and on empirical grounds, as well as an analysis of their ideological roles in the defense of biological determinist views of the human condition. Only then can we move on to show how these reductionist models may be transcended by a biology more fully in accord with the reality and complexity of the material world. Before that, however, we must examine the contradictions of the other twin planks of bourgeois ideology: the necessity for freedom and equality in the social domain. To do this, we must retrace our steps to the emergence of bourgeois society from feudalism.

Notes

1. C.B. Macpherson, *The Political Theory of Possessive Individualism* (New York: Oxford University Press, 1962).

2. This correspondence was first pointed out, in an essay that was to change the shape of the subsequent historiography of science, by Boris Hessen in *Science at the Crossroads*, ed. N. Bukharin *et al.* (Moscow: Kniga, 1931).

3. For example, J.R. Ravetz, *Scientific Knowledge and Its Social Problems* (London: Allen Lane, 1972). Also H. Rose and S. Rose, *Science and Society* (Harmondsworth, Middlesex, England: Penguin, 1969).

4. A. Sohn-Rethel, *Mental and Manual Labour* (London: Macmillan, 1978).

5. Lest there be any doubt, we should emphasize again that there are two types of criteria for understanding the scientific process. That we can show the social determinants of a particular view of the world, how and why it emerges, says nothing about the truth claims or otherwise of the scientific statements. That Joule's mechanical equivalent of heat or Einstein's matter/energy equivalence were developed in a particular facilitating social framework does not entitle one to conclude that they are thereby by definition either true or false. Criteria for judging the truth of Joule's or Einstein's claims lie between science and the real world, not between science and the social order. We are not committing the "genetic fallacy."

6. C. Dickens, *Hard Times* (Penguin Edition, 1969), pp. 48, 126.

7. On the theme of the domination of nature see W. Leiss, *The Domination of Nature* (Boston: Beacon, 1974). Also, A. Schmidt, *The Concept of Nature in Marx* (London: New Left Books, 1973).

8. A. Pope, *Moral Essays,* Epistle 1 to Lord Cobham.

9. H. Driesch, *The History and Theory of Vitalism* (London: Macmillan, 1914); also see J.S. Fruton, *Molecules and Life* (New York: John Wiley, 1972).

10. R. Virchow, *The Mechanistic Concept of Life* (1850), trans. in *Disease, Life and Man,* ed. J.K. Lelland (Stanford, Calif.: Stanford Univ. Press, 1958). Also see J. Loeb, *The Mechanistic Concept of Life,* reprinted with an introduction by D. Fleming (Cambridge, Mass.: Harvard Univ. Press, 1964).

11. Virchow's arguments worked both ways: His emphasis on "the body politic" also implied an argument that diseases of individuals were essentially socially caused rather than caused by, for instance, germs. Virchow's emphasis on social medicine, with its progressive and nonreductionist implications, is part of the contradiction between the radical social intent of much of this physiological thought in the nineteenth century and its ultimately repressive ideology.

12. K. Marx, "Theses on Feuerbach," (1845) in K. Marx and F. Engels, *Selected Works* vol.1 (Moscow Progress Publishers, 1969).

13. Stated by biochemist W. L. Byrne at a conference on "Learning disability," Kansas City, 1979.

14. F. Jacob, *The Logic of Living Systems* ((London: Allen Lane, 1974).

15. See, for example, R.M. Young, *Mind, Brain and Adaptation in the Nineteenth Century* (New York: Oxford Univ. Press, 1970).

16. S. J. Gould, *The Mismeasure of Man* (New York: Norton, 1981).

17. Any more than there are useful questions to be asked of the sperm of a septuagenarian Nobel laureate, despite Dr. William Shockley's enthusiasm for donating these fruits of his loins to a "genetic repository" in California where it may be used to inseminate the hopeful bearers of "high IQ" children.

18. B.L. Priestly and J. Lorber, "Ventricular Size and Intelligence in Achondroplasia," *Zeitschrift für Kinderchirurgie* 34 (1981): 320–26.

19. C. Lombroso, quoted in S. Chorover, *From Genesis to Genocide* (Cambridge, Mass.: MIT Press, 1979), pp. 179–80.

20. Chorover, *From Genesis to Genocide,* p. 180.

21. A. Christie, *The Secret Adversary* (New York: Dodd, Mead, 1922), p. 49.

22. For example, A.T. Scull, *Museums of Madness: The Social Organisation of Insanity in 19th Century England* (London: Allen Lane, 1979).

23. Indeed, in writing this book we have become aware of the extent to which there are still large cross-cultural differences in how norms are viewed. The U.S. educational system, it appears to us, is far more interested in categorizing the children that pass through it as "within the normal range, or alternatively as deviant from it; American parents are more likely to be told that their child falls "outside the norm" than in England, where perhaps a greater range of behavior in children is taken for granted — or less is expected of them.

24. C. Darwin, *The Expression of the Emotions in Man and Animals* (London: John Murray, 1872).

25. How would *we* explain such an anecdote? For us, it is analogous to some of the stories of amazing coincidences among separated identical twins popular today—or the search for explanations for ESP, UFOs, and bent spoons. We begin by being skeptical of the phenomena. And we point out that scientific research and explanation are concerned above all with the understanding of regularities and repeatable phenomena, not exceptions and flukes, many of which, like the apparent coincidence of behavior of long-separated identical twins, simply disappear on closer analysis.

26. F. Galton, *Hereditary Genius* (London: Macmillan, 1969).

27. For example: Gould: *Mismeasure of Man.* Also see A. Chase, *The Legacy of Malthus* (Urbana: Univ. of Illinois Press, 1980); Chorover, *From Genesis to Genocide;* and B. Evans and B Waites, *IQ and Mental Testing* (London: Macmillan, 1981).

28. For Crick on the "Central Dogma" see F. H. C. Crick, *Symposium of the Society for Experimental Biology* 12 (1957): 138–63; *Perspectives in Biology and Medicine* 17; (1973): 67–70; and *Nature* 227 (1970); 561–63.

29. For Crick, "Once information has passed into protein it cannot get out again." For Monod, "One must regard the total organism as the ultimate epigenetic expression of the genetic message itself." J. Monod, quoted in H. Judson, *The Eighth Day of Creation* (London: Cape, 1979), p. 212.

30. H. Rose and S. Rose, "The Myth of the Neutrality of Science," in *The Social Impact of Modern Biology,* ed. W. Fuller. (London: Routledge & Kegan Paul, 1971), pp. 283–94.

31. For Jacques Monod, "You have an exact logical equivalence between these two — the family and the cells. This effect is entirely written in the structure of the protein which is itself written in the DNA." Monod, quoted in Hudson, *Eighth Day of Creation*, p. 212.

32. For example, J. Hirschleifer, "Economics from a Biological Viewpoint," *Journal of Law and Economics* 20, 1 (1977):1–52.

6. Correction and Appreciation
David Matza

During the past forty or fifty years, a fundamental aspect of naturalism emerged. It was a most rudimentary aspect, and thus hardly an occasion for great cheer or self-congratulation. Still. it was consequential. Though little more than a posture, a habit of mind — an attitude — it was prerequisite to future development. This posture is an essential element of naturalism whether the world to be engaged and comprehended was that of objects or subjects. It may be termed *appreciation*.

Appreciation is especially difficult when the subject of inquiry consists of enterprises that violate cherished and widely shared standards of conduct and morality. Almost by definition, such phenomena are commonly *un*appreciated; indeed, they are condemned. Accordingly, the purpose of much research on deviation has been to assist established society ultimately to rid itself of such troublesome activities. The goal of ridding ourselves of the deviant phenomenon, however Utopian, stands in sharp contrast to an appreciative perspective and may be referred to as *correctional*.

A basic difficulty with a correctional perspective is that it systematically interferes with the capacity to empathize and thus comprehend the subject of inquiry. Only through appreciation can the texture of social patterns and the nuances of human engagement with those patterns be understood and analyzed. Without appreciation and empathy we may gather surface facts regarding a phenomenon and criticize the enterprises connected with it, but we will fail to understand in depth its meaning to the subjects involved and its place in the wider society. In this respect, as in others, the study of subjects stands in marked contrast to the study of objects, though even in the latter case a fondness for the object of inquiry is far from unknown. The difference is that in the study of subjects, appreciation and empathy are essential tools of inquiry, a basic resource without which the enormous distance between analyst and subject remains. The correctional standpoint interferes with engaging the deviant phenomenon because it is informed and motivated by the purpose of ridding itself of it. Until recently, and still in large measure today, the study of deviant phenomena has been dominated by the correctional view.

As with naturalism generally, an appreciative view is flanked on both sides by attitudes that threaten it. The desire to liquidate the phenomenon is almost as inimical to the spirit of appreciation as the frequent tendency to suppress features of the phenomenon which by conventional standards are distasteful. Curiously enough, this romantic tendency sometimes appears within a predominantly correctional perspective, but most often it accompanies appreciation. But such appreciation is only a pale imitation since it is achieved at the cost of denying essential features of the deviant enterprise.

Paupers occasionally fleece the welfare system, robbers often brutalize or otherwise molest their victims, motorcycle gangs are a terrible nuisance to policemen, prostitutes

Matza, D., *BECOMING DEVIANT*. © 1969, pp. 15–31; 37–40. Reprinted by permission of Prentice Hall, Inc., Upper Saddle River, NJ, USA.

sometimes roll their customers, drug addicts are engaged in a great deal of petty and grand theft, homosexuals are relatively promiscuous, Gypsies have been known to swindle Gentiles if a promising opportunity appears, Bohemians engage in what has been called "free love," and so on. These features — detestable by conventional standards — can hardly be denied or suppressed; they are part of what must be appreciated if one adheres to a naturalistic perspective, for they are a part of various deviant enterprises. This willingness to empathize with the deviant phenomenon in its full scope contrasts naturalism with the romanticism that superficially resembles it. The appreciative spirit was well expressed by George Borrow, the famous gypsiologist, whose writing in 1843 foreshadowed subsequent developments by eighty or ninety years. He said:

> The cause of truth can scarcely be forwarded by enthusiasm, which is almost invariably the child of ignorance and error. The author is anxious to direct the attention of the public towards the Gypsies; but he hopes to be able to do so without any romantic appeals in their behalf, by concealing the truth, or by warping the truth until it becomes falsehood.[1]

Though romanticism has hindered the growth of naturalism, the main obstacle is implicit in the correctional perspective. The correctional perspective is reasonable enough, perhaps even commendable, except that it makes empathy and understanding difficult, and sometimes impossible. Correction reflects the easily appreciated social view that persons who have strayed from moral standards ought to be persuaded by a variety of means to return to the fold, and it argues that knowledge may be put to that service. To appreciate the variety of deviant enterprises requires a temporary or permanent suspension of conventional morality, and thus by usual standards inescapable elements of irresponsibility and absurdity are implicit in the appreciative stance. Deviant enterprises, and the persons who engage them, are almost by definition troublesome and disruptive. How silly and perhaps evil, therefore, seem the appreciative sentiments of those who have been guided by the naturalist spirit. These appreciative sentiments are easily summarized: We do not for a moment wish that we could rid ourselves of deviant phenomena. We are intrigued by them. They are an intrinsic, ineradicable, and vital part of human society.

The correctional perspective

When deviant phenomena are seen and studied from the correctional perspective, the possibility of "losing the phenomenon" — reducing it to that which it is not — is heightened. The purpose of ridding ourselves of the phenomenon manifests itself most clearly in an overwhelming contemporary concern with questions of causation, or "etiology." The phenomenon itself receives only cursory attention. The ultimate purpose of liquidation is reflected in this highly disproportionate division of attention between description and explanation. With the possible exception of Sutherland's stress on behavior systems and their detailed description, and Maurer's detailed ethnography, traditional studies of deviant behavior have been highly vague and shortwinded about the phenomena they presume to explain.[2] Why bother with detailed and subtle description? The task before us, in the correctional perspective, is to get at the root causes in order to remove them and their product.

Apart from their lack of attention to detail, another noticeable consequence of many sociologists' aversion to the phenomenon itself was their incapacity to separate standards of morality from actual description. The standards intrude to assure that the phenomenon will be viewed from the outside and so described. This posture may be illustrated by two exemplary studies, pervaded by the correctional spirit, and made during the period when that spirit was still dominant. An appreciation of the correctional spirit is best gained if we go back to the decade immediately preceding the first World War, when the correctional spirit was largely unquestioned in both England and America, and was institutionalized in strong alliances among sociology, social work, and social reform.[3]

The *West Side Studies* and the *Pittsburgh Survey* both were sponsored by the Russell Sage Foundation, which was then, and is still in some measure, an influential representative of the correctional spirit. These studies, important in their time, were excellent and definitive. In them we may observe the dominant correctional attitude; additionally, however, some of the naturalistic precepts that were to appear a few years later in the Chicago school are foreshadowed. Thus, a brief consideration of these studies yields a glimpse of the correctional perspective just before its assumptions and temper were brought into question — first, inadvertently by the Chicago school and then explicitly and intentionally by two later groups.

Differences between the spirit animating the Russell Sage studies and that guiding the Chicago school can be easily exaggerated. Though there were differences, they were of degree and nuance and not clear-cut. The attitude implicit in the Russell Sage studies was not wholly correctional, just as the sentiments of the Chicago school were not wholly appreciative. The West Side and Pittsburgh surveys were already engaged in what was to become the central contribution to naturalism of the Chicago school. They, too, entered the world of the deviant but to a much lesser extent than the Chicagoans. Their main reliance was still on newspaper accounts, police folders and reports of social investigators. Some of this emphasis persisted in the work of the Chicago school, but much greater reliance was placed on the deviant subject's *own story*. Appreciation of deviant phenomena requires a consideration of the subject's viewpoint. Though it hardly requires an acceptance of that viewpoint, it does assume empathy with it. In the Pittsburgh and West Side surveys, there is a glimmer — but no more — of the connected naturalist precepts of entering the subjective world of the deviant and empathizing with the viewpoint implicit in that world. Mainly, the attitude and frame of reference for these studies were those of respectable, conventional society. Though they entered the deviant world, they did so hesitantly and without adopting the subject's point of view; though they sympathized with the plight of slum children, they hardly empathized with it; and instead of appreciating the character of the distinctive human enterprises they encountered, they condemned them and yearned for correction. The conventional and correctional assumptions that pervade these surveys are well illustrated in the following description of deviant behavior on the West Side of New York. This description is fairly typical of the attitude conveyed in the study. Only the deviant phenomena under consideration is unusual. Consequently, the implicit attitude does not pass unnoticed; usually it does.

The two chief sports of the Middle West Side — baseball and boxing — are perennial. The former, played as it always is, with utter carelessness and disregard of surroundings, is theoretically intolerable, but it flourishes despite constant complaints and interference. The diamond is marked out in the roadway, the bases indicated by paving bricks, sticks, or newspapers. Frequently guards are placed at each end of the block to warn of the approach of police. One minute a game is in full swing; the next a scout cries "cheese it." Balls, bats and gloves disappear . . . and when the "cop" appears . . . the boys will be innocently strolling down the streets. Notwithstanding these precautions, as the juvenile court records show, they are constantly being caught. In a great majority of these . . . games too much police vigilance cannot be exercised, for a game between a dozen or more boys, of from fourteen to eighteen years of age, with a league ball, in a crowded street, with plate glass windows on either side, becomes a joke to no one but the participants. A foul ball stands innumerable chances of going through the third-storey window of a tenement, or of making a bee line through the valuable plate glass window of a store on the street level, or of hitting one of the passersby. . . . When one sees the words "arrested for playing with a hard ball in a public street" written on a coldly impersonal record card in the children's court one is apt to become indignant. But when you see the same hard ball being batted through a window or into a group of little children on the same public street, the matter assumes an entirely different aspect. . . . Clearly from the community's point of view, the playing of baseball in the street is rightly a penal offense. It annoys citizens, injures persons and property, and interferes with traffic.[4]

There is little doubt that the researchers have adopted the community viewpoint and not that of the deviant subject — in this case, hard-ball players. Though the correctional temper is evident in the discussion of baseball, it is even more apparent in the discussion of the second major sport of the West Side. With regard to boxing, the investigators said:

The West Side youngster sees very little of the real professional boxers who, from the very nature of their somewhat strenuous employment, must keep in good condition . . . . But of their brutalized hangers-on, the "bruisers," who frequent the saloons and street corners and pose as real fighters, he sees a great deal; consequently, as a whole, prize-fighting must be classed as one of the worst influences of the neighborhood. It is too closely allied with streetfighting, and too easily turned to criminal purposes.[5]

The conventional commitment of the correctional perspective, as manifested in *West Side Studies,* was pervasive. Moreover, the standards espoused by the investigators are especially striking because they were so highly puritanical — so boy-scoutish. It was not simply that the ordinary member of society was entrusted with the research function; instead, perhaps, the *most moral* members served in that capacity. Note the range of values commended and stressed in the following excerpt. Note also the steady interpenetration of analysis and correctional viewpoint. Little effort is made to separate the two.

> The West Side gang is in its origin perfectly normal . . . . Its influence [on a boy] is strong and immediate . . . . Untrammelled by the perversion of special circumstances it might encourage his latent interests, train him to obedience and loyalty, show him the method and the saving of cooperation, and teach him the beauty of self-sacrifice.[6]

So pervasive and so implicit are the moral standards manifested in the correctional view of *West Side Studies* that ordinarily they are obscured from the readers notice. Occasionally, standards so demanding and so different from those of our own time emerge as dramatic manifestations of what is implicit in the entire effort. One example of this is to be found in yet another allegedly lamentable feature of slum life: "Father and children eat the same food, and the boy is accustomed to the stimulus of tea and coffee from childhood."[7]

A wholly dim view of slum life and of its close relation to diverse pathologies has been a staple of the correctional perspective, and this external perspective shaped the conclusion of the West Side investigators. "At the very outset," they suggested, "poverty destroys the possibilities of normal development."[8] In this perspective, the slum was no less — and no more — than a pathological growth in modern society. Not just crime or alcohol, but ordinary childhood activities apparent in the round of slum life — from hardball to sipping father's coffee — were, in their view, manifestations of pathology resulting in more pronounced forms of vice and evil. Many of the worse evils of the slum are to be found on the "street"; consequently a major policy recommendation of these early students of metropolitan social life was the increased construction of playgrounds.

Despite the careful detail with which slum life is depicted, the picture emerging from these studies lacks credence and fidelity. Written from the viewpoint of the conventional citizenry, it rarely transcends the limitations incumbent on the outsider. Although the observers toured the world of the West Side and sympathized with its residents, they developed little appreciation for its integrity and thus its workings. Being outsiders — and never transforming themselves — the observers were barely able to describe or comprehend the moral and social life of their subjects. Indeed, the virtual absence of moral life is taken as a cardinal feature of the West Side. They said:

> Boys start out on "crookin" expeditions, taking anything edible or vendible that they can lay their hands on . . . . Here [as in the case of stealing coal] . . . the boys have a definite point of view. They are quite non-moral and have never learned to consider the question of property. Their code is the primitive code of might and they look upon their booty as theirs by right of conquest. Further, the very pressure of poverty is an incentive to stealing for various ends . . . . When one is penniless and knows no moral code and sees one's elders acknowledging none, the temptation to adopt the tactics of the thief and the thug becomes almost irresistible.[9]

The point is not whether this interpretation is valid or not. Cultural relativism may err in the opposite direction by assuming too uncritically the moral character of deviant phenomena. That is an empirical issue that must be resolved specifically for each case. The point is that the observers of the West Side simply failed to consider the complexity of the question of moral systems. It was obvious to them that West Siders lacked a moral system because they were acting in violation of conventional precepts.

The Pittsburgh survey was guided by the same correctional spirit as the West Side studies. Most striking about correctional analysis, in the Pittsburgh survey, is the simplicity of its formulations, the lack of any sense of paradox or irony. The correctional view was — and is — pedestrian: Bad things result from bad conditions. That is almost the entire theory. Moreover there are no tricksters, no surprises in the natural world described by the Pittsburgh surveyors. As we will see, irony became a central feature of the naturalist view, especially as it was advanced by the functionalists.[10] The Pittsburgh surveyors usually felt that analysis was complete when they had succeeded in finding "some consequences of bad streets, unsanitary housing, trade accidents, and the race problem.[11] This tendency is illustrated in an assessment of conditions in Skunk Hollow, a rundown section of Pittsburgh, and the consequences of these conditions.

> Do you wish to see the housing problem? You need only follow Ewing Street the length of a city block and observe. Here are rampant the conditions generated when families with feeble resources attempt to "live," as we say, on land rendered all but valueless because to natural disadvantages have been added artificial ones which wreck home life . . . .
> Do you wish to catch glimpses of the problem of recreation, of juvenile delinquency, of the race problem, of the social evil, of liquor laws broken, of non-employment, and incapacity due to industrial causes; you need only happen in at the Hollow, and see how disintegrating forces assert themselves, when progressive ones are shut off through civic lethargy and selfishness.[12]

Of course, the authors of this study did not believe that bad conditions inevitably corrupt human nature. Here and there, families and persons could be found who withstood the corrupting influence of slum life. The surveyors were pleased to observe that "tucked in between disreputable families of the lowest type, here and there, are bright-faced thrifty Italians."[13]

The stress on the bad consequences of evil phenomena obscured the possibility of paradox and irony, obscured the possibility of evil arising from things deemed good and good from things deemed evil. Nonetheless, there was a certain advantage to such a simple perspective. It made perfectly clear that many deviant enterprises have victims. In some versions of later analysis — especially that of the functionalist — there was often a curious omission of any mention of the victims of deviant behavior. Let us briefly consider the assessments made by the Pittsburgh surveyors of the political machine, organized vice, and prostitution — phenomena which were to become the topics of functional analysis some years later.

The machine system and its political boss were given a rather negative assessment. The prime defects of the "aldermanic system" were well described. The system concentrated "appalling power" and could easily be used for oppression. Though connected with the institution of criminal proceedings, the boss's activities were unsupervised and unregulated. Moreover, it was a system in which most of the judicial officers "[were] not versed in the statutes, [were] sometimes uncouth and generally ignorant." Finally, the machine infused the judicial system with politics and thus corrupted it.[14] These points should be kept in mind when considering Robert Merton's analysis of the machine.[15]

Organized vice and the rackets are viewed even more dimly. Rooted in the "quick riches and easy spending of the successful," organized vice in Pittsburgh, the surveyors found, "attracted not only the anti-social, the unproductive and the parasitic," but also "caused a constant drift of the weak and rebellious away from the mills."[16] Those who were so tempted ceased their honest industry and joined the great mass of criminal followers. "They will live by crime, or starve serving crime."[17]

Organized crime, which preyed on human weakness, attracted not only the racketeers who administered the system, but also an "army of parasites who seek only a living — night bartenders in lawbreaking saloons, bouncers in cut-throat dives, lookouts, doormen, dealers and waiters."[18] Even more malicious were the "boosters, cappers and steerers, who work upon percentages, today the false bell-wethers to rustics at a county fair; tomorrow the fleecers of workmen."[19] Finally, Forbes pointed to the impact of the rackets on honest workmen, the sense in which the "underworld drags upon the workaday life about it."[20] He indicted, for instance, the "chuck-a-luck" machine or "wheel of fortune," which were "for many years, a favorite means for separating the workmen, especially the foreigner, from his pay. Worthless 'prizes' were given out to keep interest alive, and clever boosters . . . were employed who won the more valuable rewards."[21] This stress of victimization should be kept in mind when considering Daniel Bell's more sanguine analysis of the rackets.[22]

Prostitution, though part of the system of organized vice, was singled out for special discussion. Here too, emphasis was put on the seamy aspects and sad consequences. Though alluding to the belief of workingmen that visiting a prostitute is part of having "one big Saturday night town," Forbes would not be deceived. In his external perspective, "there can hardly be a sadder picture than the 'parlor' in a disorderly house where sit the daughters of working people soliciting debauch at the hands of youths of their class."[23] So perturbed was Forbes that he appealed to a sense of working class solidarity. He chided the labor unions of Pittsburgh for not directing their efforts toward the amelioration of this social problem. "My belief," he concluded, "is that labor unions are delinquent is not engaging aggressively in efforts to educate in their members a class consciousness without offense. A broader, more inspiring propaganda, linked to that for higher wages, should be possible to such organizations as the United Mine Workers, The Amalgamated Association of Steel, Iron and Tin Workers, and the various railroad brotherhoods. It is surely time for us to hear the last of the 'mill men's houses,' 'railroader's houses,' and so on in Pittsburgh and elsewhere."[24] Forbes' assessment and his plea to organized labor should be kept in mind when considering Kingsley Davis's analysis of prostitution.[25]

With this brief discussion of the correctional view as it appeared before the first World War, we may now turn to consider the first major American contribution to the naturalistic study of deviant phenomena — the work of the Chicago school. This school began with many of the same views and attitudes as its correctional predecessors, and in some cases never transcended those views. But its entry into deviant worlds was too profound and too dedicated to be without lasting effect. Consequently, in America, it was the Chicagoans who inspired the naturalistic study of deviant phenomena — despite their initial correctional perspective.

Appreciation and the subjective view

Appreciating a phenomena is a fateful decision, for it eventually entails a commitment — to the phenomenon and to those exemplifying it — to render it with fidelity and without violating its integrity. Entering the world of the phenomenon is a radical and drastic method of appreciation, and is perhaps a necessity when the phenomenon is ordinarily condemned. Until appreciation is instituted *as an ordinary element of disciplinary method,* first-hand contact with a deviant world seems the surest way of avoiding reduction of the phenomenon to that which it is not, thus violating its integrity. Accordingly, in the first stages of sociological naturalism, entry into the deviant worlds and appreciation of them were closely linked. Later in the development of sociological naturalism, as we will see, appreciation was essayed at a distance.

The decision to appreciate is fateful in another, perhaps more important way. It delivers the analyst into the arms of the subject who renders the phenomenon, and commits him, though not without regrets or qualifications, to the subject's definition of the situation. This does not mean the analyst always concurs with the subject's definition of the situation; rather, that his aim is to comprehend and to illuminate the subject's view and to interpret the world *as it appears to him.*[26]

The view of the phenomena yielded by this perspective is *interior,* in contrast to the external view yielded by a more objective perspective. The deviant phenomenon is seen from the inside. Consequently, many of the categories having their origin in evaluations made from the outside become difficult to maintain since they achieve little prominence in the interpretations and definitions of deviant subjects. Such was the fate of central theoretic ideas forwarded by the Chicagoans. The subversion and eventual decline of the conceptions of pathology and disorganization resulted partly from the dedicated entry into deviant worlds by the Chicagoans themselves.

Let us consider one of the peculiar worlds entered and described by researchers of the Chicago school. It will be profitable to do this for two reasons: first, because there is much of substance that may still be learned from the Chicagoans — some of their work has never been surpassed; secondly, and perhaps more important, to understand the process by which intimate knowledge of deviant worlds tends to subvert the correctional conception of pathology.

The hobo as subject

In the preface to Nels Anderson's book on homeless men, the reader is told that Anderson had long been interested in hobos, having travelled as one before developing a scholarly interest in the subject.[27] Immediately, therefore, we are alerted to the likelihood that the author will convey an inside, or interior view of the phenomenon. Through the thirties and before, hobos were considered a major social problem. Their world was not viewed as a romantic and esoteric one — as it tends to be now — and thus a correctional perspective on this phenomenon was prevalent. Indeed, Anderson's study, like most emanating from the Chicago school, was supported and partly financed by municipal agencies and commissions that were interested in ameliorating the grievous conditions associated with vice, alcohol, wandering, vagrancy, and begging. Thus, the mixture of naturalist and correctional sentiments was institutionally based as well as existing as an intellectual tension in the work of the Chicago school.

The conception of a peculiar *world,* albeit deviant, with its own logic and integrity is introduced early in Anderson's volume and occupies a fundamental place in the study. Significantly, the conception of a deviant world — unlike the looser current conception of subculture — is ecologically anchored. Deviant subjects are concentrated in a particular locale. This notion is the early and persistent link between what might appear as two disparate outgrowths of the Chicago school — ethnography and ecology. Actually, the two were closely connected. Anderson suggested the ecological segregation of the peculiar world of the hobo. Though only between one and two and a half per cent of Chicago's population consisted of homeless men, Anderson observed that they "are not distributed evenly throughout the city; they are concentrated. segregated . . . in three contiguous, narrow areas close to the center of transportation and trade."[28] Moreover, he based the development of "characteristic institutions" in the ecological concentration. "This segregation of tens of thousands of footloose, homeless . . . men is the fact fundamental to an understanding of the problem. Their concentration has created an isolated cultural area — Hobohemia. Here characteristic institutions have arisen."[29] The *isolated cultural area* was an excellent and useful conception of a peculiar world, though it perhaps posited an exact relation between ecological and moral facts about which we would be more hesitant today. Though ecological segregation facilitates the development of a peculiar world, it may not always be necessary.

The hobo's own perspective was prominent in Anderson's analysis, as he described how the ecological sectors the hobo inhabits appeared to him, and how they were utilized by him. Though pointing to the solidary features of such areas, Anderson did not romanticize the social bonds that appear. He said:

> Every large city has its district into which these homeless types gravitate . . . . Such a section is known as the "stem" or the "main drag." To the homeless men it is home for there, no matter how sorry his lot, he can find those who will understand. The veteran of the road finds other veterans; the old man finds the aged; . . . the radical, the optimist, the inebriate, all find others here to tune in with them. The wanderer finds friends here or enemies, but, and that is at once a characteristic and pathetic feature of Hobohemia, they are friends and enemies only for the day. They meet and pass on.[30]

Note that in the final part of the passage just cited, Anderson asserted a characteristic *feature* of Hobohemia. The conception of a characteristic or essential feature is central to a naturalist approach, and simultaneously, indicates a basic tension within that approach. 'To locate or assert an essential feature of phenomena is a basic part of naturalist analysis, as basic perhaps as posing a relationship between two variables is in more conventional sociological analysis. For the naturalist, the location of essential features is crucial because it is an attempt to cogently assert what the phenomenon *is*. But to assert essential features is inevitably to choose selectively from the factual world; thus naturalism, though it is anti-philosophic in temper, can hardly avoid philosophy in the form of *analytic abstraction*. The assertion of essential features is nothing less than an *analytic summary* of the phenomenon. For Anderson, the feature of *transient relations* was essential in the phenomenal world of hobos.

But the tendency to summarise the phenomenon analytically is countered in naturalism by an opposite tendency toward sheer descriptive detail; thus a tension exists. The essential features of a phenomenon are not in the facts simply waiting to be seen and catalogued. Their perception demands intuition, cogent argument, and evidence. Those preferring analytic summary resolve the tension by suggesting that the *intuitive* assertion of essential features, buttressed by evidence whenever possible, is mandatory if we are to get on with the task of social analysis.[31] From the analytic perspective, a mass of unsorted detail leads nowhere.

The opposite tendency — more dedicatedly ethnographic — appears also in the naturalist tradition. This tendency is defended partly on the grounds that analytic summary is often premature, that it must patiently await the collection of a larger and more comparative volume of fact; partly ethnography is preferred for its own sake. Detailed ethnography, bereft of analytic summary, may be preferred because of the naturalist's traditional fascination with *his* phenomenon in all its aspects. One part of the naturalist wishes to explore all the minute variations of the phenomenal realm which intrigues him. For *him,* analytic summary is tantamount to *reduction,* the high sin to naturalism. But for the analytic naturalist, *summary* is just a simplified rendition of a phenomenon in which its integrity *is not violated.*

There is no final resolution of this tension within naturalism. One need not abstractly choose between the two tendencies, and when a choice is made, it is probably a matter of personal preference. Thus, for instance, Paul Cressey in his volume on taxi-dance halls told us more about many different kinds of dance-halls[32] than I, at any rate, wish to know. But some have a higher tolerance for detail, or perhaps a more dedicated interest in dance-halls.

Whatever the threshold of tolerance, however, it is perhaps possible to agree that detailed description and classification at some point ceases to be useful. The detailed description of mundane human behavior — with virtually no attempt to assert its meaning or relevance — is the vice that attends naturalist virtue. This vice was classically summarized and assessed in Gauguin's barbed remark, directed toward the greatest of all literary naturalists. "Everyone shits," said Gauguin, "but only Zola bothers about it."

In both analytic summary and detailed ethnography, some classification or differentiation within the omnibus form is normally a feature of naturalist analysis. Such differentiation may be taken as evidence that the observer has entered the deviant world and has begun to appreciate its complexity. From the outside, deviant persons, like members of racial minorities, tend to look alike. From the inside, there is bound to be assortment and variety, observable, known, and usually designated by those who inhabit that world. Since the Chicagoans stressed the internal view of the deviant subject, it was characteristic of them to distinguish among the variable manifestations of what to the outsider seemed an omnibus form. Anderson, for instance, developed a classification of homeless men. He began with those already suggested by knowledgeable internal authorities and concluded with his own modification. Ben Reitman, a noted anarchist, intellectual, and hobo of the era, suggested that "There are three types of the genus vagrant: the hobo, the tramp and the bum. The hobo works and wanders, the tramp dreams and wanders and the bum drinks and wanders."[33]

St. John Tucker, a former President of the Hobo College in Chicago, suggested a different classification. "A hobo," he said, "is a migratory worker. A tramp is a migratory non-worker. A bum is a stationary non-worker."[34] Anderson himself accepted Tucker's distinctions but went on to distinguish between seasonal workers and hobos. The seasonal worker, he suggested, "has a particular kind of work that he follows somewhere at least part of the year. The hotels of Hobohemia are a winter resort for many of these seasonal workers whose schedule is relatively fixed and habitudinal."[35] But despite the fact that such workers live part of the year in the same areas, Anderson felt that they should not be confused with hobos, whose style and temperament were essentially different. The hobo adhered to no fixed specialty. "The hobo, proper, is a transient worker without a program. A hobo is a migratory worker in the strict sense of the word. He works at whatever is convenient in the mills, the shops, the mines, the harvests, or any of the numerous jobs that come his way without regard for the times or the seasons."[36] Though he might occasionally exploit other means of gaining livelihood, the hobo primarily worked for a living. "He may even be reduced to begging between jobs, but his living is primarily gained by work and that puts him in the hobo class."[37] Anderson added one more category to those suggested by Tucker, making a total of five classes of homeless men. The final class was termed the "home guard." "The home guard," says Anderson, "like the hobo is a casual laborer, but he works, often only by the day, now at one and again at another of the multitude of unskilled jobs in the city"[38] He estimated nearly half of the homeless men living in Hobohemia were stationary casual laborers, or home guard. Thus, in summary, the seasonal worker, the hobo, and the tramp were migratory; the bum and home guard relatively stationary; the bum and tramp were unwilling to work and lived mostly by begging and petty thieving. The seasonal worker, hobo, and home guard mainly worked for a living.

Of the five classes of homeless men described by Anderson, the home guard were most like conventional people. Yet they were viewed with contempt by the still-migratory hobo and tramp.[39] When younger, members of the home guard were frequently migratory. They had retired from wandering, but they still belonged to the world of migrants. Being migratory was highly regarded in the peculiar world of hobos and tramps, and here we have the hallmark of a moral system, however peculiar. If there are men who fall short of standards — however deviant the standards — a normative system is suggested. Anderson proceeded to describe in considerable detail the system of rules and precepts that guided hobo life. Here too, Anderson anchored the rules and regulations in an ecological base. He suggested the central role of "jungles" in the development and dissemination of hobo standards of conduct. Jungle was the name given to "places where the hobos congregate to pass their leisure time outside the urban centers."[40] These sites were on the outskirts of cities, typically near railroad crossings. Anderson described the role of the jungle in the development of a hobo morality:

> The part played by the jungles as an agency of discipline for the men of the road cannot he overestimated. Here hobo tradition and law are formulated and transmitted. It is the nursery of tramp lore. Here the fledgling learns to behave like an old-timer . . . . Every idea and ideal that finds lodgement in the tramp's fancy may be expressed here in the wayside forum.[41]

Thus, stable traditions and regulations emerged despite the transiency of the men, and despite the absence of administration. Moreover, the traditions and regulations persisted despite shifting personnel who could hardly be thought of as an enduring group. Indeed, those who were most persistent, least transient in their presence — "buzzards" — were held in lowest esteem in the jungle. Here was a world in which transiency was at a premium.

Because of the enforced transiency of the hobos no better demonstration of the key sociological thesis of the "exteriority" of norms — first made by Durkheim — can he imagined. The adherence of traditions and norms to *sites* and *situations* rather than groups was to become a central idea of the Chicago school.[42] Thus, the emergence of a hobo morality may be viewed as a most rigorous test for this central sociological idea. The transiency of personnel and the limited character of the social bonds among them were described by Anderson:

> Jungle populations are ever changing. Every hour new faces appear to take the place of those that have passed on. . . . Every new member is of interest for the news he brings or the rumours that he spreads. . . . But with all the discussion [of the road, working conditions and police] there is seldom any effort to discuss personal relations and connections. Here is one place where every man's past is his own secret.[43]

Despite the transiency and limited character of social bonds and communication, the situation and the site remain stable. Thus, according to sociological rule, regulations and traditions *naturally* emerge. An intentional breaking of jungle regulations was met by sanctions in the form of forced labor, physical punishment, or expulsion. Anderson summarized the regulations:

> Jungle crimes include (1) making fire by night in jungles subject to raids; (2) "hi-jacking" or robbing men at night when sleeping in the jungles; (3) "buzzing" or making the jungle a permanent hangout for jungle

"buzzards" who subsist on the leavings of meals; (4) wasting food or destroying it after eating . . . ; (5) leaving pots and other utensils dirty after using; (6) cooking without first hustling fuel; (7) destroying jungle equipment. In addition to these fixed offenses are other crimes which are dealt with as they arise.[44]

Thus, we see that the deviant world of hobos and tramps was socially organized. It contained differentiated *roles* which were ordered and stratified and explicit *rules* which were disseminated and enforced. Moreover, the Chicagoans stressed a third principle: Deviant worlds possessed their own peculiar satisfaction or *rewards* that were by no means limited aspects of the deviant enterprise. That deviant worlds have their own intrinsic — and to the outsider, esoteric — satisfactions was another thesis deriving from the internal, subjective view of naturalism. These satisfactions are known to the inhabitants of the deviant world and may be inferred by the perceptive observer. In Anderson's study, some of them were quite ordinary, others rather esoteric:

In the jungle the hobo is his own housewife. He not only cooks . . . but has invented dishes that are peculiar to jungle life. Chief among these is "mulligan stew." [Moreover,] the art of telling a story is diligently cultivated by the "bos" in the assemblies about the fire. This vagabond existence tends to enrich the personality and long practice has developed in some of these men an art of personal narrative that has greatly declined elsewhere.[45]

* * * * *

The neoChicagoans

Appreciation of deviant phenomena founded on taking the internal view of the subject was begun by the Chicago school and continued in the functionalist view. In some measure that appreciation has become institutionalized in contemporary sociology. But as usual, an institutionalized sentiment survives in routine form. The routinized form of appreciation is *neutrality,* which is another thing altogether. Neutrality, buttressed as it is by the philosophy of science, is the sentiment toward deviant phenomena commended by most contemporary sociologists. We are to empathize with neither the correctional enterprise nor its deviant subjects (though, according to disciplinary ethics we may, if we wish, contract with the former). Thus it would be untrue to suggest that the appreciative attitude of naturalism has simply become the stance of general sociology. To trace the continuation of the appreciative attitude, we must focus more narrowly on a smaller group: an assortment of sociologists who share a more or less similar viewpoint. Though probably premature, and perhaps even a disservice to these individual sociologists, such similarity and distinctiveness warrants saddling them with a name and conceiving them as something like a school of thought. I will call them neoChicagoans because they have revived the Chicago school's stress on direct observation and field work, have maintained and extended the relevance of the subject's view, and in a variety of other ways have indicated their appreciation of deviant phenomena and their connected enterprises. A theme that has more or less unified the neoChicagoans has been their emphasis on the *process of becoming deviant* and the part played by the official registrars of deviation in that process.[57] A small but increasing number of sociologists identify with this viewpoint. In [this volume], the discussion will focus mainly on the contributions to this viewpoint of Edwin Lemert, Erving Goffman, and Howard Becker.

Howard Becker, in *Outsiders,* pointed to the importance of the subjective view immediately. It is, he suggested, relevant to the very conception of deviation. "Outsiders" has a double meaning. The first meaning is conventional: deviates are outsiders. The second meaning is its reverse: conventional folk are outsiders, from the perspective of those involved in illicit activities. Viewing the social scene *as it appears to the persons we are trying to comprehend,* Becker explained:

> But the person who is thus labeled an outsider may have a different view of the matter. He may not accept the rule by which he is being judged and may not regard those who judge him as either competent or legitimately entitled to do so. Hence, a second meaning of the term emerges: the rule-breaker may feel his judges are *outsiders.*[58]

No inference of a complete division of opinion or a complete withdrawal of legitimacy need be drawn from Becker's statement. Its point is that we must factually ascertain the measure of consent or dissent, and to do that we must maintain the perspective of the deviant subject. A stress on the correctional perspective would be just as appropriate if the subject of inquiry were the correctors. Moreover, Becker's subjective stress need not mean that the assessments and views of deviant persons are to be taken at face value. Deviant persons may consciously attempt to mislead observers or other outsiders; they may unwittingly deceive themselves or otherwise mistake their predicament. The presenting of fronts is consistent with the capacity of subjects to use themselves in relating to their environment and the persons who compose it. The front is part of managing interaction, a conception that receives considerable attention among the neoChicagoans.[59] Just as the naturalist view avoids suppressing features of phenomena that are detestable by conventional standards, it avoids equating the subjective view with gullibility. Presenting a front, putting people on, and telling prepared sad tales are features of social life, deviant or conventional.

The misleading of the observer may be especially troublesome in the study of deviant phenomena. Since authority may frequently intervene to counteract or arrest the deviant tendency, deviant persons must frequently be devious. They are not alone in this respect, though by definition being devious seems senseless without being deviant. As a matter of degree, at any rate, conventional persons have less reason to be devious. They may *be* devious, and sometimes are, but in that case our definition rescues us — they are merely being senseless. Conversely, being devious in the presence of outsiders may be counted a normal feature of persons participating in deviant phenomena.[60] Edwin Lemert suggested that sad tales are usually told by prostitutes to clients and researchers. Less obviously, he argued that much of the literature on white-slave traffic was premised on myths emanating from the sad tales told by prostitutes.[61]

Sophisticated disbelief is not inconsistent with an appreciation of the internal view of phenomena; nor is the appreciation of the devious an insuperable obstacle to social research. Being devious is based on the fear of apprehension, the sense that others expect a justification for what is commonly regarded as a sorry lot, and the intrinsic satisfactions associated with making fools of persons ordinarily bestowed with dignity or wisdom. If those are the bases, it is primarily the outsider who will be misled. Thus, the researcher may overcome this obstacle if he is defined as a courtesy insider or if he disguises his true identity and passes.

Self-deception is more complicated than the intentional deception of outsiders, but the exploration of that possibility, too, is essential in naturalist description and consistent with the subjective view. To view phenomena internally is to stress the way they seem, or appear, to the subjects experiencing them. That appearance is relevant and consequential. But the stress on appearance in no way precludes the observation that subjects may be so situated as to glimpse the phenomenon in a special, peculiar, or distorted fashion. Their relations may be so structured as to obscure aspects of the world surrounding them. From a phenomenal standpoint, the appearance *is* a reality; but so too is distortion or refraction. Thus, for instance, juvenile delinquents may believe that others in their company are committed to the performance of delinquent acts, but partly that is because public discussion of delinquency is severely inhibited by status anxiety.[62] The subject's perspective must be comprehended and illuminated, not enshrined. The angle of vision and consequent refraction must be considered as well as the substance of what is seen.

Besides a commitment to the subjective view, qualified by an appreciation of deception, the neoChicagoans followed their predecessors in commending detailed description of the deviant phenomenon itself; correspondingly, they are probably less concerned with locating the social or personal factors allegedly leading persons to deviation than most sociologists. Indeed, as will be suggested later, there is less faith in the causal efficacy of such factors. The neoChicagoan view was well summarized by Howard Becker. Though there are a great many studies of delinquency, he observed:

> Very few tell us in detail what a juvenile delinquent does in his daily round of activity and what he thinks about himself, society, and his activities. . . . One consequence [of this insufficiency] is the construction of faulty or inadequate theories. Just as we need precise anatomical description of animals before we can begin to theorize and experiment with their physiological and biochemical functioning, just so we need precise and detailed descriptions of social anatomy before we know just what phenomena are present to be theorized about. . . . We do not . . . [then] have enough studies of deviant behavior . . . [or of] enough kinds of deviant behavior. Above all, we do not have enough studies in which the person doing the research has achieved close contact with those he studies, so that he can become aware of the complex and manifold character of the deviant activity. . . . If . . . [the researcher] . . . is to get an accurate and complete account of what deviants do . . . he must spend at least some time observing them in their natural habitat as they go about their ordinary activities.[63]

Once observed in their natural habitat, once their nefarious activities are put in proper context, once the subject is fully appreciated, the deviant person comes into proper, human focus. In what follows, we will see that the naturalist's stress on appreciation helped subvert the theoretical preconceptions that informed — or misinformed — the correctional study of deviant phenomena.

Notes

1. George Borrow, *The Zincali, An Account of the Gypsies of Spain* (New York: G.P. Putnam's Sons, 3rd ed., 1843), I, xv.

2. Edwin Sutherland and Donald Cressey, *Criminology* (New York: J.B. Lippincott Co., 6th ed., 1960), pp. 237–252. Also see David Maurer, *The Big Con* (Indianapolis: The Bobbs-Merrill Co., Inc., 1940); and Maurer, *Whiz Mob* (Gainesville, Fla.: American Dialect Society, 1955).

3. For a discussion of early British sociology and the influence of social work, or "practical philanthropy," see Donald MacRae, *Ideology and Society* (New York: Free Press of Glencoe, Inc., 1962), p 7. For a consideration of early American sociology and the great concern with pathology and its amelioration, see Jessie Bernard, "The History and Prospects of Sociology in the United States," in George Lundberg, Read Bain and Nels Anderson (eds), *Trends in American Sociology* (New York: Harper & Row, Publishers, 1929), pp. 1–71.

4. *West Side Studies* (New York: Russell Sage Foundation, 1914), I, 29–30.

5. *West Side Studies*, p. 36.

6. *West Side Studies*, p. 40.

7. *West Side Studies*, p. 75.

8. *West Side Studies*, p. 61.

9. *West Side Studies*, pp. 142–143.

10. See [Chapter 4].

11. *The Pittsburgh Survey,* ed. Paul Kellog (New York: Survey Associates, Russell Sage Foundation, 1914), V, 127.

12. Florence Lattimore, "Three Studies in Housing and Responsibility," in *The Pittsburgh Survey,* p. 124.

13. *Pittsburgh Survey,* VI, 351. In Pittsburgh, apparently it was the Italians who were the aspiring and conscientious minority at the beginning of the twentieth century. East European Jews in the same city were rather disappointing. Many of the men were to be found pimping for the whoring members of their "race." The Pittsburgh investigators report: "On a lower level [of prostitution] were the two- and one-dollar houses. These were by far the most numerous and most profitable. They were filled with young Jewesses, many of them American born, with Pennsylvania Dutch, . . . Irish and German, Canadians, and a few 'drifters' from wornout American stock. . . . In a majority of the [cheaper] brothels not operated by Negresses, the proprietresses were Jewesses, and the men who financed them were of the same race. And of the same race were a majority of the pimps or cadets who lived wholly or in part on the earnings of the women. . . ." (*Ibid.,* pp. 351, 360.) For a somewhat different picture of Jews and Italians see Jackson Toby, "Hoodlum or Business Man: An American Dilemma," in Marshall Sklare, *The Jews* (New York: Free Press of Glencoe, Inc., 1958).

14. *Pittsburgh Survey,* V, 155.

15. To be discussed in [Chapter 3].

16. James Forbes, "The Reverse Side," in *Pittsburgh Survey,* VI, 307.

17. *Ibid.,* p. 316.

18. *Ibid.,* p. 316–317.

19. *Ibid.,* p. 317.

20. *Ibid.,* p. 319.

21. *Ibid.,* p. 319.

22. See [Chapters 3 and 4].

23. *Ibid.,* p. 349.

24. *Ibid.,* p. 349.

25. See [Chapter 4].

26. As will become apparent later, a commitment to the subjective view has even more profound consequences for the direction and tenor of sociological analysis. A serious commitment to the subjective view cannot grudgingly stop with the appreciation of the subject's definition of his specific deviant predicament. It must also entail an appreciation of the ordinary subject's philosophical definitions of his general predicament. Concretely, this means that the ordinary assumptions of members of society like the capacity to *transcend* circumstances, the capacity to *improvise,* the capacity to *intend* must be treated seriously and occupy a central place in the analysis of social life. The question of transcending circumstances, and the violation of this sense in primitive sociology will be discussed later. A limited discussion of intentionality and the violation of that sense in criminology appears in my *Delinquency and Drift,* Chapters 1 and 6.

27. Nels Anderson, *The Hobo* (Chicago: University of Chicago Press, 1923).

28. *Ibid.,* p. 14.

29. *Ibid.,* p. 14.

30. *Ibid.,* p. 4.

31. Max Weber, for instance, defends this position. His rendition of the conception, essential feature, is "ideal type." See, for instance, Max Weber, *The Protestant Ethic and the Spirit of Capitalism* (New York: Charles Scribner's Sons, 1930).

32. Paul Cressey, *The Taxi-Dance Hall* (Chicago: University of Chicago Press, 1932). See, for instance, p. 18.

33. Anderson, *op. cit.,* p. 87.

34. *Ibid.,* p. 87.

35. *Ibid.,* p. 90.

36. *Ibid.,* pp. 90–91.

37. *Ibid.,* p. 91.

38. *Ibid.,* p. 96.

39. *Ibid.,* pp. 6, 10, 96.

40. *Ibid.*, p. 16.

41. Ibid., pp. 25–26.

42. Clifford Shaw and Henry McKay in *Juvenile Delinquency and Urban Areas* (Chicago: University of Chicago Press, 1942) demonstrate with great cogency the similar point that a delinquent tradition is anchored in certain neighborhoods irrespective of the shifting ethnic groups inhabiting them.

43. *Ibid.*, pp. 19–20.

44. *Ibid.*, pp. 20–21.

45. *Ibid.*, pp. 18–19.

[46–56 not included in this volume].

57. This final theme will be discussed in [Chapter 7, "Signification."]

58. Howard Becker, *Outsiders* (New York: The Free Press of Glencoe, Inc., 1963), pp. 1–2.

59. See, for instance, Erving Goffman, *Presentation of Self in Everyday Life* (Garden City, N.Y.: Doubleday and Co. [Anchor] 1959) and *Stigma* (Englewood Cliffs, N.J.: Prentice-Hall, Inc., 1963). Also see Sheldon Messinger, Harold Sampson, and Robert Towne, "Life as Theatre," *Sociometry,* March 1962.

60. In certain forms of sexual deviation, such as voyeurism, there are no insiders. Thus, being devious marks the voyeur even in the interaction with his unwitting victim.

61. Edwin Lemert, *Social Pathology* (New York: McGraw-Hill Book Company, 1951), p. 255.

62. See my *Delinquency and Drift* (New York: John Wiley & Sons, Inc., 1964), pp. 50–59.

63. Becker, *op. cit.,* pp. 166–170.

Crime, Punishment and Society

7. Deviance, Latent Functions and Society
Steven Box

For most of his adult life the seventeenth-century English philosopher Thomas Hobbes was a worried man. England was not a green and pleasant country; instead it was full of alarming sounds. There were the frightening shouts of the new middle class for more liberty, the thumping footsteps of the underprivileged on their way to Parliament, stamping out demands for more democracy, and the bells of St Peter's in Rome clanging out the Catholic Church's demand for more intervention in the affairs of the English State. These all disturbed Hobbes, for what he wanted was the peace and security necessary to pursue his beloved academic interests. How could he think with all that din going on outside?

Reduced to an acute state of anxiety, and glimpsing a historical shift back into a state of nature in which life was 'nasty, brutish, solitary, poor and short', Hobbes resolved to produce a blueprint for avoiding the impending anarchy. He reasoned that without rules people are unpredictable and untrustworthy. Only with strict and invariably enforced rules can individuals live in peace and security. Consequently Hobbes recommended a Leviathan, a Sovereign, whose primary task would be the determination of rules designed to avoid 'natural' anarchical tyranny. The Leviathan would remain above daily divisive squabbles and, in return for creating the rules to protect life and property, it would expect unquestioning subordination from citizens.

The mere existence of rules, no matter how well designed, would not solve everything, for, just as the reasonable person in the state of nature is a constant prey for the unreasonable person, so individuals under the state of political contract are constantly niggled by the thought of, and occasionally the fact that, others will not keep to the rules. Fortunately, the existence of the Leviathan is reassuring. Whereas, previously, whenever they were confronted by malevolent, brutal, unreasonable individuals, the rest had to fare as best they could — and that invariably meant subservience — they could now call and depend upon the power of the Leviathan to control and contain these ruffians.

In Hobbes' view then, individuals who break the law need to be controlled and punished, for they threaten to upset the security and stability of life made possible only under the social contract. Deviance, in other words, is dangerous. For if we conceive of society as an organic whole, and to some extent Hobbes did this, then diseases are disruptive; and in analogous translation, deviance is a disease in the social body, it is a pathology which, like a cancerous growth, has to be cut out before it spreads and kills the patient. 'Control Deviance or Die' may have been a demonstration banner that Hobbes would have carried, had he not been in a constant state of fear that to expose oneself to the public was to risk physical harm.

Steven Box: 'Deviance, Latent Functions and Society' from *DEVIANCE, REALITY AND SOCIETY* (Holt, Rinehart and Winston, 1981), pp. 25–53.

Such a view of deviance — as a disruptive and evil phenomenon — was hardly profound even in 1651, and few people could have responded, 'Eureka! So that's it.' But that is to be expected, for Hobbes, important philosopher though he may have been, was no insightful sociologist when it came to understanding the latent functions of deviance.

Sociologists have a way of looking at ordinary things and seeing them as extraordinary. Of course, everyone knows, even without reading Hobbes, that deviant behaviour can ('under certain conditions', adds the sociologist) undermine the stability of society. But only some sociologists, and those who take them seriously, also know that under certain other conditions deviant behaviour maintains, indeed is even an integral part of, social stability.

This particular irony — that deviant behaviour, both directly and indirectly, helps sustain conformity and stability — was suggested almost simultaneously by Durkheim and Marx. For quite different reasons, both of them wanted to focus their attention on the part the criminal played in maintaining existing social arrangements: Durkheim because he wanted to answer the question, 'How is society possible?', and Marx because he wanted to answer the question, 'How is capitalist society possible?'

In his early work, *Division of Labor in Society* (1893), Durkheim nicely caught the irony of deviant behaviour sustaining social integration:

> Crime brings together upright consciences and concentrates them. We have only to notice what happens, particularly in a small town, when some moral scandal has been committed. They stop each other on the street, they visit each other, they seek to come together to talk of the event and wax indignant in common. From all the similar impressions which are exchanged, there emerges a unique temper . . . which is everybody's without being anybody's in particular. That is the public temper. (1947; p. 102)

Marx, making a similar sociological observation, but this time pinning it down to a more specific historical period, namely nineteenth-century Europe, suggested that

> The criminal produces an impression now moral, now tragic, and renders a 'service' by arousing their moral and aesthetic sentiments of the public . . . the criminal interrupts the monotony and security of bourgeois life . . . he protects it from stagnation and brings forth that restless tension, that mobility of spirit without which the stimulus of competition would itself be blunted . . . crime, by its ceaseless development of new means of attacking property calls into existence new measures of defence and its productive effects are . . . great . . . in stimulating the invention of machines. (Bottomore and Rubel, 1956; pp. 159–60)

Of these complementary views of the social functions of deviance, it is the 'functional' view handed down by Durkheim and Marx which has occupied the attention of sociologists, and not the 'dysfunctional' view expounded by Hobbes. However, before going on to consider the 'fruits' of this attention, we have to consider the recent revival of interest in the 'dysfunctional' possibility shown by a number of authors who could

176

be described, for purposes of giving them some identifying label, as the neo-classic/conservative revivalists. This rather clumsy label does at least bring out two preoccupations of these writers: firstly, they have been concerned to argue in favour of the unity between offence and punishment as against the present system of individualized justice, i.e. they believe that individuals should be punished in strict accord with the seriousness of their offence, whereas individualized justice advocates treating individuals according to their *needs* and not their *deeds*. Since historically our present individualized criminal justice system came in on the shirt-tails of 'positivism' which, as a body of criminological theory and practice, rose in fashion during the nineteenth century and replaced the previously accepted 'classical' arguments of Beccaria and Bentham, it seems appropriate to call these current writers 'neo-classical'. Secondly, since they have been concerned to strengthen arguments in favour of a more-law-and-order society as against the liberal–left permissiveness which seemed to mesmerize academics, criminologists and legislators during the 1960s, it seems reasonable to refer to them as conservative. The label 'neo-classical/conservatives' having been justified, what do these authors argue?

Writing about the 'paradox of rising crime' in a period of unparallelled affluence, Wilson (1975) brings out strongly both the social disruption 'high' crime levels can bring, and the way this provokes previously law-abiding citizens to 'think again'. Thus he claims that

> Predatory crimes does not merely victimize individuals, it impedes and, in the extreme case, even prevents the formation and maintenance of community. By disrupting the delicate nexus of ties, formal and informal, by which we are linked with our neighbors, crime atomizes society and makes of its members mere individual calculators estimating their own advantage, especially their own chances for survival amidst their fellows. Common undertakings become difficult or impossible, except for those motivated by a shared desire for protection. (Coming together for protection may, of course, lead to a greater sense of mutual aid and dependence and provide the basis for larger and more positive commitments. It was out of a desire for self-defense, after all, that many of the earliest human settlements arose. But then it was a banding together against a common *external* enemy. Mutual protection against an enemy within is more difficult to achieve, less sustaining of a general sense of community, and more productive of conflict as disputes arise over who is victim and who the aggressor.) . . . what constitutes the 'urban problem' for a large percentage (perhaps a majority) of urban citizens, is a sense of the failure of community. By 'community' . . . I refer to a desire for the observance of standards of right and seemly conduct in the public places in which one lives and moves, those standards to be consistent with — and supportive of — the values and life styles of the particular individual. Around one's home, the place where one shops, and the corridors through which one walks there is for each of us a public space wherein our sense of security, self-esteem, and propriety is either reassured or jeopardized by the people and events we encounter. Viewed

this way, the concern for community is less the 'need' for 'belonging' (or, in equally vague language, the 'need' to overcome feelings of 'alienation' or 'anomie') than the normal but not compulsive interest of any rationally self-interested person in his and his family's environment. (pp. 21–22)

And he ends his book on the following chilling note:

Some persons will shun crime even if we do nothing do deter them, while others will seek it out even if we do everything to reform them. Wicked people exist. Nothing avails except to set them apart from innocent people. And many people, neither wicked nor innocent, but watchful, dissembling and calculating of their opportunities, ponder our reaction to wickedness as a cue to what they might profitably do. We have trifled with the wicked, made sport of the innocent, and encouraged the calculators. Justice suffers, and so do we all.

Empirical support for these clear views on the damage ordinary crimes, if they are perceived to be rising beyond historically recorded levels, can create — a break-down of community ties, and a rise in informal, vigilante-type protective responses which further tear a community apart — was produced by Conklin after surveying a Bostonian high-crime-rate area (the urban community of Port City) and a low-crime-rate area (the suburban Belleville). He concluded (1975), in opposition to Durkheim:

Crime generates suspicion and distrust, thereby weakening the social fabric of a community . . . Crime leads people to avoid others to take self-protective security measures, both of which actions erect barriers between the residents of a community. By diminishing social interaction and reducing natural surveillance of public areas, informal social control over potential criminals may be weakened and crime rates may increase.

When people are faced with a crime problem, they often turn to the police. When the police are unable to curb crime, citizens blame them for their ineffectiveness. One consequence is that people are less willing to report crime to the police. This diminishes the probability that offenders will be apprehended, since the police learn of most crimes from citizens. As the risk to offenders decreases, they may be more willing to commit crimes.

If people react to crime by denying personal responsibility for crime prevention and by becoming retreatist and defensive, they may be unwilling to assist victims of the crimes that they actually observe. If potential offenders become aware of citizen reluctance to become involved in the prevention of crime and the assistance of victims, social interaction and the surveillance of public spaces will have little effect on the crime problem. (p. 248)

These contemporary anguished cries of alarm and dispair for the 'loss of community' have not been emitted only from American social commentators; English authors, too, have demonstrated considerable rhetorical skills to force home the message that crime levels can damage, and are currently damaging, our community. Thus Morgan (1978), in an interesting and provocative critique of liberal and radical criminologists and all the spectrum of supporters of recent liberal legislation, such as the Childrens' and Young Persons' Act, 1969, warns us that the 'new barbarism', where

> there is an absence of value, not a distortion. When life becomes not just a cheap or exchangeable commodity, but worthless, and plunder is seemingly neither for consumption, wealth nor power, it is as petty as it is fearful, as oppressive as it is mundane. The violence, the destruction, and the youth of its perpetrators combine to produce a barbarity without splendour or honour; something tatty, haphazard and sordid, as trivial as baby talk in a world where we are increasingly sport for wanton little boys

will spread out from its present working-class enclaves to engulf us all. She writes (1978):

> Areas of low delinquency today have a habit of becoming swallowed by high delinquency ones tomorrow, and no one escapes the cost. Very many 'desirable' middle-class areas, perhaps less violent, now display an assimilating squalor in their public places, a legacy of numerous acts of petty vandalism, pilfering and filthy habits. (p. 13)

Thus,

> If the cities are to be saved as centres of a civilized urban life, and not plunged into gutted and fearful wastelands, as in some American urban centres, delinquency will have to be tackled as a problem with high priority — perhaps as *the* urban problem. City life cannot exist without security in its open spaces, some unarmed trust and reciprocity. In Britain, as on the American pattern, there is a mass exodus of skilled workers and middle-class groups from the metropolis and other inner cities revealed by studies like that of the GLC. These areas are left with heavily welfare-dependent populations: the old, the sick, the handicapped, the uneducated, the dull, the retarded and the unskilled. This represents a loss of power, voice, social skills, support and informal help and funding. What is not realised here — or is unmentionable — is that although the movement from the cities has many other long-term causes, delinquency has now ceased to be merely a symptom of urban breakdown in *this* country (if it ever was) and has become a major contributor to it. It accelerates the same vicious social circle which one can see in some schools, where those teachers who can no longer stand it leave, thus further weakening resistance to the problem by the loss of consistency, experience and familiarity. (pp. 12–13)

These writings, although clear in their denunciation of liberal–left thinkers, are unclear when it comes to a fairly obvious distinction between the dysfunction of rising crime and the dysfunction of *perceived* rising crime. The unpleasant effects, to which they all refer, are effects stemming from the common perception that crime is rising, and hence something about which one should be both frightened and protected. What relationship this perception has to actual crime rates is problematical. I do not want to be cast as one who sees no evil, but it is not clear that in objective terms our cities are now more violent, unsafe places to be in than they ever were. Of course the rates of street crime recorded by the police are, and have been, increasing, but that does not necessarily mean that crimes are actually increasing. It could be accounted for by changes in the willingness of people to report crimes to the police, or the willingness of police to accept reports. The issue is simply cloudy. But even if it were the case that actual street crimes were rising, that in and of itself would not necessarily result in frightening people more about being criminally victimized. For between the actual rising level of crime and the effects so well carved out by the neo-classical/conservative revivalists, there has to be an intervening stage; individuals have to perceive that crime is rising and that it constitutes a personal threat to them. This perceptual alternation is unlikely to spring from personal experience because, even in times of rising crime rates, individuals rarely experience directly the events which comprise these phenomena. Instead, as the Glasgow University Media Group (1976, 1980) point out, individuals' knowledge about the social world, including crime and punishment, is second hand; it is mediated not only by the media which report rising crime rates, but by their interpretation of these events, an interpretation which frequently parrots the more calculated views of ambitious politicians. The fact is that recent elections, both in America and Britain, have been partly fought, and won, on a law-and-order platform. These successes are accounted for not because the views of aspiring politicians accurately reflect what is undoubtedly a real problem of uncontrolled 'street crime' but because these very views contribute towards an amplification of such a problem. When the media report, and report again and again, the views of politicians on the worsening of street crime and the need for a strong disciplined response, it becomes real in its consequences; people begin to believe it, and consequently, many of them give their support for a political law-and-order campaign. Thus, because rising 'street crime' can be perceived by the public as both real and threatening, and something which unites everyone since we could all, by the very random and wanton nature of street crime and criminals, be victimized, its careful manipulation can be very useful to politicians seeking to mask their otherwise divisive domestic social and economic policies as well as their semi-colonial foreign ambitions. This possibility was certainly not lost on Nixon in the 1968 and 1972 elections, nor on Thatcher during the 1979 election.

We thus glimpse that behind the rhetoric of crime as dysfunctional, which is not necessarily untrue — street crime is a problem, not only for conservative but also for socialist criminologists (Crime and Social Justice Collective, 1976; Platt, 1978; Young, 1975) — there lurks a more sinister truth, namely that 'rising crime rates' are a useful ideological tool with which politicians whip up generalized public fear and hence gain electoral support for a law-and-order programme which at the same time gives political leaders a mandate — unwittingly granted — to carry out other, more socially divisive, programmes. This greater truth — *that behind the dysfunctions of crime there might be hidden benefits for a few* — can be further revealed if we turn to the phenomenon which has primarily preoccupied sociologists, namely that, ironically, crime can be functional.

Out of evil can come good. That is the ironic view which has pleased the devious sociological imagination. But again this irony, like its banal and mundane opposite —

evil causes evil — can be rendered in a simple and mystifying way. Thus to say that deviance can be functional masks more than it reveals, for, as will become apparent when we consider a number of examples, when this irony is explored it has to be extended as follows: the societal reactions to deviance can be functional, at least for the more powerful, because it contributes to the essentially ideological process of clarification, maintenance and modification of social rules. This extension becomes necessary because as the latent functions of deviance are explored, we are forced to choose between two different and competing models of society — the consensual and the conflict. Instead of viewing society as an organic body in which (deviant) parts are cancerous, we are pushed into viewing society as a precarious entity, emerging out of a constant struggle between competing subjective definitions of reality. In this arena of competition, there are some definitions of reality which direct those who accept them to behave in ways which, when viewed from other angles, are not tolerable. Whether or not this intolerable behaviour is treated as intolerable, and those who emit it labelled as deviants, depends upon the contestants' relative access to, or possession of, the power and resources for defining social reality.

If we care to follow the path of sociological irony, we start off by unmasking the deception that deviant behaviour is essentially evil, and end up viewing society as a product of a struggle between various parties, in which the victorious simply employ the conception of deviance as a strategic tool to beat down, eliminate or weaken any opposition. Those who are in authority then become necessarily less than good, and certainly not as defensible as Hobbes' Leviathan. For those who are in authority come to be so usually through employing the same principal tactics as the unreasonable person in the state of nature. They rarely need to be overtly vicious and brutal — although that is never far away; instead they engage in symbolic mystifications as a means of gaining compliance from subjects. Thus one of the daily tactics in this struggle to maintain a particular definition of reality is the artful manipulation of who is deviant, and what deviance means to our (meaning *their,* i.e. the powerful's) survival. As Reiman (1979) puts it,

> Our picture of crime — the portrait that emerges from arrest statistics, prison populations, politicians' speeches, news media and fictionalized presentations, the portrait that in turn influences lawmakers and criminal justice policy makers — is not a photograph of the real dangers that threaten us. Its features are not simply traced from the real dangers in the social world. Instead, it is a piece of creative art. It is a picture in which some dangers are portrayed and others omitted. (p. 5)

Since those crimes omitted from this creative portrait [see Chapters 3 and 6] are usually committed by the more powerful, such as governments or their agencies, multinational corporations, police forces, etc., and those included are committed more frequently by the underprivileged, the societal reaction to crime can be viewed as an artfully contrived ideological shock-wave intended to warn the middle classes that their real enemy is beneath and not above them, and to put the working classes on their guard against the dangerous criminals in their midst. The ideological message in the societal reaction to crime, the reaction which ends with the construction of a criminal population, is very clear: it is the powerless poor of whom the majority of the public should be afraid and not the powerful rich; it is the powerful rich, in the form of law-makers and law-enforcers, to whom the majority should turn dependently for protection. We are encouraged to seek protection from those who criminally victimize us most, whilst those who commit far less serious crimes are dangled before us as the real cause of our misery and the real threat to our lives, limbs and property. Thus behind the benevolent posing of the Leviathan there lurk more unpleasant realities, one of which is that it is a protector of large-scale organized corporate and government crime rather than a protector of those victimized by these crimes. It is, when viewed in this jaundiced light, an even better protection racket than that discovered by Bell (1961) in his investigation of New York's 'racket-ridden longshoremen' (pp. 175–209).

The latent social functions of (societal reaction to) deviance

Sociologists who have sought to illustrate how deviance contributes to the clarification, maintenance and modification of social rules have revealed only part of the total ironic relationship between deviance and social stability. More detailed implications of this ironic relationship still need to be drawn out. However, to do this we need to retrace the steps and simply illustrate how deviance apparently contributes to social integration.

Deviance as a clarifier of social rules

For an example of the contribution deviance can make to the clarification of social rules we can go back to a period of civil conflict which occurred during the middle period of Hobbes' life. This civil conflict, however, caused him little worry for it happened in a faraway place, Boston, Massachusetts in the 1630s.

Shortly after the New England settlers had started to build a society based upon the Puritan conceptions of the good life, strange sounds began to be heard. At first, however, no one quite knew what they were; something possibly sinister was being said, but it was too faint or surrounded by too much fuzziness for it to be heard clearly. Slowly and timorously some New Englanders began listening very carefully to what the clergy were saying; and sure enough, it was from these sacred sources that sinister sounds were being made. For when the clergy talked about the *covenant of grace* they began to do so in such a way that it resembled more and more the *covenant of works*. Could it be true? The harder they listened the more confused they became. Clearly the clergy had shifted their mood, but they expressed it in such a way that only the very astute listener between the words could comprehend the fuller implications. And when grasped, the implications were traumatic.

The root cause of this shift in the mood of the clergy, and the reason for its traumatic effects, can only be put down to a change in the context in which the New England Puritans lived. In the context of Old Europe, Puritanism was a revolutionary religious phenomenon. In its struggle with the established Catholic and Protestant Churches, the Puritan Church preached the *covenant of grace*. Grace was conceived as a condition bestowed on some men ordained by God. To be in a stage of grace was to be in receipt of an intimate and unalterable gift from God (or, possibly in blasphemous terms, a passport to the Kingdom of Heaven) with which no earthly powers, sacred or secular, could interfere. Such a conception struck a thunderous blow at the Established

182

Church's *covenant of works*. For according to this covenant only those who are virtuous, obedient and loyal, in short, only those who really work at it, will enter the Kingdom of Heaven. In the context of sixteenth-century Europe, the *covenant of works* underpinned the Established Church's authority, whilst the *covenant of grace* undermined it. 'Why', reasoned the man in a state of grace, 'obey the Catholic or Protestant Church and their officials, when God has already graced me and ordained my unearthly destiny?'

As a revolutionary religious conception, the *covenant of grace* was indeed a politically useful tool, for it justified the Puritan stand against orthodoxy. The inherent disadvantages of such a conception became increasingly clear, *at least to the clergy,* when the Puritans found themselves in a new context on the other side of the Atlantic. For in New England, Puritanism was no longer a revolutionary force encircled by religious enemies; it was instead the 'Established Church'.

In such a radically modified context the Puritan clergy, like all political leaders, began to shake off their radical views and replace them with more conservative leanings. In brief, the clergy began to feel the need for the led to be obedient and subservient; but how could this be achieved with a population suckled on the *covenant of grace*? Not giving up in despair, the clergy began to glance enviously at the authority enjoyed by their European counterparts, the leaders of the Established Churches. From being viewed as alien and undesirable, the *covenant of works* was gradually viewed as friendly, almost embraceable. But the Puritan clergy could not go that far, even if they desired such a close affinity. To have switched round completely was to have invited rebellion; to have avoided switching round was to have remained relatively powerless and without authority. To gain power and yet avoid rebellion the clergy took the only course open to them; they engaged in word-magic. They continued to preach the *language* of the *covenant of grace* but not the content. By sleight of word and intention they managed to interpose themselves, bodily and spiritually, between the Graced and the Giver of Grace.

Unable to dispose of, or in any way amend, the state of grace, the clergy resorted to the argument that *the state of grace was a condition for which one had to be prepared*; and, being peculiarly nearer to God, who better to prepare His chosen few than the clergy themselves? Thus the congregational members began to hear the message. They were told that they should be obedient to the clergy and respect their authority, because the clergy, and only the clergy, could prepare them for the Life Hereafter. The congregational members might be in a state of grace, but only the clergy knew how this state might be gracefully accepted. In return for communicating this sacred knowledge, the clergy expected secular authority.

Naturally the import of the distinction between the covenant of grace as it was understood in Europe and as it was being preached by the Massachusetts clergy in the 1630s was lost on most congregationalists. Their state of grace was not being denied them, so what was happening could not be that important. But it was. The clergy were engaged in the artful exercise of shifting the boundaries of society. Whereas subordination to the clergy was unspeakable in Europe, the clergy were beginning to speak about it in Massachusetts. They chose not to put it very clearly, but even in their distorted versions they were gradually communicating more than they intended. And it was this that was creating a growing sense of unease in New England.

It remained for one poor soul to be pushed into the limelight, to capitalize on this growing sense of unease, and nearly to suffer capital punishment for her troubles. Such a fate awaited Mrs Anne Hutchinson.

Having a slightly longer and more accurate memory, eloquence and a strong conviction in her own state of grace, Mrs Hutchinson saw through the word-magic of the clergy. She would have none of it. She declared that obedience to the clergy had nothing to do with the Will of God, since to be in a state of grace was to be without the need of earthly assistance. One's sense of conscience, one's intimate and private communion with God — these were the only guides to the good life on earth.

Mrs Hutchinson put into words the feelings many other Bostonians had sensed, but which remained unarticulated. In no time the Boston congregation preferred Mrs Hutchinson's parlour to the Church's meeting house, and the ripples of these gatherings were felt like disturbing shock-waves throughout Massachusetts. In addition to re-instructing the faithful, Mrs Hutchinson hurled one further affront at the clergy. She implied that some of them might consider themselves to be in a state of grace, but their thoughts were mistaken. In short, how could they even claim authority when their own state of grace was in doubt? At this stage the clergy could hardly allow such a challenge to pass, for clearly her behaviour had become something-about-which-something-ought-to-be-done.

But what could they do about it? She had broken no law; she had not obviously spoken heresy. Indeed, the clergy were puzzled and simply unable to find a language in which to describe her offence. Nevertheless, intensely irritated and threatened, and caught by the Queen of Heart's sense of justice, they impeached her first, and hoped to discover on what charge later. And that is exactly what happened. During the confrontation (for that is really what it was) the judge/prosecutor (there being no distinction between the two) declared her guilty of casting doubt upon the authority of the Church. By a raw display of power Mrs Hutchinson had been declared guilty of 'Hutchinsonism', no more, and certainly no less. Her views were declared to be deviant views. Anyone uttering such views in the future, therefore, ran the risk of also being declared deviant. That was the outcome of the confrontation, and with that outcome the social boundaries of the New England Settlement has been clarified and decisively shifted.

In order to put the final seal of authority on the illegality of 'Hutchinsonism', the clergy decided to subject Mrs Hutchinson to a spiritual trial. At this second hearing she was declared to be deluded in her belief that she was in a state of grace, for God reveals Himself to no man (or woman). Finally realizing her plight, Mrs Hutchinson repented. The clergy merely responded by adding the ultimate damning insult; they called her a liar because they believed her repentance insincere. On the basis of this last imputation the clergy excommunicated her. Thus, having dismissed Mrs Hutchinson's views and behaviour by declaring them to be unlawful, the clergy dismissed Mrs Hutchinson by throwing her to the devil.

By uncovering 'deviance', by publicly declaring what that deviance was, and by punishing the offender, the clergy had simply revealed *their* power — not God's. Once revealed, it was employed against the less powerful. As a consequence, the social boundaries of the New England society were clarified. The *covenant of grace* meant something different after the 1630s, and one significant implication of this difference was that the clergy had gained in temporal, as well as spiritual, authority. This institutionalization of the clergy's power might have happened without Mrs Hutchinson's help, but she focused events, drew subterranean discontents to a head, and played out her part in their settlement. What matter her suffering against the undoubted benefits of clarifying the rules of Puritan society and consolidating the authority of the clergy?

There are, of course, other implications to be drawn from this confrontation between the representatives of clerical power and those who can, in retrospect, be conveniently viewed as deviant. But the full significance of these implications is better appreciated when the other latent functions of deviance have been explicated.

Deviance as a maintainer of social rules

Contributing to the clarification of social rules is only one positive latent function of deviance. Another such function is that deviance provides an occasion for *celebrating* social rules, for realizing and confirming through action those rules which have been taken for granted. This is clearly the point Durkheim was making when he suggested that 'crime brings together upright consciences and concentrates them.' But Durkheim, and Marx and Mead for that matter, made this suggestion in a way that was too elliptical. This has misled some interpreters for, in failing to realize the elliptical rendition, they took it literally and, in doing so, failed to move beyond the surface meaning.

The key question is, are Durkheim, Marx and Mead referring to deviant behaviour and suggesting that *it* has positive social functions, or are they referring to the celebratory social euphoria which accompanies the reaffirmation of what-is-taken-for granted when someone is publicly punished for being declared guilty of a deviant act? Put this way, the question reveals its own answer, for clearly behaviour is behaviour. It might in some objective sense also be *deviant* behaviour in that it constitutes an infraction of the rules of society. But if no other persons come to know about that behaviour, or about the person who committed it, then it hardly provides an occasion on which people can come together and 'wax indignant in common'. For deviant behaviour to have a reaffirmative function, a particular societal reaction needs to occur; deviant behaviour without the reaction will not suffice.

When individuals deviate, other members of society who want the social rules maintained feel the need to respond, initially by pressuring the wayward to return to the fold and, if that fails or is thought to be of no avail, by rejecting the unacceptable. In this way, deviant behaviour provides an opportunity for the reaffirmation of social boundaries. But such reaffirmation occurs *only* if the community takes advantage of this opportunity. In other words, 'each time the community brings sanctions against a detail of behaviour . . . it sharpens the authority of the violated norm'. To put it more graphically, and to make clearer the lesson, it is only at the public scaffold that morality and immorality meet, and it is at *this point,* and not the point of legal infraction, that the line between them is sharply redrawn and social boundaries maintained.

The point is well made in the western *Hang 'em High.* The central character is himself a man of dubious morals, and is at risk of being penalized for crimes of which he is suspected. To avoid incarceration, he accepts official employment as a law-enforcement officer. His particular duty is to search for, and bring back alive, persons suspected of murder. In an important scene, the lawman is returning to town with a small group of suspects when he is attacked by one of them. Just as he is in danger of being killed, two of the other suspects come to his rescue.

The effect of the rescue is to convince the lawman, and us as the viewing audience, that these two suspects — in fact, two adolescents — are not really bad but, like good eggs in a bad omelette, have had their qualities curdled by the company they keep. Thus convinced of their essential goodness, the lawman pleads for their lives when they are later declared guilty of murder and sentenced to be hanged. The grounds on which the mayor/judge rejects this plea are illuminating for they indicate how we might add a further dimension of meaning to Durkheim's statement, 'crime brings together upright consciences and concentrates them'.

The mayor's refusal to be persuaded by the lawman is explained by him in the following manner:

> I don't doubt that those lads are not really bad, but do the people watching the gallows share our doubts? They want these men to hang because they want to feel safe. They want to be told that murderers will not get away with it — that out here, even in the wild frontier, we say murder is wrong, and we really mean business. Now if I go soft on those boys, everyone will come round to thinking the law's gone soft, and if people start thinking that, they lose their sense of direction, and before we know where we are, they'll be trigger happy and carefree, and that's anarchy. So you see, we've got to hang these lads, even if they are innocent — we've got to do it, *for the sake of the community.*

So rendered, this account of the mayor's reasons indicates how we might proceed to clarify Durkheim's position. For the logic of these reasons shifts our attention away from the *fact* of deviant behaviour to the *response* to such behaviour, *whether that behaviour be real or imagined, fancied or fabricated.* In other words, we are led to consider the possibility that it is not deviant behaviour as *such* that 'is responsible for a sense of solidarity', or 'arouses the moral and aesthetic sentiments of the public', but it is in fact a particular kind of response to deviant behaviour that creates these advantageous conditions.

What should be remembered is that most deviant offences go unnoticed and not officially recorded. In such circumstances deviant behaviour *per se* can hardly create a 'sense of mutuality among the people of a community by supplying a focus for group feeling'. Furthermore, we should not infer that *the* crucial link between deviant acts and the social function of rule support is the reportage. For even where the rate reportage is high, as in the offences of homicide, armed robbery and arson, *the fact of reportage alone cannot provide the necessary potency to arouse and reaffirm public support and recognition of the moral boundaries of society.* Only where there is a public pronouncement of the offence, drawing out its illegality and immorality, are moral boundaries reaffirmed and individually reinforced. But such pronouncements do not follow simply from the *fact* of a crime being committed. Of course where the crime is sufficiently heinous, such as police or child murders, or armed and violent robberies involving vast sums of money, it is almost certain to be widely publicized once known.

However, many more than just heinous crimes are reported and publicized; 90 per cent of media space devoted to the reportage of crimes concentrates on serious crimes such as wilful homicide, forcible rape, aggravated assault, robbery, burglary and larceny, and crimes currently fanning social hysteria, such as muggers, football hooligans, terrorists, and bombers (Chibnall, 1977; Hall, 1979; Hall *et al*, 1978). The transmission of these events usually reaches climactic proportions when there is a moral degradation ceremony, such as a criminal trial, in which a suspect is transformed from being normal into being deviant. More than any other event, it is the reportage of such moral degradation ceremonies and the publicizing of the consequences they have for the transformed person that provide the necessary potency to arouse and reaffirm public support and recognition of the moral boundaries of society.

This suggests a plausible account of the historical connection between the administration of penal sanctions and places highly visible to the public. For only in such locations can everyone, even passing strangers, observe and reflect on the meaning of such punishment. Not only the public gallows at such central points as Tyburn Corner, but also the village-pond ducking stool and the market-place stocks and pillories, are to be seen in their historical context as everyday supports of conventional morality. For gallows, ducking stools, stocks and pillories were the stage props around which the moral drama of society was played before audiences of newly instructed and re-instructed subjects.

Because penal punishments needed to be highly visible if they were to provoke subjects into considering the boundaries of proper conduct, they were carried out in front of public audiences. This consideration probably enables us to understand the historical coincidence between the decline of such grisly events and the rise of mass media. For it can be reasonably argued that these media provide a service similar to that provided by the *public* nature of penal sanctions. The media make redundant the need for large gatherings of persons to witness punishments; instead individuals can stay at home and still be morally instructed. They do this simply by reading, listening and watching mass media, a substantial part of which consists of reports on what kind of persons are being punished, and the reasons for their humiliations. The obvious consequence of such media coverage is that subjects are provoked into reflecting on the rules of society and the fate which awaits transgressors.

The reason then why deviant behaviour occupies so much media space is not because it is intrinsically interesting, but because it is intrinsically instructive. It serves to reinforce the world-taken-for-granted by restating social rules and warning subjects that violators will not be tolerated. In this way, the wayward are cautioned and the righteous are comforted.

Thus Durkheim's statement does *not* apply in the case of the vast majority of crimes, for they are unreported. Furthermore, it applies only to a small percentage of crimes which are reported, namely those subjected to much publicity. What Durkheim's proposition primarily refers to are those moral degradation ceremonies where normals are cast as deviant and their bedevilled nature exposed for all to see. From the above analysis then, it is suggested that it is not deviant behaviour *as such* that positively serves society by 'bringing together upright consciences and concentrating them', but rather it is the official publicizing of the offence and the offender.

It follows from this that so long as the punishment is public and accompanied by 'official' evaluations of the meaning of such punishable behaviour, then 'real' guilt need not be a prerequisite for reaffirming social boundaries in this manner. All that need happen is that the public are led to believe that deviant behaviour has occurred. Once that is achieved, political leaders can proceed in a Machiavellian manner to 'cure' or eliminate persons so cast.

This may all suggest a 'criminal show-trial' (Hirchheimer, 1961) rather than an ordinary confrontation in criminal courts. But that distinction is possibly one we make to comfort and mystify ourselves, whilst at the same time denigrating other political systems. For all political systems require occasions on which social rules can be publicly stated. The staging of 'scapegoat' offenders for a highly publicized trial, as the trial of seven demonstrators at the Chicago Democratic Convention illustrates (Hayden, 1970), provides such an occasion for rule reinforcement. This is not to suggest that all trials are a *conscious* confrontation between representatives of the present political order and others accused of being a threat to it. But at a *latent level,* this is just what it is — a confrontation between persons holding different definitions of reality, and in order for one definition to be reinforced, the others need to be derogated. Coser (1976) comes close to this when he writes:

> Thus the criminal, the scapegoat, the mentally ill, in their diverse ways
> allow the group to reaffirm not only its social but also its moral identity,
> for they establish signposts which serves as normative yardsticks. (p. 116)

It comes close, but in reaffirming a reified version of *the group* and its *moral identity,* Coser loses sight of the conflicts that cut between groups of 'normals' who have overlapping but different moral identities.

It should be clear from the above discussion that deviance *as such* does not directly contribute to the clarification and reaffirmation of social rules. Sociologists who have given this impression have either simply misunderstood a relationship that is not simple, or have been misunderstood by readers who have been easily impressed (Roshier, 1977).

For the case of Mrs Hutchinson, and the necessity for publicizing penal sanctions, both suggest that deviance, and the positive latent functions it provides, can be understood only in a political context. The clarification and maintenance of social rules is in essence a political competition. In this competition opponents have to be neutralized, and one technique by which this might be achieved is to label then as 'deviant'. The advantage gained by successfully labelling opponents stems from the popular conception that deviance (and those who engage in it) is dangerous. Opponents thus labelled risk punishment, ostracism and ridicule, and therein lies the political wisdom of calling them 'deviant'.

The reaffirmation of social rules is thus a political process in which the norm-enforcers (judges, magistrates and police) and norm-entrepreneurs (the legislature and pressure groups) decide the social category of persons who shall occupy the 'scapegoat' role (Chambliss, 1969; Chambliss and Mankoff, 1975; Chambliss and Seidman, 1971; Turk, 1969); on these, see [Chapter 6]. This point can be further underpinned by examining a third latent function provided by deviance, namely the modification of social rules; for when this is examined it reveals an intimate link between deviance and political considerations.

Deviance as a modifier of social rules

Deviance can act as a catalyst, or not, for social change or increased political repression, depending upon the flexibility of official, mainly governmental, response to it. This adaptive function was elaborated by Durkheim in his *Rules of Sociological Method* (1938). In this he wrote:

> Crime implies not only that the way remains open to necessary changes but that in certain cases it directly prepares these changes. Where crime exists, collective sentiments are sufficiently flexible to take on a new form, and crime sometimes helps to determine the form they will take. How many times, indeed, is it only an anticipation of future morality — a step toward what will be! According to Athenian law, Socrates was a criminal, and his condemnation was no more than just. However, his crime, namely, the independence of his thought, rendered a service not only to humanity but to his country. It served to prepare a new morality and faith which the Athenians needed, since the traditions by which they had lived until then were no longer in harmony with the current conditions of life. Nor is the case of Socrates unique; it is reproduced periodically in history. It would never have been possible to establish the freedom of thought we now enjoy if the regulations prohibiting it had not been violated before being solemnly abrogated. At that time, however, the violation was a crime, since it was an offence against sentiments still very keen in the average conscience. And yet this crime was useful as a prelude to reforms which daily became more necessary. Liberal philosophy had as its precursors the heretics of all kinds who were justly punished by secular authorities during the entire course of the Middle Ages and until the eve of modern times.
>
> From this point of view the fundamental facts of criminality present themselves to us in an entirely new light. Contrary to current ideas, the criminal no longer seems a totally unsociable being, a sort of parasitic element, a strange and unassimilable body, introduced into the midst of society. On the contrary, he plays a definite role in social life. Crime, for its part, must no longer be conceived as an evil that cannot be too much suppressed. There is no occasion for self-congratulation when the crime

> rate drops noticeably below the average level, for we may be certain that
> this apparent progress is associated with some social disorder (pp. 71–72)

Nearly 30 years later, Berger and Luckman (1967) echo these arguments. They argue that deviance has to be responded to, either by accommodation or repression, because it 'challenges the social reality as such, putting in question its taken-for-granted cognitive and normative operating procedures . . . [and hence] stands as a living insult to the Gods' (p. 117), and, it should be added, those who in *this world* claim to represent their interests. How these representatives, who in most societies also happen to be political leaders, respond to this challenge varies widely. For our purposes we can dichotomize these responses into those which *provide occasions for self-congratulation,* and those which *reflect a mood of self-examination.*

At one extreme, leaders attempt to annihilate the offender in the hope that the challenge he *symbolizes* will also be beaten. Compared with the outcome of most heresy confrontations, Mrs Hutchinson might be thought lucky — the punishment for such an offence was usually more bloody and vicious. Much more typical of the thousands of heretics who met unpleasant ends, as a result of the Inquisition and other religious persecution movements of the sixteenth and seventeenth centuries, is Tyndale. He was found guilty of unofficially translating the Bible, and for this he was first publicly hanged, and then burnt at the stake. Similarly, Russian 'political deviants' were subject to a high rate of officially induced mortality, whether they were 'Communists' under the Tzarist government, or 'Tzarists' under the Communist government. A number of recent publications (Amnesty International, 1975; Bloch and Reddaway, 1977; Lader, 1977; Medvedev and Medvedev, 1971; Wing, 1974) all suggest that many prisoners guilty of breaking state laws on religious activities, protesting against Soviet policy and being involved with clandestine literature, are confined to 'psychiatric hospitals' where they are forcibly treated for insanity; their insanity being, of course, that they are 'political deviants'.

The favoured and most frequently employed technique for eliminating the challenge symbolized in deviants' conduct has been, and probably still is, the elimination of the offender, either physically by his death, or mentally by brainwashing and induced personality change. However, this technique has not been one which necessarily resolves the challenge, for it concretizes an opponent and thereby misses the real enemy, the abstraction he symbolizes.

The limitation of this technique for handling the challenge of deviants' conduct is nicely caught in Kazan's film of the Mexican bandit-peasant leader, Emiliano Zapata, *Viva Zapata.* In the final scene, the bullet-riddled body of the bandit hero Zapata is deposited in his village's square by government soldiers. The authorities hoped this would put an end to the Morelos uprising, but in this they were mistaken. For instead of being dazed into acquiescence by this massive display of brutal authority, the peasants simply gathered around the corpse, their mood clearly captured by one expressing: 'Who are they fooling? This could be anyone. It is not Zapata. They cannot kill him. He is out there in the mountains, in the wind, in the trees — he cannot be killed, he is an *idea.'* (This 'quotation' is reconstructed from the author's notes.)

Thus the self-congratulation that follows from eliminating deviants is often hollow, for it fails to eliminate the real problem, the challenge to social reality that deviant conduct symbolizes. Political leaders, reflecting on this dire possibility, may catch themselves in a mood of self-examination, and in such a mood they may occasionally conclude that it is wiser to meet the deviant's challenge by change and accommodation.

When this occurs, deviance can be viewed as a kind of social barometer; that is, the rate of deviance becomes employed by leaders as a means of forecasting serious social disruptions. In this sense deviance is a kind of warning-light; when it reaches a certain intensity it may be taken to indicate a time when wise political leaders should consider the possibility of making a conciliatory gesture.

The most obvious gesture would be to change the formal legal position by introducing a new law, thereby making the deviant's conduct legal. One well-known and much quoted example of this political response is the repeal in 1933 of the Prohibition Amendment Act of 1919, under which the manufacture, distribution and sale of alcoholic beverages were illegal. The 1919 Amendment was the third legislative attempt to transform Americans into teetotallers. The first, in the 1850s, involved more than one-third of the states legislating against alcohol; the second, in the 1880s, involved only eight states; the third, in 1917, involved 25 states, who in turn brought about the national Prohibition Amendment. The enthusiasm of the professional abstainers was not shared by the millions of Americans who liked their booze. Almost overnight, urban and suburban dwellers, working class and middle class, whites and blacks, professionals and their clients, Protestants, Catholics and Jews, became involved in the illegal trafficking and consumption of alcoholic beverages. The mere banning of such activities was not going to curtail them.

Throughout the 1920s, despite police harassment, organized criminals made fortunes involving millions of dollars in profits, and this, plus the widespread pervasiveness of infraction, finally led the government to repeal the 1919 Act. Rather than proceed to prosecute and harass, the political leaders took the extensiveness of illegal activity as a sign that the American population would not acquiesce, and on that basis decided to change the law. Deviant behaviour had been taken as a warning light, and the government responded by modifying the legal situation rather than by continuing to persuade Americans to modify their conduct.

Legal changes, however, involve some political loss of face, particularly when these changes involve the modification or repeal of other laws which have only recently gained official approval. Thus when deviance rates indicate that some law is not acceptable, leaders frequently revert to the practice of *not enforcing* it rather than repealing it. Such a change of intention may, however, only come after a government has realized the impracticability of enforcing a law not generally accepted by the population. A clear example of this, for once showing the lighter side of deviant phenomena, is provided by the events that took place in Kent during the early part of the Second World War (Emmerson, 1968).

The miners at Betteshanger Colliery, Kent, went on strike in December 1941 because they could not reach a suitable settlement with the management on the level of pay allowances for work in a particularly difficult seam. At one stage in the negotiations the possibility of strike action seemed to recede. Unable to settle the dispute between themselves, management and labour had agreed to put the matter to arbitration, and furthermore both accepted the condition that they would be bound by the arbitration award. But when the arbitration report was published, it burst like a bomb of filth. Not only were the current rates reasonable, they were, if anything, in the arbitration board's opinion, excessive. That got right up the miners' nostrils. Four thousand men came out to get some fresh air in the Kent countryside.

Purifying as it may have been, such conduct was illegal under the National Arbitration Order which had been passed in the hope of lessening the effects of bad industrial relations on the nation's economy. But what to do about it? That was the question that perplexed authorities. The country was at war and desperately needed a high output of coal. Would there be any point in prosecuting the miners, particularly if such a response ran the risk of worsening industrial relations, ruining work morale and further reducing the amount of coal mined?

The Ministry of Labour wanted moderation, although they were not quite sure what form this might take. The Mines Department took a different view; moderation seemed to be no policy, simply a 'wait and see what happens' posture, and that meant that in the meantime no coal was being produced. Supported by the cabinet, the Secretary of Mines resolved the dilemma. He decided that the only suitable action was prosecution, and that is where events took an amusing turn.

To reduce the size of the problem the number of men to be prosecuted was quartered, so that only 1000 of the underground workers who were first involved in the dispute remained. But, with the numbers even so reduced, the prosecution was still confronted with problems. One thousand forms for serving a summons had to be found, for it was not the local custom to keep them handy in such large numbers just in case something like this happened. Eventually a stock of forms was located in London, and these had to be especially rushed down to Kent. Once they arrived, willing Justices of the Peace had to be found to sign them in duplicate. Finally, to deliver so many summonses, extra police had to be drafted into the force.

The preliminaries having been settled, thoughts turned to the actual hearings. Clearly if the men chose to be awkward and plead 'not guilty' the proceedings might take months. To avoid matters dragging out, the prosecutors approached the defendants' representatives, the union, and 'asked if they would instruct their members to plead guilty, and accept a decision on a few test cases'. Like true gentlemen, the defendants obliged and a bargain was struck.

The day of the prosecution was at first treated by the miners as though it were a festival: charabancs were hired to transport wives and children to Canterbury. Curiously, the Mines Department authorized the Regional Petroleum Officers to allow the miners petrol for this journey, even though petrol was rationed at the time. At the collieries, and throughout Canterbury where the magistrates met, bands played as if to herald war-time heroes.

But the noise of the festival died down as news of the sentences spread from the court. Although the union and its members had kept to their part of the bargain, pleading guilty and facilitating a smooth passage for the proceedings, the magistrates decided to impose harsh sentences. 'The three union officials were sent to prison. The Branch Secretary was sentenced to two months' hard labour; the local President and a member of the local executive each received one month with hard labour. Thirty-five men were fined three pounds or one month's imprisonment, and nearly one thousand were fined one pound or fourteen days' (Emmerson, 1968).

From the miners' point of view, the situation had swung from comedy to catastrophe. As the protests poured in, and sympathetic strikes were seriously canvassed, the situation threatened to become even worse, at least for the nation. But since the only men who could sanction such strike action could not do so because they were in prison and could not be contacted, the threat did not materialize.

The situation, however, did remain serious, for the men refused to return to work whilst their leaders were in prison. This meant that no coal was being produced at Betteshanger Colliery. The law had taken its course; it had led the government up the garden path only to find the coal bunkers empty. That was not what the government wanted. In an attempt to straighten things out, the Secretary for Mines, accompanied by the President of the Miners' Union, went to visit the prisoners and, after five days, was able to secure a negotiated settlement. This gave the men what they wanted in the first place, and also met the government's most urgent need — coal for the country. After the convicted men had spent 11 days in prison, the Home Secretary intervened and released them. The mine reopened, and presumably filled with a sense of victory, the miners nearly trebled the output of coal, at least for the first week.

The release of the prisoners, coupled with the payment favourable to the miners, may suggest a defeat for the government, but in fact the real government defeat and withdrawal (and the point this example is meant to illustrate) were to come a few weeks later. The Clerk to the Justices found himself in a quandary: only nine miners had paid their fine, and, not at all certain what steps to take next, he requested official guidance. Not seeing how more than 900 men could be committed to the small prison at Canterbury, and bearing in mind the enormous increase in the productivity of coal-mining in Kent, the officials in Whitehall decided that another fiasco should be averted. The Clerk was consequently advised not to enforce the Court's fines. In other words, a political decision had been made; in the face of such deviance, the government took the warning and, instead of changing the law, they decided not to enforce it. This tactic enabled some politicians to avoid too much embarrassment, for the National Arbitration Order had only recently been passed by them, and to repeal it so soon would have implied earlier political stupidity. Now the whole business could be quietly glossed over and forgotten. Although the difference between repeal and non-enforcement was significant for politicians, it was not significant for the miners. For them, one was the same as the other; but meant that the boundaries of permissible behaviour had been reshaped.

When large or strategically important sections of the community are not willing to bend their behaviour to legal requirements, then political leaders need to view this as a warning-light. Their decision on how to respond to this warning differs, but it can hardly be one that reflects indifference. As a phenomenon signifying potential danger, deviance, at least in certain forms, provides authorities with a clear indication of subjects' sense of outrage, injustice, or mere normative discontinuity; or put another way, it indicates the degree to which authorities have been prudent or foolish. For those who wish to remain authoritative, as opposed to repressive, do not foster a sense of injustice or outrage, even when they act unjustly or outrageously. As Machiavelli pointed out over four centuries ago (Marriott, 1958), as long as authorities can *appear* to be virtuous it doesn't matter how badly they actually behave. Alternatively, a government must be prepared to slip towards a more totalitarian form if it does not respond accommodatively to some widespread forms of deviance. The current British Government, and its immediate predecessors, along with other governments in industrialized countries, seems bent on this course. In Britain, the government's emphasis has become clearer recently: it is (a) not simply on more police but on quasi-military forms of policing, such as the Special Patrol Group which has increasingly been used to control and suppress political demonstrators and industrial strikers; (b) not simply on more prison officers but on quasi-military forms of controlling inmates, such as the Minimal Use of Force Tactical Intervention Squad (MUFTI) which has increasingly been used to put down effectively, and violently, prison 'rioters' who often turn out not to be rioting at all but attempting to claim their rights under prison, British and European laws (Fitzgerald, 1977; Fitzgerald and Sim, 1979); (c) not simply on more prisons, but also on transforming them into quasi-medical establishments (Box, 1981; Prewer, 1974), thus justifying such treatment-cum-punishment as brain surgery, drug therapy and control units, and at the same time extending the boundary of the catchment area so that many who would previously have not been imprisoned are now subject to the new short-sharp-shock treatment; (d) not simply on protecting state secrets but on curtailing the ability of citizens effectively to criticize the State by increasing special branch surveillance against them and by diminishing civil rights more generally, particularly in prison (Cohen and Taylor, 1978); (e) not simply on re-equilibrating justice so that the State's chances of securing convictions are 'fairer' but, by being receptive to the convenient police demands for more powers to stop, search and interrogate suspects, on making sure that previous civil and legal rights upheld under the rule of law are stripped away, thus making state prosecution and conviction rates easier to achieve.

Thus, deviance, by its volume and incidence, can indicate that social disorder on a larger scale is imminent; this requires a political response either to rectify those social injustices which often lie behind such sudden increases in 'criminal behaviour', or to shore up social control and discipline so that social disorders can be contained and controlled even if the price, which is less social democracy, is paid in full.

Societal conflicts and the latent functions of (societal reactions to) deviance

In the above discussions consideration has been given to how deviance may contribute towards social stability. The first latent function was illustrated by the example which considered how deviants might be discovered by political fiat and rejected as undesirables — thus clarifying social rules. Analysis of a second latent function revealed that social rules might be maintained by graphically and dramatically displaying 'badness', so that 'goodness' might be reaffirmed in human consciousness. Finally, a third latent function of deviance was considered. This led to the conclusion that social rules might be changed or their enforcement suspended in order that severe social conflict might be avoided. In this sense, social rules change in order that society may remain integrated and thus relatively unchanged.

It has not been the intention to consider an exhaustive list of the social functions of deviance. Further, the analysis has been confined to examining only the beneficial results that deviance can have for a society's *internal* stability. There always remains the possibility that internal stability may be achieved at the expense of increasing the risk of instability arising between a society and its *external* relationships.

The analysis of the social functions of deviance has been deliberately limited. It has not been extended because a position has now been reached where a model of society, which may enable us better to understand deviant phenomena, can now be suggested. What the analysis of the three latent positive functions of deviance reveals about the nature of society is that the *clarification, maintenance and modification* of social rules are *essentially political processes*. Rather than conceiving social rules, and the social order they help sustain, as an expression of the general will (i.e. a value-consensus position), it might be nearer the truth to view them as an expression of particular groups' interests (i.e. a conflict-of-value position). For example, a number of sociologists (Chambliss, 1964; Duster, 1970; Graham, 1972; Gunningham, 1974; Hall, 1952; Haskins, 1960; Hay *et al*, 1975; McCaghy and Denisoff, 1973; Platt, 1969; Thompson, 1975) have produced evidence consistent with the view that criminal laws reflect the interests of particular powerful groups. What the criminal law prescribes and what it omits benefit these groups much more than others. However, this position needs to be qualified. It does not maintain that all criminal laws are the direct expression of the interests of one particular interest group, such as the ruling class. It is quite clear that some individual pieces of criminal legislation reflect a temporary, rather than a permanent, victory of one interest or allied interest groups over others, and none of these may necessarily be identified or coincide with the interests of the dominant class. Yet the conflict position does not need for its support a demonstration that every piece of criminal legislation directly represents the interests of the dominant class. Some laws are passed purely as symbolic victories which the dominant class grants to inferior interest groups, basically to keep them quiet; once passed, they need never be efficiently enforced. Thus during the late nineteenth century in America, 'those segments of society economically based upon the ownership of small independent property and oriented toward small town and rural life found themselves increasingly displaced socially, politically and economically by those whose wealth and power was based upon the salaries, investments, and profits of a corporate economy' (McCormick, 1977; p. 31). Although unable to prevent the State passing legislation overtly designed to prevent certain corporate activities considered harmful to the profitability of small enterprise, this latter group was none the less able to exert enough influence severely to restrict the degree to which this legislation was enforced. Thus between 1891 and 1969, there were only 1551 cases instigated under the Sherman (Anti-Trust) Act 1890, which constitutes an extremely small annual average of 20 cases. Of these, just over two-fifths were dealt with as criminal offences; the majority were treated as administrative or civil matters, thus neatly avoiding the possibility of criminalizing either corporation or their executives. Furthermore, the earlier prosecutions were aimed primarily at trade unions and not corporations!

This unpreparedness to enforce the legislation it creates suggests that frequently the State acts in a merely symbolic manner. It reaffirms ideal cultural values — in the case of the Sherman Act those of free competition — thus providing some comfort to those sections whose position and livelihood are threatened by big monopolistic corporations, but in fact operates to realize other values held by that section of the privileged which is ascending to power.

A similar position is adopted by Pearce (1976) which criticizes Hofstadter's (1967) argument, that the anti-trust prosecutions effectively curtailed corporation misbehaviour and regulated business activity, by pointing out that the number of full-time lawyers employed by the anti-trust division and the limited budget necessarily mean that the law will be under-enforced. This means that the actual practice of law enforcement works to protect the overall activities of large industrial bureaucracies, not least by the fact that criminality does not become associated with such business enterprise.

It might be objected that even if it is possible to show that *some* criminal laws are in the interests of the dominant class, and that some others which are obviously not in these interests are ineffectively enforced, thus making them dead-letter laws, it still remains the case that laws which proscribe those types of acts which affect us most, and which set the nerve-ends of neo-classical/conservative criminologists tingling with fear and loathing, are in all our best interests. None of us want to be murdered, raped or robbed, none of us want our property stolen, smashed or destroyed, none of us want our bodies punched, kicked, bitten or tortured. In that sense, criminal laws against murder, rape, arson, robbery and assault are in all our interest; we all benefit from their existence.

This is true, but not the whole truth. For some people benefit more than others from these laws. It is not that they are less likely to be murdered, raped, robbed or assaulted, although in fact the powerful are less criminally victimized in these ways, but that by the criminal law's constructing *particular* definitions of murder, rape, robbery and assault other acts, which are in many ways very similar, are excluded, and these are just the acts more likely to be committed by more powerful individuals. Thus the criminal law defines only some types of killing as murder: it excludes, for example, deaths which result from acts of negligence such as employers' failure to maintain safe working conditions in factories and mines (Swartz, 1975); or deaths which result from governmental agencies giving environmental health risks a low priority (Liazos, 1972), or deaths resulting from drug manufacturers' failure to conduct adequate research on new chemical compounds before conducting aggressive marketing campaigns (Silverman and Lee, 1974), or deaths resulting from drunken people's driving cars with total indifference to the potential cost in terms of human lives. The criminal law includes only some types of property deprivation as robbery: it excludes, for example, the separation of consumers from part of their money that follows manufacturers' malpractices or advertisers' misrepresentations; it includes, in the words of that anonymous poet particularly loved by pre-university students of economic history, the man or woman who steals the goose from off the common, but leaves the greater villain loose who steals the common from the goose. It was to focus on such privileged exclusion that Brecht asked sarcastically, 'Which is worse, the man who robs the bank, or the man who owns it?' The criminal law includes only some types of non-consensual sexual acts as rape: it excludes sexual acts between husband and wife, no matter how much the latter is beaten by the former to exercise his 'conjugal rights'; it excludes sexual acts achieved by fraud, deceit or misrepresentation — thus a man may pose as a psychiatrist and prescribe sexual intercourse as therapy to a 'gullible' female because he knows that the law will not regard this as rape. The criminal law defines only some types of violence as criminal assault: it excludes verbal assaults that can, and sometimes do, break a person's spirit; it excludes those forms of assault whose injuries become apparent years later, such as those resulting from working in a polluted factory environment where the health risk was known to the employer but concealed from the employee; it excludes 'compulsory' drug-therapy or electrical shock treatment given to mentally disturbed patients or prisoners who are denied the civilized right to refuse such 'treatment' (Mitford, 1977; Szasz, 1970, 1977a, 1977b).

Thus criminal laws against murder, rape, robbery and assault do protect us all, but they do not protect the less powerful from being killed, sexually exploited, deprived of their property, or physically and psychologically damaged through the greed, apathy, negligence, indifference and the unaccountability of the relatively more powerful (Thio, 1978).

Of course, what constitutes murder, rape, robbery and assault varies over historical periods and between cultural groups. The changes *within* the powerful interest groups, and *between* them, and the shifting alliances of the less powerful, bring about slight and not so slight alterations in the societal power axis. But the argument here is that it is not justifiable to conclude from this that criminal law reflects a value-consensus (or even results from the State's neutral refereeing among competing interest groups). It is, however, plausible to view criminal laws as the outcomes of clashes between groups with structurally generated conflicting interests, and to argue that the intention behind such laws is to use them to reduce the ability of the less powerful even further to resist the domination of the powerful.

Viewed in this light, society is *not* an organic unity; rather, it is a problematical enterprise, a social construction of reality that at any moment may (in principle) be knocked over by the counter-realities symbolized in deviants' conduct. *At any one time,* each society has, as it were, a legalized definition of reality; it has judicial statements about which particular bundle of *possible* human behaviours will be given official approval, and which other bundles of possible human behaviour will be severely stamped on by officials. But what makes this at-any-one-time reality difficult to transpose into an at-any-and-all-time reality is the plasticity of human nature and the continuous struggle of people to break out of other-people-made worlds. Consequently, 'deviance is dangerous' (in all its various synonymous formulations) can be viewed by a cynical criminologist as a conceptual and ideological tool employed by authorities to justify punishing (i.e. eliminating, suppressing, controlling, managing) those whose behaviour puts 'social reality' into question. For if people can have the label 'deviant' (criminal, mentally ill, sexual pervert, etc.) successfully attributed to them, then there exists a prima facie justification for doing something (usually unpleasant) to them. In other words, if it is widely believed that deviance is dangerous, injurious and harmful to social stability, and that what constitutes deviance coincides nicely with all those avoidable human acts such as murder, rape, arson, assault and robbery which cause their victims — us — most pain, agony, anguish and suffering, then this very belief provides authorities with a widely accepted rationale for sanctioning, often harshly, those declared to be guilty. Isn't that exactly why they, and their media allies, spend so much time whipping up our fear about crimes of the powerless? For when they succeed, and by and large they do, then our attention is deflected on to crimes of the powerless and our applause loudest when those criminals are brutally punished. In the meantime, behind our backs, as it were, the powerful are expansively realizing their own propensity massively to harm, injure, maim and kill, although that is not conceptualized as murder, rape, arson and robbery. In other words, among other displeasing activities, politicians and their allies are in the business of convincing us that their conception of social reality (which incorporates criminal laws) is the one which should be absolutely accepted. Whilst all may be convinced some of the time, some may not be convinced all the time. And whilst a flame of defiance still flickers, there will be 'truculent, trouble-making' citizens who wish to modify the existing social reality and the structural arrangements, including criminal laws, which it helps sustain — and of course it is just this possibility that presents a challenge to those who are quite happy with the present arrangements, usually because they benefit considerably from them.

Thus, just as scientists hope to beat nature into shape in order to fit it into their scientific paradigms (Ford, 1975), so political leaders attempt to 'beat' people into shape, so that they do not step outside everyday-worlds-taken-for-granted. But this fond ambition cannot be accomplished simply by informing citizens that certain laws exist, although such information is necessary. In addition, political leaders need to demonstrate their moral (and physical) superiority by revealing what happens to people who refuse to get into line. Not only do authorities feel the need to excommunicate those labelled as 'heretics', kill those declared guilty of 'murder', imprison others found guilty of serious legal infractions, incarcerate people after having attributed 'mental illness' to them (with the alliance of the medical profession), but also they need to do so in such a dramatic style that citizens will learn what will not be officially tolerated.

In this sense, 'deviance' refers not to what a person has done, but what (from the authorities' point of view) may be justifiably done to the person to whom deviance has been successfully attributed.

Furthermore, this justification of punishment — that deviance is dangerous to us all — often serves to neutralize the moral bind of these behavioural standards which punishment supposedly seeks to preserve. Thus, because they have committed unlawful killing, murderers *may* be killed by the State, not only when under sentence of capital punishment but also when police/troops are granted a licence to kill, as they were in quelling the Attica Prison riot when 'correctional officers and state troopers stormed the prison and killed ten hostages and twenty-nine inmates' (Reiman, 1979; p. 123); because they have committed violence on others, those guilty of grievous bodily harm *may* have their own bodies grievously harmed whilst in prison, not only by various forms of extreme punishment, such as control units and drug-therapy, but also by prison staff acting brutally, as they did to quell the 'uprisings' at Hull, Albany,

Gartree and Wormwood Scrubs; those who have taken possessions which do not belong to them, or who make illegal material gain from manufacturing and selling 'illegal' substances, *may* have their own possessions, at least temporarily, but sometimes permanently, taken from them, as, for example, in the recent Julie case when the individuals found guilty of drug offences had their 'profits' confiscated. To be declared guilty is to be declared outside the protection authorities normally afford to subjects, and in such a social limbo the guilty suffer the indignities they have themselves inflicted on others.

Up to this point the impression may have been given that only *authorities* and agents licensed to maintain social control are interested in preserving social boundaries. Clearly, punishing offenders does help to preserve the concrete interests that motivate individuals and groups to become authorities; for in becoming authorities, individual and group interests can be protected. However, if the impression has been given that only the authorities are interested in maintaining social order, that impression needs to be corrected. The majority of the population are also interested, almost desperately interested, in the punishment of deviants and the preceding and/or accompanying moral degradation ceremonies. Most ordinary people are plagued by two doubts; 'Is the social world in which I live normal?' and, 'In the social world in which I live, am I normal?' In answer to both questions deviant phenomena may make a contribution, and therein lies the desperate interest in it.

Although the amount of human energy devoted to constructing social realities and combating counter-realities is considerable, it is normally exerted by only a small proportion of the population. The majority remain outside this struggle, although certainly not indifferent to its outcome, for they have been socialized into the existing world-taken-for-granted, and legitimated by higher-order realities. Individual lives, and *deaths,* are made meaningful by these realities. By accepting the existing definitions of social reality *as the* social reality, the chaos and terror of the cosmos and life are pushed out of consciousness and replaced by a conception of how to go about one's life in an orderly and proper fashion. Such orderliness, however, is put into question whenever other counter-realities are confronted, for these throw doubt on the 'normalcy' of *the* accepted reality. In the words of Berger and Luckman (1967)

> the institutional order . . . is continually threatened by the presence of realities that are meaningful in *its* terms. The legitimation of the institutional order is . . . faced with the ongoing necessity of keeping chaos at bay. *All* social reality is precarious. *All* societies are constructions in the face of chaos. The constant possibility of anomic terror is actualized whenever the legitimations that obscure the precariousness are threatened or collapse. (p. 117)

It is just this anomic terror that is symbolized in the behaviour of deviants. For in their contrary behaviour they raise the spectre of doubt, they provoke the question, 'Can my world really be normal if others behave in opposition to it?' And because such a possibility cannot be entertained, it has to be kept on the doorstep. To keep it there, the majority of the population band together in a chorus of disapproval, scorn, ridicule and, occasionally, mob hysteria. Thus, for example, homosexuality, prostitution, adultery, incest, sodomy, bestiality and pornography are all scorned; not because any of these are abnormal to human beings as a species, but because they constitute a threat to the 'normalcy' of monogamous heterosexuality. And if monogamous heterosexuality were conceived to be less than massively normal, then what would happen to all the other beliefs that constitute social normalcy? Similarly, individuals who do not behave in strict accordance with the notions of 'private property' are subject to harsh penal sanctions, not because stealing is intrinsically wrong or unnatural for human beings as a species, but because such behaviour throws into question the 'normalcy' of private property, and threatens to disturb the distribution of economic wealth which accompanies it.

The majority of the population have a vested interest in maintaining *their* social world, for it provides them, as Berger (1963) so graphically puts it, with 'warm, reasonably comfortable caves' (p. 121). By huddling with others, and by ostracizing, hospitalizing, imprisoning or killing persons whose behaviour signifies they live in another world, the majority can 'drown out the howling hyenas of the surrounding darkness' and make *their* worlds safer — although never entirely safe.

Even if the normalcy of the social world in which an individual lives is affirmed, s/he can still be plagued by one further equally significant question — his/her own normality. For an individual's normality is frequently up for review whenever any of his/her conduct, whose meaning is ambiguous, could be interpreted as improper, or whenever s/he actually does, if only momentarily, lapse into improper conduct.

It is frequently, indeed nearly always the case, that the rules governing specific social situations are ambiguous and open to numerous interpretations, such that preconceived, absolutist notions of deviance or crime are difficult, if not impossible to maintain. For example, is it the film *Last Tango in Paris* that is obscene and pornographic, or the sight of the Sevenoaks Council attempting to ban its showing in the local cinema? Are the executives who joined the Great Electrical Conspiracy (Geis, 1967; Smith, 1969) more deviant than those (few) who didn't? Is a 29-year-old feminist lesbian separatist more deviant than a 29-year-old virgin? Is the psychiatrist Daniel Ellsberg, who leaked official secrets to the press, deviant or those who later broke into his office and stole his files? Is the wife who rushed her sick husband to hospital, breaking speed limits and traffic-light signals on the way, guilty of a criminal offence? Is the university lecturer who forgets to return library books guilty of stealing. And so on, example after example of behaviour whose social meaning requires some adjudication, some authoritative resolution, before answers can be given, although doubts may not necessarily be settled.

In addition, of course, there are occasions when individuals, for a wide variety of circumstantial reasons, do commit, or perceive themselves as committing, legal infractions, such as shoplifting, traffic offences, sexual offences, occupational crimes, and tax evasions, to mention just a few. Such ambiguities and behavioural lapses provoke identity anxieties. Haunted by fears of their own bedevilment, the majority seek to exorcize these inner doubts by seeing demons residing elsewhere. As Coser (1967) puts it:

> Moral indignation against deviants serves to purge the righteous from a
> sense of their own sins and unworthiness and helps sustain their moral
> identity ... It is against the ground of criminal deviance that the righteous
> achieve the comforting affirmation of their normality. In as much as 'our'
> innocence is contingent upon 'their' guilt, dereliction by others provides
> occasion for self-congratulations. (p. 117)

The majority of the population may then often warmly embrace criminal sanctions
against others so as to express concretely their own virtuousness and to conceal or
suppress doubts about their own inclinations towards vice. In this way, the nagging
question, 'In the social world in which I live, am I normal?' is answered favourably and
affirmatively.

An examination of the functions of deviance reveals that attention should not be solely
focused on the obvious and common-sense notion that deviance can be dysfunctional.
Rather the irony that deviant behaviour contributes to society is one whose
investigation raises some interesting observations. But to focus on the social functions
brings out the further observation that it is only functional for society as it is conceived
by particular interest groups. Deviance may well clarify social rules, may well provide
occasions on which most of us can celebrate our world-taken-for-granted, and may well
enable us to avoid serious social conflict by ameliorating minor blemishes to keep the
face of society unchanged. Deviance may provide all these positive latent functions,
but, as Matza (1969; pp. 61–62) warns, these windfalls should not blind us to one vital
point. Deviance benefits some subgroups *at the expense of others*. In order that one
definition of reality, supported by and supporting some subgroups, may be maintained,
then other subgroups or social categories of persons have to keep or be kept quite. How
certain social categories are selected for this treatment, or at whose expense some
benefit, and the implications this selection has for explanations of deviant behaviour,
form the substance of [subsequent chapters].

8.　Abolition: Assensus and Sanctuary
Herman Bianchi

Part I. Major objections to the prevailing system

In order to design effective strategies of abolition and to project workable alternatives of law, we need to agree on what we are opposing.

What we in our western societies understand by a criminal law system is a state-run organization, possessed of the monopoly to define criminal behaviour, directed towards the prosecution of that behaviour which it has defined — irrespective of the wishes or needs of a possible victim or plaintiff — and which has at its disposal, pre-trial and post-trial, the power to keep its prosecutees and convicts in confinement.

Representatives and managers of the criminal law system cherish the pretension that their organization could protect society from such a dangerous threat as criminality. In fact, however, the organization, since it was established in its present form about the end of the 18th century, has, in every respect and on all counts, failed to accomplish what it promises. Quite the reverse. For a long time the criminal law organization has been escalating dangerously. Any enhancement of the punishing power of the organization has so far led to more rather than less criminality. A nation that builds more prisons and imposes more repressive punishment usually provokes criminality.

In order to do the job it has undertaken and to find continuous public support for that, the criminal law organization must always keep alive a negative stereotype of 'the criminal'. It must maintain its stigmatizing power. At best the managers of the system are unable, or unwilling, to prevent the media from feeding the negative stereotype of 'the enemy of society'.

This negative stereotype is a direct result of the system's ideology. Since the 'war against crime' is continually being waged by its managers and their supportive politicians, an 'enemy-image' is constantly being produced. When nations and their rulers prepare for warfare, they begin by invoking a negative image of the enemy: the little yellow man, the American capitalist imperialist, the Soviet communist imperialist, etc. By doing so, their people will forget that they are dealing with human beings, and almost anything goes. In a former publication I compared the way the State creates moral panic waves in order to legitimize its expansion with the myth of the Lord of the flies (*de Vliegengod,* 1967. Dutch translation of W. Golding's *Lord of the Flies,* Faber 1954.).

The origin of the negative stereotype of the offender is ominous. It stems directly from the medieval Inquisition. In the old law system of Europe there was not even a shadow of public prosecution for wrongful acts committed between free citizens. Such acts were considered to be injuries and causes of conflict, for which damage to body and

Herman Bianchi: 'Abolition: Assensus and Sanctuary' from *ABOLITIONISM: TOWARDS A NON-REPRESSIVE APPROACH TO CRIME* by H. Bianchi and R. van Swanningen (Free University Press, 1986), pp. 113–126.

property had to be repaired, and the extent of the reparation was to be fixed by negotiation. The Inquisition, however, introduced the prosecutor (ecclesiastical at first, then later on, when the state had gradually come to accept this system, a public prosecutor). The Inquisition created the image of the heretic, a subhuman enemy of the church (later, of the state) for whom there was no salvation or penitence, and against whom the most infernal punishment was permitted because he was going to hell anyway. Sooner or later the evolving European states accepted the heretic definition of social dissidence from the church (including England), called him a criminal, and gradually grew to ignore the old legal system of the country, by which most crime-conflicts were solved through negotiation. Our present criminal law system — Anglo-Saxon as well as Continental — is still based on the old Inquisition, but in a secular form.

The results of this negative image have been disastrous, and twofold. Because the old negotiation procedures of conflict-regulation fell into disuse, the prosecutee and convict cannot contribute in any regular way, and by their own free will, to the improvement of the situation. Even the most docile convict, who is prepared in the most masochistic way, and without complaint, to endure the punishment that is imposed upon him, cannot contribute to his own social salvation. From then on the stigma he received makes it impossible for him to recover the status he had before he was degraded. The victim does not profit at all from our criminal law either, for the system largely ignores him or her. Even the certainty that the criminal is being punished is not much help in gaining reparation for the harm done.

The other destructive result of this negative image is the reality that most adaptation, probation and therapy programmes have failed. Why should society take back into its midst a person who was depicted as the *enemy* of society? And most forensic psychiatry failed because it was imposed upon an unwilling 'patient' who, with good reason, did not believe that therapy would help him to be reintegrated into society, since the stigma of 'being sick' makes the original criminal stigma even worse, and is, even more difficult to wipe out. The 'criminal' stigma is always a social life sentence for any convict.

Adaptation and therapy programmes have even strengthened the destructive power of the criminal law system. That is why abolitionists do not favour the so-called 'medical model' either.

The rules of our present criminal law system are very much at variance with our general legal system. The latter is built upon the idea that the set of rules it comprises is meant for the settlement of disputes, regulation of conflicts, and the construction of society — in short, the realization of peace and justice. The criminal law system, however, is rather *destructive* to society. Its rules differ so much from the legal system that it is even ignored by authors of general introductions to the philosophy or theory of law. They do not know what to do with criminal law and where to place it. Criminal law has its own basic philosophy, entirely outside the legal system. Criminal law is like war, and this phenomenon is not treated in our legal philosophy either. That is the reason why all attempts to 'humanize' the criminal law system have failed so far: you cannot 'humanize' a war either, can you? Abolitionists do not favour the humanization of the criminal law system as a goal in itself, but as a way of recalling the legal system to deal with wrongful acts, the rule of law, and the cancelling of a derailment of the general legal system.

In fact, the present criminal law system denies human rights. During the American and French revolutions, human rights were being defined (not because there were no human rights before, but because they were in greater jeopardy then than ever before). Our present criminal law system was then definitely introduced, and these rights were declared to be inalienable, except for those being prosecuted. They received very little from this horn of plenty of human righteousness, except the right not to be cruelly punished 'unnecessarily'. Mere indictment is sufficient to deprive anyone who is prosecuted of his human dignity. He no longer has freedom of the press, no privacy for his mail, no freedom to group together or meet, no freedom for sexual and human contact. He is even deprived of the pursuit of happiness (in his case, to try to repair the harm he has done), and thereby be accepted as an honest citizen.

Our present system of criminal law prosecutes mainly those who are already the underprivileged and deprived categories of our population: racial minorities, young people, the socially weak and defenceless — and until recently (though the moral panic on AIDS can update it again) sexual deviants. For several centuries the managers of the system had been clearly showing a constant preference to prosecute the weaker, so the question may be asked if the rulers of our societies have ever been interested in real crime-control. One gets the impression that they prosecuted the weak in order to legitimize their own conduct. Rulers will never prosecute their own class associates. Or at least, it is very exceptional.

In the present structures of criminal procedures the 'criminal', or perpetrator of crime, is treated as an *object* of prosecution. Being an object is a total denial of his human dignity. Human beings should never be made into objects, since it is a basic human right to be a subject and bearer of rights. At our trials the culprit has to defend himself, not so much against his victim, as against the whole of society, which in the Netherlands is represented by an all powerful public prosecutor. Such a charge is too much for any human being. The defendant is, moreover, deprived of his natural surroundings and he is not allowed to bring in for his defence his friends and relatives. They may be witnesses, but not an intimate support group. Very few people have learned to defend themselves in such important matters without the immediate help of their kin. Only people with higher education have learned to speak up for themselves, and as a result they are less likely to be the object of prosecution because they generally have the means, and the socio-linguistic and verbal skill, of defence.

The term *trial* in the English language is living evidence of the obscure and sad origin of criminal law. *Trial* means that people had to be tried on the purity of their souls (if they ever could), and the term goes back to the days of the Inquisition and ordeal.

Part II. The aims of an abolitionist perspective

Our first aim is that criminal law should be brought back into our general legal system, back under the rule of law. The criminal law system barely deserves the beautiful name of justice, since it is a derailment of our legal system. We must learn all over again to apply the rules of a normal legal system, which for centuries, in the best of our western traditions, were used for the settlement of disputes and the regulation of conflicts between — if possible — *equal* parties. The main problems of our strategy have to be defined in legal terms. It has been the deficiency of penal reform so far that the legal system of civil and administrative law has been neglected, whereas attention has been paid exclusively to the problems of social disorganization, prison reform, psychological stress, and psychiatric therapy. As long as the present system is kept intact, all reform will be co-opted by it, and reform will eventually strengthen it, as is so vividly described by Thomas Mathiesen in his theory of positive and negative reforms (*The Politics of Abolition*, Martin Robertson, London, 1974).

Crime in abolitionist thought has to be defined in terms of *tort*. Indeed, we do not have to devise an entirely new system of rules. We already have one, waiting to be applied and adapted. Lawyers and jurists are the allies of abolitionists, since they are capable, and hopefully willing, to develop new concepts of tort which would be suitable for the regulation of crime conflicts, and rules for the settlement of disputes arising from what we used to call 'crime'. The skills of psychologists, psychiatrists, and social workers must be adapted and rewritten for conflict-regulation, whereby personality problems would become secondary — if even that. The new system would no longer be called criminal law but *reparative law*.

If a new system of rules were being tried out, we would have an excellent opportunity to 'clean up' the stereotype of the 'delinquent'. He would no longer be the — suitable enemy of society (if the managers of the criminal law system and their political friends do not place him in that role); he would no longer be a 'sick' person (if he is no longer made sick by degradation and incarceration, or labelled as sick by a psychiatry that went astray); no longer deviant (if not labelled as such by control-agencies). (See Nils Christie, 'Suitable Enemies', in H. Bianchi and R. van Swaaningen (eds.), *Abolitionism: Towards a Non-Repressive Approach to Crime,* Free University Press, Amsterdam 1986, 42–54.) In the abolitionist perspective a 'criminal', or a 'delinquent', is a person who has committed a liability-creating act, as a result of which he is in a difficult, and not always enviable, but certainly not hopeless, position in which he has to participate in a discussion on the harm he has done, and how it can be *repaired*. He is thus no longer an evil-minded man or woman, but simply a debtor, a liable person whose human duty is to take responsibility for his or her acts, and to assume the duty of repair.

To the abolitionist movement the main concepts of the system of reparative law no longer stem from guilt and culpability. We want to replace them largely by concepts like debt, liability, and responsibility. We do not deny, of course, that ethical concepts like guilt and culpability exist and are of great importance, but we doubt if they can be defined or be used in criminal law proceedings, or even be applied in legal proceedings anyway. They can most certainly *not* be used in the 'trial' proceedings as we have them now. A trial, and any other criminal procedure, is based on a false premiss of *consensus.* When, during a trial, a verdict or sentence is pronounced and a person convicted, such proceedings are based on the pretence that there is consensus on the interpretation of norms and values. This is done quite undemocratically, however, because the convict's peer and social groups have no real influence on the definition process. Those countries that have jury trials are not very much better off. What is purported to be consensus is just power exerted by one group over another. It smacks of class justice. Some radical criminologists are therefore in favour of a *dissensus* model instead of the traditional consensus model. The disadvantage of the dissensus model is, however, that it can really only be used in political trials, or those criminal proceedings which have a political character. The dissensus model is in fact a civil war *in statu nascendi,* and will turn into a consensus model whenever one of the parties has beaten the other. For abolitionist procedures an *assensus* model is preferable. Using such a model we admit that the last word on good and evil, on guilt and culpability, can never be pronounced without violence. It is better therefore to discuss these problems of ethics and morality without imposing our own views on the other person. In other publications I have tried to outline such a model *(Justice as Sanctuary: Toward a New System of Crime Control,* Indiana University Press, Bloomington, Indiana, USA, 1994). In our culture the assensus model is very common (e.g., western parliament), and in other cultures it is common in cases of harmful acts and injury. We should consider such a model for the resolution of criminalized conflicts as well. But it comprises a new set of rules, and we must first practice its use in order to master the process eventually. Once these rules are mastered, we will discover that guilt and culpability are so interwoven in our social and cultural system that we can never blame just one person, as we still do in our criminal law system. Dostoyevsky argued that each of us is guilty towards all. And we have to share responsibility. That is why a liable person has a human right to help to shoulder his responsibility. This should be a legal right as well!

The ideas of punishment and punitive response to liability acts must wither away entirely. The very thought that one grown up human being should ever have a right, or duty, to punish another grown up human being is a gross moral indecency, and the phenomenon cannot stand up to any ethical test. The punitive response should be replaced by a call for responsibility and for repair, and punishment should be replaced by reconciliation. Punishment is destructive to society because it is violent: reconciliation serves society, and is a lesson in humanity.

The institution of prison and imprisonment has to be abolished as a retributive form of punishment. No trace should be left of this dark side of human history. In our constitutions, amendments, articles, or paragraphs should be inserted to read: 'imprisonment, in whatever form, is not tolerated in this country and nation'. We can use terms that were applied when servitude and slavery were constitutionally abolished.

We must discuss answers to a number of problems, which may not be so difficult in themselves, but for which people will continue to demand an answer, and rightly so. The *first* question is: what are we going to do with the persons who create an *immediate danger* to our bodies and our lives? It is true that there are very dangerous people who are never prosecuted. Although presidents who are playing wargames in the Pacific, in Central America, and in Libya, or who are helping to terrorize European airports, are a much greater danger to people's safety than any 'ordinary criminal' whatsoever, we do not lock *them* up. We let them do their dangerous deeds in the political, military, and economic spheres. But that is not an answer to the question. I agree that we have the right, and the duty, to protect ourselves and others against danger. But at the same time I wonder if the number of dangerous people would be so great if the criminal law system no longer degraded its prosecutees, mutilating them by incarceration and mental injury; if the state no longer provoked criminality by its bad example of punitive violence; and if the media no longer whipped up public opinion against 'criminals'. Perhaps, if we improve our legal system, the number of dangerous people will be so small that, even in a large country like the United States, two or three small places of quarantine will be sufficient, and certainly not the huge store of hundreds of thousands of human beings which that country has today. The person taken into quarantine, however, would legally enjoy all medical and social help, and his treatment would be controlled by strict rules in order to avoid the abuse which could readily creep in. Any such person in quarantine would have the legal right of a trustee, a non-professional person from outside, of his own choice. Any extension of his stay would have to be controlled, not by an institutional hoard, but by the court. No extension could be imposed without plentiful legal aid for lawyers. A government deputee would have to report to parliament or the state council, annually, on any of the people in quarantine.

The *second* question that arises is: what are we going to do when a person refuses, and *continues to refuse,* to negotiate about the injury he has caused, or in which he has participated? In that case he should be invited to negotiate, not seven times, but seventy times seven. If his refusal is due to the unreasonable demands of the other party (whether the defendant refuses or the plaintiff), the case can be brought before court. If only the defendant is to be blamed for negotiations not taking place, he may be kept in custody for debts, but again under the strictest rules, lest his case be abused. The defendant must be released as soon as he or she is willing to reopen negotiations. The defendant in custody has every right to be accompanied by, or to receive, whomsoever he wishes. Such custody must be under the permanent control of a public representative. But again, in the abolitionist movement, we feel sure that if the state no longer set a bad example of violence by the repression of criminality (which is unsuccessful anyway), and if we were all able to develop a set of rules which would allow people to do justice to others and to themselves, hopefully the number of conscientious refusers would remain very small indeed.

The present system of criminal law has a very authoritarian character and is entirely devoid of democracy. Far too much power is in the hands of the prosecutor and the judge. There simply cannot be a 'fair trial', quite apart from the fact that the word trial as such must be abolished, if too much power is in the hands of one party. The abolitionist perspective wishes to bring the conflict back to the community wherever possible. This implies that we want negotiations on conflict to take place out of court as much as possible. The *third* question that arises is: are there any tasks left for *judges*? The help of a judge would only be invoked if the disputing parties were unable to come to a settlement by themselves. From the sociology of law we have learned that this is the practice already in civil and administrative cases; so why not in criminal cases? The role of the judge, therefore, would be far more that of a *mediator,* insisting that parties comply with his mediation. The judge would no longer be a person who, godlike or fatherlike, pronounces verdicts on morality, when one person, or party, is found guilty.

The role of the *prosecutor* poses the *fourth* question. It has to be redefined. He would no longer be a prosecutor, except in those cases where he would he allowed to make a public complaint, because there is no identifiable victim. In such cases a process of negotiation would be impossible otherwise. His new task, however, would be of an equalizing nature. As a public representative he would see to it that neither defendant nor plaintiff abuses the situation. If any of the parties is weaker he would stand by. The new name for his role would be that of *praetor,* a word in Roman law for the man who enabled legal action, and observed that it ran smoothly.

Fifthly, what about the *police*? In the old days, in western society, when we still had at our disposal an infra-judiciary, negotiative system of conflict solution, we could dispense with the police. As a matter of fact, there were hardly any police before 1800. But there were still old rules and customs for tracking down thieves and culprits; there were sanctuaries and asylums for outlaws; the church often offered aid in conflict regulations; and the communities were much smaller and knew people face-to-face. Our present criminal law system has only gradually crept into our society, and has become more and more anonymous.

Nowadays, social conflicts are on a larger scale and more intricate. We could not do without the police to trace those who have committed wrongful acts, and should be invited to settle the disputes. The population is too large — although more face-to-face relationships in district neighbourhood life are growing up again — and most conflicts are between more than two people. Therefore a simple convocation of the disputing parties is not always possible — but still, in a great many cases, it *is*. As long as the police do not set a bad example of violence and counter-violence (the police must be *less* violent than criminals, not *more*), so long as they are not racially biased, nor partial in class or generation conflict, nor allow themselves to be politically abused, but accept gratefully all kinds of parliamentary control and take citizen's wishes seriously in their activities and power, and do not allow the organization to be more military than at present: *then* the police would be very welcome to help the citizens to build up a better system of injury control, and to help the citizens — who will have to play an active role themselves as well — to settle their disputes.

Part III. Some guide-lines for alternatives

The abolitionist movement firmly believes that at the present time we have to have confidence that people have come of age sufficiently in order to settle their disputes by themselves, and that they are not in need of any bureaucratic organisation to take their conflict out of their hands. People were able to settle their disputes themselves in the past in our own culture, and they are still able to do so in other cultures.

Therefore we should avoid falling into the trap of bureaucracy by abolishing the existing one and handing it over to another professional bureaucracy of any kind. Professional solutions have to be very restricted in number. Servo-mechanisms have to be built into any new system we devise, such as community control and non-professional activity, in order to prevent any new professionalism from arising.

Any abolitionist movement has to be very careful not to co-opt the power of an old system which is very strong and efficient. We have seen this happen in attempts to bring 'diversion'-solutions into the old system, or, rather, half-way into it. This type of conflict solution whereby, in some cases, with the agreement of the public prosecutor, no court action will be taken so long as the parties come together to settle their disputes, e.g., by reparation, has in fact strengthened the system, because it provided the public prosecutor with the opportunity to extend his power into those areas which he had previously left unnoticed. It by no means diminished his power. He just made neighbourhood centres work for him, in order to take minor cases off his hands.

An abolitionist should not offer the authority in power an elaborate blueprint of the alternatives, because that also relieves citizens of the possibility of building up a system according to their own real needs and feelings of justice. And a blueprint is also the safest way to create a new bureaucracy of professionals (see Mathiesen's *The Politics of Abolition,* Martin Robertson, London 1974).

What follows is, therefore, not a blueprint, nor an elaborate and entirely considered system, but a few proposals whereby some answers to some questions are considered, and some new (or rather old) institutions are offered for consideration. In order to give clarity to the intricacy of the problems, we will separate the conflicts into four types.

1. *Minor cases of injury,* such as petty theft, minor robbery, insult, quarrel, and row. These are the typical cases where *neighbourhood centres* offer the best solution. The citizens who claim to be victims, and want to be plaintiffs, may settle the dispute with the defendant. Often the offenders are not detected (just like in the existing system), or are too young. If the offenders do not get punished, but simply have to repair damage and restore or return what was stolen, if they no longer have to be deterred by punishment, there is good reason to expect that this petty criminality will gradually diminish. It should be remembered how provocative the power of punishment is, certainly for young people, more so than a deterrent. Moreover, restoration of damage is a lesson in good citizenship. The word 'crime' should gradually disappear from our language. We should not forget that the stigmatizing power of language may be very harmful for good citizenship, that also implies an immediate, preventive interference at the very moment a crime is being committed.

2. *Slightly more serious cases of injury,* such as burglary and housebreaking, not too serious violence, petty fraud, swindling, arson without causing death, scuffles, scrapes, and that sort of thing. Here the neighbourhood is of great importance as well. We should not forget that most harmful acts do not stand by themselves, but are committed between people who usually know each other quite well, or between groups and in neighbourhoods. There should be boards of citizens who bring the parties together. The San Francisco *Community Board* Programme is a good example of this. We should no longer consider any party as an individual who has to defend himself or herself all alone. He should be allowed to take his intimate groups with him, because conflicts might be discussed more easily and negotiated upon in a familiar setting. In the negotiation discussions (palavers) in the neighbourhood centres, the other side of the conflict has to be party to the considerations. The other elements of the conflict will not lead to a diminution of the actors' guilt (as is now the case), since, in those discussions, it is not guilt that is under consideration but the best way of finding a solution to the conflict.

Sometimes the conflict may have difficult judicial aspects, so often lawyers and jurists will have to take part in the discussions. Here *civil law alternatives* play an important role. If the conflicting parties of defendant and plaintiff require it (although it may very often be very difficult to distinguish the one from the other), a social worker may help. But usually groups are quite capable of handling their own affairs, and feel no need to be labelled as helpless.

3. The third category are the *serious cases*, where murder or manslaughter is involved, very serious violence, rape, arson with a fatal result, and killing with political aims. These injuries are very serious, and people get very emotional about them. On the one hand an abolitionist will argue that people's emotions are whipped up by the media too often, and that politicians abuse the feelings aroused by such injuries for their own end. None the less, abolitionists agree that emotions are justified and have to be respected. They are human, and they will never disappear, and they do not need to. But emotions should not prevent attempts to bring conflict towards some kind of regulation. For long-term imprisonment does not bring the victim back to life either (to say nothing of the death penalty), and the humiliated or mutilated victim does not get his or her health back as result of this sort of punishment. And the so-called 'satisfaction', which the victim or his next of kin might receive from the certainty that the 'criminal' is suffering is far more destructive to the soul of the victim than any attempt by the actor to do some possible good, to show the slightest sign of repentance, or to try to improve the situation of his victim. The argument that severe punishment would deter criminals has been so often shown by scientific research to be entirely unjustified, in all cases of any seriousness, that it needs no further consideration in any abolitionist article, were it not that politicians still abuse that argument so often for improper purposes.

Penitence and reconciliation are, and always have been, the royal way to improve a difficult situation. It is the sole and proper way for actor and victim (and their kin) to overcome the regrettable event.

But emotions are still there, and if they do not have an outlet, or if they are not controlled and appeased, they may lead to an outburst, to lynching or to destructive and violent self-help by the people involved. Lynching takes place more often in racial repression than in cases of 'ordinary crime', and happens more often in Hollywood movies than in reality. In the old days in Europe we had a system of blood vengeance. Historical research has found evidence, however, that active blood vengeance did not occur frequently. People were far too scared of the escalatory effects of the system. There were no public prosecutors, so people had the opportunity to do justice to themselves, but they needed some kind of sting for unwilling parties: that was the threat of blood vengeance, which was usually sufficient to bring parties to the palaver hall. We should not forget that, even in cases of very serious and heinous acts, there is often much more at stake than just that act. And this has to be considered also in palavers and negotiations. Such circumstances and aspects have a better chance of being discussed there than during trials.

But emotions remain, and very often, immediately after a serious violent act, public reactions can be so violent that the actor needs some protection in order to survive for the later negotiations — not only him but his intimate group too if he has one. In the old days *sanctuary* served as a place of refuge where the perpetrator of a serious offence could go and live for a while in safety until negotiations could begin. Sanctuaries were in use in England and France until the 17th century. In the Netherlands and many other European countries they were available in a secular form until the end of the 18th century, when they were abolished to make room for our modern criminal law system. The sanctuaries were often churches, and the church often helped the parties to become reconciled. In England, and many other countries, the kings often granted to abbey churches the privilege of sanctuary, so convinced were they of its wholesome effect. We should reintroduce sanctuaries in our societies: places of refuge, having the right of immunity, outside state control, where actors of violent acts have the right of asylum whilst awaiting negotiations, either within the place of sanctuary or in a *civil court*. That would be much better than a trial. Perhaps once again there is a role for the churches here? In America revival of the *Sanctuary Movement* was initiated by the churches, which wanted to offer sanctuary to refugees from Central America. But at universities also interest in the reintroduction of sanctuaries is growing (i.e., Stastny and Tyrnauer, Universities of Vermont and Montreal). In Geneva, Switzerland, the World Alliance of Reformed Churches too has set out plans for conference on sanctuary. But why only the churches? We need secular places of refuge as well! I tried to outline some basic conditions for the establishment of sanctuaries for communal offenders in my book *Justice as Sanctuary* (1994).

4. Those cases where *no individual victim* can be found i.e., transgressions of order. These comprise such divergent acts as traffic offences, drunk-driving, offences against licensing acts, trading in contraband, economic offences, environmental offences — and, in my view also, the preparation of a war. If these offences are just the abuse of a received licence (like drunk-driving), *administrative measures* will suffice. Imprisonment is ridiculous. If a person continuously, and in spite of receiving a warning, abuses his licence he is bound to lose it. It is not such a problem. Such administrative measures seem to have more deterrent effect than imprisonment. If actors, with or without violence, claim a political excuse for their activity, they would be better to argue their case before a *political body* — like parliament — other than before a judicial body, like the court.

Although the abolitionists are in favour of handling disputes out of court wherever possible, we would still need a judiciary. For if it ever happens that negotiations get out of hand, and one of the parties is in danger of being victimized, he should have the right of appeal to a court. That too is justice.

Part IV. Action and research

The existing criminal law system is powerful. It is being backed by very powerful political and economic interests, and it is constantly being whipped up by the media, who, again, have commercial interests. For the time being we have to put up with the idea that a system which took several centuries to become what it is now will not disappear overnight, and that it will take several decades for it to be abolished and replaced by a more just, justified, and efficient system of reparation and reconciliation.

The new system has to be borne by the people, and they have to relearn what has been lost through the activity of the criminal law bureaucracy: how to cope with problems in their own community; they have to be reskilled, as Raymond Shonholtz puts it.

For the coming decades we have to live with the reality that two different systems will operate side by side — a *two-system system*. It may look odd, but for the abolitionist movement this oddness may turn out to be a benefit. Let us learn from what happened in Italy in the mid-1970s. There a group of psychiatrists, inspired by the ideas of one of them, Franco Basaglia, argued that the immense storehouse of psychiatric institutions made the patient sick instead of making him well. It is freedom that cures, they said, and our patients have to be brought back into their communities, because such communities have immense resources for healing their own deviants. All right, said the Italian government, which had been irritated for a long time by this sort of progressive thinking. And a bill was passed through parliament closing many large institutions and suspending their subsidies. The result was disastrous. The patients were simply sent back to the communities, but the latter had long since forgotten how to cope with these problems. They had to relearn what they had not been used to for more than a hundred years. The Italian government laughed up its sleeve when psychiatrists began again to beg for subsidies and the reopening of the institutions. This ill-intended generosity on the part of the government meant a serious set-back for progressive psychiatry in the country. Such a thing must not happen to the abolitionist movement of criminal law!

It is alright for criminal law to continue in those communities which are not yet well prepared to cope with their conflicts, and for the criminal law system to be available for those perpetrators of harmful acts who prefer to go on being called 'criminal' in the criminal law system, rather than being free citizens who declare themselves liable and responsible for their acts, and who want to make amends for the harm they have done. It seems to some people that the dull passivity of imprisonment is to be preferred to taking on responsibility.

A risk that may occur is that the authorities may offer subsidies for building up 'self-help' programmes in communities. There is a mortal danger in subsidies. They are quite often the most effective instrument for a bureaucracy to control the activities of its citizens (although this statement is not true of all subsidies). But subsidies lead in many cases irrevocably to professionalization, and professionals usually tend to create a new bureaucracy. Thus the system would have co-opted the abolition proposals, and neutralized them.

There is another risk; forewarned is forearmed. This is the so-called 'cave-in-model'. Penal reformers have often fallen into that trap in the last eighty years or so, as I have described in my article 'Pitfalls and Strategies of Abolition' (H. Bianchi and R. van Swaaningen (eds.), *Abolitionism: Towards a non-Repressive Approach to Crime*, Free University Press, Amsterdam, 1986, 147–56). Authorities will often argue: 'Yes, abolitionists, we think you are right. We do indeed have an inefficient and unnecessarily cruel system of crime control, and we should see to it that the smallest possible number of people are affected by it. In particular, let us prevent young people from falling victim to it: let us, for a start, save the children.' Then everyone will be happy, for we all seem to agree that children should be saved rather than adults. Several times in the last century it was like that with penal reform. The effects of this are, however, dysfunctional for abolition. For, what the authorities really have in mind is to save their prosecutors' power for what they call 'the war against hard core criminality', and it is they who define what that is. After a while, it turns out that they are prosecuting just as many people as before, because their prosecutory man-power has remained the same — or may even have increased. In the end, it turns out that just as many young people are being prosecuted as before, or even more, and they are not saved anyway. Most sweet promises by a criminal law bureaucracy to adopt an abolitionist policy, are the treacherous song of the Pied Piper.

The abolitionist movement should remain aware that, as long as the criminal law bureaucracy has the monopoly of crime definition and certainly if it remains the only authority to define hard core criminality, its power will just grow if we allow it a cave-in model. The abolitionist movement should devise its strategy for saving both violent offenders and non-violent young delinquents. Sanctuaries for serious actors are needed as much, if not more, than centres for young people, if we really want an abolitionist movement to be effective in the end.

Some people will wonder whether or not an abolitionist can still do any good within the system *without* strengthening it. Yes and no. I should like to give one illustrative example. A few years ago in the Netherlands some people were active in obtaining permission for inmates to have television sets in their cells. The prisons' administration were in favour of that, because it kept the inmates quiet, and away from any rebellious thinking. In this way it strengthened the system. But better information from the outside world will also keep them aware of their rights as citizens, make them critical of their situation, and fit to contest it. There is no doubt that the most powerful and effective action the abolitionist movement can achieve in its struggle against the prison institution is the total abolition of any restriction of human rights imposed on inmates, both on remand and after conviction. Imagine the prison authorities being obliged to grant inmates the right of free association, and not only inside their own institution or prison, but all prisoners in any one state or nation: a sort of national council of prison inmates! That would be very threatening to the system, and a lot of exertion would be needed to obtain that constitutional right. I think we must just start with — perhaps less way-out — initiatives in order to achieve the abolition of punitive laws and measures.

Many statements in this article are still in need of continued research. The abolitionist movement should try to get allies among criminological researchers, and among progressive social movements too. Criminology has predominantly been a *repressive* science. What we need in this field is a science directed towards *emancipation,* anticipating the coming changes in society.

Corporate Crime and the Comparison with Street Crime

9.   A Theory of White Collar Crime
Edwin Sutherland

A complete explanation of white collar crime cannot be derived from the available data. The data which are at hand suggest that white collar crime has its genesis in the same general process as other criminal behavior, namely, differential association. The hypothesis of differential association is that criminal behavior is learned in association with those who define such behavior favorably and in isolation from those who define it unfavorably, and that a person in an appropriate situation engages in such criminal behavior if, and only if, the weight of the favorable definitions exceeds the weight of the unfavorable definitions. This hypothesis is certainly not a complete or universal explanation of white collar crime or of other crime, but it perhaps fits the data of both types of crimes better than any other general hypothesis.

This hypothesis or other hypotheses can be tested adequately only by research studies organized specifically for this purpose and by first-hand acquaintance with the careers of businessmen. In the absence of such studies, it is necessary for the present to fall back upon data now available. The data at hand provide two types of documentary evidence, namely, biographical or autobiographical descriptions of the careers of businessmen and descriptions of the diffusion of criminal practices from one situation to another. These two types of evidence will be illustrated in the following paragraphs.

Personal documents

A young businessman in the used-car business in Chicago described the process by which he was inducted into illegal behavior.

> When I graduated from college I had plenty of ideals of honesty, fair play, and cooperation which I had acquired at home, in school, and from literature. My first job after graduation was selling typewriters. During the first day I learned that these machines were not sold at a uniform price but that a person who higgled and waited could get a machine at about half the list price. I felt that this was unfair to the customer who paid the list price. The other salesmen laughed at me and could not understand my silly attitude. They told me to forget the things I had learned in school, and that you couldn't earn a pile of money by being strictly honest. When I replied that money wasn't everything they mocked at me: "Oh! No? Well, it helps." I had ideals and I resigned.

> My next job was selling sewing machines. I was informed that one machine, which cost the company $18, was to be sold for $40 and another machine, which cost the company $19, was to be sold for $70, and that I was to sell the de luxe model whenever possible in preference to the cheaper model, and was given a list of the reasons why it was a better buy.

Edwin H. Sutherland: 'A Theory of White Collar Crime' from *WHITE COLLAR CRIME: THE UNCUT VERSION* (Yale University Press, 1983), pp. 234–256.

When I told the sales manager that the business was dishonest and that I was quitting right then, he looked at me as if he thought I was crazy and said angrily: "There's not a cleaner business in the country."

It was quite a time before I could find another job. During this time I occasionally met some of my classmates and they related experiences similar to mine. They said they would starve if they were rigidly honest. All of them had girls and were looking forward to marriage and a comfortable standard of living, and they said they did not see how they could afford to be rigidly honest. My own feelings became less determined than they had been when I quit my first job.

Then I got an opportunity in the used-car business. I learned that this business had more tricks for fleecing customers than either of those I had tried previously. Cars with cracked cylinders, with half the teeth missing from the fly wheel, with everything wrong, were sold as "guaranteed." When the customer returned and demanded his guarantee, he had to sue to get it and very few went to that trouble and expense: the boss said you could depend on human nature. If hot cars could be taken in and sold safely, the boss did not hesitate. When I learned these things I did not quit as I had previously. I sometimes felt disgusted and wanted to quit, but I argued that I did not have much chance to find a legitimate firm. I knew that the game was rotten but it had to be played — the law of the jungle and that sort of thing. I knew that I was dishonest and to that extent felt that I was more honest than my fellows. The thing that struck me as strange was that all these people were proud of their ability to fleece customers. They boasted of their crookedness and were admired by their friends and enemies in proportion to their ability to get away with a crooked deal: it was called shrewdness. Another thing was that these people were unanimous in their denunciation of gangsters, robbers, burglars, and petty thieves. They never regarded themselves as in the same class and were bitterly indignant if accused of dishonesty: it was just good business.

Once in a while, as the years have passed, I have thought of myself as I was in college — idealistic, honest, and thoughtful of others — and have been momentarily ashamed of myself. Before long such memories became less and less frequent and it became difficult to distinguish me from my fellows. If you had accused me of dishonesty I would have denied the charge, but with slightly less vehemence than my fellow businessmen, for after all I had learned a different code of behavior.

A graduate student in an urban university, in order to supplement his income, took a job as an extra salesman in a shoe store on Saturdays and other rush days. He had no previous experiences as a shoe salesman or in any other regular business. He described his experience in this store thus:

One day I was standing in the front part of the store, waiting for the next customer. A man came in and asked if we had any high, tan button shoes.

I told him that we had no shoes of that style. He thanked me and walked out of the store. The floor-walker came up to me and asked me what the man wanted. I told him what the man asked for and what I replied. The floor-walker said angrily: "Damn it! We're not here to sell what they want. We're here to sell what we've got." He went on to instruct me that when a customer came into the store, the first thing to do was to get him to sit down and take off his shoe so that he couldn't get out of the store. "If we don't have what he wants," he said, "bring him something else and try to interest him in that style. If he is still uninterested, inform the floor-walker and he will send one of the regular salesmen, and if that doesn't work, a third salesman will be sent to him. Our policy is that no customer gets out of the store without a sale until at least three salesmen have worked on him. By that time he feels that he must be a crank and will generally buy something whether he wants it or not."

I learned from other clerks that if a customer needed a 7-B shoe and we did not have that size in the style he desired, I should try on an 8-A or 7-C or some other size. The sizes were marked in code so that the customer did not know what the size was, and it might be necessary to lie to him about the size; also his foot might be injured by the misfit. But the rule was to sell him a pair of shoes, preferably a pair that fit but some other pair if necessary.

I learned also that the clerks received an extra commission if they sold the out-of-style shoes left over from earlier seasons, which were called "spiffs." The regular salesmen made a practice of selling spiffs to anyone who appeared gullible and generally had to claim either that this was the latest style or that it had been the style earlier and was coming back this season, or that it was an old style but much better quality than present styles. The clerk had to size up the customer and determine which one of these lies would be most likely to result in a sale.

Several years later I became acquainted with a man who worked for several years as a regular salesman in shoe stores in Seattle. When I described to him the methods I had learned in the shoe store where I worked, he said: "Every shoe store in Seattle except one does exactly the same things and I learned to be a shoe salesman in exactly the same manner you did."

Another young man who was holding his first position as a shoe salesman in a small city wrote an autobiographical statement in which he included the following instructions given him by the manager of the shoe store:

My job is to move out shoes and I hire you to assist in this. I am perfectly glad to fit a person with a pair of shoes if we have his size, but I am willing to misfit him if it is necessary in order to sell him a pair of shoes. I expect you to do the same. If you do not like this, some one else can have your job. While you are working for me, I expect you to have no scruples about how you sell shoes.

A man who had been a school teacher and had never been officially involved in any delinquencies secured a position as agent of a book-publishing company and was assigned to public school work. He soon learned that the publishing company bribed the members of the textbook committee in order to secure adoptions of their books. With considerable shame he began to use this method of bribery because he felt it was necessary in order to make a good record. Partly because he disliked this procedure but principally because this work kept him away from home much of the time, he decided that he would become a lawyer. He moved to a large city, registered for night courses in a law school, and secured a daytime job as a claim agent for a casualty insurance company. About two years later he was convicted of embezzling the funds of the insurance company. A portion of his autobiography describes the process by which he got into this difficulty:

> Almost immediately after I got into this business I learned two things: first, the agents who got ahead with the company were the ones who made settlements at low figures and without taking cases into court; second, the settlements were generally made by collusion with the lawyers and doctors for the claimants. Most of the lawyers for the claimants were ambulance-chasers and were willing to make settlements because they got their fees without any work. The claim agent for the insurance company got a secret kick-back out of the settlement. When I learned this was the way to get ahead in the casualty insurance business, I went in for it in a big way. Accidently I left some papers loose in my office, from which it was discovered that I was "knocking down" on the settlements. The insurance company accused me of taking money which belonged to them, but actually I was taking money which belonged to the claimants.

The following statement was made by a young man who had graduated from a recognized school of business, had become a certified public accountant, and had been employed for several years in a respected firm of public accountants in a large city.

> While I was a student in the school of business I learned the principles of accounting. After I had worked for a time for an accounting firm I found that I had failed to learn many important things about accounting. An accounting firm gets its work from business firms and, within limits, must make the reports which those business firms desire. The accounting firm for which I work is respected and there is none better in the city. On my first assignment I discovered some irregularities in the books of the firm and these would lead anyone to question the financial policies of that firm. When I showed my report to the manager of our accounting firm, he said that was not a part of my assignment and I should leave it out. Although I was confident that the business firm was dishonest, I had to conceal this information. Again and again I have been compelled to do the same thing in other assignments. I get so disgusted with things of this sort that I wish I could leave the profession. I guess I must stick to it, for it is the only occupation for which I have training.

The documents above were written by persons who came from "good homes" and "good neighborhoods" and who had no official records as juvenile delinquents. White collar criminals, like professional thieves, are seldom recruited from juvenile delinquents. As a part of the process of learning practical business, a young man with idealism and thoughtfulness for others is inducted into white collar crime. In many cases he is ordered by the manager to do things which he regards as unethical or illegal, while in other cases he learns from those who have the same rank as his own how they make a success. He learns specific techniques of violating the law, together with definitions of situations in which those techniques may be used. Also, he develops a general ideology. This ideology grows in part out of the specific practices and is in the nature of generalization from concrete experiences, but in part it is transmitted as a generalization by phrases such as "we are not in business for our health," "business is business," or "no business was ever built on the beatitudes." These generalizations, whether transmitted as such or abstracted from concrete experiences, assist the neophyte in business to accept the illegal practices and provide rationalizations for them.

The preceding documents all came from young men in subordinate positions and are in no sense a random sample of persons in such positions. Even if they came from a random sample of persons in such subordinate positions, they would not demonstrate the genesis of illegal practices by the managers of large industries. Unfortunately similar documents, even of a scattered nature, are not available for the managers of large industries. No first-hand research study from this point of view has ever been reported. Gustavus Meyer in his *History of American Fortunes* and Ferdinand Lundberg in his *America's Sixty Families* have demonstrated that many of the large American fortunes originated in illegal practices. However, these books pay little attention to the process by which illegal behavior develops in the person. Bits of information may be gleaned from biographies of men like Armour, du Pont, Eastman, Firestone, Ford, Gary, Guggenheim, Havemeyer, McCormick, Marshall Field, Mellon, Morgan, Rockefeller, Seiberling, Swift, Woolworth, and others. Many of the biographies are subscription books written on order of the businessmen for advertising purposes; criminal behavior is seldom admitted and never explained. Bouck White's *The Book of Daniel Drew* is a forthright description of an actual person but is classed in the *Dictionary of American Biography* as semi-fiction.

Diffusion of illegal practices

The diffusion of illegal practices is the second type of evidence that white collar crime is due to differential association. Business firms have the objective of maximum profits. When one firm devises a method of increasing profits, other firms become aware of the method and adopt it, perhaps a little more quickly and a little more generally if the firms are competitors in the same market than if they are not competitors. The diffusion of illegal practices which increase profits is facilitated by the trend toward centralization of the control of industry by investment banks and by the conferences of business concerns in trade associations. The process of diffusion will be considered first in relation to competition, and subsequently with reference to other relations.

The diffusion of illegal practices among competitors is illustrated in the following incident in a food manufacturing concern. A chemist who had been employed to advise this firm as to the scientific basis for claims in advertisements made the following statement regarding his experiences.

> When I got members of the firm off in a corner and we were talking confidentially, they frankly deplored the misrepresentations in their advertisements. At the same time they said it was necessary to advertise in this manner in order to attract the attention of customers and sell their products. Since other firms are making extravagant claims regarding their products, we must make extravagant claims regarding our products. A mere statement of fact regarding our products would make no impression on customers in the face of the ads of other firms.

One of the important automobile companies began to advertise the interest rate on the unpaid balance in installment purchases as six percent, when in fact the rate was more than eleven percent. Within a few weeks the other automobile companies began to advertise their interest rates as six percent, although their actual rates, also, were more than eleven percent. Again, when one automobile company published an advertisement of the price and specification of a certain car, together with a picture of a more expensive model, thus misrepresenting its cars, the other companies in the industry generally published similar advertisements with similar misrepresentation. Within a few months after the tire dealers had solemnly adopted a code of ethics in advertising, including a pledge not to use misrepresentations, one tire manufacturer announced a special cut-rate price for tires on the Fourth of July, in which the savings were grossly misrepresented; several other tire manufacturers promptly made similar announcements of cut-rate sales with similar misrepresentations. Thus competition in advertising drives the participants to the extreme, and when one corporation violates the law in this respect the other corporations do the same. The illegal behavior of the other corporations, at least, grows out of differential association.

Practices in restraint of trade are similarly diffused. One tire manufacturer made a discriminatory price on tires to a mail-order house; as soon as the other tire manufacturers and large distributors of tires learned of this arrangement, they made similar agreements for discriminatory prices, which were declared to be in restraint of trade. Sometimes definite coercion is used in forcing competitors into illegal agreements in restraint of trade. This has occurred especially in the form of threats of suits of patent infringement.

Illegal practices are diffused, also, when competition is not directly involved. This will be illustrated by the diffusion of misrepresentation in regard to the quality of gas sold by public utility corporations. The heating value of gas is customarily measured in terms of British Thermal Units, or BTU's. A BTU is the amount of heat that will raise the temperature of one pound of water one degree under standardized conditions. Until 1921, the Public Service Company of Colorado, a subsidiary of Cities Service, furnished gas in Denver with 600 BTU's. In that year this company secretly reduced the heating value of the gas, without reducing the price, until it had only 400 BTU's. The company made a statement to the Colorado State Commission that the experiment demonstrated that families consumed no more gas with the reduction of BTU's, and asked for authorization to adopt such heating values as they found to be most economical and efficient. This request was granted without an inspection of the detailed evidence and without a consultation with other authorities. This practice of reduction of BTU's, with the accompanying argument, then spread to other gas companies.

In June, 1924, the executive committee of the American Gas Association adopted a resolution that, since the Denver experiment showed no decrease in efficiency with the reduction of BTU's, the state utility commission should generally authorize the reduction of BTU's to as low as 300 without change in rates. In 1925, the Spokane Gas and Fuel Company requested authorization to reduce its gas to 450 BTU's, giving as supporting evidence the testimony of the Public Service Company of Colorado that the consumption of gas had not increased when BTU's were reduced, and with the further explanation that Alabama had adopted this standard and Illinois was considering it. The state commission of Washington, with no conflicting evidence available, granted the request. In May, 1926, the Iowa Committee on Public Utilities published a pamphlet for use in the public schools which contained the statement: "Government research has shown that the lower British Thermal Unit produces the same results in practical operation and can be more economically manufactured." In the meantime the Bureau of Standards of the federal government had been collecting evidence on this question. In 1925, it wrote a report to the effect that the efficiency of gas for heating purposes was directly proportional to the BTU's and that a decrease in BTU's was equivalent to an increase in price. This government report was discussed in 1924, before publication, with the members of the American Gas Association. The president of this Association wrote to the director of the Bureau of Standards: "Many members of the Gas Association would not want to send out a report that would indicate that the charge for gas should be inversely proportional to the calorific value of gas." A. Gordon King, a service engineer of the Gas Association, stated: "The more I study this (government) document, the less value or good to any one I see in it, and if it were possible I believe it should be suppressed."

The Bureau of Standards in 1926 asked permission to examine the data on which the Public Service Company of Colorado based their conclusions, but this request was refused. A paper on this subject was written by a gas engineer for the Bureau of Standards, which dealt specifically with the Denver situation. This paper was submitted to the Public Service Company of Colorado for criticisms. The officers of this corporation wrote to the officers of the National Electric Light Association, who wrote a personal letter to Paul S. Clapp, assistant to Secretary Herbert Hoover of the Department of Commerce, urging that the Secretary prohibit publication of the paper. Although consent to publish the paper was given to the author, both the *Gas Age Record* and the *American Gas Journal*, which had given space to the Denver claims, refused to publish this paper. It was not published anywhere until placed in evidence in 1935 by the Federal Trade Commission. This paper stated that the Public Service Company of Colorado had refused to make available the data on which they based claims that reduction of BTU's did not increase consumption of gas, that the evidence of the Bureau of Standards demonstrated the exact opposite of this, and that if the policy used in Denver were extended throughout the United States, consumers would pay $490,000,000 a year more for their gas. In 1927, the directors of the American Gas Association informed the Bureau of Standards that they did not approve of a re-investigation of this question. In July, 1928, the Association issued a news-letter to the effect that the Illinois Commerce Commission had conducted an investigation which sustained the Denver conclusion.

The Bureau of Standards appraised this Illinois study, which was made under conditions very favorable to the gas companies, as "a beautiful demonstration of an almost exact inverse proportion between the heating value and the volume of gas demanded by domestic consumers." The diffusion of these claims, which the Bureau of Standards held to be misrepresentation, was stopped by the trend toward natural gas; in fact, with the new developments, the gas companies have tended to reverse the position which they had taken during the decade of the twenties. The misrepresentation stopped as soon as it ceased to have economic value to the gas companies.[1]

Other illustrations of the diffusion of criminal practices are found in the customer-ownership campaigns of utility corporations and in the sales-quota system of many manufacturing companies. These campaigns are not in themselves criminal, but they have included fraudulent methods in so many cases that their significance is practically comparable to that of the burglar's "jimmy." It is not necessary to describe the details of the diffusion of these practices.[2]

General attitudes or mental sets, as well as specific practices, are diffused. This is illustrated in the following statement by Daniel Drew:

> With this panic year of which I am now writing (1857) a new state of affairs came about in financial circles. The panic was known as the "Western Blizzard." It put old fogeyism out of date forevermore. The men who conducted business in the old-fashioned slowpoke method — the think-of-the-other-fellow method — were swept away by this panic, or at least were so crippled up that they didn't figure much in the world of affairs afterwards. A new generation of men came in — a more pushful set. I was one of them. We were men who went ahead. We did things. We didn't split hairs about trifles. Anyhow, men of this skin, with a conscience all the time full of prickles, are out of place in business dickerings. A prickly conscience would be like a white silk apron for a blacksmith. Sometimes you've got to get your hands dirty, but that doesn't mean that the money you make is also dirty. Black hens can lay white eggs. . . . It isn't how you get your money but what you do with it that counts.[3]

Isolation

Businessmen are not only in contact with definitions which are favorable to white collar crime but they are also isolated from and protected against definitions which are unfavorable to such crime. Most of them, to be sure, were reared in homes in which honesty was defined as a virtue, but these home teachings had little explicit relation to business methods. The persons who define business practices as undesirable and illegal are customarily called "communists" or "socialists" and their definitions carry little weight.

The public agencies of communication, which continually define ordinary violations of the criminal code in a very critical manner, do not make similar definitions of white collar crime. Several reasons for this difference may be mentioned. The important newspapers, the motion picture corporations, and the radio corporations are all large corporations, and the persons who own and manage them have the same standards as the persons who manage other corporations. These agencies derive their principal income from advertisements by other business corporations and would be likely to lose a considerable part of this income if they were critical of business practices in general or those of particular corporations. Finally, these public agencies of communication themselves participate in white collar crimes and especially in restraint of trade, misrepresentation in advertising, and unfair labor practices. Thus businessmen are shielded from harsh criticisms by the public agencies of communication and remain in relative isolation from the definitions which are unfavorable to their practices.

Businessmen are shielded also against harsh criticisms by persons in governmental positions. Congress provided special implementation of the Sherman Antitrust Law and of many subsequent laws so that the stigma of crime might not attach officially to businessmen who violated these laws. This special implementation is almost, if not wholly, an exclusive feature of the laws which apply to businessmen. Moreover, the administrators select the less critical procedures in dealing with businessmen. They generally select equity procedures for businessmen accused of restraint of trade and criminal procedures for trade unionists accused of the same crime.

The less critical attitude of government toward businessmen than toward persons of lower socio-economic status is the result of several relationships. (a) Persons in government are, by and large, culturally homogeneous with persons in business, both being in the upper strata of American society. (b) Many persons in government are members of families which have other members in business. (c) Many persons in business are intimate personal friends of persons in government. Almost every important person in government has many close personal friends in business, and almost every important person in business has many close personal friends in government. (d) Many persons in government were previously connected with business firms as executives, attorneys, directors, or in other capacities. In times of war, especially, many persons in government retain their business connections. (e) Many persons in government hope to secure employment in business firms when their government work is terminated. Government work is often a step toward a career in private business. Relations established while in business, as well as inside information acquired at that time, carry over after the person joins a business firm. (f) Business is very powerful in American society and can damage or promote the governmental programs in which the governmental personnel are interested. (g) The program of the government is closely related to the political parties, and for their success in campaigns these political parties depend on contributions of large sums from important businessmen. Thus, the initial cultural homogeneity, the close personal relationships, and the power relationships protect businessmen against critical definitions by government.

The United States Steel Corporation, organized in 1900 by J. P. Morgan after he had directed the combination of many of the constituent parts, was the largest merger that had occurred in American industry. Amos Pinchot described some of the connections between this corporation and government officials which may have assisted in protecting this corporation for many years against prosecution under the antitrust laws:

> Philander C. Knox, former counsel for the Carnegie Steel Company and close personal friend of U.S. Steel director Henry Clay Frick, was U. S. Attorney General when the corporation was formed. Steel was well represented in high places throughout the administration of Theodore Roosevelt and W. H. Taft. Elihu Root, former attorney for the Carnegie Steel Company, was Secretary of State under Roosevelt and was succeeded by Knox, while Knox was replaced as Attorney General by George F. Wickersham, formerly attorney for the U.S. Steel Corporation. Truman Newberry, president of a subsidiary of U.S. Steel, was Secretary of the Navy, an important post in steel politics. Herbert Satterlee, son-in-law of J. P. Morgan, was Assistant Secretary of the Navy. Robert Bacon, a partner of J. P. Morgan and a director of U.S. Steel, was for a time Secretary of State.[4]

Although the Aluminium Company of America had the most complete monopoly of any corporation in the United States and for many years stamped out all competitors, the many complaints did not result in effective suits against this corporation for several decades. The principal power in this corporation was Andrew W. Mellon, who was a very important member of the Republican Party and a Secretary of the Treasury; it has been said that three presidents served under him. When the Democrats came into power in 1932, this corporation was not without influence in the federal government. Oscar Ewing, who had been counsel for the Aluminum Company for many years, had been treasurer of the Democratic Party and was at the time a vice-president of this party. It was understood prior to the death of President Franklin D. Roosevelt that Ewing was to be appointed Solicitor General of the United States. That plan did not materialize, perhaps because Harry S. Truman, as a member of a Senate Committee, had been very critical of the contracts secured by the Aluminum Company for the production of war materials. Other important persons were ready to assist this corporation to maintain its monopolistic position, despite the fact that it had been convicted of participating in cartels, which were a serious handicap to the efficiency of the United States in its preparations for the Second World War. The Reynolds Metal Company had developed in this emergency to assist in the production of aluminum, but great pressure was placed on the administration to restrict the sale of public power to the Aluminum Company of America. Secretary Harold Ickes testified that W. Averill Harriman, Robert R. Patterson, William S. Knudsen, and others appealed to him not to sell Bonneville power to the Reynolds Metal Company (which would leave the Aluminum Company of America as the recipient of that power), although the Bonneville Act prohibited sale of this power under conditions which would tend to create a monopoly.[5]

Harold Judson was appointed Assistant Solicitor General of the United States and in that capacity had the duty, among others, of representing the government in suits regarding the submerged oil lands of California. Judson had been an attorney for the oil companies of California and he appeared on the record as having contributed $380,500 in the California campaign of 1939. When an inquiry was made regarding this, he testified that he had not contributed any of that amount himself but all of it for oil companies in California. Although the law requires that the names of all persons making contributions either directly or indirectly be listed, Judson's name was the only one that appeared. Despite this evidence he retained his position.[6]

Another businessman who has had extensive connections with government is Victor Emanuel. He is or has been the controlling power in Standard Gas and Electric, American Aviation, Consolidated Vultee, Station WLW in Cincinnati, Republic Steel, and other large corporations. He has been affiliated, also, with a banking firm which has been reported to have had connections with I. G. Farben under the Nazi régime. After Pearl Harbor, General Aniline and Film, the principal American subsidiary of I. G. Farben, was indicted for a cartel in war materials. The German-owned patents of that corporation were seized by the Alien Property Custodian, as were other German-owned patents. The Alien Property Custodian at that time was Leo Crowley, who was also chairman of Standard Gas and Electric. In a conference of federal departments the recommendation was made that all German-owned patents be made freely available to American industry. This recommendation was unanimously approved by all participants in the conference except James E. Markham, who had become Alien Property Custodian and who was a director of Standard Gas and Electric, in which Emanuel was a powerful influence. Markham appealed to George Allen, an influential person in Washington, to oppose the recommendation of this interdepartmental committee, and Allen, too, was a director of several of Emanuel's corporations.

In some cases persons have been nominated for important positions in the government but have not been appointed when their business connections were made known. Charles Beecher Warren was nominated for the position of Attorney General of the United States in 1925, in which position he would control prosecutions under the antitrust law. It was revealed in Congressional hearings that Warren had been indicted (but not convicted) in 1910, along with the American Sugar Refining Company, which was convicted on several occasions of violations of the antitrust law, and that he had acted as an agent of that corporation from 1906 to 1925 in purchasing the stock of competing sugar corporations. His nomination was not confirmed. Also, Edwin Pauley was nominated in 1946 for the position of Under-Secretary of the Navy, which had jurisdiction over the oil reserves. Pauley had been engaged in the oil industry in California and had worked strenuously in opposition to the United States in the suits regarding submerged oil lands. He was treasurer of the Democratic Party. Secretary Ickes testified that Pauley had promised that $300,000 would be contributed to the campaign by California oil men if the government dropped the suit on submerged oil lands. Because of this publicity, Pauley's name was withdrawn.

Although some individuals may be sacrificed, those of greater power are protected. Richard Whitney, president of the New York Stock Exchange, was indicted on March

12, 1938, for stealing securities from trust funds of the Exchange, and was committed to prison on April 12, 1938. It is reported that subsequent investigations revealed that this crime was known three months before the indictment to other officers of the Exchange and to two partners of J.P. Morgan. At that earlier date Whitney made restitution to the trust funds by borrowing more than a million dollars from his brother, who was a partner of J. P. Morgan; and his brother, in turn, borrowed most of this amount from another partner, both knowing that this loan was for the purpose of restoring to the trust funds the securities which had been stolen. The New York statutes define the concealment of such knowledge as a felony. The prosecutors in the case knew that restitution had been made but made no inquiry as to the source of funds used in the restitution or as to other financiers who might have been accessory to this act. Moreover, the New York Stock Exchange, presumably with the hope of restoring public confidence, appointed Robert M. Hutchins, president of the University of Chicago, as a public representative on the Board of Governors of the Exchange. Within a short time Hutchins resigned from this Board with the public explanation that he did so because the Board of Governors refused to assist in the search for others who were implicated in the Whitney crime.[7]

Social disorganization

Differential association is a hypothetical explanation of crime from the point of view of the process by which a person is initiated into crime. Social disorganization is a hypothetical explanation of crime from the point of view of the society. These two hypotheses are consistent with each other and one is the counterpart of the other. Both apply to ordinary crimes as well as to white collar crimes.

Social disorganization may be either of two types: *anomie*[8] or the lack of standards which direct the behavior of members of a society in general or in specific areas of behavior; or the organization within a society of groups which are in conflict with reference to specific practices. Briefly stated, social disorganization may appear in the form of lack of standards or conflict of standards.

Two conditions are favorable to disorganization of our society in the control of business behavior: first, the fact that the behavior is complex, technical, and not readily observable by inexperienced citizens; second, the fact that the society is changing rapidly in its business practices. In any period of rapid change, old standards tend to break down and a period of time is required for the development of new standards.

The *anomie* form of social disorganization is related to the change from the earlier system of free competition and free enterprise to the developing system of private collectivism and governmental regulation of business. The tradition has been that a government should not intervene in the regulation of business but that free competition and supply and demand should regulate economic processes. This tradition was generally held by the people of the United States in the earlier period. While the tradition has been largely abandoned in practice, it retains great force as an ideology, which has been designated "the folklore of capitalism." In practice businessmen are more devoted than any other part of current society to the policy of social planning. This is social planning in the interest of businessmen. Social planning for the more inclusive society is criticized by businessmen as "regimentation," "bureaucracy," "visionary," and "communistic." In this transition from one social system toward a different social system, *anomie* has existed in two forms. First, the businessmen passed through a period of uncertainty. They were dissatisfied with the system of free competition and free enterprise and had no substitute on which they could agree. This period cannot be sharply limited but is located within the three to six decades after the Civil War. Second, the general public has passed or is passing through the same uncertainty, starting at a later period than did the businessman and continuing after businessmen had reached a new consensus.

Conflict of standards is the second form of social disorganization. This is similar to differential association in that it involves a ratio between organization favorable to violation of law and organization unfavorable to violation of law. For this reason it may be called, with greater precision, differential social organization rather than social disorganization. Business has a rather tight organization for the violations of business regulations, while the political society is not similarly organized against violations of business regulations.

Evidence has been presented in [previous chapters] that crimes of business are organized crimes. This evidence refers not only to gentlemen's agreements, pools, trade associations, patent agreements, cartels, conferences, and other formal and informal understandings, but also to the tentacles which business throws out into the government and the public for the control of those portions of the society. The definition of specific acts as illegal is a prerequisite to white collar crime, and to that extent the political society is necessarily organized against white collar crime. The statutes, however, have little importance in the control of business behavior unless they are supported by an administration which is intent on stopping the illegal behavior. In turn, the political administration has little force in stopping this behavior unless it is supported by a public which is intent on the enforcement of the law. This calls for a clear-cut opposition between the public and the government, on the one side, and the businessmen who violate the law, on the other. This clear-cut opposition does not exist and the absence of this opposition is evidence of the lack of organization against white collar crime. What is, in theory, a war loses much of its conflict because of the fraternization between the two forces. White collar crimes continue because of this lack of organization on the part of the public.

The explanation of crime in general in terms of social disorganization has been at the focus of attention of many criminologists for at least a generation. This has not proved to be a very useful hypothesis up to the present time. A precise definition of social disorganization has been lacking, and the concept has often included ethical implications which have interfered with its utility as an analytical concept. Also, this hypothesis cannot be tested for validity. Finally, it does not explain the content of the criminal behavior or the reasons for the conflicts of standards; the hypothesis points to and describes the conflicts of standards but provides no satisfactory explanation of the genesis of the conflicts.

Notes

1.   Federal Trade Commission, *Utility Corporations,* vol. 81A, pp. 237–244.

2. Federal Trade Commission, *Utility Corporations,* "customer-ownership" in index, vol. 84.

3. Bouck White, *The Book of Daniel Drew* (New York, 1910) pp. 144–145.

4. Amos Pinchot, "Walter Lippmann," *Nation,* 137:9, July 5, 1933.

5. Associated Press, April 15, 1945.

6. *PM,* February 19, 1945, p. 3.

7. I.F. Stone, "Questions on the Whitney Case," *Nation,* 148:55–58, January 14, 1939: "Dewey as Prosecutor," *New Republic,* 111:389–390, September 23, 1944.

8. This word was introduced into American sociological literature from the writings of the French sociologist Durkheim.

10.   Criminology and the Problem of White Collar Crime

Hazel Croall

Throughout this book many diverse views about white collar crime have been examined. Its definition is disputed and the concept itself is controversial. It is claimed to be more prevalent and serious than so-called conventional crime, yet its existence is hidden and victims are unaware of its actual or potential threat. It is generally associated with the rich and powerful yet convicted offenders tend to be the not so rich or powerful. Prosecution is rare and punishments are light, yet there is little evidence of class bias. Laws are said to reflect the interests of offenders, yet public protection is their stated aim. Suggestions for improving regulations range from decriminalization, on the one hand, to tougher punishment, on the other. Underlying these many conflicting views is the debate over whether white collar crime is 'really crime'.

It is no easy task to categorize or label these many divergent approaches. Pearce and Tombs (1990: 423), for example, have recently attacked what they describe as 'compliance theories' on the grounds that they accept that 'the illegal conduct of corporations necessarily calls for different forms of regulation than do other kinds of law-breaking'. Hawkins (1990: 445), on the other hand, argues that these criticisms amount to a 'straw man or Aunt Sally school of academic critique', by setting up an artificial theoretical position in order to criticize it. Pearce and Tombs, he argues, falsely assume that studies which attempt to describe and understand the reality of regulatory law enforcement also accept the assumptions on which it is based.

It is also difficult to associate approaches to white collar crime with current criminological approaches such as 'left idealism', left realism, or 'establishment' or administrative criminology (see, for example, Young 1986). Indeed, these categorizations themselves, especially that of left idealism, have also been attacked as creating 'straw men' (Sim *et al.* 1987). The significance of white collar crime or the crimes of the powerful to these approaches is, indeed, unclear. Young, for example, has criticized radical criminology and left idealism for its over concentration on the crimes of the powerful, which, he argues, underplays the 'real' problem of street crime, and Lea and Young (1984) call for a double thrust against both white collar and street crime. On the other hand, criminology as a whole, particularly in Britain, has been criticized for its neglect of these crimes. Much of the work often associated with radical criminology of either the left realist or left idealist variety has, with some exceptions, been concerned with the policing of lower class crime and on issues of police accountability, race and gender, rather than on corporate or white collar crime, about which much is often inferred and assumed rather than being subject to research or analysis.

Hazel Croall: 'Criminology and the Problem of White Collar Crime' from *WHITE COLLAR CRIME: CRIMINAL JUSTICE AND CRIMINOLOGY* (Open University Press, 1992), pp. 164–174.

Accordingly, no attempt will be made to attribute labels such as left idealism, left realism, or administrative criminology to the various approaches to white collar crime which have been outlined in [previous chapters], although some clear parallels are evident. Nor is it the intention, in comparing and contrasting different approaches to create yet more 'straw men' (or even women!). However, as argued in [Chapter 9] distinct approaches can be discerned which derive from very different assumptions about the nature and legal regulation of white collar crime and therefore focus on a different set of questions. Comparing these approaches can make some sense of the many divergent strands of discussion and debate.

From Sutherland's early work to the development of radical criminology, the so-called white collar crime 'debate' has hinged around its identification with high class offenders and the crimes of the powerful. This has imbued the concept with ideological connotations, and its existence became part of the critique of criminological theories which focused on the crimes of the powerless. The main underlying question is why the law and its associated agencies fail to treat white collar crime in the same way as conventional crime. Analyses focused, therefore, on the policies and practices of law enforcers, and on the law itself, both of which were seen to treat white collar crime with insufficient severity — thus perpetuating the fundamentally ideological distinction between white collar and real crime. Thus, the street and property crimes of the powerless are both legally and publicly defined as 'real crime' whereas the equally if not more anti-social activities of the powerful are not. This, in turn, was often attributed to the ability of the powerful to secure advantageous laws.

To others, often lawyers or enforcers, the main problems raised by white collar crime are the more practical ones of how it can best be regulated. Thus, what was earlier described as a 'regulatory' approach has some parallels with the concerns of what Young (1986, 1988) describes as administrative or establishment criminology. These approaches discuss the use of the criminal law and enforcement policies in the morally neutral language of cost effectiveness. The limitations of the law are seen as technical rather than ideological problems and policies of law enforcement as a response to the real enforcement difficulties posed by the offences themselves. Class bias is denied, the white collar crime debate is seen as a political one; and issues of equity and justice rendered irrelevant to those who tend to accept that the majority of white collar offences and offenders are not really criminal.

An increasing number of writers accept that both sets of questions are important. A focus on offences rather than offenders directs attention to the real difficulties of detection and prosecution to which the much maligned compliance strategies are a response. At the same time, however, the distinction implicit in both legislation and enforcement between white collar crimes and others is essentially an ideological one, and white collar offenders do enjoy many advantages in the criminal justice process. Therefore, issues of both equity and justice are important, as the failure, for whatever reason, to treat white collar crimes severely can in itself encourage their proliferation. The contrasts between these different approaches have dominated discussion of the crucial issues in the white collar crime debate — how it is to be defined; whether it is 'really criminal'; whether it constitutes a crime problem; how it is treated in the criminal justice system; and how it should best be controlled.

What is white collar crime?

It was argued in [Chapter 1] that despite its many problems, the concept of white collar crime is still useful and that the phrase is worth retaining if only on the grounds that it is widely recognized by academics, practitioners and the general public. It was also argued that its definition should be dissociated from the class, status or respectability of offenders. Subsequent analyses confirm the merits of such an approach. The automatic equation of white collar crime with high status offenders has been challenged by repeated findings that offenders come from all levels of the occupational hierarchy. By focusing on offences irrespective of the status of offenders, the concept is considerably strengthened or 'liberated' (Shapiro 1990) as it highlights the distinctive characteristics of crime committed in the course of legitimate occupational roles. The complexity and invisibility of offences which, along with the diffusion of responsibility, lead to the many difficulties of measuring, detecting and prosecuting offences are thus revealed as crucial characteristics which distinguish this kind of crime from others. Such a definition also directs attention to the 'illegitimate opportunity structures' and criminogenic characteristics of occupations and organizations which not only assists an understanding of the offences themselves but also has profound significance for their prevention.

It could be argued that such an approach denies the significance of class status and power. However, this need not be the case, and their significance has been revealed throughout analyses of offences, legislation and criminal justice. Shapiro's analysis of the social organization of trust, for example, points to the greater opportunities for abusing trust higher up the occupational ladder. It also reveals the power of those who enjoy trusted positions. Professional occupations, for example, identified as particularly 'fiddle prone' (Mars 1982; Chapter 4), may be able to control both the service which they provide and appropriate levels of remuneration (Johnson 1972). Ignorant consumers and employers are, therefore, particularly vulnerable to exploitation by the knowledgeable specialist, whether professional or not. As Hagan argues, a focus on the status of offenders

> glosses over what is potentially most salient in Sutherland's attention to differential social organization; the differential power that derives from structural location in the social organization of work.

(Hagan 1988: 20)

It has also been seen that the many structural advantages enjoyed by offenders in the criminal justice process derive from both their occupational status and economic resources.

Is white collar crime really crime?

These advantages are also affected by the perception that many offences are not really crime and this ambiguous criminal status permeates analysis of all aspects of white collar crime. It is reflected in the discourse of enforcers, legislators, sentencers and defendants, which implicitly or explicitly distinguishes many offences from 'real crime'. Thus, they are more often described as infringements or violations than as crimes or offences. They are said to be caused by mistakes or oversights rather than being the result of wickedness or scheming. They require penalties or sanctions rather than punishment. It has been seen that the whole language of regulation or compliance is very different to that of crime control and punishment. It is not only in the legal arena that such distinctions are made as the taken for granted distinctions between fiddles, perks, cons and rip-offs, and theft and fraud illustrate. These also reveal the gap between social and legal definitions of 'crime', and the extremely blurred lines between acceptable, legal, illegal and criminal activities.

But is white collar crime any 'less criminal' than other offences? Many so-called conventional crimes enjoy a similarly ambiguous status — some drug offences and motoring offences, for example, can also be seen as not really criminal. In addition, there are many arguments that white collar offences do possess the basic elements regularly associated with the definition of crime. They involve many forms of lying, cheating and stealing (Shapiro 1990), and force and fraud (Hirschi and Gottfredson 1987). Furthermore,

> as with common crime, the white collar offender clearly seeks personal benefit. This benefit may come directly to the offender or indirectly to the offender through the group or organization to which he or she belongs

> (Hirschi and Gottfredson 1987: 953).

Nonetheless, the ambiguous criminal status of offences has been a central feature of the white collar crime 'debate' with many allegations and counter allegations of ideological and political bias. Those who assert the essential criminality of white collar offences and the need to treat them as crimes are accused of political bias by those who argue that the criminal law is used primarily as an expedient against activities which are only technically criminal, an argument which in turn is attacked as ideological. To many this confirms that the very definition of crime itself is a political one.

Whatever its basis, the ambiguous criminal status of offences has enormous significance for their analysis and treatment. It gives many offenders a moral justification for law breaking and arguably, therefore, makes that law breaking more likely. It also provides the space for offenders to minimize their 'guilt' in court. To the extent that law enforcers and sentencers share a perception that the offences are not really crime, it underlies compliance strategies and sentencing decisions. Finally, it gives credibility to those who argue that business is *over* regulated, and that decriminalization and an emphasis on administrative measures rather than prosecution and tougher penalties are desirable.

Is white collar crime a problem?

Partly as a result of its ambiguous criminal status, white collar crime rarely features in public discussions of the 'crime problem'. Few questions about white collar crimes are asked in victim surveys or in Home Office studies of public estimations of crime seriousness. A recent survey of judgements of crime seriousness, for example, listed fourteen offences, of which only one, tax evasion, was a white collar offence (Pease 1988), and this was seen as one of the least serious offences. Of course, many argue that white collar crime is more widespread and has a more serious impact than conventional crime [Chapter 2]. While the well-known problems of measuring the 'real' incidence of either white collar or conventional crime make it impossible to substantiate this claim, it was seen in [Chapter 2] that its amount and impact are enormous.

However, it has been argued that however prevalent offences may be, they are not as serious as conventional crime. Their impact on victims is often trivial, they rarely involve violence, and they feature little in the public's fear of crime. Thus, Wilson (1975) has argued that conventional crime is more serious as people do not bar and nail shut their windows, avoid going out at night or harbour deep suspicions of strangers because of unsafe working conditions or massive consumer fraud. In addition Young (1986) has criticized so-called left idealists for their over concentration on elite crime which underplays the 'real' problems of street crime. None the less it can be argued that while the public may well be less likely to fear white collar crime or to define it as crime, this does not make it any the less serious.

Despite this, it could be argued that street and property crime disproportionately victimize the poor and powerless, whereas white collar crime has a diffuse effect and some offences primarily victimize those who have more to lose. Offences like insider dealing and fraud, for example, are more often directed against businesses and investors, and it was seen that institutional victims are perceived by sentencers as less victimized [Chapter 8]. However, the vulnerability of the poor to street crime is compounded by the rippling and often unrecognized effects of white collar crime (Lea and Young 1984). What makes affluent citizens less vulnerable to street crime is their ability to protect themselves by avoiding victimization by, for example, not walking on the streets in high crime areas, moving home and installing burglar alarms (Lea and Young 1984). In much the same way they can also move home to avoid pollution from the local factory and can afford to avoid buying cheap bargain goods, mass produced convenience foods or cheap second hand cars.

It has also been argued that white collar crime involves the power of the expert over the ignorant, the producer over the consumer, or the employer over the employee — even the employee over the employer. However, middle class citizens are more likely to be knowledgeable, aware of their rights and even if ignorant can seek advice. They are more likely to be readers of consumer journals and more aware of the hazards of pollution, unsafe goods or foods. This knowledge is likely to steer them away from unsafe investments, ill advised purchases and the inferior services provided by either blue or white collar 'cowboys'. They are also more able to take action to secure compensation should they be victimized. Finally, they are better able to shoulder the burden of higher prices and higher taxes which may be the result of tax evasion and employee offences. The poor and powerless, therefore are more vulnerable to exploitation and victimization from white collar, corporate and conventional crime.

Some groups, by virtue of their structural location may be specially vulnerable to particular offences. Women are arguably more vulnerable as consumers. In addition to being the main shoppers, they are more likely to buy cosmetics, perfumes or designer outfits — all of which are subject to counterfeit frauds in addition to being among those products inadequately regulated (Croall 1987). They are the main consumers of slimming aids, many of which are subsequently revealed to be dangerous and inadequately tested. They are generally assumed to be ignorant of financial and technical matters, making them particular targets for bogus investment schemes and car repair frauds. The present author has, on several occasions, been told that expensive repairs are required to her not very expensive car. It has been assumed, correctly, that she cannot judge for herself whether brake pads are worn or the suspension is faulty! Subsequent examination by a more reliable garage has found that these repairs are not required. While many male academic colleagues confess to similar ignorance, they are less vulnerable as they are assumed to be more knowledgeable. Women are also likely to be particularly vulnerable to the marketing of unsafe contraceptives and drugs as the Dalkon Shield and Thalidomide cases demonstrate (Braithwaite 1984a; Perry and Dawson 1987). Children are victimized as consumers of sweets and junk foods loaded with unsafe additives, or by cheap, attractive, but unsafe toys. Schools and hospitals have also been major purchasers of unfit meat (Croall 1987).

The apparent triviality of many white collar offences and the absence of a fear of white collar crime do not mean therefore that they are 'really' less serious. Indeed, their very invisibility underlines the vulnerability of victims. The power exercised by offenders is less naked and less violent than in many conventional offences, but preys rather on the ignorance of the victim. In addition, public indifference cannot be taken for granted. When questions about white collar offences are included in surveys of public estimations of crime seriousness, some, particularly those which result in physical injury, are rated as more serious than many conventional crimes (Levi and Jones 1985; Grabosky *et al*. 1987). This indicates that the public could take white collar crime more seriously were they to be sensitized to its dangers — an assumption underlying many of the suggestions for greater publicity (Box 1983). It can, therefore, be argued that white collar crime is a 'real' crime problem.

White collar crime and criminal justice

These arguments indicate why the treatment of offenders in the criminal justice system has been such a major source of contention. Given the serious impact of white collar crime, it seems eminently reasonable to ask why so few offenders are prosecuted and severely punished. The many debates surrounding this issue were reviewed at length in [Chapters 5, 6 and 7] and, therefore, need little re-iteration here. The major source of contention is, of course, the extent to which white collar crime can be said to be dealt with leniently and if so, whether or not this results from class bias.

It cannot be disputed that white collar crime is subject to different regulatory arrangements and that these can be interpreted as lenient — if only on the grounds that fewer are prosecuted and subjected to public as opposed to private justice. In relation to prosecution this arises largely because regulatory enforcers are more likely to take the view that they are not dealing with 'crimes' and are less concerned with issues of 'just deserts'. As Braithwaite and Pettit (1990: 191) argue:

> In every country where empirical work on business regulatory
> enforcement has been done, a similar picture of more benign enforcement
> by the regulatory agencies than by the police has emerged. One of the
> authors has done research on dozens of business regulatory agencies on

four continents without discovering one agency for which just deserts was a significant priority or even a subsidiary goal. The day the literature reports a business regulatory agency driven by desert, it will be akin to a zoologist announcing the discovery of a new species.

In addition, sentences can be described as equally benign particularly when the seriousness of offences and resources of offenders are taken into account.

Explaining this, therefore, becomes the major issue. Taking the criminal justice process as a whole, it was seen that the more extreme positions of competing approaches are largely unjustified. There is little evidence of agency bias, either on the part of 'captured' or sympathetic law enforcers, or sentencers unwilling to punish high status or elite offenders. In any event white collar offenders do not form a homogenous group. Indeed, some white collar offenders would appear to be relatively disadvantaged compared with others in respect of their relative vulnerability to prosecution and punishment. Offenders do not always receive the sympathy to which they often appeal and some can be seen as 'letting the side down'.

On the other hand, claims that current policies are justified on the grounds of efficiency, and are necessitated by the exigencies of law enforcement are equally questionable. Claims that compliance strategies are uniquely more efficient can be disputed on their own terms as it could well be argued that *more* prosecutions are necessary on the grounds of deterrence. Enforcers themselves complain about insufficiently deterrent sentences, especially in view of their highly selective prosecution policies. They further complain about the lack of resources which constrains their efforts and further limits prevention and deterrence.

It has been argued that the explanation for leniency lies in the many structural advantages enjoyed by many white collar offenders, either in comparison with other white collar or some conventional offenders. In the first place their superior resources can be used variously to avoid breaking the law, to avoid detection, to avoid prosecution and to avoid severe punishment. They can buy themselves out of prosecution by negotiating out of court settlements and out of prison by paying enormous fines. Many offenders can exploit the ambiguous criminal status of offences by providing credible arguments that they are honest, reputable business persons whose offences are isolated mistakes and who, therefore, don't deserve severe punishment, particularly as they have suffered enough already. The law itself further compounds these advantages as it encourages the use of compliance strategies and the minimal use of prosecution, provides for out of court settlements, and contains the many loopholes and ambiguities which allow defendants to minimize their culpability. It also creates categories of offences which are legitimately defined as 'not really criminal' giving yet more offenders the opportunity to deny intent, to conceal the persistence and seriousness of their offences and thus attract lighter sentences which are themselves constrained by legal maxima.

Thus, the more favourable treatment of white collar offenders cannot be attributed either to class bias or to the nature of offences alone. While the logic of compliance strategies may be justifiable to enforcers, and while sentences may appear 'fair' to sentencers, the outcome is inequitable compared to the treatment of many lower class conventional offenders. Burglars, for example, are more likely to be prosecuted and persistent burglars are likely to be incarcerated for considerably longer periods of time than persistent fraudsters, whose offences involve larger sums of money. Therefore, the outcome of the decisions of law enforcers and sentencers reinforce and reflect wider structural inequalities.

Can white collar crime be better controlled?

Criticisms of the criminal justice process are inextricably linked to criticisms of the law itself, whose many limitations were outlined in [Chapters 8 and 9]. The law is limited in scope, has many loopholes, and insufficient resources constrain enforcers. To some adherents of a regulatory approach this is less of a problem than to others, as criminal law should in any event only be used as a last resort, and better self-regulatory arrangements, coupled with market forces can be equally effective. Decreasing the use of the criminal law and the role of public enforcement, therefore, shifts the burden of preventing offences to industry and the public themselves. To Marxist and other radical theorists this, of course, is yet a further illustration of the law failing to act against the crimes of the powerful.

Increasingly, however, it is being acknowledged that the issues are more complex than suggested by *either* approach. Law represents a combination of influences, negotiations, compromises and accommodations between the conflicting interests of capitalists, individual groups of capitalists and governments, and reflects the changing priorities of these groups in response to specific political and economic pressures. None the less, its impact on white collar offending is limited, and these limitations do appear to favour business interests over those of the public, particularly in an economic and political environment in which over regulation and the high costs of compliance and enforcement dominate the political and economic agenda. However, this has not necessarily led to the deregulation which some have feared. Indeed, Braithwaite and Ayres (1991) argue that the situation is more one of regulatory 'flux', and that assertions that deregulation is on the agenda overstate the position. In addition, Pearce and Tombs (1990), from a Marxist perspective, argue that political agendas can be changed. Therefore, white collar crime need not inevitably be treated more favourably than other crimes.

Changing the present arrangements, therefore, appears possible leaving the question of what range of strategies and policies are desirable and on what grounds they are to be advocated. Clearly, they should be effective, and most accept the prioritization of public protection. Greater controversy surrounds the vexed issue of whether the interests of 'justice' require that white collar offences should be treated in the same way as conventional crimes. While accusations of direct class bias are largely unfounded, it has nonetheless been argued that offenders do enjoy a structural advantage. Any range of policies, therefore, should attempt to redress this balance, and if white collar crime is crime it ought to be treated as crime. However, this need not necessarily mean that white collar offenders should be subjected to the same kinds of punishment as conventional offenders, as conventional offenders could also be treated differently. As Braithwaite and Pettit (1990), advocating a 'republican' theory of justice argue, full implementation of just deserts for *either* white collar *or* conventional crimes is impracticable and would be prohibitively costly. Protecting the public and justice, they argue, can better be achieved by a minimal use of prosecution and punishment for *both* white collar and conventional crimes. It might be more appropriate to argue for less punitive strategies towards many conventional crimes, than more punitive strategies towards many white collar crimes.

In practice a combination of more effective self-regulation and compliance strategies and tougher laws, policing and punishment would appear to be desirable. It was seen in [Chapter 9] that such a combination can satisfy demands for both equity and cost-effectiveness. Increasing the resources of enforcers could improve their ability to protect the public and could also be deterrent. Tougher and more appropriate penalties could support these policies, and at the same time redress the balance between white collar and conventional offences. They could also underline the moral basis of the law, and if combined with publicity, would have the added advantage of sensitizing the public to the nature of offences and the possibilities of remedial action. The evidence that the public can take white collar crimes seriously, along with increasing public concern over the accountability of financial institutions, the environment, and food and health issues further indicate that efforts to increase public awareness of white collar and corporate crime could have a real effect on public tolerance.

Arguing for tougher policies need not, however, involve more white collar offenders being imprisoned, given larger and larger fines or forcefully subjected to hounding by the press. Levi (1991b), for example, points to the dangers of excessive 'shaming' and the degradations which could follow such policies. Braithwaite's analysis stresses that shaming should be re-integrative and, therefore, while punitive policies are desirable they should also be constructive. This makes suggestions for the development of white collar equivalents to probation or community service particularly appealing as they can be retributive and re-integrative.

In conclusion, therefore, it can be argued that white collar crime is a real 'crime problem'. A greater understanding of its origins and effects is, therefore, imperative, not simply to expose the crimes of the powerful and the victimization of the powerless, but to assist the development of effective policies for its control. In order for this to be done both academics and the public need to be more sensitive to the real problems involved, about which there are many misconceptions and misleading assumptions. More research needs to be carried out in order to assist an appreciation of the nature of different forms of white collar crime, their effect on victims, and the many ways in which they are culturally and subculturally tolerated. In addition, a greater understanding of how offences are structurally generated within occupational roles and organizations, and by external pressures can be of considerable value to enforcers, criminologists, and public and private organizations. Finally, it can be argued that like any other crime, it should be subject to both informal social control, and such public prosecution and punishment as is necessary to both protect the public from victimization, and underline the moral unacceptability of serious white collar offences.

11.   Crime, Power, and Ideological Mystification
Steven Box

Murder! Rape! Robbery! Assault! Wounding! Theft! Burglary! Arson! Vandalism! These form the substance of the annual official criminal statistics on indictable offences (or the Crime Index offences in America). Aggregated, they constitute the major part of 'our' crime problem. Or at least, we are told so daily by politicians, police, judges, and journalists who speak to us through the media of newspapers and television. And most of us listen. We don't want to be murdered, raped, robbed, assaulted, or criminally victimized in any other way. Reassured that our political leaders are both aware of the problem's growing dimensions and receptive to our rising anxieties, we wait in optimistic but realistic anticipation for crime to be at least effectively reduced. But apart from the number of police rapidly increasing, their technological and quasi-military capacities shamelessly strengthened, their discretionary powers of apprehension, interrogation, detention, and arrest liberally extended, and new prisons built or old ones extensively refurbished (all with money the government claims the country has not got to maintain existing standards of education, health, unemployment welfare, and social services), nothing much justifies the optimism.

The number of recorded serious crimes marches forever upward. During the decade 1970–1980, serious crimes recorded by the police increased for nearly every category: violence against the person rose by 136 per cent, burglary by 44 per cent, robbery by 138 per cent, theft and handling by 54 per cent and fraud and forgery by 18 per cent. These increases were not merely artefacts of an increased population available to commit serious crimes. For even when the changing population size is controlled statistically, crimes continue to rise. Thus in 1950, there were 1,094 per 100,000 population. This rose to 1,742 by 1960, then to 3,221 by 1970, and reached 5,119 by 1980. From 1980 to 1981 they rose a further 10 per cent, to reach an all-time record. Ironically, as 'our' crime problem gets worse, the demand for even more 'law and order' policies increases, even though these are blatantly having no effect on the level of serious crimes. At least not on the level recorded by the police.

The result, so we are told, is that the 'fear of crime' has now been elevated into a national problem. Techniques for avoiding victimization have become a serious preoccupation: more locks on doors and windows, fewer visits after dark to family, friends, and places of entertainment, avoidance of underground and empty train carriages, mace sprays or personal alarm sirens held nervously in coat pockets, a growing unwillingness to be neighbourly or engage in local collective enterprises, furtive suspicious glances at any stranger, and attempts to avoid any encounter except with the most trusted and close friends.

Steven Box: 'Crime, Power, and Ideological Mystification' from POWER, CRIME, AND MYSTIFICATION (Tavistock Publications Ltd, 1983), pp. 1–15. Reprinted by permission of Routledge.

Who are these 'villains' driving us into a state of national agoraphobia? We are told a fairly accurate and terrifying glimpse can be obtained of 'our' Public Enemies by examining the convicted and imprisoned population. For every 100 persons convicted of these serious crimes, 85 are male. Amongst this convicted male population, those aged less than 30 years, and particularly those aged between 15 and 21 years are over-represented. Similarly, the educational non-achievers are over-represented — at the other end of the educational achievement ladder there appear to be hardly any criminals, since only 0.05 per cent of people received into prison have obtained a university degree. The unemployed are currently only (*sic*) 14 per cent of the available labour force, but they constitute approximately 40 per cent of those convicted. Only 4 per cent of the general population are black, but nearly one-third of the convicted and imprisoned population are black. Urban dwellers, particularly inner-city residents, are over-represented. Thus the typical people criminally victimizing and forcing us to fear each other and fracture our sense of 'community' are young uneducated males, who are often unemployed, live in a working-class impoverished neighbourhood, and frequently belong to an ethnic minority. These villains deserve, so 'law and order' campaigners tell us ceaselessly in their strident moral rhetoric, either short, sharp, shock treatment, including death by hanging or castration by chemotherapy — 'off with their goolies' — or long, endless, self-destroying stretches as non-paying guests in crumbling, insanitary, overcrowded prisons constructed for the redemption of lost Christian souls by our Victorian ancestors. If only these ideas were pursued vigorously and with a vengeance morally justified by the offender's wickedness, then 'our' society would be relatively crime-free and tranquil. So 'law and order' campaigners tell us.

It is tempting to call all this hype — but that would be extreme! 'Conventional' crimes do have victims whose suffering is real; steps should be taken to understand and control these crimes so that fewer and fewer people are victimized. A radical criminology which appears to deny this will be seen as callous and rightly rejected. Furthermore, those crimes so carefully recorded and graphed in official criminal statistics *are* more likely to be committed by young males, living in poor neighbourhoods and so on. A radical criminology which appears to deny this will be seen as naive and rightly rejected. Finally, there are very good grounds for believing that the rising crime wave is real — material conditions for large sections of the community have deteriorated markedly. A radical criminology which remained insensitive of this would be guilty of forgetting its theoretical roots and rightly rejected. So the official portrait of crime and criminals is not entirely without merit or truth.

None the less, before galloping off down the 'law and order' campaign trail, it might be prudent to consider whether murder, rape, robbery, assault, and other crimes focused on by state officials, politicians, the media, and the criminal justice system do constitute the major part of our real crime problem. Maybe they are only *a* crime problem and not *the* crime problem. Maybe what is stuffed into our consciousness as *the* crime problem is in fact an illusion, a trick to deflect our attention away from other, even more serious crimes and victimizing behaviours, which objectively cause the vast bulk of avoidable death, injury, and deprivation.

At the same time, it might be prudent to compare persons who commit other serious but under-emphasized crimes and victimizing behaviours with those who are officially portrayed as 'our' criminal enemies. For if the former, compared to the latter, are indeed quite different types of people, then maybe we should stop looking to our political authorities and criminal justice system for protection from those beneath us in impoverished urban neighbourhoods. Instead maybe we should look up accusingly at our political and judicial 'superiors' for being or for protecting the 'real' culprits.

If we do this, we might also cast a jaundiced eye at the view that serious criminals are 'pathological'. This has been the favourite explanatory imagery of mainstream positivistic criminology. It was, however, an explanation that only remained plausible if crimes were indeed committed by a minority of individuals living in conditions of relative deprivation. For whilst this was true it was obvious, at least to the conservative mind, that 'something must be wrong with them'. However, if we look up rather than down the stratification hierarchy and see serious crimes being committed by the people who are respectable, well-educated, wealthy, and socially privileged then the imagery of pathology seems harder to accept. If these upper- and middle-class criminals are also pathological, then what hope is there for any of us! Wanting to avoid this pessimistic conclusion, we might instead entertain the idea that these powerful persons commit crimes for 'rational' — albeit disreputable — motives which emerge under conditions that render conformity a relatively unrewarding activity. Having rescued the powerful from 'abnormality' we might do the same for the powerless. Maybe they too are rational rather than irrational, morally disreputable rather than organically abnormal, overwhelmed by adversity rather than by wickedness.

If these are the lessons of prudence, then standing back from the official portrait of crime and criminals and looking at it critically might be a very beneficial move towards getting our heads straight.

However, there is an agonizing choice to make between at least two pairs of spectacles we might wear to take this critical look. We could wear the liberal 'scientific' pair, as did many young trendy academics during the 1960s and early 1970s when the stars of interactionism and phenomenology were in the ascendant. Or we might wear the radical 'reflexive' pair, whose lenses have been recently polished to a fine smoothness by those same trendy academics who have now entered a middle-age period of intellectual enlightenment! These spectacles do provide quite different views on the official portrait of crime and criminals.

Liberal 'scientism': partially blind justice

One way of getting a clear perspective on those crimes and criminals causing us most harm, injury, and deprivation is to excavate unreported, unrecorded, and non-prosecuted crimes. This can be achieved by sifting evidence from numerous self-reported crime studies and criminal victimization surveys. This is undoubtedly an important exercise for it leads us to reconsider the *validity* of official criminal statistics and the more extreme pronouncements made directly and uncritically from them.

What lessons are there to be learnt from the results of these surveys? First, there is much more serious crime being committed than the official police records indicate. The emerging consensus is that one serious crime in three (excluding burglary and car theft) is reported to the police. This knowledge can and does add fuel to the alarmist 'law and order' fire: 'its even worse than we imagined!' Second, although the official portrait of criminals is not untrue, it is inaccurate. It is more like a distorting mirror; you immediately recognize yourself, but not quite in a flattering shape and form familiar to you. Thus self-report data indicate that serious crimes are disproportionately committed by the young uneducated males amongst whom the unemployed and ethnically oppressed are over-represented, but the contribution they make is less than the official data implies. There are, it appears, more serious crimes being committed by white, respectable, well-educated, slightly older males and females than we are led to believe (Box 1981a: 56–93).

To the liberal 'scientific' mind, there are two problems here of 'slippage', one more slight than the other. Too many people fail to report crimes because they consider the police inefficient; we need to restore police efficiency in order to increase the reportage rate and hence obtain a better more reliable gauge of crime. The second, more important slippage, is that the administration of crime justice is fine in principle, but is failing slightly in practice. The police pursue policies of *differential deployment* (for example, swamping certain parts of London where the West Indian population is prominent) and *'methodological suspicion'* (that is, routinely suspecting only a limited proportion of the population, particularly those with criminal records or known criminal associates). Coupled with these practices are *plea-bargaining* (negotiating a guilty plea in return for being charged with a less serious offence) and *'judicious' judicial decisions* (which take as much notice of who you are as they do of what you have apparently done). In other words, the police, magistrates, judges, and other court officials have too much discretion. The result is too much 'street-justice', 'charge-dealing', 'plea-bargaining', and 'disparate sentencing'. In these judicial negotiations and compromises, the wealthy, privileged, and powerful are better able to secure favourable outcomes than their less powerful counterparts (Box 1981a: 157–207). This slippage between ideal and practice reveals a slightly disturbing picture. The process of law enforcement, in its broadest possible interpretation, operates in such a way as to *conceal* crimes of the powerful against the powerless, but to *reveal* and *exaggerate* crimes of the powerless against 'everyone'.

Furthermore, because a substantial section of this criminalized population is stigmatized and discriminated against, particularly in the field of employment, its reproduction is secured; many of them, out of resentment, injustice, or desperation, turn to more persistent and even more serious forms of crime. This vicious circle increases the over-representation of the powerless in the highly publicized 'hardened' criminal prisoner population.

The outcome of these processes is that the official portrait of crime and criminals is highly selective, serving to conceal crimes of the powerful and hence shore up their interests, particularly the need to be legitimated through maintaining the appearance of respectability. At the same time, crimes of the powerless are revealed and exaggerated, and this serves the interests of the powerful because it legitimizes their control agencies, such as the police and prison service, being strengthened materially, technologically, and legally, so that their ability to survey, harass, deter, both specifically and generally, actual and potential resisters to political authority is enhanced.

To the liberal 'scientific' mind, a solution of this second and more important slippage would involve a strict limitation on police and judicial discretion and less stigmatization either by decriminalizing some behaviours, or imposing less incarceration (Schur 1973). The adoption of these policies would narrow the 'official' differential in criminal behaviour between the disreputable poor and the respectable middle-class so that it approximated more closely the actual differences in criminal behaviour — at least criminal behaviour as defined by the state.

Radical 'reflexiveness': artful criminal definitions

Although an enormous amount of carefully buried crime can be unearthed by this liberal 'scientific' excavation work, we will still be denied an adequate view of those whose crimes and victimizing behaviours cause us most harm, injury, and deprivation.

Through radical 'reflexive' spectacles, all this excavation work occurs so late in the process of constructing crime and criminals that it never gets to the foundations. Those committed to self-report and victimization surveys do not start off asking the most important question of all: 'what is serious crime?' Instead they take serious crime as a pre- and state-defined phenomenon. But by the time crime categories or definitions have been established, the most important foundation stone of 'our crime problem' has been well and truly buried in cement, beyond the reach of any liberal 'scientific' shovel.

Aware that liberal 'scientists' arrive too late on the scene, radicals resolve to get up earlier in the morning. Instead of merely examining how the law enforcement process in its broadest sense constructs a false image of serious crime and its perpetrators, they suggest we should consider the *social construction of criminal law categories*. This involves not only reflecting on why certain types of behaviours are defined as criminal in some historical periods and not others, but also why a particular criminal law comes to incorporate from relatively homogeneous behaviour patterns only a portion and exclude the remainder, even though each and every instance of this behaviour causes avoidable harm, injury, or deprivation.

Some sociologist have pondered these issues and come to the conclusion that *criminal law categories are ideological constructs* (Sumner 1976). Rather than being a fair reflection of those behaviours, objectively causing us collectively the most avoidable suffering, criminal law categories are artful, creative constructs designed to criminalize only some victimizing behaviours, usually those more frequently committed by the relatively powerless, and to exclude others, usually those frequently committed by the powerful against subordinates.

Numerous researchers (Chambliss 1964; Duster 1970; Graham 1976; Gunningham 1974; Hall 1952; Haskins 1960; Hay 1975; Hopkins 1978; McCaghy and Denisoff 1973; Platt 1969; and Thompson 1975) have produced evidence consistent with the view that criminal law categories are ideological reflections of the interests of particular powerful groups. As such, criminal law categories are resources, tools, instruments, designed and then used to criminalize, demoralize, incapacitate, fracture and sometimes eliminate those problem populations perceived by the powerful to be potentially or actually threatening the existing distribution of power, wealth, and privilege. They constitute one, and only one way by which social control over subordinate, but 'resisting', populations is exercised. For once behaviour more typically engaged in by subordinate populations has been incorporated into criminal law, then legally sanctioned punishments can be 'justifiably' imposed.

In a society such as ours, populations more likely to be controlled in part through criminalization,

> tend to share a number of social characteristics but most important among these is the fact that their behaviour, personal qualities, and/or position threaten the social relationships of production. . . . In other words, populations become generally eligible for management as deviant when they disturb, hinder, or call into question . . . capitalist modes of appropriating the product of human labour . . . the social conditions under which capitalist production takes place . . . patterns of distribution and consumption . . . the process of socialization for productive and non-productive roles . . . and . . . the ideology which supports the functioning of capitalist society.
>
> (Spitzer 1975: 642)

However, this argument needs qualification. It does not maintain that all criminal laws directly express the interests of one particular group, such as the ruling class. Clearly some legislation reflects temporary victories of one interest or allied interest groups over others, and none of these may necessarily be identical or coincide with the interests of the ruling class. Yet the above argument does not demand or predict that every criminal law directly represents the interests of the ruling class. It recognizes that some laws are passed purely as symbolic victories which the dominant class grants to inferior interest groups, basically to keep them quiet; once passed, they need never be efficiently or systematically enforced. It also recognizes that occasionally the ruling class is forced into a tactical retreat by organized subordinate groups, and the resulting shifts in criminal law enshrine a broader spectrum of interests. But these victories are short lived. Powerful groups have ways and means of clawing back the spoils of tactical defeats. In the last instance, definitions of crime reflect the interests of those groups who comprise the ruling class. This is not to assume that these interests are homogeneous and without serious contradictions (Chambliss 1981). Indeed, it is just the space between these contradictions that subordinate groups fill with their demands for legal change.

It might be objected that even though *some* criminal laws are in the interests of the dominant class and that others which are obviously not in these interests are ineffectively enforced, thus making them dead-letter laws, it still remains true that laws proscribing those types of victimizing behaviours of which we are all too aware and which set the nerve-ends of neo-classical/conservative criminologists, such as Wilson (1975) and Morgan (1978) tingling with fear and loathing, *are in all our interests*. None of us wants to be murdered, raped, or robbed; none of us wants our property stolen, smashed, or destroyed, none of us wants our bodies punched, kicked, bitten, or tortured. In that sense, criminal law against murder, rape, arson, robbery, theft, and assault are in all our interests, since in principle we all benefit equally from and are protected by their existence. Without them life would be 'nasty, poor, solitary, brutish, and short'.

This is all true, but it is not all the truth. For some groups of people benefit more than others from these laws. It is not that they are less likely to be murdered, raped, robbed, or assaulted — although the best scientific evidence based on victimization surveys shows this to be true (Hindelang, Gottfredson, and Garofalo 1978) — but that in the criminal law, definitions of murder, rape, robbery, assault, theft, and other serious crimes are so constructed as to exclude many similar, and in important respects, identical acts, and these are just the acts likely to be committed more frequently by powerful individuals.

Thus the criminal law defines only some types of avoidable killing as murder: it excludes, for example, deaths resulting from acts of negligence, such as employers' failure to maintain safe working conditions in factories and mines (Swartz 1975); or deaths resulting from an organization's reluctance to maintain appropriate safety standards (Erickson 1976); or deaths which result from governmental agencies' giving environmental health risks a low priority (Liazos 1972); or deaths resulting from drug manufacturers' failure to conduct adequate research on new chemical compounds before embarking on aggressive marketing campaigns (Silverman and Lee 1974); or deaths from a dangerous drug that was approved by health authorities on the strength of a bribe from a pharmaceutical company (Braithwaite and Geis 1981); or deaths resulting from car manufacturers refusing to recall and repair thousands of known defective vehicles because they calculate that the costs of meeting civil damages will be less (Swigert and Farrell 1981); and in most jurisdictions deaths resulting from drunken or reckless people driving cars with total indifference to the potential cost in terms of human lives are also excluded.

The list of avoidable killings not legally construed as murder even in principle could go on and on. But the point should be clear. We are encouraged to see murder as a particular act involving a very limited range of stereotypical actors, instruments, situations, and motives. Other types of avoidable killing are either defined as a less serious crime than murder, or as matters more appropriate for administrative or civil proceedings, or as events beyond the justifiable boundaries of state interference. In all instances, the perpetrators of these avoidable 'killings' deserve, so we are told, less harsh community responses than would be made to those committing legally defined murder. The majority of people accept this because the state, by excluding these killings from the murder category, has signified its intention that we should not treat them as capital offenders. As the state can muster a galaxy of skilled machiavellian orators to defend its definitions, and has, beyond these velvet tongues, the iron fist of police and military physical violence, it is able to persuade most people easily and convincingly.

It may be just a strange coincidence, as Vonnegut often suggests, that the social characteristics of those persons more likely to commit these types of avoidable killings differ considerably to those possessed by individuals more likely to commit killings legally construed in principle as murder. That the former are more likely to be relatively more powerful, wealthy, and privileged than the latter could be one of nature's accidents. But is it likely?

The criminal law sees only some types of property deprivation as robbery or theft; it excludes, for example, the separation of consumers and part of their money that follows manufacturers' malpractices or advertisers' misrepresentations; it excludes shareholders losing their money because managers behaved in ways which they thought would be to the advantage of shareholders even though the only tangible benefits accrued to the managers (Hopkins 1980); it excludes the *extra* tax citizens, in this or other countries, have to pay because: (i) corporations and the very wealthy are able to employ financial experts at discovering legal loopholes through which money can be safely transported to tax havens; (ii) Defence Department officials have been bribed to order more expensive weaponry systems or missiles in 'excess' of those 'needed'; (iii) multinational drug companies charge our National Health Service prices which are estimated to be at least £50 millions in excess of alternative supplies. If an employee's hand slips into the governor's pocket and removes any spare cash, that is theft; if the governor puts his hand into employees' pockets and takes their spare cash, i.e., reduces wages, even below the legal minimum, that is the labour market operating reasonably. To end the list prematurely and clarify the point, the law of theft includes, in the words of that anonymous poet particularly loved by teachers of 'A' level economic history, 'the man or woman who steals the goose from off the common, but leaves the greater villain loose who steals the common from the goose'.

The criminal law includes only one type of non-consensual sexual act as rape, namely the insertion of penis in vagina by force or threatened force; it excludes sexual intercourse between husband and wife, no matter how much the latter is beaten by the former to exercise his 'conjugal right'; it excludes most sexual acts achieved by fraud, deceit, or misrepresentation — thus a man may pose as a psychiatrist and prescribe sexual intercourse as therapy to a 'gullible female', because he knows the law will regard this as acceptable seduction rather than rape; it excludes men who use economic, organizational, or social power rather than actual or threatened force to overcome an unwilling but subordinate, and therefore vulnerable female; it excludes the forced insertion of any other instrument, no matter how sharp or dangerous. Thus out of a whole range of 'sexual' acts where the balance of consent versus coercion is at least ambiguous, the criminal law draws a line demarcating those where physical force is used or threatened from those where any other kind of power is utilized to overcome a female's resistance. The outcome is that men who have few resources other than physical ones are more likely to commit legally defined rape, whilst those men who possess a whole range of resources from economic patronage to cultural charm are likely to be viewed by the law as 'real men' practising their primeval arts—and this is something the majesty of the law should leave alone!

The criminal law defines only some types of violence as criminal assault; it excludes verbal assaults that can and sometimes do, break a person's spirit; it excludes forms of assault whose injuries become apparent years later, such as those resulting from working in a polluted factory environment where the health risk was known to the employer but concealed from the employee (Swartz 1975); it excludes 'compulsory' drug-therapy or electric-shock treatment given to 'mentally disturbed' patients or prisoners who are denied the civilized rights to refuse such beneficial medical help (Mitford 1977; Szasz 1970, 1977a, 1977b); it excludes chemotherapy prescribed to control 'naughty' schoolboys, but includes physically hitting teachers (Box 1981b; Schrag and Divoky 1981).

The criminal law includes and reflects our proper stance against 'murderous' acts of terrorism conducted by people who are usually exploited or oppressed by forces of occupation. But it had no relevance, and its guardians remained mute ten years ago, when bombs, with the United States' and allied governments' blessing, fell like rain on women and children in Cambodia (Shawcross 1979), or when the same governments aid and support other political/military regimes exercising mass terror and partial genocide against a subjugated people (Chomsky and Herman 1979a, 1979b). The criminal law, in other words, condemns the importation of murderous terrorist acts usually against powerful individuals or strategic institutions, but goes all quiet when governments export or support avoidable acts of killing usually against the underdeveloped countries' poor. Of course there are exceptions — the Russian 'invasion' of Afghanistan was a violation of international law and a crime against humanity. It may well have been, but what about Western governments' involvement in Vietnam, Laos, Cambodia, Chile, El Salvador, Nicaragua, Suez, and Northern Ireland? Shouldn't they at least be discussed within the same context of international law and crimes against humanity? And if not, why not?

Thus criminal laws against murder, rape, robbery, and assault do protect us all, but they do not protect us all equally. They do not protect the less powerful from being killed, sexually exploited, deprived of what little property they possess, or physically and psychologically damaged through the greed, apathy, negligence, indifference, and the unaccountability of the relatively more powerful.

Of course, what constitutes murder, rape, robbery, assault, and other forms of serious crime varies over historical periods and between cultural groups, as the changes and contradictions *within* and *between* powerful interest groups, and the shifting alliances of the less powerful bring about slight and not-so-slight tilts of society's power axis (Chambliss 1981). But it is not justifiable to conclude from this that criminal law reflects a value-consensus or even results from the state's neutral refereeing among competing interest groups. It is, however, plausible to view criminal laws as the outcomes of clashes between groups with structurally generated conflicting interests, and to argue that the legislator's intention, or if that is too conspiratorial, then the law's latent function, is to provide the powerful with a resource to reduce further the ability of some groups to resist denomination. Needless to stress the point, it is a resource eagerly used to punish and deter actual and potential resisters and thereby help protect the established social order [see Chapter 6].

Nothing but mystification

Unfortunately for those committed to the radical 'reflexive' view, there is nothing but mystification. Most people accept the 'official' view. They are very aware and sensitized to muggers, football hooligans, street vandals, housebreakers, thieves, terrorists, and scroungers. But few are aware and sensitized to crimes committed by *corporate top and middle management* against stockholders, employees, consumers, and the general public [see Chapter 2]. Similarly there is only a fog, when it comes to crimes committed by *governments* (Douglas and Johnson 1977), particularly when these victimize Third World countries (Shawcross 1979) or become genocidal (Brown 1971, Horowitz 1977), or by *governmental control agencies* such as the police when they assault or use deadly force unwarrantedly against the public or suspected persons [see Chapter 3], or prison officers (Coggan and Walker 1982; Thomas and Pooley 1980), or special prison hospital staff when they brutalize and torture persons in their protective custody.

Few people are aware how men, who on the whole are more socially, economically, politically, and physically powerful than women, use these resources frequently to *batter* wives and cohabitees (Dobash and Dobash 1981), *sexually harass* their female (usually subordinate) co-workers, or *assault/rape* any woman who happens to be in the way [see Chapter 4]. But we are very aware of female shoplifters and prostitutes, and those poor female adolescents who are 'beyond parental control' and in 'need of care and protection', even though this is a gross misrepresentation of female crime and though the relative absence of serious female crime contradicts the orthodox view that crime and powerlessness go hand in hand [see Chapter 5].

Few people become aware of crimes of the powerful or how serious these are, because their attention is glued to the highly publicized social characteristics of the convicted and imprisoned population. It is not directed to the records, files, and occasional publications of those quasi-judicial organizations (such as the Factory Inspectorate in the UK or the Federal Drug Administration in the US) monitoring and regulating corporate and governmental crimes. Because of this, people make the attractive and easy deduction that those behind bars constitute our most serious criminal. As this captive audience is primarily young males amongst whom the unemployed and ethnic minorities are over-represented, it is believed that they, and those like them, constitute our 'public enemies'. Had the results of self-report/victimization surveys and the investigations of quasi-judicial agencies been publicized as much as 'official criminal statistics', and had the radical jaundiced and cynical view of criminal definitions been widely publicized, then the mystification produced by focusing exclusively on the characteristics of the prison population would not be so easily achieved. Instead, there would be a greater awareness of how the social construction of criminal definitions and the criminal justice system operate to bring about this misleading image of serious criminals.

Definitions of serious crime are essentially ideological constructs. They do not refer to those behaviours which objectively and *avoidably* cause us the most harm, injury, and suffering. Instead they refer to only a sub-section of these behaviours, a sub-section which is more likely to be committed by young, poorly-educated males who are often unemployed, live in working-class impoverished neighbourhoods, and frequently belong to an ethnic minority. Crime and criminalization are therefore *social control strategies*. They:

(i)   render underprivileged and powerless people more likely to be arrested, convicted, and sentenced to prison, even though the amount of personal damage and injury they cause may be less than the more powerful and privileged cause;

(ii) create the illusion that the 'dangerous' class is primarily located at the bottom of various hierarchies by which we 'measure' each other, such as occupational prestige, income level, housing market location, educational achievement, racial attributes — in this illusion it fuses relative poverty and criminal propensities and sees them both as effects of moral inferiority, thus rendering the 'dangerous' class deserving of both poverty and punishment;

(iii) render invisible the vast amount of avoidable harm, injury, and deprivation imposed on the ordinary population by the state, transnational and other corporations, and thereby remove the effects of these 'crimes' from the causal nexus for explaining 'conventional crimes' committed by ordinary people. The conditions of life for the powerless created by the powerful are simply ignored by those who explain crime as a manifestation of individual pathology or local neighbourhood friendship and cultural patterns — yet in many respects the unrecognized victimization of the powerless by the powerful constitutes a part of those conditions under which the powerless choose to commit crimes;

(iv) elevate the criminal justice into a 'community service' — it is presented as being above politics and dispensing 'justice for all' irrespective of class, race, sex, or religion — this further legitimates the state and those whose interests it wittingly, or otherwise, furthers;

(v) make ordinary people even more dependent upon the state for protection against 'lawlessness' and the rising tidal wave of crime, even though it is the state and its agents who are often directly and indirectly victimizing ordinary people.

Not only does the state with the help and reinforcement of its control agencies, criminologists, and the media conceptualize a particular and partial ideological version of serious crime and who commits it, but it does so by concealing and hence mystifying its own propensity for violence and serious crimes on a much larger scale. Matza captured this sad ironic 'truth' when he wrote:

> In its avid concern for public order and safety, implemented through police force and penal policy, the state is vindicated. By pursuing evil and producing the *appearance* of good, the state reveals its abiding method — the perpetuation of its good name in the face of its own propensity for violence, conquest, and destruction. Guarded by a collective representation in which theft and violence reside in a dangerous class, morally elevated by its correctional quest, the state achieves the legitimacy of its pacific intention and the acceptance of legality — even when it goes to war and massively perpetuates activities it has allegedly banned from the world. But that, the reader may say, is a different matter altogether. So says the state — and that is the final point of the collective representation [i.e., ideological construction — author].

(Matza 1969: 196)

For too long too many people have been socialized to see crime and criminals through the eyes of the state. There is nothing left, as Matza points out, but mystification. This is clearly revealed in the brick wall of indignation which flattens any suggestion that the crime problem defined by the state is not the only crime problem, or that criminals are not only those processed by the state. There is more to crime and criminals than the state reveals. But most people cannot see it.

Strain Theory and the Relationship between Crime and the Economy

12. Anomie Theory
Eileen B. Leonard

Introduction

Many sociologists view Robert Merton's anomie theory as the most influential approach to crime and deviance. His formulation first appeared in 1938 in a frequently cited article entitled "Social Structure and Anomie." My discussion will be based on this article, although I will consider the revisions, clarifications, and additions Merton offered in later years.

Merton's explanation of crime stems from the classic work of Emile Durkheim whose concept of anomie attempted to describe situations of normlessness: when the collective order has been disrupted and aspirations are unregulated and unattainable. Durkheim, however, referred to human aspirations as "natural," whereas Merton speaks of socially learned needs and restricted structural access to their attainment. Merton intended to offer a comprehensive explanation for crime and deviance; his success is still debated.

"Social structure and anomie"

Merton (1938: 672) immediately dismisses biological explanations of deviant behavior and focuses instead on the role of social structure: "Our primary aim lies in discovering how some social structures *exert a definite pressure* upon certain persons in the society to engage in nonconformist rather than conformist conduct." He analytically distinguishes between cultural goals, those aspirations or objectives that are socially learned; and institutionalized means, the distribution of opportunities to achieve these goals in normatively acceptable ways. Merton contends that it is possible for societies to overemphasize either the goals or the means. Overemphasis of the means implies an obsessive concern with correct conduct. (He refers to the "occupational psychosis" of the bureaucrat as an illustration. This is the employee who has long forgotten the ultimate objectives of the organization, but fanatically adheres to all its rules.) Merton argues, however, that in America the tendency is to overemphasize the *goals*, without sufficient attention to institutional means. He accurately specifies the overwhelming desire for monetary success and material goods in our society and contends this extreme emphasis on financial success leads to a willingness to use *any* means (regardless of legality) to see that the goal is attained. "The technically most feasible procedure, whether legitimate or not, is preferred to the institutionally prescribed conduct. As this process continues, the integration of society becomes tenuous and anomie ensures" (Merton, 1938: 674). The ideal situation, according to Merton, would be one of balance between the goals and means; conforming individuals would feel they were justly rewarded. Deviant behavior, however, results when cultural goals are accepted (people would like to be financially successful), but access to these goals is structurally limited (a lucrative job is unavailable).

Eileen B. Leonard: 'Anomie Theory' from *WOMEN, CRIME AND SOCIETY* (Longman: New York, 1982), pp. 49–63.

Merton outlines the possible reactions or adaptations that can occur when the goals have been internalized but cannot be legitimately attained. His approach is explicitly sociological since he focuses on one's position within the social system, not one's personality characteristics. The following table summarizes these adaptations (Merton, 1938: 676). Within this table, (+) refers to acceptance, (−) refers to elimination, and (±) is the "rejection and substitution of new goals and standards."

		Culture goals	Institutionalized means
I.	Conformity	+	+
II.	Innovation	+	−
III.	Ritualism	−	+
IV.	Retreatism	−	−
V.	Rebellion	±	±

Merton recognizes that the responses of individuals can change, but reactions are not random. He claims that conformity is the most common response, otherwise society would be unstable. Likewise, retreatism is least common. Merton refers to retreatists, who reject both the goals and means, as true "aliens"; they are "in the society but not *of* it" (Merton, 1938: 677). This includes psychotics, vagrants, tramps, drug addicts, and chronic alcoholics. This adaptation occurs when individuals have accepted both the goals and means and yet do not have access to legitimate and effective means. Illegitimate means are unacceptable to them, and yet they still desire the goals. Retreatism is their response: they give up on both the goals and the means. The ritualist has lost all hope of attaining the goals, but conforms rigorously to the accepted means; the rebel attempts to bring about a new social order.

Merton's major concern, however, is with the innovator: the person who uses illegitimate, but nonetheless effective, means to cultural goals. For example, the person who achieves financial success by robbing a bank, rather than by starting a savings account, is an innovator. Merton describes how the social structure encourages criminality, by pointing to specific population groups who find it extremely difficult to succeed in traditional ways. These people are asked to strive for financial success, and want to achieve it, but are denied the structural opportunities to be successful within the law. Merton notes the problem is not simply a lack of opportunity:

> It is only when the system of cultural values extols, virtually above all else, certain *common* symbols of success *for the population at large* while its social structure rigorously restricts or completely eliminates access to approved modes of acquiring these symbols *for a considerable part of the same population,* that anti-social behavior ensues on a considerable scale
> (Merton, 1938: 680).

Merton implies that the problem of crime might be corrected if everyone had equal opportunities, or, if those denied opportunities had different expectations in life (as in some cultures where the poor are simply not expected to achieve in the same way the rich are). In America, however, virtually everyone (rich and poor) aims for financial success, although not everyone has the structural opportunities to succeed. These people are then subject to enormous strain, which can result in deviant behavior. It is noteworthy that Merton maintains a value-free approach: "Whatever the sentiments of the writer or the reader concerning the ethical desirability of coordinating the means-and-goals phases of the social structure, one must agree that lack of such coordination leads to anomie" (Merton, 1938: 682). Although he notes that the American emphasis on financial success for everyone encourages "exaggerated anxieties, hostilities, neuroses and anti-social behaviour," he denies he is making a moral point (Merton, 1938: 680). Moreover, he speaks only of coordinating the system; more fundamental alternatives are ignored.

Developments in the theory

Merton concludes his article by claiming that although his discussion is incomplete, his framework can be used to explore various issues in more depth. In revisions and elaborations made in later years, he acknowledged that wealth is not the only symbol of success in American society, but he continued to stress its critical importance (1957). He also noted the absence of a stopping point in the American dream — no matter how wealthy, one can always make more money. Alternative goals (Merton mentions, for example, intellectual and artistic goals) can be actively pursued and can benefit society, particularly from a functionalist point of view, which concerns the maintenance of social order: "To the extent that the cultural structure attaches prestige to these alternatives and the social structure permits access to them, the system is somewhat stabilized" (Merton, 1957: 157). Yet the pressure toward anomie continues since the goal of monetary success is excessively extolled in America, while lack of opportunity produces strain. In addition, failure is viewed as the responsibility of the individual, not as rooted in social sources. Extreme pressure can thus push individuals in the direction of illegitimate behavior: they decide to use *any* means to gain what they and their society values. Although Merton recognizes that changes have occurred in American society and notions of equal opportunity have been qualified in light of the actual situation, he contends that the success theme still dominates.

In subsequent work, Merton admitted that all crime and delinquency are not explained in terms of anomie. However, he never specifies what is and is not explicated. He notes that social groups do not accept the success goal in precisely the same way, nor is everyone in the lower classes pushed toward deviant behavior. But he argues that some people in the lower classes *do* accept society's success goal, and they are subject to more strain than people in the upper classes. Thus, he contends subgroups suffer varying amounts of strain, but those at the bottom are most severely pressed. "Recourse to legitimate channels for 'getting in the money' is limited by a class structure which is not fully open at each level to men of good capacity" (Merton, 1957: 145). Merton admits that upper-class people can experience pressure to "innovate" and can engage in illegal business practices, but he still emphasizes that the greatest pressure (and, hence, crime) is found among the lower strata. Although opportunity can be much more rigidly restricted than it is in the United States, other systems (caste systems, for example) do not advance the same success goals for everyone and, thus, do not put as much pressure on the lower classes.

Merton (1957) expanded his thoughts on ritualism, which he sees as a private escape from cultural demands to continuously seek higher rewards. He claims this adaptation is most often found within the lower middle class, where children are strictly socialized to adhere to social rules but, at the same time, opportunities for success are extremely limited. Merton asserts that deviant behaviour is not necessarily disfunctional for the values of the group since some "innovation" can initiate patterns of behavior that succeed in goal attainment. Anomie may also result in the development of new norms, which Merton has categorized as "rebellion."

In an essay in *Contemporary Social Problems* (1966), Merton sharpened his concept of deviant behavior by distinguishing between nonconforming and aberrant behavior. This is essentially a recognition that rebellion differs from the other adaptations. For purposes of illustration, think of the behavior of a rebel such as a Black Panther, as opposed to that of a bank robber. According to Merton, nonconforming (or revolutionary) behavior involves *public* dissent (Black Panthers) whereas aberrant behavior is hidden (bank robbers). The nonconformist directly challenges the legitimacy of the social norms, which the aberrant acknowledges even as he or she violates them. Moreover, the nonconformist attempts to change the norms of society and appeals to a higher morality in the process. The aberrant simply acts in his or her own interest and wishes to avoid punishment. Finally, the nonconformist can claim to be seeking the ultimate (although unpracticed) values of society, while the aberrant is only interested in his or her private concerns (Merton, 1966: 808–810).

In this essay, Merton also discusses responses to deviant behavior. He acknowledges that people of power and authority exercise a crucial role in determining what is judged a serious violation of social standards. In a complex society, social norms are not uniformly accepted and thus opinions differ as to what constitutes a social problem. Merton (1966: 788) shuns the relativism this implies by arguing that sociologists

> ... need not become separated from good sense by imprisoning themselves in the situation of logically impregnable premises that only those situations constitute social problems which are so defined by the people involved in them. For social problems are not only subjective states of mind; they are also and equally, objective states of affairs.

Yet he agrees that the powerful set the norms, and violations are certainly not equally punished in terms of class, race, or age. Merton recognizes that deviant behavior not only involves what a person actually does, but importantly, how this behavior is perceived by those in authority.

In further clarifying anomie theory (1964), Merton maintains that continuous deviant behavior is exceptional, and conformity the modal response. He acknowledges the importance of associates in terms of innovation, rebellion, and the like: "Whether these [deviant acts] will find open expression and then become recurrent depends, in the aggregate of cases, at least as much on the responses of associates as on our own character and personality" (Merton, 1964: 219). He calls for more research on how social strains are mediated through interpersonal groups.

Criticisms of anomie theory

Merton's anomie theory is an outstanding attempt to explain deviant behavior. The vast amount of critical discussion it has elicited is, perhaps, a measure of its value and substance. It delineates the relationship between one's social position, the strain which accompanies that position, and the resulting deviant and nondeviant adaptations. Estimates of Merton's success have varied, but in examining the literature, five important criticisms emerge.

Scope and specifics

Anomie theory is not as all-embracing as Merton first hoped it would be. It cannot, for example, explain certain behavior commonly held to be deviant, such as homosexuality, or marijuana smoking among people who accept both the goals and means in society. It certainly does not adequately explain mental illness or sexual deviance. The theory is also incomplete in other respects: Cohen (1966) points out that it does not demonstrate why certain adaptations are chosen, nor does it associate different types of strain with different outcomes. Merton anticipated such criticism in his 1938 article, and although he made some improvements along these lines, the criticisms are still appropriate. Gibbons and Jones (1975) maintain that the incomplete nature of anomie theory has prevented its application to various forms of deviance, in spite of the fact that it is so popular.

The particular adaptations themselves have been criticized for their lack of specificity. Taylor, Walton, and Young (1973), for example, point out that Merton does not adequately discuss his notion of conformity, making it difficult to distinguish between conformity and ritualism, categories that should be fundamentally distinct. Clinard (1964) has commented that the concept of retreatism is imprecise and oversimplified. It is also unclear why certain people choose the adaptations they do, while others subject to strain do not succumb.

Cultural assumptions

A second cluster of arguments propose a more serious criticism of anomie theory. They maintain that the theory disregards interaction with others, which is crucially involved in deviant behavior. According to Cohen (1965), Merton overemphasizes the individual actor and does not recognize the impact of others in determining an individual's response to a situation. Cohen feels that, for this reason, anomie theory is extremely limited in explaining delinquent subcultures, particularly the nonutilitarian forms. Merton has acknowledged Cohen's criticism and argues it is justified regarding earlier versions of anomie theory. In later versions of the theory, however, he did mention that patterns of interaction should be considered. Merely dealing with this issue in passing, however, is not the same as addressing oneself to all the implications involved.

Thus, a major problem with anomie theory is its failure to explicate the intervening variables of the interactive situation. The deviant is viewed, more or less, as acted upon, rather than engaging in any type of personally meaningful behavior. Merton's lack of interest in the role of group or collective adaptations is further evidence of this difficulty.

Closely related is the criticism that Merton's entire scheme is invalid because of its basic assumptions about society, particularly the notion that universally accepted values and goals can be pinpointed in a complex modern society. Many people, like Taylor (1971), argue that goals develop within the demands of reference groups. Rather than developing the possibility that very different and even conflicting subgroups make up the whole, Merton assumes shared values throughout society. Lemert (1972) also criticizes Merton by arguing that value pluralism is an infinitely more accurate view of America than the notion of patterned values. If Lemert is correct, Merton's means–ends paradigm becomes problematic and generally insufficient in explaining deviance. Merton can be defended since he did state that different goals are possible within his scheme, but he does not consider different groups and different values; generally he posits a single source of deviance. This is unacceptable to Lemert and other critics.

Lower-class crime

Merton has been challenged for assuming that deviance is most widespread among the lower classes. He explained that the lower classes are subject to strain since they lack structural opportunities even though equality of opportunity is proclaimed. Evidence suggests, however, that deviant behavior is much more common throughout society than Merton's formula indicates. Part of the difficulty is that his theory is based on official statistics, which do indeed suggest that the bulk of deviance occurs among the lower echelons of society. But these statistics cannot be accepted at face value. They can and do reflect public concern with particular types of crime, police practices, class bias, labeling effects, and so on. Anomie theory, however, is hard pressed to explain deviance among those who are well placed in society in terms of advantage and opportunity. Why does a successful business executive, who obviously has access to legitimate means, embezzle? To discuss this would have involved Merton in a more fundamental criticism of American society since not only unsuccessful but also successful people turn to crime, indicating more serious problems within the system. Merton also has difficulty explaining why so many people in the lower classes *do* conform. Thus, anomie theory predicts both too little deviance (among the upper classes) and too much (among the lower classes).

Reaction to deviance

Another difficulty limiting the usefulness of anomie theory is its failure to deal with reactions to deviant behavior. This has been touched upon in those remarks criticizing Merton for ignoring the responses of a deviant's reference group or subculture. Along the same lines, Merton has not dealt with the results of official reaction toward the deviant. Lemert (1972) criticizes him for ignoring the role social control agencies play, particularly in the continuation of deviant behavior. The labeling perspective will be analyzed in detail later, but now it is simply observed that official reaction to deviance is largely overlooked in Merton's analysis. More informal elements, such as the stereotypes of deviants portrayed in the mass media, are also left untouched, indicating Merton's lack of interest in societal reactions and their ramifications.

Critique of society and beyond

Merton explicitly criticizes modern society, particularly American society. He disapproves of the widespread strain resulting from existing social arrangements. He sees the suffering that occurs when a society, which is, in fact, unequally structured, claims to offer equality of opportunity. Further, Merton is critical of the overemphasis placed on money, and the never-ending drive to gain more and more wealth. He sees the ritualist as an object of pity. Thus, he recognizes basic problems within our social order, and his solution is to realign our goals and means and ensure that merit meets with success.

Although Merton rejects the present system, his criticisms are not basic; they are neither as fundamental nor as extensive as they might be. For example, he does not explain the initial existence of inequality, nor the exaggerated emphasis on money making. Taylor, Walton, and Young (1973) contend that if Merton's arguments were followed through logically, they would point toward radical social change. But Merton avoids this route. He believes beneficial changes can occur within the present system. Taylor et al. retort that Merton's hopes for reforming the present system are in vain. The very reasons for inequality are rooted within the system, and serve the interests of the few. The talent and potential of the lower classes will not be salvaged through piecemeal reform:

> That the provision of sufficient jobs, of an instrumentally and expressively satisfying nature, is beyond the possibilities of the social system as we now know it, is the bitter reality of the matter. The liberal plans of sociologists such as Merton serve merely to attempt to contain and obscure this reality

> (Taylor, Walton, and Young, 1973: 104).

Thus, Merton is criticized for neglecting the cause of the dysfunction that exists between the goals and the means in our society. Instead of questioning our political economy, as Taylor et al. would have him do, he settles for supporting meritocracy. He seems confident that social problems can be alleviated within the existing system. The possibility of this will be more fully explored as we examine the explanations of crime offered by the Marxists.

Anomie and women

Merton made no attempt to apply his typology to women, and initially it seems inapplicable to them. He argues vigorously that the dominant goal in American society is monetary success, and yet he has forgotten at least half the population with this formulation. Ruth Morris (1964) accurately contends that the goals of women and girls are relational goals (successful relationships with others) rather than the financial goals sought by men. More specifically: the goal women have traditionally been taught to seek is marriage and children. A woman might legitimately achieve tremendous financial success in the business world and still find people curious to know if she is married and has a family. If the answer is no, her success is tainted. At the opposite extreme is the financially poor woman, married and raising three children. She, unlike her husband, has not completely failed in the eyes of our culture.

Although anomie theory seems inappropriate regarding women, Merton claims different goals can be considered within his framework. I will make the necessary alterations in his scheme to see if the resulting information explains the traditionally low crime rate among women and the increases presently occurring.

Women: goals and means

I accept Merton's argument that one's aspirations are socially learned, not biologically conditioned. This is accurate regarding the goals of women, in spite of any vociferous arguments to the contrary. The goal that women are traditionally socialized to desire, above all else, is marriage and a family; the accepted means is to secure the romantic love of a man through courtship. Despite the much discussed emancipation of women, the great majority of them are still taught to find primary fulfillment through marriage and children. Their main concerns revolve around family, husband, children, and home. Money and financial success are simply not as vital. This, of course, contrasts with Merton's analysis of economic success as paramount. Women are certainly interested in financial status, but this is largely seen as the responsibility of their husbands.

Low crime rate among women

Given the above revisions in terms of goals and means, Merton's anomie theory can be used, in general terms, to explain the low rate of criminal involvement among women. According to anomie theory, deviant behavior occurs when common goals are extolled for the population at large, but legitimate access is restricted. Those who lack access are under tremendous strain, and may seek alternative (and illegal) means to their objectives. This formulation assumes a very different cast when the goals of women are substituted. It becomes obvious that most women are able to marry and have a family. What is problematic is that simply *being* married and *having* children, not necessarily rewarding relationships or a skillful handling of responsibility, are expected. Seen in this light, the difficulty is that such an easily attainable goal is all that is expected of women. But given that they can usually achieve socially approved ends in a legitimate way, they avoid the types of strain Merton discussed regarding men. Therefore, the low rate of crime among women exists because they are not pressured toward deviant behavior. Women have very low aspirations and their goals are extremely accessible.

A revised anomie theory highlights the relationship between the subordinate position of women and their crime patterns. It indicates women are protected from involvement in the criminal world since they are not subject to the types of pressure and frustration men experience. On the other hand, the social expectations for women in our society (marriage and family) explain why they are severely punished for prostitution and, until recently, abortion. Why certain women initially become involved in prostitution and shoplifting is not clarified by anomie theory.

Ironically, the low crime rate among women may indicate their lack of success, in the crudest of terms, in altering their aspirations. Their limited desires in the economic realm might shield them from both financial pressures (Merton's main concern) and situational pressures (to be expanded later). Merton realized the problem he was addressing only exists when common success goals are held by the population at large.

What he neglected to mention is that possibly half our population does not primarily strive directly for financial success. Such an oversight on Merton's part is appalling; but for those who have reviewed the field of women and crime, it is not unexpected.

Increases in women's crime

Just as Merton's theory can be used, to some extent, to explain the lack of crime among women, it can, likewise, elucidate the increases that are occurring. Merton recognized (although not specifically in regard to women) that as changes occur in the social structure or goals, we can expect similar changes regarding those most severely subject to strain. If the goals of women shift, for example, toward male success goals, their rate of crime might increase, since access to such goals is typically closed to women in an unequally structured society, such as ours. Emancipation has increased somewhat, and certain women are now aiming to achieve financial success. These changes are not momentous, but they can result in disruption. Challenging traditional restrictions and expectations can lead to anomie and, hence, to an increase in female crime. It is noteworthy that the increases in women's crime have been in property offenses, mainly larceny-theft. Likewise, fraud and counterfeiting and forgery are up. Violent crime has not increased among women. In terms of anomie theory, changing expectations can bring strain, yet any new pressure on women seems to be manifest in property, not personal, crimes. This might indicate escalating financial pressure on women, but little modification in the expectations that they be nonviolent, cooperative, and even docile.

The very fact, however, that the crime rate among women has not changed drastically in the last 25 years indicates that the position of women in our society might not be radically different. The most outstanding fact about women and crime is still their limited involvement. Anomie theory explains this to a certain extent, yet there are difficulties in applying this perspective.

Problematic aspects

Anomie theory is useful in advancing the possibility that women are freer from certain strains in our society and, hence, less likely to engage in deviant behavior. Yet in applying this theory, I have posited a common goal for all women, a position that was criticized in regard to men. Anomie theory simply does not lend itself to the careful consideration of subcultures or patterns of interaction existing between the deviant and her reference group. With the existing framework, one's thinking is directed toward considering the major goal or goals in society, not toward examining subtle, although important, variations. The claim that marriage and a family is the objective of American women is accurate to a certain extent, but there are many differences among these women that should be taken into account. Furthermore, a study of the reactions (official and unofficial) to crime is not suggested by this theory, although it might be particularly important regarding women.

Anomie theory is generally helpful in explaining the low criminality among women, but when it comes to analyzing the crime that actually occurs, serious problems arise. First of all, the scheme of adaptations becomes problematic. Regarding the category of innovation, which is of major concern to Merton, it is difficult to think of illegal means to achieve the goal of marriage and family. Less than fully acceptable means can certainly be utilized (consider how our culture criticizes those who marry for money rather than love); but this is hardly illegal. Means that are illegal (purchasing a husband, marriage through force) occur seldom, if ever. Prostitution and shoplifting are certainly not alternative means to the goal. Thus, when specifically using this framework to analyze women and crime, it simply does not work. The criticisms of the theory discussed earlier become more obvious with an application to women and crime.

The imprecise nature of Merton's categories becomes clear. Prostitutes might be considered retreatists since they reject both the accepted goals and means for women. Yet, it is also possible to think of them as rebels if their primary goal is seen as financial success rather than marriage, particularly when they belong to groups that are vocal about the rights of prostitutes. Women alcoholics and drug addicts can also be called retreatists, but Merton's explanation of this category is often inapplicable. Escapism supposedly characterizes those who have given up on both the goals and means, yet many female drug addicts and alcoholics have followed the normatively accepted patterns for women and are married and have children. In addition, it is difficult to distinguish between women who are ritualists and play all the feminine games, although they have lost hope of securing a husband and family, and conformists who are still striving for this goal but are as yet unsuccessful. It is impossible to locate shoplifters anywhere within this scheme since their behavior is criminal, but they are often conformists regarding marriage and a family. Moreover, nothing helps us explain why women deviate in the way they do, nor what type of strain leads to each specific outcome.

Official statistics indicate that crime is more common among women of the lower classes, although, as mentioned above, it is difficult to relate this directly to the category of innovation. Furthermore, it is particularly troublesome to explain shoplifting among married, middle-class women in Merton's terms. Finally, a ritualistic adaptation is not more likely among lower-middle-class women, since they are not particularly restricted from the means to the accepted goal for women.

Conclusion

The application of anomie theory to women and crime has important implications regarding the theory itself, as well as crime among women and men. It clearly illustrates this theory only applies to men and mainly to the goal of financial success. This has value within limits, but it highlights the criticism that anomie theory ignores subgroups within society. When these subgroups (such as women) are examined, it is not a matter of making minor revisions; in fact the theory fails in important respects. Obviously, anomie theory must precisely categorize what it claims to explain.

Although anomie theory is deficient in analyzing the criminality of women, it is helpful in emphasizing the absence of certain types of strain experienced by women in our society, and how this relates to their low rate of crime. Merton recognized the structural inequalities that exist regarding social class, but he neglected to note similar inequalities regarding sex. Importantly, however, while women are denied lucrative careers, they are also carefully taught not to seek them (unlike lower-class males). The common symbols of success Merton discusses are not so common after all. Women are, in fact, free from certain pressures toward crime that men do not escape quite so easily. For a man, tremendous pressure typically exists to find an occupation that offers substantial rewards. Many men are broken under these demands. While they bear this burden, an analysis of anomie theory highlights a very different although equally disturbing situation for women. When revised to apply to women, the theory illuminates the astonishingly low expectations we have had for females in our society. The goal of marriage and a family is available to virtually all women, and achieving such a goal demands little talent. Merton contends that having accessible alternative goals helps stabilize the social system. Undoubtedly this is the case regarding women, but the price paid is unacceptable since it means curbing the energy and resources of fully half the population.

This does not denigrate the role of homemaker and mother, which can be a demanding and fulfilling occupation when utilized to its fullest, and certainly more challenging and rewarding than many business occupations. But being a successful homemaker or the mother of three happy, well-adjusted children is not necessarily expected. It is better to be unhappily married or even divorced than never to have married at all; better to have two neurotic children than to be childless. Just as with men, the goal is not personal satisfaction or the successful completion of any task — it is the trappings of success we seek. For men, that is money; for women, marriage and a family.

This situation ensures that we will lose a great deal of the skill and talent of the women in our society by expecting little of them and by only rewarding them for very specific and confined behavior.[1] More choice should be available,[2] but the solution does not lie in substituting traditional male success goals and increasing our crime rate. The over-emphasis on financial success for males is as problematic as the lack of challenge for females.

The application of anomie theory to women and crime has resulted in two important considerations: the lack of financial strain experienced by women and their uninspiring cultural goals.

Notes

1. The limited expectations for women are problematic in many ways. I am concentrating on the impact this has in confining women to certain roles and preventing them from exploring others. Equally dismal, however, is the situation of women who do not achieve these goals. When social expectations are so specific, those who do not fall into the conventional mold can expect to experience difficulties in our society. We refuse women socially approved alternatives. To those who do not bear children, or have not married, for any of a variety of reasons, we generally extend our pity. What is infinitely more desirable are viable alternatives (in terms of careers, living situations, varied expectations, etc.) Fortunately, the women's movement has increased our awareness that there are other goals — that we can live outside the mold with support from others and creative thinking. But I do not believe this is widely accepted in our society, as yet. And so, aside from the few strong and individualistic women (and men) who can flout social expectations at little personal expense, this situation means, very simply, that many women will suffer, and suffer unnecessarily.

2. This should include the choice of being a wife and mother, having a career, or whatever combination one prefers. Women are frequently scorned, at the present time, unless they

do it all. We are beginning to mock the woman who stays home to care for children as readily as the successful business-woman who is unmarried. What we frequently ignore is the quality of a person's life. Poorer women, of course, are locked into their class, without the luxury of discussing career options.

13. Why Should Recession Cause Crime to Increase?
Steven Box

As this chapter was being drafted, there were 'riots' in Handsworth, Birmingham, and Brixton, London, leaving a smoky trail of smouldering property and ramshackle looted shops. The inner-city face, already pock-marked by inadequate houses, crumbling schools, closed hospitals, unrepaired roads, boarded-up shops, dilapidated public services and graffiti-covered walls, was further scarred by the effects of robbery, burglary, arson and other serious crimes. But what has all this to do with the question, Why should recession cause crime to increase? If we listen to our astute politicians, the answer is simple — Nothing!

Margaret Thatcher, in a rare compassionate insight, saw the unemployed as good honest British citizens doing their best to gain employment (although she failed to add that it was despite her government's endeavours to make this practically impossible). To imply, she continued, that these people commit 'riotous crimes' is an insult which only increases the hurdles they have to overcome to earn a decent living. Gone from Mrs Thatcher's mind was the *really* 'insulting' idea, so vividly present till then, that the unemployed are 'scroungers' on whom her government has unleashed an extra couple of thousand Department of Health and Social Security inspectors to deter 'dishonest' citizens from making fraudulent claims.

Home Secretary Douglas Hurd regarded these events in Handsworth and Brixton as nothing but *crimes* committed by 'criminal elements'. They were not, in his opinion, social phenomena to be pawed over by sociologists and used as ammunition against the government and its economic policies; they were matters for the police, and beyond them, the courts.

Conservative Party Chairman Norman Tebbit, like a demonic Witchfinder General, caught a frightening glimpse of the British urban landscape being cursed by carefully orchestrated outbreaks of 'wickedness'. In the riot areas 'agitators' were sighted, 'extremists elements' were present, 'Trotskyites' and 'anarchists' were reported, 'aliens' and 'outsiders' were stirring things up, and 'drug barons' were defending their illegal business interests by fermenting anti-police sentiments. This motley ragbag of excuses rolled off the tongue with calculated ease. Anything would do, it seemed, if it obscured the social causes of crime, including the government's own contribution via its economic policies.

These views were echoed by others across the political spectrum, all anxious to avoid giving the impression that they or their party condoned outrageous riotous behaviour. There was a political chorus innocently singing in unison: unemployment is neither an excuse nor a justification.

Steven Box: 'Why Should Recession Cause Crime to Increase' from *RECESSION, CRIME AND PUNISHMENT* (Macmillan, 1987), pp. 28–67. Reprinted by permission of the publisher.

Of course, not even a sociologist, like me, would claim otherwise. Acts of violence and property destruction are wilful crimes deserving punishment commensurate with their seriousness. It is inconceivable that unemployment is such a mitigating circumstance that the offender should be regarded as absolutely blameless and without responsibility. But a demand for justice must go beyond retribution for the offence and reparation for the victim. It has to include a demand for *understanding* the offender. It needs this not in the hope that the offender will then be excused, condoned or justified. Nor does understanding the offender necessarily shift the blame to the victim. The demand for understanding is necessary because *although people choose to act, sometimes criminally, they do not do so under conditions of their own choosing.* Their choice makes them responsible, but the conditions make the choice comprehensible. These conditions, social and economic, contribute to crime because they constrain, limit or narrow the choices available. Many of us, in similar circumstances, might choose the same course of action. Furthermore, if we understand the intimate relationship between economic and social circumstances and criminal behaviour, then we might be in a better position to intervene effectively and humanely to reduce the incidence of crime.

Of course, some commentators claim we need not bother. For them, social or economic circumstances are either unrelated to behaviour or too complex and subtle ever to be captured by the sociological imagination. In their eloquent *Honest Politician's Guide to Crime Control,* Morris and Hawkins (1969, p. 45) stated bluntly that:

> the search for the cause of criminality . . . is generally thought to be an illusionary quest, not unlike the 18th Century chemists' search for the elusive hypothetical substance, phlogistic.

More specifically, James Q. Wilson (1982), the doyen of American 'policy-oriented' criminology, which argues that crimes can be prevented best by designing out the *opportunities* for their commission, claims that:

> overall unemployment seems to bear little or no relationship to crime . . . there's no basis for a prediction that a deepening or continuing of the recession will lead to increases in the crime rate.

Against these sceptical views are others detecting a relationship between economic conditions in general, and unemployment in particular, and criminal behaviour. Thus the Select Committee of the House of Lords on Unemployment, 1982, stated its belief that unemployment was:

> among the causes of ill-health, mortality, crime or civil disorder. Although this is an area where irrefutable proof is virtually impossible, we find the evidence highly indicative and we are satisfied that the link is sufficiently probable to allow the drawing of certain conclusions. We regard the connection as more than plausible. (p. 59)

Lord Scarman (1982) in providing the social background to the Brixton disorders on 10–12 April 1981, was at pains to point out that deprivations do not 'justify' attacks on the police, or 'excuse' such disorders. But at no stage did he deny that these conditions are part of the 'explanation'. Indeed, among the many deprivations he listed, unemployment figured prominently. It stood at 13 per cent in Brixton in early 1981 and 'for black people, the percentage is estimated to be higher (around 25 per cent)'. Furthermore, young blacks were even more affected, for 'unemployment among black males under 19 has been estimated at 55 per cent' (ibid, p. 27).

Clearly there is not only disagreement on whether recession in general and unemployment in particular lead to crime, but there is also confusion over the issue of 'causation' and 'excuse'. Unemployment and widening income inequality might not be an excuse recognisable in law, but that does not mean that these two features of recession do not affect the level of crime. Whether or not a 'cause' of crime is regarded as an 'excuse' is a political decision; to declare it unacceptable as an excuse is not simultaneously to effectively deny its possible contribution to the causes. Politicians like to slide over this distinction because stating that 'unemployment is no excuse' conceals the possibility that it could be a circumstance which narrows options and shapes choices to such an extent that crime becomes an attractive, maybe compelling, possibility .

So the issue of whether 'unemployment is no excuse' can be set aside while the issue of causation — Why should recession lead to more crimes? — is considered. After that trip through the tangled forest of sociological theorising, we can turn to the bewildering array of evidence relevant to assessing whether recession is linked to crime. However, before that particular fleet-footed exercise is undertaken, some issues cluttering the path have to be cleared.

In nearly all the literature on recession and crime, it is the *powerless* rather than the powerful who are portrayed as the offenders. Of course there are plausible reasons for thinking that a recession, causing widening income inequality and increasing unemployment, might result in the powerless committing more conventional crimes. But the *powerful* will also experience more temptation to commit crimes as the struggle for scarce resources intensifies and group or class tensions mount. This latter possibility seems to have been virtually ignored. Yet Bonger (1916) pointed out that, in promoting 'egoism', capitalism not only brutalises the poor, it demoralises all those caught up in the struggle and competition to survive or succeed, and makes those exploiting others particularly insensitive to the misery this produces. Echoing this point nearly sixty years later, an American criminologist David Gordon (1971) wrote:

> Capitalist societies depend . . . on basically competitive forms of social and economic interaction and upon substantial inequalities in the allocation of social resources. Without inequalities, it would be much more difficult to induce workers to work in alienating environments. Without competition and a competitive ideology, workers might not be inclined to struggle to improve their relative income and status in society by working harder. Finally, although rights of property are protected, capitalist societies do not guarantee economic security to most of its individual members. Individuals must fend for themselves, finding the best available opportunities to provide for themselves and their families. At the same time, history bequeaths a corpus of laws and statutes to any social epoch which may or may not correspond to the social morality of that epoch.

> Inevitably, at any point in time, many of the 'best' opportunities for economic survival open to different citizens will violate some of those historically-determined laws. Driven by the fear of economic insecurity and by a competitive desire to gain some of the goods unequally distributed throughout the society, many individuals will eventually become 'criminals' . . . nearly all crime in capitalist societies represent perfectly *rational* responses to the structure of institutions upon which capitalist societies are based. Crimes of many different varieties constitute functionally similar responses to the organisation of capitalist institutions, for those crimes help provide a means of survival in a society within which survival is never assured. (p. 58)

By concentrating on competition and struggle and the ethics these generate *throughout* society, it becomes easier to see that the working class have not secured a monopoly on criminal activity. Crime is endemic throughout the class structure, but this is obscured by differential law-enforcement and law-makers who prefer to regulate the powerful's worst excesses by administrative or civil law and rely on criminal law only as the final resort.

Second, the link between recession and crime seems to have concentrated on property offences, such as robbery, burglary and theft. The result is a neglect of violent crimes, such as homicide, rape, wife-battering and assault, and 'crimes of domination and repression' (Quinney, 1977, pp. 31–62) committed by the *powerful*.

This concentration on property crimes of the powerless reflects simplistic views about who gets adversely affected by recession, and what types of crimes they might commit. Although property offences appear a 'rational' response to unemployment, deteriorating living standards and widening income inequalities, the psychological effects of these experiences and how they can be transferred into 'irrational' outbursts of violence, cannot be ignored. Indeed, many feminists over the last decade have argued for there being a causal connection between inequalities and rape. Some men who experience their disadvantage as unfair or who consider themselves failures in competition with other men, may, out of frustration and anger, assault women, a vulnerable and easy target (unless they have attended self-defence classes). This is 'irrational' because sexual assaults fail to address the cause of men's oppression and, at the same time, contribute to the oppression of women. As Klein (1981) sees it:

> male physical power over women, or the illusion of power, is none the less a minimal compensation for the lack of power over the rest of one's life. Some men resort to rape and other personal violence against the only target accessible, the only one with even less autonomy. Thus sexual warfare often becomes a stand-in for class and racial conflict by transforming these resentments into misogyny. (p.72)

A similar frustration-aggression misplaced onto an accessible and vulnerable target underlies Coser's (1963) account of murder. He argues that inequalities perceived as unjust may lead to frustration, this in turn might lead to aggression which might be directed against the self but also might be directed against others, and that the rates of violence, including homicide, will be particularly high for categories of persons who experience disproportionately 'structurally induced frustrations' and for those in strata where 'internalised social controls are not strong enough to prevent . . . homicidal aggression'.

Not only might recession lead to more crimes of violence, but it obviously affects more than the economically marginalised. The two major motivations behind crime examined below — thwarted ambition and relative deprivation — are not confined to the powerless. The powerful too have problems during a recession, and these problems can and do lead to such 'crimes of domination' as corporate violations of administrative, civil and criminal law, including price-fixing, pollution, selling unsafe and untested products, ignoring health and safety regulations, and bribery. They also lead to 'crimes of repression' committed by state social control agencies, such as the police, when they brutally assault and sometimes unjustifiably kill civilians (Box, 1983; Jacobs and Britt, 1979) and commit illegal violence against strikers and sympathisers (Coulter *et al.*, 1984; Fine and Millar, 1985; Scraton, 1985), or the prison service, when prisoners are murdered or maimed (Coggan and Walker, 1982) or their legal rights violated (Cohen and Taylor, 1976; Thomas and Pooley, 1980).

Finally, there is a point, obvious once made, but which is hardly ever heard in the recession–crime debate: irrespective of the economic cycle, most crimes are committed by people *at* work! Some of these — corporate and police crimes — are discussed below, but others deserve a brief mention.

'Retrieving' a portion of one's surplus value from the employer is a fairly traditional response among employees (Ditton, 1977; Henry, 1978; Hollinger and Clark, 1983). Fiddling customers is also a way many service workers enhance their earnings, and this is not confined to those two obvious bogeymen, watch and car repairers (Mars, 1983). Nor is this 'crime at work' confined to the 'lower orders'. Embezzlement, computer fraud, professional malpractice, and government corruption are but a few of the illegalities engaged in by managers, technicians, solicitors, doctors, architects, engineers, civil servants and other 'top people' in the USA (Bequai, 1978; Douglas and Johnson, 1977; Geis and Meier, 1977; Johnson and Douglas, 1978) and the UK (Doig, 1984; Leigh, 1982; Levi, 1981). Furthermore, inflation, another feature of contemporary recession, but one which makes the middle and upper classes relatively worse off, pushes people into higher tax bands and reduces the buying power of their remaining income. Some, experiencing reduced standards of living, and not being prepared to put up with it, might turn to tax evasion, embezzlement and fraud as means of supplementing their dwindling incomes.

These crimes 'at work' have a number of characteristics: they are not frequently reported to the police since employers prefer to administer 'private justice' rather than spend time, money and energy pursuing employees through the courts (Robin, 1970); they are not feared much by the public, probably because people are less aware of such crimes; they are not part of the 'folk devil' and 'moral panic' scenario embraced by the media and politicians (Cohen, 1972; Hall *et al.*, 1978; Pearson, 1983); the police do not deploy many personnel or devote large resources to prevent, solve or prosecute these types of crime.

The outcome is that most of these 'occupationally related' crimes do not appear in the Home Office's *Criminal Statistics* or the FBI's *Uniform Crime Reports* and do not therefore penetrate the recession–crime debate. Yet not only are they widespread and committed frequently, but their monetary value far outstrips 'conventional crimes' of burglary, robbery and theft. As Ramsay Clark (1970), one time Attorney General of the USA, saw it:

> Illicit gains from white-collar crime far exceed those of all other crime combined . . . One corporate price-fixing conspiracy criminally converted more money each year it continued than all of the hundreds of thousands of burglaries, larcenies, or thefts in the entire nation during those same years. Reported embezzlements cost ten times more than bank robberies each year. (p. 38)

Clark's is not a lone voice crying out in the wilderness. Many other writers since then have estimated the physical, economic and social costs of corporate crime and have all agreed that these far outstrip comparable costs of 'conventional crimes' (Box, 1983, pp. 25–34).

Since it is 'conventional' crimes of the powerless that prey on the public consciousness and are the central focus of attention in the recession–crime debate, it is clear that many other serious crimes, crimes which undoubtedly would not fit easily into this tight, neat framework, are dismissed, ignored or forgotten. But this amnesia has to be avoided. Whatever the outcome of both theorising about and locating evidence for the recession–crime debate on 'conventional crimes', we have to remind ourselves constantly that many other crimes are being committed by people at work, often in high-status and respectable positions, and, objectively, these are more damaging to people, property and our political system.

Recession and the 'conventional' crimes of the powerless

There are numerous sociological reasons for linking recession with crime. Nearly every major sociological theory can be construed in such a way that it predicts more crime when unemployment increases and income inequalities widen. Although no one of these is totally satisfactory, it is possible to integrate them into a plausible and parsimonious theory which makes sense of a relationship between recession and crime. But first, what contributions does each major theory make to an overall integrated account?

(i) Strain theory

In strain theory, people are viewed as being essentially good and would conform were it not for stresses and contradictions in their lives. Individuals cannot ignore the problems these strains produce. In attempting to resolve or reduce them, individuals occasionally drift into deviance and crime. Two criminological strain theories — anomie, which can lead to 'thwarted ambition', and material inequalities, which can lead to 'relative deprivation' — lend themselves to the argument that recession and crime are causally linked. Both of them address the fundamental issue of motivation: Why would anyone want to commit a crime? Neither theory claims that the motive itself is a sufficient condition for crime to occur, but both claim that it is a necessary condition. Thus, blocked opportunities of work/education which might lead to 'thwarted ambition', or material inequalities which might lead to 'relative deprivation' make crime possible, but neither make it mandatory or utterly compelling. But what is important is that both these approaches stress social structure — blocked opportunities or material inequalities — as the key to understanding crime The subjective elements which form the motivation to commit crime are merely the mediating factors between structure and behaviour. This process may be absolute — 'Am I worse off than I expected or had been led to believe?' — or comparative — 'Am I worse off than others like me?'. But either way, it is triggered by external circumstances. This is not to argue that subjective elements are irrelevant; human beings are capable of attributing a variety of meanings to structural factors, such as income inequalities widening or being made unemployed. None the less, those external factors exert a 'facticity' upon the minds of most people and constrain the meanings they can attribute to them.

(a) Anomie theory

Anomie theorists argue that the motivation to commit crimes will increase whenever legitimate opportunities to achieve culturally defined success, particularly material success, are narrowed or closed off (Merton, 1957; Cohen, 1955; Cloward and Ohlin, 1960). Since in a 'meritocratic' society the major avenue for realising material success is the occupational one, it follows that during a recession when unemployment rises and levels of inequality widen, more people will experience a failure to achieve culturally defined goals of success.

In itself this 'failure' is not necessarily 'solved' by deviance or crime. Other solutions are possible. For example, some people could modify their aspirational 'fantasies' and align them to outrageous reality. What counts as 'success' could be scaled down even to the point of withdrawing from the competition altogether. But this escape route is difficult to achieve when the media, particularly TV, which ironically is a form of entertainment affordable by poorer people, pumps out 'the good life for you' every hour of the day, creating in those who haven't got it a sense of disillusionment and deprivation. Turning one's back on the competition game, 'Occupational Success', requires an effort of will, and, of course, feasible alternatives, beyond the reach of many.

Some people whose legitimate avenues to success are blocked by being unemployed or unemployable will blame themselves. They see in their inability to secure or retain the 'good job' nothing less than a flawed personality. For these self-incriminatory people, a period of anxiety and maybe depression, illness, drug addiction or suicide could be expected. Exacerbating these possibilities are other social psychological effects of unemployment: the loss of structure to one's daily life, the disruption to one's routine patterns of relating which often require more money than is now available, the growing sense of purposelessness, the loss of identity, and a deterioration in physical health (Fagin and Little, 1984; Hakim, 1982; Jahoda, 1982). And for many of those managing to avoid these extremely debilitating consequences, there is only a weary resignation and apathetic acquiescence, particularly among older unemployed persons.

So, an important conclusion for the recession–crime hypothesis is that only a minority experiencing unemployment and hence material failure will be candidates for predatory property and violent crimes. Whether they do offend depends partly on how *intensely* they feel their 'failure'.

In modern Anglo-American society, during a recession, there are many who 'fail' to achieve the cultural goal of success, but only a minority who feel so *intensely* about it that they decide to commit crimes. Thus, a sense of thwarted ambition will be exacerbated and experienced acutely by those who feel they are excluded from the avenues of success by the operation of unfair and discriminatory criterion. Intense indignation is likely to develop, given the rigged nature of competition in meritocratic capitalist societies. As Lea and Young see it, this competition takes place on a very strange racetrack:

> In reality some people seem to start half-way along the track (the rich) while others are forced to race with a millstone around their necks (for example, women with both domestic and non-domestic employment) while others are not even allowed onto the track at all (the unemployed, the members of the most deprived ethnic groups). (1984, p. 95)

Pointing out the costs of these inequalities, Blau and Blau (1982, p.118) argue that:

> inequalities for which individuals themselves can be considered responsible, even though differential advantage makes this a fiction, are held to be legitimate, whereas inborn inequalities that distribute political rights and economic opportunities on the basis of the group into which a person is born are feudal survivals condemned as illegitimate in a democracy. Such inborn inequalities exist . . . if membership in ascriptive groups, such as race, is strongly related to socioeconomic position . . . Ascriptive socioeconomic inequalities undermine the social integration of a community by creating multiple parallel social differences which widen the separations between ethnic groups and between social classes, and it creates a situation characterized by much social disorganization and prevalent latent animosities. Pronounced ethnic inequality in resources implies that there are great riches within view but not within reach of many people destined to live in poverty.

Thus, a sense of injustice, discontent, and distrust generated by the apparent contradiction between proclaimed values and norms and social experiences becomes, among certain groups, too deeply irritating and too constantly whipped up by the media to be easily shrugged off.

So the apparent relationship between recession — widening inequalities and increased unemployment/unemployability — and crime becomes compounded by a subjective element. What inequalities and unemployment *mean* becomes crucially important. Not only might this *meaning* vary between racial groups, but it might well vary between gender, age-cohorts and over time.

To the extent that individuals accept culturally defined gender roles, then men would tend to feel more discontent when unemployed because occupational success is supposed to fulfil men whereas women are argued to be more fulfilled by marital/ domestic success. However, with the rise of female employment during the 1960s and 1970s, and the increasing number of female dominated single parent families, it is *family status* — i.e., who occupies the bread-winner role — that will affect the *meaning* of unemployment. It is increasingly naive to assume that sex determines gender and therefore biological men fulfil 'male' social roles. To the extent that more women head households and need to work, then being made unemployed, particularly if it is believed to result from sexist beliefs — a woman's place is in the home with her children' — may lead to a sense of injustice. From this well of discontent might spring more crime, but its volume would be muted by female socialisation which praises passivity and recommends that suffering should be endured (Cloward and Piven, 1979). So although both unemployed male and female household heads may be motivated to commit crimes, it is likely that proportionately more men, socialised to be competitive, aggressive and domineering, will actually offend.

Similarly the young when compared with middle-aged or older persons might feel more 'putout' by unemployment because it would be more difficult for them to view this as a premature, and even welcome, release from the rigours of unfulfilling tedious work. By middle-age, most outrage and resistance will have been replaced by accommodation, displacement and passivity; the idea of crime, as a means of coping with unfulfilled ambitions long since deadened by the realities of work and domestic obligations, will simply hold little appeal. For the young, however, not yet brutalised by the harsh realities of economic and domestic life, resistance, protest and active indignation will come much easier, and with it, a preparedness to commit crimes.

Thus even in a society where the gap between culturally proscribed goals and legitimate avenues for their realisation is increasing, this might only provide a motivation for deviance/crime among small but identifiable groups of people. Others, despite a failure to achieve culturally defined success, might adopt different criteria for success, flop into a pool of self-flagellation, or adjust in the myriad ways that humans cope with the 'slings and arrows of outrageous fortune'. Although many factors shape these various responses, one in particular — *the duration of employment* — is expected to lead to criminal behaviour. The long-term unemployed, especially the young long-term unemployed who see no future before them, clearly have greater problems than those who merely slip onto and off the unemployment register because of minor friction in the labour market.

Strain theory therefore predicts more crime during a recession. Higher crime rates are the price a 'meritocratic' society pays for blocked opportunities and thwarted ambitions which increase when recession bites and are compounded by the intensified operation of ascriptive criteria, such as race, gender and age, in the allocation of employment and unemployment. These ingredients are likely to create more alienation, despair and conflict, and out of this cauldron creeps more conventional crime. But — and this is *the* point of this analysis — any relationship between recession and 'conventional' crime would only be expected to appear in particular populations: younger males more than older ones; economically independent rather than dependent women; racial minorities, particularly those with Afro-Caribbean backgrounds; working class rather than middle class. These relationships would be expected to be more pronounced in inner-city areas. Even then, other social factors might mute or encourage a criminal response. One of these — political marginalisation — will be considered in the next section, although it could equally affect the unemployed, just as the operation of ascriptive criterion in the allocation of income could lead to a sense of injustice.

(b) Relative deprivation

Closely related, and often confused with anomie theory, particularly of the Mertonian variety, is relative deprivation theory. This theory, first formulated into a rigorous body of argument by Runciman (1966), has now been adopted by a host of radical criminologists. According to Runciman:

> A is relatively deprived of X when (i) he does not have X, (ii) he sees some other person or persons, which may include himself at some previous or expected time, as having X (whether or not this is or will be in fact the case), (iii) he wants X, and (iv) he sees it as feasible that he should have X. . . . Given the presence of all four conditions, relative deprivation produces feelings of envy and injustice. (p. 10)

Although Runciman never applied this concept to the study of crime, others have done so. Thus Stack (1984, p. 231) argues that relative deprivation will occur to the extent that:

1. people lack an average income (the greater the size of this group, the greater the frequency of relative deprivation);

2. they are aware that others in a comparative reference group have incomes equal to or greater than the average (the greater this perceived gap between groups, the greater the magnitude of relative deprivation);

3. they are desirous of a higher income (this desire should increase the intensity of relative deprivation); and

4. it is historically feasible for such income redistribution to take place.

Stack believes that although relative deprivation leads to a sense of injustice it will not necessarily produce more crime. For this to occur, other conditions have to 'whip up the feelings of animosity' generated by wide and widening levels of income distribution. Essentially it all turns on whether persons experiencing relative deprivation believe the system can and will be drastically improved. To the extent that there exist free and strong trade unions and a political party committed to income redistribution, and the relatively deprived are involved in these reforming institutions and perceive the chances of success to be realistic, then crime will not necessarily increase even when income inequalities widen. However, if individuals and groups feel they are marginalised from the political process and trade-union movement, *as do many of the young unemployed and ethnic minorities,* then the relative deprivation they experience will inevitably be transformed into deviant behaviour. This is not to suggest that most property crime is an extra-legal method of achieving income redistribution. Far from it. The evidence from numerous victimisation surveys is unanimous: the vast majority of victims of these crimes are themselves poor or badly off. For example, the US National Crime Survey 1975 showed that the rate of victimisation for larceny, assault, robbery and rape, per 1,000 persons, was 93 for those earning less than $3,000, and this dropped steadily as incomes increased, to a rate of 56 for those earning more than $25,000. One conclusion is obvious: increasing property crimes are not inspired by the Robin Hood principle of robbing the rich to feed the poor; instead they result in income being redistributed amongst the poor.

Relative deprivation, at least in its more radical versions, differs from 'thwarted ambition' of anomie theory, despite the fact that both make similar, although not identical, predictions about a recession–crime relationship. Relative deprivation theory implies that only a redistribution of income brought about by progressive tax reforms, high minimum legal wages and full-employment policies can bring about humanely a reduction in the crime rate. Anomie theory, on the other hand, argues for the opening-up of blocked opportunities by more education, vocational courses, job training and counselling. The former thus argues for a more socialist society, where income differences are narrowed, the latter for a truly meritocratic society, where the cream justifiably rises to the top. Both, however, predict a relationship between recession and crime, because:

1. they predict that similar groups of people — lower class, young males, ethnic minorities — will either experience the strain of thwarted ambition as unemployment rises or relative deprivation as income differences widen; and,

2. these groups are likely to blame 'the system' for their unemployment, feel resentful about ascriptive practices excluding them, and be less involved in reformist organisation like trade unions and socialist political parties.

This is not to suggest that other groups are entirely immune from these experiences. For example, conventional crimes committed by females have increased considerably over the last decade both in the UK and USA. The most plausible reason for this is that more women have become economically marginalised during the recession. As Box and Hale (1984) argue:

> although some upper-middle-class women have made inroads into formerly male professions, the vast bulk of women have become increasingly economically marginalized — that is, they are more likely to be unemployed or unemployable or, if employed, more likely to be in insecure, lower paid, unskilled part-time jobs in which career prospects are minimal. This marginalization, particularly in a consumer-oriented and status-conscious community that is continuously conditioned by aggressive mass media advertising, is . . . an important cause of increases in female crime rates . . . Furthermore, anxieties concerning their ability to adequately fulfill the social roles of mother, wife, and consumer have been heightened during the late 1970s and early 80s because the British welfare state, on which proportionately more women than men depend, had tightened its definition of who deserves financial assistance and, at the same time, has become increasingly unable to index-link these payments to inflation. (p. 477)

Relative deprivation, particularly in an egalitarian society, is likely to increase as income differentials widen during a recession. Those who make unfavourable comparisons with others like them, or who regard their past as more rewarding economically, will have a higher rate of criminality, particularly if they do not see on the horizon any serious structural change in the allocation of rewards being attainable.

(ii) Control theory

Although strands of control theory existed before 1969, it was Hirschi's formulation that year which became the orthodox version that now straddles American mainstream criminology. The reasons for its current pre-eminence are not hard to fathom. In the first place, it is a theory which lends itself to empirical research. Indeed, over the last fifteen years it has become *the* most tested crime causation theory. But more important than that, the results have nearly all been favourable. The most that critics of its empirical adequacy have been able to come up with are minor reformulations of the relationships between social bonds. It is therefore a theory which enjoys a rare fruit in sociology: it is very well supported empirically (see LaGrange and White, 1985 and Box, 1981, ch. 5 for references). Second, it is a theory which avoids 'implicating' social structure and is therefore appealing to the established 'right' in American politics and culture. This makes it eminently attractive for research funds, and for that reason alone many scholars gravitate towards it. Control theory is therefore the dominant explanation of delinquency and 'street crime' in mainstream American criminology and therefore it has to be considered for inclusion into an 'integrated theory'.

American control theorists such as Hirschi (1969, pp. 66–75) and Johnson (1979, p.100) do not give much credence to a strong unemployment–crime link. However, it is not at all clear that their research demonstrates no relationship. In both cases the research subjects were school-children whose social class was measured by taking the father's occupation! This is inappropriate, for it is the class of *destination,* as perceived or anticipated by the school children, which affects their present behaviour.

When these weak tests are put aside and the theoretical arguments of control theory re-examined, it is contended that they do provide a bridge between the motivational element supplied by strain theorists and eventual criminal activity.

In control theory, individuals low in *attachment* to others, lacking a strong *commitment* to the future, and not holding the right *beliefs,* are predicted to be comparatively more likely to commit crimes. In other words, the level of offending will be higher among those lacking a strong emotional attachment to others, particularly family members, who do not see their future offering good prospects for achieving social or material success, and who do not subscribe to the moral principle that rules ought to be obeyed regardless of detection.

There are plausible grounds for believing that recession leads to a weakening of these social bonds and hence facilitates the commission of more crime and therefore a higher crime rate. First, it affects *attachment* because it threatens to weaken, and in some cases destroy, family relationships. The increased tension, resentment and bitterness which accompanies higher levels of unemployment and widening economic inequalities is often displaced onto the family, resulting in more wife-battering, child-abuse (Straus *et al.*, 1980) and divorce (Thornes and Collard, 1979; Colledge and Bartholomew, 1980). In turn, these fracture the love and attachment between family members who then feel freer to deviate because they care less about what other family members think of them.

Second, it affects *commitment* because unemployment casts a long shadow over those institutions formally supposed to prepare people for a job. The absence of future employment prospects delegitimises schools and results in many pupils becoming cynical, bored and rebellious. Through jaundiced eyes, the hidden purpose of school becomes redundant. Teaching kids the virtues of obedience, punctuality and ability to perform repetitive alienating tasks, becomes patently absurd if there isn't even a dull, boring, alienating job at the end of it. The new marginal youth do not have much to lose, so they become strong candidates for criminal activity, particularly when after leaving school they actually experience strain in the form of unacceptable unemployment or unemployability .

Third, recession affects individual *beliefs* in the legitimacy of conformity to conventional rules and norms because having undermined the stability of the family and the relevance of schools, both major institutions for socialisation, it damages the ability of one generation to imprint its values on the next.

Thus not only does recession produce more individuals who have a motive to deviate, but it also creates within this population a group who feel free to deviate because they do not have loved ones to whom they are sensitive, they do not view the future as sufficiently rosy to justify making a 'stake in conformity' now, and they do not believe that all law-breaking is intrinsically wrong. This does not mean that lower-class children have weak or non-existent social bonds. In all the research on control theory, the link between bonds and class has not been established empirically, and theoretically it is not predicted. However, there are a proportion of lower-class children (and middle-class children too) whose social bonds are weak. The *combination* of weak social bonds with a motive to deviate is predicted to produce higher rates of criminal activity than either the motive or weak social bonds separately. This combination is likely to be more prevalent in lower-class children not because their bonds are necessarily weaker, but because their motivation to deviate is stronger.

(iii) Societal reaction and conflict theory

Following the publication of Becker's *Outsiders* (1963), societal reaction or labelling theory became fashionable, particularly among the rising and expanding generation of young 'radical' academics, partly because it promised to explore the innovative proposition that 'social control leads to crime' whereas the mundane orthodox view was the reverse of this. However, despite its potential, labelling theory failed to incorporate structural or macro factors and there was a growing disenchantment which came with the realisation that the primary focus of attention was micro-processes of interaction, particularly between state officials and putative deviants. This tendency was further exaggerated by the incorporation of phenomenologically inspired research towards the end of the 1960s (Cicourel, 1968), which seemed to disappear up the entrails of endless analyses of half-minute video-recordings of ordinary conversations. Conflict theory developed partly in reaction to this tendency and sought to strengthen societal reaction theory by anchoring it firmly to social structure; it sought particularly to place it within the context of the establishing and maintaining power relationships through coercive means, including criminalisation (Chambliss, 1969; Chambliss and Seidman, 1971; Quinney, 1974, 1977; Turk, 1969, 1976).

As a detailed summary of social labelling and conflict theory can be found elsewhere (Box, 1981; Downes and Rock, 1982; Taylor, Walton and Young, 1973), there is no need to cover the same ground. However, there are two major arguments within labelling conflict theory which are directly relevant to the issue of recession and crime.

The first is that these are particular groups who more than others are selected for criminalisation. Those groups who fit criminal 'stereotypes' or who can cause the least trouble for those administering the criminal justice system, are more likely to be apprehended, arrested, prosecuted and severely sanctioned (Box, 1981; Chambliss, 1969; Turk, 1969). The dominant imagery of persons committing such conventional crimes as robbery, burglary [, etc., are] 'working-class' males, living in urban areas, and more likely than not to be unemployed and/or a member of an ethnic minority. Those fitting these stereotypes are more likely to be viewed with suspicion and subjected to higher rates of criminalisation. The police adopt deployment policies and methods of routine suspicion that result in the surveillance and apprehension of 'suspicious' persons — i.e., those resembling stereotypes. To the police, these policies look justified because, according to the evidence from victimisation surveys, those fitting criminal stereotypes do commit more 'conventional', mainly 'street' crimes (Hindelang, 1978, 1981). But the population under surveillance views this differently. 'Justified suspicion and warranted apprehensions', including stop and search, entry and seizure, are perceived by those on the receiving end as pure harassment and, to some, racial discrimination and prejudice. This leads a community to think of itself as 'under occupation'. It leads to the police being viewed with extreme suspicion and hostility. It inflames discontent already generated by thwarted ambition or relative deprivation. It creates an atmosphere where the unemployed and ethnic minorities feel that the forces of law and order are merely there to oppose them and therefore shore up a system of social injustice. These processes get caught up in a vicious amplification system as a deepening recession gives the civilian casualties more reason to deviate and the police and authorities more reason to be suspicious.

The second relevant feature of societal reaction theory follows from the first. Those subjected to higher rates of apprehension, arrest, prosecution and conviction are also likely to suffer from a sense of criminal injustice. This provides an additional push into further deviant acts, particularly by those who, when released from prison, find themselves so disadvantaged and discriminated against that they are unable to secure employment. This is a likely prospect even during affluent boom periods (Boshier, 1974; Buikhuisen and Dijstirhuis, 1971; Schwartz and Skolnick, 1964; Stebbins, 1971). It becomes a 'racing certainty' during recession when the levels of unemployment soar to 10 or 15 per cent of the labour force. Furthermore, stigma attached to the ex-prisoner status also creates acute problems of homelessness (Davies, 1974), and this interacts reciprocally with unemployment to create a massive push into recidivism. This in turn complicates the monocausal relationship between unemployment and crime because it is quite feasible to argue that unemployment leads to crime, but crime leads to imprisonment, imprisonment leads to unemployment (homelessness), and unemployment leads to more crime. After a while this circle obscures the original cause and the only sensible approach is to regard it as a fully interactive relationship (Thornberry and Christenson, 1984).

(iv) Theory integration

These arguments can now be summarised. During a recession, when unemployment soars and income inequalities widen, crime is predicted to rise among those experiencing 'thwarted ambition' or 'relative deprivation'. Within these groups, those not tied to the conventional order by informal bonds, or marginalised from the institutionalised organisations for social change, or alienated from the forces of law and order, are likely to have the largest and the fastest-growing rate of committing conventional crimes; those suffering *in addition* from ascriptive discrimination are predicted to commit even more conventional crimes.

Finally, these objective strains with their accompanying subjective stresses, low social controls, particularly the lack of a 'stake in conformity', and militaristic-style policing, tend to coalesce in inner-city areas. These areas, deserted by industrialists and manufacturers who find capital accumulation easier elsewhere (Wallace and Humphries, 1980), scarred by a thousand cuts in public services and amenities where alternative jobs and entertainment could have been provided (Piven and Cloward, 1982), blemished by crumbling, insanitary, overcrowded houses and high-rise flats jerry-built in the flush of post-war short-sightedness (Harrison, 1983), and polluted by the sickly smell of failure, are where the relationship between recession and crime should be most marked. It is in these areas, deserted by the professional middle class and skilled working class who find suburbs more amenable, and by governments who believe in public expenditure restraint, that the cutting edge of recession is sharpest.

The above arguments are presented in diagrammatic form in Figure 1.

Any attempt to integrate a number of strands from different theoretical traditions is bound to run into opposition. There are those like Hirschi (1979) who argue in favour of 'separate and unequal'. For him, strain and control theories are simply incompatible. Yet a constant criticism of control theory is that a motivational element is absent; it is assumed people will deviate unless social bonds prevent them. But the fact that people who are not tied by such bonds 'could' break the law does not explain 'why' they would do so. There is a distinct difference between a 'conducive' factor, which permits behaviour, and a 'generative' one which 'pushes' people towards a particular act. A motivational element therefore has to be grafted onto control theory to make it work. The above variants of strain theory seem to fit the bill.

Others might criticise the above integration scheme because it omits some theoretical traditions, such as *opportunity theory, cultural transmission theory,* and above all, *deterrence theory.* So a few words about each of these is required.

Crimes cannot be committed unless there is an opportunity to do so — this is plainly, and painfully obvious. It is also obvious how opportunity theory links recession and conventional crime. Some argue that 'the devil makes work for idle hands', and

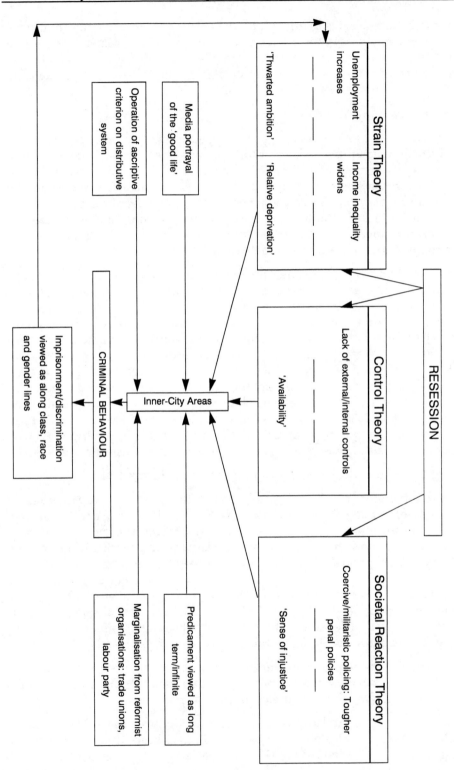

Figure 1 Causal links between recession and crime

therefore the bored unemployed with nothing to do all day are easily tempted into crime. While this may be plausible, it fails to recognise that the opportunities for 'non-conventional' crimes, such as pilfering, fraud, embezzlement and professional malpractice, exist for those *at* work. So it is not that recession increases the overall opportunities for crime; it merely shifts the balance between opportunities at work and opportunities on the street. In other words, as unemployment increases, so thefts from employers should decline, while street crimes, such as robbery and burglary, should increase.

Opportunity theory is embraced by those who consider that criminology should be directed purely by policy considerations. If car thefts increase, make cars more theft-proof. If burglaries increase, make houses more burglar-proof. There is *no* attempt to *understand* the offender. The outcome is that crime is 'displaced'. Unprotected targets become more and more attractive as more potentially lucrative targets become less and less accessible, particularly to 'amateur' offenders which is the typical 'status' for young property offenders. Those living in unprotected houses/flats are those already materially disadvantaged and often living on the razor edge of existence. What they have to lose may be little, but its replacement becomes a major problem for those on low income or supplementary benefits. Thus the 'solution' to some people's fear of crime creates conditions that feed others' fear and give them another anxiety in addition to those caused by lack of material resources. Opportunity theory is therefore doomed to sterility because essentially it recommends sticking one's finger in the crack appearing in a giant dam. Only by understanding the pressures behind these cracks can there be a chance of preventing a disastrous flood. And only in this way can the 'displacement of crime' onto those least able to cope with it be avoided.

Cultural transmission theory has not been mentioned directly in the above integrated model. However, it may well be that different cultural and subcultural heritages lead to different *meanings* being attributed to unemployment and income inequalities. Some groups may be socialised into viewing inequalities as natural and desirable — so that the brightest and fittest can be motivated to fill the most important jobs — while others have been historically conditioned to see inequalities as unnatural and undesirable — merely being expressions of greed among those who already have plenty. However, such systematic variations in meanings have already been built into the above integrated theoretical scheme, and although there is a need to trace the origin of these meanings, that particular exercise is extraneous to the present task of considering why recession should lead to more crimes.

Finally, a brief mention of deterrence theory. The idea that criminals can be deterred by increasing both the certainty of being apprehended and the severity of punishment mesmerises even those far removed from the 'Law and Order' brigade. Yet this compelling 'common sense' view overlooks a crucial distinction between 'objective' factors, such as the number and efficiency of the police, or the proportion of convicted persons sentenced to imprisonment, and 'subjective' factors, such as the *perceived* chances of not getting caught or not being severely punished even if caught (Erickson *et al.*, 1977; Jensen *et al.*, 1978; Waldo and Chiricos, 1972) .

Given the cloak of magical immunity with which many contemplating crime shroud themselves, it is not likely that the 'objective' and 'subjective' views of deterrence will overlap considerably. Thus, even if the police were to become more efficient and increase the clear-up rate, many potential criminals would either not know this fact, or consider themselves sufficiently clever and smart to avoid the longer arm of even a more efficient police force. Similarly, even if the imprisonment rate of convicted burglars increased from 30 to 40 per cent, it is unlikely that many potential burglars would be familiar with this fact, or even if they were, they would not necessarily think it altered *their* chances. Maybe there is a category mistake here. Maybe these 'objective' factors, briefly mentioned above and developed at greater length in [Chapters 4 and 5], should not be located within the deterrence debate at all. It could be that they are more suitably located within conflict theory where they become clues to the increasing tensions between groups and social classes and reflect the growing anxiety of those with the power to shape penal policy and police efficiency. In other words, maybe increased rates of arrest, conviction and imprisonment should be seen as indicators of state coercion rather than factors taken into account by people contemplating crime.

This leaves the 'subjective' version of deterrence theory. There are those (Tittle 1977, 1980) who argue that the perception of legal sanctions only has a deterrent effect if accompanied by the perception of non-legal sanctions, such as parental or peer disapproval. In the absence of the latter, the former may have little constraint on behaviour. There are others (Minor and Harry, 1982; Saltzman *et al.*, 1982; Paternoster *et al.*, 1983) whose research results were not consistent with the deterrence model. But the most sophisticated test of both formal and informal sanctions as well as normative constraints — borrowed from control theory — concluded that although these three factors interacted to produce an overall level of deterrence, it was the acceptance of conventional norms which shaped the perception of risks. In other words, an element from control theory — beliefs — was the major determinant, and the perception of legal and non-legal sanctions were variables intervening between this and criminal behaviour (Bishop, 1984). This means that weakened social bonds are likely to be accompanied by a perception that crime can be committed without incurring high prohibitive costs. Consequently, the 'subjective' version of deterrence theory is already included in the above integrated theory and does not deserve a separate entry.

Evidence in support of this integrated theory is presented in [Chapter 3]. But before moving onto the plane of 'facts', there is a further strand to this theoretical excursion.

Recession and the 'unconventional' crimes of the powerful

Of all the crimes committed by the powerful, two stand out as being particularly linked with recession. The first is corporate crime, a 'crime of economic domination', which includes bribery, corruption, espionage, arson, price-fixing, tax-evasion, fraud, false labelling and misleading advertising, paying less than legal minimum wage or not complying with health and safety regulations, pollution and environmental destruction. The second is police crime, a 'crime of repression', which includes brutality, violation of citizens' civil and legal rights such as illegal phone-tapping and surveillance, strike-breaking, false arrest and evidence-fabrication, perjury and conspiracy to pervert the course of justice.

(i) Strain theory, recession and corporate crime

Despite the pioneering work of Sutherland (1940, 1945, 1949), the study of corporate and organisational crime has only become a central criminological issue over the last decade (Braithwaite, 1984; Box, 1983; Clinard and Yeager, 1981; Conklin, 1977; Ermann and Lundman, 1982; Geis and Stotland, 1980; Hochstedler, 1984; Simon and Eitzen, 1982). This body of work, which includes such pertinent titles as *Dying For a Living* (Tataryn 1979), *Assault on the Worker,* (Reasons *et al.,* 1981) *Death on the Job* (Berman, 1978), *Unsafe at Any Speed* (Nader, 1965). *Screwing the Average Man* (Hapgood, 1974), *Massive, Hidden Agony of Industrial Slaughter* (Scott, 1974) 'Silent Killers at Work' (Swartz, 1975), and *Eating May Be Dangerous to Your Health* (Carper, 1975), documents the widespread nature of corporate and organisational crime, the seriousness of these crimes in terms of the bodies killed, maimed and injured, and the billions of pounds illegally obtained. In addition, it has developed a theoretical framework which not only seeks to explain these crimes, but also provides a basis for predicting that they will increase during a recession.

Corporations and organisations are goal-seeking entities operating in an unpredictable and contradictory environment full of competitors struggling over scarce resources. Consequently, their executives frequently find themselves in a situation where strict adherence to regulations governing their activities would not be a rational course of action to pursue. It would result in their corporation or organisation failing to achieve its goal (or goals) and maybe even going out of existence. In these dire circumstances, executives investigate alternative means, including law avoidance, evasion and violation and pursue them if they are evaluated as more likely to lead to goals being achieved. In addition, corporations form powerful and, with the right government, persuasive pressure groups to change regulations and laws originally designed to limit corporate behaviour so that employees, consumers and the general public would be better protected.

Two particular environmental uncertainties are important in the context of discussing recession and corporate crimes. First, employees organised in trade unions become an increasing problem. They attempt to restrict the numbers made redundant They struggle to prevent cuts in workers' real earnings. They fight for the maintenance and improvement in general employment conditions, particularly health and safety standards. All these threaten to maintain the unit costs of production at a level higher than that desired by corporate officials feeling the cold wind of recession on their backs. To solve this problem executives and managers consider ways of reducing the power of trade unions and regulatory agencies, such as the Health and Safety Executive in the UK, and the Occupational Health and Safety Administration in the USA, whom they perceive to be the worker's ally.

Second, competing organisations become a greater nuisance. Recession not only increases the numbers unemployed but these in turn lead to lower aggregate demand and therefore a shrunken market. In order for profit margins to be maintained, other competitors have to be controlled or eliminated to prevent prices falling as a consequence of market forces. The outcome could be illegal price-fixing or a conspiracy to drive competitors out of business. The collapse of Laker Airways in 1982 as a result of American and British airways corporations conspiring to fix prices, and which led to a $40 million settlement out of court, is a recent and dramatic illustration of this type of corporate crime.

As these two environmental uncertainties multiply during a recession, so the strain towards corporate illegalities increases. However, corporate crime need not occur. Corporations have two tactics not available to those tempted to commit conventional crimes.

In the first place, some corporations, particularly multinationals, can engage in *law evasion*. That is, they may choose, for example, to export manufacturing plants emitting too much illegal pollution. Thus a multinational asbestos corporation found that new pollution laws passed in Australia in the 1970s interfered with its production routines and raised its costs, so they closed down the plant and relocated in Indonesia — 'a country not noted for the stringency with which it enforces safety regulation to protect workers' (Braithwaite, 1980). Similarly, multinational pharmaceutical corporations might decide to flood the Third World market with drugs banned in the industrialised world. For example, the drug entero-vioform was banned in many Western countries after it was discovered that any dose above the minimum could cause a devastating syndrome of paralysis, blindness and sometimes death. Yet this drug is now being sold on the open market in many Third World countries, without warning of adverse side-effects on the labels (Bodenheimer, 1984; Braithwaite, 1984, pp. 245–78). In other words, multinationals dump some of their products, plants and practices, illegal in industrialised countries, onto undeveloped and under-developed countries. This dumping is possible because these countries are more dependent upon multinational capital investment for their modernisation and Westernisation plans, they have fewer resources to check manufacturers claims or police corporate activities, and their government officials are more susceptible to the 'folded lie' — bribery and corruption (Braithwaite, 1984, pp. 11–50; Reisman, 1979). Given these lucrative opportunities, corporations facing contraction in industrialised countries are able to avoid breaking the law by acting immorally and exporting their 'illegal' behaviour to where it is legal. By the expedient of catching a jet, a would-be burglar would not be afforded the opportunity to carry out his plans and still remain within the law. A multinational corporate executive is more fortunate!

A second strategy available to would-be corporate offenders, but not would-be conventional offenders, is that they often have sufficient economic and political clout to get law-enforcement minimised or even repealed. The history of the Occupational Safety and Health legislation in the USA is a good illustration of this.

By a conservative estimate, there were in 1980 13,000 workers killed and 22 million suffering from disabling injuries received at the workplace. Workers' increasing sensitivity to these annual colossal numbers of victims of avoidable suffering, plus a favourable political atmosphere, paved the way for the Occupational Safety and Health Act of 1970 (Donnelly, 1982). However, from its very inception, industrial leaders sought to limit the implementation and enforcement of this legislation. In 1971, according to Szasz (1984):

> Large firms and business trade associations sent their lobbyists to advise
> that management be given advance notice of inspections, that
> management be allowed to refuse entry to OSHA (Occupational Safety
> and Health Administration) inspectors, that management be allowed to
> limit inspections in the name of protecting trade secrets, and that
> inspection results be kept secret by OSHA. Industry asked for rules
> limiting the access of OSHA inspectors to company health data and
> establishing the right of management to legal counsel during inspections.
> Lobbyists also demanded that enforcement be applied to employees as well
> as management, so that employees would be equally liable for health
> practices and would be penalized for false complaints to OSHA. And
> industry continued to emphasize due process safeguards in both
> enforcement and standard-setting. (p. 107)

These manoeuvres were only partially successful and so during the 1971–4 period,
when the number of inspections and cited violations rapidly grew, industrial leaders
sought to contain the damage being committed on 'good honest business' by OSHA.
Small businesses, lacking large managerial structures, powerful Washington law firms
and wealthy trade associations, lobbied their Congressional representatives and
pursued relief through the federal court system. The latter course was more successful,
for the Supreme Court finally ruled in favour of significant limits to the enforcement
powers of OSHA. Large corporations, who were not being inspected with the same
vigour that OSHA applied to small businesses, were primarily alarmed at the prospect
of workers demanding the rights to accompany inspectors, to request inspection and to
abandon potentially hazardous sites. They were also very worried about the possible
imposition of stringent health standards, particularly those related to 'coke-oven
emissions, noise, heat stress, cotton dust, lead, pesticides and arsenic' (Szasz, 1984, p.
109).

To prevent new health standards being formulated and enforced, large businesses
practised information concealment, and when that was not entirely successful, they
insisted on 'participation', which meant in practice that they would urge caution,
demand more stringent scientific evidence and generally cause as much delay as
possible in the hope that the political climate would change. It did, when the recession
beginning 1974–5:

> cast a pall over the latter half of the decade and altered the political
> balance of forces in the debate over occupational safety and health. The
> Gross National Product fell in 1974 and 1975, the unemployment rate rose
> to 8.5 per cent in 1974, up from 4.9 in 1973, and the rate of inflation
> reached 9.1 per cent in 1975. The recession and the growing national
> economic crisis weakened organised labour and compromised public
> concern over environmental issues. (Szasz, 1984, p. 111)

Under these new circumstances large-business leaders turned from containment of
OSHA to counter-attack. Ironically, under the Carter Administration, OSHA increased
its inspections, average fines went up, and new more stringent health standards and
workers' rights were formulated. But, by then, big business felt able to challenge all

these in courts and won a major victory in 1980 when it opposed the new benzene standard. In this case, the Supreme Court declared that OSHA had to take economic factors into consideration when adopting standards and that there had to be a reasonable relationship between costs and benefits. The health and safety of workers had to be balanced against the costs to employers of supplying it. This spelt the end of any serious attempt to regulate industry. In its place, the recession succeeded an 'ideology of deregulation', which grew steadily stronger through the 1970s (Weidenbaum, 1979) and found a receptive American audience worried more about economic performance than workers' health and safety

Finally, there was the Reagan denounement. He appointed a new head of OSHA who immediately declared that 'cooperation' should replace 'punishment'. New health standards were dropped, existing ones weakened, OSHA lost 20 per cent of its inspectors, and enforcement declined and workers' rights were shelved (Calavita, 1983).

A similar deregulatory stance followed the arrival of the Conservative government in the UK in 1979. There is no need to spell this out in too much detail, but the emasculation of agencies establishing, monitoring and enforcing health and safety standards, such as the Health and Safety Commission/Executive, whose umbrella covers the Factories, Mines and Quarries, Alkali and Clean Air, Agriculture, Explosives, and Nuclear Installations Inspectorates, and the 'reform' of Wages Councils provides sufficient indicators of the government's determination to ease conditions for employers.

Just before Mrs Thatcher's first victory, Her Majesty's Factory Inspectorate had already indicated that its resources were not sufficient to perform effectively. In the *Manufacturing and Service Industry Report,* 1978, the Inspectorate wrote:

> The Factory Inspectorate . . . works against a background of increasing commitments and slender resources. There is a limit to what a force of some 900 inspectors in the field (700 general inspectors and 200 specialists) can do in practice. The Inspectorate is responsible for some 18,000,000 people at work scattered through some 500,000 or 600,000 different workplaces . . . It is obvious that an Inspectorate of its present size in relation to its responsibility cannot hope to achieve either all it would like or all the public would like it to do. (Health and Safety Executive 1980, pp. vi–vii)

Yet despite this, the Conservative government, almost immediately after taking office, required the Health and Safety Commission to *reduce* its budget for the year 1982/3 by 6 per cent compared with the 1979/80 level. The Commission's response to this loss of vital and essential resources was immediate and blunt. It replied that 'cuts of that size in our budget cannot be achieved without a reduction in our programmes directly concerning the health and safety both for workers and general public' (Health and Safety Commission Report 1980/1, 1981, p. 1). This warning, too, fell on ears only receptive to a different ideological message. Industry had to be freed from excessive regulation; market forces should be allowed to prevail. So in addition to the proposed 6 per cent cut, the government also required a further budget reduction equivalent to the loss of 150 posts. At the same time, the Commission was squeezed financially by central pay settlements exceeding the sum allowed for them in 'cash limits', a device imposed by a government concerned to reduce public expenditure — except for 'law and order.' One pertinent outcome of these funding cuts has been a dramatic loss of employees, which stands in marked and significant contrast to the expansion of both the police and prison services during the 1980s. Thus from being established in 1974, following the Health and Safety Act that year, the Executive's total staff in post rose steadily to 4,168 by April 1979, and, of these, 1,424 were field inspectors responsible for ensuring that standards and regulations were being obeyed. However, by 1984 the Executive's staff has been slashed by *one-seventh* to 3,563 and the total number of inspectors in the field dropped to 1,242. Furthermore, the projections are for more cuts. By 1986, the total inspectors in the field were expected to be around 1,200 which is the equivalent to 85 per cent of the 1979 total.

Armed with knowledge of the government's intentions and projected cuts, the Commission's plan of Work 1983/4 made gloomy reading for those concerned with health and safety at work. The Commission wrote:

> Most recently, recession, scarce resources, and rising unemployment have brought a changed focus and a new pressure to our work, raising questions about whether our activities, and those of the Health and Safety Executive are going to enhance manufacturing activity, and influencing the priority given by some groups of employers and workpeople to improving working conditions, as one objective alongside their wider objective of economic survival . . . The changing nature of economic activity and the acute problems of recession have raised fundamental questions about our activities and, more generally, the role of interventionist policies for health and safety at work. (Health and Safety Commission. 1983, pp. 1–2)

Soon after this, the Commission's director, Bill Simpson, who had been the General Secretary (Foundry Section) Amalgamated Union of Engineering Workers (1967–75) and a member of the Labour Party's National Executive Committee, was replaced by John Cullen, who had been a director of ICI (1958–67) and Rohm and Haas (1967–83). It is noticeable that the last two annual reports have not made similar complaints about resources or questioned the ability of the Health and Safety Executive to do its job.

The latest stage in deregulation of health and safety standards has been for the government to permit the Commission to 'contract out' inspection to the industries concerned. This 'self-regulation' sounds fine in principle and makes some sense when the resources of Health and Safety agencies cannot inspect a substantial proportion of establishments under its jurisdiction. But imagine the response to the suggestion that young unemployed males should monitor their own behaviour and report themselves to the police whenever they discover they have broken the law!

In addition to facilitating a reduction in production costs by weakening the effectiveness of the Health and Safety Executive and its Inspectorates, the government has directly affected wage levels by abolition of the Fair Wages Resolution in 1983 and by threatening the Wage Councils with 'reform' and abolition. The Fair Wages Resolution provided that government contractors should observe such terms and conditions for their employees as had been generally established for the trade or industry in which they operated. The argument behind this abolition was that 'fair wages' inhibited employment. However, the result, according to the Civil Service Union and the Contract Cleaning and Maintenance Association has been that both wages *and employment levels* have fallen, and they have been accompanied by a worsening in other conditions of employment.

Wages Councils, of which there are 26 covering nearly 2.75 million low-paid workers, have the power to set legally enforceable minima for wages, holidays and other conditions of employment. The government has 'reformed' these by budgetary cuts which have resulted in the number of inspectors being cut by *one-quarter* from 166 in 1979 to 129 in 1985. In a year, this handful of inspectors is only capable of inspecting 10 per cent of the 400,000 establishments under Wage Council jurisdiction. Its effectiveness, never that remarkable, has now been further reduced, and, with the threat of abolition, morale is very low. Joining the government in its desire to release market forces on the already low paid and poorly unionised, and at the same time release corporations from previously legal obligations, are the Institute of Directors, the National Federation of Self-Employed and Small Businesses, and slightly less vigorously, the Confederation of British Industries.

It would all be very different if would-be burglars urged the government to exclude supermarket stores from the category of property that could technically be burgled on the economic grounds that 'times are hard' and breaking into and taking from such stores is a rational way of making ends meet. Similarly the plea that the police should be de-established or at least dissuaded by the Home Secretary from pursuing burglars would also drop on deaf ears. But, then, would-be burglars are not respectable executives whose corporations have economic and political clout.

So, as recession deepens, the prediction that corporate crime increases has to be formulated cautiously. Large multinationals will spend more energy exporting 'crimes' to Third World countries and whittling away laws and enforcement agencies so that behaviour previously banned will now be permitted. Only in that section of industry where these two options are not so readily available will the temptation to cut corners and operate illegal practices be pronounced. Small and middle sized national companies are therefore expected to be the locus of crimes in a recession; although it has to be stressed that much avoidable suffering resulting from large multinational 'immoral' behaviour will also increase, but this will not be technically illegal.

Changing economic conditions compounding environmental contradictions and uncertainties are not the sole cause of corporate crime. There are many other factors which complete the explanation, involving personnel who are 'ambitious, shrewd and possessed of a non-demanding moral code' (Gross, 1978, p. 71), a 'subculture of structural immoralities' (Mills, 1956, p. 138) which sanitizes crimes by elevating them to a higher moral plane, a cloak of corporate respectability that shields corporations and their officials from damaging self-images and minimising negative social reaction (Benson, 1984), and an awareness that 'corporate crime pays' (Box, 1983, pp. 44–53).

However, with the exception of the last factor, these remain fairly constant throughout the business cycle. During a recession, however, environmental uncertainties increase and the costs of corporate crimes decrease because enforcement agencies are systematically weakened by government policies and the judiciary adopts a more sympathetic stance towards businessmen 'in trouble'. In these circumstances an invitation to break the law will be eagerly accepted by those for whom law evasion is not a real alternative. Corporate crime committed by small to middle-sized companies should therefore increase as a recession deepens. Evidence from research on corporate crime and its relation to changing economic conditions is reviewed in [Chapter 3].

(ii) Conflict theory, recession and crimes of repression

Conflict theorists suggest a link between recession and such crimes of repression as police killing of civilians and brutality. As Chambliss and Seidman (1971) argue:

> The more economically stratified a society becomes the more it becomes necessary for dominant groups to enforce through coercion the norms of conduct that guarantee their supremacy. (p. 33)

What they imply is that although governing elites have always had a respectable fear of hooligans (Pearson, 1983) and the 'dangerous classes', this anxiety oscillates with economic cycles. As unemployment rises, so the surplus labour force becomes a body viewed more suspiciously by the governing elite, not because it actually does become disruptive and rebellious, but because it *might*. Any widening of economic inequalities increases these fears, because the potential insubordination of the unemployed and marginalised might be actualised through militant, maybe revolutionary, organisations springing up to defend and raise the consciousness of the swelling army of the underprivileged. Under such circumstances, conflict theorists predict more state coercion.

This state coercion takes many forms. Of more relevance to criminologists is the likelihood that the state will increase the number of police and extend their powers, extend the sentencing powers of courts and encourage longer sentences for particular types of offenders, build more prisons to accommodate greater numbers being processed by a more efficient police and court system, and introduce more laws to criminalise behaviour which is seen, by some, to threaten particular economic interests, such as industrial disputes and strikes. At the same time, the state would focus these greater powers against those committing 'conventional' crimes rather than against those committing 'crimes of the powerful'.

However, all these attempts to allay respectable fears by 'sterilising' the potential ability of the subordinate surplus population to give birth to an uncontrollable rebellious movement are relatively more costly than one other simple possibility: the authorities could become more indifferent to such police crimes as unjustified arrest, evidence fabrication, brutality and even killing, particularly when the victims of these crimes are just those persons perceived to be potentially dangerous and possible recruits for political resistance.

This is not to argue that the state *directs* the police to engage in these crimes more often, or that there is a *conspiracy* to pervert the course of justice in this way. That

291

argument would be too crude and unnecessary. The logic of the situation leads to this scenario without any cigar-filled back-room meetings being necessary. As Jacobs and Britt (1979) point out:

> For inequality to lead to more lethal violence by the police it is *not* necessary to assume that elites make direct demands for harsh methods. All that is required is that elites be more willing to overlook the violent short cuts taken by the 'dirty workers' in the interests of order. Of course this interpretation fits with Hughes' (1963) argument that a willingness to remain conveniently ignorant is a fundamental explanation for much official brutality. (p. 406)

Although conflict theory provides an account of increasing police crime during a recession — the state is more willing to turn a blind eye to illegalities — this has to be supplemented by a consideration of why the police themselves would want or have a motive to commit more crimes. To understand this, the changing nature of police work during a recession needs to be examined. From the officers' perspective, police work is dangerous, socially isolating, and contains problems of authority which not only undermine efficiency, but frequently poison police–public encounters. The police regard themselves as front-line troops against certain types of violent criminals, terrorists, militant dissenters and industrial agitators.

During the last decade or so, when class tensions increased and the 'fear of crime' became a growing social problem, these police perceptions of their job and their 'symbolic assailants' sharpened. Not only were criminals viewed as becoming more desperate, as the increased use of firearms testifies, but the growing militancy of certain social groups threatened to undermine social order, the very reason for having a police force. Responding to the public fear of crime became the 'end' by which the 'means' of bending the rules were justified.

From the police's point of view, this serious situation of rising crime and public fear had to be met with equal determination. In the mounting war on crime and dissent, the police, fortified with support from the 'respectable' public, increasingly granted themselves a licence to break the law when it came to the disreputable elements. In this way the law was broken but order maintained.

This slip towards police crime, particularly brutality, was given a further nudge by deteriorating relationships between the police and that narrow section of the public on whom they concentrate most of their powers of surveillance, arrest and prosecution. When the police came to be viewed by this section of the public as an 'army of occupation', and when accounts of police brutality fanned the flames of discontent and resentment among many inner-city dwellers, then the situation was ripe for the police to feel threatened. Naturally, despite their professional training, they protected themselves as best they could, sometimes with a 'protective first strike' or by 'fitting-up' a suspect when they 'knew' the public would be better protected if he were behind bars. When politicians and some sections of the public responded by stating that 'the police are doing a wonderful job', and anyone who criticised them was very suspect indeed, then no wonder the police took this encouragement as an invitation to continue. Furthermore, the absence of an effective complaints procedure, ridiculously

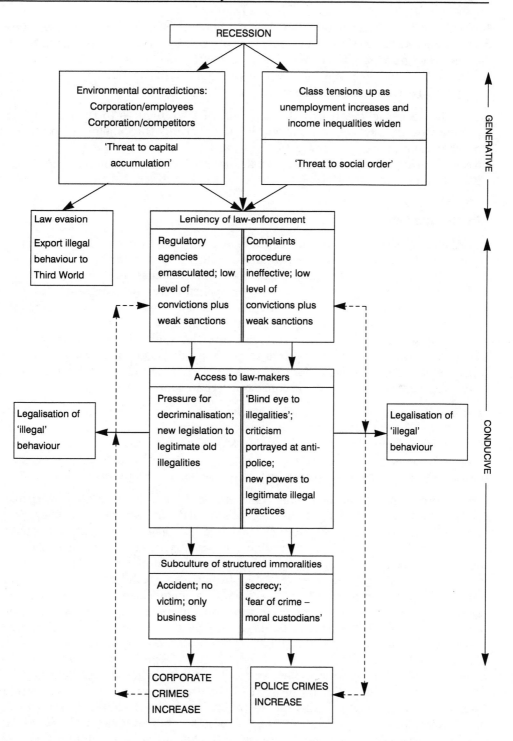

Figure 2   Recession and crimes of the powerful

low levels of prosecution and conviction, even for assault (Box, 1983, pp. 98–111; Stevens and Willis, 1981) — they wobbled between 1 and 2 per cent during the 1970s — and the growing awareness among senior police officers that they are not accountable to publicly elected local government officials (Hewitt, 1982; Spencer, 1985), simply reinforced this invitation.

Given the encouragement, and the government's willingness to turn a blind eye to irregularities if they achieve the object of defeating the 'enemy within', as Mrs Thatcher calls them, it is understandable why police crimes against civilians might increase during a recession. These ideas are presented diagrammatically here (see Figure 2) and evidence relevant to assessing their accuracy is presented in the [next chapter].

Concluding thoughts

In this chapter there has been developed an account of why people might be motivated to break the law and how other conducive factors might transform this motive into action. But to render action comprehensible is not to 'excuse' it. It may well be that the motivation to crime is a purely 'rational' response to the pressures, strains, stresses and contradictions people face. None the less, this does not make their *response* rational. Indeed, much crime is so horrendous in its victimisation, so imbued with racist and sexist overtones, and hits hardest those already on the razor edge of desperation, that it does not deserve to be excused. Legal competition and struggle under present economic conditions is bad enough, but capitalism with its clothes off is frequently beyond any human response other than condemnation.

If crimes evoke such outrage, and they clearly do, then their reduction ought to be prioritised. The 'no excuse' position is simply an impoverished response. Only when the motivation behind them, and the structural conditions, particularly inequality and competitiveness, behind the motivation are analysed can there be an appropriate point of intervention to bring about a reduction in the level of criminal activity.

Just before this chapter was finished, there were riots in Toxteth, Liverpool, and Tottenham, London. The same old tired 'folk devils' were conjured up. There was the same old refusal to admit that social causes could play a significant part in the outburst of social protest and criminal behaviour. It was the same old myopic debate that followed the riots of 1981, but with one significant difference. This time the UK government refused to set up a judicial inquiry. Clearly it did not want to receive the unpleasant news again from Lord Scarman, or someone like him, that conditions in inner-city areas were criminogenic. In place of understanding there was now only a demand for more and better tools to 'do the job' properly. Metropolitan Commissioner Newman warned the capital that next time he would not hesitate to use CS gas and plastic bullets, and water cannons were in their final testing trials. The Home Secretary promised the police a new arrestable offence of 'disturbing behaviour'. This wide discretionary power could in principle be used to protect the Asian community from racist insults, but will in practice probably be used to intensify the policing of marginalised populations. Maybe it is a sad indictment of politicians who choose not to see the legacies of their economic policies, or, if they do, refuse to admit it. Hopefully, this chapter has pointed out some of the observations or admissions politicians would make if they were more sensitive or honest. But maybe they too only make choices — to appear naive or dishonest — under circumstances not of their own choosing. If, as was hinted in the [previous chapter], these circumstances are nothing less than the 'South-Koreanisation' of the British labour force, itself brought about by the logic of international capitalism, then what politician would want to make this public? Better to take refuge in stupidity than to admit to such a policy.

Having hacked a path through the tangled forest of sociological theorising, there is now an even more daunting task — to assess the evidence relevant to testing hypotheses derived from this arduous journey into theorising.

The Subcultural Approach to Crime and Deviance

14.   Subcultures, Cultures and Class
John Clarke, Stuart Hall,
Tony Jefferson and Brian Roberts

Our subject in [this volume] is Youth Cultures: our object, to explain them as a phenomenon, and their appearance in the post-war period. The subject has, of course, been massively treated, above all in the mass media. Yet, many of these surveys and analyses seem mainly to have multiplied the confusions and extended the mythologies surrounding the topic. By treating it in terms of its spectacular features only, these surveys have become part of the very phenomenon we want to explain. First, then, we must clear the ground, try to get behind the myths and explanations which cover up, rather than clarify, the problem. We have to construct the topic first — partly by demolishing certain concepts which, at present, are taken as adequately defining it. Necessarily, this exercise of penetrating beneath a popular construction must be done with care, lest we discard the 'rational kernel' along with its over-publicised husk.

The social and political meaning of Youth Cultures is not easy to assess: though their visibility has been consistently high. 'Youth' appeared as an emergent category in post-war Britain, one of the most striking and visible manifestations of social change in the period. 'Youth' provided the focus for official reports, pieces of legislation, official interventions. It was signified as a social problem by the moral guardians of the society — something we 'ought to do something about'. Above all, Youth played an important role as a cornerstone in the construction of understandings, interpretations and quasi-explanations *about* the period. As the Rowntree study of the Popular Press and Social Change suggested:

> Youth was, in both papers [the *Daily Express* and the *Daily Mirror*] and perhaps in the whole press of the period, a powerful but concealed *metaphor* for social change: the compressed image of a society which had crucially changed, in terms of basic life-styles and values — changed, in ways calculated to upset the official political framework, but in ways *not yet calculable in traditional political terms* . . (Smith *et. al.*, 1975)

It would be difficult to sustain the argument that a phenomenon as massively present and visible as 'Youth Culture', occupying a pivotal position in the history and consciousness of the period, was a pure construction of the media, a surface phenomenon only. However, Gramsci warned us that, "in studying a structure, it is necessary to distinguish organic movements (relatively permanent) from movements which may be termed 'conjunctural', and which appear as occasional, immediate, almost accidental". The aim must be to "find the correct relation between what is organic and what is conjunctural" (Gramsci, 1971: 177).   The 'phenomenal form' — Youth Culture provides a point of departure, only, for such an analysis. We cannot

John Clarke, Stuart Hall, Tony Jefferson and Brian Roberts: 'Subcultures, Cultures and Class' from *RESISTANCE THROUGH RITUALS* (Hutchinson, 1979), pp. 9–57. Reproduced by permission of Routledge.

afford to be blind to such a development (as some 'sceptical materialists' of the old left have been, with due respect to the recent debate in *Marxism Today*) any more than we can afford to be blinded *by* them (as some 'visionary idealists' of the new left have at times been).

A. Some definitions

We begin with some minimal definitions. The term, 'Youth Culture', directs us to the 'cultural' aspects of youth. We understand the word 'culture' to refer to that level at which social groups develop distinct patterns of life, and give *expressive form* to their social and material life-experience. Culture is the way, the forms, in which groups 'handle' the raw material of their social and material existence. "We must suppose the raw material of life experience to be at one pole, and all the infinitely complex human disciplines and systems, articulate and inarticulate, formalised in institutions or dispersed in the least formal ways, which 'handle', transmit or distort this raw material, to be at the other" (Thompson, 1960). 'Culture' is the practice which realises or *objectivates* group-life in meaningful shape and form. "As individuals express their life, so they are. What they are, therefore, coincides with their production, both with *what* they produce and with *how* they produce" (Marx, 1970: 42). The 'culture' of a group or class is the peculiar and distinctive 'way of life' of the group or class, the meanings, values and ideas embodied in institutions, in social relations, in systems of beliefs, in *mores* and customs, in the uses of objects and material life. Culture is the distinctive shapes in which this material and social organisation of life expresses itself. A culture includes the 'maps of meaning' which make things intelligible to its members. These 'maps of meaning' are not simply carried around in the head: they are objectivated in the patterns of social organisation and relationship through which the individual becomes a 'social individual'. Culture is the way the social relations of a group are structured and shaped: but it is also the way those shapes are experienced, understood and interpreted.

A social individual, born into a particular set of institutions and relations, is at the same moment born into a peculiar configuration of meanings, which give her access to and locate her within 'a culture'. The 'law of society' and the 'law of culture' (the symbolic ordering of social life) are one and the same. These structures — of social relationship and of meaning — shape the on-going collective existence of groups. But they also limit, modify and *constrain* how groups live and reproduce their social existence. Men and women are, thus, formed, and form themselves through society, culture and history. So the existing cultural patterns form a sort of historical reservoir — a pre-constituted 'field of the possibles' — which groups take up, transform, develop. Each group makes something of its starting conditions — and through this 'making', through this practice, culture is reproduced and transmitted. But this practice only takes place within the given field of possibilities and constraints (See, Sartre, 1963). "Men make their own history, but they do not make it just as they please; they do not make it under circumstances chosen by themselves, but under circumstances directly encountered, given and transmitted from the past" (Marx, 1951: 225). Culture, then, embodies the trajectory of group life through history: always under conditions and with 'raw materials' which cannot wholly be of its own making.

Groups which exist within the same society and share some of the same material and historical conditions no doubt also understand, and to a certain extent share each others' 'culture'. But just as different groups and classes are unequally ranked in relation to one another, in terms of their productive relations, wealth and power, so *cultures* are differently ranked, and stand in opposition to one another, in relations of domination and subordination, along the scale of 'cultural power'. The definitions of the world, the 'maps of meaning' which express the life situation of those groups which hold the monopoly of power in society, command the greatest weight and influence, secrete the greatest legitimacy. The world tends to be classified out and ordered in terms and through structures which most directly express the power, the position, the *hegemony,* of the powerful interest in that society. Thus,

> The class which has the means of material production at its disposal, has control, at the same time, over the means of mental production, so that, thereby, generally speaking, the ideas of those who lack the means of mental production are subject to it . . . Insofar as they rule as a class and determine the extent and compass of an epoch . . . they do this in its whole range, hence, among other things rule also as thinkers, as producers of ideas, and regulate the production and distribution of the ideas of their age: thus their ideas are the ruling ideas of the epoch. (Marx, 1970: 64)

This does not mean that there is only *one* set of ideas or cultural forms in a society. There will be more than one tendency at work within the dominant ideas of a society. Groups or classes which do not stand at the apex of power, nevertheless find ways of expressing and realising in their culture their subordinate position and experiences. In so far as there is more than one fundamental class in a society (and capitalism is essentially the bringing together, around production, of two fundamentally *different* classes — capital and labour) there will be more than one major cultural configuration in play at a particular historical moment. But the structures and meanings which most adequately reflect the position and interests of the most powerful class — however complex it is internally — will stand, in relation to all the others, as a *dominant* social-cultural order. The dominant culture represents itself as *the* culture. It tries to define and contain all other cultures within its inclusive range. *Its* views of the world, unless challenged, will stand as the most natural, all-embracing, universal culture. Other cultural configurations will not only be subordinate to this dominant order: they will enter into struggle with it, seek to modify, negotiate, resist or even overthrow its reign — its *hegemony*. The struggle between classes over material and social life thus always assumes the forms of a continuous struggle over the distribution of 'cultural power'. We might want, here, to make a distinction between 'culture' and 'ideology'. Dominant and subordinate classes will each have distinct cultures. But when one culture gains ascendancy over the other, and when the subordinate culture *experiences* itself in terms prescribed by the dominant culture, then the dominant culture has also become the basis of a dominant ideology.

The dominant culture of a complex society is never a homogeneous structure. It is layered, reflecting different interests within the dominant class (e.g., an aristocratic versus a bourgeois outlook), containing different traces from the past (e.g., religious ideas within a largely secular culture), as well as emergent elements in the present.

Subordinate cultures will not always be in open conflict with it. They may, for long periods, coexist with it, negotiate the spaces and gaps in it, make inroads into it, "warrenning it from within" (Thompson, 1965). However, though the nature of this struggle over culture can never be reduced to a simple opposition, it is crucial to replace the notion of 'culture' with the more concrete, historical concept of 'cultures'; a redefinition which brings out more clearly the fact that cultures always stand in relations of domination — and subordination — to one another, are always, in some sense, in struggle with one another. The singular term, 'culture', can only indicate, in the most general and abstract way, the large cultural configurations at play in a society at any historical moment. We must move at once to the determining relationships of domination and subordination in which these configurations stand; to the processes of incorporation and resistance which define the cultural dialectic between them; and to the institutions which transmit and reproduce 'the culture' (i.e., the dominant culture) in its dominant or 'hegemonic' form.

In modern societies, the most fundamental groups are the social classes, and the major cultural configurations will be, in a fundamental though often mediated way, 'class cultures'. Relative to these cultural-class configurations, *sub*-cultures are sub-sets — smaller, more localised and differentiated structures, within one or other of the larger cultural networks. We must, first, see sub-cultures in terms of their relation to the wider class-cultural networks of which they form a distinctive part. When we examine this relationship between a sub-culture and the 'culture' of which it is a part, we call the latter the 'parent' culture. This must not be confused with the particular relationship between 'youth' and their 'parents', of which much will be said below. What we mean is that a sub-culture, though differing in important ways — in its 'focal concerns', its peculiar shapes and activities — from the culture from which it derives, will also share some things in common with that 'parent' culture. The bohemian sub-culture of the *avant-garde* which has arisen from time to time in the modern city, is both distinct from its 'parent' culture (the urban culture of the middle class intelligentsia) and yet also a part of it (sharing with it a modernising outlook, standards of education, a privileged position vis-a-vis productive labour, and so on). In the same way, the 'search for pleasure and excitement' which some analysts have noted as a marked feature of the 'delinquent sub-culture of the gang' in the working class, also shares something basic and fundamental with it. Sub-cultures, then, must first be related to the 'parent cultures' of which they are a sub-set. But, sub-cultures must also be analysed in terms of their relation to the dominant culture — the overall disposition of cultural power in the society as a whole. Thus, we may distinguish respectable, 'rough', delinquent and the criminal sub-cultures *within* working class culture: but we may also say that, though they differ amongst themselves, they *all* derive in the first instance from a 'working class parent culture': hence, they are all subordinate sub-cultures, in relation to the dominant middle-class or bourgeois culture. (We believe this goes some way towards meeting Graham Murdock's call for a more "symmetrical" analysis of subcultures.)

Sub-cultures must exhibit a distinctive enough shape and structure to make them identifiably different from their 'parent' culture. They must be focussed around certain activities, values, certain uses of material artefacts, territorial spaces etc., which significantly differentiate them from the wider culture. But, since they are sub-sets, there must also be significant things which bind and articulate them with the 'parent' culture. The famous Kray twins, for example, belonged both to a highly differentiated 'criminal sub-culture' in East London and to the 'normal' life and culture of the East End working class (of which indeed, the 'criminal sub-culture' has always been a clearly identifiable part). The behaviour of the Krays in terms of the criminal fraternity marks the differentiating axis of that sub-culture: the relation of the Krays to their mother, family, home and local pub is the binding, the articulating axis. (Pearson, 1973; Hebdige, 1974).

Sub-cultures, therefore, take shape around the distinctive activities and 'focal concerns' of groups. They can be loosely or tightly bounded. Some sub-cultures are merely loosely-defined strands or 'milieux' within the parent culture: they possess no distinctive 'world' of their own. Others develop a clear, coherent identity and structure. Generally, we deal in this volume *only* with 'sub-cultures' (whether drawn from a middle or working class 'parent culture') which have reasonably tight boundaries, distinctive shapes, which have cohered around particular activities, focal concerns and territorial spaces. When these tightly-defined groups are also distinguished by age and generation, we call them 'youth sub-cultures'.

'Youth sub-cultures' form up on the terrain of social and cultural life. Some youth sub-cultures are regular and persistent features of the 'parent' class-culture: the ill-famed 'culture of delinquency' of the working-class adolescent male, for example. But some sub-cultures appear only at particular historical moments: they become visible, are identified and labelled (either by themselves or by others): they command the stage of public attention for a time: then they fade, disappear or are so widely diffused that they lose their distinctiveness. It is the latter kind of sub-cultural formation which primarily concerns us here. The peculiar dress, style, focal concerns, milieux, etc. of the Teddy Boy, the Mod, the Rocker or the Skinhead set them off, as distinctive groupings, both from the broad patterns of working-class culture as a whole, and also from the more diffused patterns exhibited by 'ordinary' working class boys (and, to a more limited extent, girls). Yet, despite these differences, it is important to stress that, as sub-cultures, they continue to exist within, and coexist with, the more inclusive culture of the class from which they spring. Members of a sub-culture may walk, talk, act, look 'different' from their parents and from some of their peers: but they belong to the same families, go to the same schools, work at much the same jobs, live down the same 'mean streets' as their peers and parents. In certain crucial respects, they share the same position (vis-a-vis the dominant culture), the same fundamental and determining life-experiences, as the 'parent' culture from which they derive. Through dress, activities, leisure pursuits and life-style, they may project a different cultural response or 'solution' to the problems posed for them by their material and social class position and experience. But the membership of a sub-culture cannot protect them from the determining matrix of experiences and conditions which shape the life of their class as a whole. They experience and respond to the *same basic problematic* as other members of their class who are not so differentiated and distinctive in a 'sub-cultural' sense. Especially in relation to the *dominant* culture, their sub-culture remains like other elements in their class culture — subordinate and subordinated.

In what follows, we shall try to show why this *double articulation* of youth sub-cultures — first, to their 'parent' culture (e.g., working class culture), second, to the dominant culture — is a necessary way of staging the analysis. For our purposes, sub-cultures represent a necessary, 'relatively autonomous', but *inter-mediary* level of analysis. Any attempt to relate sub-cultures to the 'socio-cultural formation as a whole' must grasp its complex unity by way of these necessary differentiations.

'Youth Culture', in the singular and with capital letters, is a term we borrow from and refer to in our analysis, but which we cannot and do not *use* in any but a descriptive sense. It is, of course, precisely the term most common in popular and journalistic usage. It is how the 'phenomenon of Youth' in the post-war period has been most common-sensically appropriated. It appears to be a simple and common starting point, a simple concept. Actually, it presupposes already extremely complex relations. Indeed, what it disguises and represses — differences between different strata of youth, the class-basis of youth cultures, the relation of 'Youth Culture' to the parent culture and the dominant culture, etc. — is more significant than what it reveals. The term is premised on the view that what happened to 'youth' in this period is radically and qualitatively different from anything that had happened before. It suggests that all the things which youth got into in this period were more significant than the different kinds of youth groups, or the differences in their social class composition. It sustains certain ideological interpretations — e.g., that age and generation mattered most, or that Youth Culture was 'incipiently classless — even, that 'youth' had itself become a class. Thus it identified 'Youth Culture' exclusively with its most phenomenal aspect — its music, styles, leisure consumption. Of course, post-war youth did engage in distinctive cultural pursuits, and this was closely linked with the expansion of the leisure and fashion industries, directed at the 'teenage market'. But the term 'Youth Culture' confuses and identifies the two aspects, whereas what is needed is a detailed picture of how youth groups fed off and appropriated things provided by the market, and, in turn, how the market tried to expropriate and incorporate things produced by the sub-cultures: in other words, the dialectic between youth and the youth market industry. The term 'Youth Culture' appropriates the situation of the young almost exclusively in terms of the commercial and publicity manipulation and exploitation *of* the young. As a concept, it has little or no explanatory power. We must try to get behind this market phenomenon, to its deeper social, economic and cultural roots. In short, our aim is to de-throne or *de-construct* the term, 'Youth Culture', in favour of a more complex set of categories.

We shall try, first, to replace the concept of 'Youth Culture' with the more structural concept of 'sub-culture'. We then want to *reconstruct* 'sub-cultures' in terms of their relation, first, to 'parent' cultures, and, through that, to the dominant culture, or better, to the struggle between dominant and subordinate cultures. By trying to set up these intermediary levels in place of the immediate catch-all idea of 'Youth Culture', we try to show how youth sub-cultures are related to class relations, to the division of labour and to the productive relations of the society, without destroying what is specific to their content and position.

It is essential to bear in mind that the topic treated here relates *only* to those sections of working-class or middle-class youth where a response to their situation took a distinctive sub-cultural form. This must in no way be confused with an attempt to delineate the social and historical position of working-class youth as a whole in the period. The great majority of working-class youth never enters a tight or coherent sub-culture at all. Individuals may, in their personal life-careers, move into and out of one, or indeed several, such sub-cultures. Their relation to the existing sub-cultures may be fleeting or permanent, marginal or central. The sub-cultures are important because there the response of youth takes a peculiarly tangible form. But, in the post-war history of the class, these may be less significant than what most young people do most of the time. The relation between the 'everyday life' and the 'sub-cultural life' of different sections of youth is an important question in its own right, and must not he subsumed under the more limited topic which we address here. As Howard Parker reminds us, even the 'persistent offenders' of the delinquent sub-cultures are only occasionally preoccupied with illegal or delinquent behaviour (Parker, 1974). For the majority, school and work are more structurally significant — even at the level of consciousness — than style and music. As Paul Corrigan eloquently testifies, most young working-class boys are principally concerned most of the time with the biggest occupation of all — how to pass the time: the 'dialectics of doing nothing'.

B. Youth: metaphor for social change

We propose, in this section, to move from the most phenomenal aspects of youth sub-cultures to the deeper meanings, in three stages. We deal, first, with the most immediate aspect — the qualitative *novelty* of Youth Culture. Then, with the most *visible* aspects of social change which were variously held to be responsible for its emergence. Finally, we look at the *wider debate,* to which the debate about Youth Culture was an important, though subsidiary appendage.

We have said that an important element of the concept, 'Youth Culture', was its post-war novelty. The following quotation from Roberts reminds us to be cautious on this account; it could almost be read as referring to any of the distinctive post-war youth culture formations, though what it describes is in fact an Edwardian youth in 'the classic slum':

> The groups of young men and youths who gathered at the end of most slum streets on fine evenings earned the condemnation of all respectable citizens. They were damned every summer by city magistrates and increasingly harried by the police. In the late nineteenth century the Northern Scuttler and his "moll" had achieved a notoriety as widespread as that of any gang in modern times. He had his own style of dress — the union shirt, bell-bottomed trousers, the heavy leather belt, pricked out in fancy designs with the large steel buckle and the thick, iron-shod clogs. His girl-friend commonly wore clogs and shawl and a skirt with vertical stripes.
>
> (Roberts, 1971: 123)

It is vital, in any analysis of contemporary phenomena, to think historically; many of the short-comings in the 'youth' area are due, in part at least, to an absent or foreshortened historical dimension. In the specific area of 'Youth Culture' this historical myopia is perhaps only to be expected, for few historical studies, specifically comparing the post-war situation of youth with their situation in previous periods as yet exist (there is, of course, a growing interest in the social history of childhood and youth, and in leisure and the school, influenced by a social history perspective. Phil Cohen and Dave Robbins' forthcoming volume on sub-cultures will have a strong historical and comparative framework). The Roberts quotation clearly points to this thread of historical continuity which we cannot afford to overlook.

On the other hand, there is, also, much evidence to suggest that there *were* distinctively new historical features in the 1950s which should make us wary of the opposite fault: the tendency to adopt a static or circular view of history and so rob the post-war period of its historical specificity. The significance of the many visible structural and cultural changes of the post-war period were weighted differently by commentators and analysts at the time: but, in most calculations, the emergent 'Youth Culture' figured prominently. It was, according to emphasis, one *product* of these changes, their *epitome,* or, most sinisterly, a *portent* of future changes. But, whatever the emphasis, Youth Culture, or aspects of it, was centrally linked to how these changes were interpreted.

One important set of inter-related changes hinged around 'affluence', the increased importance of the market and consumption, and the growth of the 'Youth-oriented' leisure industries. The most distinctive product of these changes was the arrival of Mark Abrams's 'teenage consumer'; relatively speaking, Abrams saw 'teenagers' as the prime beneficiaries of the new affluence:

> . . . as compared with 1938, their *real* earnings (i.e., after allowing for the fall in value of money) have increased by 50% (which is double the rate of expansion for adults), and their real 'discretionary' spending has probably risen by 100%.
>
> (Abrams, 1959: 9)

It was but a short step from here to the view that teenagers' collective habits of consumption constituted "distinctive teenage spending for distinctive teenage ends in a distinctive teenage world" (Abrams, 1959: 10); in other words, the economic basis for a unique, self-contained, self-generating Youth Culture.

The second nexus of changes with which Youth Culture came readily to be identified, as one unfortunate by-product, were those surrounding the arrival of *mass* communications, *mass* entertainment, *mass* art and *mass culture.*

Central to this notion was the idea that more and more people were being submitted (and the passivity implied was not accidental) to ever-more uniform cultural processes. This was the result of the spread in mass consumption, plus the 'political enfranchisement' of the masses, and (above all) the growth in mass communications. The spread of mass communications was identified with the growth of the press, radio, television, mass publishing (and not with computers, internal TV and video-systems, data banks, information storage and retrieval, etc. — the commercial and managerial 'uses' which provided the real infrastructure of the communications revolution'). For those interpreting social change within the framework of what came to be called the 'mass society thesis', the birth of commercial television in Britain in the mid 1950s was a watershed event.

Youth Culture was connected with this set of changes in two ways. Firstly, and most simply, the creation of a truly mass culture meant the arrival of the means of 'imitation' and 'manipulation' on a national scale. The notion that Youth Culture was a result of such 'mindless' imitation by teenagers, fostered by shrewd and 'manipulating' commercial interests, is captured indelibly by the following quotation from Paul Johnson, probably the least perceptive commentator on Youth, in a field distinctive for its bottomless mediocrity:

> Both T.V. channels now run weekly programmes in which popular records are played to teenagers and judged. While the music is performed, the cameras linger savagely over the faces of the audience. What a bottomless chasm of vacuity they reveal. Huge faces, bloated with cheap confectionery and smeared with chain-store make-up, the open, sagging mouths and glazed eyes, the hands mindlessly drumming in time to the music, the broken stiletto heels, the shoddy, stereotyped, 'with-it' clothes: here, apparently, is a collective portrait of a generation enslaved by a commercial machine.
>
> (Johnson, 1964)

Secondly, and more sophisticatedly, some aspects of the new Youth Culture were seen, portentously, as representing the worst effects of the new 'mass culture' — its tendency to 'unbend the springs' of working class action and resistance. Hoggart, in so many respects our most sensitive recorder of the experiential nuances of working-class culture, has to be counted among the offenders here; for his portrait of the "juke-box boys . . . who spend their evenings listening in harshly lighted milk-bars to the nickelodeons" (Hoggart, 1958: 247) could almost — in its lack of concreteness and 'felt' qualities — have been written by one of the new 'hack' writers he so perceptively analyses:

> The hedonistic but passive barbarian who rides in a fifty-horsepower bus for threepence, to see a five-million-dollar film for one-and-eight-pence, is not simply a social oddity; he is a portent.
>
> (Hoggart, 1958: 250)

The third set of changes which were said to have 'produced' a qualitatively-distinct Youth Culture turned around a hiatus in social experience precipitated by the war. Generally, the argument maintained that the disruptive effects of the war on children born during that period — absent fathers, evacuation and other breaks in normal family life, as well as the constant violence — was responsible for the 'new' juvenile delinquency of the mid 50s, typified by the Teds, which was itself seen as a precursor of a more general tendency towards violence in Youth Culture. Fyvel, for example, whilst not restricting himself to this 'war' explanation, nevertheless does see the Teddy Boys as "Children of an age of violence, born during a world war . . ." (Fyvel: 1963, Preface); whilst Nuttall, more simply, identifies the single fact of the dropping of the first atomic bomb as responsible for the qualitative difference between the pre- and post-war generations:

> right . . . at the point of dropping bombs on Hiroshima and Nagasaki the
> generations became divided in a very crucial way . . . The people who had
> not yet reached puberty . . . were incapable of conceiving of life with a
> future . . . the so-called 'generation gap' started then and has been
> increasing ever since.
>
> (Nuttall, 1970: 20)

The fourth set of changes which provided an important context for the 'emergence' of Youth Culture related to the sphere of education. This interpretation pin-pointed *two* developments above all — 'secondary education for all' in age-specific schools, and the massive extension of higher education. Many things were cited as providing the impetus here: the 1944 Education Act itself, which instituted the primary/secondary division for all; the expanded 'pool of talent' consequent upon both this reorganisation and the post-war 'bulge'; the meritocratic ideology of social mobility primarily through the education system; the attempts to make a positive correlation between the country's economic growth-rate and its number of highly-trained personnel; the increased demand in the economy for technicians and technologists. But, for our purposes, the effect was singular. Quite simply, the increasing number of young people spending an increasing proportion of their youth in age-specific educational institutions from the age of eleven onwards — a quite different situation from the pre-war period when almost half the post-eleven year olds were still receiving 'secondary' education in all-age elementary schools — was seen, by some commentators, to be creating the pre-conditions for the emergence of a specifically 'adolescent society'. Coleman made the point most explicitly with his argument that an American high school pupil:

> . . . is 'cut off' from the rest of society, forced inwards towards his own age
> group. With his fellows, he comes to constitute a small society, one that
> has its most important interactions *within* itself, and maintains only a few
> threads of connections with the outside adult society.
>
> (Coleman, 1961: 3)

Last, but by no means least, the arrival of the whole range of distinctive styles in dress and rock-music cemented any doubts anyone may have had about a 'unique' younger generation. Here, as elsewhere, the specifics of the styles and music, in terms of who was wearing or listening to what, and why, were crucially overlooked in face of the new stylistic invasion — the image, depicted weekly in the new 'teenage' television shows as a 'whole scene going'. Depending on how you viewed this pop-cultural explosion, either the barbarians were at the gates, or the turn of the rebel hipster had come at last. Again, Jeff Nuttall provides us with the most extravagant and indulgent example:

> The teddy boys were waiting for Elvis Presley. Everybody under twenty all
> over the world was waiting. He was the super salesman of mass
> distribution-hip . . . he was a public butch god with the insolence of a
> Genet murderer . . . Most of all he was unvarnished sex taken and set way
> out in the open . . . The Presley riots were the first spontaneous gatherings
> of the community of the new sensibilities . . .
>
> (Nuttall, 1970: 29–30)

These explanations for the appearance of a distinct Youth Culture emerged out of a much wider debate about the whole nature of post-war social change. The key terms in this debate were, of course, 'affluence', 'consensus' and 'embourgeoisement'. Affluence referred, essentially, to the boom in working class consumer spending (though it entailed the further, less tenable, proposition that the working classes not only had more to spend, but were *relatively* better off). 'Consensus' meant the acceptance by both political parties, and the majority of the electorate, of all the measures — mixed economy, increased incomes, welfare-state 'safety net' — taken after 1945 to draw people of all classes together, on the basis of a common stake in the system. It also entailed the proposition that a broad consensus of views on all the major issues had developed, including all classes; and hence the end of major political and social conflicts, especially those which exhibited a clear class pattern. 'Embourgeoisement' gathered all these, and other social trends (in education, housing, redevelopment, the move to new towns and estates, etc.), together with the thesis that working-class life and culture was ceasing to be a distinct formation in the society, and everyone was assimilating rapidly towards middle-class patterns, aspirations and values. These terms came to be woven together into an all-embracing social myth or explanation of post-war social change. Stated simply, the conventional wisdom was that 'affluence' and 'consensus' together were promoting the rapid 'bourgeoisification' of the working classes. This was producing new social types, new social arrangements and values. One such type was the 'affluent worker' — the "new type of bourgeois worker", family minded, home-centred, security conscious, instrumentally-oriented, geographically mobile and acquisitive — celebrated in, for example, Zweig's work (Zweig, 1961). Another was the new 'teenager' with his commitment to style, music, leisure and consumption: to a 'classless youth culture'.

Thus, for both parents and their children, *class* was seen, if at all, as being gradually, but inexorably, eroded as society's major structuring and dynamic factor. Other elements were seen to be replacing it as the basis of social stratification: status, a multiply-differentiated 'pecking order' based on a complex of educational, employment and consumption-achievements; education, the new universally available and meritocratic route by which status, through job success, could be achieved; consumption, the new 'affluence' route through which status, on the 'never-never', could be bought by those failing the meritocratic educational hurdle; and age, above all age. Everything that was said and thought about working-class adults was raised to a new level with respect to the working-class young. Born during the war, they were seen as having least experience of and commitment to pre-war social patterns. Because of their age, they were direct beneficiaries of the welfare state and new educational opportunities; least constrained by older patterns of, or attitudes to, spending and consumption; most involved in a guilt-free commitment to pleasure and immediate satisfactions. Older people were, as it were, half-way between the old and the new world. But 'youth' was wholly and exclusively in and of the new post-war world. And what, principally, made the difference was, precisely, their *age*. Generation defined them as the group most in the forefront of every aspect of social change in the post-war period. Youth was 'the vanguard' of social change. Thus, the simple fact of when you were born displaced the more traditional category of class as a more potent index of social position; and the pre-war chasm between the classes was translated into a mere 'gap' between the generations. Some commentators further compounded this myth by reconstituting class on the basis of the new gap: youth was a 'new class' (see, for example: Musgrove, 1968; Rowntree and Rowntree, 1968; Neville, 1971).

Yet the whole debate depended crucially on the validity of the three central concepts we started out with — affluence, consensus and embourgeoisement; and here we must begin the task of disentangling the real from the constructed or ideological elements contained in these terms.

In general terms, the reality of post-war improvements in living standards — the real element in 'affluence' — cannot be questioned. The years 1951–64 undoubtedly saw what Pinto-Duschinsky, calls, "a steadier and much faster increase [in the average standard of living] than at any other time in this century"; using "any major indicator of performance, the 1950s and the early 1960s were a great improvement on the years between the wars and on the showing of the Edwardian period" (Pinto-Duschinsky, 1970: 56–57). However, this general rise in living standards critically *obscured* the fact that the *relative* positions of the classes had remained virtually unchanged. It was this mythical aspect of affluence, concealed under the persistent and insistent 'never had it so good' ideology, which gradually emerged when poverty — and not just pockets of it — was rediscovered, from the early 1960s onwards.

The massive spending on consumer durables obscured the fact "that Britain lagged behind almost all her main industrial competitors and that she failed to solve the problem of sterling" (Pinto-Duschinsky, 1970: 58: see also Glyn and Sutcliffe, 1972). In fact, Britain's affluent 'miracle' was *constructed* on very shaky economic foundations, "upon temporary and fortuitous circumstances" (Bogdanor and Skidelsky, eds., 1970: 8), on a 'miraculous' historical conjuncture. The Tory policy of "Bread and Circuses" — i.e., "the sacrifice of policies desirable for the long term well-being of a country in favour of over-lenient measures and temporary palliatives bringing in immediate political return" (Pinto-Duschinsky, 1970: 59) or, more succinctly, the promotion of private consumption at the expense of the public sector — was only *one possible response* to this situation, not an *inevitable outcome*.

Consensus, too, in general terms, had a real basis. The war period with its cross-class mobilisations, economic planning, political coalitions and enforced egalitarianism provided a base on which the social reforms of the post-war labour government could be mounted; and both the war and the post-war reforms provided something of a platform for consensus. Even the old free-market figure, Churchill, returned to power in 1951, had, in his own words, "come to know the nation and what must be done to retain power" (Moran, 1968: 517). In other words, Churchill, and the more astute of the Tory leadership, had come to realise that the success of their 'freedom from controls' anti-austerity programme was crucially predicated upon a 'reformed' capitalism, a socially-mindful capitalism with a 'human face'. Their electoral 'clothes stolen', and "haunted by a composite image of the potential Labour voter as quintessentially *petit-bourgeois,* and therefore liable to be frightened off by a radical alternative to Conservatism" (Miliband, 1961: 339), the Labour leadership lost its nerve, and capitulated to 'the consensus'. Official party politics were dominated in the 1950s by "the politics of the centre", whilst "the most vigorous political debates of the

1950s and 1960s were conducted independently of the party battle" (Pinto-Duschinsky, 1970: 73, 74).

However, whilst political consensus (or stalemate) was the overriding feature of the 1950s and early 1960s, the fragility of this consensus was revealed "in the nature of the party struggle" during these years. Despite "the ultimate success of the Tories in retaining office for thirteen years, the political battle was desperately close throughout the whole period" (ibid: 69). In other words, the notion of a political consensus obscures the fact that the Conservative survival was predicated constantly on the most short-term expediency imaginable (e.g., the 'give-away' inflationary budget of April, 1955, was followed by a snap April election, which was in turn followed by the deflationary Autumn 'cuts', and the stagnation of 1956). For the whole thirteen years of Tory rule, despite this vote-catching 'politics of bribery', practically half the electorate voted *against* the Tories at each election. Taken together with the finding by Goldthorpe and his colleagues, that "the large majority [of the affluent workers in their study] were, and generally had been Labour supporters" (1969: 172), echoing other sociological enquiries — it is quite possible to read 'consensus' in a different way: as betokening a waiting attitude by the British working class (often mistaken at the time for 'apathy') which an effective lead to the left by Labour at any point in the period might effectively have crystallised in a different direction (Goldthorpe *et al.* themselves make this argument: see, 1969: 190–5) .

'Embourgeoisement', the third and final term in our sociological trinity, was the product of the other two. As such, it was the most constructed term of the three, since the frailties of the other two terms were compounded in it. Even so, the 'embourgeoisement' notion, too, had some real basis, as even its critics insisted:

> Our own research indicates clearly enough how increasing affluence and its correlates can have many far-reaching consequences — both in undermining the viability or desirability of established life-styles and in encouraging or requiring the development of new patterns of attitudes, behaviours and relationships.
>
> (Goldthorpe *et al.* 1969: 163)

Yet the overriding conclusion of the Cambridge team's research, which submitted Zweig's "new bourgeois worker" to sociological scrutiny, only confirmed what their earlier paper had suggested (Goldthorpe and Lockwood, 1963):

> what the changes in question predominantly entailed was not the ultimate *assimilation* of manual workers and their families into the social world of the middle class, but rather a much less dramatic process of convergence, in certain particular respects, in the normative orientations of some sections of the working class and of some white-collar groups
>
> (Goldthorpe *et al.* 1969: 26)

In other words, 'embourgeoisement', if it meant anything at all, referred to something very different, and far more limited in scope, than anything which its more vigorous proponents, such as Zweig, envisaged. Even at the time, some of the political extrapolations made on the basis of the thesis seemed far-fetched, ideological rather than empirical in character (e.g., Abrams, 1969). Indeed, looking back at the instrumental collectivism' of Goldthorpe and Lockwood's 'affluent worker' from the perspective of the later 1960s and 1970s; at the strike-prone nature of the motor industry, and the 'leadership' which this sector of labour displayed in sustained wage militancy and militant shop-floor organisation, the whole 'embourgeoisement' thesis looks extremely thin and shaky, at least in the terms in which it was currently discussed at the time. (There is something to be said for the view that no student should read the account of the 'affluent worker' at the Vauxhall plant at Luton without setting it cheek by jowl with the experience of the Halewood plant near Liverpool, so graphically described by Huw Beynon, 1973.)

In sum, despite some significant real shifts in attitudes and living patterns, considerably overlaid by the sustained ideological onslaught of 'affluence', what comes through most strongly is the stubborn *refusal* of class — that tired, 'worn-out' category to *disappear* as a major dimension and dynamic of the social structure.

C. The reappearance of class

The various interpretations of post-war change, enshrined in the holy trinity of affluence, consensus and embourgeoisement, rested on a singular social myth — that the working class was disappearing. This postulate of the 'withering away of class' was challenged from the late 1950s onwards along two main dimensions.

Firstly, there was the rediscovery of poverty and the existence of continual, great inequalities of wealth, opened up by the critiques of the Titmuss Group (Titmuss, 1962), Westergaard (1965) and others. These showed that poverty was a structural not an accidental feature of capitalism, that wealth had been only nominally redistributed and that the main beneficiaries of the Welfare State were, in fact, the middle classes. A very small minority still owned a very large proportion of private wealth; and further, the proportions of national income going to the working and middle classes had remained roughly the same after 1945. A bedmate of the alleged move to equality in wealth — the idea that 'opportunity structures' of society had been thrown open and a new fluid social structure had arisen — was also shown to be an empty promise. Even if relative inequalities between classes had declined, the absolute distribution of life-chances had not. Certainly, changes in the occupational structure had taken place; but, as was again argued, the implications of these changes had been much exaggerated. The number of clerical jobs, for instance, greatly increased, but this was coupled with a decline in the relative status of white collar occupations produced by greater rationalisation and automation. These occupations had been stratified, leading often to a widening of the divisions between clerical 'supervisors' and the clerical 'shop-floor'. The increased unionisation and, later, the unexpected militancy of bank clerks, nurses, teachers and local government workers, was one further important development leading in the same direction. At the very least, the recent militancy among such groups suggests that the view that the rise in white collar occupations will lead to a uniform, stable, 'moderate', middle-class society is open to question.

Secondly, there was the postulate that power had been diffused via the all-round increase of wealth, the decline in relative inequality, the greater accountability of socially responsible management, and the separation of ownership from managerial control. Allied to this was the thesis that the separation of the sphere of work from the increasingly privatised sphere of home life was leading to a simple 'economic instrumentalism' in worker's attitudes to the unions (devoid of any political content it may have had); indeed, that increasing affluence had led to a permanent pacification of industrial militancy. However, Westergaard, for example, has argued convincingly that, while working-class life styles may have changed, the widening of worker's horizons and demands is a potential source of unrest rather than of stability unless the means of fulfilment are given. This is the so-called revolution of rising expectations or what Anderson called "the politics of instrumental collectivism".

Working-class resistance to anti-union and anti-strike legislation in the 1970s, like the sustained demand (through the 1960s into the 1970s) for wages to keep pace with inflation, clearly support this interpretation (though it is important to add that this defensive strategy and wage militancy has, as yet, failed to find clear political expression). In addition, resistance by sections of the working class to the incursions into the localities by property speculators and the redevelopers, and to steadily rising rents, finding its political expression in a community, non-industrial politics rather than in electoral politics and the Labour Party, has also been underplayed, devalued or ignored. Indeed, when the thesis of the 'diffusion of power' is looked at from the perspective, not of the consensual 1950s but of the polarised 1970s, it loses much of its credibility (though the shifts in the patterns of class conflict must not be overlooked). As Westergaard argues:

> . . . post-capitalism commentary has been noticeably blind to the sources of actual opposition and latent dissent to the institutions and assumptions of the current social order within the population at large: perennially prone to confuse the institutionalisation of conflict with consensus, and generally incurious about the continuing pressures under which the institutionalisation might loosen, shift or give way. The existence of those pressures should be a constant reminder of the contingent character of the present social structure, and of the limited range of assumptions from which policies conventionally are drawn which envisage little or no basic change in that structure.
>
> (Westergaard, 1974: 38)

If we had asked, at the time, 'which social group or category most immediately encapsulates the essential features of these social changes?' we would almost certainly have been given the answer — Youth: the new Youth culture. Even so perceptive an observer as Colin MacInnes could speculate that:

> The 'two nations' of our society may perhaps no longer be those of the 'rich' and the 'poor' (or, to use old fashioned terms, the 'upper' and 'working' classes), but those of the teenagers on the one hand and, on the other, all those who have assumed the burdens of adult responsibility.
>
> (MacInnes, 1961: 56)

Yet, just as the master conceptions of affluence, consensus and embourgeoisement required a more cautious and critical approach, so the evidence upon which the direction and manner of change amongst youth was based requires more detailed analysis and careful interpretation. When we look closely at some of those writers who subscribed to notions such as the generation gap, 'distinctive youth culture', welfare state youth, the 'classlessness' of youth culture, and so on, we find that the evidence they bring forward actually undermines the interpretation of it which they offer. Within the 'classlessness' interpretation, there is often a contradictory stress, precisely upon the class structuring of youth. Perhaps the best example is Abrams's work on "The Teenage Consumer" (quoted previously), which depicts a new, separate culture based on the 'teenage market'. However, if we look more closely, this teenage market is recognised by Abrams himself as having a clear class base. Abrams's 'average teenager' *was* the working class teenager:

> . . . the teenage market is almost entirely working class. Its middle class members are either still at school and college or else only just beginning on their careers: in either case they dispose of much smaller incomes than their working class contemporaries and it is highly probable, therefore, that not far short of 90 per cent of all teenage spending is conditioned by working class taste and values.
>
> (Abrams, 1959: 13)

The image of youth often carried with it the threat of 'what could go wrong'. Fyvel explained one problem group — Teddy Boys — predominantly in terms of the dislocation, caused internationally amongst all youth, by the war, increasing materialism, the stress on success, and the influence of the mass media. However his analysis also has a clear class dimension. For instance he says:

> Working-class families are (also) more vulnerable to the socially and psychologically harmful effects of rehousing, as expressed in a break-up of local community life.
>
> (Fyvel, 1963: 213)

In fact, Fyvel sees the Teddy Boy as mainly recruited from young unskilled workers whose earnings were too low and irregular for him to take part in the process of embourgeoisement enjoyed by his better-off working-class peers (ibid: 122).

It would seem reasonable to assume that the relation between the position of youth (its features and problems) and social class would receive more adequate attention in empirical sociological studies. However in the 1950s and early 1960s there were few such studies, and they largely took as their starting point the rise in delinquency rates. Those that were undertaken were mainly of an 'ecological' nature, focussed on change in working-class neighbourhoods. However the studies by Mays (1954), Morris (1957), Kerr (1958) and others all tended to be concerned with one particular aspect of these class-defined areas — the 'slum culture', and the identification of a number of 'problem families'. Often it was not clear to what degree the rest of the working class held what one writer defined as the values or 'focal concerns' of the slum-violence, excitement, fantasy, etc. (Miller, 1958). More importantly, the class analysis, though now present, was a rather technically-founded 'social' class one, (usually based on the Registrar General's classification) — a static, dehistoricised concept of class. The ecological areas were not sufficiently dynamically placed within the structure of the classes in the city and the class relations in the wider society at the time. Where a wider analysis was outlined it was largely in terms of our old friends, the triumvirate — affluence, consensus and embourgeoisement.

To replace youth within their various class formations does not, as some critics may think, give a simple uni-dimensional explanatory answer to the sub-cultures problem. Indeed explanation becomes more complex and investigation more necessary if the sub-cultures-and-class relationships are explored *without* relying on a global notion of 'the new youth leisure class'. Perhaps the most complex body of theory is the American sub-culture theorisation of the late fifties and early sixties, e.g., the work of Albert Cohen (1955), Cloward and Ohlin (1960), and its critique and development in Downes (1966). These writers did indeed try to place delinquent sub-cultures within a larger class framework. Unfortunately, in brief terms, American work envisaged the *individual* youth's class position as one rung on a single status ladder, leading inexorably to middle-class values and goals. The sub-culture problem was then presented as a problem of the disjunction between the (assumed) middle-class *goal* of success and the restricted (working class) *means* for achieving them. A youth group or sub-culture was defined as the result of status-failure, or anxiety because of rejection by middle-class institutions; or as the inability to achieve dominant goals because of blocked opportunities for success. In short there was an underlying consensual view of society based on a belief in the American Dream (of success). 'Youth culture' was a sort of collective compensation for those who could not succeed.

Significant advances upon sub-cultural theory have recently been made, especially by Murdock (1973) and Brake (1973). Following from the traditional theme that sub-cultures arise as a means of collective "problem solving" they locate youth within a quite different analysis of class relations from that of 'opportunity structures.' The major defect in Murdock and Brake's work is that their central concept — that of "problem" — is itself taken too unproblematically. Brake's version of the formation of sub-culture is neatly summarised in the following statement:

> Sub-cultures arise (then) as attempts to solve certain problems in the social structures, which are created by contradictions in the larger society. . . . Youth is not in itself a problem, but there are problems created, for example by the conscription of the majority of the young into the lower strata of a meritocratic educational system and then allowing them only to take up occupations which are meaningless, poorly paid and uncreative. Working-class sub-cultures attempt to infuse into this bleak world excitement and colour during the short respite between school and settling down into marriage and adult-hood.
>
> (Brake, 1973: 36)

Murdock's formulation is very similar:

> The attempt to resolve the contradictions contained in the work situation through the creation of meaningful styles of leisure, typically takes place within the context provided by a sub-culture . . . . Sub-cultures offer a collective solution to the problems posed by shared contradictions in the work situation and provide a social and symbolic context for the

development and reinforcement of collective identity and individual self esteem.

(Murdock, 1973: 9)

Both writers recognise the class basis of youth sub-cultures but they do not fully work out the implications this has for the study of youth. These omissions are due perhaps to the too-heavy reliance upon the concept of subcultures as "problem solving". What we would argue, in general terms, is that the young inherit a cultural orientation from their parents towards a 'problematic' common to the class as a whole, which is likely to weight, shape and signify the meanings they then attach to different areas of their social life. In Murdock's and Brakes's work, the situation of the sub-culture's members within an *ongoing* subordinate culture is ignored in terms of the specific development of the sub-culture. Thus, a whole dimension of class socialisation is omitted, and the elements of negotiation and displacement in the original situated class culture are given too little weight in the analysis.

The advance made by Murdock and Brake was to reconstruct youth cultures in class terms, thereby dissolving the mythology of a universal youth culture. Also, they stressed the role of style (its appropriation and meaning) in representing youth's class experience. Before turning to our own analysis of youth cultures and class relations we must first discuss the work of Phil Cohen whose suggestive analysis throws light on many of these key points.

D. Subcultures — an imaginary relation

Phil Cohen (1972) also offers a class analysis, but at a much more sophisticated theoretical level, placing the parent culture in a historical perspective, mapping the relations between sub-cultures and exploring the intra-class dynamic between youth and parents. His analysis was based largely on the London East End working-class community, whose strength, he suggested, depended essentially on the mutual articulation of three structures. First, the extended kinship network, which "provides for many functions of mutual aid and support" and "makes for cultural continuity and stability". The kinship system depended, in turn, on the ecological setting — the working-class neighbourhood. This dense socio-cultural space "helps to shape and support the close textures of traditional working-class life, its sense of solidarity, its local loyalties and traditions", and thus provides support "with the day to day problems that arise in the constant struggle to survive". Third, there is the structure of the local economy, striking for its diversity as well as for the fact that "people lived and worked in the East End — there was no need for them to go outside in search of jobs". As a result, "the situation of the work place, its issues and interests, remained tied to the situation outside work — the issues and interests of the community".

Cohen, then, in giving a historical context to this portrait of a traditional working-class culture, describes the impact of redevelopment and rationalisation on the family, the community and the local economy. Post-war redevelopment and rehousing led to a depopulation of the area, and the break-up of the traditional neighbourhood: this was compounded by speculative development and by a new influx of immigrant labour, producing a further drift of the local work force. The most immediate impact was on the kinship structure — the fragmentation of the traditional 'extended family' and its partial replacement by the more nucleated 'families of marriage'. "This meant that any problems were bottled up within the immediate inter-personal context which produced them; and at the same time the family relationships were invested with a new intensity, to compensate for the diversity of relationships previously generated through neighbours and wider kin . . . the working-class family was thus not only isolated from outside but undermined from within." (Cohen, 1972: 17). Redevelopment, in the shape now of the new East End estates, exacerbated the effects on working-class family and neighbourhood:

> The first effect of the high-density, high-rise schemes was to destroy the function of the street, the local pub, the cornershop, as articulations of communal space. Instead there was only the privatised space of the family unit, stacked one on top of each other, in total isolation, juxtaposed with the totally public space which surrounded it, and which lacked any of the informal social controls generated by the neighbourhood.
>
> (Cohen, 1972: 16)

Alongside this was the drastic reconstruction of the local economy — the dying of small craft industries, their replacement by the larger concerns often situated outside the area, the decline of the family business and the corner shop. The labour force was gradually polarised into two groups: the "highly specialised, skilled and well-paid jobs associated with the new technology" and "the routine, dead-end, low-paid unskilled jobs associated with the labour-intensive sections, especially the service industries". Cohen argues that the effects of these changes were most significant for the respectable part of the East End working class, who found themselves "caught and pulled apart" by two opposing types of social mobility: upwards into the ranks of the new suburban working-class elite or downwards into the 'lumpen'.

Perhaps the most significant aspect of this part of Cohen's analysis is the way in which he picks and redefines certain key themes in the affluence-consensus-embourgeoisement thesis: he discards their spectacular and ideological framework, relocates them within the specific historical relations and situation of the working class of a particular area, and arrives at a 'thesis', not about the disappearance or 'embourgeoisement' of a class, but rather about how wider socio-economic change can fragment, unhinge and dislocate its intricate mechanisms and defences. The idea of the 'disappearance of the class as a whole' is replaced by the far more complex and differentiated picture of how the different sectors and strata of a class are driven into different courses and options by their determining socio-economic circumstances. This analysis stems from the impact on the different working-class strata of fundamental economic forces, but it immediately widens into their social, familial and cultural consequences.

The changes Cohen discusses had an impact upon *both* the adult and the young members of the East End working-class community. Though the response was different according to age, position in the generational cycle and experience, the basic material and social situation which confronted them — the class problematic — was the same, for older men and women, for young workers and their families, and for the working-class teenagers. Cohen traces the impact of economic and occupational change on the young:

> Looking for opportunities in their father's trades, and lacking the qualifications for the new industries, they were relegated to jobs as van boys, office boys, pickets, ware-housemen, etc., and long spells out of work. More and more people, young and old, have to travel out of the community to their jobs, and some eventually moved out to live elsewhere, where suitable work was to be found. The local economy as a whole contracted, and became less diverse.
>
> (Cohen, 1972: 18)

He also follows this analysis through to the changed situation of the young in the family, kinship and neighbourhood situations.

For Cohen, the working-class teenager experienced these shifts and fragmentations in direct, material, social, economic and cultural forms. But they also experienced, and attempted to 'resolve' them on the ideological plane. And it is primarily to this attempted 'ideological solution" that he attributes both the rise of, and the differentiation between, the different working-class 'youth sub-cultures' of the period:

> The latent function of subculture is this — to express and resolve, albeit "magically", the contradictions which remain hidden or unresolved in the parent culture. The succession of subcultures which this parent culture generated can thus all be considered as so many variations on a central theme — the contradiction at an ideological level, between traditional working class puritanism, and the new ideology of consumption: at an economic level between a part of the socially mobile elite, or a part of the new lumpen. Mods, parkers, skinheads, crombies, all represent in their different ways, an attempt to retrieve some of the socially cohesive elements destroyed in the parent culture, and to combine these with elements selected from other class fractions, symbolising one or other of the options confronting it.
>
> (Cohen, 1972: 23)

To give one example of how this complex process worked — Cohen explains the rise of Mods in the following manner:

> ... the original mod style could be interpreted as an attempt to realise, but in an *imaginary relation* the conditions of existence of the socially mobile white collar worker. While their *argot* and ritual forms stressed many of the traditional values of their parent culture, their dress and music reflected the hedonistic image of the affluent consumer.

Cohen's general conclusion is, therefore, that:

> Mods, Parkers, Skinheads, Crombies are a succession of sub-cultures which all correspond to the same parent culture and which attempt to work out through a series of transformations, the basic problematic or contradiction which is inserted in the sub-culture by the parent culture. So you can distinguish three levels in the analysis of sub-cultures: one is the historical ... which isolates the specific problematic of a particular class fraction ... secondly ... the sub-systems ... and the actual

transformations they undergo from one sub-cultural moment to another
. . . thirdly . . . the way the sub-culture is actually lived out by those who
are [its] bearers and supports.

Cohen's analysis proposes one of the most suggestive interpretations of the
relationship between the rise of the sub-cultures and the fate of a class. It has the merit
of placing a social class formation within a whole historical framework. Its tracing
through of the links between economic and cultural change, the impact of change on a
'parent' culture, and the response of youth, is subtle and complex. Certain problems
remain unresolved. The analysis — mainly of the 1950s and early 1960s — needs now
to be extended up to the 1970s. There are problems with understanding precisely how
the impact of certain forces on a parent culture is filtered through, and differentially
experienced by its youth; and then, how and why this experience is crystallised into a
distinct youth sub-culture. What leads the Mods to explore an 'upward', the Teds or
Skinheads to explore a 'downward' option? How tight is the relation between the
actual class composition and situation of those sectors of youth choosing one or other
of these sub-cultural solutions? What accounts both for the specific sequencing, and
the specific forms which the different sub-cultural formations take? There is also a
question about how 'ideological' youth sub-cultures are understood as being. In some
ways, the most subtle and suggestive parts of the analysis relate to the way the
sub-cultures are shown to address a common class problematic, yet attempt to resolve
by means of an 'imaginary relation' — i.e., ideologically — the 'real relations' they
cannot otherwise transcend. This is a suggestive proposal — but also one most difficult

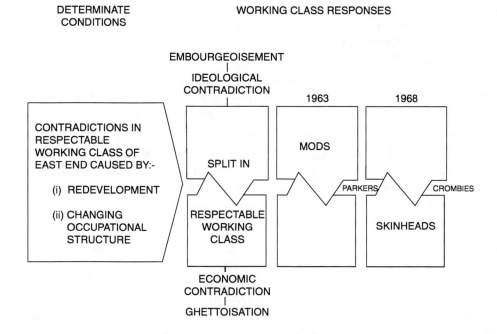

Figure 1   Class and subcultures: A version of Cohen's Model

to test and refine. The fact that men live, in ideology, an 'imaginary relation' to the real conditions of their existence is not something peculiar or limited to sub-cultures. What further things, then, provoke so highly structured, visible and tightly-bounded a response? By concentrating on the imaginary, ideological relation in which sub-cultures stand to the life of a class, the analysis may now have gone too far in the direction of reading sub-cultures 'ideologically'. Not enough account is perhaps taken of the material, economic and social conditions specific to the 'sub-cultural solution'. Despite these criticisms, the analysis remains, in our view, one of the most advanced and sophisticated of available accounts. The proposition that an 'imaginary relation' lies somewhere near the heart of the sub-cultures question is a fruitful one which — despite the problems we find in applying it concretely, we adopt and develop below.

E. Dominant and subordinate cultures

The immediate point is to note how *class* has been used by Cohen to clarify the concept of sub-culture. 'Class' does not simply *replace* sub-culture in a reductive way. Nor is class taken as a set of given, 'background', sociological variables. The relation between class and sub-culture has been placed in a more dynamic historical framework. The relations *between* classes, the experience and response to change *within* different class fractions, is now seen as the *determining* level. However, the sub-culture is seen as one specific *kind of response,* with its own meaning structure — its own "relative autonomy". Thus, the attempt to think the problem right through to the level of the social formation as a whole (where class relations are determining) is done, *not* by repressing but by *retaining* what is specific about the intermediary concept of 'sub-culture'. The social formation is not seen as a simple unity (the 'nation', 'the culture'), but as a necessarily complex, differentiated, antagonistic 'whole'. The further attempt to trace these general shifts in class relations through to their impact on particular communities, particular fractions of the class, particular local economies, is a crucial stage of that analysis.

In this section, we discuss briefly some of the broad shifts in class relations over the period as a whole, before coming to the specific question of the sub-cultures. This is a necessary first step, though, by compressing large movements into a short space, we sacrifice much of what is specific and concrete in Cohen's analysis of the East End case.

One determining level of change is the way production was reorganised and modernised in the post-war period; and the impact of this on the division of labour, on occupational cultures, on forms of working-class response , defence and resistance. The war and post-war situation accelerated changes already in train in the inter-war period. One general result was a widening of the gap between old and new sectors in the economy — old and new industries, old and new areas and regions. On the one hand, the 'new' industries, based on modern technical and electronic processes or tied to the consumer and export drives; on the other hand, the 'declining industries', the legacy of the first industrial revolution. The impact of this partial and unplanned 'rationalisation', first on skills and the division of labour, secondly on the economic life of regions and areas, was profound but quite *"uneven"*. Some areas — the South-East especially — spurted ahead; others — sometimes whole industries and regions — were impelled into a long decline. The exact shifts in the division of labour consequent on this "uneven" development, can't be charted in detail here — they remain the joker of the much-shuffled sociological 'pack' of (mainly numerical) representations of occupational mobility. Rationalisation certainly introduced new elements of fragmentation into the labour force. It also precipitated a whole 'ideological' debate — North vs. South, the 'cloth cap' vs. the white coat, etc. — which fed straight into the 'embourgeoisement' thesis, and confused it. The East End case, discussed by Cohen, demonstrates its real impact in a striking way: new economic forces penetrating, in a highly "uneven" way, into a 'backward' sector and area. The dockers caught between the casual labour pool, the state attempts to 'rationalise' and 'modernise' dock work, and the drive for containerisation is a classic instance of "combined and uneven" development, biting into a particular locality.

What matters here is not some general idea of 'social change and the working class' but, rather, the particular social and cultural composition of those sectors of the working class whose concrete situation is being restructured by quite specific economic forces. Here, changes in the economic mode of production register on a particular complex of trades, skills, workshops, a particular 'mix' of occupational cultures, the specific distribution of different class strata within them. The wider economic forces then *throw out of gear* a particular working-class complex; they dismantle a set of particular internal balances and stabilities. They reshape and restructure the productive basis, which forms the material and social conditions of life, the 'givens', around which a particular local working-class culture has developed. They disturb a particular historical network of defences and 'negotiations' (again, the complex history of the formation of the 'East End' is an excellent example).

These productive relations also form the basis of the everyday life and culture of the class. Changes in housing and in the ecology of the working-class neighbourhood are part of the same pattern; and the different facets of change react on and reverberate through each other. The impact of post-war redevelopment on traditional working-class neighbourhoods seems in general to go through three broad phases. First, the break-up of traditional housing patterns by post-war re-housing: the new housing estates and new towns. The areas left behind decay; they drift downwards towards the 'urban ghetto' or 'new slum' pattern, the prey of rack-renting, speculative landlordism and multiple occupation. The drift inwards of immigrant labour highlights and compounds the ghettoising process. Then some parts of the ghettoes are selectively redeveloped, through the combination of planning and speculative property development. The entry of middle-class families 'up-classes' certain neighbourhoods, and "planned development" (the East End scheme is, again, a classic instance here) redefines the area towards this more 'up-graded', middle-income pattern of life. Again, these are not simply forces working abstractly *on* an area. They graphically reconstruct the *real* material and social conditions in which working people live.

The forces restructuring the working-class neighbourhood and local economy also had a decisive impact on the structure of the family. Those pushed upwards and away in occupational terms were often also moving to estates and towns which prescribed, in their layout and design, a different, less extended, more 'nucleated' family pattern. Even estates rebuilt in or near the old areas have been constructed — more consistently, perhaps, than their pre-war counterparts — in the image of an 'ideal' family: that is, a more middle-class, 'nuclear' one. The working-class family did not 'disappear' under these conditions nor did working people actively subscribe to the new 'bourgeois' domestic ideal. But the family may have become more isolated; relations between children and parents, or between peers and siblings were altered, with special effect on younger family members and on women. What, in sum, was *unsettled* was the precise position and role of the working-class family within a defensive class culture. What was disturbed was a concrete set of relations, a network of knowledge, things, experiences — the *supports* of a class culture. In these circumstances, too, the 'new' gained ground precisely because it once again invaded and undermined alternative patterns of social organisation.

In the early post-war period, these changes in the intricate mechanisms and balances of working-class life and culture were overlaid by the spectacular ideology of 'affluence'. We know now what were the limits of its real impact, its uneven distribution — even in terms of wages and consumption — for most sections of the working class. There was no 'qualitative leap'. Indeed, 'affluence' assumed the proportions of a full-blown ideology precisely because it was required to cover over the gaps between real inequalities and the promised Utopia of equality-for-all and ever-rising-consumption to come. By projecting this ideological scenario, the 'affluence' myth aimed to give the working classes a stake in a future which had not yet arrived, and thus to bind and cement the class to the hegemonic order. Here, precisely, the ideology of affluence reconstructed the 'real relations' of post-war British society into an 'imaginary relation'. This is the function of social myths. The myth provided, for a time, the ideological basis of the political hegemony of the 1950s. 'Affluence' was, essentially, an ideology of the dominant culture *about* and *for* the working-class, directed at them (through the media, advertising, political speeches, etc.). Few working class people subscribed to a version of their own situation which so little squared with its real dimensions. What mattered, therefore, was not the passive re-making of the working class in one 'affluent' image, but the *dislocations* it produced — and the responses it provoked.

The full absorption of the Labour Party into its parliamentary-electoral role within the state (the completion of a long historical trajectory) and the partial incorporation into the state apparatus of the trade unions, on the back of an 'affluent' reading of the post-war situation had *real* political consequences for the working-class, [and] dismantled real defences. Other responses were unpredictable and unintended. The overwhelming emphasis in the ideology of affluence on money and consumption may well have had the unintended effect of stimulating an awareness of 'relative deprivation' and thereby contributed to the 'wage militancy' of the 1960s and 70s. The affluent workers in engineering and the motor firms pioneered the shift to work-place power, plant bargaining, shop stewards organisation and 'wage drift' — a militant 'economism' which lasted right into the period of inflation and recession, pulling the 'revolt of the lower paid' behind it. These, too, were responses to 'affluence' which its ideologies neither did nor could foresee.

To locate youth sub-culture in this kind of analysis, we must first situate youth in the dialectic between a 'hegemonic' dominant culture and the subordinate working-class 'parent' culture, of which youth is a fraction. These terms — hegemonic/ corporate, dominant/subordinate — are crucial for the analysis, but need further elaboration before the sub-cultural dimension can be introduced. Gramsci used the term "hegemony" to refer to the moment when a ruling class is able, not only to *coerce* a subordinate class to conform to its interests, but to exert a "hegemony" or "total social authority" over subordinate classes. This involves the exercise of a special kind of power — the power to frame alternatives and contain opportunities, *to win and shape consent,* so that the granting of legitimacy to the dominant classes appears not only 'spontaneous' but natural and normal. Lukes has recently defined this as the power to define the agenda, to shape preferences, to "prevent conflict from arising in the first place", or to contain conflict when it does arise by defining what sorts of resolution are 'reasonable' and 'realistic' — i.e., within the existing framework (Lukes, 1974: 23–24). The terrain on which this hegemony is won or lost is the terrain of the superstructures; the institutions of civil society and the state — what Althusser (1971) and Poulantzas (1973), somewhat misleadingly, call "ideological state apparatuses". Conflicts of interest arise, fundamentally, from the difference in the structural position of the classes in the productive realm: but they 'have their effect' in social and political life. Politics, in the widest sense, frames the passage from the first level to the second. The terrain of civil and state institutions thus becomes essentially "the stake, but also the site of class struggle" (Althusser 1971). In part, these apparatuses work 'by ideology'. That is, the definitions of reality institutionalised within these apparatuses come to constitute a lived 'reality as such' for the subordinate classes — that, at least, is what hegemony attempts and secures. Gramsci, using the example of the church, says that it preserves "the ideological unity of the entire social bloc which that ideology serves to cement and unify" (Gramsci, 1971: 328). A hegemonic cultural order tries to *frame* all competing definitions of the world within *its* range. It provides the horizon of thought and action within which conflicts are fought through, appropriated (i.e., experienced), obscured (i.e., concealed as a "national interest" which should unite all conflicting parties) or contained (i.e., settled to the profit of the ruling class). A hegemonic order prescribes, not the specific content of ideas, but the *limits* within which ideas and conflicts move and are resolved. Hegemony always rests on force and coercion, but "the normal exercise of hegemony on the now classical terrain of the parliamentary regime is characterised by the combination of force and consent . . . without force predominating excessively over consent" (Gramsci 1971: 80). Hegemony thus provides the base line and the base-structures of legitimation for ruling-class power.

Hegemony works through ideology, but it does not consist of false ideas, perceptions, definitions. It works *primarily* by inserting the subordinate class into the key institutions and structures which support the power and social authority of the dominant order. It is, above all, in these structures and relations that a subordinate class *lives its subordination.* Often, this subordination is secured only because the dominant order succeeds in weakening, destroying, displacing or incorporating alternative institutions of defence and resistance thrown up by the subordinate class. Gramici insists, quite correctly, that "the thesis which asserts that men become conscious of fundamental conflicts on the level of ideology is not psychological or moralistic in character but *structural and epistemological.*" (Our italics; Gramsci, 1971: 164.)

Hegemony can rarely be sustained by one, single class stratum. Almost always it requires an *alliance* of ruling-class fractions — a 'historical bloc'. The content of hegemony will be determined, in part, by precisely which class fractions compose such a 'hegemonic bloc', and thus what interests have to be taken into account within it. Hegemony is not simple 'class rule'. It requires to some degree the 'consent' of the subordinate class, which has, in turn, to be won and secured; thus, an ascendancy of social authority, not only in the state but in civil society as well, in culture and ideology. Hegemony prevails when ruling classes not only rule or 'direct' but *lead*. The state is a major educative force in this process. It educates through its regulation of the life of the subordinate classes. These apparatuses reproduce class relations, and thus class subordination (the family, the school, the church and cultural institutions, as well as the law, the police and the army, the courts).

The struggle against class hegemony also takes place within these institutions, as well as outside them — they become the "site" of class struggle. But the apparatuses also depend on the operation of "a set of predominant values, beliefs, rituals and institutional procedures ('rules of the game') that operate systematically and consistently to the benefit of certain persons and groups" (Bacrach and Baratz, 1962).

Gramsci believes that, in the Italian state, the dominant classes had frequently ruled without that 'natural social authority' which would make them 'hegemonic'. So hegemony cannot be taken for granted — either by the state and the dominant classes, or, for that matter, by the analyst. The current use of the term, to suggest the unending and unproblematic exercise of class power by every ruling class, and its opposite — the permanent and finished incorporation of the subordinate class — is quite false to Gramsci's usage. It limits the historical specificity of the concept. To make that point concrete: we would argue that, though the dominant classes remained massively in command during the 1930s, it is difficult to define them as 'hegemonic'. Economic crisis and unemployment disciplined, rather than 'led', the working classes into subordination in this period. The defeats suffered by the labour movement in the 1920s powerfully contributed to the coercive sway of the former over the latter. By contrast, the 1950s seem to us a period of true 'hegemonic domination', it being precisely the role of 'affluence', as an ideology, to dismantle working-class resistance and deliver the 'spontaneous consent' of the class to the authority of the dominant classes. Increasingly, in the 1960s, and more openly in the 1970s, this 'leadership' has again been undermined. The society has polarised, conflict has reappeared on many levels. The dominant classes retain power, but their 'repertoire' of control is progressively challenged, weakened, exhausted. One of the most striking features of this later period is the shift in the exercise of control from the mechanisms of consent to those of coercion (e.g., the use of the law, the courts, the police and the army, of legal repression, conspiracy charges and of force to contain an escalating threat to the state and to 'law and order'). This marks a *crisis* in the hegemony of the ruling class.

Hegemony, then, is not universal and 'given' to the continuing rule of a particular class. It has to be *won*, worked for, reproduced, sustained. Hegemony is, as Gramsci said, a "moving equilibrium", containing "relations of forces favourable or unfavourable to this or that tendency". It is a matter of the nature of the balance struck between contending classes: the compromises made to sustain it; the relations of force; the solutions adopted. Its character and content can only be established by looking at concrete situations, at concrete historical moments. The idea of 'permanent class hegemony', or of 'permanent incorporation' must be ditched.

In relation to the hegemony of a ruling class, the working-class is, by definition, a *subordinate* social and cultural formation. Capitalist production, Marx suggested, reproduces capital and labour in their ever-antagonistic forms. The role of hegemony is to ensure that, in the social relations between the classes, each class is continually *reproduced* in its existing dominant-or-subordinate form. Hegemony can never wholly and absolutely absorb the working class *into* the dominant order. Society may seem to be, but cannot actually ever be, in the capitalist mode of production, 'one-dimensional'. Of course, at times, hegemony is strong and cohesive, and the subordinate class is weak, vulnerable and exposed. But it cannot, by definition, disappear. It remains, as a subordinate structure often separate and impermeable, yet still contained by the overall rule and domination of the ruling class. The subordinate class has developed its own corporate culture, its own forms of social relationship, its characteristic institutions, values, modes of life. Class conflict never disappears. English working-class culture is a peculiarly strong, densely-impacted, cohesive and defensive structure of this corporate kind. Class conflict, then, is rooted and embodied in this culture: it cannot 'disappear' — contrary to the ideology of affluence — until the productive relations which produce and sustain it disappear. But it can be more or less open, more or less formal, more or less institutionalised, more or less autonomous. The period between the 1880s and the present shows, not a single thrust towards incorporation but a marked alternating rhythm. It is important to insist that, even when class conflict is most institutionalised, it remains as one of the fundamental base-rhythms of the society.

In old and developed industrial capitalist societies, like Britain, the culture is in fact *covered* by a network of what we might call 'institutional solutions', which structure how the dominant and subordinate cultures coexist, survive, but also struggle, with one another inside the same social formation. Many of these institutions *preserve* the corporate culture of the subordinate class, but also *negotiate* its relations with the dominant culture. These are the 'negotiated' aspects of a subordinate class culture. In work, for example, the line between workers interests and managerial power, though often blurred and overlaid by intermediary structures, never disappears. But it can be very differently *handled,* by each side, from one workplace to another, or from one historical moment to another. The informal culture of the workplace, the attempts to exercise day-to-day control over the work process, the bargaining around wage minimums from place to place, as well as the 'down-tools', the walk-out, the strike, the official dispute, the factory occupation, constitute a whole *repertoire* of working-class responses to the immediate power and authority of management and capital. They are types of counter-hegemonic power. Many of these strategies — in so far as they do not finally replace the power of capital over labour — continue to define labour as a corporate — but *not* as an incorporated — part of capitalist production. They represent a line of defence of the class, even where these defences operate within the over-determining framework of managerial power.

Working-class culture has consistently 'won space' from the dominant culture. Many working-class institutions represent the different outcomes of this intense kind of 'negotiation' over long periods. At times, these institutions are adaptive; at other times, combative. Their class identity and position is never finally 'settled': the balance of forces within them remains open. They form the basis of what Parkin has called a "'negotiated version' of the dominant system . . . dominant values are not so much rejected or opposed as modified by the subordinate class as a result of circumstances and restricted opportunities." . . . (Parkin, 1971: 92). Often, such 'negotiated solutions' prevail, not because the class is passive and deferential to ruling class ideas, but because its perspectives are bounded and contained by immediate practical concerns or limited to concrete situations. (This is the material basis and 'rational core' of working-class 'economism'.) From this arise the *situated solutions* to problems arising at a wider, more global, level, beyond the immediate class horizon. In situations where "purely abstract evaluations are called for, the dominant value system will provide the moral frame of reference; but in concrete social situations involving choice and action, the negotiated version — or subordinate value system — will provide the moral framework" (Parkin , 1971: 93). Authority, enshrined in the major institutional orders of society (e.g., the rule of the Law) may be accepted at an abstract level, but much more ambivalently handled at the face-to-face level (e.g., attitudes to the police). English working-class culture is massively orchestrated around attitudes of 'Us' and 'Them', even when this structured difference does not lead directly to counter-hegemonic strategies by the working class. Recent evidence suggests that the suspicion of property and property rights remains deeply entrenched in the class, despite the absence of any concerted thrust to abolish property relations as such (Moorhouse and Chamberlain, 1974). Even class institutions like the trade unions, which in this period were pulled a considerable distance into full collaboration with the state, nevertheless, under slightly different circumstances (legislation against fundamental trade union rights and procedures after 1970 by a Conservative Government, for example) emerged as reluctant defenders of basic working-class rights (Lane, 1974). Thus, in 'good' times as well as 'bad', contrary cultural definitions are *always* in play. These reflect the structural difference between the material position, outlook and everyday life-experience of the different classes. These discrepancies (contradictions) in situation, values and action then provide the real material and historical basis — under the right conditions — for more developed class strategies of open resistance, struggle, and for counter-hegemonic strategies of rupture and transformation. The convergence of these various strategies of negotiation by a subordinate class into a more sustained class politics requires, of course, mobilisation, politicisation and organisation. It is precisely to this distinction that Marx addressed his observations about the movement from a class 'in itself' to a class 'for itself'.

The working-class neighbourhood, which assumes its 'traditional' form in and after the 1880s, represents one, distinctive example of the outcome of negotiation between the classes. In it, the different strata of the working class have won space for their own forms of life. The values of this corporate culture are registered everywhere, in material and social forms, in the shapes and uses of things, in patterns of recreation and leisure, in the relations between people and the character of communal spaces. These spaces are both physical (the networks of streets, houses, corner shops, pubs and

326

parks) and social (the networks of kin, friendship, work and neighbourly relationships). Over such spaces, the class has come to exert those 'informal social controls' which redefine and reappropriate them for the groups which live in them: a web of rights and obligations, intimacies and distances, embodying in its real textures and structures "the sense of solidarity. . . local loyalties and tradition . . ." (Cohen, 1972). These are the 'rights', not of ownership or force, but of territorial and cultural possession, the customary occupation of the 'sitting tenant'. The institutions are, of course, cross-cut and penetrated by outside forces. The structure of work and workplace near or far, link the local labour force to wider economic forces and movements. Not far away are the bustling commercial high streets, with their chain stores and supermarkets, linking the home to the wider economy through trade and consumption. Through these structures, the neighbourhood is socially and economically *bounded*. At one level — the horizontal — are all those ties which bind spaces and institutions to locality, neighbourhood, local culture and tradition. At another level — the vertical — are those structures which tie them to dominant institutions and cultures.

The local school is a classic instance of such double-binding. (Hall, 1974a: 49–55). It is the *local* school, next to houses, streets and shops where generations of working-class children have been 'schooled', and where ties of friendship, peer-group and marriage are forged and unmade. Yet, in terms of vertical relationships, the school has stood for kinds of learning, types of discipline and authority relations, affirmed experiences quite at variance with the local culture. Its selective mechanisms of streaming, 'tracking', eleven-plus, its knowledge boundaries, its intolerance of language and experience outside the range of formal education, link the urban working-class locality to the wider world of education and occupations in ways which are connective but also, crucially, *disconnective*. It remains a classic, negotiated, or mediated class institution. In this context, we can begin to look again, and assess differently the varying strategies, options and 'solutions' which develop in relation to it: the 'scholarship' boy or girl; the 'ordinary, average-ability' kids; the 'trouble-makers'; truants and absentees; the educationally-and-emotionally 'deprived'; the actively mis-educated (e.g., E.S.N-ed black kids). Similarly, in relation to the leisure activities of the young, to peer-group culture and association, we must recognise the 'mix' of resistance and accommodation in, for example: street-corner culture, with its massively 'masculine' focus; the near-delinquent group or exploit; the Boys Brigade addict; the 'gang'; the 'football end'; the well-defined sub-culture; and so on.

Any one of these strategies in the repertoire developed by young working-class boys will stand in a complex relation to that of other 'peers'; to 'adult' strategies and solutions; to alternative positions in the same age spectrum (e.g., Skinheads vs. hippies); and to the dominant culture and its repertoire of control. The strength or absence of any of these strategies at a historical moment will depend in part on the historical conjuncture (the balance of forces between domination and subordination; the stable or changing situation of the 'parent' class, etc.). It will especially produce changes in the 'problematic' of the class — that matrix of problems, structures, opportunities and experiences which confront that particular class stratum at a particular historical moment. It will mirror changes in the material conditions in everyday life available for construction into the *supports* for one or other of the collective strategies.

Negotiation, resistance, struggle: the relations between a subordinate and a dominant culture, wherever they fall within this spectrum, are always intensely active, always oppositional, in a structural sense (even when this opposition is latent,or experienced simply as the normal state of affairs — what Gouldner called "normalised repression"). Their outcome is not given but *made*. The subordinate class brings to this 'theatre of struggle' a repertoire of strategies and responses — ways of coping as well as of resisting. Each strategy in the repertoire mobilises certain real material and social elements: it constructs these into the supports for different ways the class lives and resists its continuing subordination. Not all the strategies are of equal weight: not all are potentially counter-hegemonic. Some may even be alternatives — e.g., working-class politics and certain kinds of working-class crime. We must also recognise that a developed and organised revolutionary working-class consciousness is only *one*, among many such possible responses, and a very special ruptural one at that. It has been misleading to try to measure the whole spectrum of strategies in the class in terms of this one ascribed form of consciousness, and to define everything else as a token of incorporation. This is to impose an abstract scheme on to a concrete historical reality. We must try to understand, instead, how, under what conditions, the class has been able to use its material and cultural 'raw materials' to construct a whole *range* of responses. Some — the repertoire of resistance specific to the history of one working class — form an immense reservoir of knowledge and power in the struggle of the class to survive and 'win space'. Even those which appear again and again in the history of the class, are not fixed alternatives (reform vs. revolution), but *potential* historical 'spaces' used and adapted to very different circumstances in its tradition of struggle. Nor can we ascribe particular sociological strata of the class to particular, permanent positions in the repertoire. This, too, is quite a-historical. It is possible for the 'labour aristocracy' to provide critical radical leadership; for the unorganised or so-called 'lumpen' to organise; for 'deference voters' to lose their respect for authority; for 'affluents' to be, also, 'militants'; for 'clericals' to strike; for working wives and first generation immigrants to take the vanguard position; and so on. In the diagram below, we have tried to enforce this argument (which, we believe, follows directly from Gramsci's conception of hegemony and corporateness) by a sketch of one possible part of the strategies of negotiation, conflict and subordination. It is offered for illustrative purposes only — its value lying in the fact that it includes, within one typology, strategies which belong to the more or less adaptive poles of the spectrum, strategies developed both within and outside the formal institutionalisation of class struggle.

F. The subcultural response

We can return, now, to the question of 'sub-cultures'. Working-class sub-cultures, we suggested, take shape on the level of the social and cultural class-relations of the subordinate classes. In themselves, they are not simply 'ideological' constructs. They, too, *win space* for the young: cultural space in the neighbourhood and institutions, real time for leisure and recreation, actual room on the street or street-corner. They serve to mark out and appropriate 'territory' in the localities. They focus around key occasions of social interaction: the weekend, the disco, the bank-holiday trip, the night out in the 'centre', the 'standing-about-doing-nothing' of the weekday evening, the Saturday match. They cluster around particular locations. They develop specific rhythms of interchange, structured relations between members: younger to older, experienced to novice, stylish to square. They explore 'focal concerns' central to the inner life of the group: things always 'done' or 'never done', a set of social rituals which underpin their collective identity and define them as a 'group' instead of a mere collection of individuals. They adopt and adapt material objects — goods and possessions — and reorganise them into distinctive 'styles' which express the collectivity of their being-as-a-group. These concerns, activities, relationships, materials become embodied in rituals of relationship and occasion and movement. Sometimes, the world is marked out, linguistically, by names or an *argot* which classifies the social world exterior to them in terms meaningful only within their group perspective, and maintains its boundaries. This also helps them to develop, ahead of immediate activities a perspective on the immediate future — plans, projects, things to do to fill out time, exploits . . . They too are concrete, identifiable social formations constructed as a collective response to the material and situated experience of their class.

Though not 'ideological', sub-cultures have an ideological dimension: and, in the problematic situation of the post-war period, this ideological component became more prominent. In addressing the 'class problematic' of the particular strata from which they were drawn, the different sub-cultures provided for a section of working-class youth (mainly boys) *one* strategy for negotiating their collective existence. But their highly ritualised and stylised form suggests that they were also *attempts at a solution* to that problematic experience: a resolution which, because pitched largely at the symbolic level, was fated to fail. The problematic of a subordinate class experience can be 'lived through', negotiated or resisted; but it cannot be *resolved* at that level or by those means. There is no 'sub-cultural career' for the working-class lad, no 'solution' in the sub-cultural milieu, for problems posed by the key structuring experiences of the class.

"the naturally Conservative Nation"	"one nation"	"the two sides of industry"	"the parliamentery road"	"equality before the law"	"militancy" "extremism" "holding the nation to ransom"	"subversion" "anarchy"
deference vote	w.c. neighbourhood	Trade Union Membership	Labour Vote	'the Law'	shop steward power	the Left sects
Working Class Tory	'Us' vs. 'Them'	Trade Union Conscious-ness	Labourism	Crime Delinquency	Militant 'Economism'	Revolutionary Politics

("false conciousness") ... ("normalized repression") ... (ab-normal responses) ... (threats to state)

Figure 3 A repertoire of negotiations and responses

There is no 'sub-cultural solution' to working-class youth unemployment, educational disadvantage, compulsory miseducation, dead-end jobs, the routinisation and specialisation of labour, low pay and the loss of skills. Sub-cultural strategies cannot match, meet or answer the structuring dimensions emerging in this period for the class as a whole. So, when the post-war sub-cultures address the problematics of their class experience, they often do so in ways which reproduce the gaps and discrepancies between real negotiations and symbolically displaced 'resolutions'. They 'solve', but in an imaginary way, problems which at the concrete material level remain unresolved. Thus the 'Teddy Boy' expropriation of an upper-class style of dress 'covers' the gap between largely manual, unskilled, near-lumpen real careers and life-chances, and the 'all-dressed-up-and-nowhere-to-go' experience of Saturday evening. Thus, in the expropriation and fetishisation of consumption and style itself, the 'Mods' cover for the gap between the never-ending-weekend and Monday's resumption of boring, dead-end work. Thus, in the resurrection of an archetypal and 'symbolic' (but, in fact, anachronistic) form of working-class dress, in the displaced focussing on the football match and the 'occupation' of the football 'ends', Skinheads reassert, but 'imaginarily' the values of a class, the essence of a style, a kind of 'fan-ship' to which few working-class adults any longer subscribe: they 're-present' a sense of territory and locality which the planners and speculators are rapidly destroying: they 'declare' as alive and well a game which is being commercialised, professionalised and spectacularised. "Skins Rule, OK", OK ? But "in ideology, men do indeed express, not the real relation between them and their conditions of existence, but *the way* they live the relation between them and the conditions of their existence; this presupposes both a real and an *'imaginary', 'lived'* relation. Ideology then, is . . . the (over determined) unity of the real relation and the imaginary relation . . . that expresses a will . . . a hope, or a nostalgia, rather than describing a reality" (Althusser, 1969: 233–234).

Working-class sub-cultures are a response to a problematic which youth shares with other members of the 'parent' class culture. But class structures the adolescent's experience of that problematic in distinctive ways. First, it locates the young, at a formative stage of their development, in a particular material and cultural milieu, in distinctive relations and experiences. These provide the essential cultural frameworks through which that problematic is made sense of by the youth. This 'socialisation' of youth *into* a class identity and position operates particularly through two 'informal' agencies: family and neighbourhood. Family and neighbourhood are the specific structures which *form,* as well as frame, youth's early passage into a class. For example, the sex-typing roles and responsibilities characteristic of a class are reproduced, not only through language and talk in the family, but through daily interaction and example. In the neighbourhood, patterns of community sociality are embedded partly through the structure of interactions between older and younger kids. (Howard Parker, 1974, has commented on the role of street football as a way in which younger kids 'learn' a distinctive kind of class sociability.) These intimate contexts also refer the young to the larger world outside. Thus it is largely through friends and relations that the distant but increasingly imminent worlds of work or of face-to-face authority (the rent man, Council officials, social security, the police) are appropriated. Through these formative networks, relations, distances, interactions, orientations to the wider world and its social types are delineated and reproduced in the young.

Class also, broadly, structures the young individual's life-chances. It determines, in terms of statistical class probabilities, the distribution of 'achievement' and 'failure'. It establishes certain crucial orientations towards careers in education and work — it produces the notoriously 'realistic' expectations of working-class kids about future opportunities. It teaches ways of relating to and negotiating authority. For example, the social distance, deference, anxiety and dressing-up of parents in meetings with school teachers may confirm or reinforce the experience of school as essentially part of an alien and external world.

These are only some of the many ways in which the way youth is inserted within the culture of a class also serves to reproduce, within the young, the problematics of that class. But, over and above these shared class situations, there remains something privileged about the specifically *generational experience* of the young. Fundamentally, this is due to the fact that youth encounters the problematic of its class culture in *different sets of institutions and experiences* from those of its parents; and when youth encounters the same structures, it encounters them at *crucially different points* in its biographical careers.

We can identify these aspects of "generational specificity" in relation to the three main life areas we pointed to earlier: education, work and leisure. Between the ages of five and sixteen, education is the institutional sphere which has the most sustained and intensive impact on the lives of the young. It is the "paramount reality" imposing itself on experience, not least through the fact that it cannot (easily) be avoided. By contrast, the older members of the class encounter education in various *indirect* and distanced ways: through remembered experiences ("things have changed" nowadays); through special mediating occasions — parents' evenings, etc.; and through the interpretations the young give of their school experiences.

In the area of work, the difference is perhaps less obvious, in that both young and old alike are facing similar institutional arrangements, organisations and occupational situations. But within this crucial differences remain. The young face the problem of choosing and entering jobs, of learning both the formal and informal cultures of work — the whole difficult transition from school to work. We have already observed how the changing occupational structures of some areas and industries may dislocate the traditionally evolved "family work – career structure" — thus making the transition even more difficult. For the older members of the class, work has become a relatively routine aspect of life; they have learnt occupational identities and the cultures of work, involving strategies for coping with the problems that work poses — methods of "getting by".

In the broader context, the young are likely to be more vulnerable to the consequence of increasing unemployment than are older workers: in the unemployment statistics of the late sixties, unskilled school leavers were twice as likely to be unemployed as were older, unskilled workers. In addition, the fact of unemployment is likely to be differentially *experienced* at different stages in the occupational "career".

Finally, leisure must be seen as a significant life-area for the class. As Marx observed,

. . . The worker therefore only feels himself outside his work, and in his work feels outside himself. He is at home when he is not working, and when he is working he is not at home. His labour is therefore not voluntary but coerced: it is forced labour. It is therefore not the satisfaction of a need; it is merely the means to satisfy needs external to it.

(1964: 110–1)

In working-class leisure, we see many of the results of that "warrenning" of society by the working-class discussed above. Leisure and recreation seem to have provided a more negotiable space than the tightly-disciplined and controlled work situation. The working-class has imprinted itself indelibly on many areas of mass leisure and recreation. These form an important part of the corporate culture and are central to the experience and cultural identity of the whole class. Nevertheless, there are major differences in the ways working-class adults and young people experience and regard leisure. This difference became intensified in the 1950s and 1960s, with the growth of the 'teenage consumer' and the reorganisation of consumption and leisure provision (both commercial and non-commercial) in favour of a range of goods and services specifically designed to attract a youthful clientele. This widespread availability and high visibility of Youth Culture structured the leisure sphere in crucially different ways for the young. The equation of youth with consumption and leisure rearranged and *intensified* certain long-standing parent culture orientations; for example, towards the special and privileged meaning of 'freetime', and towards 'youth' as a period for 'having a good time while you can' — the 'last fling'. This reshaping of attitudes from within the class, in conjunction with pressures to rearrange and redistribute the patterns of leisure for the young from outside, served to highlight — indeed to *fetishise* — the meaning of leisure for the young. Thus, not only did youth encounter leisure in different characteristic institutions from their parents (caffs, discos, youth clubs, 'all nighters', etc.): these institutions powerfully presented themselves to the young as different from the past, partly because they were so uncompromisingly youthful.

Here we begin to see how forces, working right across a class, but differentially experienced as between the generations, may have formed the basis for generating an outlook — a kind of consciousness — specific to age position: a *generational consciousness*. We can also see exactly why this 'consciousness', though formed by class situation and the forces working in it, may nevertheless have taken the form of a consciousness apparently separate from, unrelated to, indeed, able to be set over against, its class content and context. Though we can see how and why this specific kind of 'generational consciousness' might arise, the problem is not resolved by simply reading it once again out of existence — that is, by re-assigning to youth a clear and simple class-based identity and consciousness. This would be simply to over-react against 'generational consciousness'. We have suggested that, though a fully-blown 'generational consciousness' served unwittingly to repress and obscure the class dimension, it did have a 'rational core' in the very experience of the working-class young in the period; the specificity of the institutions in which post-war changes were encountered, and above all, in the way this sphere was reshaped by changes in the leisure market. It may also have been located in other, material experiences of the youth of the class in this period. A 'generational consciousness' is likely to be strong among those sectors of youth which are upwardly and outwardly mobile from the working-class — e.g., Hoggart's 'scholarship boy'. Occupational and educational change in this period led to an increase in these paths of limited mobility. The upward path, through education, leads to a special focussing on *the school and the education system* as the main mechanism of advancement: it is this which 'makes the difference' between parents who stay where they were and children who move on and up. It involves the young person valuing the dominant culture positively, and sacrificing the 'parent' culture — even where this is accompanied by a distinct sense of cultural disorientation. His experience and self-identity will be based around mobility — something specific to his generation, rather than to the over-determining power of class. One of the things which supports this taking-over of a 'generational consciousness' by the scholarship boy is, precisely, his cultural isolation — the fact that his career is different from the majority of his peers. The peer group is, of course, one of the real and continuing bases for collective identities organised around the focus of 'generation'. But a sense of generational distinctness may also flow from an individual's isolation from the typical involvement in kinds of peer-group activities which, though specific to youth, are clearly understood as forming a sort of cultural apprenticeship to the 'parent' class culture. This kind of isolation may be the result of biographical factors — e.g., inability to enter the local football game where football is the primary activity of the peer group; or being a member of a relatively 'closed' and tight family situation. A young person, who for whatever reasons, fails to go through this class-culture apprenticeship, may be more vulnerable to the vicarious peer-group experience provided by the highly visible and widely accessible commercially provided Youth Culture, where the audience as a whole substitutes for the real peer group as one, vast, symbolic 'peer group': "Our Generation".

'Generational consciousness' thus has roots in the real experience of working-class youth as a whole. But it took a peculiarly intense form in the post-war sub-cultures which were sharply demarcated — amongst other factors — by age and generation. Youth felt and experienced itself as 'different', especially when this difference was inscribed in activities and interests to which 'age', principally, provided the passport. This does not necessarily mean that a 'sense of class' was thereby obliterated. Skinheads, for example, are clearly both 'generationally' and 'class' conscious. As Cohen suggested, "sub-culture is . . . a compromise solution, between two contradictory needs: the need to create and express *autonomy* and *difference* from parents . . . and the need to maintain . . . the *parental identifications* which support them" (Cohen, 1972: 26). It is to the formation of these generationally distinct working-class sub-cultures that we next turn.

G. Sources of style

The question of style, indeed, of generational style, is pivotal to the post-war formation of these youth sub-cultures. [The issue is treated at length below in the essay on "Style"; the main points only are summarised at this point.] What concerns us here is, first, how 'class' and 'generational' elements interact together in the production of distinctive group-styles; second, how the materials available to the group are constructed and appropriated in the form of a visibly organised cultural response.

Working-class youth inhabit, like their parents, a distinctive structural and cultural *milieu* defined by territory, objects and things, relations, institutional and social practices. In terms of kinship, friendship networks, the informal culture of the neighbourhood, and the practices articulated around them, the young are already located in and by the 'parent' culture. They also encounter the dominant culture, not in its distant, remote, powerful, abstract forms, but in the located forms and institutions which mediate the dominant culture to the subordinate culture, and thus permeate it. Here, for youth, the school, work (from Saturday jobs onwards), leisure are the key institutions. Of almost equal importance — for youth above all — are the institutions and agencies of public social control: the school serves this function, but alongside it, a range of institutions from the 'hard' coercive ones, like the police, to the 'softer' variants — youth and social workers.

It is at the intersection between the located parent culture and the mediating institutions of the dominant culture that youth sub-cultures arise. Many forms of adaptation, negotiation and resistance, elaborated by the 'parent' culture in its encounter with the dominant culture, are borrowed and adapted by the young in *their* encounter with the mediating institutions of provision and control. In organising their response to these experiences, working-class youth sub-cultures take some things principally from the located 'parent' culture: but they apply and transform them to the situations and experiences characteristic of their own distinctive group-life and generational experience. Even where youth sub-cultures have seemed most distinctive, different, stylistically marked out from adults and other peer-group members of their 'parent' culture, they develop certain distinctive outlooks which have been, clearly, structured by the parent culture. We might think here of the recurrent organisation around collective activities ('group mindedness'); or the stress on 'territoriality' (to be seen in both the Teddy Boys and Skinheads); or the particular conceptions of masculinity and of male dominance (reproduced in all the post-war youth sub-cultures). The 'parent' culture helps to define these broad, historically-located 'focal concerns'. Certain themes which are key to the 'parent culture' are reproduced at this level again and again in the sub-cultures, even when they set out to be, or are seen as, 'different'.

But there are also 'focal concerns' more immediate, conjunctural, specific to 'youth' and its situation and activities. On the whole, the literature on post-war sub-culture has neglected the first aspect (what is shared with the 'parent' culture) and over emphasised what is distinct (the 'focal concerns' of the youth groups). But this second element — which is, again, generationally very specific — must be taken seriously in any account. It consists both of the materials available to the group for the construction of sub-cultural identities (dress, music, talk), and of their contexts (activities, exploits, places, caffs, dance halls, day-trips, evenings-out, football games, etc.). Journalistic treatments, especially, have tended to isolate *things,* at the expense of their use, how they are borrowed and transformed, the activities and spaces through which they are 'set in motion', the group identities and outlooks which imprint a style *on* things and objects. While taking seriously the significance of objects and things for a sub-culture, it must be part of our analysis to *de*-fetishise them.

The various youth sub-cultures have been identified by their possessions and objects: the boot-lace tie and velvet-collared drape jacket of the Ted, the close crop, parker coats and scooter of the Mod, the stained jeans, swastikas and ornamented motorcycles of the bike-boys, the bovver boots and skinned-head of the Skinhead, the Chicago suits or glitter costumes of the Bowieites, etc. Yet, despite their visibility, things simply appropriated and worn (or listened to) do not make a style. What makes a style is the activity of stylisation — the active organisation of objects with activities and outlooks, which produce an organised group-identity in the form and shape of a coherent and distinctive way of 'being-in-the-world'. Phil Cohen, for example, has tried to shift the emphasis away from things to the *modes* of symbolic construction through which style is generated in the sub-cultures. He identified four modes for the generation of the sub-cultural style: dress, music, ritual and *argot*. Whilst not wanting to limit the 'symbolic systems' to these particular four, and finding it difficult to accept the distinction (between less and more 'plastic') which he makes, we find this emphasis on group generation far preferable to the instant stereotyped association between commodity-objects and groups common in journalistic usage.

Working-class sub-cultures could not have existed without a real economic base: the growth in money wages in the 'affluent' period, but, more important, the fact that incomes grew more rapidly for teenagers than for adults in the working-class, and that much of this was 'disposable income' (income available for leisure and non-compulsory spending). But income, alone, does not make a style either. The sub-cultures could not have existed without the growth of a consumer market specifically geared to youth. The new youth industries provided the raw materials, the goods: but they did not, and when they tried failed to, produce many very authentic or sustained 'styles' in the deeper sense. The objects were there, available, but were used by the groups in the construction of distinctive styles. But this meant, not simply picking them up, but actively constructing a specific selection of things and goods *into* a style. And this frequently involved [as we try to show in some of the selections in our 'ethnographic' section] subverting and transforming these things, from their given meaning and use, to other meanings and uses. All commodities have a social use and thus a cultural meaning. We have only to look at the language of commodities — advertising — where, as Barthes observes, there is no such thing as a simple 'sweater': there is only a 'sweater for autumnal walks in the wood' or a sweater for 'relaxing at home on Sundays', or a sweater for 'casual wear', and so on (Barthes, 1971). Commodities are, also, cultural *signs*. They have already been invested, by the dominant culture, with meanings, associations, social connotations. Many of these meanings seem fixed and 'natural'. But this is only because the dominant culture has so fully appropriated them to its use, that the meanings which it attributes to the commodities have come to appear as the only meaning which they can express. In fact, in cultural systems, there is no 'natural' meaning as such. Objects and commodities do not mean any one thing. They 'mean' only because they have already been arranged, according to social use, into cultural codes of meaning, which *assign meanings to them*. The bowler hat, pin-stripe suit and rolled umbrella do not, in themselves, mean 'sobriety', 'respectability', bourgeoisman-at-work. But so powerful is the social code which surrounds these commodities that it would be difficult for a working-class lad to turn up for work dressed like that without, either aspiring to a 'bourgeois' image or clearly seeming to take the piss out of the image. This trivial example shows that it is possible to expropriate, as well as to appropriate, the social meanings which they seem 'naturally' to have: or, by combining them with something else (the pin-stripe suit with brilliant red socks or white running shoes, for example), to change or inflect their meaning. Because the meanings which commodities express are socially given — Marx called commodities "social hieroglyphs" — their meaning can also be socially altered or reconstructed. The interior of the working-class home, as described, say, by Roberts (1971) or Hoggart (1958), represents one such 'reworking', by means of which things are imprinted with new meanings, associations and values which expropriate them from the world which provides them and relocates them within the culture of the working-class.

Working-class youth needed money to spend on expressive goods, objects and activities — the post-war consumer market had a clear economic infrastructure. But neither money nor the market could fully dictate what groups used these things to *say* or *signify* about themselves. This re-signification was achieved by many different means. One way was to inflect 'given' meanings by combining things borrowed from one system of meanings into a different code, generated by the sub-culture itself, and through sub-cultural use. Another way was to modify, by addition, things which had been produced or used by a different social group. Another was to intensify or exaggerate or isolate a given meaning and so change it (the 'fetishing' of consumption and appearance by the Mods, discussed by Dick Hebdige; or the elongation of the pointed winkle-picker shoes of the Italian style; or the current 'massification' of the wedge-shapes borrowed from the 1940s). Yet another way was to combine forms according to a 'secret' language or code, to which only members of the group possessed the key (e.g., the *argot* of many sub-cultural and deviant groups; the 'Rasta' language of black 'Rudies'). These are only *some* of the many ways in which the sub-cultures used the materials and commodities of the 'youth market' to construct meaningful styles and appearances for themselves.

Far more important were the aspects of group life which these appropriated objects and things were made to reflect, express and resonate. It is this reciprocal effect, between the things a group uses and the outlooks and activities which structure and define their use, which is the generative principle of stylistic creation in a sub-culture. This involves members of a group in the appropriation of particular objects which are, or can be made, 'homologous' with their focal concerns, activities, group structure and collective self-image — objects in which they can see their central values held and reflected. The adoption by Skinheads of boots and short jeans and shaved hair was 'meaningful' in terms of the sub-culture only because these external manifestations resonated with and articulated Skinhead conceptions of masculinity, 'hardness' and 'working-classness'. This meant overcoming or negotiating or, even, taking over in a positive way many of the negative meanings which, in the dominant cultural code, attached to these things: the 'prison-crop' image of the shaved head, the work-image, the so-called 'outdated cloth-cap image', and so on. The new meanings emerge because the 'bits' which had been borrowed or revived were brought together into a new and distinctive stylistic *ensemble:* but also because the symbolic objects — dress, appearance, language, ritual occasions, styles of interaction, music — were made to form a *unity* with the group's relations, situation, experiences: the crystallisation in an expressive form, which then defines the group's public identity. The symbolic aspects cannot, then, be separated from the structure, experiences, activities and outlook of the groups as social formations. Sub-cultural style is based on the infrastructure of group relations, activities and contexts.

This registering of group identity, situation and trajectory in a visible style both consolidates the group from a loosely-focussed to a tightly-bound entity: and sets the group off, distinctively, from other similar and dissimilar groups. Indeed, like all other kinds of cultural construction, the symbolic use of things to consolidate and express an internal coherence was, in the same moment, a kind of implied opposition to (where it was not an active and conscious contradiction of) *other groups against* which its identity was defined. This process led, in our period, to the distinctive visibility of those groups which pressed the 'sub-cultural solution' to its limits along this stylistic path. It also had profound negative consequences for the labelling, stereotyping and stigmatisation, in turn, of those groups by society's guardians, moral entrepreneurs, public definers and the social control culture in general.

It is important to stress again that sub-cultures are only *one* of the many different responses which the young can make to the situations in which they find themselves. In addition to indicating the range and variation in the options open to youth, we might add a tentative scheme which helps to make clear the distinction we are drawing between youth's *position* and the cultural options through which particular responses are organised.

We can distinguish, broadly, between three aspects: structures, cultures and biographies. By structures we mean the set of socially-organised positions and experiences of the class in relation to the major institutions and structures. These positions generate a set of common relations and experiences from which meaningful actions — individual and collective — are constructed. *Cultures* are the range of socially-organised and patterned responses to these basic material and social conditions. Though cultures form, for each group, a set of traditions — lines of action inherited from the past — they must always be collectively constructed anew in each generation. Finally, *biographies* are the 'careers' of particular individuals through these structures and cultures — the means by which individual identities and life-histories are constructed out of collective experiences. Biographies recognise the element of individuation in the paths which individual lives take through collective structures and cultures, but they must not be conceived as either wholly individual or free-floating. Biographies cut paths in and through the determined spaces of the structures and cultures in which individuals are located. Though we have not been able, here, to deal at all adequately with the level of biography, we insist that biographies only make sense in terms of the structures and cultures through which the individual constructs himself or herself.

15. The Adolescent Entrepreneur: Youth, Style, and Cultural Inheritance
Dick Hobbs

Working doesn't seem to be the perfect thing for me so I continue to play,
and if I'm so bad why don't they take me away?
(Popular song of summer 1968).

This chapter is concerned with the continuity of the East End's entrepreneurial inheritance, for it would be an error to switch from Victorian London to the contemporary East End without referring to the process by which culture is transmitted from generation to generation. In order that this process might be comprehended, I have focused upon youth or, more specifically, working-class youth's subcultural style. It is my argument that a close and sympathetic analysis of this phenomenon provides an opportunity to fill a gap in the area's modern history, and, more importantly, to locate youth as the crucial stage in an individual's adoption of class-specific responses to the market-place.

The culture of East London has altered in an adaptive response to changes in the 'economic ecology' of the area. This response manifests itself in specific linguistic and stylistic forms that allow for change while meeting the immediate requirements or impositions of the market. The culture is not then a static phenomenon of Victorian urban life, for as the environment changes the responses of individuals will modify accordingly within the boundaries set by precedent. As Rose (1962, p. 14) has noted, the individual can 'within the limits permitted by the culture define for himself somewhat new patterns suggested by the variation among the old ones'.

History can be seen to function as a mediating factor in the development of East End culture. The economic ecology of the area provides the dynamic for an ever-expanding environment, and the culturally defined characteristics of autonomy, independence, and entrepreneurship provide necessary sensitizing instruments for the development of a breadth of perspective that defines situations and forms a frame of reference, which in turn structures possibilities for action (Warshay 1962, p. 51; Mead 1934, p. 245).

Delinquency and dressing up

Youth can be viewed as probably the most crucial sensitizing phase in the evolution of a culture. The reason for this is best addressed by considering recent empirical work on youth and culture. During the last twenty years there have been attempts to link the study of youth to a broader analysis of culture. For example, Downes (1966) established crucial connections between delinquency and the local job market, and

Parker (1974) found that working-class youths tended to take over traditional adult practices, which is hardly surprising as the adolescents and adults of the 'Roundhouse Estate' shared most of the basic cultural constraints and social inequalities of everyday life. Paul Willis (1977) established adolescence as a period when young men learn in their daily conflicts with middle-class culture via the school, of their inherited position on the labour market.

However, it was Phil Cohen's (1972) brief paper that provided the most illuminating and far-reaching analysis of youthful style, a style that evolves in the form of a sensitizing device as a response to inherited restraint within a changing environment. Cohen identified three factors that underpin all traditional working-class communities and East London in particular, namely the extended kinship structure, the local economy, and the ecology of the neighbourhood. For Cohen, the post-war breakdown in those three interdependent elements produced a weakening of historical and cultural continuity leading to internal conflict within the newly isolated nuclear family, conflict that was decanted into generational conflict. The emergence of youthful stylistic innovations functioned as attempts at solving contradictions within the parent culture that persisted at two levels. At an ideological level the contradiction was between what Cohen calls the 'new hedonism of consumption' and traditional working-class puritanism; and at an economic level the contradiction lay between the socially mobile élite and the 'new lumpen'. Therefore, the 'respectable' working class are unable to join the trend towards upward suburban mobility as practised by the élite, and yet naturally resist sliding downward into the lumpen group.

For Cohen, and those of the Birmingham School who were influenced by his analysis, post-war British youth subcultures represent attempts to resolve these contradictions, and these attempts lead to explorations of the options facing the respectable working class, i.e. up or down. The upward option was explored symbolically by the 'Mods' while the 'skinhead' explored the downward option. However, the difficulty with these subtle interpretive schemes often lies in locating plausible empirical evidence for them.

None of my respondents was apparently aware of facing contradictions, and the initial tentative adoption of a specific style appears to have stemmed from a subsequent interest in their own appearance rather than an attempt at solving contradictions within the parent culture.

> *Mick.* I suppose I started getting interested in clothes and that when I was 11 or 12. There was a couple of kids older like who had scooters, and I suppose we looked up to them. I wouldn't say they were heroes or nothing; it was mainly the way they dressed.

While certain aspects of the style did mark an exploration of upward mobility, the central issues remained unchanged, and a specific style is only unique in terms of the clothing worn by subcultural members, and the settings in which the clothes are worn. The Mod, for example, possessed a well-defined sense of place and occasion and a line was firmly drawn between 'casual' and 'formal' social settings.

> *Ken.* But if you was going out you would wear a smart suit, maybe a tie, or I suppose [if] it was a little bit later, a short-sleeved Fred Perry. Nice

trousers like Yorkers and a decent pair of shoes. But we all used to like dressing up didn't we? I used to love wearing a suit.

These rigid formal rules regarding appearance were largely due to the unique nature of the tailoring trade in the 1960s, a trade that still fostered the small one-man business and was consequently able to produce original high-quality clothing. The Mods did not 'redefine' the suit as Hebdige (1979, pp. 52–3) has claimed; they merely redesigned it according to the fashion of the day. Hebdige ignores the fact that most men in East London regardless of occupation had their suits 'made to measure'. In the pre-boutique days of the early to mid-1960s 'off-the-peg' clothing was of inferior quality, and the suit was a regular, normally Christmas-time purchase for males of all ages. The suit was a standard item of male attire to be worn outside working hours, while at work old suits were worn by dockers and men in a wide range of jobs. Specialist working clothes were rare and labouring men wearing old lounge suits at work would appear to represent the redefinition of a commodity, or a relocation of meaning far more bizarre than the ageless pursuit of fashion by youth

Changes in youthful style can be observed as running parallel with alterations in the local socio-economic structure, and in the 1960s the sharp style of the Mods was, along with other influences, directly linked to employment opportunities. As a docker's son Mick, who left school in 1966, would have followed his father's profession, yet chose instead what Phil Cohen has termed the upward option; he became an office boy:

> *Mick.* Me old man had me name down to go in the dock when I was 18, but I never fancied it. It was good money and that but, well I never fancied labouring, 'cos that's what it is, labouring. When I left school I fancied a bit of office work. I used to fancy myself in a suit. That's all it was really, just showing out.

Also important in the formation of style was the cultural overlap of the East and West Ends of London that occurred in the 1960s as a result of alterations in gambling laws, the resultant indiscreet manifestations of East End villains in West End clubs, and the fashionable 1960s notion of classlessness. Conversely show-business personalities and members of the aristocracy flirted with East End pubs and drinking-clubs, and a cockney accent became *de rigueur* for acceptance into bourgeois society as pop stars, hairdressers, and photographers rediscovered their humble roots. For young East-Enders, this opened up a privileged and exotic domain, and they emulated their elders, taking a short trip on the Central Line to spend their wages on a Friday night. 'Going up West' was a traditional adventure for East End kids, but now with an economic base established by their elders, they were no longer tourists.

> *Bill.* I used to like Friday night the best. We'd be nicely dressed — suits — and go up West, do some of the clubs. They were good clubs, nice music, never any trouble.

The suits, music, and West End clubs represented the exploration of a successful, and very visible, masculine type, the tough, stylish, resourceful, and leisured East End male. John McVicar has cogently described this phenomenon.

341

> I graduated to the Billiards Hall and Public House, and as I established myself on the fringe of this kind of world, I became both fascinated and challenged by it . . . their rakishness, their flamboyant clothes, their tough, self-reliant manners, their rejection of conventional attitudes to sex and money — such things forced me and mesmerised me into conquering the mysteries of the world they lived in. I unconsciously modelled myself on the more successful representatives of this new society (McVicar 1979, p. 158).

Down market

By the late 1960s, the office boy came to realize that it took more than smart clothes to become a managing director:

> *Mick.* It was all right at first going on the train and that, but I got bored. I never really got on with people. They came from all over London. Some of them were well off and the way I talk, well I just never felt comfortable. I could do the work standing on me prick, but it was boring so I left.

The decline of dock-work brought about further changes in style, which in turn allowed Mick to explore and reaffirm one of the key central characteristics of East End culture: autonomy. Mick left clerical work after just eighteen months and, in Cohen's terms, proceeded to explore the 'lumpen option', working first as a plasterer's mate and then as a plasterer. As a plasterer in the early 1970s he earned up to £150 per week, but:

> *Mick.* I never liked being told what to do. I started having rucks with the guv'nors. They started checking when we started and finished and that . . . So I thought bollocks . . . I left.

At this point the tentative explorations of youth are abandoned in favour of admission to the adult world. 'Magical' solutions are made redundant in favour of conscious instrumental efforts to chisel a niche for oneself within capitalism by way of exploiting the entrepreneurial ability that is the inheritance of all East Londoners. This inheritance has been structured by market forces over many centuries, and is manifested in an exclusively working-class population largely untouched by the regimented discipline of the factory system, and forged in an environment of casual labour and small workshops that nurture independence and autonomy.

For Mick at the age of 23, certain realities became apparent. With both the 'upward' and 'lumpen' options occupationally and stylistically explored he was jobless; office work offered low wages and illusory status and the brief ascendancy of the manual worker had waned. He is now the manager of a small hardware shop, receiving a wage of £70 per week. However, he also receives a tax-free lump sum of £200 per week, thanks to negotiations between the shopowner, his accountant, and Mick. Various agreements with lorry-drivers, lucrative arrangements with customers involving VAT fraud, and his involvement in the buying and selling of stolen paint provide regular additional sums. Mick, after the explorations of youth, has cashed in his legacy.

The strategies, rules, and rituals that are first encountered in youth often become so ingrained that there is little trauma experienced when entering the adult world, for it is as malevolent, violent, and seemingly irrational as that of the teenage mugger, disco thug, or football hooligan.

Rucking and stirring

The metamorphosis of violent youth into violent adult is made apparent by the willingness of many adults to resort to violence. When Paul was 24 he was involved in a pub fight:

> *Paul.* I got me back to the bar lashing out and the landlord punches me in the back, well I thought he punched me, then he comes round the bar and has a go at the front . . . I was throwing and hitting out with bottles, glasses, anything. I got one geezer, a black bloke, with a glass and I see the blood spurt out of his forehead . . . I got outside and me back was hurting, so puts me hand there and it's soaked with blood . . . Turns up it just missed me kidney by the width of a hair.

Violence is a fact of working-class life and is not restricted to youth. The rules, strategies, and codes of violence are inherited, passed on from generation to generation. Despite Paul's close escape he reacts to violence in a similar manner some twelve years on, never slow in responding to threats with violence of his own. His understanding of the realities of East End life have led Paul to ensure that his seven-year-old son is well equipped to cope:

> *Paul.* He will just steam in and fight anybody. He was having a go with a kid with an iron bar, just standing there saying 'come on then, you want a fight' and this kid's swinging a fucking iron bar. I shouted 'oi', and then I bollocked him, and he just said 'I'm not scared of him', so I told him, 'if someone's got an iron bar, you fucking run', 'cos I teach 'im a few tricks, Dick, you know, don't fuck about, kick 'em in the bollocks [*laugh*].

While strategies are symbiotically modified, violence and the expression of tough masculinity remain resilient, ever-present features of the youth and parent cultures. Terry, at 35, is a famous local street-fighter. His head and body are covered in scars, and he has an awesome reputation for fighting which stretches back to his teens. After being involved in one affray that left him with six stitches in a scalp wound, he reflected 'and the thing is, we ain't kids. We ain't just some yobs down the road hitting each other, we're grown men, 32 and 35, and we're still fucking trying to kill each other. I mean the yobs do it and so do we'.

Fathers and sons: the inheritance of delinquent style

Stan Cohen's (1980, p. 15) emphasis on the metaphysical anomalies, particularly in the work of Hebdige, has served to shift attention away from Phil Cohen's original analysis of East London community that produced the tripartite model of traditional culture, the basis upon which the new theories are totally dependent. It is my belief that a closer examination of the concepts of kinship, ecology, and economy as they are applicable to East London will prove to be fruitful in terms of an analysis of subcultural evolution and stylistic innovation. In doing so I must question the accuracy of the historical frame within which Phil Cohen originally located delinquent subcultures. The accuracy of the ecological structure that Cohen refers to is not questioned here, nor would I query the description of East London's extended kinship networks. However, the third factor in Phil Cohen's tripartite model, the local economy, is problematic, and warrants a more detailed examination than has been given to it up to now. Cohen identifies the economy of East London as being reliant upon the docks, their accompanying distributive and service trades, and craft industries, notably tailoring and furniture-making.[1]

Furniture-making and its allied trades were traditional East End crafts and had been for many years. Hall, using 1861 census material reports that 'The biggest branch of the industry was in the inner East London boroughs of Shoreditch, Bethnal Green and Stepney' (Hall 1962, p. 72). Indeed, 31 per cent of the furniture trade's work-force were centred in the area.[2] The next ninety years saw a considerable growth in the trade[3] and the corresponding expansion of the work-force. However, with this expansion came the establishment of large factories outside East London and despite the expansion of the trade, the diffusion of manufacturing plants meant that by 1951 East London had only 17 per cent of the work-force (Hall 1962, p. 72). The 1960s witnessed actual decline in the labour force; between 1961 and 1971, 26,390 jobs were lost in London's timber and furniture industries, with traditional crafts such as french polishing all but disappearing.

In the same decade, 1961–71, the clothing and footwear industries also suffered (Hall 1962, pp. 37–70 and [Table 4]). The net effect of cheap imports, automation, and economies of scale resulted in 40,000 jobs being lost in London's clothing and footwear industries, which were centred in and around East London (Hall 1962, pp. 44–5).

Phil Cohen accurately noted this deterioration in the principal craft industries of East London, and their demise would appear to be consistent with the polarization of the work-force and the subsequent emergence of economically-specific subcultural styles. However, I feel that understating the importance of the docks in East London, and distinguishing what Cohen calls 'Dockland' is akin to separating coal-pits from mining-villages. In order that I might stress adequately the historical primacy of the docks in East London, it is necessary first to look rather more closely at events in and around the Port of London, with particular emphasis on the 1960s. The decline of London's docks began in the early 1960s due to: 'Changing patterns of trade in British ports and improvements in handling techniques which reduced labour requirements, but it only became a subject of public concern towards the end of that decade' (Hill 1976, p. 1).

Bigger ships' holds, increased use of fork-lift trucks, containerization, and palletization all contributed to this decline, particularly containerization as this enabled the man-handling involved in the preparation of loads which used to be done in the docks to be carried out elsewhere. Consequently: 'The new methods greatly reduced the demand for labour by removing the labour intensive part of dock work outside the industry altogether' (Hill 1976, p. 4). Parallel to this technological shift, capital was employed to enforce changes in labour usage. For instance, the Port of London

Authority invested £30 million in the modernization of Tilbury docks, which constituted the only location in the London system deep enough for the new containerships, while having sufficient land adjacent for the storage of container units.

Meanwhile, the employers were aware that apart from a decrease in their labour requirements, they also required fundamental changes in the day-to-day practices that had suited them admirably for the previous 100 years. However, it is doubtful if anyone could have foreseen the revolution in industrial relations that would take place as a result of those changes.

The docks had always revolved around a system of casual labour. How the system worked and the indignities it generated is vividly described by Bloomberg.

> At seven forty-five a.m. the foreman came out and stood in the road eyeing the men up and down. The registered men stood with their registration cards in their hands. All the registered men had to go to work first and any tickets left over allowed the 'nonners' as they were called, to go to work. After all the registered men had been called, everything became a shambles. Men were calling the foremen by their names: 'here John', 'over here Jack', pushing and shoving till it was impossible for the foreman to give the tickets out. Some of the foremen seemed to get pleasure from throwing the tickets on the ground and watching the men scramble and fight to pick a ticket up. Such was the system of calling men on. Is there anything more degrading?
>
> (Bloomberg 1974, pp. 16–17).

Although this process described by Bloomberg had improved somewhat by the early 1960s, with the advent of the National Dock Corporation and the 'Bomping Box' (Bloomberg 1979), the ability to hire and fire and day-to-day control over labour allocation lay firmly with the shipowner. As early as April 1963 the carrot of decasualization was being dangled in front of the dockers, against a background of falling dock registers due to 'natural wastage and retirement, not by redundancy' (Lloyd 1963).

Against this background of a declining dock register, changing patterns of trade, and alterations in handling techniques, the Devlin Report was implemented in 1967. Devlin introduced the National Dock Labour Board which administered the registered work-force. The employers paid a levy to the board and this levy paid for holidays and sick pay, and a daily wage was to be paid (44s. 4d.) instead of mere attendance money (18s. 0d.). A guaranteed weekly gross wage of £15 was agreed although, 'average earnings, unless volume of work in the docks diminishes, should be about £25 per week' (Devlin 1966, p. 18).

The avowed intention of the report was that 'the casual system should be ended, that there should be regular employment of all dock workers, and that all restrictive practices which were essentially a feature of the casual method of employment should be abolished' (Devlin 1966, p. 3). What was actually achieved was the removal of the right to hire and fire from the employer, with the effect that the employer failed to maintain power over labour allocation and disciplinary procedures.

For a brief period in the late 1960s, the docker enjoyed a measure of autonomy rare in industrial society. Those dock-workers who could resist the ever-increasing severance payments were enjoying the kind of elite position normally afforded to craftsmen. The prominent, successful masculine model for adolescents to adhere to was no longer the craftsman, white-collar worker, or to a lesser extent the successful local criminal,[4] but the docker, with money, material possessions, and an occupation that adhered to the criteria of tough masculinity that is intrinsic to all post-war youth subcultures.[5]

What I am suggesting is that rather than symbolic resistance via a magical solution, the kids were in fact performing the mundane adolescent ritual of copying their elders 'that they consider culturally unremarkable' (Corrigan 1979, p. 141). Dock reform (largely successful) increased industrial militancy,[6] and the emergence of this new industrial élite as a racist organization,[7] and the general economic decline since 1966,[8] heralded the emergence of the skinhead on the subcultural continuum. Response to contradictions in the parent culture and to the harsh facts of the labour market in a manner that confronted the state took place, not in an imaginary way, but actually on the street, at school, and at work. The skinhead style was aggressive, communal, and non-magical, rooted firmly in confronting the day-to-day problems of the manual labourer in an increasingly hostile world; just like Dad. Indeed, the lumpen option was explored by youth as a rational response to the brief cultural hegemony that manual labour enjoyed in the East London of the late 1960s.[9]

In terms of youth culture theories, a major part of the work of the 'new theorists' is to present specific subcultural styles as forms of resistance to subordination. The precise form in which this resistance is manifested is not real or actual, but symbolic or magical. Subcultural action is, as Stan Cohen (1980, p. 10) has commented, an 'historically informed response mediated by the class culture of the oppressed'.

In decoding a specific style via Lévi-Strauss, we are presented particularly in the case of Hebdige, with an interpretation that considers only the concepts of opposition and resistance, and 'this means that instances are sometimes missed when the style is conservative or supportive: in other words not reworked or reassembled but taken over intact from dominant commercial culture. Such instances are conceded, but then brushed aside' (Cohen 1980, p. 12). However, I am suggesting that in the case of East London and the emergence of skinheads, there was a genuine attempt to recreate traditional working-class community through mimicking the most readily available masculine stereotype which, as I have explained, within the parameters of East London was blatantly successful.

That East London was in decline in the late 1960s is not in dispute; rather the point is that one could hardly detect its decline in a community enjoying regular wages and into which hundreds of thousands of pounds of severance pay was being pumped. Clarke's (1976, p. 46) image of the skinheads as 'dispossessed inheritors' does not hold up in light of the militant communal action that typified the industrial struggle in and around the docks at that time. For instance, the skinhead quoted by Clarke who voices his frustrations concerning authority in general and the 'fucking bosses' in particular, is positively restrained compared with the action of dock-workers at this time. Examples can be found in an analysis of the regular shower of abuse aimed at Lord

Vestey in *The Dockworker*,[10] and the dockers' violent confrontations with the police in industrial disputes of that era (Rollo 1980, p. 178).

A Yank goes to Stepney

The 'new' theorists, following Phil Cohen, have accepted the skinhead style as being that of the 'model worker' (Cohen 1972) and I have gone to some lengths to confirm that the communal model of masculine behaviour exemplified by skinheads had its roots in manual labour. However, the notion that skinheads were copying the appearance of an imaginary (in Phil Cohen's thesis) or an actual (as I have suggested) working man is only part of the story. Workers in East London or anywhere else in Britain tended not to have their hair cropped. For work they would certainly have not worn US Army surplus flight-jackets at three times the cost of a donkey-jacket. The trousers were, for the 'hard cases', green US Army surplus. In surplus stores around the Royal Docks these were sold as 'docker's jeans' and dockers did indeed wear these, while elsewhere they were sold as 'jungle greens'.

The most significant and ambiguous item of clothing was the 'Doctor Martens' boots. These were not at the time 'industrial boots' (Brake 1980) in the sense of being common footwear for manual workers. They were too expensive[11] and the soft, light-weight leather and calf-length of the boot did not make them the most practical boot for heavy work. At this time a traditional army-style boot could be bought for less than £2. These were cheaper, heavier, and consequently a more potent weapon in a fight than the light-weight 'DMs'.

Skinheads, while inheriting the remnants of traditional behaviour from the parent culture, lacked the industrial muscle that made the dockers a potent force. Given that the community was under siege at the time — 'with all this lot against us, we've still got the yids, pakis, wogs, 'ippies on our backs' (Daniel and McGuire 1972, p. 68) — and the traditional culture to which the kids clung was changing,[12] a style of aggressive masculinity with a more visually intimidating image than donkey-jacket, monkey-boots, and sandwich-box was required. Every night on the TV news throughout the period US Marines in high-legged jungle-boots, cropped hair, and decked out in jungle fatigues leapt out of helicopters and into battle. If those concerned with symbolism can attribute special significance, for instance, to the wearing of braces, then surely the 'intellectual pyrotechnics' (Cohen 1980, p. 20) involved in the appropriation and utilization of a militaristic style to which youth had been subjected over a period of up to a decade are not beyond serious consideration.[13] In decoding style, greater attention should be paid to 'the spell cast on the young by the borrowed cultural imperialism' (Cohen 1980, p. 20) instead of 'affording exaggerated status to the internal circuit of English working-class history' (Cohen 1980, p. 12).

The Teddy Boys' 'slick city gambler' style (Jefferson 1976, p. 86), their adoption of American cars, and their use of the Confederate flag were all built around a solid wall of white American rock and roll. The Mods' utilization of black American music, and the smooth, Ivy League casual style that emerged towards the end of the Mod era, dominated British pubs, clubs, and dance-halls during this era. As Hebdige (1979, p. 81) has noted the appropriation of American 'types' was nothing new: 'the Brooklyn sharp kid had been emulated by the wartime black marketeer, the wide boy and the post-war spiv, and the style was familiar, readily accessible and could be easily worked up'. It is fair to deduce therefore that the evolution of post-war British working-class subcultures owes much to George Raft, Arthur English, and Max Miller.

Stan Cohen has criticized the 'new' theorists, and Hebdige in particular, on a theoretical level, but my main complaint is empirical — that in so many cases working-class subcultures are totally misread and distorted so as to make the working-class community of less than two decades ago unrecognizable, and its culture further detached from the reality of its participants than any writings of the 'old' school.[14] Hebdige continually confuses middle-class and working-class subcultures; the confusion is exemplified by his statement that 'Punk reproduced the entire sartorial history of post-war working-class youth cultures in cut up form' (Hebdige 1979, p. 124). Punk's origins are firmly rooted in New York via the Kings Road. Glue-sniffing, untutored rock bands, (Hebdige 1979, p. 25), and the tradition of acned rebellion passed down by James Dean and Marlon Brando, were imported wholesale, purchased, and appropriated by middle-class kids, who had left the Home Counties for West London's tried and tested version of Bohemia. This bourgeois experiment with decadence is now in its umpteenth generation[15] and has little connection with any attempt to solve problems instigated by contradictions within a deteriorating working-class community whose traditional culture is faced with extinction.

This misreading of style, while shrouded in the jargon of conflict, resistance, and change, constitutes a familiar language of contempt and patronage that the middle class, regardless of political persuasion, tend to utilize when dealing with working-class phenomena. An example is Hebdige's assertion that Punk magazines were 'deter-minedly working class' because they were 'liberally peppered with swear words' (Hebdige 1979, p. 111). So much for the richness of working-class culture. I find this attitude typical of a specific type of analysis that, while attempting to glamorize and romanticize working-class children as noble savages, succeeds merely in opening up Gouldner's Zoo (Gouldner 1968) to accommodate not only deviants, but the entire working-class population. It is less than surprising to find, pro rata, more punks at the LSE than in any East London comprehensive.

Finally, it is Hebdige's own misreading of the black influence on subcultural style that provides the most irritating attempt to comprehend the natives: 'the history of post-war British youth culture must be re-interpreted as a succession of differential responses to black immigrant presence in Britain from the 1950s onwards' (Hebdige 1979, p. 29).

The black influence on the Teds, for whom the Confederate flag was a symbol of their whiteness, is difficult to find. It was not until Haley's and Presley's whining versions of black Blues records were marketed that black music in its prostituted form was consumed in quantity by white youth.

> *Graham*. Tamla, down to anything Tamla. Martha and the Vandellas, Supremes, Stevie Wonder, Smokey Robinson, then it was Otis and Wilson Picket. Soul and Tamla. Four Tops, Marvin Gaye, that was the thing.

Their appreciation of these entertainers had nothing to do with the indigenous black population. These black American acts were smooth, cultured artists, spectacular dancers, and expensive dressers. The Mods incorporated these elements into the style of the upwardly mobile office-worker, the local villain, and the suddenly prosperous professional footballer,[16] all overtly successful, visible masculine types. Indeed ex-Mods and skinheads appear to share remarkably uniform views on blacks.

> *Mick.* But the coons made it worse. Pakis never 'ave council places do they. They buy places; a bit shrewd. But the coons I could never stand them. When I was at school there weren't any at our school. Now there's no whites. My sister-in-law still lives there, and it's like a fucking jungle, the muggings and that.

The pop-art-inspired art-school graduates may well have been inspired by black culture, although Melly's comment that 'for us the whole coloured race was sacred', which is quoted by Hebdige (1979, p. 44), tells us much about the ability of the entertainment industry to exploit black culture and little about working-class subcultures.

Indigenous black culture had little effect on working-class subcultures until the skinhead emerged. Hebdige's comments on the fusion of black and white youth cultures have more credence today, where white emulation of black style and argot are increasingly attractive to whites, who for the first time lack successful, accessible models of masculinity within their parent culture.

The 'rapport' that Hebdige (1979, pp. 53–4) refers to between black immigrant culture and white youth was negligible in the early to mid-1960s and while he quotes a Mod as claiming to 'hero worship the spades', the 'spades' were American, and Phil Cohen's upward option was not to be found in Wolfe's mystical 'noonday underground', but in the pubs along the Mile End Road where 'the chaps', the successful and not-so-successful villains, immaculately attired, could flaunt the work-ethic by boozing lunch-time, or anytime. Indeed, some of the pubs most popular with young people in the early to mid-1960s had close connections with the thriving East London underworld of that era.

> *Mick.* Mostly Black Boys, Green Gate, Bethnal Green, Globe, all them . . .
> we used to do all the usual pubs with a bit of music.

As style is inherited, so a specific youthful adaptation of working-class culture should be viewed as an exploration of the masculine options that are made available by the parent culture. Stylistically, youthful manifestations of working-class male culture survive the individual's adaptation to the labour market. The crucial point is reached when the consumer pressure of the youth market is relocated and a realistic accommodation to the labour market is made.

While Mick's various occupations can be seen to parallel Cohen's theoretical frame, the move from youth to adult life is not geared in all cases to conventional occupational choice. For many, the move out of youth marks a reaffirmation of a deviant identity that had been established in their teenage years. Bill had been involved in theft and serious violence throughout his youth. Shop-breaking, razor-fighting, and taking and driving away were regular occurrences. After he received a razor wound to his face his status among his peers was increased.

> *Bill.* Course then I do fancy myself with a nice stripe an' all. People used to look at me and think I was fucking Al Capone. If we was anywhere and there was a ruck I had to be upfront. (See Patrick 1973, pp. 40–7.)

Yet there was no real tension between Bill at his peak, and his parents. Bill was safe in the knowledge that 'the old man had been a bit of an evil bastard when he was young'. Bill's behaviour was 'normal', never contradictory to the parents' culture. Both youth and adult cultures informed and reinforced each other.

> *Bill.* I suppose he just thought I was feeling me way, . . . I used to go down the Peacock of a Sunday dinner, and he'd be in there with his brothers. They'd be talking about the good old days, and what he got up to in the army.

> One of his brothers was a real hound, got in with the Krays, shooters the lot. I remember once I was working on site, and this geezer, brickie, comes up and says 'you Johnnie Smith's boy?' So I says 'Yeah, what of it? Well he's about 40 and a bit tasty. So he says, 'Well your uncle Tom give me this', and he's got this stripe up his arm from here to here.

The essential continuity between the youthful Bill and the parent culture finally resulted in a fusion at the appropriate age of 21. While working as a builder's labourer, he was part of a 'team' that stole a quantity of sheepskin coats. The rest of the team were older and more experienced and he was paid £100 while the goods were 'put down' for a while. Bill was still owed £1000.

> *Bill.* After a couple of months me and two pals went in their drinker by Crisp Street, and I fronted them . . . and one of them says 'well if that's how you feel pal you'd better take it out of that' — you know points to his chin. So I stabbed 'im in the face . . . we managed to get out and Plod pulls us as we tried to get a cab.

Bill served three years' imprisonment. His move into adult theft and violence is of no more significance than Mick's move from plasterer to entrepreneurial shop-work. It is an adaptation to the realities of the market, an exploitative attempt at creating some measure of autonomy and achieving a lucrative reward for their endeavours. The extent of this element of autonomy, and the size of the reward, is not always made apparent by adopting a purely structural notion of class that regards the job-market as one-dimensional and static. Crime for Bill was a logical extension of his activities as a youth, and these activities were rational options that emerged from his inheritance as it was manifested in the tough macho world of the parent culture (see Patrick 1973, pp. 144–54). Mick's fiddles and fencing were entered into as extensions of the activities that the parent culture had informed him were normal. After exploring several options in his youth, he was able to express culturally defined, highly valued characteristics of autonomy and entrepreneurship.

Entrance to the East End's adult entrepreneurial world represents maturity. No longer 'magical', the adults' actions are firmly grounded in the problems that emerge from an individual's 'real' position on the labour market. The temporary appropriation of a style whose meaning is to be found by analysing youth-specific responses to the parent culture, gives way to the adoption of an entrepreneurial style that incorporates an assimilation of the entire stock of knowledge that represents the cultural precedence of working-class heritage. In East London this results in a rational and imaginative response to capitalism.

Early dealing

All respondents appeared to have shown considerable entrepreneurial promise at any early age. Mick in particular showed early indications of possessing the type of business acumen that was later to make him one of the most successful and discreet fences of stolen paint in East London. At the age of 14 Mick sold newspapers for three hours, four nights a week after school, while one night and all day Saturday he worked on a market stall selling seafood. Sundays were not wasted, as he toured the streets, pushing a hand cart.

> *Mick.* Crabs, prawns, whelks, roll-mops, everything. We'd go round ringing a bell and shouting our fucking heads off.

Much of his income, then as now, was 'fiddled'.

> *Mick.* For Friday and Saturday I used to get £2 for the market job. Sunday we'd get £3 each, which was good money. Plus we used to eat loads of prawns as we was going round, and we always had ten bob and a crab, and a couple of pints of prawns each. So Friday and Saturday I got, including fiddles, say £5. 10s.

This process of inheritance which informs individuals of the availability and viability of such practices, takes place via the oral culture generated by the immediate environment. This knowledge is transmitted by word of mouth and is highly valued as it is passed on.

> *Mick.* But the papers were the best, 'cos the fiddles I used to work with the van-boys. The bloke who did it before me told me about it and I sort of handed it down to the next kid when I left. I used to get £3 off the bloke whose pitch it was, and I was getting £5 out of the fiddle. (See Ditton 1977, p. 42.)

Mick's total income while still at school was over £5 more than his weekly wage when he entered full-time employment. This solid grounding in entrepreneurial activity is common to all generations of East Londoners. In Mick's case the uniqueness of his inheritance can, on an obvious level, be attributed to the East End's geographical location in relation to the print industry where his fiddle with the 'van-boys' originated, and from the local demand for seafood without which there would have been no market for him to exploit. However, on a wider level, the unique diversity of the area's economic base has created a precedent for individualistic action in pursuit of pecuniary reward outside the conventional contract implied by an employer–employee relationship.

Sixty-six-year-old Charlie was born into a family of costers. However, a family argument resulted in his father entering the clothing trade, but he did work on the stalls at the weekend.

> *Charlie.* It was like someone lifted a cloud off him . . . The weekend kept him going.

Charlie had done part-time jobs since he was very young.

> *Charlie.* Us kids, we always earnt money. We was always out after anyway of earning. . . I used to help the toffee-apples man . . . then when the carters came back we'd take the 'orses back to the stables. Then there was the tobacco company. It was when the big strike was on. I was only a tot, and they would throw out the big barrels . . . we'd smash-em up bundle-em up, and sell-em for firewood. If you got a shilling, well a shilling was worth pounds.

Charlie's childhood endeavours also helped formulate his adult entrepreneurial career. He went on to inherit a body of knowledge in the form of both legal and illegal practices that earned him a reasonable living throughout his working life. He was able to achieve a high degree of autonomy in his working day that can be regarded as directly attributable to his cultural inheritance and the explorations of his youth.

I am not suggesting that subculture membership forms a basis for long-term solutions to class-specific problems. Rather it is argued that the adult and youth cultures have a symbiotic relationship, each informing the other, transmitting, receiving, and interpreting information, before modifying the content and transmitting back. It is through this process of symbiosis that capitalism, in essence an exploitative and oppressive regime, might be negotiated.

Youth prepares individuals for the labour market, and youth is constantly informed about appropriate behaviour by the parent culture. Upon maturation and establishment on the labour market, the experimentations of youth are sifted and sorted, and specific central issues located in youth are brought to bear and utilized in adult life (Becker 1964, p. 52). In this way men can be seen to be both carriers and creators of culture. The culture changes, but alterations are carried out by individuals with a powerful sense of history, insulated from intrusive middle-class cultural influences, but vulnerable to the whims of the market and the mobility of capital.

The entrepreneurial model offers the East-Ender a way of maintaining the vitality of youthful experimentation, while constructing a strategy that does not threaten the existence of capitalism but makes it considerably more bearable. The essence of this strategy is to be found 'in the subtle manipulation of everyday life rather than in the dramatic or revolutionary gesture' (Cohen and Taylor 1976).

The symbiotic relationship between the youthful and adult world is a crucial stage in a continual adaptive response to alterations in the economic ecology of an area, and the stylistic forms that are readily observable within the relationship represent sensitizing devices that function to explore possibilities for action within an expanding environment. These stylistic formats explore past experiences as well as present interactions, and as a consequence tease out both those possibilities for action set by cultural precedent and those set by current and prospective interactions.

The common characteristics that structure possibilities for communal action in East London are autonomy, independence, and entrepreneurship — tried and tested adaptive responses to the marketplace.

Notes

1. Cohen (1972). Cohen also mentions 'the markets', but he fails to elaborate on what is meant by the term 'markets'. Whether this refers to the street-markets that proliferate in the area or to specialized wholesale institutions such as Billingsgate and Spitalfields, is not made clear. Consequently I shall avoid speculative analysis and concentrate on the docks and craft trades.

2. Samuel (1981 p. 97). Arthur Harding notes that the furniture trade was a family affair. 'You brought up your family to do it.'

3. Harding also indicates the expansion in the furniture trade: 'A bedroom suite was the first furniture I bought when I got married in 1924, to keep the clothes clean of bugs.' He also notes that: 'Wardrobes were practically unknown when I was a child. You put the same things on the next day. It was a question of sticking them on a chair when you went to bed of a night. If you had any best clothes you kept them in the pawnshop' (Samuel 1981, p. 199).

4. Throughout the 1960s Reggie and Ronnie Kray and their associates were rich, successful, respected, and most importantly, conspicuous manifestations of private enterprise, certainly more approachable and immitable than other local doyens of capitalism of that era such as Lord Vestey, or the chairman of Tate and Lyle. However, since most of the 'firm' were arrested in May 1968, local villains have tended to specialize and maintain low profiles and, on becoming successful, move out of the area, usually to suburban Essex.

5. Brake (1980, pp 148–54) has pointed out that while subcultures are used to establish one's gender, the stress on masculinity makes subcultural membership essentially one-sided. Brake continues to argue that within a patriarchal society male-bonding, and the exaggeration of masculinity, are essential strategies in maintaining power over women, while distancing themselves from what are regarded as the restrictions of domesticity.

6. The militant attitudes of dock-workers, and London dockers in particular, are noted by Hill (1976, pp 103–8) The disputes of the late 1960s, however, were of a particularly aggressive and occasionally spectacular nature, a case in point being the attempts by dockers to impose 'scheme' conditions of work to Chobham Farm container depot. A full blow-by-blow account of these disputes can be found in *The Dockworker, 1968–70*.

7. In April 1968, Enoch Powell gave a speech on race relations that prophesized racial warfare and called for repatriation. Powell was sacked from the Tory Shadow Cabinet and the first demonstration of support from the electorate came in the form of a march by London dockers to stake the claim of 'Enoch for PM'. While only a small proportion of the work-force took part, the dockers were one of the few groups with the self-confidence and motivation to demonstrate a point of view that, according to Schoen (1970, p. 37) was shared by between two-thirds and three-quarters of the electorate.

8. Employment figures indicate that unemployment remained steady from 1961 to 1966 and, 'With two brief intermissions have gone up every year since then'. David Donnison, ex-director of the Supplementary Benefits Commission in *New Society,* 22 Jan. 1981, p. 153. See also *Social Trends* 1981, Table 5.16 (Unemployment).

9. The benefits reaped by decasualization were, however, short-lived. From 1967 to 1970, 7,085 jobs were lost, and considerable sums were being paid in severance payments as inducements to those wishing to leave the industry. Those dockers whose length of service did not warrant an acceptable severance payment transferred to Tilbury; as a consequence East London lost an entire generation of dockers and their attendant skills and traditional work-practices. This occupational inheritance had fostered a tangible and pervasive historical perspective among dock-workers, as was noted by a pre-Devlin Official Report which stated, 'few industries are so burdened with the legacy of the past. We have been struck by the extent to which many facets have to be understood against the background of history. Practices and attitudes can often be traced back a long way; old traditions die hard' (Report of a Committee of Inquiry into the Major Ports of Great Britain (1962)).

    There was massive investment in the 'super scab ports' (*The Dockworker* 1973, no. 15) such as Felixstowe and Colchester. Employers had a free hand in these ports; for instance any dangerous cargoes such as asbestos and bone-meal that would have provoked a flurry of wage and conditions negotiations in London, were unloaded in unregistered ports by unorganized casual labour at great personal risk.

    The ability of the employers to transfer capital to the smaller unregistered ports is demonstrated by the increased tonnage both containerized and general cargo at one port, Felixstowe. In 1967, the year that Devlin was implemented, Felixstowe's total tonnage was 1,242,678 tons and by 1970 this figure had nearly doubled to 2,259,981 tons.

10. Lord Vestey, the chairman of Scruttons Maltby Ltd., one of the docks' major employers was a particularly unpopular individual with London's dockers. His regular clashes with unions and individual dockers led to his private telephone number being published in *The Dockworker* and an obscene picture of him being circulated among his employees.

11. In the late 1960s 'Dr Martens' cost about £5 a pair.

12. Phil Cohen's model of a declining social structure, despite my misgivings concerning his treatment of the docks, is an invaluable study.

13. Two publications that feature pictures of American servicemen looking like Canning Town skinheads are: *G.I.s Speak out Against the War* by Fred Halstead (New York: Merit 1970, pp. 2 and 10) and *War*, ed. by A. Leventhal (London: Hamlyn 1973, pp. 224–51).

14. S Cohen (1980, p. 30) notes that the key texts remain A.K. Cohen (1955); R. Cloward and L. Ohlin (1960); and D.M. Downes (1966).

15. J. Young in Cohen (1971. p. 32) notes the self-instigatory nature of the middle-class Bohemian's existence.

16. I. Taylor in Cohen (1971, pp. 134–64) notes the change in status within the working-class community for professional footballers that came with the abolition of the maximum wage in 1961.

The Labelling Approach

16. Misunderstanding Labelling Perspectives
Ken Plummer

The past decade has seen striking changes in the prominence given to sociological theories of deviance. Most notable is the changing status that has been accorded to labelling theory. Whilst far from new[1], in the early sixties it was seen as a radical, underground theory, attracting the 'young Turks' of sociology who used it as a basis for developing critiques of the dominant paradigms in deviancy analysis. By the late sixties (in America at any rate),[2] the theory had been co-opted into the mainstream of sociological work — enshrined in formal statements, texts, readers and Ph.D. theses, taught widely on undergraduate sociology and criminology programmes, and absorbed into much 'positivistic' social research (cf. Cole, 1975; Spector, 1976). This acceptance of the theory has been followed most recently by the growth of criticism of it from a number of contrasting perspectives, most notably ideologues who are critical of its biases, limitations and liberal assumptions (e.g., Manders, 1975), and 'positivistic' researchers who find it empirically falsified (e.g., Gove, 1975). In just ten years, labelling theory has moved from being the radical critic of established orthodoxies to being the harbinger of new orthodoxies to be criticised. Yet as one recent defender so forcefully put it:

> The sheer volume of the critics could easily lead one to presume that labelling theory is dead and already buried. But when the criticisms are considered one at a time labelling theory emerges as a still lively and viable theory. Indeed, to the extent that the criticisms call for clarification and specification of the theory it may be fairly claimed that labelling theory is strengthened by going through the process of challenge and response. The volume of criticisms may be seen as a tribute to the power of the theory. (Conover, 1976. p, 229)

In this article, I wish to consider some of these criticisms that have engulfed labelling theory in recent years and to show that they have far from succeeded in dealing the death blow to it. I will begin by considering precisely what labelling theory is, and will argue that it is most usefully conceived as a perspective *whose core problems are the nature, emergence, application and consequences of labels*. I will suggest that there can be many differing theoretical approaches within this perspective, and will go on to argue that the failure to be precise about the kind of theory one is using has led to many confusions. Symbolic interactions is only one such theory, and hence criticisms of such a theory should not be seen as synonomous with criticisms of labelling theory. My own preference, however, is for an interactionist theory of labelling; my subsequent comments will therefore be erecting a dual defence.

Ken Plummer: 'Misunderstanding Labelling Perspectives' in *DEVIANT INTERPRETATIONS*, edited by D. Downes and P. Rock (Martin Robertson, 1979), pp. 85–121. Reprinted by permission of Basil Blackwell Limited.

The main body of the discussion will then centre on three clusters of criticism: the charge of *confusion* especially over definitional and value problems; the charge of *bias and limitations*; and the charge that the theory has been shown to be *empirically falsified*. My goal throughout is to clarify the foundations of the labelling perspective so that it may continue to grow as a most fruitful approach to the study of deviance.

What is 'labelling' — a perspective, a theory or a proposition?

Because the labelling perspective is seen alternately and simultaneously as a perspective, a theory and a proposition, it becomes an easy target for attack and a ready refuge for defence: it is all things to all men. In looking at this muddle, I will identify those sociologists most commonly viewed as labelling theorists, locate their views on the nature of the theory, consider why confusions arise and propose some standardisation of terms.

First, who are the labelling theorists?[3] In a review of twenty standard books and articles at hand, I found four groups of theorists referred to as labelling theorists:

(a) Becker and Lemert — mentioned by nearly everyone;

(b) Tannenbaum, Kitsuse and Erickson — mentioned by well over half;

(c) Goffman, Schur, Garfinkel and Scheff — given between six and eight references each;

(d) a diverse sprinkling of names referred to only once or twice — Matza, Waller, Platt, Lofland, Lorber, Simmons, Sudnow, Piliavin and Briar, Cicourel and Quinney.

Now if one takes this list as representative, it is clear that 'labelling' can only be a perspective; there is no unanimous proposition that these writers are testing (cf. Erickson (1966) on issues of boundary maintenance; Becker (1963) on moral enterprise and deviant careers; Schur (1963) on victimless crimes; Platt (1969) on the historical origins of delinquency categories; Wilkins (1964) on deviancy amplification; Matza (1969) on techniques of neutralisation and signification; Piliavin and Briar (1964) on the screening process), and there is considerable theoretical diversity — functionalism (Erickson), dramaturgy (Goffman), phenomenology and the sociology of law (Quinney), systems theory (Wilkins and Scheff), naturalism (Matza), interactionism (Becker) and ethnomethodology (Kitsuse and Garfinkel).[4] The same conclusion is reached by looking at both the main exponents of labelling theory, Lemert and Becker. Neither restricts his analysis to a major proposition, and while one is a symbolic interactionist, the other is only reservedly so (Lemert, 1967, p. v; 1974). On this score, then, 'labelling' is a perspective, which raises a series of problems and suggests a few themes.

Further, none of the theorists above actually began by identifying himself as a labelling theorist: rather ironically, they had that label thrust upon them by others and only later came to incorporate it into their own sociological identities (cf. Kitsuse, 1972; Goode, 1975). Thus neither Becker nor Lemert seems at all happy with being identified as a labelling theorist; neither used this tag in his earlier work. Indeed, by the early 1970s Becker was publicly stating his preference for being known as an interactionist rather than a labelling theorist (Becker, 1974). p. 44), while Lemert was disassociating himself from the 'conceptual extrusions' and 'crudities' of labelling theory (Lemert, 1972, p. 6). Goode's review of the field also concludes that Becker and Lemert (as well as Erickson and Kitsuse) cannot be called labelling theorists (Goode, 1975, p. 571). It is important to stress both this lack of self-recognition by labelling theorists and their diverse theoretical concerns: *for the labelling perspective has only emerged from the retrospective selection of a few select themes largely from diverse theoretical projects.* They are united by some common substantive problems but not common theories. There are often much wider discrepancies than overlaps. Erickson's brand of functionalism can hardly be equated with Cicourel's ethnomethodology, while Lemert's focus on putative deviation (which implies a non-putative or objective deviance) jars markedly with Kitsuse's relativistic 'imputed deviance' (which denies an objective reality of deviance) (cf. Rains, 1976).

What are these common substantive problems? Becker suggests the following: 'We [should] direct our attention in research and theory building to the questions: who applied the label of deviant to whom? What consequences does the application of a label have for the person so labelled? Under what circumstances is the label of a deviant successfully applied? (Becker, 1964, p. 3).

While these questions have certainly received much attention from labelling theorists in recent years, they are unnecessarily narrow (and in practice Becker dealt with a wider range of problems). Since the theme of the tradition is 'labels' we should seek to discover all that we can about this phenomenon and not just a limited portion. Basically, therefore, labelling theory should centre on asking:

1. What are the *characteristics* of labels, their variations and forms?

2. What are the *sources* of labels, both societally and personally?

3. How, and under what *conditions,* do labels get applied?

4. What are the *consequences* of labelling?

All would seem clear: the labelling perspective constitutes neither theory nor proposition, but is a useful series of problems designed to reorientate the former mainstream study to the consideration of the *nature, emergence, application,* and *consequences* of deviancy labels. Yet it remains unclear because of (i) the confusions of labelling proponents themselves, and (ii) the narrow orientation for their critics.

Labelling proponents have added to the confusion by either rejecting the tag of labelling theorist or by seeking to co-opt it into one narrow kind of theoretical stance. Since their first allegiance was never to a reified, academic 'labelling theory', but to 'social control processes', 'interactionism', etc., they have not seen fit to defend it. Thus Lemert equates labelling theory with interactionism, and sees his own intellectual task as altogether more eclectic (Lemert, 1972, p. 6; Lemert, 1974); while Becker equates the general orientation with interactionism, and then opts to call it 'an interactionist theory of deviance' (Becker, 1974, p. 44). So for these writers labelling theory is not an orientation; rather, it is synonymous with interactionism. But if this is so, we cannot include Lemert, Erickson, Garfinkel, Scheff, Matza or Cicourel so clearly under that banner anymore. Schur, who also views it as an orientation embracing different theories (phenomenology, conflict, functionalism, and prediction theory), seems to assume an interactionist base.[5] But if it is an orientating series of problems, it does not have to entail a commitment to one theory. The problems of labelling may be dealt with by Marxists, ethnomethodologists, functionalists or positivists, there is no endemic link to interactionsm, and it is interactionist imperialism to suggest otherwise.

More muddling than labelling theorists themselves are critics of the theory. While most vaguely acknowledge labelling to be a conception, the attacks are actually levied either at its interactionist base (e.g., Taylor, Walton and Young, 1973a; Gouldner, 1968; Warren and Johnson, 1972) or at a narrow proposition attributed to it (e.g., Mankoff, 1971; Davis, 1972). Of the four problems I have mentioned above, critics usually focus primarily upon only *one* possible answer to the third and fourth questions — the independent and dependent variable issue (cf. Gove, 1975). They suggest that labelling theory may be characterised by the following proposition 'that societal reaction in the form of labelling or official typing, and consequent stigmatisation, leads to an altered identity in the actor, necessitating a reconstitution of the self' (Davis, 1972, p. 460); Or: 'Rule breakers become entrenched in deviant roles because they are labelled deviant by others and are consequently excluded from resuming normal roles in the community' (Mankoff, 1971, p. 204); or, most crudely: 'People go about minding their own business, and then 'wham', bad society comes along and slaps them with a stigmatising label. Forced into the role of deviant, the individual has little choice but to be deviant' (Akers, 1973, p.24).

Through these propositions, labelling theory is vulgarised into a narrow theory which can be readily refuted. It can be easily shown that many people become 'deviants' without being directly labelled by others (cf. Mankoff, 1971; Becker, 1963, ch. 3), or are labelled because of their behaviour and not merely because of the contingencies that surround them (cf. Williams and Weinberg, 1971). Yet any criticism based upon this limited view is grossly unfair, because it tends to suggest that labelling theory is concerned with labelling that is overt, public, direct and unrelated to the act: and this is simply not the case. It is true that a few studies have *implied* this kind of limited argument (e.g., Scheff, 1966), and that some illustrations have been unfortunate (e.g., Malinowski, 1926) in Becker, 1963, but in general labelling theorists do recognise a multiplicity of answers to the problems of the conditions and consequences of labelling. Thus, for example, even the classic writings are not guilty of all that has been attributed to them. Becker's own statement of 'marijuana use and social control' does not deal with matters of formal control, as labelling critics would have us believe. As Paul Rock astutely notes: [6]

> Becker's becoming a marijuana user dealt entirely with its significance to the self. It had no reference to official control, but concentrated instead on the way in which significance was built up introspectively. I have always found that critics have neglected this basic article, and persistently misread the significance of the self-identifying activity.

In addition to these classic statements, there is now much writing on the issue of self-labelling and deviance avowal (cf. Turner, 1972; Rock, 1973a; Rotenberg, 1974; Levitin, 1975); of neutralising deviance labels (e.g., Ball, 1966; Reiss, 1962; Rains, 1971; Warren, 1974b); of changing deviance labels (e.g., Lofland, 1969; Trice and Roman, 1970); and of labelling as a means of preventing as opposed to accelerating deviance (e.g., Cameron, 1964; Thorsell and Klemke, 1972; Tittle, 1975). Recently Rogers and Buffalo have furthered this kind of work by delineating nine possible adaptations of deviance to deviant labels — thereby reinforcing the view that people don't *have* to become deviant because of labelling, and furthering the sophistication of the labelling paradigm (Rogers and Buffalo, 1974).

The labelling perspective and the search for theoretical purity

Labelling, then, should not be equated with a theory or a proposition but should be seen as a perspective in deviancy research. And because of this it can harbour several diverse theoretical positions. There is thus a great potential for the perspective to contain theoretical contradictions, and to be eligible for criticisms from all theoretical sides. Incompatible theories may get welded together. They may also be pitted against each other. Thus, as an illustration of the first point, interactional sociologists may use a drift-voluntaristic model to explain primary deviance, whilst succumbing occasionally to a deterministic, over-socialised conception of the actor in looking at secondary deviance (Broadbent, 1974); as illustration of the second, phenomenological sociologists can find much in labelling which violates the canons of their theoretical work. Seeking to take seriously the examination of 'meanings of morality and immorality as acted out in every day life' (Warren and Johnson, 1972, p. 70),[7] they argue that labellists have been too behaviourist and not taken these meanings seriously enough. Yet for critical criminologists it is precisely these concerns which are viewed disapprovingly. Thus, Taylor, Walton and Young wish to move away from the relativistic idealism of labelling into analyses which pay proper attention to 'structured inequality in power and interest which underpin the processes whereby the laws are created and enforced' (Taylor *et al*, 1973, p. 68). They wish to move away from a microscopic concern with those who are labelled and those who apply labels to build a fully social (and grand) theory of crime. They eschew microscopic ethnography in favour of global assertion (cf. Manders, 1975). Now, which is it to be? Is the labelling perspective voluntaristic or deterministic, behavioural or idealistic? Since it harbours within it diverse theories, it can, of course, be both. Putting the problem more generally, the labelling perspective generates some of the oldest dilemmas in sociological theory: how to weld analyses of the structural with those of the situational; how to reconcile phenomenonalism with essentialism, absolutism with relativism, idealism with materialism, formalism with *Verstehen;* and how to abstract and generalise without reification. Imbedded in the labelling perspective are the unresolved tensions of generations of social theorists. How they may be resolved, or at least how working resolutions may be obtained between them, remains a major issue for those working in the labelling perspective.

Illustrative of one kind of resolution is that provided by Rock, but it is a resolution which only a phenomenalism or interactionism-inclined sociologist could favour. Taking the intellectual claims of phenomenalism seriously, and seeing phenomenalism as a major motif of the new deviancy perspectives, he charts some of the tensions that I have located above. That is, he notes a tension between the *essentialism* found in the formalism of interactional sociologists, the deep rules of ethnomethodologists and the structural theories of Marxists, and the *phenomenalism* found in theories of *Verstehen* and the contextual analysis of interactional sociologists. The reconciliation of notions of structure with those of meaning is proposed through a focus on the actor's definition of structure:

> I shall argue that a systematic description of commonsense ideas of social structure affords the sociologist of deviance access to areas which have previously been denied him. This description will offer him the materials upon which a phenomenological analysis of social structure can be built. For instance, he will be able to explore the import of such phenomena as social class without committing himself to the belief that social class is an autonomous or 'real' entity. (Rock, 1973b, p. 19)

Such a solution hardly resolves the basic dilemma of whether there is a 'real world' out there, and it keeps Rock tottering on the brink of solipsism. Nevertheless, from his point of view it is a consistent way in which to cope with problems of structure and could give rise to one version of labelling theory fully grounded on phenomenalism. Alternative versions of labelling could also be constructed by those who seek a more essentialist and/or structural account, in which, presumably, some absolutist notion of deviancy will ultimately have to be imported. Since the labelling perspective contains a variety of theories, these need to be rendered explicit and consistent.

Symbolic interactionism and labelling theory: an aside

Although it is only one of several possible theories that could be applied to problems of labelling, symbolic interactionism has the closest affinity with labelling theory. Its central problem — the construction of meaning — is clearly closely allied to problems of labels. Indeed, many of the criticisms that are levied at labelling theory are in fact directed towards symbolic interactionism. Since Paul Rock has defended the symbolic interactionists' account of deviance at length elsewhere [in this volume], it would serve no useful purpose to produce an extended discussion of the symbolic interactionists' enterprise here. I would, however, like to digress from my main arguments and make a few suggestions of my own.

The interactionist's distinctive view of the social world — a view which is quite unlike that of any other sociology or psychology — can be seen as a fusion of several intellectual (sometimes anti-intellectual) traditions, such as pragmatism, formalism, romanticism, mild libertarianism and humanism.[8] Taken collectively, such traditions focus upon the never-ending flow of emerging experience. The human being is both subject and object. The importance is stressed of the localised setting and context, the uncertainty of knowledge and the ambiguity and fragility of meaning — as well as the inexorable tension between the shapeless stream of human life and the shaping structures of the wider society. The intellectual traditions which have given rise to interactionism are important to understand as, without such comprehension, interactionism can easily be seen as a lightweight, passing, theoretical fad of the affluent sixties rather than as a well-established position flowing from strong philosophical arguments. Many of the criticisms made of interactionism in fact rest upon a misunderstanding of the interactionist problematic and a shallow comprehension of its philosophical background. They assume that because interactionism looks at certain theoretical problems while ignoring others, studies certain topics at the expense of others, and uses certain methodologies rather than others, it could only be doing this through ignorance and not reason. There are many criticisms of interactionism derived from postures which are radically different but from which it is assumed that the critics' position is unquestionably superior. Given adequate knowledge, we would all be structuralists or behaviourists, we would all study politics and the class structure and we would all use historical or quantitative methods. The intellectual enterprise is thus rendered closed and monolithic.

Yet the philosophical foundations of interactionism portray a world which is markedly at odds with the absolutism of structuralists, Marxists, positivistic criminologists and the like. Viewed collectively, pragmatism, formalism, romanticism, libertarianism and humanism have played an important formative role in the shaping of a distinctive interactive vision of the social world. Highlighting the endless flux of human experience, welded and shaped through the transforming power of synthetic *a priori* categorisation, and focusing upon the dereified phenomenal world where knowledge is always limited and uncertain, the interactionists have come to portray an image that is at odds with most other academic theories. It is not, thus, a vision that many academics or sociologists can be content with, since it brings in its wake a strong anti-intellectual commitment, totters frequently on the brink of self-defeating arguments and seems to revel in a multitude of irresolvable paradoxes.

The anti-intellectualism is a product of the commitment that reality is inexhaustible, that the noumena can never be grasped and that the only firm flowing truth is that which emerges in the local situated experience: abstract, analytic reasoning and global theorising that attempts to grasp absolute transcendental truths, or vast classificatory edifices that are not firmly anchored in experienced life have no room in the interactionist scheme of things. Yet such a position — while cumulatively sponsored and often well argued — leads to a number of tottering paradoxes. It is difficult to conduct intellectual work on a foundation which denies its very possibility.

Thus interactionists might want to defend their position with abstract philosophical reasoning, but the very possibility of this is denied them by their pragmatist heritage. They may wish to produce systematic codified statements of their theory, but the very possibility of this is denied them by their phenomenalist heritage. They may wish to generalise, even produce universal statements, but the value of this is questioned by the romantic base of their position. They may wish to be messianic, absolute, imperial propagandists of an élite interactionist expertise, but their libertarianism forces them to a piecemeal eclecticism. They may wish to be objective external observers of the world, but their humanistic bent constantly hurls them towards the subject and the possibility of solipsism. The paradoxes of the interactionist heritage are great indeed. Interactionists have to live with contradiction and ambiguity, knowing that any argument they make could be self-defeating.

It is not surprising, given this, that interactionism has generally been seen as a marginal theory within sociology and that interactionists have often been 'marginal men'. For much of its history it has been submerged in an oral tradition, lacking the formalisation and proselytisation that accompanies most other theories. Only recently have texts and readers been spawned, but these have emerged alongside the tradition of phenomenology which seems almost instantly to have superseded it. The Mullinses, in their admittedly curious study, 'Theory Groups in American Sociology', could actually say by 1973 that 'it is clear that the original ideas that developed within symbolic interactionism have run their course intellectually and socially. As a change maker and general orientation for sociology and as the loyal opposition to structural functionalism however it has come to an end' (Mullins and Mullins, 1973, p. 96).

Grounded in ambiguity and contradiction, floundering in irony and paradox, lacking a strong formal training ground, built by 'marginal men' and now given the death wish, it is amazing that interactionism has managed to survive at all. But is has, and I personally hope that it will continue to do so even in the face of criticisms from all sides and from within. Its view of the world may be quirky and its contradictions may be intellectually unsatisfying; it may find few sympathisers willing to stay with it for long — it is a phase one may pass through on their way to loftier enterprises. But — even in the face of all that — the interactionist does continue to provide an alternative vision of the world. It is a necessary and radical, though modest, counterbalance to most traditions of thought. Its final irony is that whilst it is consistently rejected as a valid approach to the world in academic writing, it is consistently acknowledged, most of the time, in our daily lives. The problematic meaning, ambiguity and flux which is the focal concern of interactionist thought is also the focal concern of many lives. It gels with empirical reality. Thus while interactionism may never be a dominant sociology, it has much to offer as a subversive tradition of thought within mainstream sociology (cf. Rock, forthcoming).

Two general problems in labelling and deviance theory

Before looking at some of the major limitations and biases which critics have levied at the labelling perspective, it would be useful to examine two objections which are not so much criticisms of labelling theory *per se* but problems to be found throughout the whole of the sociology of deviance. The two matters I refer to are, first, the problematic nature of defining deviance and, second, the problem of values. I will deal with each in turn.

The problem of definition

One major set of muddles occurs over the problem of defining deviance. The main source of these muddles is Becker's own classic statement (1963) where he starts his discussion of outsiders by first dispensing critically with definitions of deviance that evoke statistical, pathological or dysfunctional criteria before going on to suggest his own: 'Deviance is not a quality of the act a person commits, but rather a consequence of the application by others of rules and sanctions to an offender' (Becker, 1963, p.9). That he does not see deviance as *solely* the manufactured product of societal responses is demonstrated a few pages later, when he introduced his equally famous typology of deviance, using the additional yardstick of rule violation. Thus, combining rule violation with society responses, the following typology is produced (ex. Becker, 1963, p.20):

	Obedient behaviour	Rule breaking behaviour
Perceived as deviant	Falsely accused	Pure deviant
Not perceived as deviant	Conforming	Secret deviant

Now, locked within Becker's definition and typology are muddles indeed, some of which Becker himself addressed in a recent paper (Becker, 1974). What are the muddles, and how may they be resolved?

First, and most simple, it is argued that Becker has not provided a definition of deviance at all. As Sagarin noted:

> Becker's statement is not a definition and should not be confused with one. It merely delineates the self-other process by which the placing of a person, or a group of persons, in the category of deviant is made, but it fails to note the characteristics that deviants have in common, and those which are utilised by oneself and others to give persons that label. (Sagarin, 1967, p.9).[9]

Thus it is possible to say the same things as Becker about almost any other form of behaviour: conformity is behaviour that people so label, silliness is behaviour that people so label, and beauty is a state that people so label. Without specifying the criteria by which such labels can be recognised, the statement of Becker's remains a vacuous tautology.

This criticism is not so valid of other labelling theorists. For example, Lemert utilises a conception of deviance which straddles the statistical and the norm violation (Lemert, 1951, p.27). Further, some work has devoted attention to the problem of the contents of deviant labels, the criteria used being such as (a) essentialist themes and (b) stigmatising or devalued meanings (Scott, 1970).

A second line of criticism suggests that labelling theory is 'relativistic in the extreme' (Gibbs, 1966, p.10). Since nothing is intrinsically deviant, anything could be called deviant and nothing has to be. By this argument, child molesters, strippers, dwarfs or 'flat earthers' may be called normal if one so chooses, and routine marriage, hard work and average intelligence may be called deviant. Nothing is deviant but naming makes it so.

Now there are several real advantages of such an approach. It highlights the ambiguity of a world no longer divided into a series of neat types, the black and the white, the good and the bad, the normal and the mad: the continuity between normality and deviancy is stressed. It opens up the field of inquiry so that it is possible to discuss a range of areas hitherto neglected — blindness (Scott, 1969), subnormality (Mercer, 1973), fatness (Maddox, Black and Liedermann, 1968), and interpersonal relationships (Denzin, 1970) — thereby enabling both the foundations for a formal theory of deviance as a social property and a method for understanding the routine and the regular through the eyes of the ruptured and the irregular. And it provides the potential for a constant challenge to hitherto taken-for-granted categories and an impetus for a radical definition of those categories supported by master institution of power.

Yet this enlarging of the field has not been without difficulties. Most notably, it flies in the face of empirical reality, where we commonsensically know that some acts are more deviant than others. Deviance as a social category, and as opposed to a sociological category, is simply not as variable as the labelling theorists often seem to imply. As Taylor, Walton and Young say:

> Our objection to one assumption of the societal reaction position is this: we do not act in a world free of social meaning. With the exception of entirely new behaviour, it is clear to most people which actions are deviant and which are not deviant . . . We would assert that *most deviant behaviour is a quality of the act,* since the way we distinguish between *behaviour* and *action* is that behaviour is merely physical and action has meaning that is socially given.
>
> (Taylor *et al.* 1975a, p. 147).

What these writers assert is that behaviour is embedded in wider social contexts composed of systems of meaning which are pre-given: they cannot be neatly wished away. These contexts of meanings provide the resources out of which members fashion their interpretations of given behaviour, and are far from being capable of instant transformation. Thus, for example, in this culture 'everybody knows' that murder is illegal, that homosexuality is at least different and that blindness is a handicap. Our routine contexts simply do not permit us to say that murder, homosexuality or blindness are 'normal' and to argue such a case is to commit sociological mystification.

A second problem arising from the labelling theoreticians' relativism argues that their relativism notwithstanding, their work is directed at fields which are in fact commonly recognised as deviant: despite all disclaimers, it remains true that sociologists of deviance study strippers, drug users and criminals and not more mundane activities (Liazios, 1972). Their relativism is dishonest, since their work is informed by absolute categories commonly sensed as deviant. And closely allied to the above, the point is made that their work often serves to reinforce the apartness and 'deviantness' of certain groups (cf. Lofland, 1969). By studying the mentally ill as deviant, the sociologist tacitly concurs with public definitions of deviance. Further, when such categorisation is also combined with the sociologist's insistence on ambiguity or relativism, he may not only *reinforce* existing categories of deviance but also *create* new ones. Any work the sociologist of deviance performs is likely either to reinforce labels of deviance or to create new ones.

A third (now standard) definition muddle arises from Becker's typology cited earlier, in which there arise logically contradictory cells. More specifically, given Becker's relativistic, definitional approach to deviance, it is hard to see how two categories on his typology can exist. For if deviance is a matter of identifying and labelling, then clearly there can be no 'secret deviance' or 'falsely accused'. It is not possible to have people called 'deviant' who are not so identified, and it is not possible to have people called 'non-deviant' who are not so identified. There can only, therefore, be deviants and non-deviants.

Now all three of the criticisms outlined above pose problems (cf. Kitsuse, 1972; Becker, 1974; Gibbs, 1972; Pollner, 1974). Basically, the problems stem from a need to reconcile the irreconcilable: how to blend an absolutist conception of deviance with a relativist one. There are a number of ways in which such a tension might be partially resolved, depending upon one's theoretical posture. The solution that I feel most easy with is to define deviance as a conceptual field within sociology (not the social world) that is marked out by two criteria: that of rule violation and that of the imputation (by self or others) of stigma and devaluation. The issue of rule violation leads to the problems of which rules and whose rules — which in turn leads to the analytic distinction between *societal* and *situational* deviance. By *societal deviance* I refer in a shorthand way to those categories that are either (a) commonly sensed by most of society's members to *be* deviant, or (b) lodged in some abstract meanings,[10] such as the law or reified norms, and not to be wished away by individual members. Such deviance implies a high degree of consensus over the *identification* of the deviance, even if there is subsequently much dissention about the *appropriateness* of such a label. Thus it would be hard for anyone to say that being blind, committing armed robbery or being a transvestite were publicly acknowledged as 'normal events', even though it is clear that many people may view their designation as deviant to be utterly inappropriate. By *situational deviance* I am referring not to abstract meaning systems (perceived or real), but rather to the actual manner in which members of society go about the task of creating rules and interpreting rule violations as 'deviance' (although, of course, they would hardly use such a word) in *context*. Clearly, much of this rule making and deviancy interpretation will be contingent upon the abstract societal system I have located above. But the point remains that in situations members are freer to (i) neutralise or reject the societal version of deviance and (ii) construct rules and definitions at odds with those commonly sensed to belong to 'society'. While, in one sense, societal deviance steers towards absolute categories of deviance, situational deviance steers towards a more relativistic stance. Two examples may help to clarify some of these distinctions.

First, take the situation of routine, informal interaction on a production line (or any other conventional situation, such as routine marital interaction, peer interaction, or interaction in a club setting, etc.) (cf. Roy, 1954; Bryant, 1974, pt. 1). Such routinisation becomes possible through the co-ordination of conduct and the development of a network of tacit rules. Now, neither in society's minds nor in any dominant abstract system of values in society could such routine work be identified publicly as deviant. Routine work is not societal deviance. Yet it should also be clear that through the co-ordinated rule system, violation of such rules — or perception of violation — becomes a possibility. When such violation occurs — or is perceived as occurring — situational deviance emerges.

A second example can be drawn from the homosexual subculture (cf. Warren, 1974a). In this culture homosexuality must be viewed as societal deviance. All members of society must acknowledge (even if they strongly disagree) that homosexuality is commonly regarded as deviant; alternatively, it is hard to posit an objectified, abstract set of values in this society according to which homosexuality is not viewed as in some sense a marginal (sinful, sick, sad) state. Yet to acknowledge that homosexuality is societal deviance is not to acknowledge that it is situational deviance. Thus in situated contexts members of society or homosexuals themselves may create rules which normalise homosexuality. Homosexuality is no longer viewed as deviant. However, focusing for example, on the rule systems of the homosexual subculture, the violation (or perceived violation) of this system becomes a possibility. Homosexuals themselves may create a category of deviance within their own ranks. For instance, homosexuals may come to view the 'too camp and swish' role, the 'too straight' role, or the 'too promiscuous' role of other homosexuals as deviant. Here we have compounded complexity: societal deviance becomes 'normal' situation becomes situational deviance.

The problem of values

A major issue with any sociology of deviance must be its explicit awareness of the problem of values and, concomitantly, its own value bias. At least superficially, the labelling perspective fares well here. Most of the writings of labelling theorists seem to lack the moral disapproval of sociologists of earlier decades, and many of their writings devote space to the value debate (e.g., Becker, 1963, 1964, 1967, 1974). However, while it may be unfair to accuse the labellists of lacking awareness of value problems, this by no means precludes criticism of their particular resolutions to the problems. Two issues may be raised here: the issue of bias and the issue of solipsism.

From all sides, Becker *et al.* are accused of bias. To the Right, labelling theory is seen as deeply subversive of the *status quo* — challenging orthodox absolutist definitions of deviance and taking seriously the viewpoint of the deviant. It is biased in favour of the deviant. To the Left, labelling theory is seen as strongly supportive of the *status quo* — smuggling in taken for granted categories of deviance, focusing attention on lower-level functionaries while neglecting the oppressive power élites behind the dominant master institutions, and masking all these activities under a gentle radical guise. It is biased in favour of the oppressors, and provides a good example of the way in which the oppressive system of democratic capitalism is able to absorb potential academic threats. Now, these opposing criticisms may either simply be taken to represent the particular value positions of their proponents, or they may be taken as academic arguments about the nature of bias in scientific work.

In the former the critic has started out from a series of moral and political assumptions which the labelling theorist is shown not to support. Debates about these assumptions can ultimately only be conducted in the area of politics or philosophy, and while they must inform sociology, they are not coterminous with it.

The second issue is more germane to sociological (as opposed to purely political or moral) work. The issue here centres largely on what constitutes bias. Becker (1971) distinguishes two forms: (a) work is biased when it presents statements of fact that are demonstrably incorrect; (b) work is biased when its results favour or appear to favour one side or another in a controversy. Becker suggests that 'we cannot avoid being subjected to the charge of bias in the second sense', but that the former 'isn't in principle an unattainable goal and is worth striving for' (Becker, 1971, p. 13). Thus, taking Goffman's account of becoming a mental patient as an illustration, this work may be accused of bias because it gets the picture of what it is like to be a mentally ill person wrong, or because it tacitly sympathises with the patient, criticises the custodians and ignores the wider power structure. If the former is true, then the work is misleading and possibly dangerous — and should be rejected. But the latter could be true — until the unlikely day arrives when the sociologist is able to grasp the totality of 'all sides' in the situation at once (cf. Becker, 1967, p. 247). Those who make the charge of bias do so primarily in this second sense, which once again allows the sociologist to make clear on which side he perceives the bias to be generated.

Thus, assuming good 'objective' work is to be done, the problem becomes that of distinguishing how the work of labellists may be biased towards certain groups. In general, they do have an underdog bias; they do try to get the record straight on behalf of these groups who are conventionally perceived as troublesome, and hence challenge mainstream studies which view deviance through the eyes of the establishment and the correctionalist. Yet at the same time this 'unconventional sentimentality' is very often congruent with establishment definitions, because the very categories studied by the labellist remain those which are designated deviant by official groups. The labellist studies homosexuals not heterosexuals, criminals not law-abiders and prostitutes not heterosexual couples. In doing this the labellist tacitly confirms the establishment portrait of deviants. And in focusing — frequently — on the more exotic aspects of these deviant life styles, he also tends to emphasise the differentness of these groups. The bias of the labelling theorist to date, then, has been double-barrelled: supporting the deviant but not challenging the *status quo* (cf. Liazios, 1972; Warren and Johnson, 1972; Mankoff, 1971; Thio, 1973).[11]

Now this charge of bias — of seeming to 'take sides' — can often lead to a much more serious epistemological problem: that of solipsism. For in the work of some labelling theorists (notably those of an interactionist or ethnomethodological variety), there is a strong tendency to take seriously the persons, meanings or labels of the world and to ignore the possibility of any external referent. In the words of two extreme proponents of this view: 'Nothing in the social world has an inherent meaning. Meaning consists only of that which is imputed by people to persons and objects, as they go about their daily lives trying to make sense of the world' (Lyman and Scott, 1970, p. 26).

Thus, tacitly in some instances and explicitly in others, the sociological task becomes that of describing first one world view, then another and so on, through the entire social world. But there can be no way of reconciling these differing world views: each one has to be considered in its own terms. We study the delinquent as he experiences the world in his natural habitat and we document as accurately as possible this experience — taking very seriously the boy's own account and rejecting any concern for forces shaping his behaviour which are unperceived by the boy, or the possibility that the boy's account may not be 'right'.

In some ways this has been a most important development in sociology, for in the past sociologists have been trained *not* to take the individual's own accounts seriously but instead to go in pursuit of the causal factors unperceived by him. After listening to what the respondent says, the sociologist then sets about trying to find the *real* explanation for that behaviour, whether it lies in unconscious motivations, behavioural conditioning, the maintenance of needs or the consequence of economic forces. How the person defines his or her motives has been ignored in a pursuit of 'real' motives.

And such 'real' motives are generally located in some absolutist metaphysic around which the entire world seems to revolve.

Now the beliefs upon which this 'orthodox' have largely been built have all come under much fire recently. It can no longer pass unchallenged that there is surely a world of causation apart from actors' intentionality, that actors' meanings and talk can ultimately be translated through the medium of some universal constant, or that an absolutist metaphysic can be adhered to which explains the world by a few grand principles.

Yet a problem with much of this well-founded criticism is that it becomes guilty of 'rejection by reversal' and of what Sorokin has analysed as the 'fads and foibles' effect (Sorokin, 1956). By 'rejections and reversal' I mean the tendency to construct an alternative theory by simply reversing the major features of an opponent's theory. Thus absolutism turns into relativism, objectivism turns into subjectivism and value-free sociology becomes a value-committed sociology. By 'fad and foibles', Sorokin indicated the tendency of sociologists — in their hectic pursuit of new ideas and discoveries — to ignore what was good in past theories and to posit too radical a break with the past.

Now phenomenological labelling theory (in its preoccupation with actors' meanings) can be led to a defencelessly uncritical posture in which there are no external standards by which to appraise the individual's situation. When the homosexual tells us he or she is sick and needs treatment, when the poor tell us they are 'well off' and content, when the delinquent boy informs us that his delinquency is a product of a broken home, we can do nothing more than record this situation. A total solipsism emerges. Its rejection of absolutism reinforces this intellectual impotency.

Any work that fully espouses the principles of subjectivism and relativism must inevitably render its own findings, along with all others, incapable of possessing claims to be listened to or taken more seriously than anything else. While some of the phenomenological sociologists would go this far, interactionists walk a tightrope between social behaviourism and phenomenological idealism, and their intellectual origins in formalism and pragmatism certainly permits the incomplete grasping of localised truths. There is no inevitable connection between interactionism and 'mindless relativism' as some critics suggest (cf. Lewis, 1976). And, of course, for other — more structural or positivist versions of labelling theory — the relativist problem is bypassed.

The biases and limitations of labelling theory

A number of biases and limitations have been detected in labelling theory to date. It ignores the sources of deviant action; has too deterministic a conception of the labelling process; has relevance to only a limited range of deviant activities (cf. Reiss, 1970, pp. 80–2; Schur, 1971); ignores power; neglects structure; avoids history; focuses upon individuals to the detriment of interactional (Ward, 1971, p. 287) and organisational factors (Davis, 1972); has a 'methodological inhibition serving to limit the field to an ethnographic, descriptive, overly restrictive sociology' (Davis, 1972, p. 466), as well as a tendency to look only 'at the visible end of the selection process', ignoring 'those cases which do not develop into "career" deviants' (Bordua, 1967, p. 154). Because of restricted space, I will deal only with the first five here, but they can all be shown to be largely unfair.

The neglect of becoming deviant [12]

The first and most frequently cited limitation of labelling theory is that is fails to provide any account of the initial motivations towards deviance; it ignores the origins of deviant action and thereby frequently denudes the behaviour of meaning (Gibbs, 1966; Bordua, 1967; Mankoff, 1971; Taylor, Walton and Young, 1973a; Davis, 1972). These criticisms seem to be both fair and unfair. They are unfair in so far as they attack the perspective for not doing what it manifestly does not set out to do. A theory of labels does not have to be a theory of behaviour, although at those points where the theory suggests that the behaviour is shaped by the labels or the labels are shaped by the behaviour the two areas do interact.

However, a number of the criticisms are fairer, because while labelling theorists do not have to account for the initial deviance *in principle,* they very often do *in practice.* What critics are actually attacking is a tacit theory of primary deviance. Let me briefly give a few instances of how the problem of initial deviance has been dealt with in labelling theory (some are more successful than others).[13] In a number of studies the analysis picks up from the stage when the 'deviant' has been identified and follows the interactions from there on (e.g., Emerson, 1969; Sudnow, 1965); these simply ignore the problem. In others the analyst may provide a summary of extant eclectic work on deviant origins before embarking upon his own study of the impact of labelling (e.g., Schur, 1963). And in some an open-ended proposition is made about the sources of deviance, which acknowledges the importance of initiating forces other than labelling but elects to ignore them (e.g., Lemert, 1951, p. 67; Plummer, 1975). All of these seem to me to be reasonable positions: no theory explains everything and the analyst is entitled to set his boundaries. Yet there are some theorists, most notably Becker, who do tacitly produce theories of initial motivation. While they do not develop these, the theories lie dormant in their accounts awaiting explication. The two accounts most frequently criticised seem to be ones in which:

(1) the labels themselves are seen as the initiator of the deviant behaviour; in other words, the deviance is created by societal reaction alone;

(2) the impulse towards deviant activities is regarded as ubiquitous and widespread in society; in other words, all people would be deviant if there were not good reasons to be otherwise.

The first proposition is one frequently used by critics for the purpose of attack, but I do not think any labelling theorist would endorse it (cf. Schur, 1971, p. 5; Rock, 1973a, p. 66). Yet despite the fact that no labelling theorist seems to espouse the 'label creates behaviour' view, it is very often developed by critics. Mankoff, for instance, has shown how in a number of empirical instances (including Becker's own marijuana smokers, and Lemert's own 'naive check forgers'), that 'societal reactions seem to be neither a necessary nor a sufficient condition for career-achieved deviance' (Mankoff, 1971, p. 211): there can be career deviance without societal reactions. Now, while in a few limited instances labelling theorists may argue that it is the societal reactions which sets a deviant off on his career, these are extremely untypical cases. Lemert, Becker and Schur have all denied that careers necessarily start with societal reactions, although it remains unclear where, according to their argument, careers do commence (cf. Stebbins, 1971).

It is, I think, a gross misreading of the interactionist version of labelling theory to impute the initiation of deviant careers to labelling. It is also a misreading to believe that labelling can only be evidenced by direct formal labelling. While, however, the critics' first attack on labelling theory's account of initial motivation can be faulted because no labellist would argue that position, the butt of the second criticism can certainly be evidenced in labellist writings.

This proposition is built right into the very heart of Becker's account. As Becker says: 'There is no reason to assume that only those who finally commit a deviant act actually show the impulse to do so. It is much more likely that most people experience deviant impulses frequently. At least in fantasy, people are much more deviant than they appear' (Becker, 1963, p. 26); or later: 'Instead of deviant motives leading to the deviant behaviour, it is the other way round, the deviant behaviour in time produces the deviant motivation. Vague impulses and desires — in this case — are transformed into definite patterns of action through the social interpretation of a physical experience which is in itself ambiguous' (Becker, 1963, p. 42). Becker's view has much in common with control theory. However, critics have pointed to the possibility that this theory can trivialise the actor's initial reasons for getting into deviant activities. As Young says: 'Thus human purpose and meaning are taken from the deviant; his project is not one of importance to him, rather, it is a product of experimentation and the "accident" of labelling' (Young, 1974, p. 165). Walton (1973) has exemplified this argument by providing a case study of a highly politicised deviant group — the Weathermen — in which the initial motivation for the acts can be seen as powerful. As he says: 'The aim of this paper has been to demonstrate that some deviants exhibit purposefulness, choice, and commitment in a very different manner from that allowed in the societal reaction approach' (Walton, 1973, p. 179).

Walton has successfully demonstrated that in some instances deviant choice may be much more wilful than that which is conventionally discussed by labelling theorists. But, in effect, both Young and Walton's critiques are rather one-sided. Labellists have generally played a major role in restoring choice and meaning to the deviant's activity (cf. Matza, 1969). And this they have done primarily by constructing processual models of becoming deviant, rather than static-state/causal snapshots. In the interactionist account of labelling, people do not become deviant 'all at once' but rather — through a series of shiftings and negotiations — gradually build up a deviant self. Minor but *meaningful* fantasies may gradually emerge in deviant action. Both Young and Walton seem to seek to close this processual model and return it to a picture of person who — at a certain moment in time — suddenly seeks a clear-headed, wilful, deviant activity (in Young's case it is the hedonism of the marijuana smoker and in Walton's it is the political commitment of the Weathermen). Yet a cumulative, sequential account of 'becoming' is largely incompatible with a model that postulates powerful initiating forces. At least in the interactionist variant of labelling, human life is constantly being pieced together through conjoint action and ambiguous interpretation: it is not hammered out by clear, unilateral motives.

It must be stressed, however, that to retain choice and process is not necessarily to see these processes as 'random' and 'accidental'. Processes may stem from different systems and choice may depend on different sets of contingencies. So while it may be true that in some parts of his writing Becker seems to imply a randomness of initial motivations towards deviance, I do not think this should be seen as a necessary feature of labelling theory. Indeed, at this point the most common postulate for explaining primary deviance maybe evoked. This states simply that the early stages of deviant careers may be constructed from diverse sources. Thus for Scheff 'residual rule breaking' arises from 'fundamentally diverse sources' — 'organic, psychological, external stress, and volitional acts of innovation of defiance' (Scheff, 1966, p. 40), while for Lemert, 'differentiation' is accounted for by biology, demography, technology, groups, psychic processes and 'drift' (Lemert, 1951, ch. 2; Lemert, 1967, ch. 2). It is true that these amount to little more than open-minded confessions of ignorance, but as I have noted before it is basically unfair to criticise a theory for what it does not set out to do.

In sum, I do not find the criticisms of labelling theory, on the ground of its neglect of initial motivation, very convincing, since there is no reason of internal consistency why it should address itself to the problem of initial motives. However: (a) in practice, labelling theorists have often implicitly addressed themselves to these problems in the past, and these theories do need critical examination and elaboration; (b) some researchers (though not necessarily labelling theorists) need to focus more directly upon the possible range of links between initial motives and labels (cf. Turner, 1972).

The 'man on his back' bias: a determinism of societal reactions

Closely linked to the above is the argument that labelling theorists have rescued the deviant from the deterministic constraints of biological, psychological and social forces only to enchain him again in a new determinism of societal reactions. Thus Bordua suggests that labelling theory 'assumes an essentially empty organism or at least one with little or no autonomous capacity to determine conduct' (Bordua, 1967, p. 154), and Gouldner comments that it has 'the paradoxical consequence of inviting us to view the deviant as a passive nonentity who is responsible neither for his suffering nor its alleviation – who is more sinned against than 'sinning' (Gouldner, 1968, p. 106).

This argument has been most clearly documented by Schervish, who suggests that there is a philosophical bias in existing labelling studies which work from 'pessimistic and fatalistic assumptions that an imputed labelee is both *passive* and stands alone as an *individual*' (Schervish, 1973, p. 47). This has come about partly because it is methodologically easier to study relatively formal situations where the powerful label the weak, and partly because of the liberal assumptions of sociologists, as a consequence of which more aggressive political deviance tends to get ignored. Schervish is optimistic that although this bias has existed in the past, 'labelling theorists should now be able to move beyond their carefully drawn social psychological studies of individuals and begin to explore group, organizational, and societal levels of labelling conflict, (Schervish, 1973, p. 55).

Now while Schervish's optimism at least allows for a place for labelling theory in the future, I do not think that the 'man on his back' criticism is particularly well founded.

First, even those studies which *seem* to provide the most crude model of labelling ('no deviance →slam label→ deviance') are often firmly within a humanist tradition which sees the labelled person as sensitively playing a part under the weight of the deviant label. Goffman's mental patients are classic examples of people who have a label which is not internalised thrust upon them (Goffman, 1968). Secondly, there are a number of instances in the labelling literature of members working to fight off labels and neutralise their possible impact. Reiss's boy prostitutes, who develop normative systems which insulate them from homosexual self-conceptions, constitute one early instance of this tradition, and there have been many such accounts since that time (Reiss, 1962; McCaghy, 1968). Thirdly, studies are now developing of deviants who actively seek out the deviant label rather than having it cast upon them by others. The Braginskys' theory of mental illness centres on the idea that people seek out labels of madness in order to resolve problems of everyday life (Braginsky and Braginsky, 1969); and Rock has presented a discussion of expressive, politicised and entrepreneurial deviants, all of whom, for varying reasons, find it important to present themselves publicly as deviant (Rock, 1973a). In other words, although there may be instances of 'passive labelling' both in the literature and in the empirical world, there are also many instances where the passive picture of the man on his back simply does not apply.

I find this criticism an especially curious one when it is levied against the interactionists' account of labelling, for it is so clearly antithetical to some of the basic tenets of interactionist theory. To take a theory that is sensitive to self, consciousness and intentionality and render it as a new determinism of societal reaction could only be possible if the theory were totally misunderstood in the first place.

The irrelevance of labelling theory to certain problem areas

A third, and much less frequent, argument against labelling theory is raised by those who suggest that it is simply inapplicable to large areas of deviant behaviour. Thus the labelling model is not suitable for the analysis of impulsive crimes such as violence, physical deviance such as blindness or mild deviations which involve few overt labellers and low normative and physical visibility, such as premarital intercourse (cf. Reiss, 1970, pp. 80–2). These criticisms are generally based upon crude models of labelling, arguing either that the behaviour exists in the first place, before the application of a societal reaction (whereas presumably in areas where labelling theory is applicable, the behaviour has to be caused by labels), or that the non-existence of specific others to react to the deviance makes the model inappropriate (whereas presumably in areas where labelling theory is applicable, there have to exist specific others, like control agents, who respond to the deviance). These criticisms are based upon misconceptions of labelling theory. No labelling theorist argues that societal reactions bring about the behaviour: only that labels alter the nature, shape and incidence of the experience. And few labelling theorists believe that all the labelling has to flow from specific others: it may also stem from abstract rules and self-reactions. Labelling theory is, in principle, applicable to any area of social life, deviant or nondeviant, and key studies have already emerged in those areas often attacked as being irrelevant (e.g., Scott, 1969; Mercer, 1973; Edgerton, 1967; Rains, 1971; Christensen and Carpenter, 1962).

The neglect of power

The most serious objection to the labelling perspective which 'radical' or 'critical' criminologists have raised appears to be that it is insufficiently political. Their arguments, made forcefully in the early 1970s, take two major forms.

First, it is argued that labelling perspectives 'tend to incline sociologists toward focusing on deviance committed by the powerless rather than deviance committed by the powerful' (Thio, 1973, p. 8). Most notably, they concentrate upon the 'sociology of nuts, sluts and perverts' at the expense of 'covert institutional violence' (Liazios, 1972, p. 11). And as a result of the general acceptance of this criticism amongst 'radical' criminologists (certainly in England, though to a much lesser extent in America), there has been a drastic revision of the field in the past few years towards the study of 'crimes of the powerful' (cf. Pearce, 1976) and offences against 'human rights' (cf. Schwendinger and Schwendinger, 1975).

Secondly, it is argued that while many labelling theorists 'mention the importance of power in labelling people deviant', 'this insight is not developed' (Liazios, 1972, pp. 114–15). In particular, labelling theorists focus upon interpersonal relationships and so-called 'caretaker institutions', but fail to look at the broader economic structures in which deviance emerges. Again, as a result of the general acceptance of this criticism among radical criminologists (in England), there has been a reorientation of the field towards 'the political economy of crime'.

The consequence of these criticisms can only be viewed positively. It is important that sociologists should study the crimes of the powerful and the political economy of deviance. But while the consequences of the criticisms are sound, the criticisms themselves are weak. Both of the criticisms mentioned above flow from an ignorantly insensitive and dogmatically assertive assumption of the rightness of an absolutist position. The criticisms come close to denying the rightness of any theoretical posture or problematic other than their own. They generally imply that sociologists who look at these 'powerless' areas do so out of blindness, stupidity, ignorance or plain conservatism rather than reason. I will consider these two objections in turn.

First, the issue of a focus on the powerless. At first sight this criticism would seem to have great force. Almost without exception sociologists have focused upon the deviance of the powerless. This granted, however, it still seems to me that 'radical' critics have failed to comprehend four things: the sociology of deviance is *not* criminology; the study of deviance *is* the study of the powerless; the symbolic interactionist problematic is *not* the Marxist problematic; and the politics of libertarianism *directs* one to work with the victims of state power. These four statements are interconnected, but I will unpack each one separately.

First, the sociology of deviance is *not* criminology. This is a distinction that was much discussed during the mid-sixties, with the advent of the 'new deviance' theories. The rejection of so-called positivistic criminology ushered in the sociology of deviance; but this sociology not only changed the theoretical base for the study of criminals, it also brought in its wake a dramatic restructuring of empirical concerns. Sociologists turned their interests to the world of expressive deviance: to the twilight, marginal worlds of tramps, alcoholics, strippers, dwarfs, prostitutes, drug addicts, nudists; to taxi-cab drivers, the blind, the dying, the physically ill and handicapped, and even to a motley array of problems in everyday life. Whatever these studies had in common, it was very clear that it was not criminology. Of course, some of these same students continued to study crime, but only as one instance of deviance — an uneasy coexistence was established.

This uneasy coexistence has rarely been directly confronted, but it does serve as one root dividing point between the recent critical criminologists and the interactionist labelling theorists. The former gravitate towards criminological concerns; the latter gravitate away from them. Yet the former are unwilling to relinquish their affinities with deviance study. Thus even the title of their magnus opus *The New* Criminology — *For a Social Theory of* Deviance (my emphasis) captures the inherent confusion. For the book as a whole is about crime, criminals and the law; nowhere in the book is there to be found a concern for the blind, the stutterer, the subnormal, the physically handicapped, the physically ill, the religious deviant, the nudist or the interpersonal problems of families. It is essentially a book on criminology, but it is unwilling to relinquish its claim to be the study of deviance.

Now this is not nit-picking. Of course, I do not want to defend the arbitrary construction of academic boundaries and the creation of sterile demarcation disputes. But is it vital to recognise that the concerns of the sociology of deviance (and I am not here particularly concerned with what the concerns of criminology are — I am no criminologist) send one *necessarily* on a mission to study powerless groups. It is not capricious whimsy but theoretical necessity that leads the sociology of deviance to study powerlessness. And the reason should be so obvious that one wonders how the attacks could ever have been so seriously accepted. *For the study of deviance is the study of devalued groups, and devalued groups are groups which lack status and prestige.* Now, of course, it may be useful — for a full account of deviance — to study 'top dogs' who maintain their prestige in order to understand the mechanisms by which prestige and stigma gets allocated. It is theoretically relevant to understand why it was so long before Nixon was placed in a devalued role. But a sociology of deviance which does not focus centrally on powerless groups is likely to be a very odd sociology of deviance.

Given that deviance is concerned with devalued groups, it is also possible to suggest that there is an affinity between symbolic interactionism and the study of deviance. That interactionists have readily studied deviance is apparent; that there are good theoretical grounds for doing so is perhaps less clear. Yet if it is agreed that the interactionists' problematic is fundamentally the analysis of the ways in which members construct meanings — of self and of the social world — and of how such social constructions are pervaded with ambiguity, then it becomes clear that the topic of deviance provides an unusually complete set of illustrations for such analysis.

376

Thus the interactionists' persistent (although often tacit) concern with ambiguity may be greatly illuminated by an examination of those situations where incongruity and equivocations are central features. An ironic consequence is that such illumination may also serve to clarify the less ambiguous, more routine situations of the social world. In either case the study of deviant groups and deviant situations affords an unusually stimulating pathway to such understandings. Thus, for instance, to look at the world through the eyes of a hermaphrodite or a transvestite will tell us much about the ambiguity of gender roles and the way in which such precarious gender meaning becomes stabilised (Garfinkel, 1967; Kando, 1973; Feinbloom, 1976).

Further, the interactionists' desire to remove themselves from abstract generalities or reified theorising and to immerse themselves in the understanding of small, local contexts inevitably leads them to notice the diversity and plurality of small social worlds. All the world is not deviant, nor are there only limited realms which are consensually defined as deviant. It is not that the interactionist must select exotic groups, but that any group once studied closely will reveal a diversity of meanings and life styles, along with anomalies and problems that require studying. Most of the groups studied by interactionists are not really that quaint or exotic: they are you and I going about our daily tasks of walking and talking, living in families, visiting doctors and going to work, meeting friends and falling in love, making telephone calls, sleeping, dying and the like. This concern does not lead to the study of exotic groups but to the study of the commonplace situations of ordinary people. But once studied closely, the diversity and deviance of daily experience becomes more apparent.

Another affinity between interactionism and deviance stems from their direct concern with processes of identity construction. The building and negotiation of the self is, of course, a major focus of interactionist analysis and, again, it is clear that much can be learned from studying those situations where identities are changed, disrupted or put under severe stress. It is at those moments that the processes involved in the constitution of self may be most readily observed and studied. The study of deviance provides a host of such situations, while the study of covert institutional violence seems less well provided with such cases.

Understanding of why the powerless have frequently been the topic of labelling theory lies, finally, in recognition of the liberal to libertarian sympathies of many of its practitioners. They have been concerned with the excessive encroachment of technology, bureaucracy and the state upon the personal life — often in its grossest forms (the increasing criminalisation and medicalisation of deviance; the bureaucratisation of the control agencies and the concomitant dehumanisation of the lives of their 'victims'; and the direct application of technology in the service of control), but also in its more subtle forms — daily alienation, meaninglessness, despair and fragmentation (with the concomitant 'theory and practice of resistance to everyday life' (Cohen and Taylor, 1976)). Now, although critical criminologists deride such sympathies, they must at least agree that there is a political rationale behind the study of many powerless groups and that sometimes such concerns have had important practical, political pay-offs (decriminalisation, deinstitutionalisation, demedicalisation, deprofessionalisation and the creation of movements concerned with such activities).

In summary, then, the labelling perspective gravitates toward the powerless because: (a) the sociology of deviance generally directs them to *devalued* groups; (b) symbolic interactionism directs them to areas where ambiguity, marginality and precarious identities are readily available for study; and (c) libertarianism directs them to work with groups who are seriously 'up against the state'. Theoretically, sociologically and practically there are good reasons for a concern with the powerless.

Aside from the criticism that the labelling perspective studies only powerless groups, there is the more general problem that it neglects political *analysis*. This attack takes a weak and a strong form. In its weak form it implies that labelling analysts ignore the study of power; in its stronger form it asserts that their analysis is false.

The first — weak — criticism is simply wrong. One could well argue that the labelling perspective brought political analysis (back?) into deviancy study. It recognises that 'naming was a political act' (Goode, 1969 and that what rules are to be enforced, what behaviour regarded as deviant, and which people labelled as outsiders must . . . be regarded as political [questions] (Becker, 1963, p. 7).

From this it went on to produce a series of empirical studies concerning the origins of deviancy definitions in political action, e.g., drug legislation (Becker, 1963; Dickson, 1968; Galliber and Walker, 1977); temperance legislation (Gusfield, 1963); delinquency definitions (Platt, 1969; Lemert, 1970); homosexuality (e.g., Spector, 1977); prostitution (Roby, 1969); pornography (Zurcher and Kirkpatrick, 1976); political bias in the apprehension and adjudication of deviants (cf. Box, 1971); and the distribution of power in the bargaining process (cf. Scheff, 1968; Emerson, 1969; Carlen, 1976). Masses and masses of work could be cited here which shows the concern with political factors in the labelling perspective.

The first attack — since it is false — leads to a consideration of the second: whilst power is present in the labelling perspective, the analysis is weak. This criticism is too vast to consider in detail here: it basically involves a reconsideration of classic debates in political science theory between pluralist, élitist and ruling-class models of power. For it is argued that labelling perspectives ultimately approach a pluralistic conception of power (albeit a 'radical' pluralism — cf. Pearce, 1976) and that such analyses are discredited. Assuming that pluralism *has* been discredited (a gross assumption), the problem is then clear: does the labelling perspective really imply a pluralist conception of power? The answer should be equally clear: within the perspective, *any* theory can be applied (see the introductory remarks to this paper), so there is clearly no endemic link with pluralism.

Whilst this solution may be satisfactory to a few, it actually bypasses the basis of most of the criticism. This is the charge that interactionism is equitable with labelling theory, and it is this theory which is pluralistic. Some brief comments are necessary here, therefore, on the symbolic interactionism version of power.

The essence of the interactionists' notion of power highlights the *negotiated, ambiguous* and *symbolic* issues in politics. It is a view which should capture the flow of the empirically observable political situations that people find themselves involved in daily. For the political acts that we all experience are shrouded in such issues —

whether we confront them in university senates, in radical committees, in political organisations, on the shop floor, in church trustees' meetings or when working with (or against) the media.

In all these situations, the empirically observable situations are those of negotiation, disagreement and discussion, the selection of the right 'issue' and the right 'image', the behind the scenes canvassing. Interactionism can be used to study and understand politics at this level (Edelman, 1964, 1971; Gusfield, 1963; Hall, 1972). The objection that is voiced against such a view, of course, is that while it does show what goes on in situations, its astructural location of such situations neglects the real issues. The same model of power can be applied to a business corporation, a Boy Scout group, the IRA and the Women's Institute. Ultimately, as it builds into a cumulative portrait of the society, the interactionist theory has a close affinity with the pluralist model of power — with masses of apparently equally weighted pressure groups vying and wrestling for control. In practice I think that this is precisely the conception of power that underpins much interactionist work — it is probably no mere happenstance that Arnold Rose (a leading interactionist) is also the author of a major book on pluralist politics (*The Power Structure,* 1967). But in my view — and given the largely discredited nature of the pluralist theory — interactionism does not have to follow such a conception. In the same way as Scheff is ultimately able to weight the negotiation power of psychiatrist and client, so, too, wider groups in society will not have equal power. Society may be seen as a vast negotiated order constantly reproducing itself through a myriad of strategies and interpretive procedures. Masses of historically produced, intended and unintended decisions with intended and unintended outcomes gives rise to a highly ambiguous and constantly shifting social order. To that one need only add the hypothesis that the negotiations, decisions and outcomes are biased in favour of specific economic groups. The negotiated order is a stratified one. Paul Rock captures this conception neatly:

> *In complex societies* there is a substantial fragmentation of rule-making and rule-enforcing effort. There are innumerable legislating, defining and policing agencies which collectively make up the formal structure of a society's system of social control. Legislators, judges, magistrates, policemen, bailiffs, psychiatrists, prison officers and traffic wardens form a loosely co-ordinated system with shifting internal boundaries; a differentiation of power and function; and intricate linkages forged out of internal conflict, exchange and co-operation. The overall structure is *hierarchical;* chains of command fashion the flow of power and decision making. Each of the hierarchy's subsystems is shaped by its fellows. Each has the possibility of acquiring limited autonomy from the rest; each tends to have a drive towards maximising its control over resources and problem areas; and each is concerned about defending its boundaries against outsiders. The *higher strata* have a greater capacity to exert influence over the whole but they are functionally dependent on and constrained by the lower strata. (Rock, 1973a; 123)

The neglect of structure

Although it is manifestly clear that in some accounts of labelling, structural matters are well represented (as, for example, in Erickson's *Wayward Puritans,* 1966), critics who (wrongly) equate labelling processes with symbolic interactionism make the initially plausible complaint that the theory harbours an astructural bias. I say plausible because even sympathisers with the interactionist approach (such as Reynolds, Petras and Meltzer, 1975) would find this criticism a valid one. Yet it is most surely ill-founded — like most of the other critiques.

To accuse symbolic interactionism of neglecting structural concerns is to misread the interactionist enterprise. Every social science theory brings with it its own distinctive problematic and set of concerns, and to accuse theories of failing to deal with what they do not intend to deal with is unfair. A Marxist concern with the mode of production cannot be faulted for failing to deal with an account of heart disease, any more than a Freudian account of the unconscious can be faulted for failing to explain reinforcement contingencies. As Hewitt notes: 'It is not the task of social psychology, whether symbolic interactionist or some other perspective, to account in great detail for the systematic and complex interrelationships among institutions, organisations, social classes, large-scale social change, and other "structural" phenomena' (Hewitt, 1976, p. 148). However, that said, Hewitt rightly notes:

> At the same time, such matters cannot go unremarked and unstudied; the basic social processes [discussed by interactionism] take place within a larger context of social order and social change, and if it is not the job of the social psychologist to explain these macroscopic phenomena in their entirety, they must nevertheless be taken into account.
>
> (Hewitt, 1976, p. 148)

The central concern of symbolic interactionism is not with structural matters; it does, however, need to acknowledge such concerns if it is to be a remotely adequate *social* psychology. And if one inspects the work of many interactionists — including that of both Mead and Blumer — one finds this is so. Thus, for instance, Mead comments: 'We are individuals born into a certain nationality, located at a certain spot geographically, with such-and-such family relations, and such-and-such political relations. All these represent a certain situation which constitutes the "me" . . .' (Mead, p. 182). And later in *Mind, Self and Society* (1934), Mead devotes many pages to an (admittedly grossly inadequate) discussion of the economic and religious orders (cf. part 3). Any adequate interactionist account will firmly acknowledge that the action of persons does not take place in a social limbo, although it is through the actions of persons that any wider social order becomes historically constituted. Further, it is also true that the interactionist generally has a conception of persons wrestling with this wider order. Lichtman's argument that symbolic interactionism 'ultimately abandons the sense of human beings in struggle with an alien reality which they both master and to which they are subordinate' (Lichtman, 1970, p. 77) is (like much of his account) simply wrong. Most of the interactionist accounts of deviance portray the labelled deviant as someone who employs multiple patterns of resistance (Goffman's mental patients, Cohen and Taylor's prisoners, Matza's delinquents, Humphrey's liberated homosexuals, Scott's blind, etc., etc.), and the wider interactionist portrayals of everyday life in society are overwhelmingly full of themes of the self in struggle with a wider 'abstract', 'homeless', 'paramount Reality' (Zijderveld, 1972; Berger *et al.*, 1974; Cohen and Taylor, 1976).

However, even given that the interactionists acknowledge the existence of a wider social order and demonstrate the persistent struggles of individuals with that wider order, it would be correct to say that they lack a conception of this totality as a *structure*. But they do not neglect the concept of structure out of ignorance (they speak to many of the same concerns as structuralists); rather they deny its importance and relevance for the interactionist task. The notion of structure, they argue, is a reification which does not do justice to the central interactionist concerns of emergence, process and negotiation. At present I do not think the interactionists have developed a wholly satisfactory method of dealing with this denial of structures and simultaneous acknowledgement of a wider totality that is itself an emergent; but many attempts are now being made to furnish such a solution, some of which may ultimately prove effective.

Thus the wider social order may be approached through the concepts of 'the negotiated order' (Strauss *et al.*, 1964; Day & Day, 1977), collective action (Blumer, 1969), constraints (McCall and Simmons, 1966), the 'conglomerate' (Douglas, 1971; Rock, 1974), 'typifications' (Rock, 1973a), 'co-ordinated activity' (Blumer, 1969; Hewitt, 1976), and the 'generalised other' (Mead, 1934)(cf. Laver and Handel, 1977). There is no space in this article to deal with all these concepts but they all have in common an awareness of wider social formations than the individual (and the way they influence conduct) whilst managing to maintain a distance from the notion of a reified structure.

The empirical validity of labelling theory

One final group of objections suggest that labelling theory is simply wrong: under the harsh light of research scrutiny, the ideas of labelling theory are given little support. One noteworthy theory to receive critical attack is Scheff's labelling theory of mental illness (1975). This is in part because Scheff spells out his theory in proposition form and hence makes it readily available for falsification. But it is also because Scheff's theory — when dismantled from the riders and cautions that Scheff himself builds into the account — comes nearer than most to being a crude, deterministic model of labelling; that is, it seems to suggest that without formal labelling there would be no mental illness, and that formal labelling is an irreversible stigma. Gove's empirical critique suggests that both of these arguments do not hold (Gove, 1975). This same author has edited the proceedings of a conference specifically designed to test the validity of labelling theory over a wide range of areas — subnormality, alcoholism, disability, heroin addiction, sexual deviance, crime and delinquency — and has concluded: 'The evidence reviewed consistently indicates that it is the behaviour or condition of the person that is the critical factor in causing someone to be labelled deviant' (Gove, 1975, p. 295).

Now, empirical critiques such as these may be answered in several ways. First, they may be answered on their own terms. Thus Scheff's analysis of Gove's critique reinterprets the evidence and concludes that of the eighteen systematic studies of labelling theory available, 'thirteen support the theory, and five fail to' (Scheff, 1975). But second, and more generally, my answer to this form of critique would stress that the 'testers' of labelling theory usually adopt a narrow, empirical and positivistic concept of labelling theory which can only focus upon a very few limited hypotheses dealing with a narrow range of questions drawn from the labelling perspective. The 'testers' ignore the idea that labelling is a perspective serving to reorientate research towards a vast array of new concerns and propositions, and prefer to focus instead upon a vulgarised and distorting version which, while making the theory testable, also renders it trivial (cf. Kitsuse, 1975; Schur, 1975).

This last form of defence is certainly not arguing that labelling theory should not be open to testing and falsification: it is simply stressing that the contribution of labelling theory is open to inquiry into an assortment of new, competing propositions which answer the full gamut of labelling questions. Given this, it becomes useful to distinguish two versions of an empirical labelling theory: one is *limited,* and contains a narrow (generally distorting) set of propositions, and the other is *wider* and contains an array of (often competing) propositions. The limited version only deals with questions associated with the issues of application and consequences, while the broader version deals with questions of the nature and origins of labels too. However, even the two areas which the narrow version considers are treated in a limited way, while the wide version sees a broader set of propositions emerging. Thus, for the first area – labelling as a dependent variable (Orcutt, 1973), or the problem of application – a narrow version suggests two key propositions:

(1) deviant labels are applied independently of the personality or behaviour of those labelled;

(2) deviant labels are applied *directly* by *formal* control agents.

In contrast, the wider perspective extends these propositions to acknowledge that:

(1a) deviants may contribute to their own labelling in many ways requiring specification;

(2a) deviant labels may be applied *indirectly,* by *informal* as well as formal control agents, and by self-labelling.

It is clear that the research directives of the narrow propositions are simple and manageable: look at the ways in which formal control agents define deviants through contingencies. The research directives of the wider version do not lend themselves to such simple testing; the interaction between deviant and definer has to be considered, and the possibility of (symbolic) self-labelling analysed in detail. Labelling may occur without any specific intervening definer (cf. Rotenberg, 1974, 1975; Farrell and Nelson, 1975).

For the second area — labelling as an independent variable; the consequences of labelling — the narrow version suggest propositions like:

(3) labelling initiates or amplifies deviance — it has negative consequences;

(4) labels are deterministically internalised by labelees;

(5) such labels are irrevocable.

In contrast the wider perspective extends these propositions to acknowledge that:

(3a) labels may prevent (deter) or change deviance — they may also have 'positive' consequences;

(4a) labels may be voluntarily avowed and disavowed, and responded to in a variety of ways;

(5a) labels may be reversible and changeable: destigmatisation is possible.

Again, it is clear that the research directives for the latter are altogether more complex. Rather than assuming that there is only one negative response to labelling, the entire programme of possible responses has to be charted. Some important studies have made moves in these directions (e.g., Reiss, 1962; Scott, 1969; Turner, 1972; Warren, 1974b). In summary, although it is true that to date labelling theory has not usually fared well at the hands of empirical researchers, this is largely due to the narrow interpretation given to the theory by the researcher. When viewed as an orientating perspective, the approach becomes important as suggestive of a wide range of areas demanding empirical attack.

In conclusion: a personal commitment

I was first introduced to labelling theory during a criminology course in the mid-sixties. Naively I thought it was a 'new' theory and I found it appealing. It switched attention away from the aetiology of deviant conduct and started to examine the definitional process and the ways in which this altered the shape of 'deviant' experiences. At that time there were few criticisms being made of the theory and — like an innocent — I was seduced.

Slowly its appeal spread through English sociology and it served, perhaps, as the central rallying flag at the establishment of the National Deviancy Conference in England in 1968. It began to emerge from the underground of theory to become a topic for books and theses, as well as enjoying widespread incorporation in newly developing sociology of deviance courses. And as it became more widely known, so — rightly — more and more problems with it were noticed. From one small anticipation of the weaknesses of the theory (Gibbs, 1966), there developed a major industry of criticism. Perhaps the watershed of this criticism was the publication of *The New Criminology* in 1973, for it served to divide the new British tradition of deviancy study into two groups: those who still found much to be gained from working within the approach of labelling (now the new orthodoxy), and those who had turned away from such matters towards a concern with a political economy of crime. From that time onwards, the content, nature and even frequency of the meetings of the National Deviance Conference changed. In America, too, the perspective increasingly came under fire — though usually on empirical grounds rather than ideological ones (Gove, 1975).

I have no doubt now that while some of the criticisms have been largely beside the point, many of them have served useful functions — forcing a clarification of key theoretical, methodological and ideological concerns, and properly redirecting much work to new and politically important arenas. But the critics drastically overstate their case if they believe they can announce the 'death' of labelling theory or claim paramountcy of perspective, theory or method! I have tried in this paper to defend the view that labelling is essentially a perspective: the questions it raises are ones a sociology of deviance has to consider. I have gone on to argue that symbolic interactionism is only one theory that need be used within the labelling perspective, but that it has an affinity with the study of marginality and deviance and is a useful corrective to grander, more general theories. It has a useful role to play. Most of the paper has then considered more specific issues; most notably the suggestion that the labelling perspective is over-limited in its sphere of application and empirically wrong when tested. I hope to have shown the weaknesses of such arguments.

Massive criticism and countercriticism can be extremely effective in sharpening perspectives and theories. It can also become sterile when the amount of 'theorising about theorising' outstrips empirical inquiry. Labelling perspectives, symbolic interactionism and political economies of crime do not have to rival each other. They each raise their important problems and they each deserve serious attention.

Notes

1. The importance of Mead, Cooley and Tannenbaum is often acknowledged (for a recent instance, see Finestone, 1976, p. 188–91), but its history can be traced back much further (see Pearson, 1975).

2. Although the pattern is broadly similar, England followed a few years behind America. The Society for the Study of Social Problems was formed in the early fifties, but the English counterpart — the National Deviancy Conference — was not formed till the late sixties. The former may have become much more traditional over time, though, than the latter. Likewise the major American publications date from Becker's books (1963 and 1964), but in England the first statements are Cohen's (1967) paper and Young's (1970) book. England came later to the theory and rejected it more speedily.

3. Outside of America and England, more specific versions of labelling theory have been developed (e.g., Muller, 1974; Shoham, 1970). For ease of management, I am excluding these theories from the above discussion.

4. The main theoretical omission from the list is Marxism. Labelling theorists have flowered into Marxists (e.g., Young, 1970, 1975; Quinney, 1970, 1974; Platt, 1969, 1973), but Marxism does not seem to have facilitated the rise of the labelling problems.

5. Schur seems to be the most ardent contemporary defender of labelling theory (Schur, 1971), yet he is only occasionally mentioned as a labellist. While sympathetic to interactionism, all his work is theoretically eclectic.

6. In a private communication, I am very grateful to him — along with Stan Cohen, Malcolm Davies and Jock Young — for helpful comments on various drafts of this paper.

7. Warren and Johnson, in an extremely lucid phenomenological critique, have amplified this basic point. They suggest that labelling theory fails on three grounds: first, in its desire to be an original 'new school', it has thrown out much from past deviancy theory that is of value; secondly, while it appears highly critical of much past theorising, it has in fact imported through the back door, in different guise, a number of the very items it purports to attack; and thirdly, it has grappled inadequately with certain existential problems. Each of these criticisms is derived from a phenomenological concern with meanings. Thus, under the first criticism, Warren and Johnson suggest that there has been a too easy dismissal by

the labellists of notions of 'deviant conditions', of 'core values', of 'pathology' and of 'aetiology', when all these phenomena are often built into the meanings of deviance constructed by actors themselves. Thus the homosexual's own emergent set of meanings may be concerned with 'whether I'm sick or not', 'how I got to be like this', 'why society casts me apart', and 'being a homosexual'. To ignore these is to do a disservice to the actors' meanings.

Under the second criticism, Warren and Johnson point to the fact that while labellists rhetorically drop the notion of deviants as a special category, most of their work continues with unexplained notions of conventional deviance. Instead of inquiring into how members categorise acts as deviant, labellists continue to function with the perspectives of officials in locating and studying deviance. They tacitly remain on the side of the officials.

Under the third criticism, the authors write:

> Perhaps the most fundamental existential problem with labelling theory is its abstracting of reality from the context of used and situations, and its neglect of empirical investigations into how typifications of deviance are used by, and what their use means to, social actors on the actual occasions of their use. (Warren and Johnson, 1972, p. 90)

Now, all these criticisms have in common a desire to get back to the situated activities of members of interpreting and making deviance, shunning any unexplicated assumptions, the existence of broader macro-structures or the validity of official data, in favour of a highly microscopic and relativistic approach.

8. Space does not permit an expansion on such links. For some basic sources, see Rock, forthcoming.

9. Sagarin also provides a most helpful general discussion of the meaning of deviance in his (1975) book (part one), and with Birenbaum (Birenbaum and Sagarin, 1976, ch. 2).

10. I cannot expand these distinctions here. But at the least it should be noted that these two societal definitions work from drastically differing phenomenological positions. The former (a) stays on the level of the actor's definitions of the world (cf. Rock, 1973a), whereas the latter (b) moves — with some difficulty — between situated meanings and abstract meanings, in a manner derived from Berger and Luckmann (1967), and — more problematically — Douglas (1971). What both these definitions have in common, though, is a concern with some form of seemingly objective, external standards of deviance.

11. While the interactional labelling theorist is often on the side of an underdog, there is no reason why he or she has to be. Rock — in a private communication — helpfully comments:

> I cannot imagine why it is necessary to take either stance during the process. If an account of public control exists, it should deal with social meanings as a mutually orchestrated process. The decision to give an interpretation priority, to either partner, simply distorts understanding in a discussion of an encounter between a policeman and a delinquent, for instance. The individual's definition of this encounter and their conjoint definitions must both be incorporated.

12. This criticism occurs on both an individual motivation level and on a structural level. Labelling theory does not explain why people commit deviant acts (Sagarin, 1975), or why there exist different 'objective' rates of deviance (cf. Gibbs, 1972). The latter objection has the merit of being a sociological objection but the former is curiously misplaced. Why *should* a sociologist seek to explain individual motives? It is hard to imagine an industrial

sociologist seeking the motives of a striker or a political sociologist or those of a working-class voter. Yet sociologists of deviance are still supposed to seek such explanations. Paradoxically, the major attempt at a sociology of motivation has actually come from those who are broadly sympathetic to the labelling/interactional approach (cf. Taylor and Taylor, 1972).

13. For an even briefer 'list' of such accounts, see the introductory chapter in Gove (1975).

Marxism and Criminological Theory

17. Marx and Engels on Law, Crime and Morality
Paul Q. Hirst

1. Radical criminology and Marxist theory

Many radical criminologists and deviance theorists in their opposition to orthodox studies of deviance, crime and law enforcement are turning toward 'conflict' approaches to this phenomenon, and towards Marxism, which they regard as embodying in a powerful and coherent way the 'conflict' approach to social phenomena.[1] This tendency in sociology reflects two very general approaches to Marxism in the social sciences which are shared by radicals and conservatives alike. First, the identification of the conceptual structure and analytic content of Marxist theory stems less from a thorough knowledge of Marxism itself than from the 'Marxism' that forms the basis of debates in the established social sciences. This 'Marxism' reflects far more the epistemological concerns of the established social sciences, the debates about the validity of Marx's so-called 'predictions' in relation to the changes in social structure since Marx's day, and the ideological opposition to Marxism of the professional anti-communists, than it does the positions of Marx, Engels and the orthodox Marxists. Secondly, in their eagerness to adopt a Marxist 'conflictual' position, the radicals seldom question their own theoretical-ideological point of departure and its relation to Marxist theory. They do not pose or think of posing the questions crucial to any application of Marxism to this non-Marxist debate between radicals and conservatives in the social sciences. These questions are two-fold. On the one hand, is the given field, criminology, and the object of study it presupposes, compatible with the object of study and conceptual structure of Marxism? On the other hand, what is the specific epistemological difference between the position of the radicals and the conservatives in criminology?

Radical and conservative theories of deviance take as their point of departure the given actuality of crime and the law, and of ideological conflicts reflecting standpoints within that actuality. Radical deviancy theory takes as its scientific point of departure the desire to develop a critique of the orthodox positions in the field. It seeks to explain and justify the criminal as a product of social relations, to situate the criminal as the victim of processes of labelling and punishment which serve the interests and represent the values of the establishment, and to question the nature of laws and values as the property of that establishment. Radical deviancy theory, therefore, questions the value assumptions, underlying justifications of establishment interests, and the ideological stand of orthodox criminology, but it very rarely questions its own position, assumptions and interests.

It is the aim of this chapter to demonstrate that Marxism has a quite different view of

Paul Q. Hirst: 'Marx and Engels on Law, Crime and Morality' from CRITICAL CRIMINOLOGY, edited by Ian Taylor, Paul Walton and Jock Young (Routledge and Kegan Paul, 1975), pp. 203–230. Reprinted by permission of Routledge.

crime and 'deviancy' from that of the radicals; a view that abolishes this field as a coherent object of study. There is no 'Marxist theory of deviance', either in existence, or which can be developed within orthodox Marxism. Crime and deviance vanish into the general theoretical concerns and the specific scientific object of Marxism. Crime and deviance are no more a scientific field for Marxism than education, the family or sport. The objects of Marxist theory are specified by its own concepts: the mode of production, the class struggle, the state, ideology, etc. Any attempt to apply Marxism to this pre-given field of sociology is therefore a more or less 'revisionist' activity in respect of Marxism; it must modify and distort Marxist concepts to suit its own pre-Marxist purpose. 'Revisionism' should be seen to be done: it is the aim of this chapter to demarcate the Marxism of Marx and Engels from the 'Marxism' of the radicals.

2. The development of Marxist theory

The question of orthodoxy and revisionism raises the problem of which 'Marx' and which 'Marxism' we accept as the norm. Many sociological radicals seek to return to the themes of the 'young' Marx, to a Marxism free of 'monistic' and 'totalitarian' tendencies, to a Marxism concerned with man's alienation and human self-emancipation. The status of the work of the 'young' Marx, and of Marxist concepts in general, cannot be determined by a free-ranging and arbitrary choice based upon contemporary 'relevance' or the *post-hoc* political-ideological judgments which stem from the subsequent history of the workers' movement, in particular, from the history of the Communist Party of the USSR. Marx's own positions have much to tell us about the relevance of what is considered 'relevant' today. The validity of the concepts and the conceptual structure of Marxist theory cannot be determined by reading them in the future anterior, that is, of playing off the Marx of the 1844 *Manuscripts* against the Marx of *Capital,* against Lenin, or against Stalin.

It is the view of the author that Marx's theoretical development should enlighten these questions. Marx's later works (i.e., those works post-1844, that is, beginning with *The German Ideology)* contain a consistent and developed critique not only of bourgeois authors, Hegel, Feuerbach, Proudhon, Smith, Ricardo, etc., but also of the 'young' Marx who shared their theoretical positions. The author further considers that these differences can be revealed by the study of Marx's writings. These writings contain at each of the different periods a definite conceptual structure and enforce certain definite protocols on the reader. The notion that Marx's writings are open to any 'interpretation' we care to impose upon them is patently false and can be demonstrated by detailed reference to, and analysis of, the texts themselves.

It is to these texts that we now turn. Marx's positions on law and crime are of three distinct kinds and are directly related to his general theoretical position in three different periods. These periods are: (a) 1840–2, the Kantian critique of law, (b) 1842–4, the Feuerbachian period, and (c) 1845–82, the formation and development of Historical Materialism.

(a) The Kantian-liberal critique of law

The speculative use of reason in *regard to nature* leads to the absolute necessity of some supreme cause of the *world;* the practical use of reason *with respect to freedom* leads also to absolute necessity — but only to the absolute necessity of the *laws of action* for rational being as such (Kant, 1948, p. 123).

Marx's writings in 1842, in the *Rheinische Zeitung* and other works, are part of a practical-polemical struggle for democracy and genuine liberalism against the cowardly liberals of the Rhenish Parliament and the Prussian State authorities. These writings are concerned with the nature of law, the freedom of the press and 'official' morality.

Marx's theoretical standpoint in these texts is a Kantian rationalism and universalism. His political standpoint is that of a radical democrat and egalitarian. Marx adopts broadly Kantian positions; that reason is the attribute of a free being, that reason is universal and is distinct in essence from all empirical particularity (the 'positive'), of which it is the critique. Marx, therefore, contrasts mere positive law and official morality founded upon mundane interests with the true, universal and free necessity of laws and morality founded upon reason (1842a, p. 35):

> Thus so far from a law on the press being a repressive measure directed against the freedom of the press, simply a means to deter by penalties the repetition of a crime, the lack of a law dealing with the freedom of the press should rather be seen as an exclusion of freedom of the press from the sphere of legal freedom, for legally recognised freedom exists in the state as law. Laws are as little repressive measures directed against freedom as the law of gravity is a repressive measure directed against movement . . . Laws are rather positive, bright and general norms in which freedom has attained to an existence that is impersonal, theoretical and independent of the arbitrariness of individuals. A peoples' statute book is its Bible of freedom . . . .

> Where law is true law, i.e. where it is the existence of freedom, it is the true existence of the freedom of man. Thus the laws cannot prevent man's actions, for they are the inner laws of life of his action itself. . . . Thus a positive law is a meaningless contradiction.

The Marx of this passage thinks his opposition to censorship through a critique founded upon a transcendental conception of reason and law. Law and freedom are anthropological categories in so far as they are human attributes, but *man* is defined by his status as a free and rational being. In the last instance, these attributes of man are his attributes only in so far as he partakes of qualities extrinsic to himself, reason and freedom, which have an existence independent of him and define him. For Kant these attributes are truly transcendental, in that man is human (has the attributes which mark him off from the beasts) in that he partakes, partially and blindly, of the nature of God.

Thus, the theoretical position of Marx in this period is quite distinct from his position in the Feuerbachian period. Feuerbachian anthropology conceives man not through transcendental attributes but through the concrete reality of his biologically-based species characteristics. Man's species being is that of a unique *animal,* an animal conscious of itself and of its species. For the Feuerbachian man is a universal being because the individual is able to appropriate through species self-consciousness the infinite possibilities of the species.

Marx in 1842 rejects all religious systems as a limitation of freedom and reason, as the dogmatic subordination of morality to interest and to specific conceptions derived from the particular (1842b, pp. 29–30, original italics):

> The specifically Christian law-giver cannot recognise morality as a sphere *sacred* in itself and independent for he vindicates its inner universal essence for religion. Independent morality violates the universal bases of religion and the particular concepts of religion are contrary to morality. *Morality knows only its own universal and rational religion,* and religion only its particular positive morality. Thus according to this instruction the censorship must reject all the intellectual heroes of morality — Kant, Fichte, Spinoza, for example, as irreligious and violating discipline, morals and exterior respectability.

The contradiction of a transcendental ethic apart from empirical religion, which is itself a religion of ethics, and the practical anti-clericalism and atheism of Marx, clearly drove him to accept the Feuerbachian foundation of ethics and religion on a 'concrete' anthropology. Marx's strictly idealist and speculative position in the Kantian period leads him to place the independent existence of the idea above all particular empirical existence and all concrete struggles (1842b, p. 48):

> We are firmly convinced that the true danger does not lie in the practical attempt to carry out communist ideas but in their theoretical development; for practical attempts, even by the masses, can be answered with cannon as soon as they become dangerous, but ideas that have overcome our intellect and conquered our conviction . . . are chains from which one cannot break loose without breaking one's heart.

No wonder, then, that Marx expressed 'embarrassment' when he was forced to deal with 'economic questions' in the case of the abolition of the feudal rights of the Rhenish peasants to take wood from the forests. Marx here conceives economic relations as legal rights, from the standpoint of the distributive justice of absolute egalitarianism (1842d, p. 49):

> If every violation of property without differentiation or further definition is theft, would not private property be theft? Through my private property do I not exclude a third party from this property ?

Marx bases his argument on the theory of natural rights; private property violates the natural rights of others, it is a *theft* of their rights, and it destroys the natural equality of men. This argument carries the egalitarian tendency in natural rights theory further than Rousseau's *Discourse on the Origin of Inequality Among Men.* In this doctrine that property is theft Marx echoes Proudhon, who he was later to castigate for this very moralism in *The Poverty of Philosophy.*

The Rhenish liberals are condemned for capitulating to particular interests; to an inequality between the poor and the privileged which destroys the essence of law. The origin of this privilege is conceived of as an historical fact, as the result of a past conquest (ibid., p. 50):

> Mankind appears as disintegrated into particular animal races who are held together not by equality but by an inequality that regulates the laws. A universal lack of freedom requires laws that lack freedom, for whereas human law is the existence of freedom, animal law is the existence of a lack of freedom. The rights of aristocratic custom run counter by their content to the form of general law. They cannot be formed into laws because they are formulations of lawlessness.

Marx rejects the dictates of aristocratic custom as a form of slavery; as a form contradictory in its essence with the form of law, for the form of law can only answer to that necessary principle of morality established by Kant: 'Man, and in general every reasonable being, exists as an end in itself, *and not merely as means*'.

(b) The Feuerbachian period

> Thus in the first part I show that the true sense of Theology is Anthropology, that there is no distinction between the *predicates* of the divine and human nature, and, consequently, no distinction between the divine and the human *subject:* I say *consequently,* for wherever, as is especially the case in theory, the predicates are not accidents, but express the essence of the subject, there is no distinction between subject and predicate, the one can be put in the place of the other (Feuerbach, 1841, p. 37).

Marx's *Economic and Philosophic Manuscripts of 1844* are the key texts of this period, the specific bone of contention between those who assert the continuity of Marx's work, or who counterpose the theory of alienation to the 'alienating' abstractions of *Capital* and the orthodox Marxist position.

However, those who wish to found a theory of law and crime upon these texts face two serious obstacles: (a) law ceases to be an important element in Marx's argument; (b) the conceptual structure of the theory of the *Manuscripts* produces the reduction of all particular phenomena, law, the State, the family and religion, to the essential contradiction in society, that between the essence of labour as a self-realizing human activity and its alienation in an object, private property.

For Marx, as for Feuerbach, the existence of definite spheres of life, or social institutions apart from concrete human sensuous activity represents an alienation of the essential predicates of the human subject. Man has a specific essence, or nature, a set of predicates which constitute his species being, and man is the existence of the species in the individual, a conscious concrete subject.[2] Alienation represents the externalization of these predicates in an object which becomes independent of the subject and which subordinates the subject to his own externalized essence. This essence, separated from the subject, is no longer recognized by him, in its objectified form, as his essence, but as an independent principle which governs his own existence. Man is estranged from himself and subordinated to his own essence.

The object of the human sciences, of philosophy, is the critique of this separation of man from his essence; the revelation of the contradiction between the subject and its essential predicates. Religious and speculative anthropology makes this separation a part of the essential human condition, an ineradicable contradiction in man's being. For Feuerbach and Marx it is a specific separation which is the product of definite real-historical conditions which are bound up with the development of humanity itself and can be overcome at a particular stage in the development of humanity. Marx criticizes Feuerbach for having stopped in his critique at the point of demonstrating the foundation of religious alienation in human relations, at the point of revealing the Holy Family as an alienated form of the human family, and God as an alienated form of the essence of Man. He further criticizes Feuerbach for having stopped at a speculative critique, which remains within the idea, and therefore of having failed to recognize the necessity of a 'practical criticism' of alienation, the overcoming of alienation in the real by revolutionary practical activity.

Marx's theoretical critique in the *Manuscripts* necessarily reduces all particular social forms to the essential contradiction between the alienated form of man's essence in private property and estranged labour, and the concrete human subject who labours. The alienated predicates must be returned to the subject, hence no social relation can exist apart from the subject, and social relations are dissolved into the activity of the subject. Communism is the union of the subject and his essence, the practical abolition of the separation. Communism is the dissolution of all institutions into human self-realizing activity. Nothing exists apart from subjects, free relations one with another. Since all social relations are the spontaneous free actions of subjects, which entail no contradictions each with the other, law has no basis or reason for existence; even 'natural' laws become void in the union of nature and human practice (1844, p. 95):

> This communism, as fully developed naturalism, equals humanism and as fully developed humanism equals naturalism; it is the *genuine* resolution of the conflict between man and nature and between man and man — the true resolution of the strife between existence and essence, between objectification and self-confirmation, between freedom and necessity, between the individual and the species. Communism is the riddle of history solved, and it knows itself to be this solution.

The meaning of alienation in the *Manuscripts* is quite specific and is specified by a particular conceptual structure. Alienation, anthropology and man's being-toward-communism are inseparably linked by Marx's concepts. Thus to use 'alienation' as an explanation of a particular phenomenon, crime, for example, would be quite absurd for Marx, since alienation is a concept in a theory whose object is the dissolution of all phenomena. To prove the existence of alienation by interviews, indices, scales, X-rays or whatever, would be, for the Marx of 1844, an absurd alienation in itself. To introduce the concept of alienation into the modern social sciences is, therefore, either to abandon the concept of the *Manuscripts,* or to transform those social sciences into a practical-critical philosophy whose object is communism.

(c) The formulation and development of Historical Materialism

Marx and Engels's specific positions on law and crime in this period will be discussed in the following sections (3–4); the purpose of this section is merely to demonstrate the difference between Marx and Engels's later writings and those of Marx in the earlier periods. This difference will be demonstrated as follows: (i) the difference of the Historical Materialist conception of the social formation, cryptically stated in Marx's 1859 *Preface,* from Marx's conception of society in 1844;(ii) the difference between Marx's natural rights conception of human equality in 1842 and Marx's positions on this form of rationalist egalitarianism in the *Critique of the Gotha Programme,* 1875 (1859, p. 361):

> In the social production of their life, men enter into definite relations that are indispensible and independent of their will, relations of production which correspond to a definite stage of development of their material productive forces. The sum total of these relations of production constitutes the economic structure of society, the real foundation, on which rises a legal and political superstructure and to which correspond definite forms of social consciousness. . . . At a certain stage of their development, the material productive forces of society come into conflict with the existing relations of production, or — what is but a legal expression of the same thing — with the property relations within which they have been at work hitherto. . . . In considering such transformations a distinction should always be made between the material transformation of the economic conditions of production, which can be determined with the precision of natural science, and the legal, political, religious, aesthetic, philosophic — in short ideological forms in which men become conscious of this conflict and fight it out.

The 1859 *Preface* has been regarded as the most reductionist of Marx's writings; as the text most open to an economic determinist reading. But, when we compare it with the thoroughgoing reductionism of the critique of separation in the *Manuscripts,* this text reveals a surprising complexity.

The social relations of production '*correspond*' to a 'definite stage of the development of . . . [the] material productive forces'. The economic structure is the '*foundation*' on 'which rises a legal and political superstructure' to which '*correspond* definite forms of social consciousness'. The economic structure of society is the condition of existence of the superstructure, it is the foundation on which this superstructure rests, and therefore prescribes certain definite limits to what can be erected upon it.

No more than this can be deduced from Marx's statements. Indeed, the very notion of 'foundation' prohibits any attempt to think the content or form of the superstructure as having a direct economic *causation* in the traditional sense (the sense of polemics which regard Marxism as a factorial theory of history). Rather, it suggests a determination of the limits of variation of the superstructure by the economic structure and says nothing about the *causation* or *origin* of superstructural forms or the ideologies which correspond to them.[3] The existence of distinct levels in the social formation, of distinct and irreducible forms of social relations, is entailed in this formulation.

This conception of the social formation would be anathema to the Marx of the *Manuscripts*. It entails the existence of distinct levels which demand the admissibility of social relations which are in no sense reducible to the practice of human subjects, the social relations of production are 'indispensable and independent of their will'. In no sense are these relations deducible from the human essence; it is not the case that 'the one can be put in the place of the other' since social relations independent of human wills, which are in no sense the *product* even the *alienated* product, of those wills, cannot be deduced from the subject as its predicates. There is no *separation* in the existence of these distinct levels since their referent is not the human subject but their mutual articulation into a social totality. The reference of the levels is their relation each to the other. The relation of the social formation to the subject is completely different in 1859 from 1844. The social formation produces specific subjects with specific conditions of existence and a specific place in that formation. The social position, material conditions of existence, and forms of thought of the subjects ('definite forms of social consciousness') are effects of the structure of the social formation.

Moreover, Marx nowhere in this text suggests that these invariant characteristics of the social formation will vanish with communism. Indeed, we are left with no option but to recognize the existence of structure and superstructure as the necessary form of all human societies. The spontaneously social self-realization of human subjects, conceived as the form of communism in the *Manuscripts,* is no longer the conception of communism in 1859. In communist society, like any other, there are structural forms independent of and indispensable to the human subjects. Communism cannot know 'itself to be . . . the solution' to the riddle of history, since it is neither a unity of individual subjects, nor is it itself a subject. Social formations do not 'know' anything, and the subjects to which they give rise, even communist subjects, only know through 'definite forms of social consciousness', that is, they know as subject only through the forms of ideology which correspond to the relations that produce them as subjects. Communist societies obey the invariant laws of the social formation.

Thus, the epistemological basis of the critique of separation in the *Manuscripts* and the goal of the critique, spontaneous communism, are ruled out by the epistemological positions of the *Preface*. The *Preface* has a scientific *object,* the social formation, but no *goal,* since the new science does not identify its knowledge of its object with an end immanent in the real. It proscribes any reference to a telos; it rejects the basis of any telos, the union of social relations and the human subject, the union which enables us to read in history the ends of man. There is in the *Preface* no essential contradiction between alienated essence and the concrete subject which is resolved of anthropological necessity. The 'separation' of structure and superstructure is no contradiction but the invariant structure of the social formation.

It will be remembered that Marx, in his first essay into 'economic questions', depended upon a natural rights conception of equality. His arguments were those of distributive justice in respect of a given quantum of 'property' and the rights of each and all in respect of that quantum. His positions here can be regarded as: (i) absolute egalitarianism, equality of 'right'; and (ii) that the 'social question' is a matter of the just and equitable distribution of property, in this case, common ownership.

In his *Critique of the Gotha Programme*, 1875, Marx was confronted with very similar positions to the above in the programme of the German Worker's Party (1875, pp. 18,21):

1. Labour is the source of all wealth and all culture, and *since* useful labour is possible only in society and through society, the proceeds of labour belong undiminished with equal right to all members of society. . . .

3. The emancipation of labour demands the promotion of the instruments of labour to the common property of society and the co-operative regulation of the total labour with a fair distribution of the proceeds of labour.

In his reply Marx castigates the abstract moralism and ethical universalism of these passages and thereby measures out for us the difference between Scientific Socialism and the Kantianism of his 1842 positions.

Marx rejects the notion that socialism is a matter of distributive justice.[4] Scientific socialism is founded on an analysis of the mode of production, the production relations and the productive forces, which enforce a definite mode of distribution in a given social formation. It is the economic structure of society which establishes a definite distribution of the conditions of production which governs the distribution of the means of consumption (1875, pp. 21, 25):

> What is 'a fair distribution' ?
>
> Do not the bourgeois assert that the present-day distribution is 'fair' ? And is it not, in fact, the only 'fair' distribution on the basis of the present day mode of production ? Are economic relations regulated by legal conceptions or do not, on the contrary, legal conceptions arise from economic ones?
>
> Any distribution whatever of the means of consumption is only a consequence of the distribution of the conditions of production themselves. The latter distribution, however, is a feature of the mode of production itself. The capitalist mode of production, for example, rests on the fact that the material conditions of production are in the hands of non-workers in the form of property in capital and land, while the masses are only owners of the personal condition of production, of labour power. If the elements of production are so distributed, then the present-day distribution of the means of consumption results automatically.

In addition, Marx rejects the egalitarianism of 'equal rights'. Marx is not interested in ethical abstractions like 'equality', abstractions marked on their very character as ideological elaborations of bourgeois relation of production, but in the social relations pertaining in capitalist and socialist societies. The problem of 'equality' under socialism is not an ethical problem but a problem enforced by the mode of production; the measurement of the value of labour, the representation of the concrete labour of members of society by an equal standard. Thus in a socialist society, given deductions for depreciation, the development of the productive forces, administrative costs and common social needs, the worker: 'draws from the social stock of means of consumption as much as costs the same amount of labour'. The direct exploitation of labour no longer exists, but the mode of production still demands the determination of rewards by labour-time (ibid., p. 24, my emphases):

> In spite of this advance, this equal right is still constantly stigmatised by a bourgeois limitation. The right of the producers is *proportional* to the labour they supply; the equality consists in the fact that measurement is made with an equal standard, labour.

> But one man is superior to another physically and mentally and so supplies more labour in the same time . . . and labour, to serve as a measure, must be defined by its duration and intensity, otherwise it ceases to be a standard of measurement. This *equal* right is an unequal right for unequal labour. It recognises no class differences, because everyone is only a worker like everyone else; but it tacitly recognises unequal individual endowment and thus productive capacity as natural privileges. *It is therefore a right of inequality, in its content, like every right.* Right by its very nature can consist only in the application of an equal standard; but unequal individuals . . . are measurable only by an equal standard in so far as they are . . . taken from one *definite* side only, for instance in the present case, are regarded only as *workers*.

The ruling principle of *communism* utterly rejects egalitarianism, it demands that individuals work to their specific capacities, and allocates means of consumption to units of consumption solely on the basis of need: 'from each according to his ability to each according to his need.' It is the communist mode of production which gives rise to such a principle, and those social relations and ideologies which it embraces form the superstructure of communist society.

It has been the subject of section 2, above, to demonstrate a very real difference between the theory of Historical Materialism and the positions of the young Marx. This difference is not the simple dissimilarity of positions of equivalent epistemological validity but 'incommensurable' assumptions; of different 'paradigms' or *Weltanschauung* which admit of a choice between them based upon ideological premises. It is a difference measured by a critique; a difference in which one theory rigorously demarcates itself from others by concepts which demonstrate their erroneous and unscientific character. It is a difference in which Historical Materialism demonstrates, by means of its scientific concepts, the ideological character of the philosophical anthropologies which underlay the positions of the Young Marx.

The remainder of the paper is devoted to an explication of Marx and Engels' post 1844 positions on law and crime; positions which derive from the concepts of Historical Materialism and the political theory of Scientific Socialism. This will be discussed as follows:

3 Crime, the law and Marxist politics

4 Organized crime and production relations.

3. Crime, the law and Marxist politics

(a) *The lumpenproletariat*

> The 'dangerous class', the social scum, the passively rotting mass thrown off by the lowest layers of the old society, may, here and there, be swept into the movement by a proletarian revolution, its conditions of life, however, prepare it far more for the part of a bribed tool of reactionary intrigue. (Marx and Engels, 1848, p. 44).

Marx and Engels's pronouncements on the criminal classes often appear savage, harsh and unthinking. It is often assumed that these views represent no more than the prejudices of two Victorian gentlemen and are passed off as expressing merely the conventional morality of their day. But Marx and Engels were rather extraordinary 'Victorian gentlemen'; they were atheists, they called for the abolition of the bourgeois family, and they castigated the very bourgeois cant which the hasty observer may attribute to them. To brush off Marx and Engels's remarks on these matters as 'bourgeois moralism' is radically to misconceive their standpoint and the reasons for these positions. Their standpoint was uncomprisingly political and based on the proletarian class position. Marx and Engels ask of any social class or socio-political activity, what is its effectivity in the struggle of the proletariat for socialism, does it contribute to the political victory of the exploited and oppressed ?

Marx and Engels always stressed that capitalist society is complex, that any specific capitalist society represents the combination of different modes of production, and that it produces class relations which are not reducible to any simple opposition between proletariat and bourgeoisie. The proletariat alone is incapable of overthrowing the political rule of the bourgeoisie and its class allies; if it does attempt to carry through a political revolution in isolation, that is, without class alliances, it will be outnumbered, cornered and destroyed as was the Paris proletariat in the desperate June insurrection of 1848. Of this hopeless and heroic uprising Marx remarked: 'On the side of the Paris proletariat stood none but itself.' Without the leadership of the proletariat, that is, of the class whose position in the relations of production makes it the only class capable of carrying through the struggle for socialism, the other progressive classes will fall victim to the ideological illusions, political demands and forms of action which result from their specific situation in production relations.[5]

Engels raises the question of the lumpenproletariat in relation to this problem of class alliances in his 1874 Preface to *The Peasant War in Germany* (Engels, 1874, p. 645):

> But even the proletariat has not yet outgrown the parallel drawn with 1525. The class that is exclusively dependent on wages all its life is still far from forming the majority of the German people. This class is, therefore, also compelled to seek allies. The latter can only be found among the petty bourgeoisie, the *lumpenproletariat* of the cities, the small peasants and the agricultural labourers.

His remarks on the political efficacy of this class are as follows (ibid., p. 646):

> The lumpenproletariat, this scum of the depraved elements of all classes, which establishes its headquarters in the big cities, is the worst of all possible allies. This rabble is absolutely venal and absolutely brazen. . . . Every leader of the workers' who uses these scoundrels as guards or relies on them for support proves himself by this action a traitor to the movement.

Why are these elements not to be relied on? First, as a parasitic class, living off productive labour by theft, extortion and beggary, or by providing 'services' such as prostitution and gambling, their class interests are diametrically opposed to those of the workers. They make their living by picking up the crumbs of capitalist relations of exchange, and under socialism they would be outlawed or forced to work (see section 4 of this chapter for a fuller account of this point). Secondly, they are open to the bribes and blandishments of the reactionary elements of the ruling classes and the State; they can be recruited as police informers and the armed elements of reactionary bands and 'special' State forces.

The 'criminal classes', Marx and Engels argue, are the natural enemies of any disciplined and principled workers' movement. Ideologically and politically, they are incapable of taking a militant socialist position, and fall victim themselves, and threaten to lead elements of the workers, to the worst deviations of putschism, commandism, and arbitrary acts of violence, theft and intimidation. Their highest forms of political action are mob agitation and street fighting. As such, they represent at best the incidental material of anarchist bands, such as those established by Blanqui, which reject an organized relation to the workers' movement and seek political power through the *coup d'état,* independent of the struggles of the working class. Mob agitation and street fighting are primitive forms of political action. Modern revolution, in countries where large-scale capitalist production prevails, demands the mass seizure and control of the means of production by the workers. The factory, and the modern forms of distribution and communication, are the objective foundation of modern capitalist society and, therefore, the objective basis of proletarian power. Without the organized support of the proletariat, and that means proletarian leadership, an insurrection would be isolated, immobilized, starved and finally crushed by the forces of order.

Marx discusses two salient examples of the reactionary role of the lumpenproletariat. In the June Days the 'special' State forces, the Guardes Mobiles, were in the forefront of the suppression of the workers' rising. This same class formed the backbone of Louis Bonaparte's 'personal' political party, the Society of 10 December. Bonaparte, a declassé adventurer, relied upon his own kind. These passages of Marx are too well known to require quotation (see Marx, 1850, p. 155; 1853, p. 295).

Marx and Engels's strong language and their strong opposition to the criminal classes and the demi-monde, far from expressing an idiosyncratic moralism, stems from a definite theoretical-political point of departure.

(b) The 'delinquent solution' and political action

But, if Marx and Engels reject the criminal classes as a reactionary force, what of the 'individual' who is driven to crime ? Surely, we see here a victim of the capitalist system, a product of forces beyond his control. As early as *The Condition of the Working Class in England in 1844,* Engels discusses the formation of criminals thus (1844, p. 163):

> The contempt for the existing social order is most conspicuous in its extreme form, that of offences against the law. If the influences demoralising the working man act more powerfully, more concentratedly than usual, he becomes an offender as certainly as water abandons the fluid for the vapourous state at 80 degrees, Réaumur. Under the brutal and brutalising treatment of the bourgeoisie, the working man becomes precisely as such a thing without violition as water, and is subject to the laws of Nature with precisely the same necessity; at a certain point freedom ceases.

In *Capital,* amongst many other passages indicating the effect of capitalist production on the worker, Marx discusses the effects of the employer's attempts to evade the Factory Acts by use of the relays system, and he remarks thus: 'The hours of rest were turned into hours of idleness, which drove the youths to the pot-house, the girls to the brothel' (1867, p. 291).

The majority of the poor wretches displaced by evictions and enclosures, by the Primitive Accumulation which separated the worker from the means of production, had little option but to become thieves, vagabonds and bandits, and as such they were mercilessly persecuted by the very class that had produced their downfall (ibid., p. 734):

> On the other hand, these men, suddenly dragged from their wonted mode of life, could not as suddenly adapt themselves to the discipline of their new condition. They were turned *en masse* into beggars, robbers, vagabonds. . . .

> Hence at the end of the 15th and during the whole of the 16th century, throughout Western Europe a bloody legislation against vagabondage.

Marx and Engels, although they constantly warned the workers' movement of the danger of the criminal classes, were far from moralizing with the bourgeoisie about the conditions which produced criminality, which filled the ranks of the criminal classes with recruits. They demonstrated that it was the very capitalist system, which the bourgeoisie put forward as the model of a just and virtuous society, that produced these threats to its own 'order', 'respectability' and 'property'.

Marx and Engels did not, however, accept the bourgeoisie's own estimation of the threat to 'society' represented by the criminal. The criminal career and the 'delinquent solution', however much enforced by the harsh necessities of capitalism, are not *in effect* forms of political rebellion against the existing order but a more or less reactionary accommodation to them. The professional criminal, like all other men, 'enters into definite relations that are . . . independent of their will'; he joins the ranks of the lumpenproletariat. Like it or not, a specific class position is forced upon him. The romanticization of crime, the recognition in the criminal of a rebel 'alienated' from society, is, for Marxism, a dangerous political ideology. It leads inevitably, since the 'criminal' is an individualist abstraction of class position, to the estimation of the lumpenproletariat as a revolutionary force.

Crime is not only the business of professional criminals; other illegal actions, machine-breaking, industrial sabotage, the murder of landlords and officials by peasants, have a more obviously 'political character. Marx and Engels remark thus about outbreaks of machine-breaking (1848, pp. 41–2):

> The proletariat goes through various stages of development. With its birth begins the struggle with the bourgeoisie. At first the contest is carried on by individual labourers, then by the workpeople of a factory, then by the operatives of one trade, in one locality, against the individual bourgeois who directly exploits them. They direct their attacks not against the bourgeois conditions of production, but against the conditions of production themselves; they destroy imported wares that compete with their labour, they smash to pieces machinery, they set factories ablaze, they seek to restore by force the vanished status of the workmen of the middle ages.

Industrial sabotage is a similar index of immediate reaction to harsh, gruelling and frustrating conditions of work. For Marx and Engels these were immediate and spontaneous forms of struggle; forms which are inadequate to transform conditions of production because they are directed toward immediate objects which result from a misrecognition of the real determinants of the workers' situation. It is the task of the workers' organizations and of the political theory of Scientific Socialism to transform such forms and ideologies of struggle. To glorify such primitive forms would be to fixate the workers' movement in its infancy.

In agrarian class societies, banditry, terrorism or the spontaneous peasant uprising are the immediate forms of struggle. Bandits appear time and again in popular mythology and police reports only to vanish again into prisons, into the service of the ruling class, or to be destroyed by the forces of order. Peasant uprisings effect their spontaneous justice and redistributions and are crushed. Both forms of struggle are quite normal incidents in the socio-political rebellion.[6] It is only with the development of capitalism, and later imperialism and with the consequent development of nationwide political movements led by the proletarian vanguard, that peasant movements, linked with the struggle, forms of organization and politics of the proletariat, develop into a genuinely revolutionary political force. The case of China illustrates this point: it was only under the political leadership of the communists, who broke with the forms of organization and ideology of banditry and the spontaneous peasant uprising that the social and political conditions of agrarian China could begin to be transformed as the result of a successful revolutionary war.

Thus the criminal 'individual', or spontaneous mass actions of an illegal character, are of interest to Marxism from the standpoint of political and ideological struggle alone. They are of interest only in so far as spontaneous mass action is the point of departure of a political critique and a political struggle which transforms it into an organised and theoretically-based politics.

(c) Political 'crimes' and the State

'Crime' is defined by State law and detected and punished by the State repressive apparatus. Marx regards the State as an instrument of class oppression; an instrument which intervenes in the class struggle on behalf of the ruling class and against the proletariat and its allies. The State intervenes in the class struggle on behalf of the ruling class and against the proletariat and its allies. The State intervenes in the class struggle with its ideological and repressive apparatus to break the power of the political movement of the workers by means of legal and extra-legal sanctions. One form of such State intervention is the stigmatization of political opponents of the bourgeoisie as 'criminals'. To stigmatize political opponents as 'common criminals' is to deny ideologically their *political* character and aims, to castigate them as bandits and adventurers. The effect of such ideological-repressive interventions, if successful, is to give the political movement a pre-political character.

Marx's response to this situation was complex. To glorify illegal struggle, to argue that the State is *only* the obedient creature of the ruling class, and to argue that all legal struggles, and all attempts to use the representative means and the political freedoms protected by State law, are a sham since the State is a *mere* expression of force, is to do the bourgeoisie's own ideological job for it. To cringe before legality and State power, on the other hand, to reject all forms of struggle proscribed by the State, is to cut the political movement off from the revolutionary road. At one time and another, trades unions, the free press and free public assembly have all been illegal forms of action, even in bourgeois 'democracies'. How does Marx resolve this dilemma, the dilemma of ultra-Leftism and reformism ? Certainly not by a return to the Kantian differentiation between rational and empirical law. He does so by the application of a rigorous class and political position. Forms of struggle, legal and illegal, which define the relation of the proletarian movement to the class State, are determined solely on the basis of their efficacy, under determinate conditions, in the proletarian struggle for socialism.

A good example of Marx's position in this respect is his intervention in a specific case of political oppression, the Cologne Communist Trial. The Prussian government, in 1851–2, in the tide of repression following the defeat of the democratic revolutions of 1848, attempted to destroy its most effective opponents, the communists, by the exposure and prosecution of an international 'conspiracy' to overthrow the established order. A 'conspiracy' which proved the implication of the Communist League in plans for revolution by the fabrication of minutes and documents. Marx worked to expose the fraud, clear the name of the Communist League and assist the victims in their defence. Marx's wife Jenny, often considered falsely and unjustly to have been at heart a reactionary and ill at ease with her husbands' doings, wrote about Marx's efforts (J. Marx, 1852, p. 72):

> You can imagine how the 'Marx Party' is active day and night. . . . All the allegations of the police are lies. They steal, forge, break open desks, swear false oaths . . . claiming they are privileged to do so against Communists, who are beyond the pale of society!

The reasons for Marx's struggle were simple and entirely political; to counter police ideology about the Communist League and to attempt to check the repression of the movement. Marx's aim was clear, to preserve the political-legal conditions necessary for open communist agitation. Marx and Engels were always determined to use the legal freedoms available in the bourgeois State to the full in order to develop the workers' movement. The greatest possible political-legal freedom could only be of advantage to the workers' movement. Thus Marx and Engels constantly promoted the demands for universal suffrage, a free press, freedom for trades unions and the abolition of arbitrary and repressive laws.

4. Professional crime and production relations

In *Theories of Surplus Value,* vol. 1 Marx discusses the role of the criminal in production relations. This passage, 'The Apologist Conception of the Productivity of all Professions', is of great interest (Marx, 1969, pp. 387–8):

> A philosopher produces ideas, a poet poems, a clergyman sermons, a professor compendia and so on. A criminal produces crimes. If we look a little closer at the connection between this latter branch of production and society as a whole, we shall rid ourselves of many prejudices. The criminal produces not only crimes but also criminal law and in addition to this the inevitable compendium in which this same professor throws his lectures onto the general market as 'commodities'. This brings with it augmentation of national wealth, quite apart from the personal enjoyment which — as a competent witness Herr Professor Roscher, [tells] us — the manuscript of the compendium brings to its originator himself.

> The criminal, moreover, produces the whole of the police and of criminal justice, constables, judges, hangmen, juries, etc.; and all these different lines of business, which form equally many categories of the social division of labour, develop different capabilities of the human spirit, create new needs and new ways of satisfying them. Torture alone has given rise to the most ingenious mechanical inventions, and employed many honourable craftsmen in the production of its instruments.

> The criminal produces an impression, partly moral and partly tragic, as the case may be, and in this way renders a 'service' by arousing the moral and aesthetic feelings of the public. He produces not only compendia on criminal law, not only penal codes and along with them legislators in this field, but also art, *belles-lettres* novels, and even tragedies, as not only Mullner's *Schuld* and Schiller's *Rauber* show, but also (Sophocles's) *Oedipus* and (Shakespeare's) *Richard the Third.* The criminal breaks the monotony and everyday security of bourgeois life. In this way he keeps it from stagnation, and gives rise to that uneasy tension and agility without which even the spur of competition would get blunted. Thus, he gives a stimulus to the production forces. Whilst crime takes a part of the superfluous population off the labour market and thus reduces competition amongst the labourers — up to a certain point, preventing wages from falling below the minimum — the struggle against crime

absorbs another part of this population. Thus, the criminal comes in as one of those natural 'counterweights' which bring about a correct balance and open up a whole perspective of 'useful' occupations.

The effects of the criminal on the development of productive power can be shown in detail. Would locks ever have reached their present degree of excellence had there been no thieves ? Would the making of bank-notes have reached its present perfection had there been no forgers ? Would the microscope have found its way into the sphere of ordinary commerce (see Babbage) but for trading frauds ? Doesn't practical chemistry owe just as much to adulteration of commodities and the efforts to show it up as to the honest zeal for production ? Crime, through its constantly new methods of attack on property, constantly calls into being new methods of defence, and so is as productive as strikes for the invention of machines. And if one leaves the sphere of private crime: would the world-market ever have come into being but for national crime ? Indeed, would even the nations have arisen ? And hasn't the 'Tree of Sin been at the same time the Tree of Knowledge ever since the time of Adam ?'

On the surface this passage appears to argue that crime has an important function in the economy, that it 'produces' many other occupations as the result of its own product and, that, in the manner of Durkheim, the criminal reinforces the bourgeois 'conscience collective'. To take the passage out of the context of the whole work, is, however, very misleading.[7] The passage is shot through with irony; the irony Marx so often uses to castigate the bourgeoisie. In this text Marx is ridiculing these vulgar bourgeois apologists who justify a 'profession' by its morality. This vulgar moralist conception of the economy divides society into the respectable and the idle, depraved, feckless and criminal. Marx teases these vulgarians with the proposition that the most upright citizens depend for their livelihood on the criminal classes.

The distinction between productive and unproductive labour in the bourgeois science of political economy is quite different; the distinction is made on the basis of the contribution of an occupation to the production of wealth, or value, variously conceived. Adam Smith, for example, uses two contradictory forms of differentiation: first, he attempts to argue that productive labour is labour which produces surplus value, but lacking the *concept* of surplus value he is unable to think the *phenomenon*. He therefore falls into a second, more ideological form of argument, that productive labour is labour which produces commodities (see Marx, 1969, pp. 155–74). Despite their failure to resolve the problem in a satisfactory manner, the theoretical political economists did attempt to give a rigorous and scientific answer.

The attitude of vulgar economics is quite different (Marx, 1969, pp. 174–5, my emphases):

> What particularly aroused these polemics against Adam Smith was the following circumstance.
>
> The great mass of so-called 'higher grade' workers — such as state officials, military people, artists, doctors, priests, judges, lawyers, etc. —

some of whom are not only not productive but in essence destructive, but who know how to appropriate to themselves a very great part of the 'material' wealth partly through the sale of their 'immaterial' commodities and partly by forcibly imposing the latter on other people — found it not at all pleasant to be relegated *economically* to the same class as clowns and menial servants and to appear merely as people partaking in the consumption, parasites on the actual producers.

Marx establishes the distinction between productive and unproductive labour as follows (ibid., pp. 399–401, also my emphases):

The result of the capitalist production process is neither a mere product (use-value) nor a *commodity,* that is, a use-value which has a certain exchange-value. Its result, its product, is the creation of *surplus-value* for capital, and consequently the actual *transformation* of money or commodity into capital — which before the production process they were only in intention, in their essence, in what they were destined to be. In the production process more labour is absorbed than has been bought. This absorption, this *appropriation* of another's unpaid labour, which is consummated in the production process, is the *direct aim* of the capitalist production process; for what capital as capital (hence the capitalist as capitalist) wants to produce is neither an immediate use-value for individual consumption nor a commodity to be turned first into money and then into a use-value. Its aim is the *accumulation of wealth, the self-expansion of value, its increase;* that is to say, the maintenance of the old value and the creation of surplus-value. And it achieves this *specific product* of the capitalist production process only in exchange with labour, which for that reason is called *productive labour.*

Labour which is to produce *commodities* must be useful labour; it must produce a use-value, it must manifest itself in a *use-value.* And consequently only labour which manifests itself in *commodities,* that is in use-values, is labour for which capital is exchanged. This is a self-evident premise. But it is not this concrete character of labour, its use-value as such — that it is for example tailoring labour, cobbling, spinning, weaving, etc. — which forms its specific use-value for capital and consequently stamps it as *productive labour* in the system of capitalist production. What forms its *specific use-value* for capital is not its specific useful character, any more than it is the particular useful properties of the product in which it is materialised. But what forms its specific use-value for capital is its character as the element which creates exchange-value, abstract labour; and in fact not that it represents some particular quantity of this general labour, but that it represents a *greater* quantity than is *contained* in its price, that is to say, in the *value of the labour-power.* ...

It follows from what has been said that the designation of labour as *productive labour* has absolutely nothing to do with the *determinate content* of the labour, its special utility, or the particular use-value in which it manifests itself. A singer who sells her song for her own account is an *unproductive labourer*. But the same singer commissioned by an entrepreneur to sing in order to make money for him is a *productive labourer;* for she produces capital.

Marx establishes a rigorous distinction between the two forms of labour: productive labour is labour which produces surplus-value. These concepts enable us to investigate the various departments of professional crime and the role they play in production relations.

(a) Theft

The thief in capitalist society appropriates material products and means of exchange; in the act of theft he neither produces commodities, nor services, nor engages in commerce, nor financial speculation. He is consequently neither a productive nor an unproductive labourer, nor is he a capitalist, rather he is strictly parasitic on the labour and wealth of society. The thief steals from the members of all social classes and from all social institutions. His interdiction of the economic relations of society is ubiquitous; he intervenes in production and circulation. The modalities of employment of these appropriated resources are varied: the thief may steal either for his own direct consumption, or for exchange to provide means of exchange for the purchase of other commodities for his consumption, or, more rarely, to capitalize an enterprise of his own. Theft, whatever its source or function for the thief, always merely redistributes the existing material production or wealth and adds nothing to the stock of material production or wealth.

Extortion is similar in its economic character to theft. The pure beggar, unlike the thief, is parasitic only upon the consumption funds of other classes. The beggar who offers some pathetic token in exchange for a donation is little different in kind.

But if the thief is an economic parasite, are not the capitalist and the policeman also parasites ? No, they are not. Whilst the capitalist is neither a productive nor an unproductive labourer his position is economically necessary in any economic system governed by capitalist relations of production. The capitalist system, based upon the separation of the worker from the means of production under conditions of private property, requires both wage labourers and capitalists as agents in its production process. The position of the capitalist is inscribed in the structure of capitalist production. The policeman, a State functionary, is necessary for the reproduction of capitalist social relations; he protects the property of capitalists and others, and secures certain of the conditions of labour discipline. The existence of the modern police force owes little to the exigencies of combating professional crime and was developed primarily as an instrument of political control and labour discipline. Capitalist economies require capitalists and policemen for their existence and reproduction, they do not require thieves. The thief is a parasite on the capitalist system of production, he has no specific position as an agent in it.

Theft is not an activity confined to capitalist societies. It is a feature of all modes of production with private property. However, the position of the thief in the various modes of production is very different. In feudal societies theft is analogous in its relation to the production process to other forms of parasitism. In feudal societies the activities of bandits and vagabonds are not different in character from the mode of appropriation of the surplus product and surplus labour-time by the ruling class; which relies for its economic basis on direct political-ideological appropriation and has no specific role in the process of production. Surplus labour, on the lord's demesne, is labour directly separate from the production of the labourer's means of subsistence and is forced upon him. The ruling class in feudal society is not an economically necessary agency; its appropriation is for its own consumption and it contributes nothing to production or reproduction. The State and the ruling class stand above a society of self-sufficient producers who control the means of production. The village, a self-sufficient unit of production, has no need of the State or ruling classes.[8]

In capitalist society the production of surplus value (the form the surplus product or surplus labour-time takes under conditions of free labour) occurs directly in the process of production, in the double character of labour. The capitalist in employing the use-value of the commodity labour-power, concrete labour, in combination with the means of production which he owns, obtains a product of a value greater than the cost of that labour-power and of the portion of constant capital which is transferred to the product. This is all strictly legal and above board. The worker sold his labour-power to the capitalist, for a wage determined by the average social cost of the reproduction of that commodity, in a free contract, and the capitalist has the full right to the use-value of that commodity. No extra economic extortion or injustice has taken place here.

The State in capitalist society appropriates a portion of this surplus-value from the capitalist class, and the taxes payed by labourers represent part of the means of subsistence (cost of labour-power) for which they sell their labour to the capitalist. The capitalist class, therefore, demands a measure of control of the State budget. Under feudal conditions the ruling class appropriate a portion of the surplus product directly from the producers; for the capitalist class under a feudal State this is an intolerable situation, akin to robbery, since they are threatened with an indeterminate extortion of their accumulation fund depending upon the rapacity and taste for consumption of the feudal class. This situation, one element of the conflict of two quite different modes of production, leads to the developing bourgeoisie overthrowing or capturing the feudal State.

Thus, theft under capitalist conditions is quite different from that under feudal conditions; the baron and the bandit are not entirely dissimilar in their relation to the process of production, the capitalist and the tax officer are quite different from the thief.[9]

To argue that private property *is* theft is an absurdity. This form of argument presupposes private property, bourgeois private-property right, as the natural form of relations between man and man. One can only steal another legal entity's property. Theft presupposes private property as a condition of its existence. To argue that private property is theft requires a conception of right and of the person in whom that right inheres which are effects of the ideological elaboration of property relations in political and legal philosophy.

But property is not a natural form of the relations between man and man (or between man and woman). Private property comes into existence in a definite form of social formation; it comes into existence with the appearance of classes, and with the appearance of the State as a guardian of class society. Primitive communism recognizes neither private property nor theft amongst the members of a particular kin-group; it recognizes only the transgression of kinship relations, and the form of relations between kin-groups, which are the relations of production and distribution in primitive communism. It recognizes only offences in respect of the rituals associated with kinship, of the rituals and mythologies which form the ideological superstructure which corresponds to this mode of production.[10] Property founded upon *appropriation* requires a definite ideological and repressive superstructure. For example, European feudal property corresponds to the ideological dominance of the Catholic church: 'This much, however, is clear that the middle ages could not live on Catholicism. . . . On the contrary it is the economic conditions of the time which explain why . . . Catholicism played the chief part' (Marx, 1867, p. 81n). In feudal societies there is a dislocation between production relations and property relations, between peasant production and the 'higher unity' of the State, which gives rise to this ideological dominance. In capitalist society there is no such dislocation since property relations are the direct product of production relations and no such ideological dominance. In developed communism the principle 'from each according to his ability to each according to his need' abolishes the very category of theft. To take from the stock of use-values distributed to a specific unit of consumption would be at best an inconvenience and would merit no more than general censure for inconsiderateness. To argue that property *is* theft is to be unable to think the specificity of the different forms of social relations. Thus, the analogy between the baron and the bandit is an *analogy* and from one definite aspect, their relation to the production process.

(b) Prostitution and illegal services

The prostitute who sells for his/her personal support is an unproductive labourer, like the tutor or the lawyer who works on his own behalf. The prostitute who provides the same services for a wage in order to make money for an entrepreneur is a productive labourer, like the singer whose performances enrich a theatre-owner — both produce surplus-value which can function as capital.

Prostitution, we are told, is 'the oldest profession'; what therefore is different about prostitution in capitalist society? Nothing; capitalist relations pre-exist capitalist social formations. This is only confusing to those historicists who believe in a history of essentially unique 'epochs' rather than the Marxist analysis of the structure of different modes of production.

The same generalizations can be made about various forms of gambling and racketeering.

(c) Criminal enterprises

Illegal forms of capitalist production, for example, the production and sale of intoxicating liquors in the USA between 1920 and 1933, have certain specific differences from legitimate capitalist enterprises. The capital of the illegal enterprise has no legal title as property. Capital that is not legal property is a contradiction that sets very definite limits to its function as capital and which restricts the economic freedom of the illegal enterprise. The accumulation of capital in such enterprises is limited by their necessarily clandestine character, and this restriction enforces the conversion of such accumulated capital into strictly legal enterprises and the employment of various subterfuges to convert it into legal property.

Illegality has certain very specific effects in respect of the employment of wage labour. Such enterprises will generally recruit labour from the industrial reserve army and the lumpenproletariat. Such labour is not strictly 'free' labour, since it is driven into a collusive relation of common criminality with the employer and is subject to coercion. The rate of exploitation may be higher than in broadly comparable branches of capitalist production. The wage labourer in such enterprises has no measure of protection from the Factory Acts or the police, and is unable to form trades unions. Such labour is very unlikely to play any part in the class struggle or the workers' movement.

The outlaw capitalist has very distinct relations to his own class and to the State. He does not enjoy the protection of the State, he is unable to defend his interests politically, and he is open to immediate State closure and appropriation. The illegal capitalist must, therefore, defend his own 'property' and develop his own repressive apparatus. Where the widespread corruption of public officials and political representatives exists, outlaw capital may enjoy great security and great privileges, at a price.

In general criminal enterprises are absent from the central forms of capitalist production, from large-scale industry, and large commercial and financial enterprises. Criminal enterprises are economically marginal compared with the productive power of modern industry.

To return, in conclusion, to Marx's 'The Apologist Conception of the Productivity of all Professions'. The ironic character of the text should now be evident. To say the criminal 'produces' crimes is to use the term in a very different sense from Marx's scientific concept of production. The criminal does not produce the law or law enforcement; the existence of private property and class society give rise to these elements of the superstructure. The production of instruments of torture and of locks has been at no period a major branch of capitalist production. 'Practical chemistry', as Marx and Engels show in many other texts, owes far more to the textile industry and the manufacture of explosives than it does to fraud. Modern industrial chemistry, as Engels demonstrated, depends on the application of modern chemical science to industry. The criminal classes are a tiny fraction of the industrial reserve army, even in these days of 'full employment'. As for the criminals' services to bourgeois morality we have seen that the ideological forms of capitalist society, and of other social formations, correspond to the mode of production and not to the exigencies of outlawing the criminal. One would have to be a vulgar apologist of the bourgeoisie to discover in this text 'the Marxist theory of crime'.

Appendix

Other writings of Marx and Engels on law

This chapter is by no means an exhaustive account of Marx and Engels's positions on law and the class struggle. It concentrates upon those aspects of their work which are most relevant to the demarcation between Marxism and radical criminology. Important aspects of their positions on law neglected here are the following:

(a) *The class struggle and law.* See, Marx, 1867, chapter 10, 'The Working Day', where Marx deals with the effects of the English Factory Acts on the hours and conditions of labour, and the workers' struggle for the legal regulation of hours of work.

(b) *The law of contract, the wage-form and surplus-value.* See, Marx 1867, chapter 12, 'The Transformation of the Value (and Respectively the Price) of Labour Power into Wages', where Marx demonstrates that the bourgeois legal rights of contract are an essential element of the wage-form, an essential ideological component of the production of surplus-value (ibid., pp. 539–40):

> The wage-form thus extinguishes every trace of the division of the working day into necessary labour and surplus labour, into paid and unpaid labour.
>
> Hence, we may understand the decisive importance of the transformation of value and the price of labour-power into the form of wages, or into the value and price of labour itself. This phenomenal form, which makes the actual relation invisible, and, indeed, shows the direct opposite of that relation, forms the basis of all the juridical notions of both labour and capitalist.

The bourgeois rights of contract are simultaneously the ideological condition of existence of the wage-form, and therefore, of exploitation, and at the same time the ideological effect of that form.

(c) *Law and the social formation.* The classic texts in this respect are: Marx, 1964a; Engels, 1884; 1876, part 1, chapters 9, 10 and 11.

Notes

1. We refer here to a general ideological tendency in the social sciences; a tendency far more marked in its widespread and spontaneous manifestations than in particular published works. It is the object of this chapter to counter this general tendency by reference to Marxism rather than to offer a specific critique of the writings of radical deviancy theorists.

2. See Jacques Rancière, 'Le Concept du critique et la critique de économie politique', in Althusser *et al.* (1965). The first two sections of this important paper have been translated in *Theoretical Practice*, nos. 1 and 2, 1971.

3. This position, which is similar in many respects to that of Godelier (1967) is clearly inadequate as a complete account of Marx's theory of the social formation. The 1859 *Preface* has certain tendencies toward relativism and factorialism in the relation of structure and superstructure. The author does not subscribe to Godelier's position or to these tendencies, but is constrained by the limitations of space from citing more scientific works of Marx. For

411

a more adequate discussion of Marx's basic concepts of the social formation, see, Althusser (1970) in particular the essay, 'On the Materialist Dialectic'.

4. Della Volpe (1970) argues that the *Critique* is an example of Rousseau's 'anti-levelling egalitarianism'. But, sophistry and rhetoric apart, Della Volpe offers no proofs whatsoever that Marx's actual position in the *Critique* and his critical attitude to Rousseau are in 'contradiction'.

5. Anyone who doubts this exposition in favour of the economistic and sectarian interpretation current in sociology should consult two outstanding texts: Marx's discussion of the proposition in the Gotha Programme that, 'The emancipation of labour must be the work of the working class, relatively to which all other classes are *only reactionary mass'*, see Marx (1875), and Engels's 1895 *Preface* to Marx's *The Class Struggles in France,* see Engels (1895).

6. For a good orthodox Marxist analysis of forms of pre-political rebellion in agrarian class societies, see Hobsbawm (1959).

7. This passage has recently been reproduced in this isolated manner in the Marxist journal *Monthly Review* and under the most misleading title, 'The Productivity of Crime'. It is also reproduced, in like fashion, in the collection of Marx's writings edited by Bottomore and Rubel, 1963, see pp. 167–8.

8. See Marx (1964a).

9. This analysis is based upon, Etienne Balibar, 'Fundamental concepts of Historical Materialism', in Althusser and Balibar (1970). However, it should be noted that the present text uses Balibar's analysis in a very partial and vulgarizing fashion.

10. For a systematic Marxist account of the social relations of 'primitive' societies, see Engels (1884), and Terray (1969).

18. The State, Law and Order in Complex Societies

Frank Pearce

Introduction

In their work *The Crisis of Democracy* (1975), Crozier, Huntingdon and Watanuki make explicit and implicit use of Durkheimian concepts to present a pessimistic picture of western society and to develop some rather conservative solutions to its political problems. Many such societies have become characterized by an 'anomic democracy' owing to a 'delegitimation' of authority, the 'excessive' demands made by 'disaggregated interests' and a 'parochialism' in international affairs. Their rather banal solutions — which are more concerned with ruling these societies than with democracy as such — are in line with the ideology of the body that sponsored the study, namely the 'Corporate Liberal' Trilateral Commission, and are of little intrinsic interest.[1] Of more moment is that, although elements of Durkheim's thought can easily be deployed in such a study, a careful reading of *Professional Ethics and Civic Morals,* the text in which he most explicitly addressed the nature of the state and of democracy, generates a more radical and socialist (see Filloux, 1971), indeed a more interesting, set of concepts.

In Durkheim's view, for an advanced complex society to work effectively and reproduce itself it must be able to develop and sustain an autonomous political identity. A political society is 'one formed by the coming together of secondary social groups, subject to the same one authority which is not itself subject to any other superior authority duly constituted' (Durkheim, 1957, p. 45) There must be clear structures of rights and obligations, codified in law and rigorously enforced, which govern the conduct of individuals, secondary associations and government agencies. In such a society subject to the rule of law both individuation and cooperation are encouraged without falling into the excesses of egoism or obligatory altruism. The importance of the individual, of particularistic collectivities such as secondary associations and the necessary coordinating role of the state can then all be recognized.

The state must be separate from the rest of society as an effective 'organizing centre'. It must be clear what it is doing, what is occurring within society as a whole and what needs to be done to make society function adequately. It must produce collective representations that are truly distinguishable 'from the other collective representations by their higher degree of consciousness and reflection' (ibid., p. 50). In fact, for Durkheim the state is ultimately defined by this deliberative role and its essence is to be found in whatever assemblies carry this out. But rational deliberation requires accurate information and in Durkheim's view this would be produced by a dialogue between the state, sub-collectivities and individual citizens. The imperative need for such a dialogue is heightened if the state is genuinely striving to act in the

Frank Pearce: 'The State, Law and Order in Complex Societies' from *THE RADICAL DURKHEIM* (Unwin Hyman, 1989), pp. 179–204. Reprinted by permission of Routledge.

collective interest, since this can only be discovered by taking account of what different groups know and want. This can only happen if there exist institutions in which groups and individuals can effectively participate and it is only under these conditions that it becomes rational for the generality of citizens willingly to cooperate with the state.

> Here, the particular advantage of democracy is that, owing to the communication set up between those governing and the citizens, the latter are able to judge of the way in which those governing carry out their task, and knowing the facts more fully, are able to give or withhold their confidence (Durkheim, 1957, p. 108)

For Durkheim, democracy, as opposed to other political systems, is less defined by its specific voting arrangements than by the fact that it is based upon the maximum openness of dialogue between the state and its subject populations. Whilst he acknowledged the importance of a general, individuated franchise, he believed that such an electorate is atomized. It is also necessary to develop mechanisms that allow for the representation of sub-collectivities as such, since secondary associations are essential components of any healthy complex society. A plurality of forms of representation will maximize communication.

Hirst has also recently argued for the need to institutionalize pluralist diversity and to develop corporatist mechanisms for 'the institutionalized representation of organized interests' so that 'those interested in an area or service may have a say in how it is run or performed even if they are not directly involved in producing or delivering it' (Hirst, 1986, p. 121).

For Durkheim a precondition for democracy is open and rational debate, which requires an openness of information and a political community composed of autonomous and informed sub-collectivities. His criticism of plebiscitary politics was based upon his belief that under such conditions demagogic manipulation is likely. His stress on the need for the relative autonomy of the state, secondary associations and the individual from each other was based upon his recognition that otherwise the state would be subject to the sway of a reactionary, unreflective conservativism and the individual to the tyranny of a forced altruistic solidarity. The experience of both capitalist and socialist societies suggests that such fears are well founded.

From this discussion and that in the [previous chapter] it is clear that large-scale socialist societies, although integrated under a hegemonic ideology incorporating certain substantive principles (e.g., equality of condition, rational rule-making procedures and a collective morality), cannot be homogeneous but comprise many different groups that will all have some success in pursuing their interests. This is not too dissimilar a picture to that painted of America by pluralists in the 1950s. This was criticized by the left on a number of grounds. First, if there are social conflicts in a capitalist system, the owners and controllers of capital both individually and collectively have disproportionately large resources to call upon and these may also be used to pre-empt the emergence of conflict. Second, the very logic of the economic system as a whole works in their favour and reproduces inequality. Third, the state and political and legal forms support and presuppose capitalistic forms of social relations and actively marginalize and delegitimate certain forms of political ideology and organization. Fourth, pluralism itself therefore serves as a legitimating ideology and contributes to the concealment of class relations (Gittlin, 1965; Bachrach and Baratz, 1962; Hayes, 1972; Wolfe, 1973). In his more recent work even Dahl has deployed his own pluralistic categories to criticize both the political and economic organization of contemporary America (Dahl, 1985).

The absence of class relations in a socialist society — and of some aspects of 'skills and organizational' exploitation (Levine, 1987) — would remove major systemic mechanisms for distributing disproportionate power and influence to minorities. The radical democratization of all institutions could make democracy more substantive and less formal and enhance the power and importance of the producers. Nevertheless, some of the issues raised by both pluralists and their radical critics retain some pertinence for a socialist society.

To argue that a society, at a national and local level, could and should be actively democratic is to suggest that all organizations should be subject to some kind of democratic control with individuals enfranchised as citizens, as workers within organizations, or as recipients of services. But democracy has no one form since many different relationships between nation and region, all-embracing organizations and more particularistic ones, modes of recruiting and controlling personnel, voting systems, etc., are compatible with its principles (Hindess, 1983). There are limitations to both popular participatory democracy and representative democracy. The former is only really viable for small-scale organizations, the latter only meaningful if elected bodies are of some consequence. Even then, many administrative decisions inevitably remain the virtual monopoly of personnel with high levels of skill and competence, who thereby exert a disproportionate influence upon social life, and this is true even if their decisions are more contestable than is usually the case now. This does not mean that since 'government . . . is always in the hands of a minority' (Durkheim, 1957, p. 85) democratic elections are 'but a means of providing personnel to bodies that serve definite functions' (Hirst, 1986, p. 46). Nor is it realistic to believe that some time in the future 'the appointments necessary to control political organs may come about . . . automatically, by the pressure of public opinion, and without . . . any definite reference to the electorate' (Durkheim, 1957, p. 108). Democratic theory has always functioned on the one hand as a critique of arbitrary power and a specification of the mechanisms by which it might be refused and, on the other, as a means of assessing legitimacy, i.e., when we should subordinate ourselves to 'power' — that of norms, laws or individuals. As both Durkheim and Hirst acknowledge elsewhere, the capacity to have some kind of veto over unacceptable arrangements is an equally essential element of democracy.

Corporatism is not without problems either. True it can complement the universal franchise (Hirst, 1988, p. 201) and overcome the atomization of its participants, but corporatism tends to acknowledge only already established and legitimated groups. The legitimacy of a system is associated with the development of a hegemonic ideology, which is always something of a compromise (articulation or conglomeration of diverse fragments from previous and more local ideologies) and thus the legitimacy of *any* socio-political order is always somewhat conditional. An advanced complex society — no matter how egalitarian — will inevitably contain diverse organizations, social categories and groups. The commitment of individuals and groups to the social order will bear some relationship to whether it realizes what they see as their legitimate interests and to the extent that they believe it to be generally valid and fair. If they feel alienated and politically ineffective they may well use deviant and even illegal methods to pursue their goals.[2]

The state and the law in socialist societies

Durkheim was understandably somewhat distrustful of the state; he did not believe that it should monopolize too many social functions or exercise too much power. It has been shown that on occasion he conceptualized the state not as an expression of a unified society but rather as separate from it with possibly different but not necessarily contradictory interests. This view seems correct but it is necessary to add that no complex society, whether capitalist or socialist, can be assumed to be unified around shared interests; nor can it be assumed that the state is itself unitary and united in the pursuit of its goals. The implication of these comments is that there is inevitably something of a tension between state and society and that it is always possible that state functionaries will pursue interests that are counter to those of some or most of the other members of society, and for that matter other elements of the state. Durkheim, like such social democratic Marxists as Renner (1949) was clear that the state and its functionaries should be subject to the 'rule of law', but he recognized that this did not automatically occur (Durkheim, 1973). It can perhaps be put more strongly: since the state is itself a source of, and the effective agency for implementing, the law, it is itself, in part, outside of the law. It is only likely to remain within the 'rule of law' if it is subject to external pressures and if each of its component elements is subject to scrutiny by other relatively autonomous elements — there is something to be said for the liberal theory of checks and balances.

If in his explicit definition of law Durkheim focused on its repressive role and ignored its formal properties in his elaborated discussion and substantive analyses, he did recognize its facilitative and even constitutive role. Moreover, it was shown earlier that the juridical relation that occurs in all societies can be distinguished from legal rules, which have certain formal properties. In Hirst's recent work there is a discussion of law that is similar to but in some ways goes beyond Durkheim's, foregrounding issues that are of immediate relevance. For Hirst, law refers to forms of definitive/regulatory rules produced by certain institutions presented as a sovereign power and enforced by specific state agencies (Hirst, 1980, p. 64). 'Sovereignty' is a necessary 'fiction', which allows for the exploration and resolution of disputes between law-issuing institutions, thereby producing some consistency within its discourses. It thus

> resolves in doctrine the paradox . . . how 'law' (legal agencies) can at once be above the activities it regulates and yet subject itself . . . It . . . prioritizes certain agencies and activities within the apparatuses of the state; these are held to express the will of the sovereign. (Hirst, 1980, p. 9)

Sovereignty is a 'symbolic function' but in reality the paradox remains. The state has no essence, no clear organizing centre that is the source of law and order; the totality of the state is not intrinsically and spontaneously limited by law. On the other hand, social order, justice and liberty depend upon the existence of a relatively consistent and predictable legal system and the effective regulation of state activities.

How then is the legal system articulated with the non-legal aspects of social relations since the nature of the state and the economic system and the forms of interpersonal relationships will surely affect its form and substantive content? Marxists, for example, would argue that in class societies the law is an element of a repressive and mystificatory system (Marx and Engels, 1845, in 1976, pp. 89–93) — legal categories, the content of laws, the forms of organization and access to legal institutions are all marked (and often materially affected) by class relations (Burton and Carlen, 1979). Against such views Hindess and Hirst (1977) have asserted the virtual autonomy of law and in particular its 'necessary non-correspondence' with economic relations. For Durkheim, on the other hand, law is an index and source of different kinds of solidarity and therefore is both determined by other social relations and also has its own causal efficacy. But, whatever the problems in Durkheim's overall conceptual schema, the combination of elements of his work with aspects of Marxism has a great deal of potential.

Woodiwiss (1985) has argued that, whilst law does not have the absolute autonomy attributed to it by Hirst and it often helps maintain oppressive class relations, nevertheless it is not simply an expression of class interests. It is better understood as

> a set of state enunciated and enforced discourses, which interpellate the subjects they address in such a way that they will be law-abiding, provided that the same subjects do not successfully resist this disciplining because of prior or other interpellations originating in and articulated within counter discourses . . . the law may be understood to produce a background ideology-effect that helps to maintain the security of the social relationships that the state also and in other ways reproduces . . .

> . . . the law places the subjects it addresses in particular positions relative to one another according to the schema to be found in its component discourses. These positions are constituted by the rights and duties that define them and which therefore determine the relations that can and should exist between them; e.g., husband/wife, employer/employee and citizen/state . . . such positions and such relations are also defined and confined by other discourses and intrinsic technologies apart from those specific to the law. (Woodiwiss, 1985, pp. 72–3)

For Woodiwiss, like Durkheim, law is both an effect of and affects other fundamental social relations. Its development and substantive concerns depend upon its own internal logic, the specific (possibly conflictual) social relations that are present within a society, and their (possibly contradictory) articulation with both each other and the law. Provided that there are adequate institutional resources through which it can be 'realized', the legal recognition or creation and enforcement or denial of capacities, powers or duties will have significant social effects. Law can be constitutive, enabling and coercive.

If social formations are conceived of as mobile, articulated combinations of elements, which have as one effect the interpellation of subjects by complementary or (possibly) contradictory discourses, then the interaction between the dynamics of the social relations and the forms of collective social organization, discourses, interpersonal relationships and ideologies will determine the form, substantive content and significance of the law. These will determine what interests are secured by it and the relative ease with which individuals will wish to, or be able to, submit themselves to the exigencies of social life and the lawful authority of the state. In a socialist society the production of a formal and substantive equality for individuals would be a major social goal realized in and, in part, through the law.

Juridical relations — i.e., the existence of structures of rights and obligations and modes of attributing responsibility to individuals or collectivities — are an endemic feature of any society. Exchange relationships of various kinds — particularly the 'equitable' exchange of goods and services — can contribute to social solidarity. One of the most significant features of these forms of relationship is that the mutual interest of the parties in current and future transactions motivates them to honour their obligations. Legal recognition and control may facilitate these relations. True, it may, on occasion, enforce obligations primarily as Durkheim argued, in a 'restitutive' manner. However, once rights and obligations become subject to legal discourse they will be evaluated according to its substantive criteria of equity and of the kind of rights and duties it recognizes and prioritizes. With the development of 'organic solidarity' only certain kinds of contracts would be recognized — those between substantively equal partners.

Since Durkheim's economics are somewhat inadequate, organic solidarity would only be achieved with a more complex system like that of the Swedish Meidner plan. This, in making socialist producers' associations the basic unit of the economy, gave some indication of a more adequate legal and economic framework. Thus the socialist jurists Abrahamson and Bromston argued for the establishment

> of a set of labour rights, which should be privileged relative to private property rights . . . with such an amendment in place the contract of employment itself would be radically changed as well as the distribution of rights within it. Moreover, remembering Marx's strictures against 'equal rights' this would be profoundly unequal since if enforced they would gradually undermine any rights of capital, in the pursuit of the material equality of need-fulfillment. (Woodiwiss, 1985, p. 64)

The valorization by the law of any specific rights means that other rights and interests may suffer; from their point of view such law is not enabling but punitive. The disadvantage that they thereby experience and the threat of sanctions if they actively oppose the operation of lawful relations vindicate the Austinian–Durkheimian view that an essential (although by no means the sole) quality of law is its potential coerciveness (Skillen, 1977, p. 100). Nevertheless, legal forms may be constitutive. They may provide the rules to determine who is qualified to fulfil which tasks and to exercise which powers. They may help organize the means by which individuals are held accountable for the fulfillment of their role-related responsibilities.

The rule of law and socialism

Durkheim argued that the development of the state, if it is itself subject to law, can increase liberty, and Hirst has argued that socialism will probably see an extension of legally regulated intervention into social life. Such an extension of state activities would only be 'progressive' if there are social forces that can control the state and if the legal institutions have some real autonomy, i.e., if they are relatively independent of other state institutions and have their own bases of power (Hirst, 1980, pp. 77–88). Such socialist constitutionalism is still somewhat limited. If the structure, ordering and priorities of the state and the content of the law are the effect of a struggle between shifting heterogeneous forces and of the attempt to produce within it one or other form of coherence, then it will not work to the benefit of everybody to the same degree. It will be unlikely spontaneously to take cognizance of the interests of newly emerging groups. Whatever efforts are made to give all interests political representation within the dominant political and legal discourse, there will probably be very little understanding of the goals or the determinants of the action of the more marginal groups and individuals. As a matter of course, at times one would expect from them some illegal behaviour, some of which would be simply criminal and some proto-political. The latter might subsequently be legitimated in the same way that Socrates' conduct came to be interpreted as based upon a higher morality (Durkheim, 1938, pp. 71–2).

Moreover, it is not necessary to subscribe to any iron 'law of oligarchy' to believe that, even with sophisticated methods of supervision, powerful functionaries can rarely be totally controlled. They are under various pressures — the exigencies of office (national security, for example), contradictory demands from different groups, etc., which usually lead them to adopt a somewhat managerialist view of the world, leading in turn to their developing separate interests from the ruled. Given the resources at their disposal, this allows them to act in a partisan way. In so far as the law does not acknowledge all interests equally and since the state may act in a partisan way then, whilst a policy of legally enforced 'social defence' may be inescapable, law-abiding behaviour cannot be seen as unquestionably good, nor law-breaking behaviour as 'reactionary', 'selfish', 'anti-social', 'pathological' or 'wicked'.

The 'constitutionalist' view was put well by US Supreme Justice Fortas when he claimed that 'Just as we expect the government to be bound by all laws, so each individual is bound by all of the laws under the Constitution' (Fortas, 1968, p. 65). To which Zinn responded:

> the government being bound by law is an exception, while the citizens being bounded by law is a fact . . . The government does pick and choose among the laws it enforces and the laws it ignores. . . . Furthermore, when the government does violate the law . . . — it has no punishing body standing over it as does the citizen; it does not and cannot accept the rule of law as final. National power prevails. (Zinn, 1968, pp. 23–4)

For, if the law is somewhat partisan, if one cannot be confident that state functionaries will stay within the law and if sovereignty is a 'fiction' (however necessary), then the 'rule of law' cannot simply become invoked — as it often was by Durkheim — to justify subservience to the state. (Subsequently, 'when his links with a notorious financial wheeler dealer in Florida were revealed' (Chambliss, 1982, p. 175) Fortas was forced to resign from the Supreme Court!) In any society, individuals may rationally choose, for moral or political reasons, to engage in illegal acts in the context of political struggle rather than as a moral gesture — Socrates' mode of civil disobedience is only one option! A legal system based upon an adequate analysis of the nature of social order will recognize the category of political crime (Moran, 1981).[3]

Capitalism, socialism and the criminal law

This section will examine law in its most coercive form, as criminal law. Now Marxists have argued that crime — whether it is overridingly destructive or a form of 'primitive rebellion' — is primarily an effect of the forms of social organization and ideologies found within class societies. Poverty and egoistic ideologies help generate street crime and greed, and the defence of privilege leads the ruling class and the state to break the law, usually with impunity (Bonger, 1916; Pashukanis, 1978, p. 212; Taylor, Walton and Young, 1973; Hirst, 1972). Since class relations have been considered the most fundamental aspect of the social order, there has been a tendency to believe that the end of class inequality will see the virtual end of anti-social behaviour of crime and the criminal law (Engels, 1845, in Marx and Engels, 1975. pp. 248–9).

In an earlier work, *Crimes of the Powerful* (1976), I also argued that inequality generates conflicts that may be expressed in criminal activity. Although that text operated with an overly instrumentalist view of the state (Jones, 1982), much of its analysis of the sources and significance of crime within capitalist societies is still sound. *Inequalities of power and wealth generate criminal conduct and provide differential protection from the criminalizing power of the state.* Moreover, whilst class relations play a major role in generating and sustaining inequalities other relatively autonomous aspects of social organization (those associated with race and gender) also generate their own forms of social inequality and anti-social conduct. Thus an equality of condition (and power) between men and women and the development of different forms of personal relations and modes of eroticism would make crimes like rape less likely, since this is, in part, *an expression of and a support for male dominance* (Clarke and Lewis, 1977; Barnet, 1974; Schwendinger and Schwendinger, 1983; Henriques *et al.*, 1984, p. 251–60).

Nevertheless, it is necessary now to reject the thesis implicit in much Marxist writing, including my own, that crime will be completely eliminated from a socialist society. There will still be criminogenic situations and the socialist position on crime must be rethought. The elimination of certain kinds of inequality may itself produce problems for the elimination of others: the extent to which individuals have their desires satisfied within socialist societies will vary considerably. Moreover in areas like drug use and drug abuse (from cigarettes to marijuana, from alcohol to heroin) where there are different forms of calculation, priorities and moralities, conflict between different groups is likely and indeed virtually unavoidable.

A useful way of considering these issues is by a brief consideration of the work of Jock Young, a sociologist who has made a significant contribution to the development of criminology and who has been strongly influenced by both Durkheim and Marx. In the *The Drugtakers* (1971) he demonstrated the relevance of a transactionalist approach to the British context. *The New Criminology* (1973), which he wrote with Ian Taylor and Paul Walton, helped transform the level of theorizing in the area. His articles on

'Working class criminology' (1974) and on 'Left idealism, reformism and beyond: from new criminology to Marxism' (1979) forced many radical criminologists to confront the destructiveness of much crime. In his recent empirical studies using crime victimization surveys (Jones, Maclean and Young, 1986) and in his related development of a 'realist criminology' (Lea and Young, 1984; Kinsey, Lea and Young, 1986; Matthews and Young, 1986) he has shown that socialists must try to discover what actually are the patterns of criminal activity and victimization. They must also be willing to assess empirically the effectiveness of different crime pre-emption, crime prevention and crime control strategies by monitoring their effects. A socialist response to crime cannot be built upon principled positions and abstract theorizing alone. Nevertheless, it is possible and useful to criticize much of his work from the perspective of a reconstituted radical Durkheimism.[4]

In his earlier writings, Young argued that capitalistic social relations are a major cause of criminal activity, that much criminal activity is proto-political and that 'the task is to create a society in which the facts of human diversity, whether personal, organic or social, are not subject to the power to criminalize' (Taylor, Walton and Young, 1973, p. 282). Subsequently, whilst retaining the first proposition, he stresses rather the destructive consequences of present-day working-class crime on working-class people (Young, 1975, 1979; Lea and Young, 1984; Kinsey, Lea and Young, 1986; Matthews and Young, 1986). In a recent book co-authored with John Lea, he has developed a somewhat unreconstituted Durkheimian characterization of criminal activity. Working-class criminals, he argues, have an egoistic orientation and have adopted 'capitalistic' values.

> ... street crime itself, far from being different in terms of values from the crimes of the powerful, displays precisely the same ethos of competitiveness and machismo. (Lea and Young, 1984, p. 74)

These individuals may experience relative deprivation but they choose to become involved in crime, 'an egoistic response to injustice' that itself 'perpetrates injustice' (ibid., 1984, p. 91). Instead of engaging in 'collectivist' political action, criminals are committed egoists, willing agents of capitalistic values, who should be caught and *punished* for the protection of working-class people. Presumably if socialistic rather than capitalistic values ('altruistic rather that egoistic values') became dominant, crime would be an unlikely — but not an impossible — option for individuals to 'choose'.

These arguments of Young can be criticized for their tendency to rely upon a culturalist neo-classicism. Frequently the assumption is made that the author has an adequate understanding of the meanings that criminals give to their activities and how they interpret their interests. There is a presupposition that a rational response would be collectivistic and that all individuals are equally able to refuse the egoistic alternative. Such arguments are voluntaristic, often overly moralistic and grounded in a negative conception of freedom.[5] What freedom we have lies not only in the possibility of refraining *from action* but also in being able *to act*, of being able to work towards one's projects (Merleau-Ponty, 1962, pp. 438–9).

It is also necessary to understand how social relations affect the possibility of the realization (or displacement) of the projects and desires of individuals and hence the degree of frustration that such individuals may experience. How stark are the choices that confront them? Must they either live a lawful frustrated life or realize their goals illegally or, for that matter, relieve some of their frustration irrationally? Are they working with sensibilities, moralities and rationalities and in social milieux that we do not grasp (Foucault, 1979a)? Whilst the ideology the individual uses to interpret his/her own activity (and by which he/she is interpellated) must be a component of any explanation of human conduct (individuals must be motivated to act), it is unlikely to provide an *adequate* explanation of the determinants of their actions. Accounts are often mere glosses and at best partial explanations (Mills, 1940; Blum and McHugh, 1971). The full determinants of an individual's activities in concrete social settings are never known.

For Freud and Lacan although the conscious/preconscious/unconscious system can never be grasped in its totality, this does not rule out all forms of individual responsibility. The individual human subject operates at the point of intersection of social pressures and also possibilities; of ideologies that he or she may be able to, in part, analyse; of a socially constituted unconscious and desire; and at the same time he/she has some capacity to control conduct. Freud formulated the issue in the imperative statement *'Wo es ist, so ich wollen'*, which was interpreted by Lacan to mean

> 'There where IT WAS ITSELF, it is my duty that I come to be. '

> The I of the formula refers to an ideal concept of a harmonious accord between subject c (the conscious) and subject u (the unconscious). (Bar, 1971, p. 260)

Duty here means a responsibility to avoid situations known to precipitate conduct that is harmful to self or others and implies *a limited freedom to seek those where the effect of the constitutive play of differences is likely to be personally and socially constructive.*

Egoism and altruism should not be viewed as mutually exclusive orientations. Individuals need to take cognizance of egoism too. Their capacity to order their conduct bears a direct, albeit complex, relationship to their ability to develop, acknowledge and satisfy their (socially constituted) 'appetites and passions'. Their socio-structural location, their emotional investments and their value commitments (McCabe, 1974, 1976; Henriques *et al.*, 1984) affect the degree to which they *need* to control their desires and particularly to control them by suppression as opposed to simply organizing their lives to satisfy them in an ordered way. The logic of these comments is that a major aim of a sophisticated socialist response to crime is *to open up the socially constructive and personally fulfilling options for those who are so often faced with the stark choice between criminal activity through which they can realize their desires (or at least release tension) and an overly repressive self-denying lawfulness.*

Now implicit in much of Young's work is a somewhat Rousseauian conception of the human subject as a fundamentally good, perfectible entity. Negative traits or activities are construed as perversions of the human essence and explained either as the effect of some outside agency, i.e., of an exploitative and oppressive society, and/or as the result of a perverse choice by the individual. Young would not deny that there is some tension between the essential nature of human beings and attempts to control them, but believes that this is generally due to the contradictions between their essential humanity and the inhumanity of capitalism. In a socialist society man's nature and social relations could be in accord. Young implies that rational individuals will be able and willing to submit themselves to a socialist normative order.

For Durkheim, the rationality of the human subject is produced and sustained by society. Society is not an expression or an extension of the subject's ontological attributes; rather it provides individuals with the capacity to follow its rules and the ability to engage in meaningful and orderly social interaction. If one can *follow a rule,* by definition one can break it. Any normative order requires of its subjects that their 'appetites and passions' be controlled and ordered. 'A community of rational co-operators' may need 'to use force against itself' (Levine, 1987, p. 136) so that its members are the rational subjects they desire to be.

A critique of judicial ideology

Before returning to the issue of the role of law and the likelihood of crime under socialism, let us explore some of the implications of these remarks. Those of high social status and income have a radically different life experience from most others. This is particularly true of the very poor, who are the most likely to be convicted of crimes. The possession of wealth guarantees that an individual can feed, clothe and shelter himself or herself more than adequately. The wealthy are able to choose the activities in which they engage and plan their participation in them in ways that are likely to match their moods and thus *although they may work hard and be disciplined nevertheless they will be able to satisfy many of their desires.* Their contacts with others will rarely if ever produce anything but the self-affirming respect of equals or the deference of inferiors. In contrast, individuals of low social status can rarely plan their lives in a satisfying way and frequently do not experience social contact of a kind that might energize them to control themselves and conform to social norms. The everyday experience of the capitalist or professional academic or judge is radically different from that of the unskilled, particularly when unemployed.

Weber argued that those with access to honour, power, possessions and pleasure were seldom satisfied with the fact of being fortunate:

> he needs to know that he has a *right* to his good fortune. He wants to be convinced that he 'deserves' it and above all in comparison with others. He wishes to be allowed the belief that the less fortunate also merely experiences his due. (Weber, 1958, p. 271)

Such a concern with the 'legitimacy' of their fortune represents not so much an aspect of human ontology as an ever-present 'political' problem: how can the 'fortunate' justify themselves to the less fortunate? One function of law enforcement in capitalist societies is the legitimation of privilege.

The legal category of 'mitigating circumstances' to some extent acknowledges that the conditions under which people live affects their ability to live lawful lives (Stevens, 1863). This poses the question: if the 'fortunate' are subject to less pressure to steal than the poor, how is it then that they feel free to condemn the lower-class criminal? Foucault paraphrases the reasoning behind their answer as follows:

> He steals because he is poor; certainly we all know that not all poor people steal. So for this individual to steal there has to be something wrong with him, and this is his character, his psyche, his upbringing, his unconscious, his desires. (Foucault, 1980b, p. 44)[6]

The argument is that, since there are poor people who do not steal, it is possible to be poor and law-abiding. And further that, if the privileged were poor themselves, they would still be law-abiding. Thus the 'deserving poor' and the privileged are supposed to have similar 'moral fibre', although the latter have additional qualities that explain their relative worldly success.

'Character' then, or some other quality of the individual that transcends social contexts, is invoked to explain and justify the different trajectories of people's lives. The category of the 'deserving poor' is more a convenient legitimating and obfuscating category than a substantive reference to a specific group of people (Palmer and Pearce, 1983). Such individualistic and 'abstract' (non-materialist) (Burton and Carlen, 1979) explanations of social action are untenable. Subjects are socially constituted and continually reconstituted through their current social relations. For example, a High Court judge with a net salary in excess of £45,000 p.a. would be unlikely to know how he would feel and act if he had the life experiences and prospects of an unemployed Black youth on £1,500 or less p.a.[7] How would he cope with insufficient money for even the bare necessities of life, with a frequent lack of fit between his desires and his opportunities, with the contempt of lower-middle-class bureaucrats, with the media's portrayal of him and 'his kind', etc? What grounds would he have to assume that if he were one of the poor he would not develop and display their qualities (or values)? In his discussion of 'the forced division of labour' Durkheim argued that in any society with inherited privileges there could not be equality of opportunity, yet the idea that in capitalist societies positions of high social status are primarily achieved in a meritocratic manner is still promulgated. This discussion of course accepts at face value the claim of the privileged that their own fortune and current conduct are lawful but it has been shown elsewhere that this can by no means be assumed (Pearce, 1976; Reiman, 1979).[8]

The implications of the above discussion are manifold. The outraged self-righteous language of the privileged when they condemn the criminality of the poor is offensive because it is misleading and ultimately self-serving. But to recognize the importance of structural factors is not to argue that criminality is always the only possible outcome of criminogenic situations. Nor does one accept at face value the idea that the law-abiding poor are merely (diluted) versions of privileged role models. Some kinds of crime and types of criminal have always been tolerated by working-class people (Foucault, 1979b; Palmer, 1976).

Crime in socialist societies

Whilst a formal legal system involves some self-consciousness about at least some elements of the normative system, the extent to which the content of legal norms is subject to collective critical scrutiny depends upon the forms of political organization and the distribution of power within a society. The more egalitarian and democratic they are, the more likely it is that the legal system will function to benefit all groups and thus win their loyalty. In everyday interaction, however, new definitions of norms are constantly generated. Even when individuals and groups have roughly equivalent power, and thus engage in non-repressive communication and negotiation (Mueller, 1970), some of their activities may become defined as deviant, leading to the frustration of some of their goals. This is particularly true in a dynamic society where new activities, norms and social organizations are continually generated. Since some of these are probably mutually incompatible, the legal valorization of some entails the suppression of others. In any society this inescapable aspect of societal management will on occasion confront criminal resistance. As Durkheim argued, a high degree of social dynamism creates the possibility of a high rate of crime.

In the same way that a society of saints is more scrupulous about its members' conduct than are laymen (Durkheim, 1938, pp. 68–9), a humane society is more demanding of its members than an inhumane society. The overriding commitment of a socialist society to an equal and humane life for *all* would mean that higher standards of performance and conduct would be expected than is true under capitalism. A genuine respect for the individual might mean more rigorously imposed safety regulations (Hirst, 1980, p. 103), and a greater respect for the collectivity might mean that:

> Frauds and injustices, which yesterday left the public conscience almost indifferent, arouse it today, and this sensitivity will only become more acute with time. (Durkheim, 1973, p. 307)

The elimination of the ruling class and of many structural contradictions would make certain kinds of destructive criminal activity and the creation of a *forced solidarity* through moral panics, scapegoating, etc. less likely. But it is clear that there are features of social life as such and particularly of a dynamic society that make it inevitable that some forms of diversity will be defined as deviant and/or criminal (*contra* Taylor, Walton and Young, 1973, p. 282). Whilst a general equality of condition would be a goal in a socialist society, the existence of diverse organizations, social categories and groups would still create variations in income and differences in life chances. A lack of social homogeneity and the existence of a plurality of values in the community mean social priorities and the content of the law will always remain contentious. (Young argues a somewhat similar position to this in *Losing the Fight against Crime* — Kinsey, Lea and Young, 1986.) Furthermore, it is clear that in many areas of social life the development of skills and capacities will be uneven and some individuals will be relatively deficient and therefore disadvantaged. I have argued that a rational orientation to the world must include, and be sustained by, both 'egoistic' and 'altruistic' elements. But there is no simple calculus determining their relative proportions, so on occasion an imbalance between them may lead to excessive individualism (cynicism, careerism, crime, 'egoistic' suicide) or excessive 'collectivism' (over-conformity, a militant search for homogeneity, altruistic suicide). Thus many problems would not simply disappear with the demise of capitalism.

Durkheim argued that for individuals to develop any form of rationality they must control, limit and order their 'appetites and passions' to what those in their social position can realistically and legitimately expect. They are aided in achieving this by the various systems of social constraint, from the most intimate and concrete nexus of rights and obligations to the most abstract system of social norms — the legal system. Constraint may be exercised by a fear of sanctions, by a somewhat compulsive sense of duty and/or by a belief in social norms grounded in desire — in a sense of self-realization based upon an identification with the collectivity. On the other hand, society can only function and be reproduced if individuals contain their appetites and passions and submit to the dynamic of social life and its regulative norms. Durkheim argued rightly that because the despot is unconstrained he is as much at the mercy of his desires as is the untutored child (Durkheim, 1961, p. 45). In a society that developed true organic solidarity individuals would be expected to demonstrate a socially responsible concern with the actual consequences of their actions and a willingness to recompense anybody suffering because of them. Similarly, if 'charity' is an aspect of the dominant ideology and it is recognized that it is not individuals alone who author actions, one would expect 'victims' to be more interested in restoring their own fortunes and in understanding how harmful acts come about than in punishing their perpetrators. In the 'Two laws of penal evolution' Durkheim argued that the increase in secularism has meant that the humanity of individuals is not so readily forgotten. Those found guilty of crimes are punished more humanely (Durkheim, 1973). As an overall characterization of the history of penal practice this is undoubtedly overly optimistic — but as a prescriptive argument it has a great deal of power. If a social order valorizes all of its members and recognizes that their actions are, in large part, an effect of social forces over which they have little control, then to respond to their criminal acts in a vindictive and overly moralistic manner is illogical.

Crime: some modest socialist proposals

Since, as I have argued, a crime-free society is a Utopia, the criminal law and its enforcement apparatuses have a role to play in both capitalist and socialist societies. There is some continuity in the dilemmas faced by all complex societies. In Durkheim's terms, capitalism and socialism are of the same *genus*. The extent to which individuals are authors of their actions can vary substantially and some recognition of this should inform socialist strategies of 'social defence', in both class and non-class societies. Durkheim not only stressed the need to control the 'passions and desires' but he also recognized that they needed some gratification. A useful *initial* assumption in reacting to criminals is that they engage in crime largely because few other courses of action that allow them to gratify their desires are open to them. This neither reduces them to the status of purely behaviourist subjects — as in the work of Pashukanis, for example[9] — nor 'elevates' them to purely transcendental subjects — as in Lea and Young (Neale, 1977).

What, then, should be the socialist attitude to crime in capitalist and post-class societies? First, there is no need to accept that all acts currently defined as crimes should be prosecuted. The repeal of some legislation may be more important than its effectiveness. Second, the whole judicial system and its panoply of coercive institutions need to be reorganized, democratized and the 'powers of the judiciary . . . redefined and redistributed' (Carlen, 1983, p. 210; Taylor, 1981). Every effort should be made to reduce the role of imprisonment. It should rarely be used, except for detention — if it is literally the only way to protect people's life and limbs — or in a denunciatory manner to demonstrate the seriousness of an offence, for example in cases of rape. If prison is not generally used for other offences it is the fact of imprisonment rather than longevity of stay that demonstrates social abhorrence (Box-Grainger, 1986, pp. 49–51).

If an anti-social crime has been perpetrated, then the state should intervene in an individual's life if he or she was *its* author. Prosecution should occur if the defendant is sane and does not successfully plead 'necessity'. If guilt is established then the individual should suffer some specified penalty, although mitigating circumstances should be able to modify a sentence. The criminalizing of certain kinds of conduct and the punishment of its perpetrators publicly signals that it is anti-social and not a viable solution to personal problems, and specifies, for example in situations of interpersonal conflict such as wife battering (and crimes such as rape, see above) that there is a criminal and a victim. A scale of penalties shows the relative seriousness of different crimes and aims to deter the more serious. It can also thereby help to reinforce positive forms of social relationships — e.g., appropriately framed and enforced laws against sexual violence can help sustain sexual equality (Taylor, 1981, pp. 191–200).

Punishment allows the criminal to expiate his or her crime and therefore to become a citizen again, i.e., to return to life as a legitimate subject in a way that pre-empts the development of vigilantism and lynch law. Furthermore, a general assumption that a defendant is a responsible juridical and legal subject limits the *right* of the state to interfere in the lives of criminals inside and outside of detention. This must imply that subjectifying disciplinary and 'therapeutic treatment' has to be in some sense voluntary — criminals ought to have enforceable rights, including the right to refuse 'treatment'.[10] However, this is not to deny that other strategies might be relevant — currently for example, in Holland and the Scandinavian countries many offenders can avoid trial and conviction if they acknowledge their guilt and attend treatment programmes for drug abuse, alcoholism, etc. (Carlen, 1983, p. 213).

Nevertheless, a socialist response to criminals and to criminogenic situations must involve the search for ways of opening up the individual's possibilities of engaging in more constructive and satisfying activities. For example, it can be argued that some criminals do suffer from an 'educational problem' — they commit offences largely out of ignorance of the way in which society operates and of their own role and motives. Although often not the case (Muncie, 1984, p. 172–8), group work with young people can be non-authoritarian, equipping them with the social skills and personality attributes to cope more adequately with their environment and to make their own decisions more rationally (Bazelgette, 1971; Jones and Kerslake, 1979). Violent men are often consumed by some kind of destructive rage and/or are interpersonally inept and should be offered the possibility of some kind of therapeutic treatment, for example, that which Jimmy Boyle received in Barlinnie (Boyle, 1977). Wife batterers, rapists and child molesters should be offered contexts to develop the understanding and social skills needed for a reciprocal egalitarian sexuality (Abel *et al.*, 1976; Yaffe, 1981). As in China during the 'cultural revolution', criminal activity should be seen not as authored exclusively by the individual but as an effect of general social relationships and often of an 'underdeveloped perspective' (Pepinsky, 1978). What is needed is a neo-classicism that is able to live up to its promise and recognize its limitations, as opposed to one that functions as a support and mask for 'disciplinary processes' (Foucault, 1978b, pp. 87–8; 1979b, pp. 183, 223).

On a more structural level an understanding and/or modification of the social contexts in which potential criminals live can make crime less likely. Thus 'resource-oriented' strategies developed to deal with criminogenic situations are worth maintaining and developing. Whilst a general improvement in living conditions and sexual equality would limit the incidence of wife battering, the continued provision of accommodation for battered women could prevent its repetition (Binney *et al.*, 1981; Wilson, 1983). Mathiesen (1976), amongst others, explains the genesis of crime and the existence of prisons primarily in terms of the production and control of surplus populations and therefore believes that the replacement of capitalism by socialism would render imprisonment anachronistic. Others such as Christie (1976) and Hulsman (1986) argue that many offences should be decriminalized and conflicts should be resolved by the protagonists rather than punished by the state.[11] There is little doubt that much would improve if these changes came about. What cannot be treated as an axiom, however, is that the role of the prison as a mode of detention, of protecting society from people who are currently dangerous, will automatically disappear. It is difficult to see what alternative there would be to preventive detention for such mass murderers as Brady and Hindley (Williams, 1968), Peter Sutcliffe (the Yorkshire Ripper — Yallop, 1981; Bland, 1984), Nielsen (Masters, 1986), or David Berkowitz (the Son of Sam — Willeford, 1980).

Even if the major aim of a sophisticated socialist response to crime is to open up constructive options for those in criminogenic situations, we cannot presume to know with *scientific* certainty why (and indeed sometimes whether) an individual committed a crime or if in future they will be a law-abiding citizen or not. Some individuals commit crime when subject to no obvious overwhelming or external pressure, as in the case of much white-collar crime. Since all subjects are socially constituted, even in these cases it is important for socialists to remember that criminals remain part of society. As individuals they should have the right to a fair trial. If found guilty they should not be treated vindictively — like all of us, they are only in part responsible for their own desires and actions and should never lose the right to humane treatment.[12] At the end of this chapter it is worth reiterating Durkheim's arguments why a genuinely civilized society, as well as sympathizing with victims, would also care about offenders.

> What tempers the collective anger, which is the essence of punishment, is the sympathy which we feel for every man who suffers, the horror which all destructive violence causes us; it is the same sympathy and the same horror which inflames this anger. And so the same cause which sets in motion the repressive apparatus tends also to halt it . . . But there is a real

and terrible contradiction in avenging the offended human dignity of the victim by violating that of the criminal. (Durkheim, 1973, p. 303)

Notes

1. The policies and politics of the Trilateral Commission are assessed in Sklar (1980) and Van der Pijl (1984).

2. I have criticized Hirst (1986) for the implicit evolutionism that he shares with Durkheim in Pearce (1987a). Recently Hirst (1988) has elaborated his arguments on the need to complement the universal franchise with corporatist institutions.

3. Whilst Hirst is critical of Thompson's naive trust in the 'rule of law' (Hirst, 1980, p. 199), he does not seem adequately to think through the implications of his own comments for a socialist society.

4. Young with Taylor and Walton was involved in a somewhat acrimonious debate with Paul Hirst (see Taylor, Walton and Young 1975; and Pearce, 1985a). Hirst (1980) sharply attacked Greenwood and Young (1976), although in Hirst (1986, p. 67) there is a strong endorsement of Young and Lea (1985). Young and Lea (1984) and other recent works have been strongly criticized by Gilroy (1982, 1987), Sim (1982), Gilroy and Sim (1985), Scraton (1985).

5. In this text, Lea and Young's analysis of social milieux is sometimes somewhat empiricist (Lea and Young, 1984, pp. 76–104; Willer and Willer, 1973, pp. 88–95).

6. James Watson drove a car along a pavement crowded with Christmas shoppers, knocking down one elderly Tottenham woman, Wood Green Crown Court heard last week.

   He was jailed for reckless driving and a string of other offences, for a total of four years and nine months after admitting he turned to crime when he lost his job.

   Recorder Douglas Blair pointed out that while many people were unemployed they did not break the law.

   Watson (31), from West Hampstead, pleaded guilty to five burglaries, four offences of deception, one of handling stolen goods and two of taking cars without consent in addition to reckless driving. He asked for another ten deceptions and two burglaries to be taken into consideration. (*The Harringey Independent*, 27 August 1987)

7. In 1988, when a High Court judge earned £68,500 p.a. (£45,633 after tax), an unemployed 18–24 year old on social security received £1,355 p.a. (*Guardian* 22 April and 19 May 1988).

8. This is not the place to explore these issues in any great depth but it is worth reiterating the point that this abstract concept of the juridical subject can function in judgements about the venality of the powerful and privileged too. They may be roundly condemned for setting a bad example, *but,* more often, the fact that judge and defendant share similar lives and 'temptations' may create an empathic understanding of the complex pressures to which individuals are subject and hence to a non-essentializing view of the relationship between these criminals and their acts. Chapman (1968, pp. 54–96) provides many examples of this differential response to criminal activity.

9. For Pashukanis the science of Marxism shows that crime and/or destructive deviance are the direct consequence of class relations, particularly capitalistic ones. *Mens rea*, motives, degrees of guilt, etc. — in short, *the juridical subject* within law — are therefore ideological constructs that have real enough effects but are of little relevance in explaining how and why people become criminals or how to deal with them. Crime is caused by class inequality

and they will therefore disappear together. If individuals commit crimes in a socialist society, then this is because it still contains 'dangerous situations' owing to an incomplete social transformation or, alternatively, because such individuals are 'medical–educational' problems. Criminality that can not be diagnosed as a symptom of social contradictions or of a lack of 'education' would then have to be a 'medical problem' needing a 'medical' response (Pashukanis, 1978, p. 187). From a neo-Durkheimian viewpoint there are two obvious problems with this position. First, as was argued in [Chapter 5], no society can exist that did not develop ways in which individuals (or collectives) are made responsible either to others or to themselves for their actions. Such 'juridical relations' are pervasive throughout social life, although the attribution of responsibility for behaviour has various meanings and consequences. Second, an essential component of the explanation of human conduct is the motives that individuals attribute to themselves and others; whilst the understanding that subjects have of their action is insufficient to explain it adequately, it is certainly not irrelevant.

10. Without such 'rights' psychoanalysis could not be meaningfully used. 'Transference', the 'treatment contract' and the moment of individuation and separation from the analyst are all important elements of the therapeutic process. In a prison setting it would be virtually impossible for the analysand *and* the analyst to work out when 'insight' was a function of transference, an unconscious wish to be agreeable in order to get out of prison, or a sign of 'individuation'. Thus, *contra* Foucault, subjectifying 'disciplines' are not *per se* modes of coercive social control; in the case of psychoanalysis at least, this is so only when they are abused. Conventional psychoanalysts have, of course, often presumed that criminal acts are necessarily symptoms of a defective personal structure and that criminals seek to be caught and punished to assuage guilt. However, even one such author, Franz Alexander, acknowledged the existence of 'normal non-neurotic criminals — professional delinquents whose superegos have criminal tendencies . . . with a moral code different from that of the rest of society' (Alexander and Straub 1956, p. xi).

Foucault has been criticized by Hirst for his ultra-leftist libertarianism, for presenting 'normatising individuation' as if disciplinary practices had some 'unity of object, content or effect' and for counterposing legal and disciplinary regulation. He thereby fails to recognize that

> law defines the status of the specialist practices . . . and sets limits to the powers
> of the agents and institutions involved in forms of discipline, doctors, teachers,
> reformatories, hospitals etc. . . . (Hirst, 1980, p. 92)

Whilst some of Hirst's criticisms are powerful, he does not recognize that a major thrust of Foucault's argument is that formal definitions of status and capacity tell us little about *how* disciplinary practices are organized and how their 'objects' — mental patients, prisoners, schoolchildren, etc. — are in practice 'subjectified'. Moreover the language of rights, duties and capacities is not adequate to describe or control what occurs, it legitimates disciplinarity and itself needs to be redefined (Foucault, 1980c, p. 105). The crucial problem then is how institutions are organized, monitored and controlled.

Foucault himself fails to discriminate between different forms of organizational structure — for him they are all equivalent because they all require the disciplining and subjectivation of their members. He thus ignores the significant differences between different kinds of subjectivities and how they allow individuals to relate to themselves and the world. A capacity for self-reflection and self-control is a precondition for any kind of rational activity and any kind of social order (Dews, 1984, pp. 94–5). Foucault's over-valorization of non-reflective modes of pursuing desire is either inherently elitist — some people will inevitably be constrained by discipline in 'the realm of necessity', and let us not forget that de Sade was a marquis and von Sacher-Masoch a count! — or it is associated with a romantic nostalgia about the world of non-commodity or petty-commodity producers. In a system of petty-commodity production there would be no 'exploitation', no 'organizational oppression' and an equality of condition. Despite the far more sophisticated concepts of which he was surely aware — he was a student of Althusser's (Althusser and Balibar, 1970, p. 323) — Foucault uses concepts akin to those of the young Man to describe exploitation and struggles against it.

> Generally, it can be said that there are three types of struggles: either against forms of domination (ethnic, social and religious); against forms of exploitation *which separate individuals from what they produce; or against that which ties the individual himself and submits him to others in this way (struggles against subjection, against forms of subjectivity and submission)*. (Foucault, 1982, p. 212)

Thus he often uncritically accepted the classical concept of law and crime (Foucault, 1979b, pp. 221, 223), which after all implicitly presupposed something like petty-commodity production. Such conditions do not obtain in capitalist societies. Therefore, by default, Foucault gave support to a 'formal and inequitable egalitarianism of the deed' (Rose, 1984, p. 175).

The argument of this book has been that in a socialist society there would be many large-scale democratic organizations, which, with other pressures, would create some inequalities of income. Therefore such an absolute equality of condition could be approximated to only [. . .] by a totalitarian deadening of social energies, i.e., a form of 'forced solidarity'. The construction of a mode of punishment that had equivalent effects on all offenders would remain a problem. The deprivation of liberty in humane conditions provides the one universal and quantifiable system. This might be a relevant mode for a society still dominated by commodity production — but its manifold problems are only too well known.

11. See the comments on Christie and Mathiesen in Taylor (1981) and on Hulsman in Lea (1987).

12. Thus in developing a policy for sentencing rapists one needs the humane but unsentimental assessments of someone like Jill Box-Grainger, who is both a feminist and involved in radical alternatives to prison. In the case of trying and sentencing individual corporate criminals, Braithwaite (1984) and Box (1987) are to be preferred to Box (1983) — see Pearce (1987b).

Realist Criminology

19.   Ten Points of Realism
Jock Young

We have to deal, indeed, with an extensive and deeply-rooted social disease, which dug itself into the very body of society like a kind of ulcer; at times even threatening its very existence, but always harmful in the highest degree. Countless crimes are committed, and millions of criminals condemned, every year. Economically, the disadvantages to society are very great . . . I think it is undeniable that crime is a source of stupendous waste of money to society. Next to the economic, we have, moreover, the still more important moral disadvantages. If criminality is closely bound up with the moral standards of a people, in return it sends out demoralizing influences towards the normal sections of the population. And when one adds to all this the damage and grief suffered by the victims of the crime, and also the constant menace which criminality constitutes to society, the total obtained is already a formidable one. Neither ought we to forget the suffering on the part of the criminal himself, who — in whatever way one may wish to judge him, is after all, a part of humanity too.

The reasons for the study of criminology should therefore be clear. Admittedly it is a science which is widely studied for its own sake, just like other sciences; crime and criminals are not a bit less interesting than stars or microbes. The element of *la science pour la science* should be present in every scientist, otherwise he will be no good in his profession; and this applies to the criminologist too. But this point of view is secondary as compared with the practical aspect, just as in the case of medical science. Indeed, comparison with the latter repeatedly suggests itself. Criminology ought before anything to show humanity the way to combat, and especially, prevent, crime. What is required more than anything is sound knowledge, whereas up to the present we have had far too much of dogma and dilettantism (Bonger, 1935: 5–7)

The roots of realism

The last 20 years have witnessed a remarkable intensification of debate in criminology. The core problem has been the consistent rise in crime occurring in many, although by no means all, advanced industrial countries despite rapidly increasing standards of living coupled with the blatant ineffectiveness of the prisons and the growing awareness that extra police would only have a limited effect on the crime rate. I have detailed this process elsewhere (Young, 1986, 1988a). Suffice it to say that the two staple paradigms of criminology, social positivism (better conditions reduce the crime rate) and neo-classicism (more, effective punishment diminishes crime), became

Jock Young: 'Ten Points of Realism' from *RETHINKING CRIMINOLOGY: THE REALIST DEBATE* (Sage Publications, 1992), pp. 24–68. © Jock Young.

increasingly untenable. There was a crisis in causality (the 'aetiological crisis') and in penality. It was in response to this that the various new criminologies developed: control theory, right realism, the new administrative criminology and left idealism. Central to all these theories was a radial reappraisal of the notion of social causality. For some the search for causes of crime were rejected outright, whereas for others causality was directed away from the political and economic structure of society to the moral climate of society or the family or on to the 'crime-prone' individual. And, whereas those on the right acknowledged, indeed exaggerated, the rise in crime while managing to disconnect this from a critique of the inequitable societies which generate crime, a wide spectrum of criminologists from the liberal centre to the left downplayed or actually denied the problem of crime.

Concomitant with this was a rise in public concern about crime. In particular a rise in sensitivity to violence occurred, with clear indications, in the case of Britain at least, that intolerance of violence increased faster than the actual rise in violent behaviour (Young, 1991). Feminists pointed to the problems of domestic violence against women, of rape, of harassment in work and public places and, more recently, the problem of child abuse. The Green movement made us conscious of pollution, of environmental blight, of the perils of nuclear contamination and of dumping: all of which have clear links with corporate crime and governmental deviance. Animal Rights activists pinpointed the violence inherent in factory farming and laboratory testing. Anti-racists and gay groups highlighted the increasing incidence of racial attacks, of 'gay-bashing' and of widespread harassment. The rise in public demand for a more humane society and for a more tolerable physical environment is a key social change of the last two decades. And if the rise in crime posed aetiological problems for criminology, so did the question of changes in what is tolerable behaviour and what could be done to achieve a more civilized society.

Public bureaucracies became the subject of increased scrutiny, both by the New Right and by Social Democrats intent on public accountability. The inefficiencies of public service provision became embodied in the notion of the public as a consumer, no longer willing to have problems bestowed upon them in the old Fabian tradition, but demanding value for money and effectiveness. The long rise of the consumer society engendered a public which demanded, not only in the private sector but in the public, qualitatively higher standards of service delivery (Corrigan *et al.*, 1988).

Thus we can trace four major processes which have transformed criminological thinking: (1) the aetiological crisis as a consequence of rising crime rates; (2) the crisis in penality in terms of the failure of prisons and a reappraisal of the role of the police; (3) the increased awareness of victimization and of crimes which had previously been 'invisible'; (4) a growing public demand and criticism of public service efficiency and accountability.

Realism explicitly attempts to tackle all of these areas and to enter into debate with the responses of new right establishment criminology and left idealism. To a differing extent all of these problems and debates have been manifest in the recent history of advanced industrial societies. Of course, there are wide variations: in a few countries there has been little increase in crime, prison unrest and palpable ineffectiveness has not been universal, the new social movements which have entered into victim advocacy have developed unevenly, feminism has stronger traditions in certain countries than in others, the size of welfare bureaucracies varies, the configuration of social democratic and new right politics exist in different combinations, and so on. And, within the academy, criminology as a discipline exists with differing traditions and strengths. Thus, although the general problems which realism seeks to answer exist internationally in advanced industrial societies, their specific configuration depends on the political and social context of each country (see Brown and Hogg, 1991). In the introduction [to this book] we have traced the particular problematic in Britain. But although realist ideas have had a particular resonance in British criminology, they are by no means rooted in this context [cf. Taylor, Chapter 4]. Nowhere is this more obvious than in Elliott Currie's seminal work, *Confronting Crime* (1985). This starts with the premise of the exceptional nature of American society as a prime cause of the extraordinarily high crime rate. This is no doubt correct, but the policy recommendations and domain assumptions which Currie makes are undoubtedly realist (see the interesting commentary by Marty Schwartz, 1990). Similarly, the recent 1990 Conference on Realist Criminology in Vancouver, hosted by Brian MacLean and John Lowman, involved debates between Australian, US and British scholars, raising mainly issues of convergence and disagreement, many of which related to different social and political contexts (see *Critical Criminologist*, 1990). But the general problematic was realist, and realism itself puts great stress, as I shall argue, on the relationship between general principles and specific conditions.

The principle of naturalism

The most fundamental tenet of realism is that criminology should be faithful to the nature of crime. That is, it should acknowledge the *form* of crime, the *social context* of crime, the *shape* of crime, its trajectory through *time,* and its enactment in *space.*

The form consists of two dyads, a *victim* and an *offender,* and of *actions* and *reactions:* of crime and its control. This deconstruction gives us four definitional elements of crime: a victim, an offender, formal control and informal control. Realism, then, points to a square of crime involving the interaction between police and other agencies of social control, the public, the offender and the victim (see Figure 1).

Figure 1

Crime rates are generated not merely by the interplay of these four factors, but as *social relationships* between each point on the square. It is the relationship between the police and the public which determines the efficiency of policing, the relationship between the victim and the offender which determines the impact of the crime, the relationship between the state and the offender which is a major factor in recidivism, etc. I shall return to this later, but suffice it to say that the relationship between the four points of the square (offender, victim, state agencies and the public) varies with differing types of crime [see Lea, Chapter 3]. Indeed, a hallmark of critical criminology is its pinpointing of the irony of the frequent symbiotic relationships between control agencies — whether formal or informal — and crime. For example, the way in which the burgled public create the informal economy which sustains burglary, or the police create, through illegalities, a moral climate which spurs delinquents into crime.

Secondly, it should be stressed that, in pinpointing to the fact that crime rates are produced by such an interaction, one is merely describing the process. It does not involve acceptance of the existing patterns of criminalization.

Crime rates are a product, therefore, of changes in the number of putative offenders, the number of potential victims, and the changing levels of control exercised by the official agencies of control and the public. No explanation which does not embrace all these four factors can possibly explain crime rates. Let us focus quite simply, for the moment, on the relationship between social control in all its manifestations, and the criminal act consisting of the dyad of victim and offender.

If we examine changes over time: realists would point to these *necessarily* being a product of changes in criminal behaviour *and* changes in the sensitivity to crime. The increase in the rate of violent crime *by definition* must involve changes in violence. None of this makes it any the less 'real': for this is exactly what crime rates *really* are. This being said, the exponential increases in crimes occurring in most western countries cannot merely be a product of increased sensitivity to crime. Any dark figure of the crime unknown to the police would have been taken up long ago by the rise in crimes known to the police, and other indices, such as homicide rates and serious property crime, indicate rises even if we use earlier thresholds as our measure. Thus present rises in rates of violence in countries such as England may well be a product of an increased sensitivity to violence *and* a rise in violent behaviour.

Realist criminology indicates that crime rates are a product of two forces: changes in behaviour and changes in definitions of what is seriously criminal. These two social dimensions are not necessarily co-variant. It is quite possible, for example, for vandalism to increase but people to become less concerned and more tolerant about litter, graffiti, etc. It is possible for acts of violence in a behavioural sense to decrease, yet people become more sensitive to violence.

The social context consists of the immediate social interaction of these four elements and the setting of each of them within the *wider* social structure. Such an agenda was set out within *The New Criminology* (Taylor *et al.*, 1973), namely, that the immediate social origins of a deviant act should be set within its wider social context and that such an analysis should encompass both actors and reactors. Realism takes this a stage further, insisting not only that actions of offenders and the agencies of the state must be understood in such a fashion, but that this must be extended to the informal system of social control (the public) and to victims (see Young, 1987).

To turn to the shape of crime: crime is a series of relationships. Each type of crime presents a different network of relationships; if we compare illegal drug use, burglary and assault we note markedly different structures (see Figure 2).

Drug dealing has a well-known pyramidal shape; burglary involves numerous victims and regular fences; assault may well be a one-off case of victimization. Furthermore, the natural history of crime involves differences in the content of these relationships. Crime involves both cooperation and coercion. In the case of drug use, every step of the pyramid is consensual; in the case of burglary, dealing in stolen goods is consensual and the actual act of stealing coercive; in the case of assault, it is a purely coercive act.

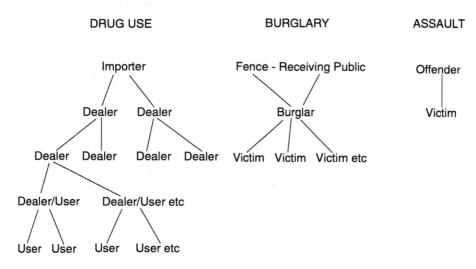

Figure 2

The temporal aspect of crime is the past of each of the four elements of the square of crime and their impact on each other in the future. A realist approach sees the development of criminal behaviour over time. It breaks down this trajectory of offending into its component parts and notes how different agencies interact. Thus we can talk of (1) the *background causes* of crime; (2) the *moral context* of opting for criminal behaviour; (3) the *situation of committing crime*; (4) the *detection of crime*; (5) the *response to the offender*; (6) the *response to the victim*. Criminal careers are built up by an interaction of the structural position the offender finds him or herself in and the administrative responses to his or her various offences. These involve both material changes in the offender's structural position and the exchange of ideas (or 'rationalizations') for offending (Cohen, 1965; Matza, 1964). But, of course, such moral careers are not confined to the offender. Other points of the square of crime change over time. Policing practices change in their interaction with offenders, the public's fear of crime in the city creates patterns of avoidance behaviour which consciously and unconsciously develop over time, victims — particularly repeated victims such as in cases of domestic violence — change the pattern of their life as a consequence of such an interaction.

The spatial dimension of crime is the material space in which this process enacts itself. All crime has a spatial dimension, and the geography of crime varies widely in terms of the specific crime. Drug dealing has an international dimension, a national distribution and a focus on specific areas of the city. Burglary occurs widely across a locality and subsists on a hidden economy which is locally based. Assault has no wider spatial dimension. It occurs, however, frequently in specific areas. For example, in terms of assault by a stranger, it has a pronounced geographical focus which is made evident, both in the incidence of assault and the fear of victimization, manifest in the avoidance of certain areas. Just, then, as specific crimes involve differing structures of relationships, they also involve particular structures in space.

Crime occurs privately and publicly and specific crimes are private at certain points of their structure and public at others. In the case of drug dealing, all aspects of the crime, apart from street level, are extremely private transactions. At the level of the opportunistic user, it is quasi-public: people must know who the dealers are, and they must, like any other 'shopkeepers', be relatively open to the public. In the case of burglary, the act itself is, apart from the brief circumspect act of breaking in, a private act: it occurs usually when the owner is out of his or her house, and when neighbours can see no suspicious activities. Subsequently the sale of stolen goods is quasi-public: it occurs publicly in shops which fence wittingly or unwittingly stolen goods or, in terms of direct public purchase, it occurs in the public areas of the pub or workplace. Assault in a public place is, by its very nature, an open event. Unlike domestic violence, it is coercion in the street, in a public house, or in some other public venue.

The principle of multiple aetiology

If we examine the square of crime, it is obvious that crime rates involve a fourfold aetiology. It involves the causes of offending (the traditional focus of criminology), the factors which make victims vulnerable (e.g., lifestyle analysis, Felson and Cohen, 1981), the social conditions which affect public levels of control and tolerance, and the social forces which propel the formal agencies such as the police. It is impossible to explain crime rates in terms of one of these causal sequences, although it is commonplace in criminological theory that such *partial* explanations are attempted. And, of course, such explanations must involve an *aetiological symmetry:* it is inadmissible, for example, to grant the police a different aetiological status than that of the delinquent. Such an explanatory scheme must detail the *immediate signs* of behaviour and set this within the *wider social origins* (Taylor *et al.*, 1973).

The present period in criminology is characterized by a retreat from a discussion of wider social causes of offending. With a few notable exceptions (Currie, 1985; Braithwaite, 1979), the social democratic tradition of making the link between social structure and offending is severed. In part, this is a response of establishment criminology to new right governments, which, quite clearly, wish to embrace theories which disconnect their policies from uses in the crime rates. The abandonment of interest in crime causation has been complex and manifold. Precisely because it covered a wide spectrum of politics and theory it was extremely effective. The British school of administrative criminology was doubtful about the validity of causes of 'dispositions' altogether. The realists of the right, such as James Q. Wilson, did not deny that there were causes of crime. Indeed, they outlined a plethora of causes (Wilson and Herrnstein, 1985). Rather, they point to the few 'causes' which can be altered without making social changes which would be politically unacceptable, which stresses the individual rather than the social causes of crime. Travis Hirschi (1969), in his influential 'control theory', abandons causation to the extent that it is identified with motivation. Cause metamorphoses from active desire into absence of restraint.

The question of aetiology was, therefore, not abandoned. What were played down were the causes of offending: the traditional focus of criminology. Other aetiologies took its place: the causes of lack of informal controls (control theory), the causes of changes in exposure to victimization (Felson and Cohen's emphasis on lifestyle), the causes of ineffective formal sanctions (Wilson's emphasis on the inadequacy of punishment). That is, the partial causality rooted in the offender characteristic of positivism, in all its varieties, became replaced by other partial causalities focused on other dimensions of the square of crime: informal social control, the victim or the formal system.

Top-down and bottom-up explanations

Such a partiality is apparent, not only in criminology of the right, but in criminology of the left. This is seen clearly in the tendency to explain changes in crime and differences in the crime rate between groups, either in terms of *top-down explanations* (changes in the administration of justice), or *bottom-up explanations* (in terms of changes in criminal behaviour). Yet if we are to have a fully developed criminology, we must logically have both a sociology of action and reaction. How can we explain, for example, the rise in the official rate of crimes of violence in the majority of advanced industrial countries in this century if we do not explain both changes in violent behaviour and changes in sensitivity to violence? A one-sided approach — so common — which focuses on one or the other is patently inadequate.

Deviance and control cannot be studied independently of each other. You cannot study changes in policing without changes in patterns of crime, the social control of women without changes in the behaviour of women, the impact of drug legislation without changes in drug use. Systems of social control profoundly affect deviance and changes in deviance patterns of control. The two items are necessary parts of the equation and both variables interact with each other.

Interpreting the criminal statistics

Such a principle must be applied also to the vexed question of the interpretation of the criminal statistics. For the left idealists the criminal statistics are an epiphenomena — they measure the activities of statistics-generating bodies (the police, the courts, etc.). They do not measure differences in criminal behaviour. Thus the differences in official crime rates between, say, working-class and middle-class delinquency, or black and white crime, or even, the differential between boys and girls, is seen as a clear indication of the prejudices of the social control agencies and little else. The best statistics, according to these authors, would be the prison statistics, for at least they give a reasonably accurate measure of who is in prison. Claims of a 'crime wave' and of significant changes in the quantity of crime over time are seen to be the product of recurrent moral panics, materially underscored by the increase in the size of police forces which inevitably generate a greater volume of statistics (e.g., Gilroy and Sim, 1985).

In contrast, for conventional criminology, crime statistics are unscientifically gathered and metaphysical in their categorization — but on the whole, and at least in their profiles of criminality which they yield, they reflect the true differences in crime between different groups and of changes in the extent of criminality over time.

For the realist the fundamental axiom is, as we have seen, that the reality of crime is a product of action and reaction. Someone acts in a given way and certain legal agencies of control react against them. This double process is central to the nature of crime and to attempt to separate one from the other and to believe that there is a true crime rate independent of the activities of reactors, is a clear fallacy. Thus the debate about whether crime statistics are either largely a function of the reaction of social control agencies or a function of the activities of offenders is chimerical. An 'either-or' approach to criminal statistics simply violates the reality of crime. Both processes must be involved and the weighting varies widely between different types of crime. It should be noted, however, that in the vast majority of serious crimes reported to the police by the public, therefore, realistically the overall criminal rate tends to be propelled more by the motor of public demand rather than by proactive policing: that is by public definition of deviancy rather than those held by the police.

Although realism would see crime rates as a product of the administration of criminal justice (the reaction to crime) and the social situation which produces criminal behaviour (the criminal act), it stresses the predominance of structure over administration. (Such an analysis would be true also of a realist approach to health or education.) To take the racial 'disproportionality' of prisons, for example, the greatest factor in the higher proportion of blacks is due to poverty, age structure and residence in the inner city rather than the bias of the system (Currie, 1985; Reiman, 1979).

Three caveats to this must be made: (a) the administrative bias against imprisoning corporate and white-collar criminals compared to those committing conventional crimes; (b) the pronounced bias in the minority of cases where proactive policy is involved (e.g., drug offences: see Blumstein, 1982); and (c) the extraordinary effect of imprisonment on long-term recidivism where, indeed, criminal justice administration becomes the major driving factor in their structural position.

Relative deprivation and crime

At this point let us turn to the substantive explanation of crime. Realism sees a major cause of criminal behaviour as relative deprivation. Crime can, therefore, occur anywhere in the social structure and at any period, affluent or otherwise — it is simply not dependent on absolute levels of deprivation or the level in the social structure of the offender [see Lea, Chapter 3]. This being said, it is clear that parts of the poor, particularly the lower working class and certain ethnic minorities who are marginalized from the 'glittering prizes' of the wider society, experience a push towards crime that is greater than elsewhere in the structure (Lea and Young, 1984).

To put an emphasis on relative deprivation as a cause of crime is not to retreat into monocausality. Of course, there are many causes of crime. Even within the tradition of anomie theory, subcultural theorists have tended to give undue emphasis to relative deprivation, the disjunction of aspirations and opportunities, over anomie as a lack of limits, a product of an individualism, where "From top to bottom of the ladder, greed is aroused without knowing where to find its ultimate foothold. Nothing can colour it since its goal is far beyond all it can attain" (Durkheim, 1952: 256). And certainly one can contrast the anomie of the disadvantaged, which is largely concerned with relative deprivation, from the anomie of the advantaged, which is often a product of a limitless pursuit of money, status and power (Young, 1974; Simon and Gagnon, 1986; Taylor, 1990). This being said, relative deprivation is an extremely potent cause of crime for it is:

1. not limited to lower working-class crime because relative deprivation can, and does, occur throughout the social structure [see Lea, this volume];

2. not merely concerned with economic crime because subcultures of violence among the poor and the violence of better-off men occur precisely as a response to relative economic deprivation;

3. not concerned with absolute poverty, and thus pinpoints the paradox of those crimes of the poor which focus on status goods. As Elizabeth Burney pointed out in her study of street robbery: 'Poverty is, nevertheless, not the immediate motive for street crime, since most offenders do not lack necessities: rather, they crave luxuries. The outstanding characteristic of young street offenders is their avid adherence to a group "style", which dictates a very expensive level of brand-name dressing, financed by crime' (1990): 63; see also Currie, 1990).

The implications of this understanding of causality are of vital importance. Specifically, we have in our cities conditions of unemployment with no foreseeable future for young people, and where the concept of 'youth' merely extends itself into those aged 30 and beyond. In such a situation relative deprivation is manifest, in the contrast with the increasingly wealthy strata of those in work, and is underscored by the gentrification of our large cities which allows comparison to be easily available and, indeed, unavoidable.

The principle of specificity

Both positivism and the new administrative criminology seek generalizations which are independent of culture. A discussion of whether maternal deprivation leads to crime, or if beat policing is effective, would be typical endeavours. Left idealism, with its sense of the obviousness of criminological generalization, enters the field of general laws with an abandon which would alarm the most staunch positivist. Of course unemployment leads to crime; it is self-evident that the recession has led to the rise in heroin use among young people, and so on. Such a mechanistic relationship between objective conditions and human behaviour is absurd. It is central to a realist position that objective conditions are interpreted through the specific subcultures of groups involved. This is the nature of human experience and social action. Generalization is possible, but only given specific cultural conditions and social understandings. Thus, absolute deprivation (poverty, unemployment, etc) is no guide to the genesis of crime. This is the central failure of positivism, both in its aetiology and its policy making. Relative deprivation, experienced injustice in certain limited political situations, is at the root cause of crime.

The utter vacuity of the general 'law': unemployment leads to crime, is displayed when one considers the majority of the human race: women, who have a very high rate of unemployment (in terms of non-domestic labour) and extremely low crime rates. But unemployment *does* give rise to crime in certain circumstances. The failure of such positivism is seen in the Home Office study of the relationship between race and crime (Stevens and Willis, 1979). Here they found a positive correlation between white unemployment and the white rate of crime. But for blacks, the relationship was puzzling: for there was a negative correlation between black unemployment and certain sorts of black crime and 'somewhat surprisingly' the *white* unemployment rate was found to correlate highly with the *black* crime rate. 'A plausible interpretation', they note, 'seems hard to find' (p. 23). For, from the point of view of positivism, it is as if one pushed one table and the table next to it moved! But as John Lea and I have argued elsewhere, such a finding is by no means strange:

> As we have argued, there are no *direct* relationships between objective factors and behaviour. The experience of blacks in areas of high white unemployment may well be that or racial discrimination and scapegoating. Such an alienated sub-culture would have a considerable reason to break its lawful bonds with the wider society; it might also experience the demoralisation which is the basis of much criminality. In areas where there is massive black unemployment there may be less basis for a comparison with whites and thus a relative lack of the frustration that leads to criminality. (1984: 160)

Such an analysis can be applied to generalization in a wide variety of areas. For example, in the field of drugs research I have argued for a socio-pharmacological approach. This rejects both the notion that the effects of drugs situation and the moral careers of drug users can be read, so to speak, positivistically from the pages of a pharmocopoeia or relativistically, that drug use is a mere function of culture alone. Rather, specific drugs have effects in particular cultural set-ups: the psychotropic nature of the drug both structures and is structured by the culture (Young, 1971). And in the field of subculture theory, Ward and Kassebaum (1966), in their pioneering study of women's prisons, cut through the debate around whether inmate subculture is transmitted on from the outside pre-prison culture of the prisoners, or is a functional product of 'the pains of imprisonment' while within the prison. By adding the crucial variable of gender to the discussion they have shown how the way in which the pains of imprisonment are experienced is a function of the gender subculture of the inmates. The 'same' prison (objective conditions) produces widely different subcultural solutions (human behaviour) dependent upon the subjective assessment of the inmates.

If we are to be wary about sociological generalizations within one nation at one time, then we should be all the more wary about general laws which attempt to cross historical periods and hop from examples in one country to another. A classic illustration of lack of specificity is Scull's decarceration thesis (1977) which empirically assumed that all forms of deviancy involving incarceration would pass through the same sequence (as if the reactions of the powerful would not vary with the specific deviance) and, even more oddly, that the British figures, which did not fully substantiate his thesis, were simply 'lagging behind' those of the United States. Here we see not only a generalization from one country to another, but from one category to another.

Thus, to be more precise, the problem of specificity refers to generalizing about crime, law or victimization from one country or one social group and assuming that one's conclusions apply to all countries or social groups. It is being unable to see how general variables come together in a very specific form in any particular situation. This results in work which is not only inadequate as a generalization, but is lacking in its ability to cope with what is special about the precise constellation of factors which delineate any particular situation. Specificity is a heuristic failure, both on the level of the general and the particular.

The three major problems of specificity which have dominated criminological thinking have operated on the level of both social category and nationality. The first is obviously the fashion in which male, working-class crime has been used to depict all criminality. We have seen how the impact of, first of all, radical and then feminist criminology has sharply dislodged such thinking. The consequences for theory have been enormous. The new empirical dimensions have far from worked themselves out yet through the maze of conventional theory.

The second is the depiction of crime in advanced industrial countries to describe crime in general. Colin Sumner, in a brilliant essay on crime and under-development (1982), rightly castigates those authors such as Clinard and Abbott (1973) who see crime in poor countries as just a replay of what has occurred in the west, and their general economic development as just a delayed natural evolution. He points to the way in which all the traditional criminological equations become overturned when one begins to look at police behaviour, crimes of the powerful, crimes of the poor and of political oppositionists within the context of global imperialism. Such work has only just begun, but it is of the utmost importance that radical criminology makes a committed attempt to tackle the problems. No one else will. Positivism never did and the new administrative criminology sees itself as producing control generalizations which will apply anywhere, from the estates of New England to the streets of Soweto.

The third problem of specificity is a relatively recent phenomenon occurring in the post-1945 period, and that is the Americanization of criminology. It is important to realize the significance of the domination of US criminology on the criminologies of the rest of the world. The central paradox is that the vast output of the United States — often involving the most innovative work in the field — emerges from a country which is extremely atypical in terms of the majority of advanced industrial countries. The homicide rate, for example, is 14 times higher in Los Angeles than in London, and if we are to look for countries which have similar rates of violence to the United States it would be to Latin America, rather than any other industrial country, east or west. There are a series of atypical characteristics of the United States which may well relate to its exceptional crime rate. For example, its lack of social-democratic politics, its extremely high commitment to the American Dream version of meritocracy, its high emphasis on formal legal equality as an ideal, its remarkable ethnic pluralism, the extent and range of organized crime, the extent of ghettoization, etc (Currie, 1985, 1990). All of these factors are likely to have a profound effect on the theory generated in such a society. The theory of differential association, Mertonian anomie theory, neo-Chicagoan labelling theory, social control theory, are all illuminated if we begin to think how they fit so well such an exceptional state. This is not an argument for theoretical isolationism. There is no doubt that the United States has, in this century, produced by far the most important developments in theoretical criminology. It is to argue, however, that these theories cannot merely be transplanted to, say, a European context; they have to be transposed *carefully*.

The contradiction, then, is that the most influential work in criminology stems from one of the most atypical advanced industrial states. The extent of this paradox can, perhaps, be illustrated if we imagine that Japan became in the 1990s the leading producer of criminological work. Japan is, of course, an extremely atypical capitalist society — and in the area of crime it is the absolute opposite of the United States. Even by European standards the changes in the crime rate are remarkable. For example, from 1948 to 1982 the crime rate in Japan declined by 36 percent compared to a rise of 348 percent in England and Wales over the same period. And this was despite dramatic changes taking place in Japanese society: massive industrialization, vast internal movements of population, urbanization and general social upheaval (Government of Japan, 1983).

It would not be difficult to imagine the types of criminological theory which would emerge from Japan if it indeed dominated the field of criminology. At the bottom line one can imagine quite 'reasonable' theories which linked a rise in the standard of living with a drop in crime. And one can visualize, perhaps, with a certain *schadenfreude*, criminologists in Berkeley or New York trying to fit the evidence of their own country in the new dominant paradigm.

To argue for specificity is not to argue against empirical generalization. It is to say that generalization is possible within particular social orders concerning particular groups. Nor is it to argue that cross-cultural theories of crime are impossible — it is to say firmly that these theories find their resolution in specific societies. For example, the notion of relative deprivation as a theory of discontent, which results in crime in certain social and political circumstances, is one of great heuristic value. But there is a big jump between how the form and content of relative deprivation is experienced among boys in the Lower East Side of Manhattan, to how it is structured in terms of girls in Florence, Japanese youth in Tokyo or corporate criminals in Switzerland .

The principle of focusing on lived realities

Realism focuses on lived realities. It is concerned with the material problem which particular groups of people experience in terms of the major social axes of age, class,

446

gender and race, and spatially with their locality. It is these structural parameters which give rise to subcultures. Realism has a close affinity with subcultural theory (Willis, 1977; Cohen, 1965). Subcultures are problem-solving devices which constantly arise as people in specific groups attempt to solve the structural problems which face them. The problems are evaluated in terms of the existing subculture and the subculture changes over time in order to *attempt* a solution to those perceived problems (see Lea and Young, 1984: ch. 3; Young, 1974). Crime is one form of subculture adaptation which occurs where material circumstances block cultural aspirations and where non-criminal alternatives are absent or less attractive.

The experiences of the public with regard to crime and policing cannot be reduced to global figures of the average risk rates of particular crimes or the 'normal' citizen's experience of policing. All evidence indicates that the impact of crime and policing is geographically and socially focused: it varies enormously by area and by the social group concerned. The reason the realists tend to select inner-city areas is to enable us to detail such experiences at the sharp end of policing, while comparing this to data derived from wider-based surveys of total cities and the country as a whole. The reason for the use of extremely high sampling is to be able to break down the impact of crime and policing in terms of its social focus: that is, on social groups based on the combination of age, class, gender and race. Such a high social focus corresponds more closely to the lived realities of different groups and subcultures of the population. Thus, just as it is inaccurate to generalize about crime and policing from gross figures based on large geographical areas, it is incorrect, even within particular areas, to talk in terms of, for example, 'all' young people, 'all' women, 'all' blacks, 'all' working-class people, etc (Schwartz, 1988). Generalizations which remain on such global levels frequently obfuscate quite contradictory experiences, generating statistics which often conceal vital differences of impact. We have shown in the *Second Islington Crime Survey* (Crawford *et al.*, 1990), for example, how the introduction of age into the analysis of fear of crime by gender changes the usual generality of men having low fear of crime and women high. In fact, older women have a fear of crime rather like men in the middle age group, and younger women have a fear rather like old men. And, in the case of foot-stops by the police, it becomes evident that differentials based on race are much more complicated than the abstraction that blacks are more likely to be stopped than whites. No older black women in our sample were stopped. Young, white, women were over three times more likely to be stopped than older black men. And even the differential between young black men and young white men becomes remarkably narrowed when class is introduced into the equation. Such an approach in realist method is termed an awareness of the specificity of generalization, the need to base analysis firmly grounded in specific areas and social groups. It is in marked contrast to the approaches which try to explain differences in experience in terms of only one of the major social axes: age, class, gender or race. Such reductionism, as exemplified by radical feminism or fundamentalist class analysis, simply does not fit the reality of social experience. This approach enables us to be more discriminate about generalization with regard to changes in modes of policing and methods of crime control. For example, in the debate about shifts from consensual to more coercive forms of policing (Lea and Young, 1984), it allows us to ascertain whether contradictory forces at work involving consensual policing of certain areas and groups

447

and more coercive methods with others. Similarly, the probable efficacy of crime control measures such as beat policing or neighbourhood watch must be grounded in specific communities and locations.

Putting behaviour into context

Realism involves the invocation of rationality rooted in material circumstances. That is, it places the behaviour of the offender, the police officer, the victim and the public at large, in the actual material circumstances that each individual experiences (Lea and Young, 1984). This is not to say that people do not make mistakes in understanding the world, whether it is the behaviour of the police officer in stop and search, or the fear of crime of the citizen. Indeed, this is *ipso facto* the very nature of rational behaviour. Rather, it sets itself against an idealism which analyses people's beliefs and behaviour, primarily as a product of free-floating ideas and prejudices, whether a product of outside influences such as the mass media, or socially detached group values, or personal psychological attributes.

Realist method relates attitudes and beliefs to actually lived experience of material circumstances. For example, it attempts to explain police behaviour, not in terms of the enactment of a group of people with, say, authoritarian personalities, or a macho culture, or rigid 'them' and 'us' attitudes engendered at training school. All of these things may or may not be true, but they are not the primary determinants of police behaviour. To take a police patrol as an example: it is the actual nature of the police task, the experiences confronted in attempting to achieve objectives in the face of the opportunities and difficulties encountered on the job which is central to understanding the behaviour of patrolling officers. In this instance of police practice it cannot be deduced from legal rules nor from a free-floating 'cop culture' nor the autonomous prejudices of individual police officers. Realism attempts to put police practice, the interpretation of rules, the generation of an occupational culture, and the attitudes of individual officers, in its context. For example, stop and search procedures are largely ineffective at dealing with the crimes to which the legislation was directed: burglary, hard drug use and carrying weapons. Direct information, either gleaned from the public, or by detective work, would be needed in order to have a high yield from such a procedure. In the absence of such information, patrolling officers equipped with stop and search powers, and wishing to have at least some yield from their work, will, of necessity, target those groups which have high offending rates, particularly young, working-class males — black and white. As most people stopped will be perfectly innocent, such a trawling of a particular social group will inevitably create a counter-productive hostility in the target groups and accusations of unfairness, selectivity and prejudice. But it is the inadequate tools for the job and an ill-thought-out piece of legislation which creates the working context for the police, not merely the enactment of personal and cultural prejudice.

Social constructionism, positivism and everyday life

Realism, then, does not deal in abstractions: the principle of specificity demands that explanation be grounded. It is not just that the concept of 'crime' embraces a motley of types of behaviour and varieties of legal regulation; each 'type' of crime and each form of regulation must be specified if we are to make any progress in understanding their interaction. Opiate addiction, for example, can mean many different things in particular subcultures. Burglary can involve the rational calculation of the professional or the opportunism of the young lad. Domestic violence can involve a variety of sub-species, each with its own life cycle. And, turning to social control, beat policing can involve many greatly different activities from the aggressive to the consensual; neighbourhood watch can be a uniting or a divisive intervention. All of this suggests the necessity of typologies which cut across legal or formal definitions, but, going further, that these typologies must be grounded in the particular lived realities of the phenomenon under investigation. It does not exclude generalization, it merely argues that generalization must be socially based and explanations which are abstracted out of context have very little chance of aetiological success because they ignore the very social context which determines them.

The principle of social control

The control of crime must reflect the nature of crime. That is, it involves informal and formal interventions on both the level of the offender and the victim. Crime occurs in a spatial situation and has a temporal sequence which involves the particular act between offender and victim and the wider social context in which this occurs. To control crime from a realist perspective involves intervention at each part of the square of crime: at the level of the factors which give rise to the putative offender (such as structural unemployment), the informal system (such as lack of public mobilization), the victim (such as inadequate target hardening), and the formal system (such as ineffective policing). In realism all points of intervention are possible and necessary. Intervention based polemically on one mode alone, whether it is argued that, for instance, more jobs or public mobilization through neighbourhood watch, or the target hardening of buildings or more effective policing, may make some gains. But intervention on one level alone — even if effective — will inevitably have declining marginal gains. A multi-pronged strategy is always desirable for this reason alone, but all the more so in that each level of intervention interacts with the others. This being said, interventions at the level of social structure (such as changes in employment opportunities) are more effective than changes in the criminal justice system. A perfect criminal justice system operating to the letter of the rule of law would still disproportionately prosecute and incarcerate the poor. Realism would, of course, acknowledge that 'on the day', without — and to a lesser extent even with — long-term structural intervention, other interventions are necessary.

Realism prioritizes structural intervention, but it concedes that interventions at all levels, from target hardening to policing, are inevitably necessary. One cannot blame the crime rate on the inadequacies of the criminal justice system; one can criticize the rampant inefficiencies, malpractices and unfairness that abound within those institutions, and point to the way in which such unfairness adds fuel to the sense of social injustice that the offender has already experienced (Matza, 1964). But the causal push which creates crime originates primarily within the social structure, not within the administration of justice.

Realists, therefore, stress the primacy of intervention in the social structure over the interventions of the criminal justice system (CJS). They neither seek to elevate the

CJS to a paramount role, nor to suggest that CJS interventions are irrelevant or inevitably counter-productive. Rather, they insist on the minimal use of the CJS while stressing its importance as the necessary body of coercively empowered institutions within a democracy which backs up informal and non-CJS institutions. For some commentators, on the right, the CJS is seen somewhat like a magic wand which, if waved more vigorously, will solve the problem of crime. For liberals, it is believed that if only the wand were waved in an impartial way, in time, with due process, the problems of crime would be greatly alleviated. And on the left, abolitionists — often, unsurprisingly, with a background in law — would seem to believe that if the wand ceased waving, crime itself would disappear and resolve itself into a series of rather minor 'problematic situations'. All of these notions are false. All evidence suggests that a more punitive response to crime is unproductive. Due process is an important goal to fight for, but it will not remedy the substantive inequalities within society which engender crime and generate the class and racial disproportions in our prisons. And, whereas one would wholeheartedly agree about the withdrawal of the CJS from minor 'problematic situations', there are far too many serious crimes which must be attended to with the use of coercive sanctions and many more which are, at present, unacted upon and neglected (cf. Hulsman, 1986).

Informal versus formal systems of control

It is a central finding of modern criminology that the criminal justice system has only a minor purchase on the overall crime rate. The rate of crime relates to changes in the social and economic structure on which the CJS has little effect.

Informal agencies of social control (the public, the family, the peer group) are the major method of controlling crime once it has occurred. A vital agency in this area is the strictures placed upon people by employment (Young, 1979). Non-policing formal agencies, such as the school or the everyday surveillance which occurs in shops, are also of great importance. The police and the CJS have a minor, yet vital, role in this process. In this, the police are largely dependent on public support in their efforts to control crime (see Kinsey *et al.*, 1986) and the effect of the CJS is, in part, predicated upon the level at which public opinion backs up state stigmatization (Braithwaite, 1989).

Left idealism and the denial of the role of the CJS

A commonplace among left idealists and others of the abolitionist persuasion is to move from the recognition of the importance of non-penal methods of controlling crime, to discarding the CJS altogether. Louk Hulsman (1986) makes the 'discovery' that the vast majority of 'crimes' are not dealt with by the CJS. He moves from this to suggest the abolition of the CJS and, indeed, the abolition of the concept of crime altogether. For him 'crime has no ontological reality'. Crime is not the *object* but the *product* of criminal policy (p. 71). The informal system of control, which deals with the majority of 'problematic situations' should be extended to tackling their totality.

Of course, only a tiny proportion of events which are potentially criminal are, in fact, criminalized. In realist terms it is even more drastic than this: a near infinity of acts could be criminalized if criminal codes were interpreted with complete abandon.

Criminalization involves the selection of certain activities in a political process which stretches from the public via the police through the courts. All of this is well documented by conventional analysis of the creation of criminal statistics (Lea and Young, 1984: ch. 1). What should be stressed is that this is not merely a top-down process, as social constructionists and left idealists would maintain, but involves a high level of grass roots public input. A large proportion of this process is based on public consensus, although there is inevitably, *as this is by necessity a political process,* argument at the edges of this consensus (for example controversy over cannabis; what or what is not pornographic; the comparative immunity of crimes of the powerful; definitions of rape, etc). That is, arguments about how the net of social control should be reduced and extended. For realists it is vital that such a process of criminalization should be democratized. It involves the public, but it does not involve the public enough. For example, that police priorities should fall in line with public priorities (Jones *et al.*, 1986). Such a recognition of the importance of criminal law in the process of democratic social control does not imply that the existing sanctions and mechanisms are accepted uncritically. On the contrary, community alternatives to prison (Matthews, 1989), the use of mediation schemes (Matthews, 1988), the advocacy of non-criminal regulation where possible (Pearce, 1990) are all high on the agenda. Realists [claim], however, that the use of criminal sanctions, albeit in a diminished fashion, is essential for the maintenance of social order and, indeed, as a back-up measure to strengthen the efficacy of informal modes of conflict resolution. The choice is not between informal or formal measures of control, nor do these measures parallel the distinction between non-coercive and coercive intervention. Informal sanctions can, of course, be more repressive than formal sanctions. Realists certainly do not criticize the repressive nature of much state control in order to replace this by the tyranny of public opinion. It is only by maintaining a balance between formal and informal sanctions that we can hope to reduce crime without descending to the totalitarian 'utopia' of the ubiquitous neighbourhood busybody and the omniscient intolerance of an 'other-directed' *Gemeinschaft*.

The police and crime

The argument that the police have little effect on the crime rate is curiously prevalent among criminologists of all parts of the political spectrum. It is held by administrative criminologists (Morris and Heal, 1981), by right realists such as Wilson (1975), who stress order maintenance rather than crime control as the prime police function, by left idealists who are certain that policing is about politics, not about crime (Bunyan, 1976), and even by sectors of the police themselves. Indeed, as Sir Peter Imbert, Commissioner of Police for the Metropolis, put it recently: 'Blaming police for the rise in crime is as absurd as blaming the fire brigade for the increase of fires.'

All of this reverses the conventional wisdom of the police as the front line in the fight against crime. We have reviewed these arguments extensively in *Losing the Fight against Crime* (Kinsey *et al.*, 1986: ch. 4). Yet while realists firmly place the major motor which produces crime in society at large and emphasize the central role of the public and of the multi-agencies, we do not let the police off the hook. The assertion that the police have little effect in crime rates frequently blurs the issues because it (a) does not recognize that most research is about the marginal effects of extra police, not about the deterrent effect of existing police levels; (b) generalizes from correlations between specific crimes (such as burglary) and particular policing practices (such as beat policing) and the general crime rate (Crawford et al., 1990: ch. 7).

Once again the principle of specificity: the deterrent effect varies with the type of crime, the type of policing (if beat policing what *type* of beat policing?), the locality and the existing relationships between the public and relevant agencies. The deterrent effect of policing is dependent on public confidence; it can be high where public support is great (as in the suburbs) and break down in the inner city, where public confidence collapses. Conversely, the power of the informal system to control crime may be great if police back-up is present, but may be radically demoralized where the police are seen as an alien force. More police can have a deterrent effect or can reduce deterrence, dependent on the context. This stress on specificity simply does not allow us to marshal blancmange figures of police staff levels correlated with general clear-up rates. Nor is it admirable to move from particular police practices and specific crimes to assertions about the deterrent effect of policing in general. The most frequent research example involves generalizations based on beat policing (largely unspecified; is it aggressive patrols which alienate the public or user-friendly policing which gives public confidence?) and the burglary rates against which beat policing is scarcely likely to have any impact in the first place.

It has been suggested recently by Mathiesen (1990) that the realist project has placed all its faith in better policing as the major mode of controlling crime. It is difficult to imagine how such a caricature has been constructed: charitably one imagines it is due to restricted reading rather than limited scholarship. In particular, it involves generalization from texts that were concerned with the intervention over police accountability (Kinsey et al., 1986). It should be clear from this chapter that the control of crime involves interventions on all levels: on the social causes of crime, on social control exercised by the community and the formal agencies, and on the situation of the victim. Furthermore, that social causation is given the highest priority, whereas formal agencies, such as the police, have a vital role, yet one which has in the conventional literature been greatly exaggerated. It is not the 'Thin Blue Line', but the social bricks and mortar of civil society which are the major bulwark against crime. Good jobs with a discernible future, housing estates that tenants can be proud of community facilities which enhance a sense of cohesion and belonging, a reduction in unfair income inequalities, all create a society which is more cohesive and less criminogenic.

It is obvious from this analysis that certain crimes are more difficult to control than others (particularly if they are consensual and in private) and that particular points of intervention in the shape of the crime present greater difficulties than others. There are resistant points and there are weak spots. Both the type of intervention and what agency is involved must be tailored to these structures.

The principle of multi-agency intervention

Multi-agency intervention is the planned, coordinated response of the major social agencies to problems of crime and incivilities. The central reason for multi-agency social intervention is that of realism: it corresponds both to the realities of crime and to the realities of social control. Social control in industrial societies is, by its very nature, multi-agency. The problem is that it is not coordinated and represents a series of other disparate policy initiatives, with little overall rationale for the allocation of resources, and institutions which are often at loggerheads with each other. Yet, as I have discussed, the multi-agencies are mutually dependent on each other and each agency is dependent on public support, whether an agency dealing with domestic violence, child abuse or juvenile delinquency. In this section I wish to deal with the relationship between (a) the agencies and particular forms of crime; (b) the agencies and the public; (c) the agencies themselves.

The agencies and crime

Different agencies are involved for different crimes and at different stages in the process of tackling offenders. If we compare burglary to child abuse we see immediately the differences between the involvement of the various agencies. Burglary will, in general, have a high police involvement in terms of the apprehension of the criminal. The local council, on the other hand, will have the greatest role in the 'target hardening' of the local estate. If the culprit is an adult, social services will be unlikely to be involved, but they will, of course, do so if the offender is a juvenile. For child abuse, in contrast, the social services will play a paramount role; the schools will be major institutions of detection, and the medical profession will play an important role in terms of corroboration. And in terms of the different stages of tackling offenders: one can see how the police role as a back-up agency for providing coercive intervention where necessary and legal evidence in the courts occurs at different times in the procedure than the long-term process of social work intervention.

Different agencies are involved at different parts of the trajectory of the offender. As we have seen, a realist approach to offenders sees the development of criminal behaviour over time. It breaks down this trajectory of offending into its component parts and notes how different agencies can and should be operative at different stages. Thus, to recapitulate these stages, we have: (1) the *background causes* of crime; (2) the *moral context* of opting for criminal behaviour; (3) the *situation of committing* crime; (4) the *detection of crime*; (5) the *response to the offender*; (6) the *response to the victim*. Let us examine these one by one, noting the factors involved and the agencies with the power to intervene.

Background causes. These lie in relative deprivation as witnessed in poverty and unemployment, in overcrowded housing conditions, in poor leisure facilities and in inadequately funded families (particularly single parent). Here central government, the local authorities, and local business have responsibility.

The moral context. Here we have in particular the family, the education system, the mass media, youth organizations and religious organizations. Here the public themselves, the councils, in their provision of education and youth facilities, the media professional in the context of the often heavy media, of adolescents, and local religious and youth leaders, have their roles.

The situation of commission. Here target hardening, lighting, public willingness to intervene and police patrols, are important. Thus the important agencies are the council, the police and the public themselves.

The detection of crime. Here, as discussed above, the cooperation of police and public is paramount, both in terms of informing the police and witnessing in courts.

The response to the offender. Here the role of the police and the courts is paramount in their dual aim of punishment and rehabilitation. A rehabilitated offender, of course, should not be a recidivist. Here social services are prominent in their role of caring for young people, but also in terms of possibilities of employment, and the shoring up of unstable family situations.

The response to the victim. Up to now I have discussed the whole process of multi-agency social intervention as it was just concerned with dealing with offenders and preventing offences. We must never forget, however, the other half of the dyad of crime: the victim. Here again, it is obvious that various agencies must be involved in tackling the problem of criminal victimization. Social services, for example, may have to deal with the after-effects of a mugging of an elderly person, the council has to repair doors after burglary, battered women's refuges have to deal with domestic violence, the police have to deal with the victims' fear on the spot. Victim Support has a vital role to play throughout. Thus our measurement of success — or failure for that matter — is not solely in terms of the levels of offending (that is, crime) but in the levels of victim support provided.

I have discussed the wide range of tasks which influence crime, which involve different agencies and which are influential at different times in the trajectory of offending. It is important to note how these agencies have different material possibilities of intervening and act within given political limits. We have to choose, then, what agencies are involved and what factors can feasibly be manipulated.

Our approach then views crime as a developing system, from its initial causes to the impact on the victim. In doing this it places the responsibility for crime control on a wide range of agencies and the public themselves.

Multi-agencies and the public

The literature on multi-agency intervention is dominated by a discussion of the relationship between the institutions involved. This analysis, quite correctly, focuses on the possibilities of cooperation and likely conflicts between the agencies. It omits, however, a crucial link in the scheme, namely the relationship between the agencies and the public. I have noted the vital role which the public plays in policing. The recognition of this is, if anything, a major part of modern criminological thinking. And we must not restrict our attention to police–public relations, but the relationships between the public and the various agencies concerned with crime control. For the social services, education, probation and the local council, no less than the police, are dependent on public cooperation.

Relationship between agencies

The democratic relationship between agencies must be based on their specialist knowledge and purchase on particular crimes. That is a division of labour predicated on the specific segment of the crime process in which the agency specializes. For example, at what point in time along the continuum of the development of crime, outlined above, is a particular agency's involvement paramount and what perspective does the agency represent? In the latter instance, a juvenile delinquent, for example, may be regarded from the point of view of whether guilty or not by the police, the context of a family with problems by the social services, and as part of a family which causes problems for others in the estate by the housing officers. There has to be pre-agreed consensus as to specialism, although in some cases more than one agency will be involved at the same point. Lighting, for example, will be under the auspices of both the local authority's architects' department and their housing officers. Different crimes will, of course, involve different multi-agency cooperation. Child abuse will involve a strong medical involvement, as well as police and social services. Domestic violence will involve the voluntary agencies as well as the more usual constituents.

Having brought together these agencies there will, despite an agreement on acknowledged specialisms, be a necessary conflict of interests. In child abuse, for example, social work will, by necessity of its brief, focus on the general welfare of the child within the family; the police more on the actual issues of culpability; the paediatrician on the extent of physical contact and harm. What is necessary, in the coordination of such expertise, is that in the final analysis a corporate decision be made, after listening to the contributions of each agency, and backed with sufficient executive power to come to an agreed decision. As it is, the agencies discuss together, yet then too often merely proceed upon their own paths with their own agenda. Such imbalances are dramatically seen where, in the case of child abuse, either medical or social services play too dominant a role, or, in the case of crime prevention, where the police take too prominent a role. It is the role of local authorities to provide this coordinating role. It is the ultimate task of national government to ascertain how the funding of resources to each agency is based on the actual cost-effective contribution of each part, rather than, as at present, allow resources to be decided by the separate agencies themselves. Such a conception of minimal policing in the context of multi-social intervention has clear implications for the second dimension of our analysis. Here there is widespread community support for such a proposal (Painter *et al.*, 1989). It does not involve a domination by the police on the multiple agencies, and, though advocating cooperation between the agencies, it does not suggest a corporatism involving a cosy level of agreement. Rather, because of the different approaches and priorities of each agency, room has to be made for a healthy debate and conflict of perspectives within a consensus delineated by public demands for the control of specific areas (cf. Sampson *et al.*, 1985). Finally, in terms of the second dimension, the public accountability of agencies — a concern hitherto largely omitted in discussion of multi-agency intervention — the priority is to ensure efficiency and the need for public bodies to fall in line with the demands of the public whose support is necessary for their effectiveness and who, out of their rates and taxes, pay these bodies for the task of achieving a reasonable level of community safety. All of this, with due regard to the three dimensions of multi-agency intervention, suggests the basis for a restructuring of these institutions so as to ensure a maximum level of service delivery in this area, while protecting the rights and dignity of the offender.

The principle of rational democratic input

Taking people seriously

The public pay for community safety; they ultimately empower the police and the local authority to make provisions for a safe environment. There is much talk, at the moment, of the quality of life, and the emergence of green issues as priorities in the platforms of all political parties. Considerable focus is given, quite correctly, to architecture, to consumer satisfaction, to creating an environment in the city which makes it a pleasure to live in. But what can be more central to the quality of life than the ability to walk down the street at night without fear, to feel safe in one's home, to be free from harassment and incivilities in the day-to-day experience of urban life?

The social survey is a democratic instrument: it provides a reasonably accurate appraisal of people's fears and of their experience of victimization. Local surveys further allow us to move beyond the abstraction of aggregate national statistics. Crime is extremely geographically focused and policing varies widely between the suburbs and the inner city. To add the crime rates for a suburban area to that of an inner-city area produces blancmange figures of little use to anyone. More invidiously, it allows politicians to talk of irrational fears of crime when compared to the actual risk rate of the 'average' citizen. The 1982 *British Crime Survey* showed that the risk of experiencing a robbery in England and Wales was once every five centuries; an assault resulting in injury, once every century; a family car stolen, once every 60 years and a burglary once every 50 years (Hough and Mayhew, 1983). But crime is extensively geographically focused and 'irrational' fears become the more rational with geographical focus on the inner city. And the often-made assertion that certain groups have an irrational fear of crime because of their supposedly low risk rates often disappears on closer examination. Ascribing irrationality to women, for example, is based on ignoring that much crime against women, such as domestic violence, is concealed in the official figures, that women are less tolerant of violence than men and that they experience harassment on a level which is unknown to most men. The latter point, particularly, is important for policing public areas. Women experience a wider spectrum of crime than men. Their range of victimization extends from harassment to serious crime. The range for men is more likely to be experienced in the more serious end of the spectrum. Because of this, men find it difficult to comprehend women's fears. The equivalent experience of sexual harassment for men would be if every time they walked out of doors they were met with catcalls asking if they would like a fight. And the spectrum which women experience is all the more troublesome in that each of the minor incivilities could escalate to more serious violence. Sexual harassment could be a prelude to attempted rape; domestic verbal quarrels could trigger off domestic violence; burglary is feared, not only as a property crime, but as a possible precursor to sexual assault. If crime deteriorates the quality of life for men, it has a much more dramatic impact on the lives of women in the inner city.

Social surveys, therefore, allow us to give voice to the experience of people, and they enable us to differentiate the safety needs of different sectors of the community. In this they often make reasonable the supposedly irrational. But it must not be thought that irrationality does not occur with regard to crime and the means of its control. Crime is a prime site of social anxiety and the mass media provide the citizen with an extraordinary, everyday diet of spectacular crimes, often of the most statistically atypical kind. It is, perhaps, not surprising that the news value of the most unusual garish offences is higher than that of the more mundane crimes that daily plague the lives of the inner-city dweller. And in a free society there is little that can, or should, be done about such media predilections. For in a real sense the most unusual examples of inhumanity tell us something of the extremes of moral depravity that are possible in today's society. The trouble occurs when the citizen comes to believe that what is typical on television is typical in his or her neighbourhood. The debate on the effects of the mass media on public attitudes is long, fraught and, in part, unresolved (Cohen and Young, 1981). What is a useful rule of thumb, however, is that the mass media have greatest influence on opinion where people have little direct knowledge of the matter in question and the least where they have direct empirical experience. Applying this to the repeated findings of victimization studies, we would expect that there is little chance of inner-city dwellers being particularly irrational about most of the common serious crimes.

When we turn to crime control, the possibility of public irrationality is considerably greater. For, although they may have experienced victimization, they have, on the whole, little knowledge as to how effective crime control occurs. It comes as a surprise, for example, that a large proportion of serious crime is solved by the public rather than by police investigation. And, as we have seen, neighbourhood watch is widely seen as a panacea for burglary, despite being largely ineffective.

Social surveys can, therefore, provide us with a democratic input into the direction and prioritization of crime control. But they cannot provide us with a blueprint. You cannot read policy directives from social surveys but neither can you provide directives without a real consumer input. The victimization survey accurately provides a map of the problems of an area. Although based on public input, it delivers what any individual member of the public is ignorant of: that is how private problems are publicly distributed. In this task, it pinpoints which social groups within the population face the greatest risk rates and geographically pinpoints where these occurrences most frequently occur. In this it directs crime intervention initiatives towards these people and places which are most at risk. It therefore reveals the concealed crime rate and it ascertains its social and spatial focus. But it goes beyond this, for risk rates alone, however delineated, do not measure the true impact of crime and hence the actual patterning of crime as a social problem. To do this we must advance beyond the one-dimensional approach of aggregate risk rates and place crime in its social context. The myth of the equal victim underscores much of conventional victimology with its notion that victims are, as it were, equal billiard halls, and the risk rate involves merely the calculation of the changes of an offending billiard ball impacting upon them. People are, of course, not equal; they are, more or less, vulnerable, depending on their place in society. First of all, at certain parts of the social structure, we have a compounding of social problems.

If we were to draw a map of the city outlining areas of high infant mortality, bad housing, unemployment, poor nutrition, etc, we would find that all these maps would coincide and that further, the outline traced would correspond to those areas of high criminal victimization (Clarke, 1980). And those suffering from street crime would also suffer most from white-collar and corporate crime (Lea and Young, 1984). Further, this compounding of social problems occurs against those who are more or less vulnerable because of their position in the social structure. That is, people who have least power socially suffer most from crime. Most relevant here is the social relationships of age, class, gender and race. Realist analysis, by focusing on the combination of these fundamental social relationships, allows us to note the extraordinary differences between social groups as to both the impact of crime and the focus of policing. It is high time, therefore, that we substituted *impact* statistics for *risk* statistics.

The principle of rational democratic output

Let us now turn to outcome. At first this would seem obvious: the *modus vivendi* of crime control is to control crime. But we must ask: what crimes are being controlled, at what cost, and where do these crimes figure in public priorities? That is, we must connect up demand with supply; what crimes the public prioritize in terms of community safety and how effective the various agencies and initiatives are at their control with an eye to cost-effectiveness. But efficiency alone is an insufficient indicator of success. It is quite possible to pour resources into a particular estate or area to good result. But the reduction of crime at a particular point in the city may have little effect on the overall crime rate. At its most acute, the individual citizen may turn his or her home into a veritable fortress of locks, bolts and guard dogs, which will undoubtedly reduce the chances of crime at a particular point in a street, but not reduce — indeed, may increase — the incidence of crime in adjacent properties. Or, on a larger scale, residents of a private estate may employ their own security guards and, by environmental means, isolate their housing from the neighbourhood. Such social sanitization may greatly reduce the incidence of crime in such privatized areas. Or, within the public realm, a local authority may select an estate and implement considerable degrees of target hardening on doors and windows, coupled with an expensive concierge system. Such 'show casing' of one estate may produce good particular results, but have little effect on the universal incidence of crime in the area. The task of an effective crime policy is to reduce crime in general. In this it is like a community health project; success is not measured by the extent to which the well-off can purchase vaccines, private health care and medicines, but the degree to which such indicators as the levels of infectious diseases are reduced, infant mortality in general curtailed, overall lifespan increased, etc.

Crime, like illness, is a universal problem. It affects all classes, ages, races; men and women. For this reason, being a prevalent and universal phenomenon, it rates very highly in people's assessment of problems of their area. More people, for example, see crime in an inner-city area such as the London Borough of Islington as a problem than they do unemployment, housing or education. This is because these latter problems, however serious, affect, most directly, only parts of the population: those who are unemployed, those with poor housing, those with children at school. But however universal a problem crime is, it affects particular parts of the population to a greater extent than others. In part, this is because the incidence of crime focuses on certain parts of the population rather than others, but also, most importantly, because the impact of identical crimes varies considerably with the vulnerability of those who are the targets of crime. To this extent, we must not only seek to reduce the crime rate universally, but we must allocate greater resources to those who suffer the most. Once again, community health provides a model. Ill-health is a universal human problem, but ill-health focuses more on certain sectors of the population than it does on others. We must, therefore, in order to reduce the general rate of crime, target our resources. Unfortunately, and this has been a general problem of welfare provision, resources are not distributed so much to those in greatest need, as to those with the greater political muscle and social persuasion. The history of the National Health Service and of state educational provisions has adequately displayed this. And, as I have argued, crime control has its parallel problems in the shape of the privatization of community safety and the 'show casing' of selected areas of public housing.

The interrelated nature of intervention

The degree of impact of an intervention about crime by one agency is dependent on the other agencies. To take a simple example; no amount of propagation by the police of crime prevention advice in terms of better locks and bolts will be effective on estates if the council does not simultaneously strengthen the doorframes of its tenants' houses. Or, of greater significance, police effectiveness is almost totally predicated on public support — it cannot function without the information flow from the informal system of social control. And the same is true of deterrence: the effect of police cautioning or sentences of the control relates closely to the degree of public stigma. That is, we must concern ourselves, not only with how effective each piece is with regard to crime control, but how these various pieces can be welded into an effective mutually supporting intervention. As an effective strategy in one agency will need support from other institutions, we can only judge the effectiveness of an innovation in practice in one area to the extent that the requisite support occurs elsewhere.

Realism about cost effectiveness in tackling crime. Realism states that any intervention has its costs. Different crime control measures have to be measured against: (a) how effective are they compared to each other? (b) how effective is the marginal increase in resources in one area rather than another? (c) what is the cost of the measure in terms of other desiderata, for example, the quality of life or the exercise of civil liberties?

Our point should now be clear. A realist policy acknowledges that there are various methods which, if properly tested, monitored and costed, can reduce crime. But any one method, however effective, will have declining marginal returns if taken too far and too exclusively. Furthermore, any one method, be it public surveillance through neighbourhood watch, extra police on the streets, or target hardening, will have costs which impact on the quality of life and the freedom of citizens. Present government policy, by putting too great an emphasis on target hardening and ignoring the conditions which give rise to crime, has created an imbalance in intervention. It has focused on reducing the opportunities for crime, not on its causes, on one half of the equation rather than on both of its sides.

Every social intervention inevitably has unintended repercussions. The cost of crime control has to be measured against the degree of displacement of crime occurring and the effect on the quality of life (from the aesthetics of target hardening to the civil liberties aspect of intensive policing). An effective intervention will have a crime displacement which is quantifiably lower, qualitatively of a less serious nature which directs crime away from the most vulnerable social groups (in the area of drug control, see Dorn and South, 1987). Its social cost will have to be weighed against any losses in the quality of life. Realistically, we have to decide politically what level of crime is tolerable when weighed against such social costs. No method of crime control will be totally effective: we must talk in terms of palpable gains rather than magical solutions.

Open and closed systems. The distinction between open and closed systems is a fundamental distinction made in the recent realist philosophy of science (Bhaskar, 1980). Most scientific laws are predicated on research carried out *in vitro,* that is closed systems, where all extraneous factors are held constant. Here causality can be traced with a degree of simplicity. But in the actual natural world, for example, in sciences such as meteorology, the degree of extraneous factors present in an open system make statement of cause and effect extremely difficult. *X* follows *Y*, depending on the contingency of circumstance: it is better, therefore, to speak of 'causal powers' which may or may not be enacted, depending on circumstance. The social world is an 'open system' *par excellence.*

To hold that an intervention in policing or other forms of crime control, in such an open system, would be instrumental in changing the crime rate begs a series of questions: namely, that the number of possible victims, offenders and public reaction to crime are constant. But changes in the social structure of the area affect all of these factors. For example:

1. increased gentrification would affect the number of victims and also by increasing relative deprivation, the number of putative offenders;

2. increased population mobility would affect the social solidarity of the area and hence the strength of public control of crime;

3. changes in the age structure, particularly of young males, would affect the number of putative offenders;

4. changes in employment and economic marginalization would affect the number of offenders;

5. changes in lifestyle by increasing, for example, the number of evenings out made by members of the public would affect the victimization rate, both in terms of risks in public space and the risks of homes unattended.

We can attempt to control for some of these, but an open system over any reasonable length of time will exhibit the movement of many of these factors. What I am pointing to is that the process which gives results to crime rates is a system of relationships, and what is more, it is an open system (see Figure 3).

The implication of such an open system is that — with the exception of short-term experiments, where a social intervention such as improvements in lighting is introduced and the effects measured (Painter, 1989) — it is extremely difficult to pinpoint cause and effect.

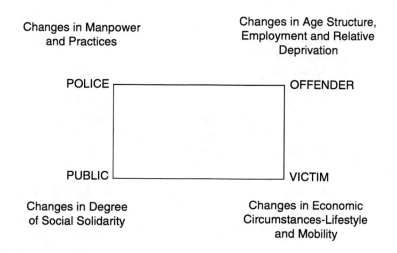

Figure 3

The principle of democratic measurement

Realism and the criminal statistics

The problem of criminal statistics is the base-line problem of criminology. It is a recognized problem which has a history as long as the discipline, stretching back to the work of Alphonse Quetelet in the 1830s. It is a concern which has haunted every theory. For if the problem of what causes crime is a conundrum, the difficulty of knowing, in the first place, what crimes occur, to what extent and where, undercuts all others. It is on the shifting sand of the statistics that the most elaborate and powerful structures of theory flounder.

The problem comes down to answering the question of what is the 'real' rate of crime and, indeed, is there such an entity? Let us dispose first of the notion that victimization studies technically solve this question by overcoming the problem of the 'dark figure'. For, despite grandiose claims for victimization data (Sparks *et al.*, 1977), all of the old problems remain, albeit in a less marked form. Victimization studies have dark figures, they are a product of research units whose conceptualization of the data from the questionnaire to the coding reflects their own values, and they ask questions of interviewees with different definitions of what constitutes a crime (Young, 1988b).

Realism propounds that rates of crime are by definition a result of the interplay of actors and reactors: of victims and offenders, on one hand, and of formal and informal control, on the other. Rates of crime change as these interacting sectors change and any satisfactory theory of crime must take cognizance of the totality of this process. The rate of crime is the result of a dynamic process of decision making, not a fixed datum 'out there' (Wheeler, 1967; Wilkins, 1964).

The simple belief that the crime rate is a gauge of offenders is wrong. The crime rate goes up, it is true, when there are more motivated offenders: but it also goes up when there are more available victims or when the police and public are more lax in their control, or more sensitive in their definition of 'intolerable' behaviour. But how does the crime rate relate to the crime statistics? How does one move from infractions in the world to tabulated data on official reports? The crime rate is not a 'natural' act, crime rates do not spring automatically out of aggregates of illegalities. Someone has to embark on an act of collecting these varied, moral infractions together. Crime rates are not naturally and automatically produced phenomena, they are second order data produced by bureaucracies: whether the police, victimization survey work or criminologists engaged in self-report studies. They involve applying a fairly consistent measuring rod (such as have you been burgled/assaulted?) to a series of actions which the public inconsistently evaluates (holding differing definitions of what constitutes burglary/assault).

Crime is, by its very nature, a product of action and reaction. It involves behaviour and the variable legal response to that behaviour: an infraction and an evaluation. Criminal statistics, whether official, self-report, or victim report are, therefore, neither an objective fact of behaviour (Eysenck and Gudjonsson 1989), nor merely a social construction dependent on the evaluation of the powerful. Different groups within society and different societies at various parts of historical time vary in their definitions of what is tolerable behaviour. The statistics of violence, as we have seen, depend on the extend of violent behaviour and the tolerance level to violence. There is no objective yardstick for crime, but a series of measuring rods dependent on the social group in which they are based. All societies and social groups, however, stigmatize a wide range of usurpation of the person and of property. At any point in time, various social groups will agree up to a point, then differ from that point onwards. The measuring rod is not — and cannot be — consensual in an absolute sense, but it has a considerable overlap of agreement (Young, 1988b). All groups, for example, abhor violence against women, but they will vary in their definition of what constitutes abhorrent violence, For this reason, criminal statistics are, by their very nature, blurred; they can never be stated with precision, although they can be more or less democratically ascertained and can make possible a real, if hazy, outline of the constraints of the problem.

The comparison of crime rates between different groups, between different countries, and over time, is, therefore, a process by which we must be clearly aware of differences in value. The so-called 'education effect', where, for example, middle-class women claim higher rates of violence than working-class women, is a case in question (Sparks, 1981). It is not, however, beyond the capabilities of researchers to ask questions on not only reported violent behaviour and to construct tolerance scales towards violence. Furthermore, there is a level of specificity here, where certain crimes, such as burglary, have less of a subjective component than does violence (Hough, 1986). But even such 'objective' crimes have clear definitional variations: note the problems in international comparisons which often blur attempted burglaries with successful break-ins. Over time, in longitudinal studies, we must be aware that a 'successful' intervention, say a housing estate which reduces the behavioural manifestations of vandalism, may result in an increased intolerance to vandalism. Because of this, the resulting post-intervention survey may indicate more acts of vandalism than before or, even more puzzlingly, because of a decrease in behaviour concomitant with an increase in intolerance, no 'change' whatsoever (Young, 1988b).

If Quetelet pointed to the existence of a dark figure of crime, realist and feminist studies have pointed to how this dark figure is qualitatively structured. The dark figure varies with what type of crime committed by whom against which victim. Such an analysis takes us one step further. The dark figure expands and contracts with the values we bring to our study: recent studies of the extent of marital rape or changes in child abuse over time clearly indicate this.

Crime as a unifier

Both radical critics of the left and the right suggest that law and order is an issue which splits the community. For left idealists (Bridges *et al.*, 1987) it involves the mobilization of state (and particularly police) definitions of crime with anti-working class and racist undertones. For the radical right, law and order is about the protection of the law-abiding from a predatory underclass. Realism sees the issue of crime as a major unifier: law and order, like health and education, are areas which affect the majority of the population, which is the constituency of social democratic politics (cf. Brown and Hogg, 1992). Right-wing law and order politics not only seek to divide the population, they are ineffective at controlling crime and would seek to privatize community safety — just as in health and education — in a fashion which would privilege the wealthy and the powerful. Furthermore, the poor suffer most from crime and, once again, as in health and education, have a priority of needs in social democratic policy. Crime is endemic throughout society, it is not a monopoly product of an underclass, although conventional crime is most endemic in the lower part of the class structure. And it is the poorer and most vulnerable sections of the population (less well-off whites, blacks, lower working-class women) against whom crimes of the powerful (from corporate crime, through lack of safety regulations, to police malpractices) and conventional crimes create the greatest impact. It is not an either/or between corporate crime and conventional crime as left idealists would maintain.

There is a widespread consensus throughout society of the importance of crime as an issue and the priority crimes to tackle. Certainly there are differences in emphasis between social groups, but research shows a consistent unity of concern, particularly with regard to crimes of violence and serious property offences (Jones *et al.*, 1986). To point to a degree of consensus within the population about the definitions of various crimes is not to seek an absolute consensus. Indeed, in realist terms, this is impossible. But the unity of interest allows us the possibility, both of a common measuring rod, and a political base which can argue for taking crime seriously.

The principle of theory and practice

> The problem goes something like this: intellectual and academic life in general and in the social sciences in particular, thrives best and depends upon a spirit of scepticism, doubt and uncertainty. Answers are provisional; thought is ambiguous; irony is deliberate. All this can best be achieved when one is free from pressures of everyday demands — especially those to be 'relevant' and to fit and tailor your ideas to serve the managers of society. Uncompromising intellectual honesty does not usually please politicians and civil servants.

> Political life, on the other hand — and in this context I include social policy, welfare, social work, social control, criminal justice — calls for some immediate commitments. Decisions have to be made, clear public statements made, bets placed, budgets drawn up, doubts temporarily laid aside. You have to respond to values that are binding and encourage neither scepticism nor irony: social justice, humanitarianism, doing good, equality, citizenship, public safety, the needs of victims. All this familiar. But the familiar is always with us. (Cohen, 1990: 10–11).

The 'interior' history of an academic discipline involves the development of intellectual traditions, each with its own problematic and involving material problems of funding and employment. The 'exterior' history involves the political context, the policy problems of the outside world, and the various prevalent social and political ideologies (Hacking, 1981; Phipps, 1987; Young, 1988). The history of criminology may be written as an interior dialogue of ideas and debates, but it exists always in an exterior world of changing problems of crime and penality, of funding from central and local government agencies, of contemporary conceptions of human nature and social order. Theories of society do not come into being out of the blue. They arise out of the hunches and intuitions of people trying to make sense of the world around them: they arise out of real problems facing people in the social world which confronts them. The academic refines, develops and systemizes theory, but the agenda is set for him or her by the actual problems of the world outside the ivory tower and the text is largely pre-written by the social currents and fashions of the time. Whatever textbooks write about the 'interior' history of a discipline, as if it developed as the accumulated wisdom of the free exchange of ideas and criticism, the 'exterior' history of a subject, engendered by the practical problems of the outside world is, in fact, paramount.

The exterior world always penetrates the academic interior, whether it involves the most armchair radical theorist or the establishment criminologist working as a civil servant for a government bureaucracy. But, paradoxically, all are cocooned from reality by their social distance from their subjects, their obdurate preconceptions and myopia and, above all, by their political impotence. It is my contention that the achievement of a creative relationship between the interior and exterior worlds is essential to a mature criminology, albeit that it creates many dangers and pitfalls.

Theory is divorced from practice: theoreticians are divorced not just from practitioners, but from those who are the objects of their study. This is particularly true in criminology: criminologists live in different areas than criminals, they work in an academic milieu: the world of street crime or corporate crime, for that matter, is socially distant from them. They share little sympathy for the cop on the beat, they have a culture which is instinctively suspicious of both the bureaucrat in the town hall and the politician. Yet if we are to engage in a subcultural analysis of the police officer, the victim, the offender and the various publics constituting society, we cannot spare the criminologist from subcultural scrutiny. The fifth point in the square of crime is the criminologist [see Ruggiero, Chapter 5]. A reflexive sociology must ground the academic in his or her milieu. As Gouldner put it:

> If every social theory is thus a tacit theory of politics, every theory is also

464

a personal theory, inevitably expressing, coping and infused with the personal experience of the individuals who author it. Every social theory has both political and personal relevance which, according to the technical causes of social theory, it is not supposed to have. Consequently, both the man (sic) and his politics are of presumably 'autonomous' social theory.

Yet, however disguised, an appreciable part of any sociological enterprise devolves from the sociologist's effort to explore, to objectify, and to universalize some of his own most deeply personal experiences. Much of any man's (sic) effort to know the social world around him is prompted by an effort, more or less disguised or deliberate, to know things that are personally important to him; which is to say, he aims at knowing himself and the experiences he has had in his social world (his relationship to it) and at changing this relationship in some manner. Like it or not, and know it or not, in confronting the social world the theorist is also confronting himself. . . .

Whatever their other differences, all sociologists seek to study something in the social world that they take to be real; and, whatever their philosophy of science, they seek to explain it in terms of something that they feel to be real. Like other men (sic), sociologists impute reality to certain things in their social world. This is to say, they believe, sometimes with focal and sometimes only with subsidiary awareness, that certain things are truly attributable to the social world. In important part, their conception of what is 'real' derives from the domain assumptions they have learned in their culture. These culturally standardized assumptions are, however, differentiated by personal experience in different parts of the social structure. Individually accented by particular sentiment-generating experiences, the common domain assumptions in time assume personal arrangements; they become part of a man's personal reality. (1971: 40–41)

In this vein C. Wright Mills documents the underlying assumptions of small town society which textbooks of this period carried. Such domain assumptions involve preconceptions and blindness. The root of partiality: the emphasis upon only one part of the explanation in crime is both culturally and materially based. The classic example is that pointed to by David Matza:

The scholar's or scientist's way of becoming partially blind is, inadvertently perhaps, to structure fields of injury in such a way as to obscure obvious connections or to take the connections for granted and leave the matter at that. The great task of disconnection — it was arduous and time-consuming — fell to the positive school of criminology. Among their most notable accomplishments, the criminological positivists succeeded in what would seem the impossible. They separated the study of crime from the workings and theory of the state. That done, and the lesson extended to deviation generally, the agenda for research and scholarship for the next half-century was relatively clear, especially with regard to what would *not* be studied. (1969: 143)

It is extraordinary that establishment criminologists who are the most politically constrained in their work can view themselves as politically neutral scientists *par excellence*. But radicals, as well, carry with them preconceptions and blindness. Their culture of scepticism, so rightly prized, is sceptical only in certain areas: it is naive in others. What are we to make of the arch-sceptic Michel Foucault when he comments:

> At the end of the eighteenth century, people dreamed of a society without crime. And then the dream evaporated. Crime was too useful for them to dream of anything as crazy — or ultimately as dangerous — as a society without crime. No crime means no police. What makes the presence and control of the police tolerable for the population, if not fear of the criminal? This institution of the police, which is so recent and so oppressive, is only justified by that fear. If we accept the presence in our midst of these uniformed men, who have the exclusive right to carry arms, who demand our papers, who come and prowl on our doorsteps, how would any of this be possible if there were no criminals? And if there weren't articles every day in the newspapers telling us how numerous and dangerous our criminals are? (1980: 7)

There are, as Edward Thompson remarked about left idealist positions on law and order 'In secure and secluded places, some marvellously abstract notions afloat' (1980: 173). And political conceptions tacitly held are reinforced by the social distance of the criminologist from his or her subject matter. It is this social distance which was largely to account for the 'great denial' of the rise of crime among liberal criminologists in the late 1960s and early 1970s, which makes it difficult for male academics to understand the problem of crime and sexual harassment for women, and which was the moving force in the realist argument against both administrative criminology and left idealism. And the underestimation of the problem of crime by the latter criminologies became, of course, the basis for the initial slogan of realist criminology: to take people and crime seriously.

The bridge between the academic milieu and the deviant is constructed in two ways by research and, more rarely, by involvement in practical interventions. It is here that preconceptions should alter and myopia becomes unblinkered. But the material and cultural limitations are difficult to shake off and often not recognised. Research demands funding, seldom are there no strings attached, particularly if the researcher wishes the contracts to be renewed. Grants, like lunches, are seldom free. In all western countries the major research funding is central government, and this alone severely structures preconceptions and blindness (Young, 1988c). Radical sources of funding exhibit precisely the same problems. Taboo issues such as race and crime are systematically ignored by the liberal establishment (Wilbanks, 1985).

Both quantitative and qualitative research frequently involves a *projection* of the researcher's preconceptions on interviewees. Crime surveys, for example, typically provide a questionnaire menu of options which simply do not correspond to the lived experience of those interviewed. The modal type of crime for a middle-class male, for example, is the burglary: this generates a discrete 'event-orientation' which fails to encompass 'incessant' violence experienced by lower working-class groups (Genn,

1988), the continuous nature of domestic violence (Mooney, 1991) or the spectrum of harassment experienced by women in public spaces and working-class Asians in inner-city housing estates. Yet the 'bridge' between theory and data, for quantitative researchers, is regularly experienced as a row of figures on a computer printout: a small army of interviewers shielding the preconceptions of the theorist. Qualitative research, much heralded as being more intimate and reflexive, frequently involves a simple projection of the researcher's preconceptions. Margaret Mead was not alone in being deceived and deceiving herself. Stan Cohen, in his introduction to the revised edition of *Folk Devils and Moral Panics* (1980), trenchantly notes how radical ethnographers frequently treat subcultures like Rorschach blots.

If empirical research frequently involves the projection of preconceptions on its subject matter, criminological practice displays a welter of unmonitored projection. If there is anything one can agree with in the work of Wilson it is his dictum: 'Above all we can try to learn more about what works and in the process abandon our ideological preconceptions about what *ought* to work.' It must be said, however, that Wilson, in a typical act of inversion and partiality, ushers one set of ideological preconceptions out of the door simply to make room for another. But the dictum remains true; put simply: politicians of all persuasions throw money at crime problems. Millions of pounds, dollars and yen are spent every year on crime prevention with scarcely a thought as to cost effectiveness. Monitored research is rare and is, as I have argued, much more difficult than is usually acknowledged. Most practice is divorced from theory on all but a rudimentary level. A considerable part of criminological theory is, in fact, the critique by armchair theorists of other people's practice. To an extent this is a necessary and vital intervention. For if theoreticians, in their research, constantly face the problem of substantiating their preconceptions, practitioners within their own ideological and material context have a pronounced tendency to self-congratulation. As Dennis Rosenbaum notes in his exhaustive and meticulous examination of community crime prevention programmes:

> Despite all the impressive statistics and laudatory accomplishments attributed to community prevention programs, the standard evaluations in this field, which structure the foundation of public opinion about the success of these programs are seriously wanting.

> The endorsement of community crime prevention programs extends from many quarters, including federal state and local government agencies as well as community organizations. The enthusiastic embracing of community crime prevention is perhaps most apparent at the grass-root level, where practitioners acclaim the utility of their efforts through popular press articles and numerous homespun program publications, newsletters, and guidebooks that also serve to assist interested communities in the planning and implementation of programs.

> Not everyone has the same level of interest in presenting the 'hard facts'. To obtain program funding from public or private sources, grant applications often have a strong motivation to convince the funding agency that it will be investing in a proven, highly effective program for

preventing crime in their community. Likewise, the granting agencies, although wanting to remain neutral in the absence of hard data, also want to believe that they were supporting a good 'product'. Moreover, the media are very interested in success stories inasmuch as our losses in the seventeen-year 'war against crime' have greatly outnumbered our victories. Consequently, we have witnessed literally hundreds of media stories about the proven successes of community crime prevention over the past decade. Given this state of affairs, the primary 'checks and balances' must come from the academic community, armed with evaluation research skills and disinterested in the direction of the outcome. (1986: 19, 22, 23).

And, of course, Rosenbaum is talking about US research, where he can find less than 20 satisfactory monitored pieces of intervention. In Britain the situation is much bleaker — most community crime prevention programmes are simply not monitored, or if they are, are monitored using patently inadequate data and measures of success and failure.

Theory and practice are, thus, both our subjects of investigation. They both belong to the orbit of criminology.

Conclusion: the scope of criminology

The problem which faces criminology is not insignificant, however, and, arguably, its dilemma is even more fundamental than that facing sociology. The whole *raison d'être* of criminology is that it addresses crime. It categorizes a vast range of activities and treats them as if they were all subject to the same laws — whether laws of human behaviour, genetic inheritance, economic rationality, development or the like. The argument within criminology has always been between those who give primacy to one form of explanation rather than another. The thing that criminology cannot do is deconstruct crime. It cannot locate rape or child sexual abuse in the domain of sexuality or theft in the domain of economic activity or drug use in the domain of health. To do so would be to abandon criminology to sociology; but more importantly it would involve abandoning the idea of a unified problem which requires a unified response — at least, at the theoretical level. However, left realist criminology does not seem prepared for this. (Smart, 1990: 77)

Good criminology, of course, does precisely this: relate rape or child sexual abuse to the domain of sexuality, theft to the domain of economic activity, and drug use to the domain of health. But neither can the sociology of sexuality, economies or health studies remain within their watertight domains. Good work in these areas rarely does. But what Smart would seem to argue is that the domain of criminology should be cut up and disposed of between the various, more fundamental domains. Because it addresses a series of disparate behaviours? Is this not true of the domains of sexuality, economics and health? Illicit drug use is an economic activity, it is a health problem and, in the case of certain drugs, it has clear sexual connotations. To which domain should we reduce our studies? But enough of such demarcation disputes. Realist criminology starts from the deconstruction of the criminal act into its fundamental components: law and state agencies, the public and various institutions of civil societies, the victim and the offender. This is the domain of criminology. It is these formal relationships — which encompass disparate substantive behaviour and which involve different aetiologies. And central to realist criminology is that all parts of the square of crime must be linked up from the micro-level of interaction, to the mezzo-level (such as the nature of police bureaucracies or the informal economy in burgled goods) to the macro-level. From *The New Criminology* onwards we have consistently argued that criminology cannot remain on the micro-level, it must connect up with the wider domains, particularly the economic and the political.

This being said, many of the points of realism are applicable to other social science disciplines. The difficulty of social intervention is scarcely one which is limited to criminology. Indeed, the key problematic of realism is rooted in the shortcomings of social democratic attempts to engineer a more equitable social order.

20.   Realism and Corporate Crime

Frank Pearce and Steve Tombs

Realists have shown some recognition of the importance of white-collar and corporate crime (Matthews, 1987; Young, 1986, 1987), and have provided an examination of the relative impact of corporate crime and street crime on people's lives. In a discussion of some depth and subtlety of the similarities and differences between these two kinds of crime, Lea and Young (1984) argue that while both display 'the same ethos of individualism, competitiveness and machismo', the former

> . . . is the most transparent of all injustices. It is a starting point for a double thrust against crime on all levels. If we concentrate on it alone, as the political right would wish, we are actively engaged in a diversion from the crimes of the powerful. If we concentrate solely on the latter, as many on the left would have us do, we are omitting what are real and pressing problems for working class people, and lose the ability to move from the immediate to encompass the more hidden, and thus demonstrate the intrinsic similarity of crime at all levels of our society. (Lea and Young, 1984: 75)

Undoubtedly many on the left invoke the category of corporate crime as an alibi for downplaying the impact of street crime. They fail to explore it in any depth; nor do they unpack it, nor isolate causal sequences, nor specify the kinds of non-reformist reforms that could limit its occurrence now, and which may have a transformative potential (Gorz, 1980). In truth, much of the recent empirical and theoretical work on the crimes of the powerful has been undertaken by social democrats and liberals rather than by Marxists (Clinard and Yeager, 1980; Braithwaite, 1984; Box, 1983, 1987; for some exceptions see Snider, 1989; Barnett, 1983; Pearce and Tombs, 1989, 1990, 1991). Yet despite the attempts of realism to take crime seriously, there are significant problems with the way that realists have dealt with both street crime and with the crimes of the powerful.

Realism and corporate crime

Unfortunately, some of the references in the realist literature to corporate and white-collar crime are as gestural as those made by 'left idealists'. Matthews (1987: 376), for example, may make reference to these, but when he analyses the relationship between criminal offenders and the victims of crime he restricts his analysis to street crime (1987: 387–8). This inconsistency is not surprising because in practice realism has tended to focus on the more immediate interpersonal anti-social conduct — that is, *on crimes between subjects.*

Frank Pearce and Steve Tombs: 'Realism and Corporate Crime' in *ISSUES IN REALIST CRIMINOLOGY,* edited by R. Matthews and J. Young (Sage Publications, 1992), pp. 70–101. © Frank Pearce and Steve Tombs.

'Crime is a social relationship. It is institutionalised; it is imbued with meaning; both offenders and victims are predictable, and above all *they relate to one another*' (Young, 1987: 344, emphasis added). Young's characterization of the nature of crime does not adequately describe the anonymous relationship between a manufacturer and a consumer using a faulty or dangerous product. It does not capture the extent to which acts of omission are what cause harm in many such cases or in those involving dangerous pollution, nor that it is the failure of employers to fulfil their statutory managerial duties that lead to many workplace injuries and deaths. *Corporate crime is poorly described or understood if we stay within a conceptual framework restricted to interpersonal relations between subjects; moreover, within this framework it is equally unlikely that methods will be found to control it.* This leads one to wonder if, in analysing subjects like murder realists would routinely include an examination of the statistics for deaths caused by workplace accidents and occupationally caused diseases (Boyd, 1988). Would a realist analysis of the violence and harassment suffered by women at work include a discussion of corporate violence and the particular forms it takes against women?

Realism in its present state of development fails to engage in such analyses — yet we do not want to argue that it cannot do so. Rather, taking corporate crime seriously requires a modification of realism's conceptual categories and a broadening of its field of interest. Such analyses might thus very easily draw upon some of realism's strengths. For example, it is possible to adapt some of its research methods to explore aspects of 'commercial crime'. The *Second Islington Crime Survey* included questions relating to commercial crime, health and safety and pollution. Although these results will be discussed in detail elsewhere (Pearce, 1990b), it is worth noting here that they do indeed indicate a great deal of criminal activity by some of the more 'respectable' classes'. For example, of those respondents giving definite answers about their experience of buying goods and services during the previous 12 months: approximately 11 percent had been given misleading information, 21 percent believed that they had been deliberately overcharged and 24 percent had paid for what turned out to be defective goods or services. This indicates that the incidence of commercial crime is high both relatively and absolutely: during the same period, approximately 4 percent of respondents giving definite answers had had a car stolen, 7 percent suffered from a burglary and 7 percent from an actual or attempted theft from their person.

'Left realism', the police and regulatory agencies

Important for the focus of this chapter is the belief that we can build upon some 'left realist' arguments on policing to interrogate the conduct of those agencies entrusted, at least symbolically, with the regulation of commerce, health and safety and pollution. 'Left realist' analysis of the agencies of social control has been developed by studying the nature of and determinants of the modus operandi of the police and by questioning the extent to which they are responsive and democratically accountable to local communities (Kinsey *et al.*, 1986). Very similar questions can be raised about the agencies which regulate the conduct of businesses in relationship to each other, to investors, customers, employees and the local community. These agencies tend to try and achieve 'compliance' through persuasion rather than a 'policing' strategy which uses legal sanctions against businesses and executives found to be in breach of the law.

For some this is not a problem; for many others, such as ourselves, it is a major reason why they are in practice so ineffective.

The most fundamental principle of new left realism is that crime really is a problem. Arguing that realism 'must neither succumb to hysteria nor relapse into a critical denial of the severity of crime as a problem' (Young, 1986: 25), the realists state that 'the major task of a radical criminology is to seek a solution to the problem of crime and that of a socialist policy is to substantially reduce the crime rate' (p.28). This, then, requires that they engage in an analysis of both the formal organization and the modus operandi of the police, to consider ways in which this institution might better address 'the problem of crime'.

Reference to the 'problem' of crime is important. Realists do not believe that increasing crime rates are simply a function of increased police activity, as some 'left idealists' would have it, but rather that these rates reflect reality: that is, the problem of crime has been, and continues to be, a growing one. Moreover, it is one that the police, despite continual (almost exponential) increases in resources, have proved hopelessly inept at tackling.

Lea and his colleagues (1987), for example, note that in the period 1961–1985, the number of police officers serving in England and Wales increased from 75,800 to 120,700, while the numbers of crimes reported to the police rose from 871,000 to 3,612,000. That is, the number of crimes per police officer rose from 12 to 30 (Lea *et al.*, 1987: 32). Focusing on a more recent period, 1979–86, when 'there has been a considerable increase in police resources at every level ', the number of crimes cleared has risen by 18 percent — but the increase in crimes reported to the police has been 52 percent (Lea *et al.*, 1987: 34).

This relative decline in clear-up rates is at the heart of realism's focus on police resourcing and practice. Rejecting arguments for even greater resources for the police, the realists state that such increases tend only to 'disappear into an ever expanding bureaucracy' (Lea *et al.*, 1987: 39). More importantly the key problem is not one of the police themselves, but of police – public cooperation. Thus,

> The typical crime is reported to the police by the public and is solved through public cooperation . . . Over 90% of serious crime in Britain is reported by the public to the police; this rises to over 95% in inner-city areas. The information usually consists of the facts of the crime and a very good indication of who did it. (Lea *et al.*, 1987:40)

For these reasons, realists conclude that: 'the flow of information from the public to the police is crucial. Where the public support the police, they will maintain the flow. When that flow of information dries up successful policing becomes tremendously difficult' (Lea *et al.*, 1987:40).

In an explicitly prescriptive section on 'The theory and practice of democratic policing', Kinsey *et al.* (1986: 186–215) develop a number of proposals which are based on the earlier argument that the police are hopelessly inefficient in dealing with a rapidly rising crime rate, and thus that the inadequate flow of information from the public to the police gives substance to police claims that they can in fact do little about this crime rate. Their proposals focus around two guiding principles, namely 'maximum public initiation' and 'minimum necessary coercion', these principles protecting the rights of individuals and thus providing 'effective guarantees of an *efficient* and socially *just* system of policing' (Kinsey *et al.*, 1986: 193).

'Maximum public initiation' of police action is urged at both the collective and individual level. In this way, it is hoped to minimize the autonomy of police occupational culture and political attitudes in the drawing up of criteria for deciding when to intervene and when not to. 'Minimum necessary coercion' by the police requires a strict limit on police powers. The premise of police work is thus that it is for the police to cooperate with and respond to the demands of the public, rather than vice versa. The realists then go on to set out the legislative framework of minimal policing, which would seek:

1. to define the limits of minimum necessary coercion;

2. to define the precise limits of police powers of intervention and interference in private lives and liberty, and to reduce the scope of police discretion;

3. to minimize the role of police-initiated activity while maximizing that of public-initiated activity.

For the realists, then, minimal policing appears to offer the basis for a 'radical reorganisation of the police and a limitation on their powers, while providing for an efficient and effective system of policing in line with public needs' (Kinsey *et al.*, 1986: 207). We should be clear about the status of these reforms. Following Ryan, we would argue that these policy proposals are liberal rather than socialist in nature: 'Young *et al.* have increasingly — though, in fairness, not exclusively — justified their law and order policies as socialist ones on the basis of making sure that the police are responsive to the needs of working-class communities. This *responsiveness,* is, primarily, what makes their policies *socialist'* (Ryan, 1986: 30).

We agree with Ryan that 'such a restrictive emphasis is hardly sufficient. Moreover, it is possible that the practical effects of such arguments might be, in certain contexts, profoundly anti-democratic. Nevertheless, to preview the argument to be set out below, it is important to recognize the differential effect of implementing realist-type reforms in the context of safety, health and environmental regulation. For *such an implementation would entail empowering workers and local communities against capital,* and thus these reforms may have a transformative potential, thereby being 'non-reformist reforms' rather than 'mere' or 'liberal' reforms.

To begin to consider the relevance of realist arguments for the enforcement of regulatory law in the spheres of safety, health and the environment, we need to note the objective differences between this context and that with which the realists are concerned, namely street crime.

The regulation of safety, health and the environment

Police officers police local communities. Thus there is no a priori distinction between those to whom 'protection' is being offered (potential victims) and those who might be the object of police action (potential offenders). Indeed, in some of the areas focused on in the realists' crime surveys, the existence of very blurred boundaries between victims and offenders, particularly among the young, is likely. This is very different from the relationship between many regulatory agencies and the groups with whom they interact. While some health, safety and environmental law obviously places duties and obligations upon workers and members of local communities, it is clear that the object of regulation is business. Moreover, it is equally clear that those in whose interests the regulations exist, and for whose protection they should be enforced, are workers and local communities.

This key difference leads us on to a very closely related point. Regulatory law will need to be enforced less 'minimally' than the kinds of law with which the realists are concerned, precisely because of the immense inequalities in power between the regulated — business — and those whom the regulations exist to protect — workers and local communities. (A recognition and full understanding of this imbalance of power also necessitates academic work, in terms of an adequate theorization of the nature of the offenders under regulatory law, namely corporations.) When the realists discuss 'public initiation of police action', we not only endorse this with respect to worker and local community initiation of regulatory inspectorate action, but would add that the imbalance of power in this latter sphere requires the development of much more formal mechanisms to encourage, facilitate and render effective such initiation. Just as the realists constantly argue for more democratic means of controlling policing, this need is more urgent with respect to the activities of regulatory agencies. (This, after all, has been a central concern of the 'capture' literature of the last two decades within social science literature on regulation.)

Thus, while realism urges that policing become much more reactive and much less proactive, we would resist this exigence in the sphere of regulatory law. One reason for this is simply that there are some differences between the types of offence that fall within the ambit of the police, on the one hand, and regulatory agencies on the other (though this should not be overemphasized — see below). Regulatory violations are often easily observable, ongoing states of affairs, rather than discrete often concealed acts. For these reasons, a proactive presence by the factory or pollution inspectorate can be more productive in that the chances of an inspector uncovering violations on a site visit are clearly much greater than a police officer happening across an assault, burglary, car theft, and so on (although, of course, this does occur).

Two points follow from this. One is that in the sphere of regulatory law, to the extent that workers and local communities are presented with the formal mechanisms whereby they can initiate inspectorate attention/action, to the extent that they develop trust in those inspectorates, and as far as they themselves develop confidence and expertise, then the need for a proactive inspectorial commitment may decline. But this is to take a very long-term view. Moreover, the need for a proactive presence will never disappear completely — those in unorganized workplaces, for example, will continue to be particularly vulnerable, while the lack of a subjective perception of harm on the part of a local community from a local site/company may be less a consequence of the absence of objective harm, more a consequence of 'unpolitics' (Blowers, 1984; Crenson, 1971; Smith, 1989; Lukes, 1974).

The second point that follows is that demands for an increase in numbers of inspectors are perfectly legitimate in a way that, as realists argue, demands for increased police resources are not. In contrast to the increase in the numbers of police officers in England and Wales over the past decade, the same period has witnessed a considerable decline in the numbers of factory inspectors in particular (the same is true of the US), while at the same time the number of workplaces to be inspected has risen dramatically and (European Community-inspired) legislation has meant a significant increase in the range (and, indeed, nature) of laws to be overseen by the Health and Safety Executive in general (Tombs, 1990a).

Thus the central thrust of the above is that while we wish to adopt the realist argument for democratization and maximum public initiation of action in the context of reforming the organization and activities of regulatory agencies, the different circumstances within which these and the police operate mean that arguments for 'minimal coercion', to the extent that this implies strict limitations on agency powers, are wholly inappropriate within the context with which we are concerned.

Before we go on to consider at length the modus operandi of the regulatory agencies in the sphere of health, safety and environmental laws, one further point, as yet unmentioned, needs to be emphasized from realist writing on police work. Realist work on the police has addressed directly the 'problem' of discretion. Many writers on police work have wrestled with the question of how to minimize the exercise of police discretion. But the realists have adopted a slightly, but significantly, different position on this issue. Thus they have emphasized that *policing not only is, but must be, inherently political. The exercise of discretion is not only inevitable but desirable,* allowing the ends in the name of which the police exist to be explicitly considered. This might be one way in which realist proposals can be developed in a socialist rather than simply liberal direction:

> Discretion is thus not to be seen as a failure, nor as inevitably prejudicial to the powerless, nor — precisely because of this — as a matter for the police to determine as they will. Discretion, by definition, cannot be limited by law. At the moment, however, the politics of the police are buried within their existing organisational structures, and ideologically denied in the rhetoric of police professionalism. We have argued that a politics of the police is inevitable, and a certain politics desirable. Changes demand a recognition of these facts and a radical institutional reorganisation which would allow the inevitable to accord with the desirable. (Kinsey *et al.*, 1986: 168)

Again, in the context of debates on health, safety and environment, a recognition of the political nature of the questions involved is important. But so often it is precisely this fact which is at best understated, at worst denied. Questions of how safe is safe enough, what are acceptable costs and benefits of industrial activity, what determines 'reasonable practicability', and so on, are explicitly political issues; they are certainly not technical questions. A recognition of this must be progressive, and indeed is a precondition of the transcendence of a technocratic rationality which pervades much of industry and serves as a barrier to the kind of 'maximum public initiation' which was spoken about above.

Theories of regulation

The first question that must be dealt with is whether regulatory violations should even be considered to be equivalent to street crimes. Capitalists and corporate executives, many judges and regulators, some economists and political scientists and, indeed, many legal theorists and criminologists have argued that regulatory and white-collar offences are inherently different from such activities. James Q. Wilson, appropriately, has claimed 'predatory street crime to be a far more serious matter than consumer fraud, anti-trust violations, etc . . . because predatory crime makes difficult or impossible the maintenance of meaningful human communities' (1975: xx). More recently, in his book with Richard Herrnstein, *Crime and Human Nature,* he has retained a focus on street crime because — 'Robbery, stealing, incest and factory pollution were condemned by overwhelming majorities in every society' (1986: 22). What is bizarre about this work is that in it, he studiously and with no explanation, avoids any discussion of the last and ultimately potentially expansive category of 'factory pollution'.

Proponents of a 'compliance' (as opposed to a 'policing') regulatory strategy argue that the nature of corporate illegalities calls for different forms of regulation than is the case for other kinds of lawbreaking. Businesses and particularly corporations are not, as many would have it, typically 'amoral calculators', but rather 'political citizens' who may indeed sometimes err but more because of 'organizational incompetence' than deliberate wrongdoing. Thus they need advice rather than chastisement: regulatory agencies should act as consultants rather than 'policemen' (Kagan and Scholz, 1984: 68). Although some corporations sometimes act as if they are 'amoral calculators', this is neither necessary nor typical; where regulations are violated, this is usually the result of factors other than pure economic calculation. Corporations can and do have a primary commitment to act in a socially responsible fashion, are not essentially criminogenic, and will not cease to commit violations because of attempts at deterrence (Kagan and Scholz, 1984: 67–8; see also Hawkins, 1984: 110, Hutter 1988: 45–7,80; Richardson *et al.,*1983: 125–49). To accept a view of the corporation as an amoral calculator entails a corresponding view of the most appropriate regulatory response to such corporations, namely, 'strict enforcement of uniform and high specific standards, backed by severe penalties', with regulatory officials acting quite literally as 'policemen' (Kagan and Scholz, 1984: 72).

In their view, this is quite wrong, because legal infractions by business are unsuitable for criminalization. In the case of pollution there is a need 'to preserve a fragile balance between the interests of economic activity on the one hand and the public welfare on the other' (Hawkins, 1984: 9), and, relatedly, it is 'the inherent nature and circumstances of factory "crime" ' that 'necessarily engender a compliance response' (Jamieson,1985: i). Not only is *mens rea* inapplicable in most cases of regulatory violations, particularly since such deviance occurs within an organizational framework (Richardson *et al.,* 1983: 56–7), but there is an inherent injustice in the use of a standard of strict liability, and, anyway, many regulatory offences involve acts or omissions, which are *mala prohibita* rather than *mala in se.* Regulatory violations differ from 'traditional' or 'consensual' crimes in that the former are 'morally problematic' (Hawkins, 1984: 11), lack 'self-evident moral blameworthiness'

(Jamieson, 1985: 30) or are characterized by 'moral ambivalence' (Hutter, 1988: 10–11).

These controversies, of course, are not new. In the 1940s Sutherland and Tappan debated the status of the concept of 'white-collar crime' (Sutherland, 1940, 1941; Tappan, 1947) and recently Blum-West and Carter (1983) have vindicated many of Sutherland's arguments by showing that there are no substantive differences between torts and crimes. Glasbeek and Rowland have convincingly developed detailed legal arguments as to why killing and injuring at work should be treated as typical crimes of violence (Glasbeek, 1984, 1988; Glasbeek and Rowland, 1979) and, elsewhere, we have addressed the issue of the status of such regulatory offences by drawing out an analogy between such health and safety violations and motoring offences (Pearce and Tombs, 1990). It is clear that these activities can be criminalized, particularly, as we show below, with some relatively minor changes in company law.

Let us then, for the moment, turn to the argument that corporations are not amoral calculators. In our view the claim that corporations can do anything other than attempt to maximize long-term profitability is theoretically untenable. It is the basic rationale for, indeed constitutive of, their very existence. For any corporation to have a primary commitment to social responsibility would entail ignoring both its rationale and the nature of the existing economic system. This is *not* to argue that such rational calculation necessarily means that all regulations are ignored by corporations, nor that any particular corporation will in practice succeed in either a correct interpretation of what is rational, nor be able to act in accordance with that interpretation. Clearly, then, corporations will, at times, act 'irrationally' — what the 'compliance school' calls incompetence and political citizenship are both perfectly compatible with a concept of corporations as amoral calculators. Nor is it to imply that business firms or the individuals who hold positions of power and take decisions within them will all act criminally. It is simply to recognize that, as Box has argued, the nature of the capitalist mode of production forces corporations to attempt to exert as much control as possible over their operating environments, this pushing them into violating those regulations which seek to prevent individual corporations from using their corporate power to exert certain forms of control over consumers, workers, governments, other corporations, and so on (Box, 1983).

A more plausible view, then, is that of Edwin Sutherland (1983) who argued that corporations are 'rationalistic, amoral and nonsentimental ':

> The corporation probably comes closer to the 'economic man ' and to 'pure reason' than any person or any other organization. The executives and directors not only have explicit and consistent objectives of maximum pecuniary gain but also have research and accountancy departments by which precise determination of results is facilitated . . .
>
> . . . the corporation selects crimes which involve the smallest danger of detection and identification and against which victims are least likely to fight. . . . The corporations attempt to prevent the implementation of the law and to create general goodwill. . . . (Sutherland, 1983: 236–8)

Indeed, although recent theorists differ somewhat about the appropriate models for describing business organizations, few, if any, give any credibility to the notion of the 'soulful corporation' (Pearce and Tombs, 1989, 1991).

In the view of economists of the Chicago school, for example, everybody's pursuit of self-interest in the free market produces an efficient allocation of resources, enhances individual self-satisfaction and promotes liberty and freedom of choice. Such self-interest, they argue, is much more likely to produce a satisfactory social order than is the invocation of such vague goals as social responsibility: 'If businesses do have a social responsibility other than making maximum profits for share holders, how are they to know what it is? Can self selected private individuals decide . . . how great a burden they are justified in placing on themselves of their stockholders to serve the social interest?' (Friedman, 1962: note 26, pp. 133–4). In their view, management's desire to take account of social interests — the community, consumers, employees — would be merely a ploy to give them some autonomy from shareholders. (For examples see the debate about 'corporate responsibility' in the Sunday *New York Times* during March 1990).

Although, as we will show, such economists tend to agree with the compliance school about the appropriate status of regulatory offences, they raise some interesting questions. In their view in the relationship between economic activity and the state there are tremendous dangers to the working of market rationality and efficiency. Since all economic actors, including corporations and state agents, are motivated by self-interest although state activities are justified because they are alleged to correct allocative problems due to market failure, in fact, they primarily function to redistribute resources by interfering with the normal working of the market. The major beneficiaries are usually small groups of highly motivated and well-organized economic actors — iron triangles of established companies, regulators and politicians. Control is achieved through the regulatory apparatus favouring such companies directly or by imposing prohibitive costs on potential competitors by, for example, demanding expensive safety standards. Consumers also suffer because they have to pay higher prices. In other words, they are very cynical about the autonomy of regulatory agencies and their utility for achieving any kind of social goals (cf. Stigler, 1971; Peltzman, 1976).

Thus, in their view, 'social regulation ' is something best achieved by a combination of market forces and litigation rather than by governmental regulation. Optimum realizable health and safety standards, for example, are likely to be reached when employers find the level of expenditure on safety which is just marginally less than the expenditure incurred by accidents made up of the damage to property, of training new workers, of increased insurance premiums, of workmen's compensation, of litigation and of paying workers increased wages because they know that they are engaging in relatively dangerous work. The most that regulatory agencies can realistically do is to set performance hazard standards or develop injury taxes (Oi, 1977). First, let us note that the very idea that one can distinguish between 'social regulation' and 'economic regulation' is ideological. For example, the 'regulation of hazardous products is the soft underbelly of economic regulation, precisely because it deals ultimately with who will bear the hidden costs of new products and production processes' (Doern, 1977: 17).

479

Then, for insurance and workmen's compensation to have any effect compensation levels must be high. For an injury tax to work, the tariff must be significant. For litigation to be effective courts must be sympathetic to those who are injured, resources must be made available to equalize them and employers in the competition for legal help, and settlements must be substantial. For workers to know about injury rates and for them to be able to demand higher wages it is essential that they have access to accurate information about company affairs. All of these require a combination of substantial legal aid, the coercive power of regulatory agencies and strong trade unions — exactly what such theorists wish to avoid!

Wilson is sympathetic to the arguments of these economists but he is also critical of them for certain oversimplifications. He suggests that not all regulatory agencies are captured by those that they are meant to regulate, and therefore a more complex model is required of the relationship between state agencies and the different social groups competing to influence them. First there are not one, but four, political situations. He redefines as *client politics* the situation where costs are widely distributed and benefits concentrated (as in state licensing laws). *Majoritarian politics* occur when both costs and benefits are widespread (as in the Social Security and Sherman Acts). *Interest group politics* exist when both costs and benefits are narrowly distributed and hence negotiation and compromise can occur (as in the labour laws). Finally, *entrepreneurial politics* occur when benefits are widely distributed and costs are highly concentrated (as in environmental and motor safety regulation). Secondly, while it is true that some regulatory officials are politicians ambitious for higher appointive or elective office, others are careerists motivated by organizational bureaucratic concerns, and yet others are professionals responsive to the norms and interests of their wider occupational community. Thirdly, although in economics what is relevant is not what individuals want or why but only consumers 'revealed preferences' known through market conduct; in politics values often only emerge in the course of the political process and efforts are continuously made to change people's wants so that they are in accord with the emerging political programme:

> Both economics and politics deal with problems of scarcity and conflicting preferences. Both deal with persons who ordinarily act rationally. But politics differs from economics in that it manages conflict by forming heterogeneous coalitions out of persons with changeable and incommensurable preferences in order to make binding decisions for everyone (Wilson, 1980: 363)

This, in Wilson's view, had become a serious problem in the 1970s since unqualified, irrational political actors — trade unionists and 'bureaucrats, professionals, academics, the media, those whose political position depends upon controlling resources other than wealth and whose motivations are more complex than wealth maximization' — sometimes interfere with both market forces and the internal workings of the professionally run corporation. Unreasonable laws can be passed, excessive damages awarded, unworkable regulations promulgated, and product certification unfairly denied. Such individuals and attitudes — a belief in a risk-free society, for example — can gain excessive influence within democratic assemblies, in the courts, in juries and can capture regulatory agencies. There can be another iron triangle of regulatory entrepreneurs, regulatory agencies and, for example, environmentalist politicians (Wilson, 1980; Weaver, 1978).

Although some of the specific points made by Wilson, about the different kinds of regulatory political situations for example, are not without value, it is clear that he fails to attend to the wider structural context of the situations that he explores or to examine long-term outcomes. There is a need to examine the significance of both the Social Security Act of 1935 and the 1890 Sherman Act, and ask why the former presaged such a minimal welfare state in the US (the development of which has been subject to such tremendous vagaries and extraordinary resistance — cf. Block *et al.*, 1987) and why the latter, and subsequent legislation, have not stopped the economic system becoming increasingly oligopolistic (Coleman, 1989: 14; Jones, 1982). He provides no explanation of why environmentalists and trade unionists advocating a healthy and safe environment within and without the workplace were successful in developing effective regulation for only three or four years in the mid-1970s. In fact, *contra* Wilson and David Vogel (cf. Vogel, 1989), their short-term victory — as a result of heightened social conflict and a profound but temporary crisis in the legitimacy of the American political and economic order (Donnelly, 1981) — but speedy defeat, is testimony, not to the plural nature of the US political system, but rather to the resources, resilience and power of business which was able to launch the massive counterattack associated with deregulation (Calavita, 1983; Szasz, 1984, 1986a, 1986b).

One can reinterpret some of the arguments of compliance theorists to make this point, albeit after making some pretty fundamental criticisms. Bardach and Kagan, for example, make two objections to the 'regulator-as-policeman' strategy. First, it engenders rigidity and/or legalism, which in turn generates 'regulatory unreasonableness' and 'unresponsiveness' (Bardach and Kagan, 1982: 58). Here the regulatory inspector is seen as something akin to an automaton, compelled towards the prosecution of each and every violation detected. Such a representation is not only stereotypical, echoing Thatcherite and Reaganite 'anti-statist' rhetoric, but is based upon a misconception of what the police actually do. Because of the necessarily wide range of laws that they exist to enforce and for operational/practical reasons, police officers regularly and routinely exercise discretion, as an indispensable (Lustgarten, 1987), and even desirable (Kinsey *et al.*, 1986), part of their work. Their second, and more telling, objection is that this strategy stimulates 'opposition and the destruction of cooperation' (Kagan and Scholz, 1984: 73). Business may resort to legalistic counter-measures, organize politically and attack the agency at the legislative level, jeopardizing 'the agency's legal mandate, its funding, and its very existence' (Kagan and Scholz, 1984: 74).

On the one hand, they imply that if regulators were only more reasonable — both British and US occupational health and safety inspectors were instructed in being more polite when visiting businesses, and business executives were asked to comment on their conduct to the inspectors' superiors (Wilson, 1985) — then compliance would be the normal outcome. On the other hand, they argue, and themselves find it a reasonable state of affairs that: regulation is viable only when it prevents the *avoidable* harmful side-effects of wealth creation and an inspectorate's mandate would be withdrawn if it were seen to be overzealous; regulations are only passed which do not pose a fundamental challenge to an industry's economic viability and industry is powerful enough to resist the enactment or enforcement of overrestrictive regulations. *The legitimacy of a capitalist economic system and the illegitimacy of its being policed are in fact starting-points for such analyses.* There is, however, no reason for us to endorse any such view. Their own analysis suggests that there are two distinct inequalities of power — those that derive from an imbalance in resources, including knowledge and expertise, and those that derive from corporate ideological hegemony. As we have shown elsewhere (Pearce and Tombs, 1990), while 'compliance theorists' recognize that the enforcement realities/necessities they describe are defined and limited by the 'needs of business' they consistently fail even to attempt to transcend or subvert the limitations placed upon 'realistic' possibilities by this de facto dominance. Dominance, of course, implies struggle and resistance and it is important to recognize deregulation and other Reaganite policies, for example in relation to welfare, as a recuperative counterattack against some real historical gains (Block *et al.*, 1987). Ironically, recently, a contingent event, the Bhopal disaster, has made it possible to reopen the debate about these issues. Indeed, if the workings of the capitalist system and its empowering of the major corporate actors is the omnipresent context of all political situations this does not mean that it is in total control of its own destiny. It does not automatically secure its economic, political or ideological conditions of existence. It is the unpredictability and uncontrollability of the US economy, rather than the nature and function of regulatory agencies, that has been the major focus of Kolko's work for the last 20 or so years (Kolko, 1962, 1963, 1984).

Kolko's work is relatively compatible with a conception of regulatory bodies as more hegemonic apparatuses than captive agents. In this view a stable capitalist social order depends upon one fraction of capital achieving leadership — in both the state and civil society — over both other fractions of capital and the subordinate classes. In order to do this it does all that it can to disarm these other groups while winning their consent through (limited) compromises with their interests. In the 'relatively autonomous' state there is established an 'unequal equilibrium of compromises' and an 'unequal structure of representation'. Regulatory agencies always involve representation of fractions of capital, of the wider state and, sometimes, of other social interests: 'Like other parts of the state apparatus, these institutions represent the interests of a specific fraction [of capital] — but in a particular way, as they are effectively combined with the long term interests of the hegemonic fraction. That is, they simultaneously represent and regulate (Mahon, 1979: 155).

This means that such apparatuses may give *some* privileges to businesses already operating in an area and may give partial recognition to the interests of subordinate groups. However, the overall control exercised over the state and civil society by the hegemonic fraction means that such concessions are likely to be strictly circumscribed, at least in the long run. Rianne Mahon has shown how this can be achieved through the medium of the hierarchical relationship that exists between the different state apparatuses — specialist regulatory agencies can be located in relatively weak government departments and/or their activities can be subject to the review of other state agencies which more closely reflect the interests or rationales of the hegemonic fractions of capital. In the US the Office of Management and Budget fulfilled this latter function in the 1980s (Horwitz, 1989: 208–11). Mahon's work (1977, 1979, 1984), which we have only been able to sketch here, represents the beginnings of an alternative and more sophisticated analysis of regulatory agencies.

For Wilson, however, it is bureaucratization and inefficiency that are characteristic of state activities. Thus the fewer the demands that are made on the state — and the less political activity there is — the better. There is little point in trying to change anything because 'the relationship between electoral needs and policy outcome is problematic' (1980: 390). He produced a similar argument with somewhat different conclusions, of course, in the case of street crime, since here he argues that nothing can be done about the social causes of crime, which anyway are unknowable, but deterrence remains very much on the agenda (Wilson, 1975: xiv–xv; Young, 1986: 9–12). Yet, while usually he claims that the less regulation the better, in his article with Rachal (1977), he argued that regulation can in fact be very effective but only if it is private enterprise that is being regulated and not government bureaucracies. He makes unfavourable comparisons between the effective and ineffective regulation of private and public housing, hospitals and utilities, respectively. Although there are indeed *difficulties* in regulating state activities (cf. Hirst, 1986), generally what Wilson claims are that examples of the *impossibility* of such regulation are due rather to a failure to supply governmental agencies with sufficient funds and adequate guidelines — for example, to maintain public housing and both to provide cheap electricity *and* control pollution. It is conservative hostility to public enterprise that is the problem, not public enterprise itself. It is also worth noting that it is impossible adequately to regulate some markets because adequate regulation makes them economically unviable for private enterprise, and conversely they can only be viable if they are inadequately regulated. Szasz's (1986b) discussion of the regulation of hazardous waste disposal and Campbell's (1987) of the state and nuclear waste are instructive in this regard. Indeed, overall it is only too clear that:

> In the end, the politics of regulation turns less on the dynamics of coalition formation, the behavior of regulatory officials, or the rulings of the courts, important as these are, than on the dominant vision of the larger society in which nationally organized interests, policy entrepreneurs, bureaucrats, and courts are merely highly specialized, and unrepresentative manifestations. That vision encompasses a conception of the good society and of the place of the citizen in that society, a notion of the proper boundaries between public and private, and of the appropriate domains of community norms and individual decision. That vision, whatever its content, ultimately prescribes the tolerance within which conventional regulatory politics can be conducted. (Schuck, 1981: 723)

Different kinds of economics and different forms of analyses are also forms of politics. While claiming objectivity they are tied to particular interests, while guiding and justifying actions they can also obscure what is occurring.

Amoral calculators: some empirical evidence

That most corporations are not amoral calculators, and thus that their adherence to regulations is not conditional upon their short-term or longer-term self-interest, is, as we have seen, a central tenet of the arguments of those advocating compliance strategies. Bardach and Kagan (1982) even attempt to quantify the proportion of all corporations which are amoral calculators, or 'bad apples'. They assume, 'for analytical purposes', that at most they 'make up about 20 per cent of the average population of regulated enterprises in most regulatory programs' (Bardach and Kagan, 1982: 65). If the theoretical argument for viewing corporations as amoral calculators is unconvincing, the empirical evidence as to the spread of illegalities among all types of corporations seems, *contra* Bardach and Kagan, in favour of a view which sees the commitment of corporations to regulations as essentially contingent.

We will illustrate these points by a brief analysis of the state of occupational health and safety in the UK. This is not because there exist no useful analyses of the state of health and safety in the US (Coleman, 1989) or Canada (Glasbeek, 1988; Goff and Reasons, 1986) but for reasons of space. Currently in the UK more than 600 people die in work-related accidents every year, and in excess of another 18,000 suffer major injuries from work-related incidents. Moreover, after a long period of decline in the numbers injured at work in Britain, the 1980s have seen dramatic increases in major injuries in certain industrial sectors (HSE, 1987). About 750 people each year are officially recorded as dying per year from occupational diseases, but these are based upon very narrowly drawn categories. Trades unions have estimated that 20,000 people die each year partly as a result of work-related ill-health (Work Hazards Group, 1987), and this figure is given significant support by the Royal Commission on Civil Liability (1978) which estimated that what are recorded as occupationally related illnesses may be only 20 percent of the true figure of such illnesses.

Moreover, in report after report, the Health and Safety Executive and its Inspectorates state that management bears primary responsibility for these accidents, for example: 75 percent of maintenance accidents in the chemical industry (HSE, 1987), '2 out of 3 deaths in general manufacturing' (HSE, 1983), '3 out of 5 farm deaths' (HSE, 1986), 78 percent of fatal maintenance accidents in manufacturing (HSE, 1985b), 70 percent of deaths in the construction industry (HSE, 1988), and so on. *In other words, in more than three out of five cases of fatal accidents, managements were (fatally) in violation of the Health and Safety at Work Act 1974 in terms of their General Duties to employees (Sections 2 and 3).*

Further, *contra* Bardach and Kagan, existing empirical evidence suggests that regulatory deviance is not confined to a tiny proportion of firms. Carson's (1970) work on the Factory Inspectorate found that whatever their size every one of the 200 firms visited in the course of his research violated health and safety laws at least twice, and the average number of violations per firm was 19. Few however were legally sanctioned. Recent HSE industry 'blitzes' have also revealed widespread regulatory violations. One recent blitz on the textile industry, for example, found that *191 of 300 premises inspected were not even registered with local regulatory agencies, as required by law* (Health and Safety Executive, 1985a). Similarly, when, in the summer of 1987, the work of about 4500 contractors on construction sites was inspected, 868 prohibition notices were issued to stop work immediately because of dangerous conditions. In other words, as a result of one set of inspections conditions on one in five building sites visited were so bad that work had to be stopped immediately

(*Occupational Safety and Health*, December 1987). Moreover it is not only small and 'fly-by-night' firms that engage in such violations. Violations are widespread among companies of all sizes and in all sectors of the economy (Pearce 1990a; Pearce and Tombs, 1991; Clinard and Yeager, 1980: 130; Carson, 1982). Although these data are not conclusive as to the common-place and routine nature of regulatory deviance with respect to health and safety law, they are surely enough to call into question empirically that which we had earlier questioned theoretically — namely, the claim that only a minority of corporations should be treated as if they are amoral calculators.

Corporate illegalities, corporate organization and corporate responsibilities

We have argued that the distinction between 'traditional' criminals and corporate offenders contains both real and ideological aspects. It describes certain aspects of reality in that business is an activity which has certain socially useful consequences. But it remains largely ideological in that it implies that the corporation can have a primary commitment to act in a socially responsible manner; it is ideological in that illegalities are currently considered to form a marginal element of business activity; and it is ideological in its acceptance of business's own definitions as to what constitute 'reasonable' regulations.

Once these assumptions which underpin the distinction between 'traditional' and 'regulatory' offenders, and the different regulatory responses engendered by this distinction, are problematized, then both the distinction itself and the arguments against the 'policing' of industry are greatly weakened. This allows us to reopen the question of the most 'appropriate' regulatory strategy for dealing with corporate violations of health and safety laws, to transcend at least some of the ideological 'understandings' within which both the questions we may pose and the answers we can find are presupposed.

On this basis, we have been able to consider eminently practicable strategies for controlling corporate activities, including the use of automatic penalty points as one among a wider range of sanctions available to regulatory agencies, and the application of the principles of licensing in this sphere (which has in fact become a reality recently in a number of US states — this for explicitly political reasons) (Pearce and Tombs, 1990). Thus the transcendence of the assumption that corporations cannot be policed allows serious consideration to be given to the practicalities of such a strategy — and many of the practical problems are, indeed, attested to usefully in the work of the 'Compliance school'. Yet there is no need to conflate the immediately practicable with either the once-and-for-all possible or desirable forms of regulation. Avoiding this conflation is indeed crucial once it is recognized that what is 'feasible' is in fact a political issue, and thus subject to change.

Let us consider one of the allegedly key practical difficulties in 'criminalizing' regulatory deviance. Because regulatory deviance occurs within an organizational framework, it has been alleged that there are overwhelming practical difficulties in prosecuting businesses (Richardson *et al.*, 1983: 56–7), so we need to show that it is or could be feasible to prosecute corporate offenders. Certainly, until very recently, it has been the case in the UK that where a company is prosecuted for regulatory violations it is the corporate entity that is charged — rather than particular individuals such as senior executives — with the company being represented in the court by the company secretary, usually to face a fine which in practice is little more than a tax. Company law, while increasingly specific about financial responsibilities (and with a possibility of criminal prosecution for negligence as in Section 89 of the 1986 Insolvency Act), is extremely vague about those concerned with occupational safety and environmental damage, thus creating problems in determining individual and collective responsibility for disasters and accidents. Nevertheless, there are possibilities both in current law, and in relatively minor law reform, to make directors and chief executives legally as well as morally responsible for accidents and disasters while still providing them with a reasonable defence if they are not in fact to blame. This will also make prosecution easier and hence a more rational option for the Inspectorates.

The problem of establishing corporate culpability in the UK context is exemplified by the important Appeal Court Decision on the Zeebrugge disaster. The court found that a Corporation can be indicted for manslaughter, when the *mens rea* and *actus reus* of manslaughter can be established against those who are identified as the embodiment of the corporation itself. The court determined, however, that the evidence (available to the coroner) did not support a prosecution in this case (Law Report, *The Guardian*, 15 October 1987). However, the DPP eventually issued eight summonses for manslaughter, arising out of the Zeebruggge tragedy. These included two issued against company directors and one issued against P&O European Ferries (Dover) Ltd (formerly Townsend Car Ferries). With this latter summons is raised again the issue of corporate manslaughter. A company may well be held liable through the doctrine of identification, on the grounds that the acts and omissions of certain 'controlling individuals' may be seen as the acts and omissions of the company itself. Thus a company is held personally liable. The crucial issue here, as yet unresolved, is whether the corporate guilt of a company can be established by 'aggregating the actions of various different officers which on their own do not amount to manslaughter' (James, 1989: 4). Of equal importance is the fact that 'the notion of corporate manslaughter is now entering the popular vocabulary' (Wells, 1988), opening the possibility of reforming how corporations are organized and behave. Both the law and sentencing could be used to force companies to improve their organizational structure, their management of health and safety and to attend to 'total quality control' in these kind of activities as well as with respect to finished products.

In the US many companies have developed sophisticated systems that monitor safety and clearly define the responsibilities of managerial personnel (Braithwaite and Fisse, 1987) and it is surely no coincidence that some have also been successfully prosecuted for manslaughter and murder (Coleman, 1989). Moreover, and *contra* Braithwaite (1985), even rigorous self-regulation will only ever work if there is an effective external inspectorate. Since there is no reason to believe that companies would be rigorous about recording incidents and accidents (Di Mento, 1986: 56; Tombs, 1990b) independent monitoring is essential. It is only the fear of effective legal sanctions that will begin to make management genuinely safety-conscious.

On the basis of the preceding, and our work presented elsewhere, we believe that a punitive policing strategy is necessary, desirable and practicable. Such policies obviously will be resisted by capital and its allies (Snider, 1989) and will only be forced upon corporations by other social groupings, such as workforces, local communities and consumers. Although the parameters of capitalist social relations place real limits on how far such reforms can proceed, that some reforms can proceed should now be clear enough. In the next section, we aim to show that one important means of bringing pressure to bear on capital is by challenging corporations to justify their claim that they are responsible political citizens.

Calling the corporate bluff

When large corporations claim to be socially responsible they rarely spell out the conditions that, given their primary goal of profit, would be necessary for them to consistently act in a responsible way. How realistic, for example, would it be for them to show genuine concern about the impact of their operation on occupational and community health and safety if their competitors did not do the same? Even in this limited area they could only act responsibly if they accepted significant changes in their own and their competitors' forms of organization and operating environments; if they acknowledged the importance of environmental impact assessment and social accounting; and if they accepted the public's right to know. Let us look at corporate arguments to see how they often both proclaim social concern and at the same time avoid what it would really mean.

Corporate executives claim to do everything reasonably practicable to make a profit by using safe and efficient production processes to make safe and useful products which are then sold in highly competitive markets. Essentially they can be trusted to be self-regulating although they will work with regulatory agencies. These agencies are useful when they are responsive to government, industry and other legitimate interest groups and when they impose appropriate standards on a minority of, usually small, incompetent or dubious businesses. Although the typical corporation accepts reasonable state intervention, unfortunately unreasonable laws can be passed, excessive damages awarded, unworkable regulations promulgated, and product certification unfairly denied. Less external regulation, then, is usually the preferred and more reasonable option. Corporations, after all, are responsible political citizens.

Thus, we find that in 1988, the chairman and chief executive of Monsanto announced that his company 'abandoned a possible substitute product for asbestos . . . because a whole generation of lawyers had been schooled in asbestos liability theories that could possibly be turned against the substitute' (Mahoney, 1988). In the 1970s, the chemical industry had opposed a proposed federal PVC standard because it would cost two million jobs and $65 billion. It 'was simply beyond the compliance capacity of the industry' (Rattner, 1975). Pro-business analysts calculated that in 1976 the overall administrative cost of regulation in the US was $3.2 billion and the compliance cost $62.9 billion — a total of $66.1 billion. In 1975 federal regulations had increased the average price of a car by $449.41 forcing the car industry and consumers to spend an additional $3.025 billion on cars, money that both industry and consumers could have spent more productively elsewhere (Weidenbaum and de Fina, 1978). However, if we look more closely at these examples we can draw quite different conclusions. First, one reason for high settlements in asbestos cases — Johns-Mansville had to pay approximately $2.5 billion to 60,000 claimants (*Los Angeles Times*, 22 February 1989)

— is that, from the 1920s onwards, the major companies concealed from their workers and the public a mass of accumulating evidence of the dangers of asbestos (Brodeur, 1985). Secondly, when an approximately equivalent PVC standard was eventually adopted industry developed new technology, continued to flourish, without job losses and at only 5 percent of the expected cost (Wilson, 1985: 15–16). Thirdly, although health and safety and environmental regulations are expensive to implement they also cut down on the destruction of property and on the cost of deaths and injuries to individuals, their families and the community as a whole — air pollution control saved something like 13,900 lives per annum and reduced property damage by nearly $6 billion (Freeman 1979; see also Wilson, 1985). Similarly, making cars less dangerous may simply be an additional cost for car manufacturers but this is not true for the community as a whole. The additional $3.025 billion spent on the purchase of cars helped save $2.5 billion through exhaust fume control, and over £5.5 billion from reductions in accidents even if we restrict ourselves to insurance and litigation-based estimates of the value of life and limb. From the point of view of the rest of the community — including some corporate executives — then there was a net benefit from this regulation of about $5 billion.

Expenditure on pollution control may simply be a cost for polluting industries but it may often stimulate economic growth. In the US in the 1970s 'some 20,000 employees were put out of work because of plant closings, but over 600,000 were employed in various pollution related activities' (Marcus, 1980). The absence of pollution control may inhibit development. Recently, William Waldegrave admitted that 'Inferior environmental regulations and a lack of government support is undermining the £2 billion plus [British pollution control] industry' *(The Guardian,* 2 May 1987). In the US where industries have been forced to monitor and register emissions of dangerous chemicals, 'savings from controlling waste and improving processes efficiencies often more than outweigh the costs' (Elkins, 1989: 3).

But this is by no means necessarily true. Many pollution control and some health and safety measures *will* involve industry in significant additional expense. For example in 1975 and 1976 the US chemical industry spent approximately 9 and 12 percent of capital expenditure on pollution control equipment and although it was expected to decrease subsequently it remained nearly double the expected expenditure overseas (Castleman, 1979; and see Wilson, 1985). A key political issue, then, is who will bear the costs of safe production? Furthermore, there are a number of situations where profits and safety are necessarily at odds with each other. One is where there is a declining market, and hence fixed costs may be cut to maintain profitability. Another is where companies keep extending the life of plant and machinery by replacing parts, even when they have already received a good return on their investment. Yet another is when in an expanding market a relatively undercapitalized corporation, wishing to maintain its market share, may dangerously overutilize both plant and personnel. Bhopal serves as an example of the first situation, US airline passenger services of the second and Boeing aircraft production of the third (Pearce and Tombs, 1989; *The Guardian,* 27 and 31 January 1989). What may be economically rational behaviour from the point of view of the corporation certainly is not from the point of view of workers, consumers, the community or even from the point of view of a market economy as a whole — if it is truly competitive, that is. It is only a countervailing ethical commitment of the corporation to act in another way or the threat of sanctions that under these circumstances would lead a corporation to act in a socially responsible manner.

The previous discussion shows that whereas corporations are usually reluctant to submit themselves to effective regulation, it is sometimes possible to pressurize them to do so and that at times their resistance may be weakened by appealing to the long-term self-interest of both corporate executives and their major shareholders. This suggests the necessity and feasibility of developing strategies to challenge the corporations to live up to their self-representation as 'responsible political citizens'. We should stress, however, that any victories won through such strategies may well be temporary. Corporate capital will fight back — industry can emigrate, laws can be changed, regulatory agencies can be captured, starved of funds, or disbanded. As long as corporations and capitalistic social relations remain there will be a continuous struggle. This is no reason to despair but rather to develop ever-new strategies. Pressure can be brought on corporations both externally and internally — corporations are not themselves internally homogeneous.

In some ways the rational actor model of the corporation is an oversimplification. First it leaves unresolved the issue of the relationship between short-term and long-term profitability. Corporate raiding is intimately connected with the demand by some shareholders that short-term profitability should be maximized even if this involves the selling of assets which are essential to long-term profitability. An example would be land (owned by a corporation) which has increased in value and hence could be sold at a substantial profit, but is earmarked as the prime site for new plant when a new product goes into volume production a few years down the line. Here there is a conflict of interest between those — both management and certain key investors — concerned with the long-term viability of a corporation and those merely concerned with the turnover of their money. To make matters even more complicated most large companies themselves now engage in speculative investments in money markets, in addition to actually producing and selling commodities. Whatever, these different pressures tend to strengthen the power of the accounting and purely financial departments of corporations over and above sales or production. Furthermore, this dominance is perfectly compatible with the trend in recent years, noted by Kreisberg (1976), for many corporations to decentralize decision making and goal setting away from head office to local management while specifying standard operating procedures. What Kreisberg does not mention, however, is that this is often accompanied by the setting of strict financial targets by the head office. This, incidentally, is an inherently criminogenic relation. First, it demands certain levels of profit independently of the specific difficulties in operating safely and legally in particular operating environments. Secondly, it is very easy for the chief executives to avoid knowing or at least to refuse to acknowledge how profits are actually made and thus avoid liability for any wrongdoings. The events at Bhopal can be read as a tragic outcome of just such an arrangement (Pearce and Tombs, 1989) and on a more mundane level the Tesco judgment implicitly encourages higher management to be 'wilfully blind' about what happens at lower levels (Fife and Machin, 1982; Wilson, 1979).

Both the 'rational actor' and this 'organizational process' model of corporate structure can be viewed as sub-types of 'bureaucratic politics' in which the corporation is viewed as a site of struggle between different groups (Kreisberg, 1976). These groups can be defined by, for example, the ownership or non-ownership of capital, by sectoral employment or by professional affiliation. Any resolution of this struggle is dependent upon the relative resources available to different groups and the operating environment of the organization. This means that although certain groups or alliances of groups become dominant this is not necessarily a stable arrangement, and there are always compromises since all groups have some power (cf. Foucault, 1982). If currently accountants and major shareholders dominate the corporation, professional engineers, *qua* professional engineers, can still have some influence. It may be possible to mobilize these in conjunction with organized labour and citizens' groups to demand that corporations attain certain environmental and health and safety standards.

So, for our purposes, a number of questions need to be addressed. First, given capitalistic social relations, what kind of legal framework could be set up to pressurize corporations, corporate executives and engineers to be responsible citizens while still engaging in productive business activity? Secondly, how could engineers and other employees committed to high standards of health and safety and pollution control, press the board of their companies to act responsibly and how would they in turn persuade their shareholders? We know that because of the demand for high immediate returns on investments, the threat from corporate raiders and so on, many executives are finding any kind of long-term planning and investment problematic, never mind those associated with health and safety and pollution control. Thirdly, how could other corporations and corporate executives who wished to act unethically (and often thereby steal a competitive advantage) be stopped from doing so? In other words, how could the ethical be empowered to be responsible without being disadvantaged vis-a-vis irresponsible (albeit 'instrumentally rational') competitors and colleagues?

To be a genuine political citizen whether of the world community or more local ones such as a common market, nation state or locality, means to be committed to the continued viability of this community, to bring immediate (net) benefits and to help secure its future. The major transnational corporations are all based in democratic countries. To prove that this is not merely a happenstance, corporations, as members of democratic political communities, should be challenged to recognize that workers, consumers, etc, have a right to participate freely in the political process and to know to what dangers they are being exposed. Corporations should accept responsibility for the dangerous side-effects of their productive processes, products and waste, and they should recognize that calculations of cost and benefit also include the costs and benefits to present and future members of communities.

Industry must be challenged to acknowledge that the community has a right to call all its members to account, whether by market mechanisms, litigation or regulatory agencies. This necessitates readily available detailed information about the nature of corporate activities and products and about the decisions and decision-making processes of corporations. There must exist the capacity effectively to bring corporations and their executives to account for their actions. Industry must be forced to accept the need for effective external regulation.

There is good evidence that when corporations organize production safely it is not primarily because of a commitment to safe production for its own sake but also because a safe firm is often an efficient firm and vice versa. Braithwaite's analysis of the 'organizational characteristics' that 'make for safe mining' apply equally well to all large-scale manufacturing, namely, 'clout for the safety department, clearly defined accountability for safety imposed on line managers, top management commitment to and monitoring of safety performance, programs for guaranteeing safety training/supervision, effective communication and, most important of all, effective plans to cope with hazards' (Braithwaite, 1985: 71).

Yet if, as we have seen, there are some situations where there will be financial advantages in engaging in less than safe production, then if a corporation puts safety first it needs to know that competing and potentially less scrupulous corporations are unlikely to risk cutting corners. The only way that a corporation could routinely behave ethically and not be disadvantaged would be for irresponsible corporations to be publicly sanctioned. The issue was put clearly by an executive vice-president of Dow when he pointed out that by resisting expenditure on air pollution control, some companies are able 'to establish a margin of advantage over their competitors. Such conduct is hurting the rest of industry and should not be defended or tolerated' (cited in Brown, 1987: 242). It is thus quite understandable that in her study of pollution control Brittan found that firms whose discharges complied with water control standards 'favoured a hard line on enforcement' (1984: 79).

Regulatory agencies that have effective powers and adequate financing can, however, equalize the market conditions to which all are subject. This is the rationale informing the support by the Chemical Manufacturers' Association of the USA, of 'the adoption and enforcement of the hazardous materials regulations by State and Local governments' (Smith, 1986: 83). They may also raise the cost of engaging in a particular business to the advantage of the well-resourced larger corporations. Perhaps this is part of the reason why 'Britain's biggest waste tip operator . . . dismissed regulations . . . covering the passage of dangerous wastes across national frontiers as a "dramatic failure" to control hazardous waste imports . . . [and] called for a US-style environmental protection agency to take over all aspects of policy-making, legislation, and enforcement of regulations' (The Guardian, 9 September 1988). This is one situation where if private enterprise is used it can be to the advantage of the public that it is a large corporation.

Moreover, to be cynical, if something does go wrong corporations will try to shift blame — on to employees and on to regulators. This has been no more clearly demonstrated than when Union Carbide, having sought out a weakly regulated country, attempted to blame Sikh extremists, employees and the Indian government for the Bhopal disaster. They alleged that the latter may have granted 'a licence for the Bhopal plant without adequate checks on the plant'; the 'agencies responsible for the plant were grossly understaffed, lacked powers and had little impact on conditions in the field'; 'the Bhopal department of labour office had only two inspectors, neither of whom had any knowledge of chemical hazards' (Muchlinski, 1987: 575). However inadequate the regulation, as we have argued elsewhere, the major responsibility for the disaster clearly remains with Union Carbide (Pearce and Tombs, 1989).

This reminds us that it is only if we have effective regulation nationally and internationally, thus equalizing the conditions under which corporations compete, that the same safety standards might apply throughout the world. This could generate new markets, force technological development and help sustain and enhance the quality of life. In the context of the current development of large trading blocs there exists the possibility of producing adequate regulatory frameworks which will have some binding effect on the major corporations if they wish to produce for and sell in their major markets. The safety-conscious public is not without leverage.

It is no coincidence that in its eagerness to gain access to the profitable French agricultural producer markets Union Carbide agreed to French trade union demands that in its pesticide plant at Béziers expenditure on safety would increase to 20 percent from the usual 3.5 percent (Dinham *et al.*, 1986). Thus if corporations are serious about their social responsibilities they will accept the kinds of changes that have been advocated in this chapter. They would not be painless or cost-free. But if corporations do not accept the need for change then we can only assume that their self-representation as socially responsible organizations and as 'political citizens' committed to the long-term interests of the communities in which they operate is little more than a public relations ploy. The suggestions in this chapter, then, should be construed as both a set of practical measures and as a challenge.

Conclusion

In this chapter we first explored, challenged and then modified some of the arguments of left realism as a prelude to exploring the phenomenon of corporate crime and to developing strategies to combat it, or at least to regulate it more effectively. We were critical of the individual-centred nature of much left realist writing and showed how this inhibited their study of 'crime in the suites'. We then referred briefly to an example of left realist empirical work on commercial crime, namely the *Second Islington Crime Survey,* before turning to the topic of corporate crime. That section of the chapter provided an extensive criticism of those who write on corporate crime from the point of view of the compliance school and entailed a refutation of their view that corporate illegalities are not 'real crimes' and that corporations should be assisted rather than policed. We then provided detailed examples of what this could mean in practice; in doing so, we attempted to develop elements of the realist arguments for the reform of the policing of street crime, which we had considered earlier. Finally we explored the conditions under which those corporations that represent themselves as responsible could be forced actually to behave in a responsible manner. This entailed both challenging them to live up to their self-portrayals and exploring the unacknowledged conditions that make this more likely. The most important of these is that 'responsible corporations' need strong independent regulatory agencies to police their own and their competitors' conduct in order to equalize the conditions of competition. Even if corporations refuse to accept these suggestions they have the great advantage that by taking the corporations at their word and by accepting the existence of a competitive capitalist economy they challenge the corporations on their own terrain. Furthermore, since they involve the restructuring of corporations, the empowering of different groups and the assertion of collective rights over those of private property they could be the basis of non-reformist reforms.

Despite some of our reservations concerning the descriptive and prescriptive work of the realists on crime and policing, the spirit underlying the argument developed here for the policing of corporations is strictly congruent with the realist exigence that crime be taken seriously. In attempting to indicate the extent of the commonplace victimization from corporate crimes, and to develop practical strategies for ways in which workers and local communities may both be protected and be empowered to protect themselves from such illegalities, we hope that we have at least begun to stimulate realist work in a further, much neglected and often inadequately treated, area of crime.

Note

The research upon which this chapter is based was made possible in part by grants from both Queen's University and Wolverhampton Polytechnic.